THE WORKS OF JONATHAN EDWARDS

VOLUME 1

Perry Miller, General Editor

Jonathan Edwards

Freedom of the Will

EDITED BY PAUL RAMSEY

PROFESSOR OF RELIGION, PRINCETON UNIVERSITY

New Haven

YALE UNIVERSITY PRESS, 1957

LONDON: OXFORD UNIVERSITY PRESS

Portrait of Jonathan Edwards by Joseph Badger.
Yale University Art Gallery

A careful and ſtrict

ENQUIRY

INTO

The *modern* prevailing Notions

OF THAT

FREEDOM of WILL,

Which is ſuppoſed to be eſſential

TO

Moral Agency, Vertue and *Vice, Reward* and *Puniſhment, Praiſe* and *Blame.*

─────────────────────────

By JONATHAN EDWARDS, A.M.

Paſtor of the Church in *Stockbridge.*

─────────────────────────

Rom. ix. 16. *It is not of him tvat willeth──*

─────────────────────────

BOSTON, N. E.

Printed and Sold by S. KNEELAND, in Queen-ſtreet.
MDCCLIV.

GENERAL EDITOR'S NOTE

WITH PAUL RAMSEY's edition of *A Careful and Strict Enquiry into the Modern Prevailing Notions of . . . Freedom of Will* the Editorial Committee for the Works of Jonathan Edwards presents the first volume of the Yale University Press edition. The project, undertaken with the generous support of the Bollingen Foundation, has been launched with the purpose not only of republishing all of the printed works of Edwards but also of publishing the massive manuscript materials in which much of Edwards' most profound thinking and finest prose have been concealed.

It is appropriate that *Freedom of the Will* should appear as Volume 1, for although it is not the first in the Edwards chronology, it is the work through which his fame has been most widely spread abroad, even to the multitudes who have known the book only by hearsay.

At the outset we hope it will be understood that while we approach this towering edifice with veneration, we do not expect to find among all students a unanimity of interpretation, or uncritical endorsement of Edwards' views. He is too majestic a figure to yield to every observer a single, simple meaning, and was too rigorous a critic himself to demand servile adherence. Hence it is the policy of the Committee to put each volume into the hands of a different editor, for him to expound and evaluate in his own terms. If out of these several treatments various and sometimes contradictory interpretations emerge, we shall greet that result as a documented attestation to the range and complexity of Edwards' mind.

We therefore seek uniformity only in editorial integrity: our aim is meticulous faithfulness to the words of the original text, whether printed or manuscript, within the limits of a format acceptable to modern eyes. Only a few general editing conventions have been established. Apart from these, each editor will cope with special problems as seems best to him according to the demands of his own text.

The very existence of the project is itself testimony to the deepening appreciation in the mid-twentieth century of the importance of Edwards to the intellectual as well as the religious history of America. A generation or so ago, outside a restricted circle of professional theologians, he was popularly known only as one who had preached a distasteful and happily outmoded brand of hell-fire and brimstone. There was, in fact, a general disposition to pass him over as an anachronism, as retrograde. Recent events in world history have no doubt stimulated drastic re-examination of such complacent assumptions. Whether because of that prodding or because of the logic of intellectual development, we find today a new urgency to confront and reinterpret the historic philosophical and theological cruxes with which Edwards grappled so courageously.

This is not to imply that today the precise doctrines that Edwards maintained, in the language in which he cast them, have been or should be extensively revived; indeed it is quite beside the purpose of this edition to promulgate them. But as Professor Ramsey's account of the provenience of the *Inquiry* and of the immense issues involved in it helps us to comprehend, Edwards—the greatest philosopher-theologian yet to grace the American scene—deserves to be heard. He has waited long for the monument we propose to erect to him, the only one he would have been at all interested in: a clear and fair exhibition of his thought.

PERRY MILLER

CONTENTS

WHEN first compiling the memoirs of Jonathan Edwards, Samuel Hopkins wrote that "President Edwards was one of those men of whom it is not easy to speak with justice without seeming, at least, to border on the marvelous, and to incur the guilt of adulation." [1] The same is true when anyone undertakes to speak of the single work *A Careful and Strict Inquiry into the Modern Prevailing Notions of the Freedom of Will,* which with ample reason has been called Edwards' greatest literary achievement. The book was first published in 1754, near the midpoint of the six years Edwards was pastor of the local church and missionary to the Indians at Stockbridge, Massachusetts. If it be true that whoever reads the *Inquiry* [2] "should remember that many a chapter must have been temporarily laid aside while the great theologian paused to catecise the Indian boys or to set them a spelling lesson," [3] he will find few if any faults here to remind him of this fact. The subject was one to which Edwards had directed his considerable powers of mind throughout his life, beginning no doubt when he was a student of science, philosophy, and theology at Yale College when first under the influence of Locke, and continuing during the three decades from his election as tutor at Yale to the publication of the *Inquiry,* and—with increasing awareness of the importance of the problem—even during the years of the Revival and other tumults at Northampton. Into the writing of it he poured all his intellectual acumen, coupled with a passionate conviction that

1. Samuel Hopkins, *The Life and Character of the Late Reverend Mr. Jonathan Edwards* (Boston, 1765) in *The Works of President Edwards* (8 vols. Worcester, 1808, cited below as Worcester ed.), *1,* 9.

2. This abbreviated citation was the one most frequently used by JE himself when he had occasion to refer to this work.

3. Clarence H. Faust and Thomas H. Johnson, *Jonathan Edwards* (New York, American Book Co., 1935), p. xiv. The only internal evidence of the circumstances of JE's writing (unless his "drunkard" illustrations be such) is a reference to the Mohawk language (below, p. 423).

the decay to be observed in religion and morals followed the decline
in doctrine since the founding of New England. The jeremiads, he
believed, had better go to the bottom of the religious issue! The
product of such plain living, high thinking, funded experience and
such vital passion was the present *Inquiry,* a superdreadnaught which
Edwards sent forth to combat contingency and self-determination (to
reword Swenson's praise of one of Kierkegaard's big books) and in
which he delivered the most thoroughgoing and absolutely destructive criticism that liberty of indifference, without necessity, has ever
received. This has to be said even if one is persuaded that some form
of the viewpoint Edwards opposed still has whereon to stand. This
book alone is sufficient to establish its author as the greatest philosopher-theologian yet to grace the American scene.

1. *Edwards' Life while Writing the* Inquiry

If we may rely on Edwards' biographer, Sereno Dwight, seven years
passed between Edwards' first recorded indication of his plan to write
on the freedom of the will and the execution of this purpose. In the
course of the year 1747, Dwight tells us, "an epistolary correspondence was commenced between Mr. Edwards and the Rev. John
Erskine," minister of the Church of Scotland, which continued for
more than ten years until Edwards' death. In a postscript to his first
letter to Erskine, written sometime during the summer of 1747, Edwards mentioned the *Treatise Concerning Religious Affections* just
published, and then he sketched a plan for the treatise which he intended to be his next major work: "I have thought of writing something particularly and largely on the Arminian controversy, in distinct discourses on the various points in dispute, to be published successively, beginning first with a discourse concerning the Freedom
of the Will, and Moral Agency; endeavouring fully and thoroughly
to state and discuss those points of Liberty and Necessity, Moral and
Physical Inability, Efficacious Grace, and the ground of virtue and
vice, reward and punishment, blame and praise, with regard to the
dispositions and actions of reasonable creatures." [4]

Thus Edwards planned to join argument with Arminianism precisely on the ground of its greatest strength, i.e. the importance of
the ethical and the human for understanding the relation between
God and man. Arminianism (a name derived from that of the Dutch

4. Sereno E. Dwight, *The Life of President Edwards,* in *The Works of President
Edwards* (10 vols. New York, 1829), *1, 250.*

theologian Jacobus Arminius, 1560–1609) was a movement of revolt
against the doctrine of irresistible grace in Calvinism. While still
asserting the inability of man to exercise saving faith or do anything
really good without regeneration by the Holy Spirit, or without
prevenient grace, the early Arminians nevertheless taught that the
Divine decrees were conditional, or dependent on God's foreknowledge of the faith in believers, and that Christ's atonement made possible, although not actual, the salvation of everyone. Grace, they
believed, was indispensable at every moment in the life of believers,
but it was not irresistible. Grace, they were confident, would prove
sufficient for continual victory over temptation; but they refused to
express this confidence by the "necessary" perseverance of the saints.
As irresistibility was the distinguishing mark of Calvinism, so was
conditionalism of Arminianism. The Arminians of the early seventeenth century, however, placed great stress upon God's side of the
divine-human relationship. Nevertheless, their teaching that the
grace of God might be resisted opened the way to an increasing emphasis upon the ethical and the human among later Arminians. This
passed over easily into Pelagianism, which dwells more upon the
example of Christ than upon his atoning work, and into deism or
natural religion, in which the ethical and the human gain complete
ascendancy. Thus "Arminianism" became but a loose term for all
forms of the complaint of the aggrieved moral nature against the
harsh tenets of Calvinism. In the eighteenth century there was probably more in common between Edwards' defense of orthodoxy and
the restored Arminianism of Arminius, which emerged with new
strength and warmth in the Wesleyan revival, than between the latter
and some of the "Arminians" whom Edwards opposed. In any case,
Edwards proposed to combat this viewpoint by showing that "the
modern prevailing notions" of freedom of will, of human action and
moral responsibility, were simply erroneous, and that nothing about
the ethical and the human, properly grasped, required the adoption
of loose notions concerning the governance of God.

This design was interrupted by a remarkable series of events which
compress most of the travail of Edwards' lifetime. First came the
death of David Brainerd, the fiancé of Edwards' second daughter,
Jerusha, and shortly thereafter the death of Jerusha herself, in her
eighteenth year. From Northampton, August 31, 1748, Edwards wrote
to Erskine: "I have for the present, been diverted from the design I
hinted to you, *of publishing something against some of the Arminian*

Tenets, by something else that Divine Providence unexpectedly laid in my way, and seemed to render unavoidable, viz. publishing Mr. Brainerd's Life, of which the enclosed paper of proposals gives some account." [5] Again on October 14, 1748, he wrote: "As to my writing against Arminianism; I have hitherto been remarkably hindered; so that probably it will be a considerable time before I shall have any thing ready for the press; but I do intend, God allowing and assisting, to prosecute that design: and I desire your prayers for the Divine assistance in it." [6]

An Account of the Life of the Late Reverend Mr. David Brainerd was published in 1749, but in that same year a controversy began with his Northampton parishioners over the qualifications for communion. This led to writings upon that subject and finally to Edwards' dismissal from the church. How steadfast his purpose was, however, is to be seen from a letter to Erskine on July 5, 1750, written from the midst of turmoil just five days after he preached his farewell sermon: "The books you sent me, were entertaining to me, and some of them will be of advantage to me, if God should give me opportunity to prosecute the studies I had begun on the Arminian Controversy." [7] Indeed, in this same letter he indicates his conviction that the affair of his dismissal was not unrelated to doctrinal disagreements more basic than qualifications for communion, when he describes one of the leaders of the opposition, "my grandfather Stoddard's grandson, being my mother's sister's son," Joseph Hawley, as "a man of lax principles in religion, falling in, in some essential things, with Arminians," and "very open and bold in it." In Edwards' view, conjoined with the dangers of merely formal church membership there seemed "to be the utmost danger, that the younger generation will be carried away with Arminianism, as with a flood"; and he expressed the fear that under the circumstances the people of Northampton in choosing his successor would "be more likely to be thorough in their care to settle a minister of principles contrary to mine, as to terms of communion, than to settle one that is sound in the doctrines of grace." [8]

In spite of these interruptions Edwards was all the while deeply engaged in study, and no doubt writing in his notebooks, upon the

5. Ibid., p. 251.
6. Ibid., p. 270.
7. Ibid., pp. 405–6.

subject of the freedom of will. "An end is put, for the present, by these troubles," continues this same letter to Erskine, "to the studies I was before engaged in, and my design in writing against Arminianism. I had made considerable preparation and was deeply engaged in the prosecution of this design, before I was rent off from it by these difficulties, and if ever God should give me opportunity, I would again resume the affair. But I am now, as it were, thrown upon the wide ocean of the world, and know not what will become of me, and my numerous and chargeable family." [8]

Edwards moved to Stockbridge in 1751, there to preach to and instruct the Housatonnuck Indians with the assistance of John Wonwanonpequunnonnt, one of their countrymen, as interpreter.[9] There, too, he learned again the wisdom of words written as a young man in his diary on Saturday night, June 6, 1724 (such gloom in youth may perhaps be understood from the fact that this was the week he entered upon the office of tutor at Yale College): "I have now, abundant reason to be convinced, of the troublesomeness and vexation of the world, and that it never will be another kind of world." [1] For the opposition followed him, finding new occasion in the new duties and administrative problems of the Indian mission. There, too, he found his pen could not yet rest from the controversy over the qualifications for communion. The reply to Solomon Williams had to be written. "I had begun to write something against the Arminians, before the late controversy," he wrote on July 1, 1751, to Thomas

---

8. Ibid., p. 410–11. To another minister in Scotland, July 6, 1750: "Arminianism, and Pelagianism, have made a strange progress in a few years." Edwards correctly discerned that this was the principal danger confronting religious life in America in the mid-eighteenth century, following upon the breach made in religious leadership by controversy over the revivals, rather than the triumph of Stoddardism in the matter of church membership of which JE was personally a victim. In his farewell sermon (July 1, 1750, following action of the church council on June 22) JE warned the congregation concerning Arminian tenets, saying that "the progress they have made in the land, within this seven years, seems to have been vastly greater, than at any time in the like space before: and they are still prevailing, and creeping into almost all parts of the land. . . . And if these principles should greatly prevail in this town, as they very lately have done in another large town I could name [Boston], formerly greatly noted for religion, and for so long a time, it will threaten the spiritual and eternal ruin of this people, in the present and future generations" (ibid., pp. 649, 650).

9. Ibid., p. 452.

1. Ibid., p. 103.

Gillespie in Scotland, "and now lately, Mr. Williams has written a book, in answer to mine on that subject; which I think myself obliged to answer, if God give me opportunity." [2]

How quickly Edwards' mind, when given opportunity, returned to the subject he regarded as most important of all may be seen from a letter one year later, July 7, 1752, to Erskine:

> The last week, I sent away my Answer to Mr. Williams. If I live till it is published, I will endeavour to send one to you, and some other friends in Scotland. I hope now, in a short time, to be at leisure to resume my design, of writing something on the Arminian controversy. I have no thought of going through with all parts of the controversy at once; but the subject, which I intended, God willing, first to write something upon, was *Freewill and Moral Agency;* endeavouring, with as much exactness as I am able, to consider the nature of that freedom of moral agents, which makes them the proper subjects of moral government, moral precepts, councils, calls, motives, persuasions, promises and threatenings, praise and blame, rewards and punishments: strictly examining the modern notions of these things, endeavouring to demonstrate their most palpable inconsistency and absurdity; endeavouring also to bring the late great objections and outcries against Calvinistic divinity, from these topics, to the test of the strictest reasoning; and particularly that great objection, in which the modern writers have so much gloried, so long triumphed, with so great a degree of insult towards the most excellent divines, and in effect against the gospel of Jesus Christ:—viz. That the Calvinistic notions of God's moral government are contrary to the common sense of mankind. In this essay, I propose to take particular notice of the writings of Dr. Whitby, and Mr. Chubb, and the writings of some others, who, though not properly Pelagians, nor Arminians, yet, in their notions of the freedom of the will, have, in the main, gone into the same scheme. But, if I live to prosecute my design, I shall send you a more particular account of my plan, after it is perfected.[3]

It is evident that by this time Edwards' argument had taken its full shape in his mind, together with the selection of the writings he meant to refute. This may, indeed, have been the case some years

2. *Ibid.*, p. 468.
3. *Ibid.*, pp. 497–8.

earlier before leaving Northampton, since we know that from the beginning of their correspondence and following the first announcement of his design to write upon this subject Erskine sent him copies of the books of "the more considerable Arminian divines," some of which he had already acquired with this end in view.[4]

In August 1752 Edwards began the actual drafting of the *Inquiry,* only to be interrupted again by a high point of his continuing difficulties at Stockbridge. He explained to Erskine, November 23, 1752: "I began the last August, to write a little on the Arminian controversy, but was soon broke off: and such have been my extraordinary avocations and hindrances, that I have not had time to set pen to paper about this matter since. But I hope that God, in his providence, will favour me with opportunity to prosecute the design." [5]

When next the project is mentioned it is nearing completion. "After many hindrances, delays, and interruptions, Divine Providence has so far favoured me, and smiled on my design of writing on the Arminian controversy," Edwards wrote Erskine, April 14, 1753, "that I have almost finished the first draft of what I first intended; and am now sending the proposals for subscription, to Boston, to be printed." [6] Thus the treatise was ready for publication in 1753, perhaps by the middle of the year. Actual publication was delayed until early in the year 1754, in order to allow time to enlist subscribers in Scotland.[7]

Dwight estimates that in the actual composition of the *Inquiry* Edwards spent only four months and a half, and concerning this he exclaims, "So far as I am aware, no similar example, of power and rapidity united, is to be found on the annals of Mental effort." [8] With no desire to expunge this record from the annals of mental effort, perhaps we should not regard it as such an astonishing accomplishment, recalling that the author had given the subject his strongest, if intermittent, attention for many years prior to 1752–53, and remembering also that he habitually spent more than twelve hours a day in some form of study and that his usual method of study was to formulate and arrange his thoughts upon some problem *by writing*. More-

4. Ibid., pp. 250, 507.

5. Ibid., p. 511.

6. Ibid., p. 533.

7. Ibid., pp. 534, 537. Forty-two of the 298 subscribers to the original edition are listed as residing in Scotland.

8. Ibid., p. 533.

over, Edwards was on the verge of the golden age in the production
of his works. The following years, 1754 and 1755, were probably
spent in the composition of *A Dissertation Concerning the End for
Which God Created the World* and *A Dissertation Concerning the
Nature of True Virtue* (posthumously published),[9] and in 1756 he
began his treatise *The Great Christian Doctrine of Original Sin Defended*,[1] which was published early in 1758, shortly before his death.
These three works, with the *Inquiry*, are not wholly undeserving of
such high praise as "four of the ablest and most valuable works,
which the Church of Christ has in its possession." [2]

Perhaps we should say that the *Inquiry into the Modern Prevailing
Notions of the Freedom of Will* is not the greatest of Edwards' works
but the greatest *of its kind*. For his *Treatise Concerning Religious
Affections* (1746) in defense and criticism of the Revival stands without many peers among writings on the philosophy and psychology of
religion, as does *The Nature of True Virtue* among books on ethics.
And the "Miscellanies" are often described as the greatest of Edwards'
works. All these, and other writings that might be mentioned, have
high merit each in its own kind, and there is not much profit in comparing them with each other in order to find a summit. There is more
grandeur in a range of many summits, and in the scope of the many
kinds of interests and competence that are to be found in the writings
of Jonathan Edwards. Uncompleted at the time of his death, his
system of thought is nevertheless more complete than that of most
other men.

2. *The Theological Issue*

Edwards' argument in this treatise rests upon two pillars: the proof
from biblical revelation and the proof from reason. "Whether these
things are agreeable to Scripture," he writes, "let every Christian, and
every man who has read the Bible, judge: and whether they are agreeable to common sense, let everyone judge, that have human understanding in exercise" (p. 326). He supposes himself herein to have to
do both with "such as own the truth of the Bible" (p. 239) and with
such as exercise human understanding. The contemporary reader
who may be apt to dismiss the authority of the former should give
attention to the fact that the longest chapters in this book deal with

9. Ibid., pp. 542, 544.
1. Ibid., p. 556.
2. Ibid., p. 447.

such subjects as the scriptural evidence for God's certain foreknowledge of the volitions of moral agents, which certain knowledge is
then proved inconsistent with contingency (Pt. II, Secs. 11, 12), and
with showing that the acts of the will of the human soul of Jesus
Christ were necessarily holy, yet were virtuous, praiseworthy, and
rewardable (Pt. III, Sec. 2). Of these passages, the first provides the
capstone to the argument of the first two parts, which up to this point
consist wholly of philosophical clarification and reasoning. Moreover, the philosophical reader will do himself disservice if he imagines that Edwards' reasoned position may be grasped from the early
sections alone. The casual reader may as easily give up where Chubb
is being flayed as where Scripture is quoted; but he that perseveres
to the end will have his reward. Edwards returns again and again to
philosophical analysis.

For Edwards as a theologian the issue is a simple one: either contingency and the liberty of self-determination must be run out of
this world, or God will be shut out. "If there be no absurdity or
difficulty in supposing one thing to start out of nonexistence, into
being, of itself without a cause; then there is no absurdity or difficulty
in supposing the same of millions of millions" (p. 183). Indeed exactly this happens according to the hypothesis Edwards is opposing:
"millions of millions of events are continually coming into existence
contingently, without any cause or reason why they do so, all over the
world, every day and hour, through all ages. So it is in a constant
succession, in every moral agent" (pp. 183–4). When Edwards thinks
of a single action of the human will causing the state of mankind to
be vastly different from what it would otherwise have been for all
succeeding generations, he immediately points out how this volition
itself depended on countless other men's volitions of the same and
preceding generations (pp. 248–50). If these volitions each and all
together start out of nothing into existence, then truly the moral and
historical world is so unordered as to be repugnant both to sound
reason and true divinity. In such a situation, God "must have little
else to do, but to mend broken links as well as he can, and be rectifying his disjointed frame and disordered movements, in the best manner the case will allow. The supreme Lord of all things must needs
be under great and miserable disadvantages, in governing the world
which he has made, and has the care of, through his being utterly
unable to find out things of chief importance, which hereafter may
befall his system; which if he did but know, he might make season-

able provision for" (p. 254). The end of the natural world is the moral world, and in any case the consequences of a single human volition, when traced out, are so immense as to destroy the providence of God if the will determines itself. Therefore Edwards believes "it is indeed as repugnant to reason, to suppose that an act of the will should come into existence without a cause, as to suppose the human soul, or an angel, or the globe of the earth, or the whole universe, should come into existence without a cause" (p. 185).

Liberal theology in the modern period might have gained in firmness and substance if it had stopped to answer Edwards.[3] Indeed, in the present day one wishes that theologians who affirm God's prescience without predetermination would elaborate this view against Edwards' refutation of it—and his reduction of God's certain knowledge to his knowing the certainty inherent in events—in Pt. II, Sec. 12, and many places that follow in this treatise. Until this has been done, it will be suspected of those who adhere to "the supposed rational and generous principles of the modern fashionable divinity" (p. 430), today no less than in 1754, that "their differing from their fathers with such magisterial assurance, in these points in divinity, must be owing to some other cause than superior wisdom" (pp. 437–8).

3. By far the best reply was the first, by James Dana of Wallingford in his *An Examination of the Late Reverend President Edwards's "Enquiry on Freedom of Will"* (Boston, 1770) and *The "Examination of the Late Reverend Edwards's Enquiry on Freedom of Will," Continued* (New Haven, 1773). These works of Dana have the great merit of taking at face value JE's analysis of an act of volition as a matter of motivation and pointing out that this does not yet settle the question what causes this or that motive to be, or appear, strongest (*Examination*, Pt. I, sec. 1, pp. 1–9). He also accepts the Lockean distinction between "volition" and "agent" and contends that the subject or agent determines *himself,* rather than the will (or a property of agents) determining *itself* (*Examination Continued*, p. 148). Thus Dana defended a type of self-determination that was not so easily refuted by JE's reduction of the position to an infinite regress, and he was able to begin a counterattack: JE's "reasoning on self-determination may be well summed up thus: Because a man cannot take the second step without the first; therefore he cannot take the first without a previous one" (*ibid.,* p. 134). After Dana, the opponents of JE more and more had recourse to faculty psychology and a tripartite distinction between understanding, will, and appetite in human nature (F. H. Foster, *A Genetic History of the New England Theology,* University of Chicago Press, 1907, pp. 224–69; despite Foster's approval of the development of theology after JE, it simply restated self-determination in its weakest form).

3. *The Philosophical Argument*

When Edwards applies to those who have "human understanding in exercise," he constructs a reasoned argument upon the subject of free will that deserves much admiration for its tight, logical connection and its vigorous statement. Indeed, from the point of view of the history of ideas, as well as from the perspective of persons who are persuaded that the latest is bound to be the most advanced philosophy, it is striking that two hundred years ago Edwards was saying the same thing that is being said today, with variation and often not so well, by the latest analysts of the determinist school. A brief summary of the agreement between Edwards' opinions and those of many present-day philosophers needs to note at least the following crucial points: (1) Since ordinary language is notoriously inexact, "freedom" and all other terms to be used in this discussion must be carefully defined. Freedom means the ability to do what we will, or according to our pleasure. (2) That men indubitably have such freedom, and only such freedom, can be demonstrated by an exhaustive analysis of an act of volition. In defining freedom and analyzing the nature of an act of volition, questions about what *goes before* an act of willing should not be raised. By *placing brackets around* all such questions and removing them from consideration,[4] we can be sure of sticking close to the actual *experience* of freedom and not be tempted to import into the discussion notions of freedom that are the product of confused metaphysical speculation. (3) Not only is the determination of action by will, motive, or pleasure of the agent consistent with morality, but morality actually requires determinism, since law and commandment, praise and blame apply to the motive or inclination inherent in the willing agent. (4) There can be no event without a cause. (Here, consciously or unconsciously, the brackets are removed and both Edwards and contemporary determinists introduce consideration of events before the act of willing.) There are no grounds for supposing a "pure ego" intervening from without to influence the course of voluntary action. (5) In speaking of causation, however, it is

---

4. In the following exposition, the term "bracketing" is not used in the ordinary sense of "coupling with" but with precisely the opposite meaning of "excluding something from" consideration. This meaning was given the word by the philosopher Husserl, who for the sake of clear and exhaustive analysis of phenomena in human experience "bracketed" scientific and metaphysical questions, i.e. removed them from view.

the *connection* or *correlation* between antecedent and consequent rather than efficient causation that we should have in mind. (6) Moreover, *moral* necessity needs to be distinguished from *natural* necessity, and *determinism* from *compulsion*. Determinism and moral necessity are consistent with praiseworthiness and blameworthiness (indeed, they require it), while compulsion and natural necessity are not.

Now, Jonathan Edwards was not merely a rationalist; Puritanism was also his heritage. He even states that he "should not take it at all amiss, to be called a Calvinist, for distinction's sake: though I utterly disclaim a dependence on Calvin" (p. 131). Therefore, the foregoing summary of the agreement between Edwards and present-day determinists perhaps suggests the question whether after all "the wonderful one-hoss shay, / That was built in such a logical way / It ran a hundred years to the day" ever actually "went to pieces all at once,—/ All at once, and nothing first,—/ Just as bubbles do when they burst." Does not a wheel or a splinter off the Deacon's Masterpiece continue on among philosophical determinists today? One may raise this question without forgetting their heritage from Spinoza, Hobbes, and Hume, and without ignoring the original repair work Edwards did on the "shay." Then the question is: Is there a hidden defect somewhere, or is there about the whole of it still "a general flavor of mild decay, / But nothing local, as one might say," or is this the "truth" that "keeps its youth"? [5] Nowhere better than by an examination of Edwards can one find this out. It is still true, as Tappan wrote more than a hundred years ago, "There is no work of higher authority among those who deny the self-determining power of the will; and none which on this subject has called forth more general admiration for acuteness of thought and logical subtlety. I believe there is a prevailing impression that Edwards must be fairly met in order to make any advance in an opposite argument." [6]

DEFINITION OF LIBERTY

". . . there is a vast indistinctness and unfixedness," writes Edwards, "in most, or at least very many of the terms used to express things pertaining to moral and spiritual matters" (p. 316). Especially is this true when men speak of volition and moral ability; and a large part of Edwards' treatise is given over to a definition of terms, whether

5. Oliver Wendell Holmes, "The Deacon's Masterpiece."
6. Henry Philip Tappan, *A Review of Edwards's "Inquiry into the Freedom of the Will"* (New York, 1839), p. xi.

by trying to find out the proper meaning in experience of a word as it is commonly used or by inventing "terms of art," i.e. technical terms improving "the benefit of language, in the proper use and design of names" (p. 130). The terms "moral necessity" and "philosophical necessity" are given meaning by Edwards as "terms of art," while "freedom" has the meaning he finds it to have in ordinary language.

Freedom of the will pertains to those acts of volition in which a man is "free from hindrance or impediment in the way of doing, or conducting in any respect, as he wills" (p. 163). Such

> power and opportunity for one to do and conduct as he will, or according to his choice, is all that is meant by it; without taking into the meaning of the word, anything of the cause or original of that choice; or at all considering how the person came to have such a volition; whether it was caused by some external motive, or internal habitual bias; whether it was determined by some internal antecedent volition, or whether it happened without a cause; whether it was necessarily connected with something foregoing, or not connected. Let the person come by his volition or choice how he will, yet, if he is able, and there is nothing in the way to hinder his pursuing and executing his will, the man is fully and perfectly free, according to the primary and common notion of freedom [p. 164].

In other words, a man is free to do what he wills, but not to do what he does not will.

This definition of liberty as the freedom to do what we will was imbedded in Aristotle's distinction between voluntary and involuntary acts. Calvin also thought of it, but refused "to decorate a thing so diminutive with a title so superb," and so threatening to divine sovereignty, as "freedom." [7] Edwards' understanding of freedom is similar to Spinoza's, and to Hobbes', who wrote of Bishop Bramhall in their controversy on the subject of free will that anyone who "cannot understand the difference between *free to do if he will,* and free *to will,* is not fit . . . to hear this controversy disputed, much less to be a writer in it." [8] In his *Inquiry* Edwards says that "it hap-

7. John Calvin, *The Institutes of the Christian Religion*, Bk. II, ch. 2, sec. 7; trans. John Allen (2 vols. Philadelphia, Presbyterian Board of Christian Education, 1936), *1*, 287.

8. *The English Works of Thomas Hobbes*, ed. Sir William Molesworth (11 vols. London, 1839), *5*, 51.

pens I never read Mr. Hobbes" (p. 374). This may not be quite true, since he refers to Hobbes in the "Notes on Natural Science" written while at Yale.[9] What, if much at all, he read of Hobbes we do not know, and whether his mind was much affected by "Hobbistical" views may be questioned. Unlike Locke's works, Hobbes' were certainly not textbooks at Yale; therefore his observation about never reading Hobbes may be substantially correct. There is greater parallelism, perhaps, between Edwards and David Hume, who, like Edwards, endeavors to show that according to any reasonable sense of the terms "liberty" and "necessity," "all mankind have ever agreed in the doctrine of liberty as well as in that of necessity, and that the whole dispute, in this respect also, has been hitherto merely verbal." Hume also defines liberty as "a power of acting or not acting, according to the determination of the will." [10] In this and other respects in the development of modern ideas, Edwards is to Locke as Hume is to Locke. Since there is no evidence that Edwards read Hume before writing the *Inquiry*,[1] their thoughts on freedom and necessity were

9. Dwight, *Life,* in Dwight ed., *1,* 724. Faust and Johnson, p. lxxii, err in referring to this as from "The Mind."

10. "Of Liberty and Necessity," *An Enquiry Concerning Human Understanding* (1748), Sec. VIII, pt. 1.

1. At a later date, Dec. 11, 1755, JE wrote to Erskine: "I had before read that book of Essays, having borrowed Mr. Bellamy's, and also that book of Mr. David Hume's, which you speak of. I am glad of an opportunity to read such corrupt books, especially when written by men of considerable genius; that I may have an idea of the notions that prevail in our nation" (Dwight ed., *1,* 550; Dwight also states, without giving the date or his source for this information, that Hume "appears to have read several of the works of Edwards," p. 543). This indeterminate reference to a time "before" December 1755 when he read Hume itself permits one to conclude that JE *may* have read Hume as early as the period in which he was composing the *Inquiry*. If it was only afterward that he actually did so, we know that the occasion of his immediate interest in Hume was his reading of Lord Kames' *Essays* (see below, Related Correspondence). In JE's MS "Catalogue of Books," p. 37, there are two entries which may be dated late in 1754 or early in 1755 because they have between them an entry taken from the Boston *Gazette* of Nov. 12, 1754, and because the last entry on page 37 is from the same paper on April 28, 1755; these entries mention Kames' use of Hume: (1) "Treatise of human nature: The Author of the Essays on the Principles of Morality and Natural Religion, p. 103, speaking of this Treatise of Human Nature says 'The Figure which this Author deservedly makes in the Learned world is too considerate to admit his being past over in silence.'" (2) "The same Author in the same Book of Essays, p. 222, says of this Book, 'I have an high opinion of the Authors acuteness and Penetration.' . . . The Author of

original, separate achievements, like the metaphysical idealism of
Edwards and Bishop Berkeley on which there has been so much comment.

Edwards plainly admits, even contends, that whether a man is determined in his choice by some prior cause or by no cause at all does
not enter into the definition or the experience of freedom. If a person is able to do what he wills or chooses, he is free, no matter how
he came to make this choice. In his "Remarks on the *Essays on the
Principles of Morality and Natural Religion,* in a Letter to a Minister of the Church of Scotland," [2] Edwards in 1757 repeated his
definition of freedom (this time in terms of pleasure) and again he
brackets from view, and removes from discussion, questions about
the causes preceding the free act of volition itself: "Liberty," he
writes, "is the power, opportunity, or advantage, that anyone has to
do as he pleases, or conducting in any respect, according to his pleasure; without considering how his pleasure comes to be as it is."
Choosing as one pleases he also understands "without determining
how he came by that pleasure."

Perhaps it should be observed that any philosopher holds *some*
view of what goes before volition. Some will rely very much upon

---

the Essays last [mentioned] mentions & quotes another Book of the author of
the Treatise of Human Nature, called 'Philosophical Essays concerning Human
Understanding' pp. 283 and 353." Again, however, it is not impossible that JE
knew Kames' *Essays* (and so had renewed interest in Hume) at an earlier date
than these entries, and earlier than his correspondence with Erskine concerning
them. JE wrote Erskine in his "Remarks on Lord Kames' *Essays"* that the "intimations" Erskine had given JE concerning the controversy in Scotland and the
use being made of the *Inquiry* to support Kames' position "has occasioned my
reading this Author's *Essays* on that subject with particular care and attention."
This may mean his first reading or a second, careful reading. The question of
JE's knowledge of Hume before or while writing the *Inquiry* turns on the interpretation to be given of an earlier entry in his "Catalogue of Books," p. 22: "A
Treatise of Human Nature being an attempt to introduce the experimental
method of Reasoning into moral subjects, wherein the nature of the understanding & passions is examined & explained in 2 vols. Octavo . . ." There is
some reason to believe that this entry was made sometime between 1750 and
1752, but this and the other entries may mean only that JE was interested in
getting hold of this highly commended author. He probably read Hume as late
as 1755, or nearly two years after finishing the *Inquiry*. (I am indebted to Thomas
Schafer, of Duke University, for the substance of this note, and for the text of
several subsequent citations from the "Miscellanies.")

2. See below, Related Correspondence.

the structures of reality (the *logos*) as determinative in every case of rational volition, others upon the moving continuum of moral incentives and motives for the controlling influence in volition, both distinguishable from natural necessity or compulsion. By designating the meaning of freedom and then analyzing an act of volition, Edwards merely places in brackets—he does not set entirely aside— his belief in divine determination, or what causes the strength of motives, or his confidence that all events, even moral events, have their causes. His definition of liberty and his account of voluntary action have the clarity and force of a phenomenological analysis. This analysis may be consistent with various metaphysical views, such as determinism or indeterminism, which were bracketed.

THE ACT OF VOLITION

Edwards sets the same limits around accounts of the nature of voluntary action. "If a man does something voluntarily, or as the effect of his choice, then in the most proper sense, and as the word is most originally and commonly used, he is said to act: but whether that choice or volition be self-determined, or no, whether it be connected with foregoing habitual bias, whether it be the certain effect of the strongest motive, or some extrinsic cause, never comes into consideration in the meaning of the word" (p. 347). This is the focus of Edwards' picture of the exertion of an act of will. He seeks to catch the agent in the very act of willing or choosing, and to give an accurate report of what goes on in the soul or mind in the state of willing and at the time of willing or in the state of freedom at the time of freedom (pp. 206–7), without consideration of what went before or comes after.

With this alone in view, Edwards observes that "in every act, or going forth of the will, there is some preponderation of the mind or inclination, one way rather than another; and the soul had rather have or do one thing than another, or than not to have or do that thing" (p. 140). To suppose that indifference to any degree cuts down the preponderance of inclination means only that the mind is not yet choosing or we have not yet focused our attention upon what happens when it actually gets to the point of making a choice. It is absurd "to suppose the will, at present, to be otherwise than, at present, it is" (p. 161). "Present choice can't at present choose to be otherwise: for that would be *at present* to choose something diverse from what is *at present* chosen" (p. 305). If inclination cannot at present change itself, this is only because, being what it is, it àt present cannot incline to change itself. " 'Tis absurd to suppose that a man should directly, properly and sincerely incline to have an inclination, which at the same time is contrary to his inclination: for that is to suppose him not to be inclined to that which he is inclined to" (p. 312). There may be contradiction among our "weak, dull and lifeless wouldings," [3] which do not yet begin to raise us much above a state of indifference; but there can be no contradiction among inclinations when the soul gets to the point of actually inclining one way. It may be that the mind is torn between competing motives until it comes to a decision, but the least interval of time that separates such a state of indecision from an act of choice is of no more importance for what happens in the choosing than if the mind had ceased to be subject to competing motives twenty years before the volition began. It may be "the mind is indifferent until it comes to be not indifferent" (p. 196), but the least interval of time that separates the state of indifference from an act of choice is of no more importance for what happens in choosing than if the mind had ceased to be indifferent twenty years before the action began. Indifference "can't reach the action," or the volition (p. 207). Even the very beginning of choice, the least preponderance of inclination one way, is not a state of indifference (p. 207). The soul cannot choose without choice or prefer without preference. "The mind is not indifferent when it determines itself, but *had rather* do one thing than another, had rather determine itself one way than another" (p. 197).

This leads Edwards to say that the will always *is* as the greatest apparent good *is* (pp. 144, 217), or *is* as the last dictate of the understanding *is* (p. 222), or *is* what the strongest motive *is*. He does not say that the will is *determined* by the greatest apparent good, by the last dictate of the understanding, or by the strongest motive, except in occasional lapses in manner of expression which may manifest on Edwards' part, or mislead him to, a belief that more could be proved by this analysis of voluntary action than can actually be proved by it. "I have rather chosen," he writes, "to express myself thus, that the will always *is* as the greatest apparent good, or as what appears most agreeable, is, than to say that the will is *determined* by the greatest apparent good, or by what seems most agreeable; because an appearing most agreeable or pleasing to the mind, and the mind's preferring or choosing, seem hardly to be properly and perfectly

3. *Treatise Concerning Religious Affections* (1746), in Worcester ed., *4*, 16.

distinct" (p. 144). He agrees with Clarke that the last dictate of the understanding is not at all diverse from the act of the determination of the will itself, that willing is not *connected* with (or caused by) that dictate, but *is* as the last judgment of the understanding *is* (p. 222). When he speaks of the "strongest motive," he does not mean the strongest among still competing motives, but he writes, "I have respect to the strength of the whole that operates to induce to a particular act of volition, whether that be the strength of one thing alone, or of many together" (p. 141). Present will *is* as the present preponderant inclination or motive *is*. "And indeed it comes to just the same thing: to say, the circumstances of the mind are such as tend to sway and turn its inclination one way, is the same thing as to say, the inclination of the mind, as under such circumstances, tends that way" (p. 328). Not quite the same, we may note, if the former manner of expression leads the reader to assume that the will or mind is inclined by the sway or determination of something that is not within the agent's present act.

The word "determined" may properly be used only to designate the connection between the internal act of choice and some concomitant or following external action, or to indicate the connection between some preceding state of affairs and present inclination, apparent good, or last dictate (i.e. choice). What appears most agreeable does not *determine* choice; it determines the external voluntary action following as a consequence of choice (p. 144). But this is the same as saying that *choice* determines the external action, since the choice that comes before action *is* as what appears most agreeable *is*. Inclination or motive do not determine the will; they determine the action consequent upon an act of willing. But this is the same as saying that the will determines the action, since the act of willing *is* as preponderant inclination *is*.

Edwards also uses the word "determined" when speaking of the connection that links present volition with *prior* conditions. While the act of choice *is* as what appears most agreeable or pleasing to the mind, an act of choice is *determined* by whatever in or about the object viewed or in or about the mind's view causes something to be agreeable. He mentions briefly the kinds of things which would explain what causes something to seem agreeable (or what causes the strength of motives): "not only what appears in the object viewed, but also the manner of the view, and the state and circumstances of the mind that views" (p. 144). By the "state" of the mind that views, he takes into account how character and personality influence what one finds agreeable. However, this sort of speculation about the determination of the strength of motives is of quite subordinate concern to the author when first introduced. He writes: "Whether I have been so happy as rightly to explain the thing wherein consists the strength of motives, or not, yet my failing in this will not overthrow the position itself; which carries much of its own evidence with it, and is the thing of chief importance to the purpose of the ensuing discourse" (p. 148). The position itself, which carries much of its own evidence with it, is "that the will is always determined by the strongest motive, or by that view of the mind which has the greatest degree of previous tendency to excite volition" (p. 148). Surely here is a lapse in language. What is self-evident is that a man wills those actions which appear most agreeable to him, or that he wills what his heart inclines to. This much, and this alone, can be established by analyzing the nature of an act of volition. His will *is* his strongest motive or inclination, but—to go beyond phenomenological analysis —this in turn may be assumed to be determined by whatever (in or about himself or the object in view) causes the strength of motives.[4]

Or we may say that the willing is determined by whatever explains the successive changes in the mind's ideas, by which succession alone the mind is sensible to any movement in time. "That which happens

---

4. James Dana quite clearly saw the point at issue here: "If, therefore, it was of any importance to show . . . what determines the will, and to prove that the strongest motive doth it; it was at least of equal importance to point out, what it is that causeth such motive to be, or appear, strongest" (*Examination,* pp. 4–5). "To speak of the *preponderation and prevalency* of motive implies that the mind is already determined; that its choice is made. And hence a preponderating, prevalent motive is not the determiner of the mind's election. The cause of this is still to be sought somewhere else" (*Examination Continued,* p. 31 n.). JE in fact grants Dana's point, that it has still to be shown what determines the strength of motives, but this was for him a minor point in comparison with showing that nowhere among motives is there the slightest room for self-determination strengthening one motive against another. He supposed that once self-rule was excluded, Christian theologians would not be in doubt as to who was the Ruler of the moral and historical, no less than the natural, world. More clearly than JE or Dana, Stephen West in his defense of JE endeavored to remove any remaining ambiguity due to the use of the words "cause" or "determine" when speaking of motives. The word "motive" (he wrote; see Dana, *Examination Continued,* p. 145) "importeth nothing different from the real choice of the mind. . . . When motive is considered as *cause* or *antecedent,* its *correlative* is *outward action.*"

in the unsearchable course of things, to which the mind yields itself, and by which it is guided, is not anything that comes to pass without a cause; and the mind in determining to be guided by it, is not determined by something that has no cause. . . . The involuntary changes in the succession of our ideas, though the cause may not be observed, have as much a cause, as the changeable motions of the moats that float in the air, or the continual, infinitely various, successive changes of the unevennesses on the surface of the water" (p. 200). In the foregoing statement the brackets are removed, and Edwards wraps the unsearchable in a hypothesis that as such does not arise from an exhaustive inspection of the nature of voluntary action.

Giving attention only to the moment of present volition, and without raising questions about the genesis of this choice or about possible impediments to its consequent action, "not only is it true, that it is easy for a man to do the thing if he will but the very willing is the doing; when once he has willed, the thing is performed; and nothing else remains to be done. Therefore, in these things to ascribe a nonperformance to the want of power or ability, is not just; because the thing wanting is not a being *able,* but a being *willing*" (p. 161). There is no way for the will to determine an act than by willing and choosing it (p. 190). Obviously a man has the power to will as he does will. What he wills, he wills (p. 193). In this sense a man may choose as he pleases.

PRAISEWORTHINESS AND BLAMEWORTHINESS

In the second and third parts of the *Inquiry* Edwards answers the objection that praise for the goodness and blame for the badness of an action are appropriate only if the will be free with a freedom of indifference. The "sum total" of such ethical judgments, he says, is the assertion of "a person's having his heart wrong, and doing wrong from his heart" (p. 357) or doing right from his heart. "The common people don't ascend up" any further in gathering in their notion of praise or blameworthiness (p. 357). Of course, they "do suppose it is the person's *own act.*" But all that belongs to this is that it be "something done by him of choice" (p. 358). They "do suppose that the man does it in the exercise of *liberty.* But then their notion of liberty is only a person's having opportunity of doing as he pleases. They have no notion of liberty consisting in the will's first acting, and so causing its own acts." In fact, "such a notion of liberty is what none have, but those that have darkened their own minds" (pp. 358–9).

If this be the proper meaning of the terms in ordinary language, Edwards' understanding of free volition is wholly consistent with moral praise or blame. A person may be praised or blamed insofar as he had voluntary *engagedness* in the action. "When a thing is *from* a man, in that sense, that it is from his will or choice, he is to blame for it, because his will is *in it:* so far as the will is *in it,* blame is *in it,* and no further" (p. 427). Edwards gives an even stronger statement of the meaning of moral engagement and responsibility when he writes that actions are subject to ethical judgment "not so properly because they are *from* us, as because we are *in them,* i.e. our wills are in them; not so much because they are from some *property* of ours, as because they are our *properties*" (p. 428). "The *soul* of virtue and vice" is "a certain beauty or deformity that are *inherent* in that good or evil will" (p. 340). This is the meaning Edwards finds in such ambiguous phrases as "being the cause," "being the author," "having a hand" in responsible action, that a person be the *doer* of the deed and "the immediate agent, or the being that *is acting, or in exercise* of that act" (pp. 342, 399). Morality means our willing love of virtue and for this we are properly to be praised, and not because "by some method or other" we "wrought ourselves into the love of it" (p. 340).

The viewpoint Edwards is opposing means, by contrast, that the more the soul has "disengagedness in its actings, the more liberty" (p. 272): the more liberty the more disengagedness, and if perfect liberty, then complete disengagement and no responsibility. Unless man wills according to the dictates of reason, the agreeableness of the good to him, and from his own disposition and character, it is not choice that determines his act; "it is therefore a contingence, that happens to the man, arising from nothing in him; and is necessary, as to any inclination or choice of his; and therefore can't make him either the better or worse, any more than a tree is better than other trees, because it oftener happens to be lit upon by a swan or nightingale; or a rock more vicious than other rocks, because rattlesnakes have happened oftener to crawl over it" (pp. 326–7). He would be liable "to act altogether at random, without the least connection with, or restraint or government by, any dictate of reason. . . . as destitute of perception as the smoke that is driven by the wind!" (pp. 272–3). Ethical judgment upon human behavior would then become perfectly meaningless. "For how was man to blame for perfect accident, which had no cause, and which therefore, he (to be sure) was not the cause of . . . ?" (p. 414).

Edwards supports this point of view by an appeal to the common opinion which correlates the higher praise and more vigorous condemnation with the stronger inclination to virtue or vice. Affirming that "endeavors can have no more goodness in 'em, than the will which they are the effect and expression of" (p. 315), he concludes that "the stronger the inclination, and so the further from indifference, the more virtuous the *heart,* and so the more praiseworthy the *act* which proceeds from it" (p. 320). The "universal sense of mankind" is that there is sincerity of virtue only in "actions which proceed from a heart *well disposed* and *inclined,*" and greater virtue "the *stronger,* and the more *fixed* and *determined* the good disposition of the heart." Actions that spring from perfect indifference and coldness of heart, if there were any such, would "have no sincere goodness in 'em, having no virtue of heart in 'em" (p. 321). Indeed, in regard to certain "flagitious horrid iniquities" "the being indifferent, for a moment, would be highly vicious and vile" (p. 322). "For the mind to be in a state of indifference with respect to 'em, is to be next door to doing them . . . for equilibrium is the next step to a degree of preponderation; and one, even the least degree of preponderation (all things considered) is choice." From indifference one would "be full as likely to choose 'em as to refuse 'em, to do 'em as to omit 'em" (p. 322).

According to the Arminian notion of freedom of indifference there can be "no such thing as any virtuous or vicious *quality of mind*" (p. 325). Either this notion of freedom must be run out of the world, or else virtue and vice will be wholly excluded from it. For the strength of a man's good or evil inclinations, wherein consist his moral goodness or wickedness, must, according to Arminian self-determination, be actually inconsistent with goodness or wickedness (p. 310).

Finally, unless there is some cause connected with the motives of men, there would be no utility in means for influencing their behavior. "For the end of laws is to *bind to one side;* and the end of commands is to turn the will one way: and therefore they are of no use unless they turn or bias the will that way" (p. 304). If indeterminism were true, it would be "in vain to set before them the wisdom and amiableness of ways of virtue, or the odiousness and folly of ways of vice" (p. 331). These things are represented to the understanding in order to determine choice. Considerations such as these lead Bertrand Russell to say, "While, therefore, as a philosopher I hold the principle of universal causation to be open to question, as a commonsense individual I hold it to be an indispensable postulate in the conduct of affairs. For practical purposes we must assume that our volitions have causes, and our ethics must be compatible with this assumption. Praise and blame, reward and punishment, and the whole apparatus of the criminal law, are rational on the deterministic hypothesis, but not on the hypothesis of free will." [5]

IS THE WILL INDEPENDENT AND SELF-MOVED?

Up to this point the present summary of Edwards' position in the *Inquiry* has been informed by my belief that it is misleading to suggest that the presupposition of its argument is that all events, including moral events, have their causes and occur by some sort of necessity.[6] No doubt this was Edwards' opinion, from which he never

5. *Human Society in Ethics and Politics* (New York, Simon and Schuster, 1955), p. 79. Cf. Austin E. Duncan-Jones: "If the particular decision that I make, within a certain range, is not determined, then my previous life might have had the precise character that it actually had and I might none the less have made a different decision: I am therefore not responsible for having made this precise decision. And so on. *A fortiori*, unrestricted indifference is inconsistent with responsibility. We therefore have a simple constructive dilemma. If determinism is true, people are not responsible, and if the liberty of indifference is true, people are not responsible; but either determinism or the liberty of indifference is true; therefore people are not responsible." "Freedom: an Illustrative Puzzle," *Proceedings of the Aristotelian Society*, new ser. *39* (1938–39), 108. See also Pt. VII, "Moral Freedom, Guilt, and Responsibility," of *Readings in Ethical Theory*, ed. Wilfred Sellars and John Hospers (New York, Appleton-Century-Crofts, 1952); C. D. Broad's inaugural lecture, *Determinism, Indeterminism, and Libertarianism* (Cambridge, Cambridge University Press, 1934); Gilbert Ryle's chapter "It Was to Be" in *Dilemmas* (Cambridge University Press, 1954); and the article by the University of California Associates on "The Freedom of the Will" in *Readings in Philosophical Analysis*, ed. Herbert Feigl and Wilfred Sellars (New York, Appleton-Century-Crofts, 1949), pp. 594–8—all provide interesting parallel reading to JE and make evident the fact that contemporary philosophers have not succeeded in going much beyond him. In defense of a sort of freedom JE might have opposed, the reader may want to consult C. Arthur Campbell's inaugural lecture *In Defense of Free Will* (Glasgow, Jackson, Son and Co., 1938) and his *Criticism and Construction* (London, George Allen and Unwin, 1931); Nicolai Hartmann, *Ethics* (London, George Allen and Unwin, 1932), Vol. *3;* E. F. Carritt, *Ethical and Political Thinking* (Oxford, Clarendon Press, 1947); H. D. Lewis, *Morals and Revelation* (London, George Allen and Unwin, 1951); and that most remarkable metaphysics of the will, Austin Farrer's *Finite and Infinite* (Westminster, England, Dacre Press; Glasgow, University Press, 1943).

6. Faust and Johnson, p. xliv.

wavered. He writes that the causal principle "seems to be the first dictate of the common and natural sense God hath implanted in the minds of all mankind" (p. 181). But this was not and ought not to have been a primary postulate introduced at the beginning or in the course of the argument, since this is precisely what Edwards sets out to prove. He has to demonstrate that the principle of universal *causation,* or, if this be granted and a distinction made, universal *necessary* causation, applies to acts of the will. The pillars upon which his thought is erected in this treatise are his definition of liberty, his analysis of the nature of an act of volition, and (consistent with these) his interpretation of an agent's responsibility for an act when his will is *in it*. He correctly reasons that "if volition comes to pass by perfect contingence, and without any cause at all, then it is certain, no act of the will, no prior act of the soul was the cause, no determination or choice of the soul, had any hand in it" (p. 271). This may all be granted while still keeping in brackets questions about what causes the soul's own determinations.

Moreover, Edwards succeeds in refuting self-determinism if this means that in a *preceding* action the soul determines to determine or chooses to choose. The Arminian cannot escape by contending that self-determinism involves no preceding *act,* since the only way to determine to choose is by *acting* voluntarily. But what if the *act* of self-determination is no *preceding* act but rather one which takes place *in the willing* itself? This possibility Edwards mentions in framing certain possible replies to his own argument: "If it should be said, that although it be true, if the soul determines its own volitions, it must be active in so doing, and the determination itself must be an act; yet there is no need of supposing this act to be prior to the volition determined; but the will or soul determines the act of the will *in willing;* it determines its own volition, *in* the very act of volition; it directs and limits the act of the will, causing it to be so and not otherwise, *in* exerting the act, without any preceding act to excite that." Of three possible interpretations of the meaning of this objection, the second has some merit: "that the soul's determining the act of volition is the same thing with its exerting the act of volition" (p. 177). Obviously such a viewpoint approaches Edwards' own, so long as he sticks to analyzing the nature of free volition and moral responsibility; and it is therefore not surprising that his answer to this suggestion seems singularly weak (pp. 177–8; the possibility is significantly omitted from a later rapid summary of this same list of objections, p. 191). Edwards simply *demands* that the self-determinist not speak in this way. In describing the soul's being conversant about its own inner action, he must continue to make the same separation between volition and action as when speaking of the soul's being conversant about an external action. This will set him off on a path of *preceding* internal acts that will soon lead him out of this world; but if the self-determinist agrees to this, he will be doing at Edwards' insistence what elsewhere in abundance Edwards accuses him of doing, namely using of the soul's volitions language suitable only for discourse about external actions.

Thus we owe to Edwards himself the suggestion of a type of self-determinism which may be able to withstand the onslaught of his own attack; and which he was better able to formulate as an objection than his opponents were able to advance as a contention. In any case, so far as moral and volitional experience are concerned, and on Edwards' own penetration of these matters so long as he does not allow concepts not directly involved in them to intrude, there may be self-determination *in the willing*. Then one need not suppose action to be without the causation of the will or without the determination of the agent, or suppose that action results from the will being lit upon by swans and nightingales or crawled over by rattlesnakes. Nor need one suppose volition to be caused by involuntary changes in the succession of our ideas, which in turn have as much a cause (and our yielding to them as much a cause) as the changeable motes that float in the air, or the continual, infinitely various, successive changes of the unevennesses on the surface of the water.

In any case there is nothing in Edwards' account of an act of free, responsible volition which precludes it from being independent and self-moved. This may be inferred from what Edwards says elsewhere about God's volition. "If there be any such thing at all, as what we mean by *acts of will* in God; then he is not indifferent whether his will be fulfilled or not. And if he is not indifferent, then he is truly gratified and pleased," or has pleasure in it.[7] If there be an end for which God created the world, in that voluntary action God took real delight. In like manner with men's acts of will, "we must suppose that God before he created the world, had some good in view, as a consequence of the world's existence that was originally agreeable to him in itself considered, that inclined him to create the world, or

7. *Dissertation Concerning the End for Which God Created the World,* Ch. 1, sec. 4, *ans.* 2 to *obj.* 1; in Worcester ed., *6, 47.*

bring the universe, with various intelligent creatures into existence
in such a manner as he created it." [8] We may justly infer what God
intended, or was inclined to, by what he actually does.[9] In other
words, in speaking of God's will Edwards employs the principle of
analogy which has its point of departure in what we know of human
volition. This principle he plainly states in *The Nature of True
Virtue.* "This is the only way," he says, "that we come to be capable
of having ideas of any perception or act even of the Godhead. We
never could have any notion what understanding or volition, love
or hatred are, either in created spirits or in God, if we had never
experienced what understanding and volition, love and hatred, are
in our own minds. Knowing what they are by consciousness, we can
add degrees, and deny limits, and remove changeableness and other
imperfections, and ascribe them to God. Which is the only way we
come to be capable of conceiving of any thing in the Deity." [1] Yet in
the *Dissertation Concerning the End for Which God Created the
World* he writes:

> There is something in that disposition in God to communicate
> goodness, which shows him to be *independent and self-moved* in
> it, in a manner that is peculiar, and above what is in the benef-
> icence of creatures. Creatures, even the most gracious of them,
> are not so independent and self-moved in their goodness, but that
> in all the exercises of it, they are excited by some object that they
> find; something appearing good, or in some respect worthy of re-
> gard, presents itself, and moves their kindness. But God, being all
> and alone, is *absolutely self-moved.* The exercises of his com-
> municative disposition are absolutely *from within himself,* not
> finding any thing, or any object to excite them or draw them forth;
> but all that is good and worthy in the object, and the very *being*
> of the object, proceeding from the overflowing of his fullness.[2]

It is obvious that Edwards (in saying that God in his volitional action
is independent and self-moved yet motivated and inclined by what
pleases him, while man chooses what pleases him yet is not self-

8. Ibid., Intro.; *6,* 16.
9. Ibid., Ch. 1, sec. 1, no. 6; *6,* 28.
1. *The Nature of True Virtue,* ch. 5; in Worcester, ed., *2,* 440.
2. Ch. 1, sec. 4, *obj.* 4, no. 2 (final italics JE's); in Worcester ed., *6,* 59–60.
See below, Pt. 5, no. 18, of this Introduction, for JE's notion of God's "arbitrary"
action.

moved) simply adds degrees and denies limits, and removes change-ableness and other imperfections. Otherwise, what might be said of the divine will would be univocal with the account of human volition. On the other hand, statements about divine and human volition would be equivocal, and we would be able to say nothing at all about acts of will in God, if Edwards went so far as to deny that these acts, no less than human volitions, are a matter of preponderant in-clination or pleased-ness. So much we know from the analysis of an act of choice, and may ascribe to God from the experience of choice in our own minds. Edwards' belief that self-determinists are wrong in ascribing self-motion to man arises, then, not from any description of willing in itself or as it is *within* the agent *himself,* but from a justifi-able fear that "they who thus plead for man's liberty, advance princi-ples which destroy the freedom of God himself." [3] For Edwards there is only one "causal progenitor" in the history of the world; all other beings and events have "causal ancestors." [4]

THE ORIGIN OF ARMINIAN NOTIONS OF LIBERTY AND
NECESSITY, AND THE SHAPE OF EDWARDS' REPLY

In an act of willing, the soul, according to Edwards, is conversant not with some remote object or goal, but with the immediate action to be done. Still this is an *external* action, and the volition from which it arises is an inward matter. The language of ethical discourse has been formed to refer to this situation, and as a consequence the words we use and the characteristic statements we make express two assump-tions that are correct only in cases of the production of external con-duct. (1) There is a distinction properly made between the willing subject and the act performed, and we speak correctly of a causal connection between these two different things when we say that the self determines its action. The volition is different from the effect it produces. This shapes what we ordinarily mean by "agency" and "liberty" (including Edwards' definition). (2) There is a supposable opposition between endeavors of the volition and impediments to action in the external world. This shapes what we ordinarily mean by "ability" and "inability," or "necessity."

A fatal mistake is made when self-determinists begin to speak of

3. "Miscellaneous Observations Concerning the Divine Decrees in General, and Election in Particular," No. 21; in Worcester ed., 5, 369.

4. Cf. Broad's inaugural lecture *Determinism, Indeterminism, and Libertari-anism,* p. 35.

the soul's being conversant about its own inner volition. Using language first formed by man's experience in determining overt action, they fail to make the needed alteration in meaning when this is used to characterize his inner world.

> First, these terms "action" and "necessity" are changed from their original meaning, as signifying external voluntary actions, and constraint . . . to signify quite other things, viz. volition itself, and certainty of existence. And when the change of significance is made, care is not taken to make proper allowances and abatements for the difference of sense; but still the same things are unwarily attributed to "action" and "necessity," in the new meaning of the words, which plainly belonged to 'em in their first sense; and on this ground, maxims are established without any real foundation, as though they were the most certain truths, and the most evident dictates of reason [p. 389].

As regards volition itself, the abatement that needs to be made is in recognition of the fact that in the act of willing itself there is no distinction to be made between the original volition and the effect it produces. There is only one thing that happens in the will: an act of willing inwardly performed. The self-determinists Edwards opposed did not make this allowance. They spoke of a self determining itself as if the acting self were prior to the self acted upon. They spoke of an act of the will prior to the willing, choosing to produce its own choice. The Arminians, we may say, emphasized the hyphen in the expression "self-determination," thus splitting the indivisible volition into an act prior to the act on one side of the hyphen and the consequent willingness on the other.[5] Of course, there may be a

5. JE does not, in the *Inquiry,* follow out the suggestion of his youthful notes entitled "The Mind," where, analyzing the nature of *human* consciousness in contrast to animal inclination in terms of self-relatedness, he himself places the hyphen within the self or within the mind:

[16.] CONSCIOUSNESS is the mind's perceiving what is in itself,—ideas, actions, passions, and every thing that is perceptible. It is a sort of feeling within itself . . .

[59.] . . . The main difference between Men and Beasts is, that Men are capable of reflecting upon what passes in their own minds. Beasts have nothing but direct consciousness. Men are capable of viewing what is in themselves, contemplatively.

A very great difference between Men and Beasts is, that Beasts have no voluntary actions about their own thoughts. . . . It is the act of the Will, in bringing its ideas into Contemplation, and ranging and comparing of

present volitional endeavor to influence *future* volitions (p. 161), and in this case a distinction may be drawn between a volition and the later volition it is conversant with. But in the case of present volition no such thing may be supposed: the will wills what it wills and cannot *now* incline to will or choose otherwise. We have seen that Edwards' answer to another sort of self-determinism—which comes close to his own position by affirming that the soul's determining the act and its exerting the act of volition are the same thing—is simply to demand that the hyphen be restored to its place of proper importance.

Edwards' refutation of the cruder type of self-determination takes the form of a *reductio ad absurdum*. This means that the form of his reply is shaped by the same misuse of language that accounts for Arminian errors. He adopts their manner of speaking, importing into the inner world of volition language first formed by the experience of voluntary, external, bodily action, in order to show what absurdities this comes to. Let volition once split apart upon the hyphen into will*er* and will*ed,* and this must be supposed to happen in an infinite series of preceding acts of volition until free volition is run out of this world, or else we come to rest in a first act of the will which was not free in this notion of freedom. The high point of Edwards' ridicule is perhaps found in the celebrated passage about the traveler from Tierra del Fuego who reported seeing there an animal (free will) "that begat and brought forth itself, and yet had a sire and a dam distinct from itself; that it had an appetite, and was hungry before it had being; that his master, who led him, and governed him at his pleasure, was always governed by him, and driven by him as he pleased; that when he moved, he always took a step before the first step; that he went with his head first, yet always went tail foremost; and this, though he had neither head nor tail" (p. 346).

---

them in Reflexion and Abstraction. The minds of Beasts, if I may call them *minds,* are purely passive with respect to all their ideas. The minds of Men are not only passive, but abundantly active. Herein probably is the most distinguishing difference between Men and Beasts. Herein is the difference between Intellectual, or Rational, Will, and mere Animal Appetite, that the latter is a simple Inclination to, or Aversion from, such and such Sensations, which are the only ideas that they are capable of, that are not active about their ideas: the former is a Will that is active about its own ideas, in disposing of them among themselves, or Appetite towards those ideas that are acquired by such action.

[67.] . . . All Acts of the mind, about its ideas, are not themselves mere ideas [Dwight ed., *1*, 680, 682, 683].

Perhaps the most powerful and comprehensive statement of the *reductio ad absurdum* argument itself, however, occurs in the following passage, which, while it is more compressed than any in the *Inquiry* or than Edwards' himself likely would have published, is worth quoting at length:

> Their notion of liberty is, that there is a sovereignty in the will, and that the will determines itself, so that its determination to choose or refuse this or that, is primarily within itself; which description of liberty implies a self-contradiction. For it supposes the will, in its first act, choosing or refusing to be determined by itself; which implies that there is an antecedent act of the will to that first act, determining that act. For, if the will determines its own first act, then there must be an act of the will before that first act (for that determining is acting), which is a contradiction. There can be no fallacy in this; for we know that if the will determines its own act, it does not determine it without acting. Therefore, here is this contradiction, viz. that there is an act of the will before the first act. There is an act of the will determining what it shall choose, before the first act of choice; which is as much as to say, that there is an act of volition before the first act of volition. For the will's determining what it will choose, is choosing. The will's determining what it will will, is willing. So that according to this notion of liberty, the will must choose before it chooses, in order to determine what it will choose. If the will determines itself, it is certain that one act must determine another. If the will determines its own choice, then it must determine by a foregoing act what it will choose. If the will determines its own act, then an antecedent act determines the consequent; for that determining is acting. The will cannot determine without acting. Therefore I inquire what determines that first act of the will, viz. its determination of its own act? It must be answered, according to their scheme, that it is the will by a foregoing act. Here, again, we have the same contradiction, viz. that the first act of the will is determined by an act that is before that first act. If the will determines itself, or determines its own choice, the meaning of it must be, if there by any meaning belonging to it, that the will determines how it will choose; and that it chooses, according to that, its own determination how to choose, or is directed in choosing by that its own determination. But then I would inquire,

whether that first determination, that directs the choice, be not itself an act or a volition; and if so, I would inquire what determines that act. Is it another determination still prior to that in the order of nature? Then I would inquire, what determines the first act or determination of all? If the will, in its acts of willing or choosing, determines or directs itself how to choose, then there is something done by the will prior to its act of choosing that is determined, viz. its determining or directing itself how to choose. This act determining or directing, must be something besides or distinct from the choice determined or directed, and must be prior in order of nature to it. Here are two acts of the will, one the cause of the other, viz. the act of the will directing and determining, and the act or choice directed or determined. Now, I inquire, what determines the first act of the will determining or directing, to determine and direct as it does? If it be said, the will determines itself in that; then that supposes there is another act of the will prior to that, directing and determining that act . . .[6]

And so on *in infinitum,* or until the Arminian runs himself out of his own assertion (p. 338). Edwards' point is simply that if the will *chooses* its choice, it must be supposed to *choose* to choose this choice, and before that it would have to *decide* to choose to choose this choice, and so on.

Perry Miller has written that although the *Inquiry* was Edwards' "most sustained intellectual achievement," it was not written "to be an integral part of the 'Rational Account,' but for a prologue, to clear the ground for the construction of his monument." [7] While this is true, the prologue was not merely the *sine qua non* to the construction of the rest of the system, nor did the *Inquiry* merely lay down an argument which could be used again and again in the writings whenever the question of free will appeared. With only slight alteration this same argument was also most effectively employed by Edwards when he was dealing with matters more substantive to his projected, full-length defense of Christianity. Therefore the *argu-*

6. "Miscellaneous Observations Concerning the Divine Decrees in General, and Election in Particular," No. 22; in Worcester ed., *5,* 370–1.

7. *Jonathan Edwards* (New York, William Sloane Associates, 1949), p. 251. JE planned to write a full-length exposition and defense of Christian doctrine, a whole system of philosophical theology. This was his "uncompleted summa" (Miller, p. 285), which we possess only in fragments in the great treatises that followed the *Inquiry.*

ment of the *Inquiry,* if not the treatise itself, was not just preparatory but truly integral to the "Rational Account." Part of the reason Edwards relies so heavily on this argument is that by it he hoped to give incontrovertible refutation of self-determinism and also at the same time to command the very citadel of other issues. "On the determination of this one leading point," Edwards writes in one of the treatises intended as a part of his "Rational Account," "depends the issue of almost all controversies we have with such divines"; and he says,

> I stand ready to confess to the forementioned modern divines, if they can maintain their peculiar notion of *freedom,* consisting in the *self-determining power of the will,* as necessary to *moral agency,* and can thoroughly establish it in opposition to the arguments lying against it, then they have an impregnable castle, to which they may repair, and remain invincible, in all the controversies they have with the reformed divines, concerning Original Sin, the sovereignty of grace, election, redemption, conversion, the efficacious operation of the Holy Spirit, the nature of saving faith, perseverance of the saints, and other principles of like kind. However at the same time I think this same thing will be as strong a fortress for the *deists,* in common with them.[8]

The shape of Edwards' argument on some of these issues is often the same as that which we have been explicating, even though the matter be no longer the question of free will. By essentially the same contention he hoped to command the citadel of these other issues. This can be illustrated from what he says about true virtue, original righteousness, and original sin. By the common agreement of all mankind, and in agreement with the principles of Christian morality, there can be no virtuous act unless it arise from virtuous love and consent in the heart. Yet—and here comes Edwards' characteristic argument—"there can be no act done from love, that shall be the cause of first introducing the very existence of love."[9] It had been John Taylor's contention that Adam could not have been "originally righteous," since he could not have been righteous until after he had *chosen.* Edwards' reply is that unless he was originally righteous he

8. *The Great Christian Doctrine of Original Sin Defended* (1758), Pt. IV, ch. 1; in Worcester ed., *6,* 423.

9. "Miscellaneous Observations Concerning Efficacious Grace," No. 49; in Worcester ed., *5,* 456.

could never become so by prior choice or self-determination, which act by definition has as yet no virtue in it. "But if he were wholly without any such thing as love to God, or any virtuous love, how should he come by virtue? The answer doubtless will be, by act of choice: He must first choose to be virtuous. But what if he did choose to be virtuous? It could not be from love to God, or any virtuous principle, that he chose it; for, by the supposition, he has no such principle in his heart: And if he chooses it without such a principle, still, according to this author, there is no virtue in his choice; for all virtue, he says, is to be resolved into that single principle of love." [1] Thus according to these confused notions, virtuous love, as the principle of all virtue, must go before virtuous choice and be the principle and spring of it; and yet this same virtuous love must come after choice and be the result of it. This is the same inconsistency into which Edwards drives the self-determinist on the metaphysical question of free will.

> The nature of virtue being a positive thing, can proceed from nothing but God's immediate influence, and must take its rise from creation or infusion by God. . . . It cannot begin, or take its rise from . . . our choice, or voluntary diligence. For if there exist nothing at all of the nature of virtue before, it cannot come from cultivation; for by the supposition there is nothing of the nature of virtue to cultivate, it cannot be by repeated and multiplied acts of virtuous choice, till it becomes a habit. For there can be no virtuous choice, unless God immediately gives it. The first virtuous choice, or a disposition to it, must be immediately given, or it must proceed from a preceding choice. If the first virtuous act of will or choice be from a preceding act of will or choice, that preceding act of choice must be a virtuous act of choice, which is contrary to the supposition. For then there would be a preceding act of choice before the first virtuous act of choice. And if it be said the first virtuous act of choice is from a preceding act of will which is not virtuous, this is absurd. For an act of will not virtuous, cannot produce another act of will of a nature entirely above itself, having something positive in it which the cause has nothing of, and more excellent than it is; any more than motion can produce thought or understanding; or the collision of two bodies

1. *The Great Christian Doctrine of Original Sin Defended*, Pt. II, ch. 1, sec. 1; in Worcester ed., *6, 263.*

can produce thought; or stones and lead can produce a spirit; or nothing can produce something.[2]

When it is a question of *choosing* choice or *choosing* virtue, that antecedent choosing is for Edwards only a nothing out of which nothing comes. This is the meaning he draws from the verse that stands as a motto on the title page of the *Inquiry:* "It is not of him that willeth . . ." (Rom. 9:16).

MORAL AND NATURAL NECESSITY

Edwards' understanding of "causation" has some similarity, on one side, with that of David Hume and, on the other, it has even more agreement with Leibniz' principle of sufficient reason.[3] "Beyond the constant *conjunction* of similar objects, and the consequent inference from one to the other, we have no notion of any necessity or connection," Hume had written six years before Edwards. He said, "A cause is *that* after which *anything* constantly exists. . . . This is, indeed, all we know of the matter. And this constancy forms the very essence of necessity, nor have we any other idea of it." Our "faculties can carry us no further in our knowledge of this relation than barely to observe that particular objects are *constantly conjoined* together," and that the mind customarily makes the transition from the one to the other.[4] "Therefore," Edwards writes in a somewhat similar vein, "I sometimes use the word 'cause,' in this inquiry, to signify any antecedent, either natural or moral, positive or negative, on which an event, either a thing, or the manner and circumstance of a thing, so

2. "Miscellaneous Observations Concerning Efficacious Grace," No. 42; in Worcester ed., 5, 453.

3. This conjunction of ideas rather nonplussed earlier commentators. James Dana notes, regarding JE's notion of cause and effect, that "whenever he uses the former word for any *antecedent,* or the *occasion* of an event or thing, and the latter for the *consequence* of another thing (as he tells us he sometime doth) he so far agrees with Mr. Hume in *words* as well as sense"; and he affirms that Hume is an author of first distinction "whose essays on some moral subjects are so nearly akin to Mr. Edwards on necessity, that a reader might think the latter copied from the former" (*Examination,* pp. vi, 126). Yet Dana charges JE with a "promiscuous use of the words *cause, ground, reason*" (p. 28 n.); and in his appendix exhibiting in parallel columns the "coincidence between the principles of Mr. Edwards' book and those of ancient and modern Fatalists," it is remarkable how quotations from Hume and Leibniz alternate with each other.

4. David Hume, "Of Liberty and Necessity," Sec. VIII, pt. 1, of *An Enquiry Concerning Human Understanding* (1748).

depends that it is the ground or reason, either in whole, or in part, why it is, rather than not; or why it is as it is, rather than otherwise; or in other words, any antecedent with which a consequent event is so connected, that it truly belongs to the reason why the proposition which affirms that event, is true; whether it has any positive influence, or not. . . . Having thus explained what I mean by cause," he goes on to say, "I assert, that nothing ever comes to pass without a cause" (pp. 180–81). He says that he is going to use the word in "a sense which is more extensive, than that in which it is sometimes used" (p. 180).

Of course, in associating Edwards at all with Hume's view of causation we have to distinguish (as is commonly done) between the definition of cause as conjunction or connection and Hume's *uncertainty* as to the constancy of the connections or their being grounded in things. For Hume conjunction was constant only in experience up to the present, while Edwards was sure of it for the future because the connection was a part of God's great system where whatever is has sufficient reason. Their views are alike in rejecting the older notions of efficient causation in favor of cause as conjunction; although, with Leibniz, Edwards believes causation to be the ground or reason inherent in the world, because of the principle of sufficient reason in acts of will in God. This explains why Edwards moves uncertainly in the Humean direction, and why he writes of metaphysical or philosophical necessity that it is "nothing different from certainty," not "the certainty of knowledge, but the certainty that is in things themselves, which is the foundation of the certainty of the knowledge of them." At every point Edwards seems to draw back from having gone so far in the direction of Hume: philosophical necessity, he says, is "that *wherein lies the ground* of the infallibility of the proposition which affirms them" (p. 152; italics mine).

Yet his rejection of efficient causation of one event by another ought first to be stressed, together with his replacement of this traditional notion of causation by the idea of constant conjunction or connection. Edwards invariably speaks of the necessity that links some future event with an eternally necessary being, or with something in the past or present that has already made sure of existence, as "a necessity of consequence and connection." It may therefore be suggested that Edwards means by "connection" something not unlike Hume's "constant conjunction." Indeed, Edwards' argument that the divine decrees or predetermination do not at all increase the certainty already implied by divine foreknowledge rests finally upon this new understanding that "causation" or determination itself means constant correlation of events. The whole is a grand system of harmonious connections.

> God decrees all things harmoniously, and in excellent order; one thing harmonizes with another, and there is such a relation between all the decrees as makes the most excellent order. Thus, God decrees rain in drought because he decrees the earnest prayers of his people; or thus, he decrees the prayers of his people because he decrees rain. I acknowledge, to say God decrees a thing "because," is an improper way of speaking about God. God decrees the latter event because of the former no more than he decrees the former because of the latter. But this is what we would: when God decrees to give the blessing of rain, he decrees the prayers of his people; and when he decrees the prayers of his people, he very commonly decrees rain; and thereby there is an harmony between these two decrees, of rain and the prayers of God's people. . . . But this I say, it's improper to make one decree a condition of another, as make the other a condition of that; but there is a harmony between both.[5]

Moreover, when using the word "necessity" in a philosophical sense Edwards explains that he means by it "really nothing else than the full and fixed connection between the things signified by the subject and predicate of a proposition, which affirms something to be true" (p. 152). Here again, the idea of necessary connection is far re-

---

5. "Miscellanies," No. 29; cf. Worcester ed., 5, 353–4. I judge that F. H. Foster errs when he stresses efficient causation and the operation of secondary causes in JE's view, and when he charges the Edwardeans (including JE, Jr.) with "straining his language" to accord with "the Berkeleian idealism which pervaded . . . the whole New England school at this point in its history" to the point of teaching that cause has no efficient power (*A Genetic History*, p. 239). Earlier Foster noted that there is another interpretation of JE "founded upon the ambiguity of the word 'cause' in his philosophy" (p. 71, note 17), and himself affirmed that JE "wrapped up in one term both efficient and occasional causes," his own idealism and the occasionalism of Malebranche having much to do with this. This was, according to Foster, an ambiguity that was to make the whole structure of JE's thought "insecure to the highest pinnacle" (p. 64). There was by no means such ambiguity. JE's rejection of efficient causation was quite thorough, and he speaks only of what "makes" things to be what they are because of the strength of his immediate personal consciousness of God and because he believed things have their ground in the sufficiency of the divine wisdom. There, but for the grace of God, went Hume!

moved from the traditional concept of efficient causation, or what *makes* something to be true. The connection, Edwards writes, *"lies in, or may be explained by* the connection of two or more propositions one with another" (p. 153; italics mine). It *consists in* "an infallible connection of things signified by the subject and predicate of a proposition" (p. 156). Later on, when Edwards takes up the problem of God's knowledge of the future existence of any event, consisting in an indissoluble connection in his mind between the subject and the predicate of the proposition that affirms its future existence, he explains, "The subject is that possible event; the predicate is its future existing: but if future existence be firmly and indissolubly connected with that event, then the future existence of that event is necessary" (p. 265).

Now, either moral events or physical events can be designated by the subject of a proposition affirming future existence, and from this it follows that there is a significant, qualitative difference between moral and natural necessity. Philosophical necessity, as we have just noticed, lies in or may be explained by the firm and unalterable connection between the subject and predicate of the proposition affirming the future existence of an event. Necessity, so understood, needs to be distinguished as "moral necessity" and "natural necessity," according to whether the subject of the proposition infallibly affirming future existence designates a moral or only some natural happening. By this distinction in quality between moral and natural necessity Edwards replies in advance to the charge that every form of necessity or determinism makes men blocks or stones.

Edwards' distinction between moral and natural necessity is a cardinal point insisted on by contemporary determinists under the heading of the difference they point out between "determinism" and "compulsion." If the question be asked whether every event is caused or determined, the answer forthcoming from Edwards and very many modern thinkers is doubtless yes; but if it be whether every event is compelled, the answer is clearly no. Free acts are uncompelled acts, not uncaused or undetermined acts. Edwards associates himself with this distinction—in fact he was among the first to formulate fully and adequately this distinction—between determinism and compulsion. This he does not only in his discussion of moral and natural necessity as such, but also (with greater verbal similarity) where he speaks of *constraint,* force, compulsion, or "coaction" (pp. 164, 213, 269, 277, 280, 295, 296, 297), which is a person's being "necessitated" to act *contrary* to his will, and which he regularly contrasts with philosophical or moral necessity, and the latter with constraint.

By moral necessity is meant a necessity of connection and consequence which arises from "moral causes," inclinations, motives, etc. (p. 156). The difference Edwards points out between moral and natural necessity "does not lie so much in the nature of the connection, as in the two terms connected. The cause with which the effect is connected, is of a particular kind; viz. that which is of a moral nature; either some previous habitual disposition, or some motives exhibited to the understanding. And the effect is also of a particular kind; being likewise of a moral nature; consisting in some inclination or volition of the soul, or voluntary action" (p. 158). In fact the difference may be said to consist wholly in the terms connected and not at all in the nature of the connection, when we remember that the extent to which Edwards approximates to Hume's definition of causation as constant conjunction pertains as much to natural necessity as to moral, and when we notice his assertion that "the effect may be as perfectly connected with its moral cause, as a naturally necessary effect is with its natural cause" (p. 157). Edwards always speaks of a "firm," "indissoluble," "sure" and "infallible" connection between antecedents and consequents in the case of moral necessity, or rather of a firm, indissoluble, sure and infallible connection between the subject and predicate of the proposition which affirms future existence of the moral event.

The origin of Arminian errors with regard to their use of such terms as "necessity," "inability," "impossibility," etc. is the same as was noted before. The language of ordinary discourse has been shaped for the purpose of expressing the voluntary production of effects in external behavior. There is always supposable an opposition between the inward endeavors of the will and the difficulties of —impediments to and constraints upon—successful action in the external world. When we say that an action is difficult, we ordinarily mean that there is some "natural difficulty" against which the will needs to put forth special effort. When we say it is impossible, we mean that no strength of volition can accomplish it. When we say the action is necessary and we are unable to do otherwise, we mean that there is a "natural necessity" by which it is bound to come to pass, do what we will and oppose it how we will. In short, all such words in ethical discourse are shaped to the end of expressing the situation of the will in the face of natural necessity, compulsion, or constraint against which the will is supposed to be putting forth opposing effort. In common use these terms are "relative"—relative to supposable opposition (p. 352).

To continue to use these words in the same sense when conversant about the internal act of volition itself makes perfect nonsense, for here there is no supposable opposition. If a man wills, he wills or is preponderantly inclined. Whatever impediments may confront him when he goes into action, there is no natural difficulty or necessity or inability about the willing itself. Yet the words continue from long association to call up notions of opposition that may be irresistible. For want of abatements and changes in the meaning of words adapted to their new usage and "for want of due consideration, men inwardly entertain that apprehension, that this [moral] necessity must be against men's wills and sincere endeavors. They go away with that notion, that men may truly will and wish and strive that it may be otherwise; but that invincible necessity stands in the way" (p. 354). This is the mistake Arminians make when they dispute with Reformed divines. Edwards wants it observed that, consistent with his definition of philosophical, moral necessity, all such words are used "in some new sense, diverse from their common use." They are contrived "terms of art."

If men do something that is very wicked or very good "from a necessity that is without their wills, or with which their wills have no concern or connection," it is none of their responsibility. If "the necessity is such, that it is all one whether they will them, or no; and the reason why they are done, is from necessity only, and not from their wills; 'tis a very plain dictate of common sense that they are not at all to blame" (p. 350). Moreover, natural difficulty partially excuses; and this means any "difficulty prior *to,* and not at all consisting *in* will and inclination itself, and which would remain the same, let the inclination be what it will." Edwards excludes from the meaning of the necessity with which he is chiefly concerned any "natural propensity in the state of things, to the thing to be done, or effect to be brought to pass, abstracted from any consideration of the inclination of the heart" (p. 351). From this it may be inferred that moral necessity is not without the will or abstracted from consideration of the inclinations, and is not *prior to* but *consists in* will and inclination; and that events that are necessary with a moral necessity do not come to pass whether one wills or not. This is the necessity he shows to be consistent with liberty. There can be no distinction more crucial for understanding this treatise than "whether the impossibility were natural and against the will, or moral, lying in the will . . . whether the difficulty, or approach to necessity be natural against the will, or moral, lying in the propensity of the will" (p. 360).

Someone who no longer uses the word in its ordinary sense may still have objection to the perfect nature of the connection entailed in Edwards' notion of philosophical necessity; and indeed it is only what the relations have in common that warrants Edwards' use of the one word "necessity" for relations between terms of such different character. This he points out:

> In "necessity," that which is *vulgarly* so called, there is a strong connection between the thing said to be necessary, and something antecedent to it, in the order of nature; so there is also in "philosophical necessity." And though in both kinds of necessity, the connection can't be called by that name, with relation to an opposite will or endeavor, to which it is *superior;* which is the case in vulgar necessity; yet in both, the connection is *prior* to will and endeavor, and so in some respect *superior.* In both kinds of necessity there is foundation for some certainty of the proposition that affirms the event [p. 354].

Putting several of the foregoing statements together, we may conclude that for Edwards, natural necessity is *prior* to the will from *without* the will, superior to supposable opposite endeavor of the will, and does not at all consist in the will; while moral necessity is a connection *lying in* the will that also exists in some sense prior to the will and endeavor, and so is in some respect *superior,* though not superior to any supposable opposition from the will with which it consists.

When drawing near this mystery, men may well take off their shoes, for it has an ancient lineage in western theology. What we may call *theological* necessity, lying in the will and not compelling men whether they will or no, is an idea which goes back at least to St. Augustine. "It does not follow," Augustine writes, "that, though there is for God a certain order of causes, there must therefore be nothing dependent on the free exercise of our own wills, for our wills themselves are included in that order of causes which is certain to God. . . . How, then, does an order of causes which is certain to the foreknowledge of God necessitate that there should be nothing which is dependent on our wills, when our wills themselves

have a very important place in the order of causes?" [6] Augustine likewise distinguishes natural necessity from a connection of the soul
with God that might well be called moral necessity:

> For if that be called *our necessity* which is not in our power, but
> even though we be unwilling effects what it can effect—as, for in-
> stance, the necessity of death—it is manifest that our wills by
> which we live uprightly or wickedly are not under such a neces-
> sity; for we do many things which, if we were not willing, we
> should certainly not do. This is primarily true of the act of willing
> itself—for if we will, it *is;* if we will not, it *is* not—for we should
> not will if we were unwilling. . . . Our wills, therefore, *exist* as
> *wills,* and do themselves whatever we do by willing, and which
> would not be done if we were unwilling.[7]

"For He who foreknew did not foreknow nothing," Augustine continues, but something; and He who determined did not determine
nothing, but something, even the power of our wills and the willing
itself which, were we now unwilling, would not now be willing. "It
is certain that it is we that *will* when we will, but it is He who makes
us will what is good, of whom it is said, 'The will is prepared by the
Lord.' " [8] Here is a necessity that lies in the propensity of the will
itself.

Luther's meaning was the same, in his distinction between a "necessity of compulsion" and the "necessity of immutability."

> I could wish, indeed, that we were furnished with some better
> term for this discussion, than this commonly used term, *necessity,*
> which cannot rightly be used, either with reference to the human
> will, or the divine. It is of a significance too harsh and ill-suited
> for this subject, forcing upon the mind an idea of compulsion,
> and that which is altogether contrary to *will.* . . . for Will,
> whether divine or human, does what it does, be it good or evil,
> not by any compulsion, but by mere willingness or desire, as it
> were, totally free. [Yet God's immutable will rules over all, and
> to speak of this:] where the term fails to express the idea required,
> the understanding of the reader must make up the deficiency,
> knowing what is wished to be expressed. . . . the *necessity of*

6. *The City of God,* Bk. V, ch. 9.
7. Ibid., Bk. V, ch. 5.
8. *On Grace and Free Will,* ch. 32.

immutability, though neither is that sufficiently grammatical, or sufficiently theological.

But, by *necessity,* I do not mean *compulsion;* but (as they term it) the *necessity of immutability,* not of *compulsion;* that is, a man void of the Spirit of God, does not evil against his will as by violence, or as if he were taken by the neck and forced to it, in the same way as a thief or cut-throat is dragged to punishment against his will; but he does it spontaneously, and with a desirous willingness. . . . On the other hand, when God works in us, the *will,* being changed and sweetly breathed on by the Spirit of God, desires and acts, not from *compulsion,* but *responsively,* from pure willingness, inclination, and accord. . . . All this we do willingly and desiringly, according to the nature of *will:* for if it were forced, it would be no longer *will.* For compulsion is (so to speak) *unwillingness.*

Heaven was not made for geese.[9]

And Luther reminds Erasmus that he is speaking of the *necessity* of the thing consequent, not the *compulsive* necessity of the thing consequent.[1]

In fact, no theologian of any stature who believed in divine determinism, or in *any degree* of efficacy in the operation of divine grace upon the soul, has ever failed to distinguish such determinism or efficacy from compulsion. This may be enough to suggest that in the history of western ideas secular scientific and philosophical notions of causation and determinism are rooted in theological determinism. To the extent that this is true, it is not less but more evident in systems of thought which carefully distinguish between causation and compulsion, between determinism and force, or between philosophical or moral necessity and physical necessity.

Very much in the manner of Augustine or Luther, Edwards writes that the "determining act of the soul is not denied, but supposed, as it is the effect we are speaking of, that the influence of God's Spirit determines." [2] Of course, he was never in any doubt as to who that Being is who knows the secret of determining the determining act

9. Martin Luther, *The Bondage of the Will* (1525), trans. Henry Cole (Grand Rapids, Michigan, Wm. B. Eerdmans Publishing Co., 1931), Secs. x, xxv, xxvi.
1. Ibid., Sec. xcvii.
2. "Miscellaneous Observations Concerning Efficacious Grace," No. 72; in Worcester ed., 5, 480–1.

of the soul and inclining the human heart without nullifying its will. The remainder of his system completes the motto of this work: "It is not of him that willeth, nor of him that runneth, but of God that showeth mercy" (Rom. 9:16). The relationship between God and the soul he sometimes expresses in traditional theological language as a spiritual infusion of the Spirit of God.[3] Sometimes he expresses it in the terms of Platonic, Johannine, and Augustinian illuminism: "The light of the Sun of righteousness does not only shine upon them, but is so communicated to them that they shine also, and become little images of that Sun which shines upon them," and so men become *"lightsome* bodies."[4] Sometimes, adopting John Locke's understanding of the natural frame of the human mind, he expresses the bearing of God's mighty power upon the will as His impressing upon the mind "what some metaphysicians call a new *simple idea* . . . an entirely new kind of principle . . . also entirely a new kind of exercises . . . which the soul knew nothing of before, and which no improvement, composition, or management of what it was before conscious or sensible of, could produce," i.e. which is not the product of what Locke calls "reflection" varying and compounding ideas and inclinations drawn from natural impressions.[5] Sometimes, as in the present *Inquiry,* Edwards prepares the way for all this by attempting to show that volitions do not produce other volitions but rather come to pass out of a philosophical necessity which determines that "something" which is the determining act of the soul itself. We come, there-

---

3. *Treatise Concerning Religious Affections,* Pt. III, no. 1; in Worcester ed., *3,* 125.

4. Ibid., p. 128 (italics mine).

5. Ibid., p. 134 (italics mine). These three consecutive references drawn from the *Treatise Concerning Religious Affections* demonstrate, I judge, how wrong it is to reduce JE's system to that of John Locke, while ignoring the traditional doctrine of infusion and not giving equal weight to his Augustinian doctrine of illumination. Insofar as Locke had great influence, it was not to make JE some sort of religious naturalist or sensational empiricist, but to provide him with a different philosophical manner of stating the truth contained in these earlier theological points of view. Locke had destroyed the possibility of crediting "traditional revelation," since this can afford no new simple ideas; but, as a proper empiricist, he left open the possibility of an "original revelation," or "that first impression which is made immediately by God, on the mind of any man, to which we can not set any bounds" (*An Essay Concerning Human Understanding,* Bk. VI, ch. 18, no. 2). Jonathan Edwards elaborated his system of religious thought within this opening, and upon the surprising work of God in the Great Awakening.

fore, to the borders of the suggestion that contemporary determinists, whose views upon the *Sitz im Leben* of human volition have so much in common with Edwards, perhaps should examine whether their views "ben't" more inadequate without Edwards' God than with Him.

Edwards is not altogether unwavering in his use of such words as "necessity," "inability," and "impossibility" as "terms of art" with the definition we have seen he assigns them. It is significant that the points at which he seems to deny himself the legitimate use of the words "necessary" and "inability" are when he is strongest in his insistence that moral necessity and moral inability are consistent with liberty because the will is *in it*. It is not just that the terms in their vulgar sense do not apply to acts of the will, but Edwards seems to acknowledge that even in the contrived sense they are somehow inappropriate, or at least that better terms might be chosen or devised rather than these to bear his meaning. When first introducing the extraordinary definition of "necessity" and "inability" in their philosophical sense, it is not clear that the new meaning will remove entirely all the "perfect insignificance and nonsense" there is in saying, when the words still have their ordinary significance, that it is "necessary" for a man to choose virtue during the time that he actually prefers it, or that it is "impossible" for him to choose otherwise so long as the same choice continues (p. 151). If "the thing wanting is not a being *able,* but a being *willing*" (p. 162), then the thing present is not a being *unable,* but a being *unwilling*.

It is true that Edwards always contends that a virtuous woman may be morally unable to commit adultery; and the more virtuous the further from able. Of course, she can do what she wills: shall we then call this "ability"? But she can't do what she won't, or wills not: shall we then call this "inability"? Either word seems wrong. " 'Tis true, a man's evil dispositions may be as strong and immovable as the bars of a castle. But who can't see, that when a man, in the latter case, is said to be 'unable' to obey the command, the expression is used improperly, and not in the sense it has originally and in common speech?" (p. 363). In these instances the thing lacking is not a being able, but a being willing; and the thing present is not a being unable, but a being unwilling.

The more Edwards' analysis of an act of free volition exerts its full force, the less appropriate it seems to use such words as "inability" etc.; yet it is precisely the phenomenological limits placed around his analysis that compel one to agree that a man cannot choose otherwise so long as the same choice continues and his heart is so inclined.

The dispute about grace's being resistible or irresistible, is perfect nonsense, for the effect of grace is upon the will. So that it is nonsense, except it be proper to say that a man can with his will resist his own will, or except it be possible for him to desire to resist his own will; that is, except it be possible for a man to will a thing and not will it at the same time. Or if you speak of enlightening grace, and say this grace is upon the understanding, it is nothing but the same nonsense in other words. For then the sense runs thus, that a man, after he has seen so plainly that a thing is best for him that he wills it, yet he can at the same [time] nill it. If you say he can will anything he pleases, that is most certainly true. For who can deny that a man can will anything he doth already will? That a man can will anything that he pleases, is just as certain as that what is, is.

Wherefore, it is nonsense to say that after a man has seen so plainly a thing to be so much the best for him that he wills it, he could not have willed it if he had pleased. That is to say, if he had not *willed* it he could *not have willed* it. That is certain, that a man never doth anything but what he can do. But to say, after a man has willed a thing, that he could not have willed it if he had pleased, is to suppose two wills in a man: the one to will, which goes first, the other to please to will. Wherefore, to say that the man could have willed otherwise if he had pleased, is just all one as to say (only a hundred times as nonsensically spoken) that if he *had* willed otherwise, then we might be sure he *could* will otherwise.[6]

A man cannot properly be said to awaken from sound sleep "irresistibly," since he would have to be awake to resist. Nor was Adam formed out of the dust "irresistibly," since before he was, he was not there to resist. "Whoever supposed that the term *irresistible* was

6. "Miscellanies," No. *o* (Probably written when Edwards was tutor at Yale. Perhaps the passage should read, at several points, "could have nilled it," "could not-have-willed it" or as JE, Jr. emended the text, "could have not willed it." See "Miscellaneous Observations Concerning Efficacious Grace," No. 36; in Worcester ed., 5, 448).

properly used with respect to that power by which an infant is brought into being; meaning, irresistible by the infant?" [7] These cases parallel the first exertion of an act of will. The necessity conversant with that volition cannot properly be said to be irresistible, nor the will be said to be unable.

I am aware that when Edwards says that certain expressions are used "improperly," he means only that they are used without their *own* or their common meaning. This is the case again when in his "Remarks on Lord Kames' *Essays*" [8] he summarized and defended his *Inquiry* by pointing out, "I have largely declared, that the connection between antecedent things and consequent ones . . . which is called moral necessity, is called by the name 'necessity' improperly." In this letter Edwards goes on to say that "such a necessity as attends the acts of men's wills, is more properly called 'certainty,' than 'necessity'; it being no more than the certain connection between the subject and predicate of the proposition which affirms their existence." "Certainty" was used, in fact, throughout the *Inquiry*. Thus Edwards tended sometimes to remove the very word "necessity," after spending so much time giving it new meaning, in favor of another whose "original and proper meaning" was more suitable.

Besides this, the reader may well regard it as significant, and a subject worthy of further scrutiny, that (1) in showing liberty to be consistent with necessity, Edwards uses an ordinary meaning in the one case and a technical meaning in the other, and that (2) there is a convergence upon the conclusion aimed at (i.e. the consistency of freedom with necessity) resulting from the two shifts to be observed in Edwards' usage. On the one hand, his analysis of an act of volition leads him to say that the will *is* as the greatest apparent good *is* or as preponderant inclination *is;* yet he frequently lapses into saying the will is *determined* by these things, and hence he appears to draw from the will itself grounds for determinism. On the other hand, beginning with a technical definition of "moral necessity," when he stresses the fact that a man *can* do what he wills more than the fact that he *cannot* if he does not will, Edwards tends to suggest the removal of "unable" and its cognates from use in this connection, and hence he appears to find within necessity itself greater room for freedom. And

7. "Miscellaneous Observations Concerning Efficacious Grace," No. 45; in Worcester ed., 5, 454.

8. See below, Related Correspondence, p. 456.

finally one may observe that (3) however consistent freedom may be with the idea of necessity, the experience of freedom can never afford us an inference concerning necessity, nor the necessity that operates in the rest of the natural world with any inference concerning human freedom. As Hume said in another connection, the consistency need not be absolutely denied, only the inference.

4. *Edwards and John Locke*

1. Sereno Dwight tells us that "in the second year of his collegiate course, while at Wethersfield, [Edwards] read Locke on the Human Understanding with peculiar pleasure. . . . From his own account of the subject, he was inexpressibly entertained and delighted with that profound work, when he read it at the age of fourteen; enjoying a far higher pleasure in the perusal of its pages, 'than the most greedy miser finds, when gathering up handfuls of silver and gold, from some newly discovered treasure.' " [9] To understand Edwards' inquiry into the modern notions of freedom it will be helpful to search again into the relation between his thought and that of John Locke (1632–1704), as set down particularly in the chapter "Of Power" in the *Essay Concerning Human Understanding*.[1] After all that has been written upon the subject of Edwards' Lockean views, insufficient attention has been given to the present work in this regard. A close study of it will add both clarity and puzzlement to the problem of Edwards' philosophical lineage.

The question of the freedom of the will is, in the opinion of both Edwards and Locke, a question badly posed. "To talk of liberty," writes Edwards, "as belonging to the very will itself, is not to speak good sense. . . . For the will itself is not *an agent* that has a will. . . . He that has the liberty of doing according to his will, is the *agent* or *doer* who is possessed of the will; and not the will which he is possessed of." It is the bird, and not the bird's power of flying, that "has a power and liberty of flying" (p. 163; italics mine).

In this Edwards' thought and language follow Locke closely. The British philosopher wonders whether his analysis of power and the definition of liberty as a power of the soul "may not help to put an end to that long agitated, and, I think, unreasonable, because unintelligible question, viz. *Whether man's will be free or no?*" and he gives as reason for this expectation the fact that

9. Dwight, *Life, 1,* 30.
1. Bk. II, ch. 21; Ed. A. C. Fraser (2 vols. Oxford, 1894), *1,* 308–80.

The question itself is altogether improper; and it is as insignificant to ask whether man's *will* be free, as to ask whether his sleep
be swift, or his virtue square. . . . Liberty, which is but a
power, belongs only to *agents,* and cannot be an attribute or
modification of the will, which is also but a power [no. 14]. . . .
Liberty . . . is the power a *man* has to do or forbear doing [no.
15]. . . . The will is nothing but one power, and freedom another
power or ability; so that, to ask whether the will has freedom, is
to ask whether one power has another power, one ability another
ability. . . . For who is it that sees not that powers belong only
to agents, and are attributes only of substances, and not of powers
themselves? So that this way of putting the question (viz. whether
the will be free) is in effect to ask, whether the will be a substance,
an agent, or at least to suppose it. . . . But if any one should ask,
whether freedom were free, he would be suspected not to understand well what he said; and he would be thought to deserve
Midas's ears, who, knowing that rich was a denomination for the
possession of riches, should demand whether riches themselves
were rich [no. 16]. . . . It is the mind that operates, and exerts
these powers; it is the man that does the action; it is the agent
that has power or is able to do. For powers are relations, not
agents: and that which has the power or not the power to operate,
is that alone which is or is not free, and not the power itself [no.
19]. . . . I think the question is not proper, *whether the will be
free,* but *whether a man be free* [no. 21].

In like manner Edwards maintains that it is the agent, and not his
will, that has the power or liberty of doing according to his will. One
suspects, however, that he lacks some degree of thoroughness or consistency in directing attention always to this question which he and
Locke agree is at issue—namely, whether a *man* be free or no? Instead, Edwards' polemic against the definition of freedom as a self-
determining power (shaped as it is by the view he is opposing) leads
him to reduce this question back again to the one from which Locke
departed—namely, whether the *will,* not the man, has the power,
or whether the *will* be free by prior act of will to determine itself?

2. This agreement of Edwards with Locke upon the matter of
attributing freedom (however it be understood) to the soul or mind
and not to an attribute or power or faculty of the soul is based on
their common rejection of the division of the person into various

distinct faculties, such as the tripartite distinction between the reason, the will, and the appetites in traditional psychology. In short,
we have here a conception of the fundamental unity or coinherence
of human capacities. "The ordinary way of speaking," writes Locke,
"is, that the understanding and will are two *faculties* of the mind; a
word proper enough, if it be used, as all words should be, so as not
to breed any confusion in man's thoughts, by being supposed (as I
suspect it has been) to stand for some real beings in the soul that
performed those actions of understanding and volition. . . . I suspect, I say, that this way of speaking of *faculties* has misled many into
a confused notion of so many distinct agents in us" (no. 6). This is
the same as to suppose that there is a speaking faculty, a walking
faculty, a dancing faculty, etc.; and "we may as properly say that it is
the singing faculty sings, and the dancing faculty dances, as that the
will chooses, or that the understanding conceives" (no. 17), and we
may as properly speak of a digestive faculty or an expulsive faculty
as of motive, intellectual, and elective faculties (no. 20).

Of course, on the verbal level it is impossible to avoid altogether
the use of such words as "understanding" and "will" to refer to different functions of human nature or different relations into which
its powers enter. Thus Edwards writes, "If it be possible for the
understanding to act in indifference, yet to be sure the will never
does" (p. 197), "every act of the will is some way connected with the
understanding" (p. 217), and he seems to believe that Clarke too
much "confounds the understanding and will, and makes them the
same" (p. 223). Such statements as these may indicate something
below the level of language that demands to be acknowledged. Therefore John Locke says concerning the terms of faculty psychology
that "such words . . . are to have their place in the common use
of languages" since "it looks like too much affectation wholly to lay
them by." Concerning the ideas behind the terms, he also writes,
"Not that I deny there are faculties, both in the body and mind:
they both of them have their powers of operating" (no. 20). His view
requires only that the faculties of the mind be carefully redefined as
powers, and as such they are still clearly distinguishable: "For these
being all different powers in the mind, or in the man, to do several
actions, he exerts them as he thinks fit: but the power to do one
action [e.g. willing] is not operated on by the power of doing another
action [e.g. perceiving, understanding]" (no. 18).

Joining with Locke in placing the powers formerly called faculties
in the mind or *in the man,* Edwards goes beyond Locke in abolishing

differentiation between them. This is manifest in Edwards' judgment that the will and the understanding cannot properly be said ever to oppose each other in regard to the same thing. This was possible according to the older faculty psychology.

Even deeper diremptions were placed in the mind or *in the man* by the theological literature on the bondage of the will within the Pauline-Augustinian-Calvinist tradition which Edwards continues and reformulates. One thinks here of St. Paul's "I do not do the good I want, but the evil I do not want is what I do" (Rom. 7:19), and of St. Augustine's cry, "I it was who willed, I who was unwilling. It was I, even I myself. I neither willed entirely, nor was entirely unwilling. Therefore I was at war with myself, and destroyed myself." [2] According to Augustine it is possible for a man to will and "nill" the same thing at the same time. No such conception of the self-contradiction *in the will* is to be found in Edwards. Yet Edwards' variance from Augustinianism on this matter is in large measure verbal and arises from the fact that his view in the main consists of an analysis of an act of effective volition or choice in which any contradiction *in the man* is supposed to be past. What Augustine calls contradiction in the will Edwards takes into account in what he says about simultaneous "consent to being" and "dissent from being":

> It is naturally agreeable to Perceiving Being that Being should consent to Being, and the contrary disagreeable. If by any means, therefore, a particular and restrained love overcomes this General Consent;—the foundation of that Consent yet remaining in the nature, exerts itself again, so that there is a contradiction of one consent to another. . . . And by inclining or doing that, which is against his natural inclination as a Perceiving Being, he must necessarily cause uneasiness, inasmuch as that natural inclination is contradicted. And this is *Disquiet of Conscience.* . . . But when there is no sense of any such dissent from Being in general, there is no contradition to the natural inclination of Perceiving Being.[3]

If these youthful notes are to be credited as part of Edwards' mature system, it is evident that the war between the will or love to God and the will or love to lesser beings in Augustine's view was expressed by Edwards in terms of a conflict between man's basic con-

2. *The Confessions,* Bk. VIII, ch. 10.
3. "The Mind," No. 14; in Dwight ed., *1,* 701.

sent to being in general and his dissent from being when consenting only to more restricted being. Edwards simply does not locate this conflict among the acts of the will, since for him "an act of the will is the same as an act of choosing or choice" (p. 137), the conflict being supposed to be overcome before ever the mind chooses, or else out of a multitude of contending inclinations the least preponderation one way he defined as an act of will. Augustine could never choose or act rightly because before grace he could never *will entirely;* while, according to Edwards, an act of will is by definition the entire mind acting. Nevertheless, a man cannot actually will or act entirely unless his inclinations and consent to being have been made captive to the beauty of Being itself. For, according to both men, consent or love to any lesser being cannot possibly be whole-hearted, on account of the unacknowledged but ineradicable foundation of consent or love to God in the human heart.

The fact that Edwards understands human nature in terms of a more thoroughgoing unity than even Locke did is made evident by the objections he raises against certain of Locke's views. In the first section of the *Inquiry,* Edwards disagrees with Locke's suggestion that the word "preferring" may not be precisely the equivalent of a "choice" or "act of volition" (no. 21), and with his stronger statement that "the will is perfectly distinguished from desire" (no. 30). Edwards argues that on closer inspection it will be found that (1) "will" and "prefer" and (2) "will" and "desire" mean the same thing. The quotation cited from Locke on the second point, distinguishing will from desire, is preceded in his text and introduced by a definition of volition which seems to forestall Edwards' objections to his hesitancy in the first instance to using the word "preferring." "Volition," Locke writes, "is nothing but that particular determination of the mind, whereby, barely by a thought, the mind endeavors to give rise, continuation, or stop, to *any action which it takes to be in its power*" (no. 30; italics mine). Both men, then, agree in substance that properly to will requires, in Edwards' words, "a concurring habitual expectation that it will be so; having ever found by experience, that on such an immediate preference, such sensations and motions do actually instantaneously, and constantly arise" (p. 138).

Locke, however, seeks a different term for the mind's relation to what is *not* "nextly chosen" or for what is *not* the "next and immediate object of the will" (p. 138); or rather, he judges that the word "prefer" somewhat and the word "desire" more emphatically suggest our attitude toward an impossible or a remote end which may not now be willed or chosen. Edwards simply wants no such distinction of terms, although he does not explicitly deny that human motivation, in the whole of it, includes what Locke directs attention to by means of these distinctions. Edwards telescopes these meanings and finds as a consequence that will and preference and will and desire always agree in respect to the same thing, whether this be an immediate or a remote object. These powers or relations of the mind to its ends are believed to run counter only by a confusion in thinking in cases where the immediate and remote objects of action are different. This is to say that, strictly speaking, will and desire or preference never run counter. The reader may judge which of these views accords the more with ordinary language, to which Edwards frequently makes appeal, or which is more to be preferred as a product of that capacity of mankind "to improve the benefit of language, in the proper use and design of names, given to things which they have often occasion to speak of, or signify their minds about" (p. 130).

A more important, because more than verbal, issue is whether Edwards' refusal to follow Locke in adopting or devising terms that have different shades of meaning does not lead him to adopt, or reveal in him, a too extreme conception of the unity of human powers or a too monolithic view of the motivations to action. "This insistence that will, preference, desire . . . are all merely different names for the act of the will, closed, so Edwards hoped, all the loopholes by which his opponents might drag in some notion of freedom under the guise of opposition among the affections." [4] Edwards went beyond Locke in order to stop the mouths of his New England opponents who, even as they too were absorbing Locke, continued to use the jargon of faculty psychology and found room for freedom in the interstitial spaces left open by such a view of human nature. Edwards wanted to stop all crevices in the argument. As Tappan remarks, "Edwards' analysis is more nice than Locke's, and his whole development more true to the great principle of the system—necessary determination. Locke, in distinguishing the will from the desire, seems about to launch into a different psychology, and one destructive of the principle." [5]

4. Faust and Johnson, p. xlvii.
5. *A Review of Edwards's "Inquiry into the Freedom of the Will,"* p. 86.

3. Another important aspect of Edwards' relationship to Locke which can be clarified by a study of this treatise appears in the author's discussion, in Pt. I, Sec. 2, of the question whether the will be determined by the strongest motive, i.e. by the greatest apparent good. Here he affirms that since the word "good" includes in its signification the removal of what is disagreeable or evil, his own view of the determination of the will always by greater good succeeds in including that "uneasiness" which "Mr. Locke supposes determines the will" (p. 143). Whether this be so or not may be questioned; but before entering upon a discussion of this subject we need briefly to call to mind the radical difference between the first and the second editions of Locke's great work, particularly in the extensive revision of the chapter "Of Power."

In the second and subsequent editions of the *Essay Concerning Human Understanding,* "upon a stricter inquiry" (no. 35) Locke inserted his "second thoughts" (no. 31) concerning the liberty of the will, substituting nos. 28–62 of this chapter for nos. 28–38 of the first edition (1690). The revision was retained in the third and fourth editions printed in Locke's lifetime, in the French translation supervised by him, and of course in the many editions published after his death in 1704. When writing the present treatise, Edwards used a copy of the seventh edition, as he indicates in the footnotes. This was the first octavo edition, in two volumes, published in London in 1716. However, Edwards may have studied the *first* edition of Locke's *Essay* when he was a student and later tutor at Yale College. The so-called "Dummer Library," a catalogue of books given to Yale College in January 1713, lists among the donations of Elihu Yale a copy of the 1690 edition. If Edwards originally became acquainted with Locke's first edition, and this was the form in which Locke's thought first made its impact upon him, that would explain why Edwards' views on freedom of the will correspond so closely in substance to Locke's "first thoughts" on the same subject, together with a strange reluctance on Edwards' part to take issue directly with important elements of the sweeping revision incorporated in the edition he actually used in composing his own *Inquiry*. Against such an hypothesis, however, one of his notes on "The Mind" makes objection to Locke's view, introduced into the second and subsequent editions, that willing always arises from uneasiness, for, says Edwards, a man's "voluntary refusal is an act of the Will, which does not arise from any uneasiness in his present circumstances." [6] This demonstrates that Edwards must have known the second or some subsequent edition of Locke's *Essay* (perhaps even the seventh he used in writing the *Inquiry*) sometime during the years 1717–20 when he composed these notes.

"Good, then, the greater good, is that which determines the will"— this is what Locke said (no. 28) in the first edition of this chapter, and Edwards says the same thing now. The shift in Locke's thought from the second edition onward was from the greater good to felt uneasiness as the motive of willing. It may be questioned whether Edwards, in adopting in effect the position of Locke's first edition, does in fact include without significant alteration what Mr. Locke, upon second thought concerning the question, supposed determines the will. For while Locke admits that the avoiding or removal of uneasiness is in every case good, not every acknowledged good produces motivating uneasiness on account of its absence. He writes: "The greater visible good does not always raise men's desires in proportion to the greatness it appears, and is acknowledged to have: though every little trouble moves us, and sets us on work to get rid of it. . . . All present pain, whatever it be, makes a part of our present misery: but all absent good does not at any time make a necessary part of our present happiness, nor the absence of it a part of our misery. If it did, we should be constantly and infinitely miserable; there being infinite degrees of happiness which are not in our possession" (no. 45).

Here again the difference in their viewpoints turns upon Locke's readiness and Edwards' refusal to devise a term, or appropriate and refine one in common usage, for the mind's relation to remote good. For Edwards requests it be "carefully observed" that he is speaking only of "the direct and immediate object of the act of volition" (p. 143). From this restriction Edwards', and Locke's first, view follows unavoidably. Moreover, *this* is never denied in Locke's second and later editions:

> For, as to *present* happiness and misery, when that alone comes into consideration, and the consequences are quite removed, a man never chooses amiss: he knows what best pleases him, and that he actually prefers. Things in their present enjoyment are what they seem: the apparent and real good are, in this case, always the same. For, the pain and pleasure being just so great

6. No. 70; Dwight ed., *1*, 693.

and no greater than it is felt, the present good or evil is really so much as it appears. And therefore were every action of ours included within itself and drew no consequences after it, we should undoubtedly never err in our choice of good: we should always infallibly prefer the best [no. 60].

These words are good commentary upon Edwards' illustration of the drunkard, but Locke did not think this admission opposed to the conclusion that present uneasiness motivates action, and not the mind's total apprehension of the good. Thus Locke distinguishes between the greatest apparent good (which, though objectively good, may be remote and unappealing) and the good that makes itself felt in uneasiness or dissatisfaction. Edwards joins together what Locke put asunder. He needs only one term to describe the motivations to voluntary action and the appearance of good to the mind.

We have seen that one of the numbers in "The Mind" explicitly opposes Locke's theory of uneasiness. It seems likely, therefore, that other numbers which do not expressly mention Locke reveal the young Edwards at work constructing (or reconstructing) a verbally more simplified, monolithic account of the powers and motivations of men. As a consequence Edwards was able to adopt language similar to Locke's first edition without explicitly denying (what Locke needed more than one word to express) that there may be remote and objective good not at present part of the soul's apprehension:

[21.] THE WILL. It is not that, which appears the greatest good, or the greatest apparent good, that determines the Will. It is not the greatest good apprehended, or that which is apprehended to be the greatest good; but the Greatest Apprehension of good. It is not merely by judging that any thing is a great good, that good is apprehended, or appears. There are other ways of apprehending good. The having a clear and sensible idea of any good, is one way of good's appearing, as well as judging there is good. . . . And that Good, of which there is the greatest apprehension or sense . . . is chosen by the Will. And if there be a greater apprehension of good to be obtained, or evil escaped, by doing a thing, than in letting it alone, the Will determines to the doing of it. . . . The degree of apprehension of good, which I suppose to determine the Will, is composed of the degree of good apprehended, and the degree of apprehension.

[60.] WILL, ITS DETERMINATION. The greatest mental existence of Good, the greatest degree of the mind's sense of Good, the greatest degree of apprehension, or perception, or idea of [our] own Good, always determines the will.

. . . the degree of the ideal perceptive presence of the good in the mind. . . .

It is utterly impossible but that it should be so, that the inclination and choice of the mind should always be determined by Good, as mentally or ideally existing.[7]

The foregoing notes (which, if studied in their entirety, provide excellent supplementary explanation of what Edwards means in the *Inquiry* by "the manner of the mind's view") demonstrate again that Edwards' position consists simply of a clear analysis of an act of volition: The will *is* as the greatest *apprehension* of the good *is,* or the degree of such apprehension. The will *is* as *is* the degree of the ideal perceptive presence of the good in the mind.

The difference between Edwards and Locke appears again on p. 148, where Edwards states that "the will always follows the last dictate of the understanding." In doing so he takes "understanding" in "a large sense" to mean the mind's whole *present* or efficacious apprehension of the greater good, which might as well be called a "narrow" sense excluding reference to the *remote* good except insofar as this plays a part in present uneasiness—which comes down to saying that the mind is now motivated by present motivation. Locke, on the other hand, took the "last dictate of the understanding" in the other meaning and was forced to revise his view. The only way Edwards can deny the correctness of his doing so is in terms of the terms; for, as he points out, "If by the dictate of the understanding is meant what reason declares to be best or most for the person's happiness, taking in the whole of his duration, it is not true, that the will always follows the last dictate of the understanding" (p. 148).

Beneath the terms each man uses, more than terminology is at issue. At least by the time of the *Inquiry,* the idea of a remote or objective good somehow known by the mind alongside of the lively apprehension of good by the will plays no effective role in Edwards' thought; and as a consequence he has no need of the distinction between the powers of understanding and will except in the ordinary usage he occasionally adopts. A clear distinction between the "facul-

7. "The Mind," in Dwight ed., *1,* 691-3.

ties" of understanding and will was written into the complete title of the notes on "The Mind," [8] and this distinction was useful when he wanted to set apart the mind's power of merely judging that any-thing is a great good (or the appearance of greatest good as an idea in the understanding) from the will or inclination of the mind (or the "greatest apprehension" of good). In the *Inquiry,* however, no actual distinction is made between "the degree of good appre-hended" (by the understanding) and "the degree of apprehen-sion" of good (by the mind's power of willing). The degree of good apprehended and the degree of apprehension, the nature and circumstance of the object and the state and manner of the mind's view, are now completely telescoped into one. If a remote or objective good is not effectively present in the mind's apprehen-sion, it should not be regarded as actually present at all so far as the analysis of action is concerned. In place of the remote good actually appearing as "a clear and sensible idea" in the judgment of the understanding but perhaps not forcefully present in the degree of apprehension, there is only a good blurred and weakened in the *present* but distant scene before the mind's eye. The degree of good that appears and the degree of apprehension of the good are one. So are understanding the good and willing the good. The direction in which Edwards' thought was to move was forecast in the conclud-ing words of the note on "The Mind" just quoted: "For we mean nothing else by Good, than *that which agrees with the inclination and disposition of the mind.* And surely that, which agrees with it, must agree with it. And it also implies a contradiction, to suppose that that good, whose mental or ideal being is greatest, does not always determine the Will; for we mean nothing else, by Greatest Good, but that which agrees most with the inclination or disposition of the soul. It is ridiculous to say, that the soul does not incline to that most, which is most agreeable to the inclination of the soul." [9] Therefore Tappan remarks upon how completely Edwards "makes mind and object to run together in choice, or how perfect a unition of the two, choice is." [1]

<hr/>

8. "The Natural History of the Mental World, or of the Internal World: Being a Particular Enquiry into the Nature of the Human Mind, with Respect to Both Its Faculties—the Understanding and the Will—and Its Various In-stincts, and Active and Passive Powers," Dwight ed., *1,* 664.

9. "The Mind," No. 60; in Dwight ed., *1,* 693.

1. *A Review,* p. 31.

It is interesting to observe that Isaac Watts, who before the mid-eighteenth century was with Edwards outstanding among orthodox theological writers as a purveyor of Lockean ideas, discusses at some length these same principles—uneasiness, the greatest apparent good, and the last assent of the understanding—as determiners of the will. Like Edwards he cannot discover much difference between these proposals. "The removal of this present uneasiness is itself the greatest apparent good, and if the will be determined to act thus or thus for the removal of its present uneasiness, then it is still determined by the greatest apparent good." But he takes more cognizance than Edwards of the distinction Locke himself had drawn, saying that he does not see in it "ground enough for that great opposition between his doctrine in this point, and the common doctrine, which he seems to represent in two whole sections." Like Edwards, Watts contends that he has included in the other principles what Locke says motivates the will. Watts, however, takes precisely the wrong turn in interpreting Locke when he asks "Does it not then follow, that uneasiness is the remote mover of the will, and desire of good the proxime mover of it?" [2] And, as we shall see, he denies that any one or all three of these principles gives sufficient explanation of every movement of the will, while Edwards contends that properly understood, "the greatest apparent good" subsumes the rest and comprehends the whole meaning of motivation.

4. It was his making a distinction between things or *objects* chosen and *acts* of choice which led Locke to a radical reconstruction of his views on the liberty of the will. He writes, "A very judicious friend of mine, since the publication, suspecting some mistake in it, though he could not particularly show it me, I was put upon a stricter review of this chapter. Wherein lighting upon a very easy and scarce observable slip I had made, in putting one seemingly indifferent word for another, that discovery opened to me this present view, which here in this second edition, I submit to the learned world" (no. 73). What this slip was, of one seemingly indifferent word for another, is shown by Locke's correspondence with Molyneaux, July 15, 1693: "By observing only the mistake of one word (viz. having put *things*

2. *An Essay on the Freedom of Will in God and in Creatures* (1732), in *The Works of the Reverend and Learned Isaac Watts, D.D.,* selected and compiled by David Jennings and Philip Doddridge in 1753 (6 vols. London, 1811), *6,* 248–9.

for *actions*) which was very easy to be done in the place where it is,[3] I got into a new view of things, which, if I mistake not, will satisfy you and give a clearer account of *human freedom* than hitherto I have done." [4] Observing this distinction led Locke to *abandon* his former view that the will is determined by the greater good, while Edwards employs exactly the same distinction in the course of his argument to the opposite consequence of strengthening his contention that *in the moment of the action* the will *is* as the greatest apparent good is. "The very act of volition itself is doubtless a determination of the mind . . . coming to a choice between two things, or more, proposed to it. But determining among external *objects* of choice, is not the same with determining the *act* of choice itself, among various possible acts of choice" (p. 178). This is Edwards' typical reply to writers like Watts who, beyond the inclination of the will according to the last dictate of the understanding apprehending the greater good in one object rather than another, endeavor to produce concrete illustration of cases in which the will determines itself to choose between two or more perfectly indifferent things, between two pieces of cake exactly alike, or touching one spot rather than another on a chessboard.

> Indeed the man chooses to *take* or *touch* one rather than another; but not because it chooses the *thing* taken, or touched. . . . The case may be so, that of two things offered, a man may, for certain reasons, choose and prefer the taking of that which he *undervalues,* and choose to neglect to take that which his mind *prefers.* In such a case, choosing the thing taken, and choosing to take, are diverse. . . . And therefore the arguments which they

3. First edition, ch. 21, no. 28 (ed. Fraser, *1,* 375): "We must remember that volition or willing, regarding only what is in our power, is nothing but the preferring the *doing* of anything to the not *doing* of it; action to rest, and *contra.* Well, but what is this preferring? It is nothing but the being pleased more with one than the other. Is then a man indifferent to be pleased, or not pleased, more with one *thing* than another? Is it in his choice, whether he will or will not be better pleased with one *thing* than another? And to this I think every one's experience is ready to make answer, No." (The italics in this passage have been altered to indicate how Locke slips from "preferring the *doing*" to being "better pleased with one *thing,*" across the words at the midpoint of the passage which, in respect to this distinction, are indeterminate; "the being pleased more with *one* than the *other.*")

4. See Fraser's note to no. 73 of Bk. II, ch. 21 (*1,* 366).

bring, in order to be to their purpose, ought to be to prove that the mind chooses the action in perfect indifference, with respect to that *action;* and not to prove that the mind chooses the action in perfect indifference with respect to the *object* [p. 201].

Notice also that in the language and thought of this passage precisely the same lines of opposite development insist on emerging which Locke followed out, namely, the use of the word "prefer" with exactly the same meaning (diverse from "will" or "choice") which Edwards rejected in Locke at the outset, and the use of the word "undervalue" which implies a possible opposition between the judgment of the understanding concerning the greatest apparent good (which attaches the more to choiceworthy *objects*) and motives to *action* from felt uneasiness or some other motive. Edwards manages to suppress the tendency of thought to move in this direction from his own and Locke's first position, while Locke commits himself to this inherent development. Although Locke would have agreed with Edwards that there is an important distinction between whether the will be "conversant about the *objects presented*" or "the *acts* to be done" (p. 201), he came to the quite opposite conclusion that in being conversant about acts to be done, the will is mainly conversant about felt uneasiness and not primarily "nextly" or immediately about the mind's apprehension of the greater good (which has more to do with the *thing* presented).

5. He judged also that in being conversant about actions, the will is conversant about the possibility of *suspending* action. This brings us to the other outstanding aspect of Locke's revised viewpoint, and to the question of Edwards' relation to Locke's new view of freedom. The mind, Locke believed, has in most cases "a power to *suspend* the execution and satisfaction of any of its desires; and so all, one after another" (no. 48). "This is the hinge on which turns the liberty of intellectual beings," this is "the great inlet and exercise of all the liberty men have": "that they can suspend their desires, and stop them from determining their wills to any action, till they have duly and fairly examined the good and evil of it." We can "hold our wills undetermined" (no. 53).

Locke explains this view of freedom in explicit contrast with his earlier (and Edwards') viewpoint in a paragraph (no. 57) that was introduced into Coste's French edition and thence into the posthumous editions, including the seventh Edwards used. The passage opens with a definition of the freedom of will which *was* Locke's and *is* Edwards': "Liberty, it is plain, consists in a power to do, or not to do; to do, or forbear doing, *as we will.*" This cannot be denied, yet it is inadequate. For, says Locke, this definition of freedom seems "to comprehend only the actions of a man *consecutive to volition*" (italics mine); and it must always be inquired further, "Whether he be at liberty to will or no?" In other words, in being conversant about *actions,* is not a man conversant about acts of *willing* as well as about acts of *doing* as he wills?

In answering this, Locke still allows that "in most cases, a man is not at liberty to forbear the act of volition."

> But yet there is a case wherein a man is at liberty in respect of willing; and that is the choosing of a remote good as an end to be pursued. Here a man may *suspend* the act of his choice from being determined for or against the thing proposed, till he has examined whether it be really of a nature, in itself and consequences, to make him happy or not. For, when he has once chosen it, and thereby it is become a part of his happiness, it raises desire, and that proportionably gives him uneasiness; which determines his will, and sets him at work in pursuit of his choice on all occasions that offer [no. 57].

As for the question which greatly exercised the Arminians, and Edwards in his answer to them, namely the question what condition of the will warrants praise or blame, reward or punishment, Locke's blunt retort is: *"He had a power to suspend his determination."*

Now, the striking and puzzling thing about Edwards' *Inquiry* is that, with all this before him in Locke, he nevertheless introduces the theory of suspension quite anonymously, or as if it were a formulation or possible objection he himself has made up, in the fashion of philosophical and theological writings at that time, in order to assist and complete his own argument. Why does Edwards not single out John Locke for refutation? He had in him an opponent worthy of his polemical powers, and moreover a proponent of the freedom to suspend whose philosophical outlook had largely become Edwards' own. Instead, he opens the matter with the words, *"If any should suppose,* that these difficulties and absurdities may be avoided, by saying, that the liberty of the mind consists in a power to suspend the act of the will, and so to keep it in a state of indifference, till there has been opportunity for consideration . . . I say, *if anyone* imagines that this helps the matter, it is a great mistake" (pp. 209–10; italics mine). Is this not an extraordinary reticence? If Edwards' argument from this point on to the end of Sec. 7 of Pt. II be valid, it has the power to force Locke into "gross inconsistencies" and "impertinence" —more effectively, it may be suggested, than the largely verbal fashion in which Whitby's statements [5] are made to bear witness against themselves in Sec. 5 of this part, where they are flanked by essentially the same argument. For however naive Whitby may be in not distinguishing between *"willing* what we will" and *"acting* what we will or please," precisely because he has not done so his language in defining liberty as *"doing* what we will" cannot be construed to mean "acting" in distinction from "willing" what we please, or be made to bear witness against itself and in behalf of Edwards. Because Locke probes so deeply as to make this distinction, it occurs to him to say that the will is conversant with itself in suspending the act of willing; and herein he opens himself to Edwards' reply.

Toward the end of the *Inquiry* (Pt. IV, Sec. 7, note 2) Edwards quotes at length from Locke's *Essay* in support of his view that a perfect moral being, such as we suppose God to be, will always be determined by the highest good. The opening words are, " 'Tis not a fault, but a perfection of our nature, to desire, will and act, according to the last result of a fair examination." It should be pointed out that this is the concluding sentence of no. 48, in which Locke has just introduced for the first time, against the background of an analysis of *uneasiness* as the motive for action, his notion that the power to suspend action is "the great inlet and exercise of all the liberty men have" (no. 53). Edwards completely ignores the significance of the expression "the last result of a fair examination" in the context of the idea of suspension, and instead moves on to the following passages that were taken over by Locke largely unrevised from his first edition. Was it only a slip of the pen when, later on in this footnote, Edwards copied "wise *determinations*" instead of Locke's words "wise *considerations*"? This is not to suggest that Locke's reformulation ought to have been more thorough, depicting God holding his will undetermined between a higher and a lesser good, or that Edwards' citation on the whole is mistaken or irrelevant. It simply shows how Edwards looks the other way rather than find the notion of suspension in Locke, and face up to it there in the context of a

5. See below, Pt. 5, no. 11 of this Introduction.

philosophy more sophisticated than many of the Arminian theologians, and more like his own.

The argument between whose jaws Locke might have fallen, had he been a living Arminian rather than a dead mentor, is that the suspend*ing* of volition is but another act of volition. This will*ing* to suspend is, then, subjected by Edwards to the same analysis as any other act of volition.[6] In willing to suspend, are we free simply in the sense that, *consecutive* to this volition, we are able to do what we will, or is there a prior freedom or power to fetch forth this very will to suspend, without already, in the time of volition, a preponderation that way? The search for a will behind every act of willing "drives the exercise of freedom back *in infinitum;* and that is to drive it out of the world" (p. 211); nor in any case is it a proper explanation of the original freedom of the will to suspend, from which we have actually departed in the course of this reasoning. In thus running the will "out of the world," Edwards really asks and answers the question whether the will—and not whether the man— be free.

6. The form and substance of the above contention recur throughout Edwards' *Inquiry*. It is logically undeniable, and moreover set forth the more effectively in Edwards' rhetorical style with its piling up of long yet perfectly clear sentences with punctuation apparently only, as it were, for breath. A final aspect of the relationship of Edwards to Locke which should be noted is that the germ, and more than a germ, of this argument he might have found in Locke. Especially was this true of the first edition, if this was one of the editions Edwards studied at Yale, Puritanism in him being thereby awakened from its scholastic slumber; but it is still there in the edition Edwards had by him when writing.

6. Anthony Collins, *A Philosophical Inquiry Concerning Human Liberty,* 1717 (3d ed. 1735, republished with a preface by Joseph Priestley, Birmingham, 1790), in contrast to JE, refers to Locke when dealing with the theory of suspension (p. 26), and his reply is the same as JE's: ". . . He is not less determined to will, because he does often suspend willing or choosing in certain cases: for *suspending to will,* is itself an *act of willing;* it is willing to *defer willing* about the matter proposed. . . . A man, who suspends a will about any matter, wills doing nothing in it at present, or rejects for a time willing about it. . . . So that willing, or choosing, *suspension,* is like all other choices or wills that we have" (p. 27).

> Besides to make a man free after this manner by making the
> action of willing depend on his will, there must be another
> antecedent will, to determine the acts of this will, and another
> to determine that, and so *in infinitum:* for wherever one stops,
> the actions of the last will cannot be free [no. 23].

The foregoing passage of the first edition, which may have been
studied by Edwards at Yale, was retained by Locke in the three other
editions published during his life. It was, however, stricken from the
French, and the hand of Locke may have been in this; nor does it
appear in the posthumous editions, i.e. in the seventh, which Edwards used—perhaps because of the sound judgment of the editor
that it could not be assimilated by Locke's "second thoughts" concerning liberty. Yet an equally forceful passage was allowed to
remain:

> To ask whether a man be at liberty to will either motion or rest,
> speaking or silence, which he pleases, is to ask whether a man
> can will what he wills, or be pleased with what he is pleased
> with? A question which, I think, needs no answer: and they who
> can make a question of it must suppose one will to determine
> the acts of another, and another to determine that, and so *in
> infinitum* [no. 25].

Here only the concluding words "an absurdity before taken notice
of" were eliminated, for editorial consistency with no. 23 which, as
we have noted, was posthumously altered. So the foregoing could have
been read by Edwards at the time of his writing. And in all editions,
i.e. both the first and the seventh, Locke writes:

> It is plain that a man that is walking, to whom it is proposed to
> give off walking, is not at liberty, whether he will determine him-
> self [7] to walk, or give off walking or not: he must necessarily prefer
> one or the other of them; walking or not walking. . . . The

7. In the French edition: "n'est plus en liberté de *vouloir vouloir* (permittez
moi cette expression)," on which Leibniz comments, "Si nous voulions vouloir,
nous voudrions vouloir voiloir, et cela irait à l'infini." Bk. II, ch. 21, no. 24 (ed.
Fraser, *1,* 327). Essentially the same argument might, of course, occur to anyone
without the assistance of Locke, as it did to Luther: "But may we suppose, that
this power is a kind of medium, between the will itself and the action itself; such
as, that by which the will itself allurs forth the action itself of willing or not
willing, or by which the action itself of willing or not willing is allured forth?"
The Bondage of the Will (1525), trans. Cole, Sec. XLII.

mind, in that case, has not a power to forbear *willing:* it cannot
avoid some determination concerning them, let the consideration
be as short, the thought as quick as it will, it either leaves the man
in the state he was before thinking, or changes it; continues the
action, or puts an end to it . . . thereby either the continuation
or change becomes *unavoidably* voluntary [no. 24].

This is enough to make abundantly clear not only the possible source
in Locke for one of Jonathan Edwards' main arguments but also the
fact that statements of Locke concerning liberty of will might have
been made to testify against themselves much more readily than the
statements of some of the Arminians that Edwards selects for this
purpose.

5. *Edwards and His Antagonists*

The philosophy of Jonathan Edwards in the *Inquiry* must also be
considered in relation to the books he takes up for refutation in the
course of this writing. Three authors are of chief concern here:
Thomas Chubb, Daniel Whitby, and Isaac Watts. If in all that has
been written about Edwards as a Lockean insufficient attention has
been given to the actual relation between the *Inquiry* and Locke's
chapter "Of Power," it may be said that the relation between Edwards and his chief antagonists in this work has been passed over even
more lightly. An examination of Edwards' treatment of the writings
of Chubb, Whitby, and Watts, far from adding unnecessary detail,
will actually advance us a great distance toward an adequate comprehension of Edwards' views. Without this, indeed, what he says in
connection with these authors may seem but an ancient battle of
words which at this date can safely be read over rapidly without careful attention to how the argument stands between them.

Why Edwards selected these three and not others for refutation is,
of course, now past finding out. Samuel Clarke, for example, was at
least equally renowned in that day and from the perspective of a
later age he was obviously of far greater importance as a thinker; yet
Edwards accords him only an occasional reference in the text and an
occasional quotation in a footnote toward the end of the *Inquiry.*
Edwards' selection may have been due simply to the paucity of books
in the backwoods of New England. Yet it is easy to exaggerate this
factor; and as we have seen, by prodigious labor of correspondence
with Erskine and other leading divines and by recording references

to books drawn from every available source, Edwards kept himself
well informed about events in the scholarly world. It is wrong to suggest that he chose only spokesmen of an extreme type of Arminianism
upon whom, by exposing their absurdities, he could bring a more
devastating defeat. It is also incorrect to suggest that Edwards' argument surreptitiously depends on the doctrine of original sin (or that
consequently he proves only that the will has no self-determining
power *to the good* and not that it has no self-determining power);
and that he selected authors who knew least that this was the issue,
and unfortunately was never answered by anyone who undertook to
uncover this silent assumption. Edwards does not bring the corruption of the will decisively into the issue because, quite simply, he
thought he had no need to do so in order to show that nothing about
the human or the ethical gave any ground for the Arminian rejection
of the determining grace of God.

These three opponents represent sufficient diversity of opinion to
be representative of the thought prevailing at the time; and it would
be easy to show that if Edwards' argument against them is really
sound, it can be applied with equal force to other proponents of free
will. In fact, in the range of opinion and churchmanship among them
is to be found the best reason for their selection. Chubb was a deist
(to which extreme position, Edwards believed, Arminianism was
bound to come if any opening be given it), Whitby was a minister of
the Church of England, and Watts was a dissenting minister and
theologian, representing Edwards' own tradition in theology in
which serious breach was being made. To refute these three authors
effectively was to direct a line of fire all along the battle front, and
to serve the cause of truth in the church generally. In any case, Edwards can be fully understood only by recapturing the original force
of the *Inquiry* upon readers who were as familiar with the writings
of Chubb, Whitby, and Watts as we today are with the live options
to Christian orthodoxy in certain persuasive statements of the philosophy of naturalism, humanism, and liberalism.

THOMAS CHUBB

1. Thomas Chubb (1679–1747), a journeyman all his life who nevertheless attained considerable reputation as a writer on theological
and philosophical subjects, was to the leading lights of the eighteenth
century a constant object of condescension and wonder. He was the
assistant to a tallow chandler, a seller of candles, and—his eyesight

permitting—a glovemaker, who made his living by these employ-
ments and by receiving help from various benefactors, and who, for
the rest, spent his time in study and writing and in chairing a small
discussion group in the town of Salisbury, England. He began his
authorship with a defense of Arianism, entitled *The Supremacy of
the Father Asserted: or, Eight Arguments from Scripture to Prove
that the Son Is a Being Inferior and Subordinate to the Father, and
that the Father Alone Is the Supreme God* (1715), having been stimulated to undertake this writing by reading the historical preface to
William Whiston's *Primitive Christianity Revived* (1711); and
Whiston himself secured the publication of Chubb's first tract. His
fellow townsmen expected him one day to rival Locke, which he
never did. Yet his treatises, which it is said were once praised by Vol-
taire, apparently were widely read, especially in the American part
of "this nation." Pope called him a "wonderful phenomenon" and
said of his collected *Tracts* published in 1730 (the book Edwards used
in writing his *Inquiry*) that he "read the whole volume with admiration of the writer, though not always with approbation of the doctrine."

Beginning as an Arian and a disciple of William Whiston and
Samuel Clarke, Chubb thereafter moved rapidly on to a variant of
deism, and wrote a number of works in this vein. It has recently been
pointed out that in the eighteenth century "in point of fact, the first
disturbances to agitate English opinion . . . were within the bodies
of the old Christian churches—chiefly, the debate about the Trinity.
Deists only poured in through a breach already opened by good Christians." [8] Chubb poured with them. Whiston himself observed that
Socinianism or unitarian rationalism was only a short step from
deism, but he neglected to notice the easy passage from his own
Arianism to Socinianism. Chubb, however, made rapid strides, as
did Thomas Woolston and John Toland. His deistic writings fall
mainly after what Leslie Stephen calls "the culminating point of the
deist controversy," [9] and he was never so influential as Tindal or
Toland. That is to say, the deistic movement had passed beyond the
"critical" stage to "constructive deism" which, it soon became apparent, had little to say for itself. The inability of deists to agree upon

8. Roland N. Stromberg, *Religious Liberalism in Eighteenth Century England*
(New York, Oxford University Press, 1954), pp. 5–6.
9. *History of English Thought in the Eighteenth Century* (New York, 1876),
ch. 3, no. 73.

those moral and religious truths apprehended by the universal "religion of nature" and by the consciences of all mankind proved fatal to it. Nobody doubted the religion of nature until the deists undertook to say what it was, just as before that, according to the remark of the deist Anthony Collins, nobody doubted the existence of God until Dr. Clarke strove to prove it, and before that "nobody doubted the doctrine of the Trinity until William Sherlock tried to demonstrate it mathematically." [1] In this age constructive Trinitarianism, constructive theism, and constructive deism put themselves to the test and were successively found wanting. Thomas Chubb participated in a small way in the breaking up of deism, or rather he produced a bit of the evidence to which historians refer when they speak of the confusion and failure of "constructive deism," by publishing in 1745 an attack upon Rutherforth's theory of self-love, called *The Ground and Foundation of Morality Considered.* Thus from the Trinitarian controversy to the evident disorder and lack of positive content in deism, Thomas Chubb summed up in his person most of the currents of the age. Yet he remained a Christian and a churchgoer. The question, however, which should have been argued, writes Leslie Stephen, was "the utility of maintaining the Christian embodiment of deistic doctrines." [2]

2. Edwards singles out, as he says in the preface, only one of Chubb's views for refutation in the present work; and he takes care not to blacken the Arminian divines who agree with Chubb upon this point by associating them with his other doctrines which they doubtless held in abhorrence. "The dogmatic assertion of Free-will," Stephen points out, "became a mark of the whole deist and semi-deist school." [3] This is the point of Edwards' attack; and as a matter of fact Chubb's tracts to which he refers were all published before the author's semi-deism fully developed.

Nevertheless, attention should be given to Edwards' reading of the movement of thought in his century. While he acknowledges that "it would be unjust, in many instances, to charge every author with believing and maintaining all the real consequences of his avowed doctrines," still it is important to know what are "the consequences of the doctrine really." Edwards believed that "the leading article in the

1. Stromberg, pp. 10–11.
2. *History of English Thought,* ch. 3, no. 73.
3. Ibid., ch. 1, no. 33.

Arminian scheme . . . if pursued in its consequence, will truly infer, or naturally lead to all the rest" of Mr. Chubb's opinions (p. 132). The freedom of will was, as Edwards saw it, the breach through which deism poured, and the abandonment of Christianity. Having done what he could in this work to stop the breach, Edwards indicates in his conclusion the consequence he expected his argument to have for strengthening belief in all the other doctrines of orthodox Calvinism. This should not be neglected if we are to understand Edwards. If instead we use plastic surgery on his thought with a view to giving it a more pleasing visage before modern eyes, we shall not understand even what he conceived himself to be undertaking in discussing the freedom of the will, on which all the rest depended. In this connection, it is significant to note that in his letter of Oct. 19, 1757 to the trustees of the College of New Jersey (now Princeton) in answer to their invitation to him to become president of the college (and before mentioning his projected "great work, which I call a *History of the Work of Redemption,* a body of divinity in an entirely new method"), Jonathan Edwards wrote of

> laying out many things in my mind to do in this matter, if God should spare my life, which my heart hath been much upon: particularly many things against most of the prevailing errors of the present day, which I cannot with any patience see maintained (to the utter subverting of the gospel of Christ) with so high a hand, and so long continued a triumph, with so little control, when it appears so evident to me, that there is truly no foundation for any of this glorying and insult. I have already published something on one of the main points in dispute between Arminians and Calvinists: and have it in view, God willing, (as I have already signified to the public) in like manner to consider all the other controverted points, and have done much towards a preparation for it.

Edwards may describe more or less correctly the current of thought in his century, so well illustrated in Chubb's life as an author, and yet he might have mistaken the source from which it flowed.[4] A con-

4. The historical sequence of the chief subjects of controversy in the eighteenth century, which has been sketched above, is a correct account of the developments in England and in Chubb's thought. Things happened somewhat differently in New England. Here "the religious" constituted a more compact minority whose unity was first decisively broken by the bitter dispute over the Great Awakening.

temporary historian writes that " 'original sin' was doubtless the real
nub of the whole controversy involving free will" and "the truth is
that this age inclined to the Arminian side because it did not have
that profound sense of man's worthlessness on earth which leads to
the Augustinian-Calvinist position." [5] By contrast, Edwards seems to
believe that free will was the real nub of the controversy over original sin and over the other doctrines of Calvinism; and it was his
judgment that because the age inclined to the Arminian side on the
question of freedom of will it was losing all sense for the meaning of
original sin and its grasp upon the other principles of historic Christianity. For this reason he wrote the present *Inquiry* before his *The
Great Christian Doctrine of Original Sin Defended* in answer to John
Taylor. For Edwards the refutation of Arminian notions of free will
was the thing upon which hinged everything else of importance for
the religious thought of his century, as the impression of grace upon
the soul was the foundation of the religious life. *If* the former was an
error in historical judgment, it was one into which he was betrayed
by the combination in his mind of Lockean and Newtonian speculation with the shift—that had already taken place in the development
of Calvinism—by which the doctrine of predestination was moved
into a place of importance it never before occupied in constructive
Christian theology, as that from which the other heads of doctrine
derive rather than itself perhaps being derived from more basic
doctrines or experience.

Before concluding that he was in fact mistaken in this judgment
one ought carefully to examine the reason Edwards believed the
Arminian doctrine of the freedom of will to be the first step along
the path of abandoning Christianity in other, more essential respects;
and why he thought the destruction of this view its chief defense.
When this is done it will be found that there is a sure and certain—
one might almost say an organic—connection between views of sin
(and associated aspects of the Christian scheme of redemption) and
the conception of the will held in any age. This connection manifests
itself in the fact that it is precisely by taking refuge in the autonomy

---

This opened the breach through which poured the controversy over free will. Only
after the American Revolution were Anti-Trinitarian viewpoints widely expressed
in high quarters. See Conrad Wright, *The Beginnings of Unitarianism in America*
(Boston, Beacon Press, 1955), passim. Edwards was concerned with doctrines in
the order of their logical dependence.

5. Stromberg, pp. 116, 117–18.

of their wills that people, and the thought-forms of any age, avoid full-scale confession of sin. Men perhaps acknowledge the sins they are conscious of themselves producing by self-determining acts of will. But once they begin to search only for self-determined acts they are likely to find nothing at all to confess, and this is precisely the virtue of such an understanding of sin and of freedom. There is no such thing to be found in human experience as choosing to choose the sinful act, and so, on these terms, no sin to confess; or at least very little in comparison with confessing sin to be a fixed and stated quality of human nature and a steady cause among the causes of all the actions of natural man. Thus the self-determining power of the will was, in Edwards' belief, an "escape clause" the Arminians wanted to write into man's covenant with God by which to avoid, or diminish the severity of, what piety requires. The step "from piety to moralism" [6] was attractive to many people because moralistic conceptions cutting sin down to the size of self-determination seemed so plausible to them; and, moreover, thus to deny or diminish the disease was always more pleasant than to seek its radical cure from grace. The ground had to be removed from under such moralism before piety could be restored. The escape clause had to be expunged in order that the ancient covenant might regain its former force. The exit into autonomy of the will had to be stopped, or else people would never again need to halt where they are and make, on the spot, full confession of their utter sinfulness and seek a determining power not their own for righteousness' sake.

That such was Edwards' conviction, and his undertaking in the *Inquiry,* is evident from his extensive remarks to this effect in a letter to Rev. John Erskine, August 3, 1757.[7] Nothing is more necessary,

6. Cf. Joseph Haroutunian, *Piety versus Moralism: the Passing of the New England Theology*, New York, Henry Holt, 1932.

7. This letter mentions JE's letter of July 25, 1757, remarking upon Lord Kames' *Essays*, and concludes with Erskine the arrangements whereby it was to "be printed in Scotland, if it be thought best," as "A letter from me to a minister in Scotland." JE looked on these letters, both that of July 25 and that of August 3, as of special importance and sent duplicates of both, lest one copy of either should fail to arrive. Dwight remarks concerning the letter of August 3 quoted above that it also "might well have been published at the time, and circulated through the Church at large" (ed. Dwight, *1, 558*). Certainly JE's "Remarks" upon Lord Kames' *Essays* add little that was not clearly and fully stated in the *Inquiry*, while that of August 3 throws a great deal of light upon JE's viewpoint that is not to be found elsewhere in his writings. See below, Related Correspondence.

writes Edwards, for evangelical humiliation and salvation than for men to be brought to thorough conviction of their sin. Yet "the thing, that mainly prevents this, is men's excusing themselves with their own inability, and the moral necessity of those things, wherein their exceeding guilt and sinfulness in the sight of God, most fundamentally and mainly consists." Of course, it may be that they often dwell upon *particular acts* of sin, to which they seem to have determined themselves, and are not at all disinclined even to "think of some instances of lewd behavior," etc.

> But the grand principles of iniquity, constantly abiding and reigning, from whence all proceeds, are all overlooked. Conscience does not condemn them for those things, because *they cannot love God of themselves, they cannot believe of themselves,* and the like. . . . These things are very much, for want of being thoroughly instructed, in that great and important truth, *that a bad will, or an evil disposition of heart, itself, is wickedness.* It is wickedness, in its very being, nature and essence, and not merely the occasion of it, or the determining influence, that it was first owing to.[8]

If sin be hardness of heart, then plainly the more obdurate the heart the more is it sinful. The more a man cannot do otherwise from moral inability, or the more he simply cannot feel at all inclined to do otherwise, the more sinful he is. Belief in the self-determining freedom of will, however, would lead us to conclude the exact opposite: that the harder the heart the less guilt of sin. If on the occasion of some mighty "awakening" or general "attention" to religion men feel themselves prone to confess sin, they will invariably be prevented from doing so by false notions of freedom, since according to these notions men must first search out only those sins to which they have determined themselves.

> This notion of their inability to help it, excusing them, will keep them from proper conviction of sin herein. . . . When they find how hard their hearts are, and how far from a proper sensibility and affection in things of religion; they are kept from properly condemning themselves for it, from the *moral necessity,* or *inability,* which attends it. For the very notion of hardness of heart, implies moral inability. The harder the heart is, the more dead

---

8. This and several subsequent quotations are from the letter mentioned above. See below, Related Correspondence, pp. 467–9.

it is in sin, and the more unable to exert good affections and acts. Thus the strength of sin, is made the excuse of sin.

If growing good by a number of self-determined acts is all that is required or to be expected, there can properly be no such thing as being wholly converted to Christ. If growing wicked by a number of self-determined acts is all that is meant by sin, there can properly be no such thing as abasement of the soul before the divine holiness on account of wickedness beyond man's power to remove. Therefore, Edwards contends,

> These notions of liberty of indifference, contingence and self-determination, as essential to guilt or merit, tend to preclude all sense of any great guilt for past or present wickedness. As has been observed already, all wickedness of heart is excused, as what, in itself considered, brings no guilt. And all that the conscience has to recur to, to find any guilt, is the first wrong determination of the will, in some bad conduct, before that wickedness of heart existed, that was the occasion of introducing or confirming it. . . . And *how small a matter does this at once bring men's guilt to,* when all the main things, wherein their wickedness consists, are passed over. And indeed *the more these principles are pursued, the more and more must guilt vanish, till at last it comes to nothing* [italics mine].

Edwards' view that freedom of the will, and the views of certain historians of thought that sinfulness, was the hinge upon which the door swung open into the intellectual history of the eighteenth century, are not actually opposed to each other. Ideas in that age, Edwards discerned, were in flight *to* freedom, and at the same time in flight *from* confession of sin and from engagement in other grand moments of the Christian scheme.

In this connection, it is significant that quite a number of Chubb's *Tracts* with which Edwards deals [1] were written by Chubb in the

1. Thomas Chubb, *A Collection of Tracts on Various Subjects,* London, 1730. In the citations below, and in JE's text, page references from p. 249 through p. 277 of these *Tracts* are from Treatise XX, "A Vindication of God's Moral Character"; those to pp. 303–25 are from Treatise XXIII, "Five Letters Relating to the Fourth Proposition of Mr. Barclay's Apology," Pt. 1, "An Examination of Mr. Barclay's Principles with Regard to Man's Natural Ability since the Fall"; pp. 349–70, from Treatise XXVI, "Scripture Evidence Considered: in a View of the Controversy, betwixt the Author and Mr. Barclay's Defenders" (one page reference to this work in the original, being plainly in error, has been corrected

course of a controversy between himself and certain defenders of the fourth proposition of Robert Barclay's *An Apology for the True Christian Divinity, as the Same Is Held Forth, and Preached, by the People, Called in Scorn, Quakers* (1676). This proposition states that

> All Adam's posterity . . . is fallen, degenerate, and dead; deprived of the sensation (or feeling) of this inward testimony, or Seed of God, and is subject unto the power, nature, and Seed of the Serpent, which he sows in men's hearts . . . from whence that not their words and deeds only, but all their imaginations are evil perpetually in the sight of God, as proceeding from this depraved and wicked seed. Man, therefore, as he is in this state, can know nothing aright; yea, his thoughts and conceptions concerning God, and things spiritual (until he be disjoined from this evil seed, and united to the Divine Light) are unprofitable both to himself and others. Hence are rejected the Socinian and Pelagian errors, in exhalting a natural light.

Repelled by this, Chubb was propelled to develop his own notions concerning the competence, liberty, and goodness of natural man. (Add to this his strong desire to "vindicate God's moral character" generally.) It is true Chubb was not, first off, propelled by a view of man's liberty of will (which opinion was already firm and well-elaborated in his mind) to dismiss the traditional doctrine of sin and to become, in other respects as well, a deist. Yet he was stimulated to develop or embrace such notions of freedom as the one safe way of avoiding the traditional doctrine of sin. The same was true of the origin of Whitby's concern with the problem of freedom.

The tactic Edwards adopted in the first flurry of the Arminian controversy was a direct rational defense of great Christian truths. In two successive public lectures in the latter part of 1734 he preached discourses on justification by faith alone, and he was promptly criticized for voicing positive (i.e. controversial) opinions, not only by his opponents but by others who thereby showed how hesitant they had become to express such convictions or to hear them openly expressed.[2]

---

to the proper place; and the one remaining reference may also be wrong but it is too brief to tell); pp. 371–82, from Treatise XXVII, "Reflections on Natural Liberty"; and pp. 385–97, from Treatise XXVIII, Pt. 1, "Some Farther Reflections on Natural Liberty."

2. Dwight, *1*, 122, 140–1. This discourse was first published in 1738 among five discourses prefixed to the *Narrative of Surprising Conversions;* and JE quotes

By this direct approach Edwards touched off the Great Awakening in Northampton; but following the controversies over that event it soon became evident that Arminianism was stronger than before. The Puritan stronghold could not be defended, nor a stop be put to defection from the ranks, unless the exit into the freedom of autonomous self-determination was blocked forever. This was Edwards undertaking in the *Inquiry*, and this is also why he regarded this treatise as necessary preparation, but only as preparation, for the complete rational defense of Christianity.

3. Is it altogether incorrect to suspect that Edwards did not relish the plebeian flavor surrounding this interloper among scholars? He certainly held Chubb's views the more in contempt for being more removed from orthodox Christianity than those of the other writers selected for refutation in this work. In any case, I shall have to point out that he does not succeed in refuting Chubb's position because he does not effect a meeting with it—although this is not to say that Chubb's ideas are either adequate or self-consistent in themselves.

Certainly Edwards does not everywhere take Chubb's meaning for what it is; and this can be seen at the first place he brings him into consideration (p. 226). When Chubb writes that "no action can take place without some motive to excite it," he does not mean that, when motive excites, the action will always take place; or, in Locke's language, that given the motive, the action becomes "unavoidably voluntary." He means rather that motives "invite" the will to act. Motives that are the indispensable or necessary condition may not be a sufficient condition for action. Therefore, this first cluster of quotations do not themselves directly contradict those Edwards cites in the immediately following paragraph; and the opposition set forth between these two paragraphs disappears, together with the asserted inconsistency in Chubb's views. It is true that Chubb "abundantly speaks of motives as 'excitements of the acts of the will,'" and as Edwards says, "to excite, is positively to *do* something." Yet Edwards' account of what motives do obscures rather than grasps Chubb's meaning: "To create, is to cause to be created; to make, is to cause to be made; to kill, is to cause to be killed; to quicken, is to cause to be quickened; and *to excite, is to cause to be excited*" (pp. 236–7). Yes, Chubb might well reply, in the sense that to "invite" is to cause to be invited, to

---

from it when citing his own previously printed words about Arminianism, in the *Inquiry*, below, p. 300.

"address" is to cause to be addressed, to "court" the will is to cause
it to be courted, to "stimulate" is to cause to be stimulated. He may
be abysmally in error as to the truth and human experience in this
matter when he writes that no volition can take place without some
motive to induce it and yet asserts that among competing motives the
will or "active faculty" may choose the weaker and not the stronger
motive (p. 229). But there is no verbal inconsistency or *logical* absurdity in saying so, since this plainly means that while there is *some*
previous ground and reason for the action proposed by each of the
motives there is never in motive alone *sufficient* ground or reason for
any one action. "Both of these," motive and will, Chubb writes, "are
absolutely necessary to constitute a *moral agent.*" [3]

4. Chubb frequently calls motives the *"passive* ground" or *"passive*
reason" of action, which Edwards describes as "a remarkable phrase;
than which I presume there is none more unintelligible, and void of
distinct and consistent meaning, in all the writings of Duns Scotus,
or Thomas Aquinas" (p. 228). He then goes on to convict Chubb of
inconsistency in affirming the very same motive to be both previous
and consequent to the action of the will. Yet Chubb's meaning in the
use of the word "passive" is not so difficult to grasp. It is a relative
term. Of course, motives *accomplish* something, they stimulate the
will, and in this they are *active.* But when the "active faculty" or will
comes into play, in relation to it they become passive. Edwards' real
contention against Chubb should be that he separates too completely
the faculties of will and understanding (or perception, which takes
in motives), a point he fails to score in his eagerness to play second
to a duel between Chubb's words. By calling previous motive the
"passive ground" of voluntary action Chubb does not mean "first
acted upon" by volition in such a fashion that the will originally determines to fetch forth its own initial motivation. Rather is "passive"
a term indicating the relationship between two things both already
in existence, neither prior or consequent to the other, namely, the
will and its environing motives taken in by the understanding. "Man
is a compound being, consisting partly of *understanding,* and partly
of *appetite,*" whence come motives, and "the active faculty." [4] Volition does "act toward" motive in choosing to yield to it. With regard

3. Chubb, *Tracts,* p. 311.
4. Ibid., pp. 256–7.

to perceptions of the fitness of things gathered by the understanding, the whole man is "so far passive" that if he *attend* to these things, he cannot judge otherwise than according to the greater good. Yet moral action springs from both motive *and* will; and the action is "done by a *power,* in the exercise of which I am not *passive* but *active*" [5]—

> the motive that prevails being not a *power,* or *active cause,* but barely a *passive reason* of, or an excitement to the action, or to the refraining from acting. There being this apparent difference between *motive* and *physical necessity,* viz. the one *forces,* the other does but *invite:* one is an *address* to an *active,* the other is *acting upon* a *passive being:* the one supposes *liberty,* the other *passiveness* in the subject influenced or wrought on by them. And consequently man has *power,* and is as much at *liberty* to reject the motive that *does prevail,* as he has power and is at liberty to *reject* those motives that do not.[6]

When Chubb speaks of motive as the ground for the *exertion* of an act of the will (cited by Edwards, p. 228), this is thrown significantly into a subordinate clause, and Edwards does not take into account the remainder of the statement: "Whereas, in the case of *liberty,* tho the self-moving power will not be exerted, unless some motive be the ground or reason of it; yet action does not *necessarily* follow the perception of such a motive, but a man is at liberty to *exert* or *suspend* the exertion of that power, notwithstanding." [7] Here, discussing the question whether the will is necessarily determined to the greater good, Chubb rests liberty in a power to suspend; and this means that, if the will exerts itself to suspend action, *previous* motives so far become, in relation to it, *passive.* The parallel with Locke is apparent; and Edwards' reduction of the act of suspending to an act motivated like all the rest seems equally applicable to Chubb or to Locke. Edwards' effort to force Chubb to testify against himself is largely verbal, and dependent upon taking what he says about motives as previous ground for action in a different sense from Chubb's usage.

Edwards might perhaps have scored a direct hit upon Chubb's admission that motives or "ideas that take place in the understanding"

5. Ibid., p. 260.
6. Ibid., p. 257.
7. Ibid., p. 391.

are the ground or reason not only of action (in the sense of inviting to action) but also "of the suspending the exercise of that power." [8] Yet even here the positions presuppose themselves and never meet in open or decisive encounter. For Chubb admits, nay even contends, that the act of suspending action, *when motivated* through the understanding, has nothing to do with liberty. If man be "at *liberty* to *examine* whether what appears to him to be his greatest self-good be, in reality, so, or not; then, that appearance has no . . . *necessary* effect upon the active faculty. . . . But if *examination* could come into this scheme, it would not help the case; because examination would be as *necessary,* and as *unavoidable,* as the actions would be, which would follow upon it. For as there must be the *appearance* of a probability of error, or the intervention of *some motive,* to be the *foundation* for such examination; so where that probability appears, or such motive intervenes, man . . . must *necessarily* and *unavoidably* examine whether what appears to be his greatest self-good be, in reality, so, or not." [9] This truly Edwardean argument serves only to show that Chubb's liberty is, in Edwards' sense, "out of this world" of motives and that liberty to interrupt action (or for that matter to begin it) Edwards supposes can be reduced again to motivation, while Chubb supposes it cannot. For Chubb supposes there actually is a liberty of the will to suspend motivation which in many instances is not itself motivated through appetite, perception, or understanding.

5. Edwards is on sounder ground when he argues, pp. 232–3, that if the will can choose to act from the weaker motive, it could choose to act from no motive at all; and that this in fact, as Chubb allows, is not the case. But then we must raise the question whether Chubb's statement, that no volition takes place without some motive to induce it, be not simply a *description* of what is ordinarily the case in human actions. No doubt his language to this effect, and the frequency of these assertions, support Edwards' interpretation. Yet this is hardly sufficient to draw from Chubb the conclusion that "the will can't stir at all without some motive" (p. 233). In one of the treatises cited, Chubb reasons that while God *can* do evil, we may rest assured he *will* not do so "because we are sure nature does not afford a motive, which will be the ground or reason of such a choice." He then says that "though *a free being can act without a motive,* with respect to

8. Ibid., p. 310.
9. Ibid., p. 374.

any *necessity* he is under to the contrary; yet, I think, it is evident *he will not,* because, I think, there must be some *motive,* to be the ground and reason of his choice." [1] Here "I think" evidences Chubb's uncertainty about the universal necessity of motives accompanying or stimulating free action. Again he speculates that the will *can* choose evil; but since *"nature* does not afford a *motive* which will be the *ground* or *reason* of such choice . . . it will follow, not that a man *cannot,* but that he *will not* choose evil, as such." [2]

Near the end of his *Inquiry,* Edwards calls Chubb to witness that God does no evil because he "necessarily perfectly knows what is most worthy and valuable in itself" (p. 418). Chubb does write that by saying "it is morally impossible for God to do evil" is meant that "the moral unfitness of such a conduct affords a motive, which, by its persuasive influence, will as effectively prevent God from doing evil, as any physical impossibility, that is, as any impossibility arising from physical impediments can do." These things are equally certain. Yet Chubb's *certainty* concerning God's moral character differs from Edwards' in that "morally impossible" or "moral unfitness" have not for him quite the same meaning as the "moral necessity" of the opposite, since he does not, like Edwards, use the word "necessity" interchangeably with "it is impossible that it not be." Therefore, he says, "the ground of this knowledge, viz. that God will not do evil, does not arise from our knowing that he wants either power *or liberty* to do evil" or from our knowing "that the forementioned motive will always *necessarily* prevent *every* intelligent being from acting thus, and thereby that it is strictly impossible" for a good will to do evil.[3]

Moreover, there is one sort of case in which the will always wills without a motive. Rigorously separating understanding from appetite, Chubb writes that "motives arising from the *same branch* of the constitution, may be greater or less; but motives, which arise from *different branches* of the constitution, admit of *no* comparison." Whenever reason and appetite come in competition, then, "it is not greater or less motive, but a *freedom* of *election* which is the foundation of action." In such instances of men's actions, "whichsoever of these *they do follow,* that is, whichsoever of these is to them the *ground* or *reason* of action, that, in that instance, they call the *strongest motive;* and the motive whose persuasive influence they *reject,*

1. Ibid., p. 381.
2. Ibid., p. 385 n.
3. Ibid., pp. 261–2 (italics mine).

that, in this instance, they call the *weakest*," [4] i.e. the strongest motive
is the one "prevailing in the event" which is from the will and not the
motive. Here clearly, in a passage Edwards does not refer to, the will
as a free cause fetches forth its own motive, or acts without a motive;
and this does seem to be inconsistent with Chubb's more frequent
statements that there must be some motive. These latter, however,
taken by themselves, entail no inconsistency, since Chubb only means
to assert by them that almost always (or even as a statistically universal fact) acts of the will spring from the self-activating faculty only
in the context of environing motives. Again it is evident that Edwards should disprove Chubb's faculty psychology and not try to
catch him in an inconsistency.[5]

6. Another instance of Edwards' reduction of Chubb's notion of
a free act to "a heap of contradictions" rests upon the latter's statement, "When the self-moving power is exerted, it becomes the *necessary* cause of its effects" (p. 235). The continuation of this quotation
is sufficient to place it in proper context: "yet as a man is *free* and
voluntary, in the exertion of that power; that is, he is not under a
necessity, from the constitution of things, to exert, or not exert it, to
exert it this way, or that way, tho there may be more reason for the
one than the other: so, in that respect, it is said to be a *free cause,* and
those *effects* are likewise said to be *free,* which are produced by it." [6]
The effects are necessary consecutive upon willing; but, according to
Chubb, *to exert* the will, from which effects follow, is not.

It is all the more important to extend the foregoing quotation—
with its resting of the exertion of the will upon free election—because Edwards makes so much of what might appear to the reader to
be innumerable statements by Chubb where he seems to say that
motives cause the *exertion* or the *production* of an act of will. There

---

4. Ibid., p. 396.

5. This same objection continued to be made against JE by his New England
opponents. Thus Samuel West wrote in his *Essays on Liberty and Necessity* (New
Bedford, Mass., 1795), Pt. II, p. 5: "To enable us to determine which is the
strongest, the motives compared must all belong to the same faculty of the soul;
and if they belong to different faculties of the mind, no comparison can be made
between them." In the light of the continued sway of faculty psychology even
after Locke's views had been widely but superficially accepted, we can understand
JE's endeavor to drive home the new conception of the human mind by adopting an even more unitary view than Locke's.

6. Chubb, *Tracts,* p. 389.

is one passage in which, in an exceptional use of the words "production" and "exertion," Chubb does give this meaning to the influence
of motive upon action; [7] and here he falls between the jaws of Edwards' argument (pp. 237–8). Yet it should be pointed out that this is
the one place in all the treatises Edwards cites in which Chubb writes,
with the meaning Edwards takes from it, that motives are necessary
for the *production* of action or the *exertion* of the will. His usual
meaning is simply that "motives are only the *ground* or *reason,* why
we suspend or exert the self-moving power, or why we exert it, in
one way, or at one time, rather than in another way, or at another
time, but are not causes of either. Motives are merely *passive,* if I
may so speak, in the production of action. That is, they have no
causality, in the production of it." [8] By passive ground Chubb ordinarily means what "causes the will to be *invited.*" This passage in
which he goes the length of saying that motives are necessary for the
exertion of will or the production of action should be counterbal-
anced by his speculation at the opposite extreme from his usual position, that there may actually be such a thing as a wholly unmotivated
will.[9]

DANIEL WHITBY

7. Daniel Whitby (1638–1726) was a polemical Church of England
divine who first came to public attention because of his anti-Romist
tracts, such as *The Idolatry of Host Worship* (1679). Because he
proved to be not so polemical on the other side he lost somewhat in
favor among fellow churchmen, with the anonymous publication of
*The Protestant Reconciler, Humbly Pleading for Condescension to
Dissenting Brethren in Things Immaterial.* To this an ironic reply
was made in the form of a "letter of thanks" purporting to come from
the Anabaptists at Munster; and the University at Oxford condemned
his proposition that, in order not to offend the weaker brethren, laws
should not be enacted requiring conformity in "things indifferent";
his books were burned, and he was forced to retract. His greatest
work was a paraphrase and commentary on the New Testament, in
two volumes (1703), which Philip Doddridge (the dissenter, and
protégé and literary executor of Isaac Watts) regarded as "preferable
to all others."

7. Ibid., p. 317.
8. Ibid., p. 389.
9. Ibid., pp. 381, 385, 396; and see above, Pt. 5, no. 5, of this Introduction.

In 1710 Whitby became engaged in refuting the Calvinism of John Edwards, who had been forced in 1670 to resign from St. John's College at Cambridge because of his views. Anthony Collins in his *Discourse of Free-Thinking* was able to list on the Calvinist side, no one among the Anglicans worth naming except John Edwards.[1] Collins and Whitby both observe that most Anglicans were Arminians. An Anglican of the eighteenth century was surprised to learn that until about the time of Archbishop Laud the clergy were universally Calvinist, and that in those days the anti-Calvinists were the despised "Anabaptists." Arminianism permeated the eighteenth century, and in mild form the whole of the Church of England in this century, becoming in a sense not heresy but orthodoxy.[2] But still there was John Edwards, who in retirement after 1686 and till his death in 1716 made the press rather than the pulpit the means of diffusing his opinions; and in the course of polemic against him in particular and against Calvinism in general Whitby wrote the *Discourse on the Five Points,* first published in 1710, on which Jonathan Edwards in America comments. Ranked as an Arminian, Daniel Whitby soon went beyond this position. Apparently he was much shaken by the views of Samuel Clarke upon our Lord's deity, which came out in 1712; and his "retractation," published "by his express order" posthumously, evidences an Arian and unitarian tendency.

8. The "Discourse on the Five Points" is Jonathan Edwards' abbreviated citation throughout to refer to Daniel Whitby's *A Discourse Concerning I. The True Import of the Words Election and Reprobation; and the Things Signified by Them in the Holy Scripture. II. The Extent of Christ's Redemption. III. The Grace of God; Where It Is Enquired, Whether It Be Vouchsafed Sufficiently to Those Who Improve It Not, and Irresistibly to Those Who Do Not Improve It; and Whether Men Be Wholly Passive in the Work of Their Regeneration? IV. The Liberty of the Will in a State of Trial and Probation. V. The Perseverance or Defectibility of the Saints; with Some Reflections on the State of Heathens, the Providence and Prescience of God* (2d ed. 1735). First published in 1710, this work contains in the second edition an additional Discourse VI in answer to three objections, and a Postscript in reply to John Edwards' refutation of Whitby's earlier exposition of biblical texts relevant to the controversy.

1. Stromberg, *Religious Liberalism,* pp. 111–12.
2. Ibid., p. 110.

Even though Jonathan Edwards refers on p. 222 to most of the "heads" of Whitby's discourses, and the conclusion shows that his *Inquiry* has in view the defense of Calvinism under these same heads, by far the greater number of Edwards' citations are to Discourse IV, "The Liberty of the Will of Man in a State of Trial and Probation." It may not be altogether wrong to see in Edwards' use of the word "heads" not only a characteristic literary device for designating the main points of an outline, but also an acknowledgment that Whitby's discourses correspond by way of opposition to the five canons or "heads of doctrine" formulated by the Calvinist Synod of Dort (1619), and in substance to the five articles of the Arminian Remonstrance (1610). The title of Whitby's book listed in the Dummer catalogue as a gift to the library of Yale College in 1713 reads "Discourses on the Quinquarticular Controversy"; and Edwards may have first read it there. In any case, the controversy was a "five-pointed" or five-headed one, in which the various points held together.

For the most part, Whitby's book is hardly more than a tessellation of quotations from the Bible and the early Church Fathers. Still it is important to deal with his point of view in substance, even if summarily, as background for understanding Edwards. It should be noted in general terms that the addition to the "quinquarticular" controversy of an explicit and full-length defense of the freedom of the will in the fourth discourse by the Anglican divine reflects a significant development in Arminianism during the century since the Remonstrance (1610). In the original charter of Arminianism all five articles were more decisively theological without autonomous anthropological speculation upon the freedom of will.

9. Also, Whitby's strenuous denial of the imputation of Adam's sin to the rest of mankind had already carried him beyond the ordinary, or at least the traditional, Arminian position. On pp. 299–300 Edwards detects Whitby in the inconsistency of affirming both that nothing necessary can be sinful or blameworthy and that our natures never had the power to continue innocent as Adam did in his day. This may be a correct observation; yet it is more likely that here Whitby only inadvertantly seems to say there is some sort of necessity of sinning in fallen man. For what he is endeavoring to do in this passage is to show that no disability we have on Adam's account ought ever to be called "sin" or blamed upon us. He is objecting to the notion that our solidarity with Adam's sin renders it just for God

to punish us, on the ground that we had "Strength sufficient" in our first parent Adam, and "therefore may be dealt with as if we had it still." "They who then were not, were not in *Adam*," Whitby writes, "To say our Nature was in *Adam,* and so our Power and our Will might also be in him, is also false; for *Adam* was a particular Man, an *Individuum,* and therefore could have only an individual and particular Nature, and therefore only a particular Will and Power. . . . In a word, the Question is not concerning the Justice of condemning the Nature of *Adam,* but concerning the Justice of condemning *our Persons*" for not doing that which it was impossible for us to do" (final italics mine).[3] This necessity Whitby would not ordinarily call sin. In the preface to his work Whitby announces, indeed, that "that which first moved me to search into the Foundation of these Doctrines, viz. *The Imputation of* Adam's *Sin to all his Posterity,* was the strange Consequences of it"—namely, that this doctrine in the eighteenth century seemed "as contradictory to the common Reason of Mankind, as any thing could be, and so contained as strong an Argument against the Truth of *Scripture,* if that Doctrine was contained in it, as any could be offer'd for it." [4] Whitby's point of view is therefore adequately represented by the second quotation Edwards cites in the paragraph on p. 299: "That if we be necessitated, neither sins of omission nor commission, would deserve that name."

10. He who has not much meditated upon God, the "confirmed" angels, and the damned spirits may possibly make a thriving earthworm, but will most indubitably make a blundering appraisal of how the argument stands between Edwards and Whitby. In spite of an earlier footnote (Pt. II, Sec. 7, note 1) containing a concise and accurate statement of Whitby's views, Jonathan Edwards seems greatly astonished (p. 277) that Dr. Whitby himself allows that God is without the sort of freedom assigned to man. God's morally necessary acts, Edwards observes, are not praiseworthy if a man would not be esteemable under a like moral necessity; "so that, putting these things together," Whitby will be forced to say that "the infinitely holy God, who always used to be esteemed by God's people," is not virtuous or praiseworthy. Yet in Whitby the emphasis always falls on the concluding words of the title of his fourth discourse, "The Liberty of the Will *of Man in a State of Trial and Probation.*" There is no am-

3. Whitby, *Discourse on the Five Points,* pp. 164 f.
4. Ibid., pp. i, ii.

biguity in what he means by human "freedom" under such conditions. It is quite different from the "unavoidably voluntary" actions of God and other beings in the heavenly or diabolical hierarchy, or of men who have passed beyond their probationary existence.

There is, however, a failure on Whitby's part to distinguish between the praise or blameworthiness of human actions and the "praise" that may appropriately be made of God, the angels, and the actions of men when their original freedom to do otherwise has finally reached consummation in a perfect freedom not to do otherwise than they continually do in heaven. When Whitby discusses the liberty of the will, he always stresses what is praise or blameworthy in a creature "in a state of trial or probation." Therefore it is fair to observe that (since Whitby was doubtless as devout as an eighteenth century Anglican divine need be) he no doubt also had in mind some such distinction as Kant's between God's *holy* and man's *good* will, both praiseworthy because not distinguished from each other so entirely as to make the word "praise" completely equivocal in the two cases. Edwards is not responsible for never considering this possibility, since it is not elaborated by Whitby; but his not doing so surrounds with some doubt his attempt to show that Whitby's notion of *human* freedom *in a state of trial* is inconsistent with praise to God. Whitby makes it quite plain that the human freedom of which he speaks is no very great thing. There are higher forms of freedom than this, in comparison with which the liberty of the human will is only an inferior good, and not at all a sovereign power eternally in the possession of man. "The Liberty belonging to this Question, is only that of a lapsed Man in a State of Trial, Probation and Temptation. . . . *This Liberty is indeed no Perfection of Human Nature;* for it supposes us imperfect . . . and when we are advanced to *the Spirits of just Men made perfect,* or to a fixed State of Happiness, will, with our other Imperfections *be done away;* but yet it is a Freedom absolutely requisite . . . to render us capable of Trial or Probation . . . nor is this Liberty essential to Man *as Man,* but only necessary to Man placed in a State of Trial, and under the Power of Temptation." [5] This should have been enough to notify Edwards that Whitby believed the freedom of God, of angels, and of "confirmed" human souls more praiseworthy still than choices made by men during their pilgrimage toward this end. The contention of the next following section (Pt. III, Sec. 2), that Jesus Christ was actually in a state of

5. Ibid., pp. 299–300 (first and final italics mine).

trial and so was praiseworthy for his goodness and yet that it was
morally impossible for him to have willed otherwise than he did, has
more force against Whitby. Within the terms in which the debate
was then set, Edwards rightly regarded the latter argument "as a
point clearly and absolutely determining the controversy between
Calvinists and Arminians," or at least between himself and Whitby
(p. 289, and Pt. III, Sec. 2, note 2).

Edwards appeals to what Whitby allows to be true concerning
devils and damned spirits to support his contention that Arminians
also make God in some sense the author of evil and of the sinful wills
of these beings, and that they therefore also find it necessary to distinguish between God's disposing or determining will and his revealed or preceptive will. "Our doctrine, in its consequence," Edwards writes, "makes God the author of men's sin in this world, no
more, and in no other sense, than his doctrine, in its consequence,
makes God the author of the hellish pride and malice of the devils.
And doubtless the latter is as odious an effect as the former" (p. 398).
Whitby does say that the devil and damned spirits, "tho they are not
determined to Evil Actions in Particular, are yet determined to do
Evil in General and not Good." But this is a punitive consequence
of their sin in some prior "State of Trial," [6] and hence I suppose that
Whitby would have no difficulty with the thought that God is the
efficient author of the wickedness to which they are given up, or (for
him the same thing) that he is the *deficient* author of this wickedness
in that the divine assistance is not given to them which would be
absolutely necessary to their avoiding evil. The crucial point for
Whitby is that God makes no applications to such devils and damned
spirits to reform and hearken to his exhortations. "No Promises are
made to the confirmed *Angels,* no Motives offered to engage them
to chuse the Good, no Evils are threatened to the *Devils* or the
damned Spirits to deter them from doing Evil." [7] To men in a state
of probation *to whom these things are proffered,* it is all one whether
God be the *efficient* or the *deficient* cause of their sin, since in either
case they necessarily cannot respond to his commands and promises.
The presence or absence of divine exhortations for his creatures to
will otherwise makes for Whitby the vast difference between God's
determining what becomes unavoidably voluntary in the after life

6. Ibid., pp. 302, 300.
7. Ibid., pp. 304–5.

and his so determining the human will now. He has no objection to divine determination *as such,* whether by directly disposing or by permitting something to happen by withholding the grace necessary to avoid it.

Of course, Edwards is correct when he writes, "Be sure Dr. Whitby's words do plainly suppose and allow" that God gives some of his creatures up to their own necessary wickedness (p. 409). But that this in turn supposes a distinction between God's *secret* and his *revealed* will in Edwards' sense may be questioned; and Edwards' contention that it does again deflects rather than faces the full force of Whitby's analysis of that inferior freedom man has while under probation. "Confirmed" beings (angels, devils, saved or damned spirits) have lost the lesser liberty *ad utrumvis* they formerly had. They are now under necessity of doing evil or good, "yet do it voluntarily." But Whitby has steadfastly in mind that such freedom, however much more desirable (or horrible) than that we have now, deserves no further reward or punishment. He goes so far as to say that if the devils "are to suffer any thing on account of their Temptations of Men to do Evil . . . they so far lie under no necessity of doing this, but might abstain from those Temptations." [8] In the relation of God to their state of punishment, therefore, there is implied no distinction between God's *secret* will *determining* and *disposing* them to the end they have earned in a previous state of trial and his *revealed* or *preceptive* will disapproving of what they did or of what they do. It is one thing to argue, with St. Augustine, that further wickedness may fittingly be the penal consequence of sin. This Whitby allows. It would be quite another thing to argue that this sin, which is the punishment for sin, deserves blame in the same sense the first sin did. This Whitby denies; and in so doing denies also that God secretly determines the wills of his creatures in ways which, it is revealed to them during their probation, he disapproves.

11. Enough has perhaps been said in connection with Locke about Whitby's shallowness in not distinguishing between *doing* what we will and *willing* to will. Then it is not quite right to suppose that his statements, and the "sayings of the fathers, which he quotes as his vouchers" (p. 192) actually bear witness to Edwards' notion of the will's freedom as the power to act consecutive upon willing. Sec. 5

8. Ibid., p. 300.

of Pt. II shows not so much the impertinency and inconsistency of Whitby the Arminian as it does Edwards' great powers commanding his own view to emerge from an incidental use of words he quotes.

12. Edwards states that Whitby alleges the agreement of Stoics and other pagan philosophers sometimes as a point in favor and sometimes as a point against a viewpoint he is opposing (pp. 372–3). It may be well to call attention to the not so wholly arbitrary way in which this is done. When Whitby cites the Stoics with approval it is in order to say that the Christian faith can and should make the fullest possible use of "reason," for example when he quotes Seneca and writes,

> Nor ought these Arguments to be slighted as being only the Sayings of *Philosophers,* guided by the dim Light of Reason, when they deliver only that in which the common Notions of Mankind have long agreed; for that would be of dreadful Consequence to the whole *Christian* faith: for our Belief of it must bottom upon some rational Inducements, and common Principles of Reason, which if they may be false, *Christianity* may be a false *Religion;* if they be evident and certain Truths, whatsoever contradicts them must be false: If therefore any Article of our Faith should to the best of our Judgments plainly contradict them, it must shock the Foundation of our Faith by engaging Men to believe that false which alone engaged them to believe that Faith was true.[9]

On the other hand, when Whitby identifies a point of view he opposes with an objectionable or heathen position, this may not be the *reason* he asserts its falsity. It is true that Whitby abruptly dismisses the opinions of his adversaries because of their affinity with those of Hobbes. Nevertheless, his concern with "the Fate of the Philosophers" of ancient times is simply to point out that in this they were "condemned by the Christian Fathers," copiously quoted.[1] In short, he seeks to demonstrate that "these late Notions, concerning the Liberty or rather Servitude of the Will of lapsed Man, were generally condemned by the Primitive Christians.[2] This is a *historical* point as to what, in fact, is Christian teaching; and this approach was not ordinarily confused by Whitby with the issue as to truth which

9. Ibid., pp. 327–8.
1. Ibid., pp. 350 f.
2. Ibid., p. 363.

should be argued rationally. The tradition of the church, Whitby was able to write in another connection, "gives no unquestionable assurance of the truth or [for that matter, of the] derivation of these customs from our Lord and His Apostles, for haply the Church embraced them upon other motives." [3] And Anthony Collins quotes Whitby as saying "We should call no Man Guide, or Master upon Earth, no Fathers, no Church, no Council." [4] Unless for one man to be reasonable renders another less so, to call attention to this is in no sense to underrate the powerful and untroubled reasonableness with which Edwards, from Pt. IV, Sec. 6 on, calls upon his readers to disavow no idea because it happens also to have been held by some bad man.

ISAAC WATTS

13. The theological inheritance of Isaac Watts (1674–1748), hymn-writer and the only dissenter among the authors Edwards opposed, was closer to that of Edwards than any of his other antagonists. He was also the only one of the three who had important direct connection with the intellectual life of the American colonies. For both these reasons, it is necessary to make more extended comment upon the relation between Watts' thought and Edwards' argument in the *Inquiry*.

Watts was "a study in hesitant Calvinism." [5] He lived among third and fourth generation nonconformists in England, after "the Protestant ethic" had time to accomplish its work and the beginning of its own demise. The Mark Lane meeting, where Watts had been assistant pastor for a number of years, was "the most aristocratic dissenting meeting in London." [6] Watts followed in this pastorate Isaac Chauncy, son of President Charles Chauncy of Harvard College and uncle of the Charles Chauncy, pastor of First Church, Boston, who was to

3. Paul Elmer More and Frank L. Cross, eds., *Anglicanism: the Theory and Practice of the Church of England, Illustrated from the Religious Literature of the Seventeenth Century* (Milwaukee, Wis., Morehouse Publishing Co., 1935), p. 117.

4. *A Discourse of Free-Thinking* (London, 1713), pp. 45–6.

5. Thus Stromberg, *Religious Liberalism*, p. 116, describes Watts' *The Ruin and Recovery of Mankind*, which (with Edwards' treatment of the same theme) was one of the attempts to answer John Taylor's treatise on original sin.

6. Arthur Paul Davis, *Isaac Watts: His Life and Works* (Columbia University Ph.D. dissertation, privately published 1943), p. 23.

oppose Edwards' part in the revival; but because of poor health Watts was active in this post for only a few years. Thereafter he retired to his books upon the benefit of patronage. For eight years he lived in the house of Thomas Hollis, who founded the first professorship of mathematics and natural philosophy at Harvard (and with some advice from Watts picked Isaac Greenwood to be the first occupant of the chair), endowed a chair of divinity, and at his death left a considerable additional sum of money to the college (naming Watts a trustee of the fund). Another patron was Sir Thomas Abney, alderman and one-time Lord-Mayor of the city of London, a typical "saint" of Watts' group of dissenters, with whose household he lived for thirty-six years.

In the *Lives of the Poets,* Dr. Johnson writes concerning Watts: "Every man acquainted with the common principles of human action, will look with veneration on the writer, who is at one time combating Locke, and at another making a catechism for children in their fourth year. . . . He has provided instruction for all ages, from those who are lisping their first lessons, to the enlightened readers of Malebranche and Locke." Yet in Johnson's opinion "his devotional poetry is, like that of others, unsatisfactory. . . . It is sufficient for Watts to have done better than others what no man has done well." [7] A later generation will likely reverse this preference of Johnson's for Watts' instruction and distaste for his poetry and hymns. He provides a good illustration of the fact that a man may be a very good hymn writer and only an indifferent theologian or philosopher. Despite the erotic mysticism and preromanticism of much of his verse, hymns such as "Our God, Our Help in Ages Past," "Joy to the World, the Lord is Come," "When I Survey the Wondrous Cross," "Jesus Shall Reign Where're the Sun," etc. have more enduring significance than his logic which was once used by students at Oxford and Cambridge or the *Philosophical Essays, on Various Subjects* such as "Mr. Locke's Notion of Substance Considered" and "Of Innate Ideas: the Common Opinion Well Refuted by Mr. Locke."

Watts' moderate and reconciling temper in religious disputes is well illustrated by the titles of three of his works, *The Harmony of All the Religions Which God Ever Prescribed, The Arian Invited to the Orthodox Faith,* and *Orthodoxy and Charity United in Several Reconciling Essays on the Law and the Gospel, Faith and Works.*

7. Samuel Johnson, *The Lives of the Most Eminent English Poets, Concluded,* in *The Works of Samuel Johnson, LL.D.* (11 vols. London, 1787), *3,* 185, 187 f.

Upon the last Dr. Johnson remarked that "it was not only in his book, but in his mind, that *orthodoxy* was *united* with *charity*." [8] From perusing his writings, a G. K. Chesterton might observe that Watts suffered from charity in the wrong place: charity has moved from the heart, from the organ of ambition, and settled upon the mind, the organ of conviction, where it was never meant to be. For such a judgment there is, indeed, enough evidence to be found in Watts' life and work. He proposed to unite the independents and the baptists by asking the former to give up infant baptism and the latter to give up immersion! He explained the doctrine of election so that it became consistent with the possibility of universal salvation: If God guarantees the salvation of a certain number of saints, there is then no reason "why the strictest calvinist should be angry, that the all-sufficient merit of Christ should overflow so far in its influence, as to provide a conditional salvation for all mankind, since the elect of God have that certain and absolute salvation, which they contend for, secured to them by the same merit." [9] This popular Baxterian formula expressed the mood of numerous dissenters who wished neither to cast off their Calvinistic traditions nor to accept them in all their original severity. So Watts accepted election while rejecting reprobation. Thus, "the rigorous Calvinistic doctrine that some are saved and some are damned had become the rather flabby suggestion that some are just more saved than others." [1] A recent biographer of Isaac Watts sums up the consequence of his compromising temper:

> Watts accepted Locke's philosophy, but he also clung to the theory of "innate ideas"; he wrote a *Guide to Prayer* to tone down dissenter enthusiasm in prayer, but he published *An Exhortation to Ministers* to arouse warmth in nonconformist preaching; he rejected the Trinity of the Athanasian Creed because it was illogical; yet he refused to be classed with the Unitarians; he exalted reason in his non-religious essays and depreciated the sufficiency of reason in the religious; he had the usual Neo-Classic horror of enthusiasm, but he spent a lifetime trying to infuse it into the religion of his age; he believed in the certain election of a chosen few, but at the same time he insisted that all men have free will. Watts probably never felt the inconsistency of these

8. Ibid., *3*, 185.
9. *The Ruin and Recovery of Mankind*, in *Works, 6*, 152.
1. Stromberg, p. 113.

opposing views, because he could defend each of them to his own satisfaction on what were for him perfectly rational grounds.[2]

It was frequently remarked by Watts himself that "a moderate man must expect a box on both ears." [3] He often received what he expected.

This failure—if failure it was—completely to systematize his thought upon all subjects was surely the result of a sensitive and inquiring mind. A letter to Benjamin Colman thanking him for the gift of a picture makes evident Watts' generous spirit and the scope of his interests: "I have put it in a frame that it may hang in the same rank with Dr. Increase and Dr. Cotton Mather, in the front of my study. I have there near eighty philosophers and divines surrounding me; their spirits are copied in their books, and their faces adorn my beloved place of retirement. There Heathens and Christians, Papists and Protestants, Calvinists and Arminians, Presbyterians and Episcopalians, all meet in silence and peace. Were you to see my cohabitants, you would say I was a man of catholicism. Most of them I hope to meet in the regions of peace and love." [4] If Watts' catholicity sometimes left him holding his weary head in his hands, still it was a thinking head he held there. In short, like most theologians he shared the confidence in reason common in the eighteenth century. This was not necessarily a supine or exuberant confidence. It often meant rather that "if there was a great gamble in the reliance on reason it was an inevitable one: the other games were all closed out." [5]

Shortly after Watts' death there arose a furious controversy over the memory and reputation of this venerable man. Some asserted that before he died he became an outright unitarian, and that his literary executors, Jennings and Doddridge, willfully suppressed this fact by destroying the evidence for it in the writings he left unpublished. The orthodox denied this, either directly or, granting the fact, by affirming the old man had become senile before adopting such views. To demonstrate derangement Augustus Toplady published posthumously a verse by Watts which he said showed the weakness of old age—which proved, however, to be rather the weakness

2. Davis, p. 222.

3. Jeremy Belknap, *Memoirs of the Lives, Characters and Writings of Dr. Isaac Watts and Dr. Philip Doddridge* (Boston, 1793), p. 24.

4. Sept. 16, 1736. Belknap, p. 17.

5. Stromberg, p. 24.

of youth, it having already been published by the author years before! The truth seems to be that Watts never was completely orthodox on the doctrine of the Trinity as this was understood in the controversy with Whiston and Clarke. In his many writings upon the subject Watts displayed a strong desire to reconcile the Arians with the orthodox, for example by his belief that the human soul of Jesus Christ pre-existed the creation of the man; and in "The Author's Solemn Address to the Great and ever-blessed God, on a Review of what he had written in the Trinitarian Controversy," published posthumously, he held his head in his hands: "Forbid it, O my God, that ever I should be so unhappy as to unglorify my Father, my Saviour or my Sanctifier, in any of my sentiments or expressions concerning them. . . . Help me, heavenly Father, for I am quite tired and weary of these human explainings, so various and uncertain." [6]

But I suspect that the views of Isaac Watts in general would today be defended as the *essence* of the orthodox position to a greater extent than they seemed to be in his own time. He strove to get behind the ontological formulations of the creeds to a more "scriptural and oeconomical" explanation, relating chiefly to the "characters and offices" of the three persons in our salvation, and he said that in terms of their function and work (*ad extra,* traditional theology would say) the three were one and the same, equally divine. And to Thomas Bradbury, that breath of old Calvinism, he wrote "I have often freely declared, and still declare, that I allow the greatest distinction possible between the sacred three in the divine nature, which does not arise to three distinct conscious minds or spirits. Make it as great as you will short of this and I acquiesce. But then since three distinct conscious minds is the idea of three proper literal persons, whatever falls short of this can be but an analogical personality: yet if any man will call this a proper divine personality, though it is but similar to human personality, I will not contend about words and names." [7] This is reminiscent of Augustine's words when he was engaged in shaping the meaning of the terms to fit the meaning he believed was basic to the Christian faith: "The Father, Son, and Holy Spirit cannot be named by our words, which certainly are bodily sounds, except in their own proper intervals of time, divided by a distinct separation, which intervals the proper syllables of each word occupy," and his exclamation: "Therefore they are called three

6. *Works, 4,* 673.
7. 1725. Belknap, p. 112.

persons, or three substances, not in order that any difference of essence may be understood, but that we may be able to answer by some word, should any one ask what three, or what three things?" [8] Still it may be that in these regions every theologian is open to the fate which Colman said was Watts': "My dear Watts has looked so long at the sun as to weaken his sight." [9]

14. It is important to have in mind Watts' views on the Trinity, as well as his Arminian position on the freedom of the will, when reading Edwards. Before Edwards wrote his *Inquiry*, Watts may have been regarded as somewhat heterodox in his other opinions. If so, it would have been a conclusion drawn from his published writings, and likely not yet from the storm that broke out after his death over the possibility that this pious man had gone on to adopt still more extreme views. This came not immediately after his death in 1748 but following the publication of his collected works by Jennings and Doddridge in 1753, one year before Edwards' *Inquiry*. However, it has been suggested that the reason Edwards never refers to Isaac Watts by name, but only as "the author of *An Essay on the Freedom of Will in God and the Creature*," is that his New England opponents would then simply have disavowed Watts' views and thus have escaped refutation by denying they believed any such opinions as were held by him on any subject. This suggestion will not stand in face of the fact that Edwards assumes when he first mentions this work in the preface that everyone knows who the author is, and has a high regard for him; and we shall have to find another explanation for why he so studiously avoided naming Watts. Edwards' page references are to the tract in an issue separate from other works; or at least the pagination begins with page one, which would still have been the case if he were using a copy of this work bound (as was commonly done) with Watts' *An Essay toward the Proof of a Separate State of Souls between Death and the Resurrection,* published the same year. Edwards speaks of the author with great respect, hesitating even to call him an Arminian, even though he agrees with the principal point of their doctrine. He plainly has in mind the author's great reputation for piety and learning, "his name and character," and calls him a "good divine . . . in many respects"; and he says that the essay "is commonly ascribed" (p. 132) to a known author.

8. *On the Trinity,* Bk. IV, ch. 21; Bk. VIII, preface.
9. In the year before Watts' death. Belknap, p. 29.

From Edwards' manner of speaking it is evident that Watts' piety and not his heterodoxy would be in the minds of most readers; and that everyone knew who was the author. One is reminded of the degree to which Edwards was in fact defeated by this same popular renown— by the charge that in the *Inquiry* concerning freedom of will Edwards involves himself in absurdities regarding the saintly Watts. "By which Rate Dr. Watts is the Arminian," wrote Chauncy Whittelsey, "and Mr. Lock the Calvinist." [1] Such power comes from being the maker of a nation's songs.

Edwards' citation of Watts under the incognito of "the author" may trace back to the circumstance of the original publication of the essay. There are two possibilities, the simplest of which is that Watts' essay was originally issued anonymously and that, even though its authorship was well-known,[2] Edwards limits himself to the form of citation warranted by the original title page. The second possibility is that Watts' essay on the freedom of will was originally issued in England in 1732 with his name on the title page, but that most if not all of the copies known in the colonies were specially printed with no ascription of authorship, for a reason which will be suggested in a moment. At this late date it seems impossible to prove definitely either that all copies of the 1732 edition were anonymous or that some were attributed to Watts. Extant copies, so far as I have been able to discover, seem all to be without the author's name; but this in itself does not demonstrate that all were similarly printed.[3] Yet it

1. Franklin B. Dexter, ed., *Extracts from the Itineraries and Other Miscellanies of Ezra Stiles, D.D., LL.D.* (New Haven, 1916), p. 592.

2. The essay was included in Vol. *6* of the collected works of Watts, compiled and issued by Jennings and Doddridge in 1753, one year before JE's publication of his rejoinder to it. Even before this no one could have doubted that Watts was the author, since he took no trouble to hide the fact, or to dissociate himself from the views expressed.

3. Extant copies in the libraries at Yale, Princeton, and Harvard do not have Watts' name printed on them; nor does the copy in Dr. Williams's Library, London (which is the copy cited in a list of the works of Watts on display in London during the Bicentenary in 1948), nor the two copies in Edinburgh. There are no copies in the Bodleian, Oxford, or at Mansfield College; nor are there any at St. Andrews, Dublin, or Aberdeen. Advertisements in the journals of the period might offer some corroborative evidence one way or the other, but the presence or absence of the author's name in such advertisements can hardly be considered final proof. The question must be left unsettled, particularly in the light of Watts' practice of having many copies of his acknowledged works printed with pseudo-anonymity.

is not impossible that Watts' essay on the freedom of will was originally issued in England with his name on the title page, and that it
was never in any sense an anonymous publication. For Watts apparently distributed a number of copies of several of his works, especially to his friends and to the college libraries in America, *without*
his name printed on them.

The relation between Jonathan Edwards and Isaac Watts must be
viewed in the light of the latter's keen interest in New England. In
later life Watts came to know many of the leaders of the colonies.

> His home in London became a sort of clearing house for Ameri-
> can problems. He acted as literary agent for Benjamin Colman,
> Elisha Williams, and others; sent books to the libraries of Har-
> vard and Yale; collected money for missionary work among the
> Indians; found donors for Harvard; acted as trustee for two of
> her important funds; helped to pick her text-books and pro-
> fessors; counselled New England's governors; wrote catechisms,
> hymns, and other texts which were used in the New England
> churches and schools; and took part in the Great Awakening Con-
> troversy. Without a doubt Watts entered as fully into the life of
> New England as any Englishman of his day.[4]

The first known contact between Edwards and Watts came as a result
of the publication by Watts and John Guyse of the work sent them
by Colman, *A Faithful Narrative of the Surprising Work of God in
the Conversion of Many Hundred Souls in Northampton, in a Letter to Reverend Dr. Benjamin Colman, of Boston, Written by the
Rev. Mr. Edwards, Nov. 6, 1736.* The preface, signed by Watts and
Guyse Oct. 12, 1737, contains the following protestation of Calvinistic orthodoxy, although it was written five years after Watts
published his Arminian treatise on freedom of will: "If our Readers
had Opportunity (as we have had) to peruse several of the Sermons
which were Preached during this glorious season, they should find
that it is the common plain Protestant Doctrine of the Reformation,
without stretching towards the Antinomians on the one Side, or the
Arminians on the other, that the Spirit of God has been pleased to
honor with such illustrious success."

The two London ministers apparently felt that because of its
"enthusiasm" the *Narrative* contained certain excesses, and they
took the liberty of toning down certain passages. Edwards protested

4. Davis, *Isaac Watts*, pp. 49–50.

this through Colman, and Watts answered, "We can bear with satisfaction all the reproaches we sustain here, both in conversation and in newspapers, but we hope we shall receive no addition from New England of anything that should make us uneasy." [5] Watts' attitude toward the Revival was always an ambivalent one. One rare occasion when he disagreed with Philip Doddridge was over the latter's admitting Whitefield to his pulpit. Yet he defended Edwards and the "raised affections" against Chauncy's attacks in a series of letters to Chauncy and to Colman.[6]

Before this, at an early age, Edwards began to know the writings of Watts. On the back of an envelope addressed to him "at Yale-Colledge," in what became a growing and more permanent "Catalogue of Books" in which he was interested, Edwards notes "Mr. Watts Poems" and "Mr. Watts Sermons"—the former crossed through by a line, the latter not, which may mean he had read the poems but not the sermons (although in this same list "Lock of human Understanding" is not crossed through).[7] *The Essay on the Freedom of Will in God and in Creatures* was, of course, published after Edwards' years at Yale as student and tutor.

This work, bound with *An Essay toward the Proof of a Separate State of Souls* came to the Yale College library as a gift from the author in 1733, the next year after publication. These works had no name printed on the title page, although another volume given at the same time had the initials "I.W." In either case it was plain who sent them and who wrote them. The explanation of Watts' curious reticence about naming himself the author is to be found in his modesty, or his mock-modesty. He protested that his printers and book-sellers would never supply him enough of these semidisguised copies, and to Colman he complained that of such printings he could not obtain enough copies "to oblige a quarter" of his friends. On sending to Harvard at the same time copies of the same books given to Yale, Watts wrote Colman: "I have here sent the College two or 3 books as a friend, not as an author, which I own I approve with relation to the subjects on which they treat. . . . I have ventured to expose myself heretofore perhaps too much with regard to current Orthodoxy where I have set my name. But as to these books I think

5. Ibid., p. 51.
6. Ibid., p. 52.
7. T. H. Johnson, "Jonathan Edwards' Background of Reading," *Publications of the Colonial Society of Massachusetts,* 28 (1930–33), 203.

they are tolerably orthodox, tho I ever own myself a Protestant, and claim a right to think freely and to judge for myself." [8] Notice here a use of the word "Protestant" with a different meaning from what it has in the expression "the common plain Protestant Doctrine of the Reformation" when later prefacing Edwards' *Narrative*. One may notice also a certain hesitancy over the doubtful orthodoxy of his views expressed in these works, perhaps concerning freedom of the will; but this was not sufficient to outweigh pride of authorship and his conviction as to the truth of his opinions on these subjects. It may have been the case that for many years the only copies of a number of the works of Watts that were available in America were anonymous as to authorship on the title page; but that this was on account of the author's peculiar method of distributing his writings through channels to his friends or to the institutions he befriended, and not for the purpose of avoiding identification. Indeed, Watts' purpose would have been defeated had he not been identified as the actual author. It may not be incorrect, therefore, to apply here the remark of his biographer that all his friends agreed "that Watts had one trait in perfection, modesty. The quality certainly grew with age. In later years it became so extreme as to arouse suspicions concerning its genuineness." [9]

If we find in this the explanation for Watts' reluctance to name himself the author of gift-copies of his books, it only remains to explain, if this be possible, why Edwards himself was similarly unwilling to name the author everyone knew. It is not likely to have been the odor of heterodoxy associated with some of Watts' views. Chubb was more so; and Watts is introduced with a tribute to his reputation for piety and for soundness in other respects than the point at issue. There is left only the possibility that Edwards simply complies with and does not violate the literary form of anonymity with which Watts modestly clothed himself (or that he respects the formal anonymity of the entire first edition, if this was the way it was issued). It is not unlikely that the copies then available in the colonies were mainly or exclusively those that came by donation. It is an interesting question, of course past finding out, whether, if ever, before or after Watts' preface to his *Narrative*, Edwards himself was the recipient of one of these gifts of books, and whether he may

8. June 29, 1733. Anne Stokely Pratt, *Isaac Watts and His Gifts of Books to Yale College* (New Haven, Yale University Press, 1938), p. 24.

9. Davis, *Isaac Watts*, p. 16, and cf. pp. 220–2.

not have worked from a personal copy of *An Essay on the Freedom of Will in God and in Creatures* given him by "the author."

15. Concerning freedom of will *in the creature,* man, the argument between Edwards and Watts is fairly joined; and Edwards states both his own position and that of his opponent so clearly that little further comment is needed. On pp. 186–9 Edwards deals with Watts' contention that because the soul is of an *active* nature, in contrast to passive material substance, its acts may come to pass spontaneously, of themselves, without a cause. One suspects that here the two points of view presuppose themselves and that what Edwards demands that Watts explain could be "explained" to Edwards only by reference to a cause. "Cause" meant for Edwards "sufficient reason." It is of course true that the general activity of the soul does not tell us why the soul diversifies itself one way rather than another. For Edwards to ask why it acts one way rather than another is to demand a causal (or a sufficient) explanation; while Watts, having *described* the soul's activity so as to locate there the source of new emergents, is quite content to wait for the soul in each act to determine itself one way spontaneously.

On pp. 195–201 Edwards considers Watts' principal point, namely that there are things perfectly indifferent in the mind's view concerning which the will determines without, in these cases, reference to prevailing motive or greater good. Here it is that by using the distinction Locke also made between *things* to be chosen and *acts* to be done, Edwards contends that in being conversant about actions to be done the will always has some reason or motive for its choice even in cases where the *things* chosen may be perfectly indifferent. On pp. 271–2 Edwards fastens upon Watts' distinction between chance and design, and finds in this opportunity to wedge him between chance or a design *in infinitum* behind the design of the will as principles explanatory of human action. This argument was Edwards' trademark.

16. When we come to the freedom of will *in God,* there is need for additional comment upon the issue between the two men. For precisely when the sovereign freedom of God is in question are we best able to see the two directions in which theological reflection may move, and these are clearly and vigorously represented by these two spokesmen for the traditions of the Reformation. On the one hand, the divine will may be thought to manifest itself in a vast

concatenation of events, no one of which might not have been since all are ordained for the best. This is Edwards' view. To Watts, such a scheme makes "the blessed God a sort of almighty minister of fate"; [1] and instead he was driven to think of the almighty freedom of God in terms of the absolute and radical contingency of the created world. For Edwards, the will of God guarantees that everything is necessarily what it is according to his purpose. For Watts, the free will of God guarantees that nothing but his will need be, and that every created thing might not have been or might have been otherwise than it is. Determinism according to the pattern of eternal ideas or some inscrutable yet ruling good *or* the radical contingency of the created world may each, and either of them with equal fitness, be the correlate of the divine sovereignty.

Thus contingency just as well as metaphysical necessity may be the logical consequence of exalting the sovereign freedom of God. One thinks here of the radical contingency of the world that was insisted on by nominalists and other late medieval voluntaristic thinkers who traced all explanation home to the will of God, and of the account of the divine determination as not bound to make use of "secondary causes" in Calvin and the Reformation generally. Watts might well claim to stand in this tradition; and there can be no doubt that the inner *motif* of his thought was such piety as the Reformation fostered and a willingness in everything to say "the Word of God is not bound." This is his concern when he insists that there are a great many things "perfectly indifferent" to God which yet he may choose to enact.

> As, What sort of system of beings he would make, and whether minds, bodies, or both? What should be the precise shape, and what the precise place of every corporeal being in the world? Whether this whole universe, or the sun in our system, should have one atom in it more or less? Whether the whole or any part of it should have been created one moment sooner or later? In what precise spot of our solar world Jupiter or Saturn, or any of their satellites, or this earth or its moon should be first placed; or whether any of them should have one particle of matter more or less in them, than they have, or this or that particle lie in any other situation? Whether this single atom of mould or clay should be part of the glebe at Taunton or York; or whether this grain

1. *An Essay on the Freedom of Will in God and in Creatures,* in *Works, 6,* 272.

of sand or pebble should be found on the shore of Deal or Dover, or on the coasts of Africa or the East Indies? Whether this particle of water should belong to the Severn or the Thames, or should be flowing this moment in the Atlantic or the Mediterranean sea; or whether this particle of air should be found in Essex, or Hertfordshire, or in America, on this day, this hour, and this second of time? On what particular branch such a bird should sit at such a minute, and what notes it should sing; and how many leaves should grow on such a bough, and how many indentings on the edge of each leaf: How many colors should grow on the cheek of such a tulip, or yellow seeds lie in the bosom of a rose: Whether this particular human soul should be united to a body born in Lapland or Russia, Britain or China; or this child should be created for a tall stature or a dwarf, or be brought into the world in the seventh or seventeenth century: Whether this drop of rain should fall upon a ploughed field or a rock, or this bright sunbeam light on me or my neighbor, on the earth or the moon? And perhaps ten thousand other things, and that of much greater importance in their consequences, may have no superior fitness or unfitness in themselves, but are all equal and all indifferent. And here the will of God, by and of itself, as a free and sovereign power, determines itself in its choice, and as it were makes it so far more agreeable and good to himself by his own choice and determination, and he delights in his own will and purpose, and in the correspondent works of his hands.[2]

The contrary assumption that God can only act according to the fitness of things, writes Watts, must mean that:

God could not have abstained from making this our world at all, nor from making it just such as it is, nor withheld his hand from creation one moment longer: Then he could not have made one more planet or star, or one less than he has done; nay, not so much as one atom or dust more or less in any star or planet, nor have placed them in any other form. He could not have given the sun one more beam, nor any morning since the creation one more gleam of light, or one less shade of darkness. Then the everblessed God could not have been happy one moment longer in solitude, or without creatures, nor begun to form any part of this universe, or this globe, earlier or later than he did; nor could he

2. Sec. 4, *prop.* 14; ibid., *6*, 256–7.

have caused one spire of grass to grow on this earth, nor one drop of water in the sea, nor one sand more or less at the bottom of it. He could not continue the material world, nor any atom of it, a moment longer in existence, nor have fixed the periods even of the minutest beings any otherwise than he has done. Not a drop of rain could fall, not a particle of water flow, nor a dusky atom of smoke ascend, in any other manner, nor at any other minute than it doth; nor could the great God have decreed it otherwise in the least punctilio, so far as mere corporeal nature is concerned therein, because each of these was supremely fit, together with the original train of causes which necessarily produced them. . . . The Americans and the Hottentots could not have been formed otherwise than under such special disadvantages; nor could Great Britain have had the gospel withheld from it one moment longer. Nor, indeed, according to this scheme, could God have withheld his Son from being sent to redeem the world, nor withheld his Spirit with all its gifts and influences from the inhabitants of this globe, nor have omitted any one miracle towards the propagation of this gospel; for the will of God was absolutely determined to do this by its superior fitness.[3]

Watts goes on to speak of God under these conditions being but "a sort of almighty minister of fate," a passage quoted several times by Edwards (pp. 375 and 381).

Now, let us at once grant Edwards the accolade for his argument against all this: that Watts wrongly thinks of spatial parts of time and indeed of eternity as but a greater space in which God creates (pp. 385–7), that even minute differences have great consequences in the whole of it (pp. 392–3), and that when Watts speaks about one "numerical identity" exactly like another between which God chooses, he talks profound nonsense (pp. 390–2). It is true, the spirit of Watts' praise of the blessed and sovereign will of God who for no reason other than his will alone holds in being everything that has being and which but for his will would instantly not be—such a conception of the radical contingency of the created world has very much in common with Edwards' Enfield sermon. Nevertheless, the issue between Edwards and Watts hinges upon Edwards' concept of the moral necessity of an act of will in God, or the rational deter-

3. Sec. 7, *dif.* 1; ibid., *6*, 271–2.

mination of the divine *arbitrium,* and Watts' assertion that in no
sense does the word "necessity" apply to God's voluntary acts.

Edwards writes that Watts imagines "there is some sort of privilege or dignity in being without such a moral necessity, as will make
it impossible to do any other, than always choose what is wisest and
best" (p. 377). With only this statement before him, the reader might
suppose that Watts believes that God sometimes chooses the unfit or
what is not best, or at least that Watts emphasized less than Edwards
his goodness in choosing the fit. This would not be a correct interpretation. Over and over again Watts writes that wherever and whenever there actually is any superior fitness in things God always wills
the best. What he insists upon is that so far as human thought can
probe such matters, we must suppose there are *also* innumerable acts
of the will of God choosing between perfectly indifferent alternatives. And he contends further that, this being so, such decisions,
retroactively so to speak, make it plain that when God does will what
is "wisest and best" when there *is* some superior fitness in things it
was not necessary for him to do so but he did so out of sovereign freedom and uncaused free causation. In either type of divine choice
there is then equal "privilege and dignity." Citing a number of these
assertions of Watts that "wheresoever there is such an antecedent
superior fitness of things, God acts according to it," Edwards tried to
force Watts to testify that there is in his view no virtue nor anything
of a moral nature in such voluntary choices (p. 382). This also will
not do, since Watts believes that when God acts in accordance with
antecedent fitness he does so from transcendent freedom and not from
any necessity; and that in a sense we know this from pious reflection
upon the contingent and perfectly indifferent creatures and events
he often wills to be.

Indeed, precisely in connection with God's moral government
Watts marshalls what he takes to be evidence that there is much which
God wills without there being antecedent or inherent fitness in his
doing so, and that he then takes delight in what he pleases.

> The will of God by and of itself determines and chooses what
> positive laws, what duties he will command or prescribe to his
> creatures, and he makes the thing which he prescribes more fit
> and good for us to practice merely by his own choice, determina-
> tion, and command: As whether the tabernacle of Moses should

have just such a number of boards or curtains, pins or tacks in it; whether every board or every curtain should be just so long and so broad, to the thousandth part of an inch. . . . In short, I would ask whether every point and tittle of every ceremony and positive duty which God has appointed from the beginning of the world to this day, had in itself and in the nature of things, such a superior fitness, that it could not be determined otherwise? *Surely it is much more becoming and proper for us to think and say, that God has determined these things by his own will and self-determining power and free choice:* for it seems to me a very harsh and bold affirmation, that not one of all these punctilios could ever have been otherwise appointed by God himself.[4]

And concerning God's dealings with men:

It lays a just foundation of praise and thankfulness for all the free actions of his goodness and kindness to his creatures, according to those degrees of mercy and bounty which he distributes among them; because he is not obliged to all those particular actions or objects by a necessary and superior fitness, since he might have chosen to neglect those objects, or to manifest equal or superior goodness to other creatures, or to do it in much less degrees, or in other ways and manners, any of which might have been equally fit and proper: As for instance, God might have brought forth the soul of an American savage in the British islands, surrounded with light and knowledge; or have produced me among the savages in America, in gross darkness, as well as in Great Britain, a land of light. My soul might have been united to a body born of African idolaters: He might have made me blind and a cripple, as well as given me health and eye-sight; I might have had the brain of an idiot, and have been bred up without knowledge, as well as enjoyed my share of intellectual powers and advantages of learning; he might have formed me the child of a beggar, made me an heir to filth and wretchedness, and trained me up to ask my bread from door to door, instead of the comfortable circumstances which I enjoy, and the parents from whence I came. We cannot but suppose it possible for the great God to have found a way to have made these things comport with his grand scheme and counsels in the universe, if he had so pleased; but he has chosen and determined better things for me

4. Sec. 4, *prop.* 16 (italics mine); ibid., *6*, 258.

from his own free-will and sovereign goodness, and blessed be his name.[5]

The contrary scheme makes void God's providence in the moral government of men:

> Will not this destroy, or at least vastly abate the reasons of gratitude and love to God in those who receive his favours, when kings and slaves, rich men and beggars, strong men and cripples, creatures whose life is filled with pain and poverty, or whose whole period of life is affluence and ease, were distinguished only and necessarily by the superior fitness of their circumstances? What is there of free mercy in his disposal of benefits? . . . And have not Abraham the friend of God, David the king, Paul the apostle, Sir Isaac Newton the philosopher, Judas the traitor, Irus the cripple, Davus the slave, and Jack Adams the idiot, all equal reason of thankfulness to the free bounty of their Maker, since so far as he acted in their composition of mind or body, or in their original circumstances of life, he determined each in such a particular manner, because his own will was thus necessarily determined, and therefore he could not have done otherwise? [6]

So far does Watts glory in the unbounded freedom of God and in the radical contingency of the moral no less than of the natural world. In both cases, "if you ask why he should create this sort of world rather than another, and this sort of creatures rather than others, which may be equally fit, he borrows the reason for it only from himself; his own good pleasure is a sufficient reason: He doth it because he will: Nor is any other reason necessary besides his own self-determining power. It is supremely fit he should do what he pleases." [7] Thus Watts believes there is very much that is virtuous and of a moral nature, and much in God's free mercy to be thankful for, when God acts beyond the antecedent fitness in things; and from glorying in this we can pass to the admiration of God's ordaining the wisest and best where there *is* some inherent superior fitness, without, even in these instances, imagining his freedom ever to be subjected to any necessity.[8]

5. Sec. 5, *adv.* 8; ibid., *6*, 262.
6. Sec. 7, *dif.* 2; ibid., *6*, 274.
7. Sec. 6, *ans.* to *obj.* 2; ibid., *6*, 266.
8. Wright, *The Beginnings of Unitarianism in America*, pp. 91–114, affirms that the confusion in JE's argument, and in the discussion that followed, was due

17. Edwards refers to passages such as have just been cited when he opposes Watts' opinion that "a necessary determination of the divine will by a superior fitness . . . derogates from the *freeness* of God's *grace* and *goodness,* in choosing the objects of his favor and bounty, and from the obligation upon men to *thankfulness* for special benefits." Edwards answers that "it derogates no more from the goodness of God, to suppose the exercise of the benevolence of his nature to be determined by wisdom, than to suppose it determined by chance" (p. 393); and in referring to random chance and perfect accident it may be suspected that he evades rather than meets Watts' account of events that come about by will. A second reply makes use of the distinction previously noted between objects or *things* chosen and *acts* to be willed. Of course, no man as an object can merit God's favor rather than another nor ought he to think that the grace bestowed on him is fit and properly belongs to him. Yet God, in being conversant about acts to be done, may be supposed to find in some actions a "natural fitness" to answer some wise design of his own

---

to the fact that neither JE nor his New England opponents saw clearly that they were in no disagreement as to the determination of the will by the understanding and in accordance with the greatest apparent good. Only Watts denied this. The point of real disagreement, Wright affirms, was whether an inherited taint of sinfulness dictates what a man apprehends to be good. There may be some truth in this analysis, but Wright obscures, as did JE's opponents, the question whether in responding to the greatest apparent good there is (leaving sinfulness aside) real spontaneity in the human will, and a capacity for the production of new, original determinations in the will. More than the doctrine of sinfulness, the sovereignty of God was at issue; and which of these two was the more crucial point can be seen by answering the question, Did not JE and the New England Arminians propose different accounts of an act of will in Adam before the Fall? If this be so, then their views of the moral necessity of man's acts of will must have been inherently different, however much they agreed as to acts of will in God being necessarily wise and holy. When JE showed that the human will always is in accord with man's present apprehension of the good, this (or so he believed) pointed toward the conclusion that motives are what they are primarily because of the withdrawal or the presence of grace. The only alternative was to assert that the self determines itself in the willing *and in its apprehension* of the good. JE may not be held responsible if only Watts (and Chubb?) clearly affirmed this to be the case. He set himself the task of showing that it is inconsistent to say (as did Clarke, Whitby, and certain New England divines) *both* that the will is determined by reason and that the will determines itself, since the latter must mean that the agent in some sense is also the uncaused causal progenitor of his own understanding of the good. Such ultimate power JE attributed to God alone, in the operations of grace upon the whole man or the whole mind.

(p. 394). Thus God's own act, which is the proper and immediate object of his volition, may always be from some prevailing motive according to the wisest and best design; and yet men who are objects of his favor in these acts may have in themselves no more fitness than others who are not. How far does this differ from Watts' view that the will of God, by and of itself, as a free and sovereign power, determines itself in its choice, and as it were makes that which is objectively indifferent so far more agreeable and good to himself by his own choice and determination? Perhaps only in that Edwards enters more into the heart of the divine decision and gives an analysis of the act of choice itself.

In answering the foregoing objection Edwards displays no more compassion for "Jack Adams the idiot," or no more softness in facing the *prima facie* arbitrariness of arrangements in the moral world, than does Watts. It is a strength of Calvinism, and perhaps at the same time its weakness, that it faces the facts with an attitude of unflinching empiricism. Instead of defining what God ought to do from some sweet anterior conception of divinity, it defines what God is from what God actually does in the world that he has made and providentially governs. The difference between the two men is found in that Edwards interprets the phenomena as manifestations of God's will which always is determined to accord with some inscrutable wisdom or fitness, while Watts believes it more to the glory of God to say that both the natural and the moral world in their radical contingency simply manifest God's will in a great many things that are themselves perfectly indifferent, in God's own view of the alternatives no less than in ours.

18. The fundamental issue between Edwards and Watts may be located at the point whether there be a "moral necessity" significantly different from "natural necessity." Edwards affirms that Watts takes the wrong turn into the belief that "this moral necessity and impossibility is in effect *the same thing* with physical and natural necessity and impossibility" (p. 381; italics mine). It is true that Watts writes, "in philosophical strictness and the truth of things, this moral necessity and impossibility, and this metaphysical necessity and impossibility will appear to be very *near akin:* and although there may be *some difference* between these two necessaries, viz. moral and metaphysical, *as to the immediate and proxime cause and reason of their necessity,* yet the necessity of both of them is a physical or nat-

ural necessity, *they are both equally strong and unalterable,* and the original cause and reason why both of them are necessary lies in the very *nature* of things. I might say the same also concerning their *impossibility.*" [9] One suspects that during the course of writing his *Inquiry,* and by the time he takes up Watts on this point, Edwards has allowed to develop in his own thinking a sharper distinction between natural and moral or philosophical necessity than he established at the outset. In Part I, Sec. 4, Edwards introduces this distinction from philosophical discussions then current without undertaking, he says, himself "to inquire whether this distinction be a proper and perfect" one (p. 156). He defines "moral necessity" as a necessity of connection and consequence which arises from moral causes, such as inclinations and motives (p. 156). Moreover, Edwards affirms that "moral necessity may be as absolute, as natural necessity" (p. 157). He asks that it be observed that "When I use this distinction of moral and natural necessity, I would not be understood to suppose, that if anything comes to pass by the former kind of necessity, the *nature* of things is not concerned in it, as well as the latter" (p. 157; italics mine); and he tries to explain why ordinary language distinguishes too sharply between "choice" and "nature" (p. 158). How different is this from what Watts says of the distinction in the preceding quotation? Understanding quite well what was meant by moral necessity, Watts simply does not believe that this is different enough from natural necessity to be compatible with human freedom or with moral virtue in the will.

19. After reading what Edwards says in reply to Watts, one may be surprised to learn that elsewhere Edwards himself speaks of God's relation to the world as an immediate and *arbitrary* operation. What then is the difference between Edwards' and Watts' conceptions of the arbitrariness of God's action?

When defending the proposition that God imputes Adam's sin to man in later generations because they are truly one with him and consequently the sin "is *truly* and *properly* theirs, and on that *ground,* God imputes it to them," [1] Edwards set forth the view that

9. *An Essay on the Freedom of Will in God and in Creatures,* in *Works, 6,* 275, Sec. 7, *ans.* to *dif.* 3 (italics mine). The difference between the two views appears in that, where Watts regularly links *metaphysical* with *natural* necessity, distinct from moral, JE always joins his *philosophical* with *moral* necessity, distinct from natural.

1. *The Great Christian Doctrine of Original Sin Defended* (1757), Pt. IV, ch. 3; in Worcester ed., *6,* 458.

personal identity or the continuity of any finite substance through time depends wholly on God's operation, and in this connection he spoke of God's action in thus sustaining his creatures in the world as a perfectly arbitrary action. "God's *preserving* created things in being," or his preserving in a man an individual consciousness identical with the infant he once was, are "perfectly equivalent to a *continued creation*, or to his creating those things out of nothing at *each moment* of their existence." Without a new exertion of divine power they would at once "drop into nothing." A thing's existence in the present moment and into the following moment depends not in any degree upon its *antecedent* existence, or upon powers or laws inherent in the nature of secondary causes and effects: "*God* produces the effect as much from *nothing*, as if there had been nothing *before*." [2] The continuity of the created world may be compared to the duration of an image in a mirror:

> The image constantly renewed, by new successive rays, is no more numerically the same, than if it were by some artist put on anew with a pencil, and the colors constantly vanishing as fast as put on. And the new images being put on *immediately* and *instantly*, do not make them the same, any more than if it were done with the intermission of an *hour* or a *day*. The image that exists this moment, is not at all *derived* from the image which existed the last preceding moment; as may be seen, because, if the succession of new *rays* be intercepted, by something interposed between the object and the glass, the image immediately ceases; the *past existence* of the image has no influence to uphold it, so much as for one moment. Which shows that the image is altogether new made every moment; and strictly speaking, is in no part numerically the same with that which existed the moment preceding. And truly so the matter must be with the *bodies* themselves, as well as their images. . . . If so, the existence caused is every instant a new effect, whether the cause be *light*, or immediate *divine power*, or whatever it be. [3]

Of course, bodies and persons (which are the images and shadows of divine things) and the entire state of the created world moment after moment follow preceeding bodies and persons and momentary states of the same kind "in an established order" which we call the order and course of nature. Yet, "the course of nature is demonstrated, by

2. Pt. IV, ch. 3; ibid., *6*, 451.
3. Pt. IV, ch. 3; ibid., *6*, 453 n.

late improvements in philosophy, to be . . . nothing but the established order of the agency and operation of the author of nature." [4]

This operation is not only immediate and constant but *arbitrary*. Why then does Edwards' reject Watts' account of God's arbitrary action? His words in a "Miscellaneous Observation" concerning "Gods immediate & Arbitrary Operation," closely resemble those of Watts:

> If we ascend with Respect to Time, and go back in the series of Existences or Events in the Order of their succession to the beginning of the Creation . . . we shall come to arbitrary operation. The creation of the matter of the material world out of Nothing [,] the Creation even of every individual atom, or primary particle, was by an Operation perfectly arbitrary.
>
> After the creation of the matter of the world out of nothing, the Gradual bringing of the Matter of the World into order was by an arbitrary Operation [.] It was by arbitrary divine [operation] that the primary particles of matter were put in motion, and had the Direction & Degree of their Motion determined, and were brought into so beautiful and useful a situation one with respect to another [.] [5]

And if Edwards can affirm of the oneness of every man with Adam that "a *divine constitution*," indeed an *arbitrary* divine constitution, "is the thing which *makes truth,* in affairs of this nature," [6] might not Watts reply that he but says the same thing: that an arbitrary divine constitution *makes* the true and the real to be what they are when it is a question of locating atoms, and *makes good* whatever God pleases?

The answer is that of course Edwards affirms (with Watts) the radical contingency of the created world, but that (despite his use of the term) he opposes Watts' view of God's arbitrary action. The word "arbitrary" was frequently used by philosophers in the eighteenth century in the sense of the Latin *arbitrium,* which simply means "judgment" or "decision." Edwards held a different view from that of Watts on the nature of God's *arbitrium,* will, or decision. Again it becomes evident how much Edwards' position simply consists of an

4. Pt. IV, ch. 2; ibid., *6,* 433.
5. "Miscellanies," No. 1263.
6. *The Great Christian Doctrine of Original Sin Defended* (1757) Pt. IV, ch. 3; in Worcester ed., *6,* 454.

analysis of an act of volition (in God, and opposed to Watts' analysis) and how internal to the willing is what he calls moral necessity. The distinction between the two men is one that lies between rationalism and extreme voluntarism in all speculation about God and man. "When I call this an *arbitrary constitution,* I mean, it is a constitution which depends on nothing but the *divine will;* which divine will depends on nothing but the *divine wisdom.* In this sense, the whole *course of nature,* with all that belongs to it, all its laws and methods, and constancy and regularity, continuance and proceeding, is an *arbitrary constitution.* In this sense, the continuance of the very being of the world and all its parts, as well as the manner of continued being, depends entirely on an *arbitrary constitution.*" [7] In brief, whenever Edwards says that the divine operation is arbitrary he always adds, "in every other respect, excepting that it is regulated by divine wisdom." [8] This was the import of the opening definitions in the "Miscellaneous Observation" previously quoted: "When I speak of Arbitrary operation, I don't mean Arbitrary in opposition to an operation directed by wisdom, but in opposition to an Operation Confined to & limited by those fix'd establishments & Laws commonly called the Laws of Nature [.] The one of these I shall therefore, for want of better Phrases, call *a natural Operation* [,] the other *an arbitrary operation.*" [9]

There is a moral necessity in God's acts of will that can be said to govern the divine will, just as surely as his will is regulated by his divine wisdom. Yet his will remains arbitrary in the sense that no sort of necessity imposes itself upon him from the outside. If we say that God necessarily wills the best, this does not mean that the will of God is subject to anterior or exterior conceptions of the good. Arminians, such as Watts in this essay, seemed to Edwards to exhalt the divine will, free of all necessity, above the divine wisdom to the point of making almightiness irresponsible; and all for the purpose of inferring a corresponding freedom of indifference (however limited) in man the created image of God. Thus, voluntarism in theology was only of quite questionable aid to piety in apparently subjecting everything in heaven and earth to God's will, for the final conclusion from such theology was that man, too, has an ungoverned will.

Yet Edwards meant for his account of God's arbitrary action to be

7. Pt. IV, ch. 3; ibid., *6,* 453.
8. Pt. IV, ch. 3; ibid., *6,* 456.
9. No. 1263.

applied *mutatis mutandis* to the analysis of human volition. "When we come to the highest Ranks of Creatures," he writes, "we come to them who themselves have the greatest Image of God's Arbitrary operation, who 'tis therefore most fit should be the subjects of such operations," or to "greater Degrees of an Arbitrary Intercourse" between God and the soul that indefinitely transcend all natural necessity and every one of "those fix'd establishments & Laws commonly called the Laws of Nature." [9] So far was Edwards from having succumbed to the Newtonian world view and the binding operation of secondary causes (which many commentators have concluded from the tone of the *Inquiry*)! God's *arbitrium* has at every point immediate governance of the world of moral and historical events where men have the highest degree of intercourse with Him.

20. Commenting on the puzzle about God's placing the globes (which was a point at issue between Edwards and Watts), Samuel West remarks that "as many determinations in the Divine mind, about placing the globes, are necessary, as in the human mind about touching the squares." [1] This suggests a correlation between the analysis of God's "arbitrary" yet rationally and morally necessary volition in creating the globes in their places and the analysis given by Edwards (pp. 198 ff.) of man's free yet morally motivated and necessary volition to touch one square on a chessboard. In neither case is this a question about *objects* to be chosen. There is no more reason in one square than in another why it should be chosen, just as there is no objective merit in the elect which gives ground for their being chosen while God passes over Jack Adams the idiot. Nevertheless, there may be a *natural fitness* of such a determination of the *act* of God's goodness to answer some design of his own (cf. p. 394). Edwards supposes the principle of *sufficient motivation* still to be operative in every one of the choices of the human or the divine mind; for in "making up one's mind" in each case, it is a question of the mind being conversant about *actions* to be done. The mind chooses the action which, in its view, is better. If we suppose the steps in God's willing to create the globes or atoms where they are to be the same as the steps taken by a man in touching one square, the following account might be given: The first step is God's *general* determination that he will create an atom or a globe somewhere. The

1. *Essays on Liberty and Necessity* (New Bedford, Mass., 1795), p. 18. Cf. pp. 16–18, 87.

next step is another *general* determination to give himself up to
accident, in some certain way; as to create at the spot that happens
to be most in his mind when he counts to three, or to some other
like accident. The third and last step is a *particular* determination
to place the globes in a certain individual spot, even that place, which,
by that sort of accident the divine mind has pitched upon, has actually offered itself beyond others (cf. p. 199). Now, the foregoing
story of creation does not do God much honor, and it may be in-
credibly naive in many of the ways Edwards points out against
Watts. Yet this is certain: it satisfies the conditions Edwards lays
down for the sufficient motivation of an act of volition, since in none
of these several steps did the mind of God proceed in absolute indifference, but in each of them he was influenced by a preponderating
inducement (cf. pp. 204–6). In each of these determinations of his will,
(being conversant about *actions* to be done and not about indifferent
objects) God acted in accordance with what was pleasing and good.
Truly, on this reading there is not much discernible difference between Edwards' position and that of Watts. How then shall one
choose between them, unless Watts be right in saying that the will
can actually choose in instances such as this where there is no discernible difference between alternatives?

21. It is not enough to analyze an act of will in God in terms of
sufficient motivation or inclination. This (the mind being conversant about the suitableness of *actions* to be done and not about
the worth of *objects* to be chosen) may be supposed, as in the foregoing story of creation, to be a matter of subjectivity and caprice and
yet the will be determined in it. Edwards, therefore, has another
string to his bow. Indeed, this is his principal point with regard to
acts of will in God: the analysis of an act of willing in terms of the
principle of *sufficient reason,* and herein it is plain "how completely
he makes mind and object to run together in choice, or how perfect
a unition of the two" God's "choice is." [2]

This is his real answer to Watts. It is wholly unreasonable to suppose that God ever chooses between two actions (or objects in their
total context) so much alike that they are actually *identical* in every
respect, for in such a case there would be no *ground* or *reason* for
his choice. Two atoms or globes "are two in no other respects than
those wherein there is a difference" (p. 388). If we presume two

2. Tappan, *A Review,* p. 31.

effects to be brought to pass "without any difference," they "are therefore just the same" (p. 389); and there is no sufficient reason for the divine wisdom or will to elect to do any such thing. To suppose God made an atom "without anything really aimed at in so doing" is just as unreasonable as "to suppose that he made the planet Jupiter without aim or design" (p. 392). "And it might as reasonably be asked, why, when God first caused it to thunder, he caused that individual sound to be made, and not another just like it? Why did he make choice of this very sound, and reject all the infinite number of other possible sounds just like it, but numerically differing from it, and all differing one from another? I think everybody," concludes Edwards, "must be sensible of the absurdity and nonsense of what is supposed in such inquiries" (p. 391).

Thus in replying to Watts, Edwards gains the victory by an eloquent and masterful statement of the principles of *sufficient reason* and the *identity of indiscernibles,* which may be compared to the views of Leibniz in his *Theodicy* and in his lengthy correspondence with Samuel Clarke. In fact, Edwards gives the same rejoinder to Clarke, Whitby, and Watts in the present *Inquiry* which only forty years earlier Leibniz made to Clarke in their correspondence.[3]

"The principle in question," wrote Leibniz, "is the principle of the want of a sufficient reason; in order to any thing's existing, in order to any event's happening, in order to any truth's taking place." [4] The identity of indiscernibles cannot, of course, be known by discerning that they are identical. It is rather, for both Edwards and Leibniz, an inference from the principle of sufficient reason, or but another way of stating that principle. Things *indifferent,* like placing three bodies perfectly alike in any order whatsoever, "will never be placed in any order, by him who does nothing without wisdom. But then he being the author of things, no such things will be produced by him at all; and consequently there are no such things in

3. *A Collection of Papers Which Passed between the Late Learned Mr. Leibniz and Dr. Clarke* (1715–16), trans. into English by Clarke himself and originally published in 1717; in *The Leibniz-Clarke Correspondence,* ed. H. G. Alexander, Manchester University Press, 1956. Foster, *A Genetic History,* p. 48, n. 3, says that "Leibnitz's correspondence with Clarke was a common book" available in New England. The possibility that JE may have read it, or the *Theodicy,* cannot be ruled out. JE's "Catalogue of Books," however, contains no evidence that he knew Leibniz' works.

4. *A Collection of Papers,* Fifth Paper, no. 125.

nature." [5] Since God does nothing without reason, and there can be no reason for arranging identical objects in nature in one way rather than another, there can be no things in nature between which there is not some discernible difference—to his mind's view. Otherwise, he would discern the indiscernible, or choose without discerning and be pleased with one thing that cannot please more than another. God will never choose among indiscernibles, because there is no reason for it. Because God does what is wisest and best and acts always with sufficient reason, two things that are indiscernible from each other can never be found in the world. They can only be abstractly supposed.[6]

It is not surprising to find also that Leibniz' views on the subject of necessity are quite similar to those of Edwards: "God *can* do everything that is possible," i.e. he *can* produce whatever does not imply a contradiction, "but he *will* do only what is best." [7] "For God chooses among possibles, that is, among many ways, none of which implies a contradiction." But within the broad expanse of what is logically or metaphysically possible, or possible in the nature of things, he chooses with a *moral necessity* what is good. "But good, either true or apparent; in a word, the motive, inclines without necessitating; that is, without imposing an absolute necessity. For when God (for instance) chooses the best; what he does not choose, and is inferior in perfection, is nevertheless possible," [8] even though it is not *morally* possible for God to will it. And when a wise being chooses what is best, he is not less free on this account. Therefore, "moral necessity," Leibniz believes, "does not derogate from liberty." [9]

Unfortunately Edwards never had occasion to elaborate his point of view in contrast to that of Leibniz. Yet his earlier correspondence with Thomas Gillespie suggests that in the last analysis there is a great difference between his own views and those of the exponent of this, the best of all possible worlds. Even though Romans 8:20 affirms that "all things work together for good to everyone who is called," this does not mean that each of the elect should conclude from this

5. Ibid., Fourth Paper, no. 3.
6. Cf. ibid., passim, but esp. Fourth Paper, nos. 1, 3, 5 f., 13, 15, 18 f.; Fifth Paper, nos. 15, 21, 23–6, 60, 66–70.
7. Ibid., Fifth Paper, no. 73. Cf. no. 76.
8. Ibid., no. 8.
9. Ibid., no. 7.

that the circumstances of his life are in every respect the best possible, or even the best "compossible." "The meaning" of this verse, writes Edwards, "cannot be that God's actual dispensations towards each Christian are the best for him *of all that are possible;* or that all things which are ordered for him . . . are in all respects better for him than any thing which God could have ordered or done . . . for that implies that God will confer on every one of his elect, as much happiness as he can confer, in the utmost exercise of his omnipotence, and this sets aside all those different degrees of grace and holiness here, and glory hereafter, which he bestows according to his sovereign pleasure."

Instead, the meaning is that "there is a certain measure of holiness and happiness, to which each one of the elect is eternally appointed, and all things that relate to him, work together to bring to pass *this appointed measure of good,*" and "all things will tend to, and work together to accomplish that degree of good which God has purposed to bestow upon them, and not any more." To suppose otherwise the saints would have to convince themselves, contrary to reason and experience, that "it is for their good to have no more good, or that it is for their happiness to have no more happiness here and hereafter." At the same time, "the sovereignty of God will also be seen, with regard to the measure of the good or benefit aimed at, in that some other things, if God had seen cause to order them, would have produced an higher benefit." [1] We may conclude from this, so far as concerns the individual's place in the "heavenly temple" or the scheme of things God is preparing, that there are *possibilities* which go beyond what God actually intends, and the individual might have had another place bestowed on him according to God's "sovereign pleasure." Thus Edwards expresses man's faithful acceptation of sovereign divine determinations which, as Watts emphasized, always might *for him* have been otherwise.

It is with respect to the entire scheme of things, the "heavenly temple" itself including the location of any "stone" in it, that Edwards believed (it would appear, contrary to Watts) that God has his own reasons for whatever he wills. The faithful acceptance or consent to being as a whole requires an acknowledgment of the ultimate wisdom of God in all that he does, yet without denying that he might have ordered "an higher benefit" than he has for any specific indi-

1. Letter to Thomas Gillespie, September 4, 1747, from Northampton; ed. Dwight, *I*, 237–8.

vidual. With respect also to the entire scheme or heavenly temple itself, we may find the chief point of disagreement with Leibniz' position. For there was for Edwards no structure of possibilities above and beyond God's providence and superior to his sovereignty. While God need not bring to pass all the good that is possible for each individual, the good of the whole which he brings to pass suffers no limitation from any realm of in-compossibility external to his own rational will. A world over which God rules is no doubt a good world, even the best world; but it is not to be termed the best *of all possible worlds,* nor on the other hand are we to say it is *not* the best that might have been chosen of all the possibilities. It is simply God's world in the whole of it. God suffers no limitation "in the utmost exercise of his omnipotence," either from the fact that he could not assign a different weight of glory or happiness to any individual, or from the fact that the whole scheme of things was made up out of what was compossible. This shows again "how perfect a unition" of reason and will, mind and object, God's choice is, and how Edward's position simply consists of an analysis of an act of will *in* God. However, a world in which there is bestowed on a certain individual one weight of glory or happiness is a different world (and not only different for the individual) from the one which would have existed had he been given a different degree of happiness. Therefore, God's "carrying on of his own designs in everything" and "not carrying on that which is not his design" entails a choice, from among possible worlds, of the one he determines to actualize. Edwards' view seems, then, indistinguishable from Leibniz'. Perhaps it was inevitable that, in maintaining the perfect unition of mind and will in God, he should say so much that is similar to Watts and so much that is similar to Leibniz; and that a commentary on Edwards which magnifies his disagreement with Watts and ignores his frequent expression of nearly the same opinions would be in danger of supposing more agreement with Leibniz than the evidence warrants. Edwards' letter to Gillespie serves to warn us that Edwards somehow stops short of Leibniz' form of rationalism because of his effort to take due account of the voluntaristic element in God's sovereign "arbitrary" action.

Two remarks may be made in conclusion. (1) If Edwards' analysis of the determination of an act of volition in God be truly susceptible to the interpretations given in the last two numbered paragraphs (20 and 21), the question may be raised whether "sufficient motivation" and "sufficient reason" have actually the same meaning (as both

Edwards and Leibniz believed). To ask the reason may not be the same as to ask the motive or the cause of voluntary action. (2) At the same time, it should now be evident that Edwards moved in two directions when abandoning the notion of efficient causation. One of these directions, it has already been pointed out, was toward a definition of cause as "connection," and in this he was like Hume. Yet unlike Hume he believed in the *certainty* of connection and that the certainty is inherent in things connected because it is a certainty sustained there by the rational will of God, and in this he moved in the direction of supplementing crude efficient causation with Leibniz' principle of sufficient reason, or the idea of cause as ground.

6. *Note on the Text*

Jonathan Edwards' *A Careful and Strict Enquiry into the Modern prevailing Notions of That Freedom of Will, Which Is Supposed to Be Essential to Moral Agency, Vertue and Vice, Reward and Punishment, Praise and Blame* was first published in Boston by S. Kneeland in the year 1754. This was the only publication of the work in Edwards' lifetime, and the present volume has been edited from this original edition.[2] A second and third edition were brought out by publishers in London in 1762 and 1768 in the decade following Edwards' death in 1758. To the third edition the "Remarks" on Lord Kames' *Essays* was added for the first time. The fourth English edition appeared in 1775, and in 1790 two more British editions. In 1774

2. An "advertisement" printed at the end of the index of the first edition announces that "upon a cursory review of these sheets, the *errata* observed in the press-work appear of so little importance, as not to be worth the formality of noting them for correction." Yet there is such a *printed* list of twelve *errata* pasted in the copy of the *Inquiry* given to the Yale library in 1756 by Nathan Beers, and also in the copy that belonged to JE, Jr. The type used in printing these *errata* looks suspiciously like that of the original publisher, who may therefore have changed his mind about simply appealing to the "candid reader" to "allow of the usual excuses for such imperfections, almost unavoidable in printing books of any length." In any case the *printing* of a list of corrections must have been done shortly after the original issue; and JE himself may have drawn up the list. The surprising thing is that earlier editors seem not to have known of these corrections. Instead, they reprinted the same errors, or else altered the passage in an effort to make sense some other way. These corrections—some of them of considerable significance—have all been incorporated into the present edition. This same printed list of errata is pasted in JE, Jr.'s copy of his father's book, the flyleaf inscribed Nov. 1, 1764. JE, Jr. added in ink errata of his own, and six of these corrections are adopted in the present edition.

the *Inquiry* was published in a Dutch translation from Utrecht, and in that same year the fourth edition was brought out in America. This accounts for all the editions within the eighteenth century.

During the first half of the nineteenth century there were ten separate editions, four brought out in America and six in Great Britain; and in 1865 there was published an edition in Welsh. This makes a total of nineteen separate editions brought before the scholarly world during the first hundred years after its original publication,[3] without taking into account the inclusion of the *Inquiry* in Edwards' collected works, among the eight volumes of the Leeds edition of 1806–11, in the Worcester edition of eight volumes in 1808 with its many reprintings, and in the works published in ten volumes by Sereno E. Dwight, 1829–30. The Worcester edition has been most generally available in this country. The present volume then may perhaps be called the twentieth (or the twenty-third) edition of Edwards' *Inquiry*. Its publication is a consequence of the growing interest during recent years in the study of American intellectual history in general and of Edwards in particular, and also a consequence of the revival of interest in theology which has awakened the present generation to the importance of great theologians of the past. Not for the past hundred years has serious work been done on Edwards' texts, nor has there been much concern to keep his writings readily available to the republic of readers. In comparison with the frequent publication of Edwards' writings during the first hundred years, we have been exceedingly improvident of our heritage.

Two goals have been set before each of the editors of the various published works of Jonathan Edwards in preparing them for the Yale Edition of his collected works. The first is to provide the modern reader with a text he can easily read. To this end, peculiarities in the printing of the original edition that simply impede vision are here removed or modernized. In accordance with modern usage excessive capitalization—of stressed substantives, for example—is removed and lower case used wherever possible. In a number of instances, dashes following periods, and thus separating sentences, are deleted when they seem to serve no purpose. The dash is replaced by a series of dots when this indicates that Edwards omitted words from a quotation. The words "it Self," "my Self," "any Body," "every Where," and "any Thing" are printed as one word. The printing of

3. See Thomas H. Johnson, *The Printed Writings of Jonathan Edwards 1703–1758* (Princeton, Princeton University Press, 1940), pp. 64–72.

whole clauses or sentences in capital letters is abandoned, and in most of these instances italics are used instead. The word "and" is used instead of the ampersand.

Idiosyncratic spelling is modernized so that the eye of the reader need not halt over single words; thus "chuse" becomes "choose" and "perswasion" "persuasion." American spelling is preferred to British, for example "inquire" rather than "enquire." The apostrophe in possessives such as "our's" and "it's" is taken out. Contractions which are merely orthographic are silently lengthened: "tho'" is changed to "though," "tho't" to "thought," and "will'd" or "confess'd" to "willed" or "confessed." " 'Till" and " 'til" are replaced by "till," but never lengthened to "until." However, contractions such as "don't" and "ben't" are retained. The words "spake" and "shew" are exceptions to the regular modernization of spelling, because in these instances to retain the older spelling may preserve the authentic tone of the original as much as in the case of the contractions just mentioned. The preferred modern spelling of "subtle" and "subtlety" is used instead of "subtile" and "subtilty," because these older and nonpreferred forms no longer convey to the reader a difference in audible tone, but only the impression of a mistaken or rare spelling.

The use of italics, often excessive in eighteenth-century publications, is greatly reduced: proper names are not italicized; words referred to as words are enclosed within quotation marks rather than italicized. Quotation marks are, of course, used for actual quotations where Edwards regularly uses italics for this purpose; and his use of italics for indirect quotations is omitted. Frequently, italics used for emphasis are shortened, and not repeated so often. It is enough for the modern reader to have the stress placed upon the distinction between *natural* and *moral* necessity once in a paragraph, or even at the opening of a continuous passage discussing this subject, without repeating the italics every time the expressions occur.

Significant corrections inserted into the text are always enclosed within brackets, and in many instances the source of the correction is given in a footnote. The addition or deletion of a single "s" is made without notification. Small corrections are also silently made in punctuation, pagination, and Scripture references within the text. In a number of instances a colon is used in our sense of "as follows." Sometimes I use a dash at the end of a paragraph instead of the period, to indicate how rapidly Edwards moves from stating an objection in a long *incomplete* sentence to answering it in the next paragraph. Once, more than two lines of words referred to as words are simply set off by dashes rather than enclosing each of them in quotation marks. Abbreviations of the titles of biblical books and "pp.," "Arg.," and "Corol." are standardized. Punctuation around the numbering of items or paragraphs is regularized; thus, the period in "(1.)" and punctuation marks before such parentheses are removed. Where the parenthesis occurs within a sentence, commas and other punctuation marks before the parenthesis [,( ] or before the closing of a paren-thesis [,) or ;)] are placed afterward [ ), or);], using the strongest mark in case two are dropped. In the case of a pair of substantatives italicized in the original, when enclosing these words in quotation marks (to indicate that they are referred to as words) Edwards' comma after the first word is omitted, in the belief that the use of quotation marks provides sufficient pause for the modern reader. Thus *'willing,* and *choosing'* is changed to ' "willing" and "choosing." ' For the same reason, commas before and after the proper name in 'the appellation "Arminian" in this treatise' and sur-rounding the quoted words in 'the phrase "moral necessity" is used variously' are dropped; and sometimes also the comma after "must" in 'if I explained the word "must" by there being a necessity.' It is believed that these alterations will facilitate reading without any loss for those who relish Edwards' style.

With a view to allowing Edwards to speak for himself, editorial footnotes explaining or commenting on the text are held to a mini-mum. Instead of multiplying critical footnotes at the bottom of the pages, the reader is simply referred at various points in the text to numbered paragraphs in the foregoing parts of this Introduction, where the editor has undertaken to supply necessary background in-formation and to give an analysis of Edwards' argument or comment upon it. Thus the "critical notes" may be read before, after, or while reading Edwards. The editor's notes that remain at the bottom of the page are always placed in brackets to distinguish them from Ed-wards' own, except that where Edwards' too brief citations have simply been lengthened, it was thought unnecessary to separate his from the editor's part in the reference. Brackets are also used for one or two insertions into the text. Edwards' own citations, both in the text and in the notes, have been lightly styled to conform to the style established for the edition.

Perhaps this is the place to call attention to the fact that Edwards was by no means persuaded by our modern idea that a scholar should always be meticulously exact when quoting from another author. He often changes the tense of the verb or the number of the subject of a sentence or modifies its opening words to be continuous with the words by which he has himself introduced the quotation. At times he comes close to paraphrase. Yet he does not scruple to italicize these statements or enclose them in quotation marks. The editor has checked these instances of Edwards' use of other books and in no instance has found him unfaithful to the original author's meaning, or, between the quotation marks, unfair to him. To correct his quotations so as to make them formally quite exact would mutilate the text with bracketed insertions, and to repeat the quotation accurately in a footnote would needlessly burden the page.

The second aim that has guided the editor of this volume is a desire to provide the contemporary reader with a text that preserves the authentic tone and style of Edwards' eighteenth-century writing. If the only test had been to provide a readable text from which the substance of Edwards' *philosophical* point of view might most readily be apprehended, the text could have been put forth in completely modern form. However, students and teachers of English literature have a legitimate interest in Edwards as a writer, and the ordinary educated reader needs to go away from a study of the *Inquiry* impressed by more than Edwards' thought. Therefore, the editor attempted to present Edwards in all essential respects as he wrote and was read in the mid-eighteenth century. To this end, expressions such as "independent on" and "if it be never so great," and a manifold use of "at all" for emphasis, stand as Edwards spoke, wrote and printed them. Contractions that are not purely orthographic, i.e. those that have value in indicating tone or that affect pronunciation if read aloud, have all been retained, for example " 'tis," " 'twas," " 'em," "e'er," "can't," "don't," "ben't," "han't," "mayn't." The Worcester edition and all later printings as a rule try to improve Edwards in most of these respects. "At all" was frequently stricken out and Edwards was softened and smoothed as a consequence; "if it be ever so great" was preferred, and all the contractions mentioned were lengthened.

In addition to the substitution of "ever" for "never," and the deletion of "at all," the Worcester edition rewords certain passages or rearranges the order of words in them. A comparison with the original edition shows that by making these changes, on the whole, more was lost from Edwards' characteristic style than was gained.

Original edition, 1754	*Worcester edition, 1808*
for the Strength of the Will, let it be never so great, don't at all enable it to act one Way	for the strength of the Will, let it be ever so great, does not enable it to act one way
So that the Will acts not at all, does not so much begin to act in the Time of such Liberty.	So that the Will does not so much begin to act in the time of such liberty.
they are not worthy to be rewarded or praised; or at all esteemed, honoured or loved on that Account.	they are not worthy to be rewarded or praised, esteemed or loved on that account.
God's Actions, and particularly those which he exerts as a moral Governour, have moral Qualifications, are morally good in the highest degree.	God's actions, and particularly those which are to be attributed to him as moral governor, are morally good in the highest degree.
a Choice preceeding all Volitions, which are thus caused, even the very first of them	a choice preceding all Volitions which are thus caused, even the first of them
If this be their Meaning, then all this mighty Controversy about Freedom	If this be their meaning, then this mighty controversy about freedom
free from actual Possession, and vacant of Predetermination, so far, that	free from, and vacant of predetermination, so far, that
govern and determine them every one.	govern and determine them.
it would be very long to mention particularly	it would be tedious to mention particularly
And such Success, such Victory, and such a Reign and Dominion is often expressly foretold	And such a victory, and such a dominion is often expressly foretold
which are what originally	which are originally
Hence some Metaphysicians have been led unwarily, but exceeding absurdly, to suppose	Hence some metaphysicians have been led unwarily, but absurdly, to suppose
Such Kind of Terms in their original use	Such terms in their original use
they would be able more easily to compare them with their original and common Sense; and so would not be so easily cheated by them. The Minds of Men are so easily led into Delusion by no Sort of Terms in the World, as by Words of this Sort.	they would be able more easily to compare them with their original and common sense; and so would not be so easily led into delusion by words of this sort.
the certainer such Determination is	the more certain such determination is
so far as natural Inclination has had a Hand in determining their Wills	so far as natural inclination has influence in determining their Wills

Original edition, 1754	*Worcester edition, 1808*
such an Objector, if he has Capacity and Humility and Calmness of Spirit, sufficient impartially and thoroughly to examine himself	such an objector, if he has capacity and humility and calmness of spirit, and sufficient impartiality, thoroughly to examine himself
that might be reduced to more, and more demonstrable Inconsistencies	that might be reduced to more demonstrable inconsistencies

In only one instance was a bit of rewriting perhaps justified:

may be the Effect of some other Cause, besides the Liver, or the Being that lives, in whom Life is caused to be	may be the effect of some other cause, besides the being that lives, in whom Life is caused to be

Once this procedure led to mistaking Edwards' meaning:

the more he does either with full and strong inclination	the more he does either with or without full and strong inclination

A number of instances in which words were doubtless accidentally omitted here and there from the Worcester and other editions have been corrected by editing from the original, without, it is hoped, the loss of others from the text. A case in point is:

There is no Medium between suspending to act, and immediately acting; and therefore no Possibility of avoiding either the one or the other one Moment; and so no Room for Deliberation before we do either of them.	There is no medium between suspending to act, and immediately acting; and therefore no possibility of avoiding either the one or the other one moment.

The procedure of rewriting Edwards was carried out even more extensively by the Dwight edition,[4] in comparison with which the Worcester edition, indeed, seems quite accurate verbally. Where Edwards wanted two words to express his full meaning, in such expressions as "agreeable or pleasing," "consequence and fruit," "choosing or preferring," Sereno Dwight frequently judges that one word of each of these pairs is enough. The final "is" of "the Will is as the greatest apparent Good is," and similar statements, he simply omitted. He would let nothing have "an Hand in"; and he troubled a great deal to avoid a preposition at the end of a sentence or phrase:

4. The "advertisement" printed in the first volume of the Dwight edition states that "According to the original plan, the negligences of language in the published works were to be corrected; and this plan was not relinquished, until the slow process of correcting them with the pen, on the printed page, was far advanced towards completion."

Original edition, 1754	*Dwight edition, 1829*
and not some Object that the Act of Will has not an immediate, but only an indirect and remote Respect to	and not some object to which the act of Will has only an indirect and remote respect

"The" was deleted from "the calling some professing Christians" or "the thus distinguishing." Most notable of all Dwight's revisions was his dropping words, phrases, and even sentences in order to secure a simplified text, or rearranging words so extensively as in effect to rewrite entire passages. This can be seen in the preface (not printed at all in the Worcester edition):

may not imply, nor infer any more than that there is a Difference, and that the Difference is such as we find we have often Occasion to take Notice of, and make Mention of. That which we have frequent Occasion to speak of (whatever it be, that gives the Occasion) this wants a Name: and 'tis always a Defect in Language	may not imply any more, than that there is a *difference;* a difference of which we find we have often occasion to take notice: and it is always a defect in language
That the Difference of the Opinions of those, who in their general Scheme of Divinity agree with these two noted Men, *Calvin,* and *Arminius,* is a Thing there is often occasion to speak of, is what the practice of the latter it self confesses	That there is occasion to speak often concerning the difference of those, who in their general scheme of divinity agree with these two noted men, *CALVIN* and *ARMINIUS,* is what the practice of the latter confesses

Such extensive rewriting continues beyond the preface in Dwight's edition. The reader has a right to expect greater fidelity to the text.

I am sensible that such things as Edwards' spelling, his purely orthographic contractions, and his use of italics, which in this edition are sacrificed for the sake of presenting a more readable page, are also a part of his literary style. Yet when we remember the importance of the oral tradition in English and American literature in Edwards' day and the influence the practice of reading aloud still had upon the written language, surely the modifications made in this edition are not so essential to the taste and relish of Edwards' style as the vigorous expressions stricken out by the Worcester and Dwight editions and the contractions that have been retained in this edition.

Allied with these is the matter of the integrity of Edwards' use of rhetorical instead of syntactical punctuation, which had already begun to suffer alteration at the hands of the editor of the Worcester edition. In general it is hoped that in this edition Edwards has been more radically modernized, when it is a question of dispensable forms or of orthography—while at the same time the flavor, tone, and vigor of his writing have been conserved more fully—than in any other edition since the early nineteenth century editors set themselves the task of improving him. The aim, at least, has been to offer the contemporary reader a volume in which, with many obstacles to his vision removed, he may "hear" Edwards speaking and writing to him as he did to people in 1754.

Eighteenth-century punctuation seems to have had a rhetorical or oratorical rather than a grammatical or syntactical basis, as does usage today. Commas, semicolons, colons, and periods formed a series of rests arranged in increasing length or finality. They provided pauses for breath when reading aloud. Thus the colon was almost never used to mean "as follows" or "for example" as we so frequently use it today. It was used rather to introduce into a sentence a pause of the greatest duration or with the highest sense of finality short of a period. In like manner, the comma provided a rest of the shortest degree; it was frequently used between the subject and the predicate of a sentence, and with no distinction between restrictive and nonrestrictive clauses for which we use the comma today. Any attempt to alter rhetorical punctuation in the direction of grammatical punctuation would have been impossible to carry through consistently; it would also many times have distorted Edwards' meaning and would always have interrupted the rhythms of his literary style.

The editor of the Worcester edition, noting that a comma fell at the end of a clause, many times introduced a comma also at its beginning where none was, thus transforming it into a nonrestrictive clause according to the rules of grammatical punctuation; or else he omitted the final comma and by so doing eliminated the pause or rest Edwards provided and made the clause grammatically restrictive. Thus, where Edwards wrote "there being nothing in the Squares in themselves considered, that" the Worcester edition inserts a comma after "squares"; and again after "mind" in "and the Mind in determining to be guided by it, is not determined," etc. Expressions such as "therefore," "in other words," "by the supposition," "in like manner," "in general," "in some respects" were frequently set off by commas where Edwards usually does not so punctuate his sentences. Edwards often allows a series of adjectives or verbs to flow together without separating commas, as when he wrote "every prepossessing fix'd Bias," "moral Inability, consisting in that which is stated habitual and general," and "Men may truly will and wish and strive."

Although Samuel Austin in editing the Worcester edition took out many of Edwards' commas, on balance there are many hundreds more commas in the Worcester edition than in the original. Why should the reader stagger through the reading of such a sentence as "Let us, for clearness sake, suppose, that God had, at the beginning, made two Globes" when what Edwards printed was "Let us for Clearness sake suppose, that God had at the Beginning made two Globes"?

Edwards' rhetorical punctuation was also often given different rhythm and interrupted by the wrong pauses when Austin demoted a colon to a semicolon or comma or a semicolon to a comma and when he promoted the colon to a period. In the sentence "For 'tis absurd, to suppose the same individual Will to oppose it Self, in its present Act; or the present Choice to be opposed to, and resisting present Choice: as absurd as it is to talk of two contrary Motions, in the same moving Body, at the same Time," both cadence and meaning hinge upon the medial colon which ought not to have been changed to a rest of the same duration as that provided by the preceding semicolon. The same may be said of the substitution of commas for both semicolons in "If it should be asked, why the Soul of Man uses it's Activity in such a Manner as it does; and it should be answered, that the Soul uses it's Activity thus, rather than otherwise, because it has Activity; would such an Answer satisfy a rational Man?"

Before concluding these notes on the text of the present edition, it may be in order to remark upon the flexibility, vigor, clarity, and swift movement writers gained from their use of rhetorical punctuation in the eighteenth and earlier centuries in contrast to the grammatical punctuation of the nineteenth and twentieth centuries. When Edwards tells a story in illustration of a point, he writes:

> If a child has a most excellent father, that has ever treated him with fatherly kindness and tenderness, and has every way in the highest degree merited his love and dutiful regard, being withal very wealthy; but the son is of so vile a disposition, that he inveterately hates his father; and yet, apprehending that his hatred of him is like to prove his ruin, by bringing him finally to poverty and abject circumstances, through his father's disinheriting him, or otherwise; which is exceeding cross to his avarice and ambition; he therefore wishes it were otherwise: but yet remaining under the invincible power of his vile and malignant disposition, he continues still in his settled hatred of his father [p. 314].

The reader can readily give himself over to be borne along by the swift moving rhythms of Edwards' style, and yet at no point in the reading of these rather long and complex sentences need he be confused as to their meaning or unclear about the appositions or connections within the sentence. To tell such a tale, a modern writer would doubtless have to employ in the course of it a number of colorless new beginnings, like "The son, however, had such a vile disposition," "He was," or "But besides this." What is true of Edwards' story telling is equally true of the expression of his philosophical thought. Style and punctuation are internally related to the persuasiveness and force of his argument, allowing as it does for the eloquent piling up of swift-moving, long, rhythmic, yet perfectly clear sentences. He was able to wring an Arminian's neck the more effectively, in part at least, because single sentences wrapped back upon themselves, closing every loophole, and carried every detail forward in pulsations separated by a gradation of rests without any loss of lucidity.

There remains for me the pleasant duty of acknowledging the help I have received in the course of preparing this work of Edwards for publication. Perry Miller of Harvard has encouraged and guided me at many points beyond the call of duty as general editor. He and John Smith and Norman Holmes Pearson of Yale University and Thomas Schafer of Duke University (and on behalf of the Editorial Board, Sidney Mead of the University of Chicago and Sydney Ahlstrom of Yale) have read the Introduction and have given me the benefit of their criticisms. I am grateful also to James Ward Smith and John W. Yolton of Princeton and Bernard Wand of Carleton College, Ottawa, Canada, for their comments upon parts of the Introduction. Two former students of mine at Princeton, Wendel Dietrich and Horace Allen, have hewn wood and drawn water with me in collating and preparing the text, and checking footnotes. W. D. White of Baylor University checked the final page proofs, and Edward Smolensky helped me prepare the Index.

I shall be grateful if these introductory comments find somewhere "that individual, whom with joy and gladness I call my reader," for then if only in a very small measure I shall have paid some of my indebtedness to historical scholarship. However, if the reader opens this volume just at this page and his eyes light first upon these words, he is sincerely invited not to turn back but to read Jonathan Edwards.

PAUL RAMSEY

Princeton University
February 6, 1957

MANY find much fault with the calling professing Christians, that differ one from another in some matters of opinion, by distinct names; especially calling them by the names of particular men, who have distinguished themselves as maintainers and promoters of those opinions: as the calling some professing Christians "Arminians," from Arminius; others "Arians," from Arius; others "Socinians," from Socinus, and the like. They think it unjust in itself; as it seems to suppose and suggest, that the persons marked out by these names, received those doctrines which they entertain, out of regard to, and reliance on those men after whom they are named; as though they made them their rule: in the same manner, as the followers of Christ are called "Christians"; after his name, whom they regard and depend upon, as their great Head and Rule. Whereas, this is an unjust and groundless imputation on those that go under the forementioned denominations. Thus (say they) there is not the least ground to suppose, that the chief divines, who embrace the scheme of doctrine which is by many called Arminianism, believe it the more because Arminius believed it: and that there is no reason to think any other, than that they sincerely and impartially study the Holy Scriptures, and inquire after the mind of Christ, with as much judgment and sincerity, as any of those that call them by these names; that they seek after truth, and are not careful whether they think exactly as Arminius did; yea, that in some things they actually differ from him. This practice is also esteemed actually injurious on this account, that it is supposed naturally to lead the multitude to imagine the difference between persons thus named and others, to be greater than it is; yea, as though it were so great, that they must be as it were another species of beings. And they object against it as arising from an uncharitable, narrow, contracted spirit; which, they say, commonly inclines persons to confine all that is good to themselves and their own party, and to make a wide distinction between themselves and others, and stigmatize those that differ from them with odious names. They say moreover, that the keeping up such a distinction of names has a direct tendency to uphold distance and disaffection, and keep alive mutual hatred among Christians, who ought all to be united in friendship and charity, however they can't in all things think alike.

I confess, these things are very plausible. And I will not deny, that there are some unhappy consequences of this distinction of names, and that men's infirmities and evil dispositions often make an ill improvement of it. But yet I humbly conceive, these objections are carried far beyond reason. The generality of mankind are disposed enough, and a great deal too much, to uncharitableness, and to be censorious and bitter towards those that differ from them in religious opinions: which evil temper of mind will take occasion to exert itself, from many things in themselves innocent, useful and necessary. But yet there is no necessity to suppose, that the thus distinguishing persons of different opinions by different names, arises mainly from an uncharitable spirit. It may arise from the disposition there is in mankind (whom God has distinguished with an ability and inclination for speech) to improve the benefit of language, in the proper use and design of names, given to things which they have often occasion to speak of, or signify their minds about; which is to enable them to express their ideas with ease and expedition, without being incumbered with an obscure and difficult circumlocution. And the thus distinguishing persons of different opinions in religious matters, may not imply, nor infer any more than that there is a difference, and that the difference is such as we find we have often occasion to take notice of, and make mention of. That which we have frequent occasion to speak of (whatever it be, that gives the occasion) this wants a name: and 'tis always a defect in language, in such cases, to be obliged to make use of a description, instead of a name. Thus we have often occasion to speak of those who are the descendants of the ancient inhabitants of France, who were subjects or heads of the government of that land, and spake the language peculiar to it; in distinction from the descendants of the inhabitants of Spain, who belonged to that community, and spake the language of that country. And therefore we find the great need of distinct names to signify these different sorts of people, and the great convenience of those distinguishing words, "French" and "Spaniards"; by which the signification of our minds is quick and easy, and our speech is delivered from the burden of a continual reiteration of diffuse descriptions, with which it must otherwise be embarrassed.

That the difference of the opinions of those, who in their general scheme of divinity agree with these two noted men, Calvin, and Arminius, is a thing there is often occasion to speak of, is what the practice of the latter, itself confesses; who are often, in their discourses and writings, taking notice of the supposed absurd and pernicious opinions of the former sort. And therefore the making use of different names in this case can't reasonably be objected against, or condemned, as a thing which must come from so bad a cause as they assign. It is easy to be accounted for, without supposing it to arise from any other source, than the exigence and natural tendency of the state of things; considering the faculty and disposition God has given mankind, to express things which they have frequent occasion to mention, by certain distinguishing names. It is an effect that is similar to what we see arise, in innumerable cases which are parallel, where the cause is not at all blameworthy.

Nevertheless, at first I had thoughts of carefully avoiding the use of the appellation "Arminian" in this treatise. But I soon found I should be put to great difficulty by it; and that my discourse would be so encumbered with an often repeated circumlocution, instead of a name, which would express the thing intended, as well and better, that I altered my purpose. And therefore I must ask the excuse of such as are apt to be offended with things of this nature, that I have so freely used the term "Arminian" in the following discourse. I profess it to be without any design, to stigmatize persons of any sort with a name of reproach, or at all to make them appear more odious. If when I had occasion to speak of those divines who are commonly called by this name, I had, instead of styling them Arminians, called them "these men," as Dr. Whitby does Calvinistic divines; it probably would not have been taken any better, or thought to show a better temper, or more good manners. I have done as I would be done by, in this matter. However the term "Calvinist" is in these days, among most, a term of greater reproach than the term "Arminian"; yet I should not take it at all amiss, to be called a Calvinist, for distinction's sake: though I utterly disclaim a dependence on Calvin, or believing the doctrines which I hold, because he believed and taught them; and cannot justly be charged with believing in everything just as he taught.

But lest I should really be an occasion of injury to some persons, I would here give notice, that though I generally speak of that doctrine, concerning free will and moral agency, which I oppose, as an Arminian doctrine; yet I would not be understood, that every divine or author whom I have occasion to mention as maintaining that doctrine, was properly an Arminian, or one of that sort which is commonly called by that name. Some of them went far beyond the Arminians: and I would by no means charge Arminians in general with all the corrupt doctrine, which these maintained. Thus for instance, it would be very injurious, if I should rank Arminian divines in general, with such authors as Mr. Chubb. I doubt not, many of them have some of his doctrines in abhorrence; though he agrees, for the most part, with Arminians, in his notion of the freedom of the will.[1] And on the other hand, though I suppose this notion to be a leading article in the Arminian scheme, that which, if pursued in its consequences, will truly infer, or naturally lead to all the rest; yet I don't charge all that have held this doctrine, with being Arminians. For whatever may be the consequences of the doctrine really, yet some that hold this doctrine, may not own nor see these consequences; and it would be unjust, in many instances, to charge every author with believing and maintaining all the real consequences of his avowed doctrines. And I desire it may be particularly noted, that though I have occasion in the following discourse, often to mention the author [2] of the book entitled, *An Essay on the Freedom of the Will, in God and the Creature,* as holding that notion of freedom of will, which I oppose; yet I don't mean to call him an Arminian: however in that doctrine he agrees with Arminians, and departs from the current and general opinion of Calvinists. If the author of that essay be the same as it is commonly ascribed to, he doubtless was not one that ought to bear that name. But however good a divine he was in many respects, yet that particular Arminian doctrine which he maintained, is never the better for being held by such an one: nor is there less need of opposing it on that account; but rather is there the more need of it; as it will be likely to have the more pernicious influence, for being taught by a divine of his name and character; supposing the doctrine to be wrong, and in itself to be of an ill tendency.

I have nothing further to say by way of preface; but only to bespeak the reader's candor, and calm attention to what I have written.

1. [See above, Introduction, Pt. 5, no. 1.]
2. [See above, Intro., Pt. 5, nos. 13, 14.]

The subject is of such importance, as to *demand* attention, and the most thorough consideration. Of all kinds of knowledge that we can ever obtain, the knowledge of God, and the knowledge of ourselves, are the most important. As religion is the great business, for which we are created, and on which our happiness depends; and as religion consists in an intercourse between ourselves and our Maker; and so has its foundation in God's nature and ours, and in the relation that God and we stand in to each other; therefore a true knowledge of both must be needful in order to true religion. But the knowledge of ourselves consists chiefly in right apprehensions concerning those two chief faculties of our nature, the *understanding* and *will*. Both are very important: yet the science of the latter must be confessed to be of greatest moment; inasmuch as all virtue and religion have their seat more immediately in the will, consisting more especially in right acts and habits of this faculty. And the grand question about the freedom of the will, is the main point that belongs to the science of the will. Therefore I say, the importance of this subject greatly *demands* the attention of Christians, and especially of divines. But as to my manner of handling the subject, I will be far from presuming to say, that it is such as *demands* the attention of the reader to what I have written. I am ready to own, that in this matter I depend on the reader's *courtesy*. But only thus far I may have some color for putting in a *claim*; that if the reader be disposed to pass his censure on what I have written, I may be fully and patiently heard, and well attended to, before I am condemned. However, this is what I would humbly *ask* of my readers; together with the prayers of all sincere lovers of truth, that I may have much of that Spirit which Christ promised his disciples, which guides into all truth; and that the blessed and powerful influences of this Spirit would make truth victorious in the world

PART ONE

Wherein Are Explained and Stated Various Terms and Things Belonging to the Subject of the Ensuing Discourse

SECTION 1. CONCERNING THE NATURE OF THE WILL

It MAY possibly be thought, that there is no great need of going about to define or describe the "will"; this word being generally as well understood as any other words we can use to explain it: and so perhaps it would be, had not philosophers, metaphysicians and polemic divines brought the matter into obscurity by the things they have said of it. But since it is so, I think it may be of some use, and will tend to the greater clearness in the following discourse, to say a few things concerning it.

And therefore I observe, that the will (without any metaphysical refining) is plainly, that by which the mind chooses anything. The faculty of the will is that faculty or power or principle of mind by which it is capable of choosing: an act of the will is the same as an act of choosing or choice.

If any think 'tis a more perfect definition of the will, to say, that it is that by which the soul either chooses or refuses; I am content with it: though I think that 'tis enough to say, it's that by which the soul chooses: for in every act of will whatsoever, the mind chooses one thing rather than another; it chooses something rather than the contrary, or rather than the want or nonexistence of that thing. So in every act of refusal, the mind chooses the absence of the thing refused; the positive and the negative are set before the mind for its choice, and it chooses the negative; and the mind's making its choice in that case is properly the act of the will: the will's determining between the two is a voluntary determining; but that is the same thing as making a choice. So that whatever names we call the act of the will by—choosing, refusing, approving, disapproving, liking, disliking, embracing, rejecting, determining, directing, commanding, forbidding, inclining or being averse, a being pleased or displeased with—all may be reduced to this of choosing. For the soul to act voluntarily, is evermore to act electively.

137

Mr. Locke [1] says, "The will signifies nothing but a power or ability to prefer or choose." And in the foregoing page says, "The word 'preferring' seems best to express the act of volition"; but adds, that "it does it not precisely; for (says he) though a man would prefer flying to walking, yet who can say he ever wills it?" [2] But the instance he mentions don't prove that there is anything else in "willing" but merely "preferring": for it should be considered what is the next and immediate object of the will, with respect to a man's walking, or any other external action; which is not his being removed from one place to another; on the earth, or through the air; these are remoter objects of preference; but such or such an immediate exertion of himself. The thing nextly chosen or preferred when a man wills to walk, is not his being removed to such a place where he would be, but such an exertion and motion of his legs and feet, etc. in order to it. And his willing such an alteration in his body in the present moment, is nothing else but his choosing or preferring such an alteration in his body at such a moment, or his liking it better than the forbearance of it. And God has so made and established the human nature, the soul being united to a body in proper state, that the soul preferring or choosing such an immediate exertion or alteration of the body, such an alteration instantaneously follows. There is nothing else in the actings of my mind, that I am conscious of while I walk, but only my preferring or choosing, through successive moments, that there should be such alterations of my external sensations and motions; together with a concurring habitual expectation that it will be so; having ever found by experience, that on such an immediate preference, such sensations and motions do actually instantaneously, and constantly arise. But it is not so in the case of flying: though a man may be said remotely to choose or prefer flying; yet he don't choose or prefer, incline to or desire, under circumstances in view, any immediate exertion of the members of his body in order to it; because he has no expectation that he should obtain the desired end by any such exertion; and he don't prefer or incline to any bodily exertion or effort under this apprehended circumstance, of its being wholly in vain. So that if we carefully distinguish the proper objects of the several acts of the will, it will not appear by

1. [John Locke, *An Essay Concerning Human Understanding* (1690), Bk. II, ch. 21, no. 17; ed. A. C. Frazer (2 vols. Oxford, 1894), *1*, 321. JE cites the 7th ed. London, 1716.]

2. [Ibid., no. 15; p. 320.]

this, and suchlike instances, that there is any difference between "volition" and "preference"; or that a man's choosing, liking best, or being best pleased with a thing, are not the same with his willing that thing; as they seem to be according to those general and more natural notions of men, according to which language is formed. Thus an act of the will is commonly expressed by its pleasing a man to do thus or thus; and a man's doing as he wills, and doing as he pleases, are the same thing in common speech.

Mr. Locke says,[3] "The will is perfectly distinguished from desire; which in the very same action may have a quite contrary tendency from that which our wills set us upon. A man (says he) whom I cannot deny, may oblige me to use persuasions to another, which, at the same time I am speaking, I may wish may not prevail on him. In this case 'tis plain the will and desire run counter." I don't suppose, that "will" and "desire" are words of precisely the same signification: "will" seems to be a word of a more general signification, extending to things present and absent. "Desire" respects something absent. I may prefer my present situation and posture, suppose sitting still, or having my eyes open, and so may will it. But yet I can't think they are so entirely distinct, that they can ever be properly said to run counter. A man never, in any instance, wills anything contrary to his desires, or desires anything contrary to his will. The forementioned instance, which Mr. Locke produces, don't prove that he ever does. He may, on some consideration or other, will to utter speeches which have a tendency to persuade another, and still may desire that they may not persuade him: but yet his will and desire don't run counter at all: the thing which he wills, the very same he desires; and he don't will a thing, and desire the contrary in any particular. In this instance, it is not carefully observed, what is the thing willed, and what is the thing desired: if it were, it would be found that will and desire don't clash in the least. The thing willed on some consideration, is to utter such words; and certainly, the same consideration so influences him, that he don't desire the contrary; all things considered, he chooses to utter such words, and don't desire not to utter 'em. And so as to the thing which Mr. Locke speaks of as desired, viz. that the words, though they tend to persuade, should not be effectual to that end, his will is not contrary to this; he don't will that they should be effectual, but rather wills that they should not, as he desires. In order to prove that the will and desire may run

3. [Ibid., no. 30; p. 332. See above, Intro., Pt. 4, no. 2.]

counter, it should be shown that they may be contrary one to the other in the same thing, or with respect to the very same object of will or desire: but here the objects are two; and in each, taken by themselves, the will and desire agree. And 'tis no wonder that they should not agree in different things, however little distinguished they are in their nature. The will may not agree with the will, nor desire agree with desire, in different things. As in this very instance which Mr. Locke mentions, a person may, on some consideration, desire to use persuasions, and at the same time may desire they may not prevail; but yet nobody will say, that desire runs counter to desire; or that this proves that desire is perfectly a distinct thing from desire. The like might be observed of the other instance Mr. Locke produces, of a man's desiring to be eased of pain and so forth.

But not to dwell any longer on this, whether desire and will, and whether preference and volition be precisely the same things or no; yet, I trust it will be allowed by all, that in every act of will there is an act of choice; that in every volition there is a preference, or a prevailing inclination of the soul, whereby the soul, at that instant, is out of a state of perfect indifference, with respect to the direct object of the volition. So that in every act, or going forth of the will, there is some preponderation of the mind or inclination, one way rather than another; and the soul had rather have or do one thing than another, or than not to have or do that thing; and that there, where there is absolutely no preferring or choosing, but a perfect continuing equilibrium, there is no volition.

SECTION 2. CONCERNING THE DETERMINATION OF THE WILL

B Y "determining the will," if the phrase be used with any meaning, must be intended, causing that the act of the will or choice should be thus, and not otherwise: and the will is said to be determined, when, in consequence of some action, or influence, its choice is directed to, and fixed upon a particular object. As when we speak of the determination of motion, we mean causing the motion of the body to be such a way, or in such a direction, rather than another.

To talk of the determination of the will, supposes an effect, which must have a cause. If the will be determined, there is a determiner. This must be supposed to be intended even by them that say, the will determines itself. If it be so, the will is both determiner and determined; it is a cause that acts and produces effects upon itself, and is the object of its own influence and action.

With respect to that grand inquiry, what determines the will, it would be very tedious and unnecessary at present to enumerate and examine all the various opinions, which have been advanced concerning this matter; nor is it needful that I should enter into a particular disquisition of all points debated in disputes on that question, whether the will always follows the last dictate of the understanding. It is sufficient to my present purpose to say, it is that motive, which, as it stands in the view of the mind, is the strongest, that determines the will.—But it may be necessary that I should a little explain my meaning in this.

By "motive," I mean the whole of that which moves, excites or invites the mind to volition, whether that be one thing singly, or many things conjunctly. Many particular things may concur and unite their strength to induce the mind; and when it is so, all together are as it were one complex motive. And when I speak of the "strongest motive," I have respect to the strength of the whole that operates to induce to a particular act of volition, whether that be the strength of one thing alone, or of many together.

Whatever is a motive, in this sense, must be something that is extant in the view or apprehension of the understanding, or perceiving faculty. Nothing can induce or invite the mind to will or act anything, any further than it is perceived, or is some way or other in the mind's view; for what is wholly unperceived, and perfectly out of the mind's view, can't affect the mind at all. 'Tis most evident, that nothing is in the mind, or reaches it, or takes any hold of it, any otherwise than as it is perceived or thought of.

And I think it must also be allowed by all, that everything that is properly called a motive, excitement or inducement to a perceiving willing agent, has some sort and degree of tendency, or advantage to move or excite the will, previous to the effect, or to the act of the will excited. This previous tendency of the motive is what I call the "strength" of the motive. That motive which has a less degree of previous advantage or tendency to move the will, or that appears less inviting, as it stands in the view of the mind, is what I call a "weaker motive." On the contrary, that which appears most inviting, and has, by what appears concerning it to the understanding or apprehension, the greatest degree of previous tendency to excite and induce the choice, is what I call the "strongest motive." And in this sense, I suppose the will is always determined by the strongest motive.

Things that exist in the view of the mind, have their strength, tendency or advantage to move or excite its will, from many things appertaining to the nature and circumstances of the thing viewed, the nature and circumstances of the mind that views, and the degree and manner of its view; which it would perhaps be hard to make a perfect enumeration of. But so much I think may be determined in general, without room for controversy, that whatever is perceived or apprehended by an intelligent and voluntary agent, which has the nature and influence of a motive to volition or choice, is considered or viewed *as good;* nor has it any tendency to invite or engage the election of the soul in any further degree than it appears such. For to say otherwise, would be to say, that things that appear have a tendency by the appearance they make, to engage the mind to elect them, some other way than by their appearing eligible to it; which is absurd. And therefore it must be true, in some sense, that the will always is as the greatest apparent good is. But only, for the right understanding of this, two things must be well and distinctly observed.

1. It must be observed in what sense I use the term "good"; namely, as of the same import with "agreeable." To appear good to the mind, as I use the phrase, is the same as to appear agreeable, or seem pleasing to the mind. Certainly, nothing appears inviting and eligible to the mind, or tending to engage its inclination and choice, considered as evil or disagreeable; nor indeed, as indifferent, and neither agreeable nor disagreeable. But if it tends to draw the inclination, and move the will, it must be under the notion of that which *suits* the mind. And therefore that must have the greatest tendency to attract and engage it, which, as it stands in the mind's view, suits it best, and pleases it most; and in that sense, is the greatest apparent good: to say otherwise, is little, if anything, short of a direct and plain contradiction.

The word "good," in this sense, includes in its signification, the removal or avoiding of evil, or of that which is disagreeable and uneasy. 'Tis agreeable and pleasing, to avoid what is disagreeable and displeasing, and to have uneasiness removed. So that here is included what Mr. Locke supposes determines the will. For when he speaks of uneasiness as determining the will, he must be understood as supposing that the end or aim which governs in the volition or act of preference, is the avoiding or removal of that uneasiness; and that is the same thing as choosing and seeking what is more easy and agreeable.[1]

2. When I say, the will is as the greatest apparent good is, or (as I have explained it) that volition has always for its object the thing which appears most agreeable; it must be carefully observed, to avoid confusion and needless objection, that I speak of the direct and immediate object of the act of volition; and not some object that the act of will has not an immediate, but only an indirect and remote respect to. Many acts of volition have some remote relation to an object, that is different from the thing most immediately willed and chosen. Thus, when a drunkard has his liquor before him, and he has to choose whether to drink it, or no; the proper and immediate objects, about which his present volition is conversant, and between which his choice now decides, are his own acts, in drinking the liquor, or letting it alone; and this will certainly be done according to what, in the present view of his mind, taken in the whole of it, is most agreeable to him. If he chooses or wills to drink it, and not to let it alone; then this action, as it stands in the view of his mind,

1. [See above, Intro., Pt. 4, nos. 3, 4.]

with all that belongs to its appearance there, is more agreeable and pleasing than letting it alone.

But the objects to which this act of volition may relate more remotely, and between which his choice may determine more indirectly, are the present pleasure the man expects by drinking, and the future misery which he judges will be the consequence of it: he may judge that this future misery, when it comes, will be more disagreeable and unpleasant, than refraining from drinking now would be. But these two things are not the proper objects that the act of volition spoken of is nextly conversant about. For the act of will spoken of is concerning present drinking or forbearing to drink. If he wills to drink, then drinking is the proper object of the act of his will; and drinking, on some account or other, now appears most agreeable to him, and suits him best. If he chooses to refrain, then refraining is the immediate object of his will, and is most pleasing to him. If in the choice he makes in the case, he prefers a present pleasure to a future advantage, which he judges will be greater when it comes; then a lesser present pleasure appears more agreeable to him than a greater advantage at a distance. If on the contrary a future advantage is preferred, then that appears most agreeable, and suits him best. And so still the present volition is as the greatest apparent good at present is.

I have rather chosen to express myself thus, that the will always *is* as the greatest apparent good, or as what appears most agreeable, is, than to say that the will is *determined* by the greatest apparent good, or by what seems most agreeable; because an appearing most agreeable or pleasing to the mind, and the mind's preferring and choosing, seem hardly to be properly and perfectly distinct. If strict propriety of speech be insisted on, it may more properly be said, that the voluntary action which is the immediate consequence and fruit of the mind's volition or choice, is determined by that which appears most agreeable, than the preference or choice itself; but that the act of volition itself is always determined by that in or about the mind's view of the object, which causes it to appear most agreeable. I say, in or about the mind's view of the object, because what has influence to render an object in view agreeable, is not only what appears in the object viewed, but also the manner of the view, and the state and circumstances of the mind that views.—Particularly to enumerate all things pertaining to the mind's view of the objects of volition, which have influence in their appearing agreeable to the mind, would be a matter of no small difficulty, and might require a treatise by itself, and is not necessary to my present purpose. I shall therefore only mention some things in general.

I. One thing that makes an object proposed to choice agreeable, is the apparent nature and circumstances of the object. And there are various things of this sort, that have an hand in rendering the object more or less agreeable; as,

1. That which appears in the object, which renders it beautiful and pleasant, or deformed and irksome to the mind; viewing it as it is in itself.

2. The apparent degree of pleasure or trouble attending the object, or the consequence of it. Such concomitants and consequents being viewed as circumstances of the object, are to be considered as belonging to it, and as it were parts of it; as it stands in the mind's view, as a proposed object of choice.

3. The apparent state of the pleasure or trouble that appears, with respect to distance of time; being either nearer or farther off. 'Tis a thing in itself agreeable to the mind, to have pleasure speedily; and disagreeable, to have it delayed: so that if there be two equal degrees of pleasure set in the mind's view, and all other things are equal, but only one is beheld as near, and the other far off; the nearer will appear most agreeable, and so will be chosen. Because, though the agreeableness of the objects be exactly equal, as viewed in themselves, yet not as viewed in their circumstances; one of them having the additional agreeableness of the circumstance of nearness.

II. Another thing that contributes to the agreeableness of an object of choice, as it stands in the mind's view, is the manner of the view. If the object be something which appears connected with future pleasure, not only will the degree of apparent pleasure have influence, but also the manner of the view, especially in two respects.

1. With respect to the degree of judgment, or firmness of assent, with which the mind judges the pleasure to be future. Because it is more agreeable to have a certain happiness, than an uncertain one; and a pleasure viewed as more probable, all other things being equal, is more agreeable to the mind, than that which is viewed as less probable.

2. With respect to the degree of the idea of the future pleasure. With regard to things which are the subject of our thoughts, either past, present or future, we have much more of an idea or apprehension of some things than others; that is, our idea is much more clear,

lively and strong. Thus, the ideas we have of sensible things by immediate sensation, are usually much more lively than those we have by mere imagination, or by contemplation of them when absent. My idea of the sun, when I look upon it, is more vivid, than when I only think of it. Our idea of the sweet relish of a delicious fruit is usually stronger when we taste it, than when we only imagine it. And sometimes, the ideas we have of things by contemplation, are much stronger and clearer, than at other times. Thus, a man at one time has a much stronger idea of the pleasure which is to be enjoyed in eating some sort of food that he loves, than at another. Now the degree, or strength of the idea or sense that men have of future good or evil, is one thing that has great influence on their minds to excite choice or volition. When of two kinds of future pleasure, which the mind considers of, and are presented for choice, both are supposed exactly equal by the judgment, and both equally certain, and all other things are equal, but only one of them is what the mind has a far more lively sense of, than of the other; this has the greatest advantage by far to affect and attract the mind, and move the will. 'Tis now more agreeable to the mind, to take the pleasure it has a strong and lively sense of, than that which it has only a faint idea of. The view of the former is attended with the strongest appetite, and the greatest uneasiness attends the want of it; and 'tis agreeable to the mind, to have uneasiness removed, and its appetite gratified. And if several future enjoyments are presented together, as competitors for the choice of the mind, some of them judged to be greater, and others less; the mind also having a greater sense and more lively idea of the good of some of them, and of others a less; and some are viewed as of greater certainty or probability than others; and those enjoyments that appear most agreeable in one of these respects, appear least so in others: in this case, all other things being equal, the agreeableness of a proposed object of choice will be in a degree some way compounded of the degree of good supposed by the judgment, the degree of apparent probability or certainty of that good, and the degree of the view or sense, or liveliness of the idea the mind has, of that good; because all together concur to constitute the degree in which the object appears at present agreeable; and accordingly volition will be determined.

I might further observe, the state of the mind that views a proposed object of choice, is another thing that contributes to the agreeableness or disagreeableness of that object; the particular temper which the mind has by nature, or that has been introduced and established by education, example, custom, or some other means; or the frame or state that the mind is in on a particular occasion. That object which appears agreeable to one, does not so to another. And the same object don't always appear alike agreeable to the same person, at different times. It is most agreeable to some men, to follow their reason; and to others, to follow their appetites: to some men, it is more agreeable to deny a vicious inclination, than to gratify it; others it suits best to gratify the vilest appetites. 'Tis more disagreeable to some men than others, to counteract a former resolution. In these respects, and many others which might be mentioned, different things will be most agreeable to different persons; and not only so, but to the same persons at different times.

But possibly 'tis needless and improper, to mention the frame and state of the mind, as a distinct ground of the agreeableness of objects from the other two mentioned before; viz. the apparent nature and circumstances of the objects viewed, and the manner of the view: perhaps if we strictly consider the matter, the different temper and state of the mind makes no alteration as to the agreeableness of objects, any other way, than as it makes the objects themselves appear differently beautiful or deformed, having apparent pleasure or pain attending them: and as it occasions the manner of the view to be different, causes the idea of beauty or deformity, pleasure or uneasiness to be more or less lively.

However, I think so much is certain, that volition, in no one instance that can be mentioned, is otherwise than the greatest apparent good is, in the manner which has been explained. The choice of the mind never departs from that which, at that time, and with respect to the direct and immediate objects of that decision of the mind, appears most agreeable and pleasing, all things considered. If the immediate objects of the will are a man's own actions, then those actions which appear most agreeable to him he wills. If it be now most agreeable to him, all things considered, to walk, then he now wills to walk. If it be now, upon the whole of what at present appears to him, most agreeable to speak, then he chooses to speak: if it suits him best to keep silence, then he chooses to keep silence. There is scarcely a plainer and more universal dictate of the sense and experience of mankind, than that, when men act voluntarily, and do what they please, then they do what suits them best, or what is most agreeable to them. To say, that they do what they please, or what pleases them, but yet don't do what is agreeable to them, is the same thing as to say, they do what they please, but don't act their pleasure; and that is to say, that they do what they please, and yet don't do what they please.

It appears from these things, that in some sense, the will always follows the last dictate of the understanding. But then the understanding must be taken in a large sense, as including the whole faculty of perception or apprehension, and not merely what is called reason or judgment. If by the dictate of the understanding is meant what reason declares to be best or most for the person's happiness, taking in the whole of his duration, it is not true, that the will always follows the last dictate of the understanding. Such a dictate of reason is quite a different matter from things appearing now most agreeable; all things being put together which pertain to the mind's present perceptions, apprehensions or ideas, in any respect. Although that dictate of reason, when it takes place, is one thing that is put into the scales, and is to be considered as a thing that has concern in the compound influence which moves and induces the will; and is one thing that is to be considered in estimating the degree of that appearance of good which the will always follows; either as having its influence added to other things, or subducted from them. When it concurs with other things, then its weight is added to them, as put into the same scale; but when it is against them, it is as a weight in the opposite scale, where it resists the influence of other things: yet its resistance is often overcome by their greater weight, and so the act of the will is determined in opposition to it.

The things which I have said may, I hope, serve, in some measure, to illustrate and confirm the position I laid down in the beginning of this section, viz. that the will is always determined by the strongest motive, or by that view of the mind which has the greatest degree of previous tendency to excite volition. But whether I have been so happy as rightly to explain the thing wherein consists the strength of motives, or not, yet my failing in this will not overthrow the position itself; which carries much of its own evidence with it, and is the thing of chief importance to the purpose of the ensuing discourse: and the truth of it, I hope, will appear with greater clearness, before I have finished what I have to say on the subject of human liberty.

SECTION 3. CONCERNING THE MEANING OF THE TERMS NECESSITY, IMPOSSIBILITY, INABILITY, ETC.; AND OF CONTINGENCE

THE WORDS "necessary," "impossible," etc. are abundantly used in controversies about free will and moral agency; and therefore the sense in which they are used, should be clearly understood.

Here I might say, that a thing is then said to be necessary, when it must be, and cannot be otherwise. But this would not properly be a definition of necessity, or an explanation of the word, any more than if I explained the word "must" by there being a necessity. The words "must," "can," and "cannot" need explication as much as the words "necessary" and "impossible"; excepting that the former are words that children commonly use, and know something of the meaning of earlier than the latter.

The word "necessary," as used in common speech, is a relative term; and relates to some supposed opposition made to the existence of the thing spoken of, which is overcome, or proves in vain to hinder or alter it. That is necessary, in the original and proper sense of the word, which is, or will be, notwithstanding all supposable opposition. To say, that a thing is necessary, is the same thing as to say, that it is impossible [it] should not be: but the word "impossible" is manifestly a relative term, and has reference to supposed power exerted to bring a thing to pass, which is insufficient for the effect; as the word "unable" is relative, and has relation to ability or endeavor which is insufficient; and as the word "irresistible" is relative, and has always reference to resistance which is made, or may be made to some force or power tending to an effect, and is insufficient to withstand the power, or hinder the effect. The common notion of necessity and impossibility implies something that frustrates endeavor or desire.

Here several things are to be noted.

1. Things are said to be necessary *in general*, which are or will be notwithstanding any supposable opposition from us or others, or from whatever quarter. But things are said to be necessary *to us*,

which are or will be notwithstanding all opposition supposable in the case *from us*. The same may be observed of the word "impossible" and other suchlike terms.

2. These terms "necessary," "impossible," "irresistible," etc. do especially belong to the controversy about liberty and moral agency, as used in the latter of the two senses now mentioned, viz. as necessary or impossible *to us,* and with relation to any supposable opposition or endeavor *of ours.*

3. As the word "necessity," in its vulgar and common use, is relative, and has always reference to some supposable insufficient opposition; so when we speak of anything as necessary *to us,* it is with relation to some supposable opposition of our wills, or some voluntary exertion or effort of ours to the contrary. For we don't properly make opposition to an event, any otherwise than as we voluntarily oppose it. Things are said to be what must be, or necessarily are, *as to us,* when they are, or will be, though we desire or endeavor the contrary, or try to prevent or remove their existence: but such opposition of ours always either consists in, or implies opposition of our wills.

'Tis manifest that all suchlike words and phrases, as vulgarly used, are used and accepted in this manner. A thing is said to be necessary, when we can't help it, let us do what we will. So anything is said to be impossible to us, when we would do it, or would have it brought to pass, and endeavor it; or at least may be supposed to desire and seek it; but all our desires and endeavors are, or would be vain. And that is said to be irresistible, which overcomes all our opposition, resistance, and endeavor to the contrary. And we are to be said unable to do a thing, when our supposable desires and endeavors to do it are insufficient.

We are accustomed, in the common use of language, to apply and understand these phrases in this sense: we grow up with such a habit; which by the daily use of these terms, in such a sense, from our childhood, becomes fixed and settled; so that the idea of a relation to a supposed will, desire and endeavor of ours, is strongly connected with these terms, and naturally excited in our minds, whenever we hear the words used. Such ideas, and these words, are so united and associated, that they unavoidably go together; one suggests the other, and carries the other with it, and never can be separated as long as we live. And if we use the words, as terms of art, in another sense, yet, unless we are exceeding circumspect and wary, we shall insensibly slide into the vulgar use of them, and so apply the words in a very inconsistent manner: this habitual connection of ideas will deceive and confound us in our reasonings and discourses, wherein we pretend to use these terms in that manner, as terms of art.

4. It follows from what has been observed, that when these terms "necessary," "impossible," "irresistible," "unable," etc. are used in cases wherein no opposition, or insufficient will or endeavor, is supposed, or can be supposed, but the very nature of the supposed case itself excludes and denies any such opposition, will or endeavor; these terms are then not used in their proper signification, but quite beside their use in common speech. The reason is manifest; namely, that in such cases, we can't use the words with reference to a supposable opposition, will or endeavor. And therefore if any man uses these terms in such cases, he either uses them nonsensically, or in some new sense, diverse from their original and proper meaning. As for instance; if a man should affirm after this manner, that it is necessary for a man, and what must be, that a man should choose virtue rather than vice, during the time that he prefers virtue to vice; and that it is a thing impossible and irresistible, that it should be otherwise than that he should have this choice, so long as this choice continues; such a man would use these terms "must," "irresistible," etc. with perfect insignificance and nonsense, or in some new sense, diverse from their common use; which is with reference, as has been observed, to supposable opposition, unwillingness and resistance; whereas, here, the very supposition excludes and denies any such thing: for the case supposed is that of being willing, and choosing.

5. It appears from what has been said, that these terms "necessary," "impossible," etc. are often used by philosophers and metaphysicians in a sense quite diverse from their common use and original signification: for they apply them to many cases in which no opposition is supposed or supposable. Thus they use them with respect to God's existence before the creation of the world, when there was no other being but he: so with regard to many of the dispositions and acts of the divine Being, such as his loving himself, his loving righteousness, hating sin, etc. So they apply these terms to many cases of the inclinations and actions of created intelligent beings, angels and men; wherein all opposition of the will is shut out and denied, in the very supposition of the case.

Metaphysical or philosophical necessity is nothing different from certainty.[1] I speak not now of the certainty of knowledge, but the cer-

1. [The 1754 ed. reads *"their* certainty." Here I follow JE, Jr., in correcting the text. See the list of errata added to the printed list in his copy of his father's book, Rare Book Room, Sterling Memorial Library, Yale University.]

tainty that is in things themselves, which is the foundation of the
certainty of the knowledge of them; or that wherein lies the ground
of the infallibility of the proposition which affirms them.

What is sometimes given as the definition of philosophical necessity, namely, that by which a thing cannot but be, or whereby it cannot be otherwise, fails of being a proper explanation of it, on two
accounts: first, the words "can" or "cannot" need explanation as
much as the word "necessity"; and the former may as well be explained by the latter, as the latter by the former. Thus, if anyone
asked us what we mean, when we say, a thing cannot but be, we
might explain ourselves by saying, we mean, it must necessarily be
so; as well as explain necessity, by saying, it is that by which a thing
cannot but be. And secondly, this definition is liable to the forementioned great inconvenience: the words "cannot" or "unable" are
properly relative, and have relation to power exerted, or that may be
exerted, in order to the thing spoken of; to which, as I have now observed, the word "necessity," as used by philosophers, has no reference.

Philosophical necessity is really nothing else than the full and fixed
connection between the things signified by the subject and predicate
of a proposition, which affirms something to be true. When there is
such a connection, then the thing affirmed in the proposition is necessary, in a philosophical sense; whether any opposition, or contrary
effort be supposed, or supposable in the case, or no. When the subject and predicate of the proposition, which affirms the existence of
anything, either substance, quality, act or circumstance, have a full
and certain connection, then the existence or being of that thing is
said to be necessary in a metaphysical sense. And in this sense I use
the word "necessity," in the following discourse, when I endeavor to
prove that necessity is not inconsistent with liberty.

The subject and predicate of a proposition, which affirms existence
of something, may have a full, fixed, and certain connection several
ways.

(1) They may have a full and perfect connection *in and of themselves;* because it may imply a contradiction, or gross absurdity, to
suppose them not connected. Thus many things are necessary in their
own nature. So the eternal existence of being generally considered,
is necessary in itself: because it would be in itself the greatest absurdity, to deny the existence of being in general, or to say there was
absolute and universal nothing; and is as it were the sum of all con-

tradictions; as might be shewn, if this were a proper place for it. So God's infinity, and other attributes are necessary. So it is necessary in its own nature, that two and two should be four; and it is necessary, that all right lines drawn from the center of a circle to the circumference should be equal. It is necessary, fit and suitable, that men should do to others, as they would that they should do to them. So innumerable metaphysical and mathematical truths are necessary in themselves; the subject and predicate of the proposition which affirms them, are perfectly connected of themselves.

(2) The connection of the subject and predicate of a proposition, which affirms the existence of something, may be fixed and made cer tain, because the existence of that thing is already come to pass; and either now is, or has been; and so has as it were made sure of existence. And therefore, the proposition which affirms present and past existence of it, may by this means be made certain, and necessarily and unalterably true; the past event has fixed and decided the matter, as to its existence; and has made it impossible but that existence should be truly predicated of it. Thus the existence of whatever is already come to pass, is now become necessary; 'tis become impossible it should be otherwise than true, that such a thing has been.

(3) The subject and predicate of a proposition which affirms something to be, may have a real and certain connection *consequentially;* and so the existence of the thing may be consequentially necessary; as it may be surely and firmly connected with something else, that is necessary in one of the former respects: as [2] it is either fully and thoroughly connected with that which is absolutely necessary in its own nature, or with something which has already received and made sure of existence. This necessity lies in, or may be explained by the connection of two or more propositions one with another. Things which are perfectly connected with other things that are necessary, are necessary themselves, by a necessity of consequence.

And here it may be observed, that all things which are future, or which will hereafter begin to be, which can be said to be necessary, are necessary only in this last way. Their existence is not necessary in itself; for if so, they always would have existed. Nor is their existence become necessary by being made sure, by being already come to pass. Therefore, the only way that anything that is to come to pass hereafter, is or can be necessary, is by a connection with something that is necessary in its own nature, or something that already is, or has

2. [The 1754 ed. begins a new incomplete sentence.]

been; so that the one being supposed, the other certainly follows. And this also is the only way that all things past, excepting those which were from eternity, could be necessary before they came to pass, or could come to pass necessarily; and therefore the only way in which any effect or event, or anything whatsoever that ever has had, or will have a beginning, has come into being necessarily, or will hereafter necessarily exist. And therefore this is the necessity which especially belongs to controversies about the acts of the will.

It may be of some use in these controversies, further to observe concerning metaphysical necessity, that (agreeable to the distinction before observed of necessity, as vulgarly understood) things that exist may be said to be necessary, either with a *general* or *particular* necessity. The existence of a thing may be said to be necessary with a general necessity, when all things whatsoever being considered, there is a foundation for certainty of its existence; [3] or when in the most general and universal view of things, the subject and predicate of the proposition, which affirms its existence, would appear with an infallible connection.

An event, or the existence of a thing, may be said to be necessary with a particular necessity, or with regard to a particular person, thing or time, when nothing that can be taken into consideration, in or about that person, thing or time, alters the case at all, as to the certainty of that event, or the existence of that thing; or can be of any account at all, in determining the infallibility of the connection of the subject and predicate in the proposition which affirms the existence of the thing; so that it is all one, as to that person, or thing, at least, at that time, as if the existence were necessary with a necessity that is most universal and absolute. Thus there are many things that happen to particular persons, which they have no hand in, and in the existence of which no will of theirs has any concern, at least, at that time; which, whether they are necessary or not, with regard to things in general, yet are necessary to them, and with regard to any volition of theirs at that time; as they prevent all acts of the will about the affair. I shall have occasion to apply this observation to particular instances in the following discourse. Whether the same things that are necessary with a particular necessity, be not also necessary with a general necessity, may be a matter of future consideration.

3. [The 1754 ed. reads *"their* existence." Here again I follow JE, Jr.'s correction.]

Let that be as it will, it alters not the case, as to the use of this distinction of the kinds of necessity.

These things may be sufficient for the explaining of the terms "necessary" and "necessity," as terms of art, and as often used by metaphysicians, and controversial writers in divinity, in a sense diverse from, and more extensive than their original meaning, in common language, which was before explained.

What has been said to shew the meaning of the terms "necessary" and "necessity," may be sufficient for the explaining of the opposite terms, "impossible" and "impossibility." For there is no difference, but only the latter are negative, and the former positive. Impossibility is the same as negative necessity, or a necessity that a thing should not be. And it is used as a term of art in a like diversity from the original and vulgar meaning, with necessity.

The same may be observed concerning the words "unable" and "inability." It has been observed, that these terms, in their original and common use, have relation to will and endeavor, as supposable in the case, and as insufficient for the bringing to pass the thing willed and endeavored. But as these terms are often used by philosophers and divines, especially writers on controversies about free will, they are used in a quite different, and far more extensive sense; and are applied to many cases wherein no will or endeavor for the bringing of the thing to pass, is or can be supposed, but is actually denied and excluded in the nature of the case.

As the words "necessary," "impossible," "unable," etc. are used by polemic writers, in a sense diverse from their common signification, the like has happened to the term "contingent." Anything is said to be contingent, or to come to pass by chance or accident, in the original meaning of such words, when its connection with its causes or antecedents, according to the established course of things, is not discerned; and so is what we have no means of the foresight of. And especially is anything said to be contingent or accidental with regard to us, when anything comes to pass that we are concerned in, as occasions or subjects, without our foreknowledge, and beside our design and scope.

But the word "contingent" is abundantly used in a very different sense; not for that whose connection with the series of things we can't discern, so as to foresee the event; but for something which has absolutely no previous ground or reason, with which its existence has any fixed and certain connection.

SECTION 4. OF THE DISTINCTION OF NATURAL AND MORAL NECESSITY, AND INABILITY

THAT NECESSITY which has been explained, consisting in an infallible connection of the things signified by the subject and predicate of a proposition, as intelligent beings are the subjects of it, is distinguished into moral and natural necessity.

I shall not now stand to inquire whether this distinction be a proper and perfect distinction; but shall only explain how these two sorts of necessity are understood, as the terms are sometimes used, and as they are used in the following discourse.

The phrase "moral necessity" is used variously: sometimes 'tis used for a necessity of moral obligation. So we say, a man is under necessity, when he is under bonds of duty and conscience, which he can't be discharged from. So the word "necessity" is often used for great obligation in point of interest. Sometimes by "moral necessity" is meant that apparent connection of things, which is the ground of moral evidence; and so is distinguished from absolute necessity, or that sure connection of things, that is a foundation for infallible certainty. In this sense, "moral necessity" signifies much the same as that high degree of probability, which is ordinarily sufficient to satisfy, and be relied upon by mankind, in their conduct and behavior in the world, as they would consult their own safety and interest, and treat others properly as members of society. And sometimes by "moral necessity" is meant that necessity of connection and consequence, which arises from such *moral causes,* as the strength of inclination, or motives, and the connection which there is in many cases between these, and such certain volitions and actions. And it is in this sense, that I use the phrase "moral necessity" in the following discourse.

By "natural necessity," as applied to men, I mean such necessity as men are under through the force of natural causes; as distinguished from what are called moral causes, such as habits and dispositions of the heart, and moral motives and inducements. Thus men placed in certain circumstances, are the subjects of particular sensations by necessity: they feel pain when their bodies are wounded; they see the objects presented before them in a clear light, when their eyes are opened: so they assent to the truth of certain propositions, as soon as the terms are understood; as that two and two make four, that black is not white, that two parallel lines can never cross one another: so by a natural necessity men's bodies move downwards, when there is nothing to support them.

But here several things may be noted concerning these two kinds of necessity.

1. Moral necessity may be as absolute, as natural necessity. That is, the effect may be as perfectly connected with its moral cause, as a naturally necessary effect is with its natural cause. Whether the will in every case is necessarily determined by the strongest motive, or whether the will ever makes any resistance to such a motive, or can ever oppose the strongest present inclination, or not; if that matter should be controverted, yet I suppose none will deny, but that, in some cases, a previous bias and inclination, or the motive presented, may be so powerful, that the act of the will may be certainly and indissolubly connected therewith. When motives or previous bias are very strong, all will allow that there is some difficulty in going against them. And if they were yet stronger, the difficulty would be still greater. And therefore, if more were still added to their strength, to a certain degree, it would make the difficulty so great, that it would be wholly impossible to surmount it; for this plain reason, because whatever power men may be supposed to have to surmount difficulties, yet that power is not infinite; and so goes not beyond certain limits. If a man can surmount ten degrees of difficulty of this kind, with twenty degrees of strength, because the degrees of strength are beyond the degrees of difficulty; yet if the difficulty be increased to thirty, or an hundred, or a thousand degrees, and his strength not also increased, his strength will be wholly insufficient to surmount the difficulty. As therefore it must be allowed, that there may be such a thing as a sure and perfect connection between moral causes and effects; so this only is what I call by the name of "moral necessity."

2. When I use this distinction of moral and natural necessity, I would not be understood to suppose, that if anything comes to pass by the former kind of necessity, the nature of things is not concerned in it, as well as in the latter. I don't mean to determine, that when a

moral habit or motive is so strong, that the act of the will infallibly follows, this is not owing to the nature of things. But these are the names that these two kinds of necessity have usually been called by; and they must be distinguished by some names or other; for there is a distinction or difference between them, that is very important in its consequences: which [1] difference does not lie so much in the nature of the connection, as in the two terms connected. The cause with which the effect is connected, is of a particular kind; viz. that which is of a moral nature; either some previous habitual disposition, or some motive exhibited to the understanding. And the effect is also of a particular kind; being likewise of a moral nature; consisting in some inclination or volition of the soul, or voluntary action.

I suppose, that necessity which is called natural, in distinction from moral necessity, is so called, because "mere nature," as the word is vulgarly used, is concerned, without anything of choice. The word "nature" is often used in opposition to "choice"; not because nature has indeed never any hand in our choice; but this probably comes to pass by means that we first get our notion of nature from that discernible and obvious course of events, which we observe in many things that our choice has no concern in; and especially in the material world; which, in very many parts of it, we easily perceive to be in a settled course; the stated order and manner of succession being very apparent. But where we don't readily discern the rule and connection (though there be a connection, according to an established law, truly taking place), we signify the manner of event by some other name. Even in many things which are seen in the material and inanimate world, which don't discernibly and obviously come to pass according to any settled course, men don't call the manner of the event by the name of nature, but by such names as "accident," "chance," "contingence," etc. So men make a distinction between "nature" and "choice"; as though they were completely and universally distinct. Whereas, I suppose none will deny but that choice, in many cases, arises from nature, as truly as other events. But the dependence and connection between acts of volition or choice, and their causes, according to established laws, is not so sensible and obvious. And we observe that choice is as it were a new principle of motion and action, different from that established law and order of

1. [The 1754 ed. begins a new incomplete sentence. A correction seems to be needed at this point, although I ordinarily retain JE's longer incomplete sentences characteristically beginning with "Which."]

things which is most obvious, that is seen especially in corporeal and sensible things; and also that choice often interposes, interrupts and alters the chain of events in these external objects, and causes 'em to proceed otherwise than they would do, if let alone, and left to go on according to the laws of motion among themselves. Hence it is spoken of, as if it were a principle of motion entirely distinct from nature, and properly set in opposition to it—names [2] being commonly given to things, according to what is most obvious, and is suggested by what appears to the senses without reflection and research.

3. It must be observed, that in what has been explained, as signified by the name of "moral necessity," the word "necessity" is not used according to the original design and meaning of the word: for, as was observed before, such terms "necessary," "impossible," "irresistible," etc. in common speech, and their most proper sense, are always relative; having reference to some supposable voluntary opposition or endeavor, that is insufficient. But no such opposition, or contrary will and endeavor, is supposable in the case of moral necessity; which is a certainty of the inclination and will itself; which does not admit of the supposition of a will to oppose and resist it. For 'tis absurd, to suppose the same individual will to oppose itself, in its present act; or the present choice to be opposite to, and resisting present choice: as absurd as it is to talk of two contrary motions, in the same moving body, at the same time. And therefore the very case supposed never admits of any trial, whether an opposing or resisting will can overcome this necessity.

What has been said of natural and moral necessity, may serve to explain what is intended by natural and moral *inability*. We are said to be *naturally* unable to do a thing, when we can't do it if we will, because what is most commonly called nature don't allow of it, or because of some impeding defect or obstacle that is extrinsic to the will; either in the faculty of understanding, constitution of body, or external objects. *Moral* inability consists not in any of these things; but either in the want of inclination; or the strength of a contrary inclination; or the want of sufficient motives in view, to induce and excite the act of the will, or the strength of apparent motives to the contrary. Or both these may be resolved into one; and it may be said in one word, that moral inability consists in the opposition or want of inclination. For when a person is unable to will or choose such a thing, through a defect of motives, or prevalence of contrary motives,

2. [The 1754 ed. begins a new incomplete sentence.]

'tis the same thing as his being unable through the want of an inclination, or the prevalence of a contrary inclination, in such circumstances, and under the influence of such views.

To give some instances of this moral inability: A woman of great
honor and chastity may have a moral inability to prostitute herself to
her slave. A child of great love and duty to his parents, may be unable
to be willing to kill his father. A very lascivious man, in case of certain opportunities and temptations, and in the absence of such and
such restraints, may be unable to forbear gratifying his lust. A
drunkard, under such and such circumstances, may be unable to
forbear taking of strong drink. A very malicious man may be unable
to exert benevolent acts to an enemy, or to desire his prosperity: yea,
some may be so under the power of a vile disposition, that they may
be unable to love those who are most worthy of their esteem and
affection. A strong habit of virtue and great degree of holiness may
cause a moral inability to love wickedness in general, may render a
man unable to take complacence in wicked persons or things; or to
choose a wicked life, and prefer it to a virtuous life. And on the other
hand, a great degree of habitual wickedness may lay a man under an
inability to love and choose holiness; and render him utterly unable
to love an infinitely holy Being, or to choose and cleave to him as
his chief good.

Here it may be of use to observe this distinction of moral inability,
viz. of that which is general and habitual, and that which is particular
and occasional. By a *general and habitual* moral inability, I mean an
inability in the heart to all exercises or acts of will of that nature or
kind, through a fixed and habitual inclination, or an habitual and
stated defect, or want of a certain kind of inclination. Thus a very
ill-natured man may be unable to exert such acts of benevolence, as
another, who is full of good nature, commonly exerts; and a man,
whose heart is habitually void of gratitude, may be unable to exert
such and such grateful acts, through that stated defect of a grateful
inclination. By *particular and occasional* moral inability, I mean an
inability of the will or heart to a particular act, through the strength
or defect of present motives, or of inducements presented to the view
of the understanding, on this occasion. If it be so, that the will is
always determined by the strongest motive, then it must always have
an inability, in this latter sense, to act otherwise than it does; it not
being possible, in any case, that the will should, at present, go against
the motive which has now, all things considered, the greatest strength

and advantage to excite and induce it. The former of these kinds of moral inability, consisting in that which is stated habitual and general, is most commonly called by the name of "inability"; because the word "inability," in its most proper and original signification, has respect to some stated defect. And this especially obtains the name of "inability" also upon another account: I before observed, that the word "inability" in its original and most common use, is a relative term; and has respect to will and endeavor, as supposable in the case, and as insufficient to bring to pass the thing desired and endeavored. Now there may be more of an appearance and shadow of this, with respect to the acts which arise from a fixed and strong habit, than others that arise only from transient occasions and causes. Indeed will and endeavor against, or diverse from present acts of the will, are in no case supposable, whether those acts be occasional or habitual; for that would be to suppose the will, at present, to be otherwise than, at present, it is. But yet there may be will and endeavor against future acts of the will, or volitions that are likely to take place, as viewed at a distance. 'Tis no contradiction, to suppose that the acts of the will at one time, may be against the acts of the will at another time; and there may be desires and endeavors to prevent or excite future acts of the will; but such desires and endeavors are, in many cases, rendered insufficient and vain, through fixedness of habit: when the occasion returns, the strength of habit overcomes, and baffles all such opposition. In this respect, a man may be in miserable slavery and bondage to a strong habit. But it may be comparatively easy to make an alteration with respect to such future acts, as are only occasional and transient; because the occasion or transient cause, if foreseen, may often easily be prevented or avoided. On this account, the moral inability that attends fixed habits, especially obtains the name of "inability." And then, as the will may remotely and indirectly resist itself, and do it in vain, in the case of strong habits; so reason may resist present acts of the will, and its resistance be insufficient; and this is more commonly the case also, when the acts arise from strong habit.

But it must be observed concerning [3] moral inability, in each kind of it, that the word "inability" is used in a sense very diverse from its original import. The word signifies only a natural inability, in the proper use of it; and is applied to such cases only wherein a present

3. [The 1754 ed. reads "concern*ed*." Corrected from the *printed* list of errata. See Intro., Pt. 6, "Note on the Text," note 2.]

will or inclination to the thing, with respect to which a person is said to be unable, is supposable. It can't be truly said, according to the ordinary use of language, that a malicious man, let him be never so malicious, can't hold his hand from striking, or that he is not able to shew his neighbor kindness; or that a drunkard, let his appetite be never so strong, can't keep the cup from his mouth. In the strictest propriety of speech, a man has a thing in his power, if he has it in his choice, or at his election: and a man can't be truly said to be unable to do a thing, when he can do it if he will. 'Tis improperly said, that a person can't perform those external actions, which are dependent on the act of the will, and which would be easily performed, if the act of the will were present. And if it be improperly said, that he cannot perform those external voluntary actions, which depend on the will, 'tis in some respect more improperly said, that he is unable to exert the acts of the will themselves; because it is more evidently false, with respect to these, that he can't if he will: for to say so, is a downright contradiction: it is to say, he *can't* will, if he *does* will. And in this case, not only is it true, that it is easy for a man to do the thing if he will, but the very willing is the doing; when once he has willed, the thing is performed; and nothing else remains to be done. Therefore, in these things to ascribe a nonperformance to the want of power or ability, is not just; because the thing wanting is not a being *able,* but a being *willing.* There are faculties of mind, and capacity of nature, and everything else, sufficient, but a disposition: nothing is wanting but a will.

SECTION 5. CONCERNING THE NOTION OF LIBERTY, AND OF MORAL AGENCY

THE plain and obvious meaning of the words "freedom" and "liberty," in common speech, is power, opportunity, or advantage, that anyone has, to do as he pleases. Or in other words, his being free from hindrance or impediment in the way of doing, or conducting in any respect, as he wills.[1] And the contrary to liberty, whatever name we call that by, is a person's being hindered or unable to conduct as he will, or being necessitated to do otherwise.

If this which I have mentioned be the meaning of the word "liberty," in the ordinary use of language; as I trust that none that has ever learned to talk, and is unprejudiced, will deny; then it will follow, that in propriety of speech, neither liberty, nor its contrary, can properly be ascribed to any being or thing, but that which has such a faculty, power or property, as is called "will." For that which is possessed of no such thing as will, can't have any power or opportunity of doing according to its will, nor be necessitated to act contrary to its will, nor be restrained from acting agreeably to it. And therefore to talk of liberty, or the contrary, as belonging to the very will itself, is not to speak good sense; if we judge of sense, and nonsense, by the original and proper signification of words. For the will itself is not an agent that has a will: the power of choosing, itself, has not a power of choosing. That which has the power of volition or choice is the man or the soul, and not the power of volition itself. And he that has the liberty of doing according to his will, is the agent or doer who is possessed of the will; and not the will which he is possessed of. We say with propriety, that a bird let loose has power and liberty to fly; but not that the bird's power of flying has a power and liberty of flying. To be free is the property of an agent, who is possessed of powers and faculties, as much as to be cunning, valiant,

1. I say not only "doing," but "conducting"; because a voluntary forbearing to do, sitting still, keeping silence, etc. are instances of persons' conduct, about which liberty is exercised; though they are not properly called "doing."

163

bountiful, or zealous. But these qualities are the properties of men or persons; and not the properties of properties.

There are two things that are contrary to this which is called liberty in common speech. One is *constraint;* the same is otherwise called force, compulsion, and coaction; which is a person's being necessitated to do a thing *contrary* to his will. The other is *restraint;* which is his being hindered, and not having power to do *according* to his will. But that which has no will, can't be the subject of these things.—I need say the less on this head, Mr. Locke having set the same thing forth, with so great clearness, in his *Essay on the Human Understanding.*[2]

But one thing more I would observe concerning what is vulgarly called liberty; namely, that power and opportunity for one to do and conduct as he will, or according to his choice, is all that is meant by it; without taking into the meaning of the word, anything of the cause or original of that choice; or at all considering how the person came to have such a volition; whether it was caused by some external motive, or internal habitual bias; whether it was determined by some internal antecedent volition, or whether it happened without a cause; whether it was necessarily connected with something foregoing, or not connected. Let the person come by his volition or choice how he will, yet, if he is able, and there is nothing in the way to hinder his pursuing and executing his will, the man is fully and perfectly free, according to the primary and common notion of freedom.

What has been said may be sufficient to shew what is meant by liberty, according to the common notions of mankind, and in the usual and primary acceptation of the word: but the word, as used by Arminians, Pelagians and others, who oppose the Calvinists, has an entirely different signification. These several things belong to their notion of liberty: 1. That it consists in a self-determining power in the will, or a certain sovereignty the will has over itself, and its own acts, whereby it determines its own volitions; so as not to be dependent in its determinations, on any cause without itself, nor determined by anything prior to its own acts. 2. Indifference belongs to liberty in their notion of it, or that the mind, previous to the act of volition be, *in equilibrio.* 3. Contingence is another thing that belongs and is essential to it; not in the common acceptation of the

2. [Locke, *Essay,* Bk. II, ch. 21, nos. 14–21; *1,* 319–24. See above, Intro., Pt. 4, no. 1.]

word, as that has been already explained, but as opposed to all necessity, or any fixed and certain connection with some previous ground
or reason of its existence. They suppose the essence of liberty so
much to consist in these things, that unless the will of man be free
in this sense, he has no real freedom, how much soever he may be at
liberty to act according to his will.

A moral agent is a being that is capable of those actions that have
a moral quality, and which can properly be denominated good or
evil in a moral sense, virtuous or vicious, commendable or faulty. To
moral agency belongs a moral faculty, or sense of moral good and
evil, or of such a thing as desert or worthiness of praise or blame, reward or punishment; and a capacity which an agent has of being
influenced in his actions by moral inducements or motives, exhibited
to the view of understanding and reason, to engage to a conduct
agreeable to the moral faculty.

The sun is very excellent and beneficial in its action and influence
on the earth, in warming it, and causing it to bring forth its fruits;
but it is not a moral agent: its action, though good, is not virtuous
or meritorious. Fire that breaks out in a city, and consumes great
part of it, is very mischievous in its operation; but is not a moral
agent: what it does is not faulty or sinful, or deserving of any punishment. The brute creatures are not moral agents: the actions of some
of 'em are very profitable and pleasant; others are very hurtful: yet,
seeing they have no moral faculty, or sense of desert, and don't act
from choice guided by understanding, or with a capacity of reasoning
and reflecting, but only from instinct, and are not capable of being
influenced by moral inducements, their actions are not properly sinful or virtuous; nor are they properly the subjects of any such moral
treatment for what they do, as moral agents are for their faults or
good deeds.

Here it may be noted, that there is a circumstantial difference between the moral agency of a ruler and a subject. I call it circumstantial, because it lies only in the difference of moral inducements they
are capable of being influenced by, arising from the difference of
circumstances. A ruler acting in that capacity only, is not capable of
being influenced by a moral law, and its sanctions of threatenings
and promises, rewards and punishments, as the subject is; though
both may be influenced by a knowledge of moral good and evil. And
therefore the moral agency of the supreme Being, who acts only in
the capacity of a ruler towards his creatures, and never as a subject,

differs in that respect from the moral agency of created intelligent beings. God's actions, and particularly those which he exerts as a moral governor, have moral qualifications, are morally good in the highest degree. They are most perfectly holy and righteous; and we must conceive of him as influenced in the highest degree, by that which, above all others, is properly a moral inducement; viz. the moral good which he sees in such and such things: and therefore he is, in the most proper sense, a moral agent, the source of all moral ability and agency, the fountain and rule of all virtue and moral good; though by reason of his being supreme over all, 'tis not possible he should be under the influence of law or command, promises or threatenings, rewards or punishments, counsels or warnings. The essential qualities of a moral agent are in God, in the greatest possible perfection; such as understanding, to perceive the difference between moral good and evil; a capacity of discerning that moral worthiness and demerit, by which some things are praiseworthy, others deserving of blame and punishment; and also a capacity of choice, and choice guided by understanding, and a power of acting according to his choice or pleasure, and being capable of doing those things which are in the highest sense praiseworthy. And herein does very much consist that image of God wherein he made man (which we read of Gen. 1:26, 27 and ch. 9:6), by which God distinguished man from the beasts, viz. in those faculties and principles of nature, whereby he is capable of moral agency. Herein very much consists the *natural* image of God; as his *spiritual* and *moral* image, wherein man was made at first, consisted in that moral excellency, that he was endowed with.[3]

3. [These two things, the natural and the spiritual or moral image of God in man, are not to be identified but distinguished in JE's thought. By the natural *imago Dei* man is capable of moral agency. By the spiritual *imago Dei* he was originally endowed with moral excellence in the exercise of that agency. Thus JE writes, "As there are two kinds of attributes in God . . . his moral attitudes, which are summed up in his holiness, and his natural attributes of strength, knowledge, etc. that constitute the greatness of God; so there is a twofold image of God in man, his moral or spiritual image, which is his holiness, that is the image of God's moral excellency (which image was lost by the fall) and God's natural image, consisting in man's reason and understanding, his natural ability, and dominion over the creatures, which is the image of God's natural attribute": *Treatise Concerning Religious Affections*, Pt. III, sec. 3; in *The Works of President Edwards* (8 vols. Worcester, 1808, cited below as Worcester ed.), *4*, 189–90. "When God made man at first, he implanted in him two kinds of principles. There was an *inferior* kind, which may be called *natural,* being the principles of mere human nature. . . . Besides these, there were *superior* principles, that were

spiritual, holy, and divine, summarily comprehended in divine love; wherein consisted the spiritual image of God": *The Great Christian Doctrine of Original Sin Defended*, Pt. IV, ch. 2; in *Works, 6,* 428. Again in *A Dissertation on the Nature of True Virtue*, ch. 5, in *Works, 2,* 439, he writes that "an inclination to agree with ourselves" in moral matters and to live by some consistent scheme of action "is a natural principle," while "an agreement or union of heart with the great system, and to God the head of it, who is all in all in it, is a divine principle."]

PART TWO

Wherein It Is Considered Whether There Is or Can Be Any Such Sort of Freedom of Will, as That Wherein Arminians Place the Essence of the Liberty of All Moral Agents; and Whether Any Such Thing Ever Was or Can Be Conceived of

SECTION 1. SHEWING THE MANIFEST INCONSISTENCE OF THE ARMINIAN NOTION OF LIBERTY OF WILL, CONSISTING IN THE WILL'S SELF-DETERMINING POWER

HAVING taken notice of those things which may be necessary to be observed, concerning the meaning of the principal terms and phrases made use of in controversies concerning human liberty, and particularly observed what liberty is, according to the common language, and general apprehension of mankind, and what it is as understood and maintained by Arminians; I proceed to consider the Arminian notion of the freedom of the will, and the supposed necessity of it in order to moral agency, or in order to anyone's being capable of virtue or vice, and properly the subject of command or counsel, praise or blame, promises or threatenings, rewards or punishments; or whether that which has been described, as the thing meant by liberty in common speech, be not sufficient, and the only liberty, which makes, or can make anyone a moral agent, and so properly the subject of these things. In this part, I shall consider whether any such thing be possible or conceivable, as that freedom of will which Arminians insist on; and shall inquire whether any such sort of liberty be necessary to moral agency, etc. in the next part.

And first of all, I shall consider the notion of a self-determining power in the will: wherein, according to the Arminians, does most essentially consist the will's freedom; and shall particularly inquire, whether it be not plainly absurd, and a manifest inconsistence, to suppose that the will itself determines all the free acts of the will.

Here I shall not insist on the great impropriety of such phrases, and ways of speaking, as "the will's determining itself"; because actions are to be ascribed to agents, and not properly to the powers of agents; which improper way of speaking leads to many mistakes, and much confusion, as Mr. Locke observes.[1] But I shall suppose that the Arminians, when they speak of the will's determining itself, do

1. [See Intro., Pt. 4, no. 1.]

by the will mean "the soul willing." I shall take it for granted, that
when they speak of the will, as the determiner, they mean the soul
in the exercise of a power of willing, or acting voluntarily. I shall
suppose this to be their meaning, because nothing else can be meant,
without the grossest and plainest absurdity. In all cases, when we
speak of the powers or principles of acting, as doing such things, we
mean that the agents which have these powers of acting, do them, in
the exercise of those powers. So when we say, valor fights courageously, we mean, the man who is under the influence of valor fights
courageously. When we say, love seeks the object loved, we mean,
the person loving seeks that object. When we say, the understanding
discerns, we mean the soul in the exercise of that faculty. So when
it is said, the will decides or determines, the meaning must be, that
the person in the exercise of a power of willing and choosing, or the
soul acting voluntarily, determines.

Therefore, if the will determines all its own free acts, the soul
determines all the free acts of the will in the exercise of a power of
willing and choosing; or, which is the same thing, it determines them
of choice; it determines its own acts by choosing its own acts. If the
will determines the will, then choice orders and determines the
choice: and acts of choice are subject to the decision, and follow the
conduct of other acts of choice. And therefore if the will determines
all its own free acts, then every free act of choice is determined by a
preceding act of choice, choosing that act. And if that preceding act
of the will or choice be also a free act, then by these principles, in
this act too, the will is self-determined; that is, this, in like manner,
is an act that the soul voluntarily chooses; or which is the same thing,
it is an act determined still by a preceding act of the will, choosing
that. And the like may again be observed of the last mentioned act.
Which brings us directly to a contradiction: for it supposes an act
of the will preceding the first act in the whole train, directing and
determining the rest; or a free act of the will, before the first free act
of the will. Or else we must come at last to an act of the will, determining the consequent acts, wherein the will is not self-determined,
and so is not a free act, in this notion of freedom: but if the first act
in the train, determining and fixing the rest, be not free, none of
them all can be free; as is manifest at first view, but shall be
demonstrated presently.

If the will, which we find governs the members of the body, and
determines and commands their motions and actions, does also

govern itself, and determine its own motions and acts, it doubtless
determines them the same way, even by antecedent volitions. The
will determines which way the hands and feet shall move, by an
act of volition or choice: and there is no other way of the will's determining, directing or commanding anything at all. Whatsoever
the will commands, it commands by an act of the will. And if it has
itself under its command, and determines itself in its own actions, it
doubtless does it the same way that it determines other things which
are under its command. So that if the freedom of the will consists in
this, that it has itself and its own actions under its command and
direction, and its own volitions are determined by itself, it will
follow, that every free volition arises from another antecedent volition, directing and commanding that: and if that *directing* volition
be also free, in that also the will is [self-]determined; [2] that is to say,
that directing volition is determined by another going before that;
and so on, till we come to the first volition in the whole series: and
if that first volition be free, and the will self-determined in it, then
that is determined by another volition preceding that. Which is a
contradiction; because by the supposition, it can have none before it,
to direct or determine it, being the first in the train. But if that first
volition is not determined by any preceding act of the will, then that
act is not determined by the will, and so is not free, in the Arminian
notion of freedom, which consists in the will's self-determination.
And if that first act of the will, which determines and fixes the subsequent acts, be not free, none of the following acts, which are determined by it, can be free. If we suppose there are five acts in the
train, the fifth and last determined by the fourth, and the fourth by
the third, the third by the second, and the second by the first; if the
first is not determined by the will, and so not free, then none of
them are truly determined by the will: that is, that each of them are
as they are, and not otherwise, is not first owing to the will, but to
the determination of the first in the series, which is not dependent
on the will, and is that which the will has no hand in the determination of. And this being that which decides what the rest shall be, and
determines their existence; therefore the first determination of their
existence is not from the will. The case is just the same, if instead of
a chain of five acts of the will, we should suppose a succession of ten,
or an hundred, or ten thousand. If the first act be not free, being determined by something out of the will, and this determines the next

2. [Corrected from *printed* list of errata.]

to be agreeable to itself, and that the next, and so on; they are none of them free, but all originally depend on, and are determined by some cause out of the will: and so all freedom in the case is excluded, and no act of the will can be free, according to this notion of freedom. If we should suppose a long chain, of ten thousand links, so connected, that if the first link moves, it will move the next, and that the next; and so the whole chain must be determined to motion, and in the direction of its motion, by the motion of the first link; and that is moved by something else: in this case, though all the links, but one, are moved by other parts of the same chain; yet it appears that the motion of no one, nor the direction of its motion, is from any self-moving or self-determining power in the chain, any more than if every link were immediately moved by something that did not belong to the chain. If the will be not free in the first act, which causes the next, then neither is it free in the next, which is caused by that first act: for though indeed the will caused it, yet it did not cause it freely; because the preceding act, by which it was caused, was not free. And again, if the will ben't free in the second act, so neither can it be in the third, which is caused by that; because, in like manner, that third was determined by an act of the will that was not free. And so we may go on to the next act, and from that to the next; and how long soever the succession of acts is, it is all one; if the first on which the whole chain depends, and which determines all the rest, ben't a free act, the will is not free in causing or determining any one of those acts; because the act by which it determines them all, is not a free act; and therefore the will is no more free in determining them, than if it did not cause them at all. Thus, this Arminian notion of liberty of the will, consisting in the will's self-determination, is repugnant to itself, and shuts itself wholly out of the world.

SECTION 2. SEVERAL SUPPOSED WAYS OF EVADING THE FOREGOING REASONING, CONSIDERED

I F TO EVADE the force of what has been observed, it should be said, that when the Arminians speak of the will's determining its own acts, they don't mean that the will determines its acts by any preceding act, or that one act of the will determines another; but only that the faculty or power of will, or the soul in the use of that power, determines its own volitions; and that it does it without any act going before the act determined; such an evasion would be full of the most gross absurdity. I confess, it is an evasion of my own inventing; and I don't know but I should wrong the Arminians, in supposing that any of them would make use of it. But it being as good a one as I can invent, I would observe upon it a few things.

First, if the faculty or power of the will determines an act of volition, or the soul in the use or exercise of that power, determines it, that is the same thing as for the soul to determine volition by an *act* of will. For an exercise of the power of will, and an act of that power, are the same thing. Therefore to say, that the power of will, or the soul in the use or exercise of that power, determines volition, without an act of will preceding the volition determined, is a contradiction.

Secondly, if a power of will determines the act of the will, then a power of choosing determines it. For, as was before observed, in every act of will, there is choice, and a power of willing is a power of choosing. But if a power of choosing determines the act of volition, it determines it by choosing it. For 'tis most absurd to say, that a power of choosing determines one thing rather than another, without choosing anything. But if a power of choosing determines volition by choosing it, then here is the act of volition determined by an antecedent choice, choosing that volition.

Thirdly, to say, the faculty, or the soul, determines its own volition, but not by any act, is a contradiction. Because for the soul to direct, decide, or determine anything, is to act; and this is supposed; for the soul is here spoken of as being a cause in this affair, bringing something to pass, or doing something; or, which is the same thing, exerting itself in order to an effect, which effect is the determination of volition, or the particular kind and manner of an act of will. But certainly, this exertion or action is not the same with the effect, in order to the production of which it is exerted; but must be something prior to it.

Again, the advocates for this notion of the freedom of the will, speak of a certain sovereignty in the will, whereby it has power to determine its own volitions. And therefore the determination of volition must itself be an act of the will; for otherwise it can be no exercise of that supposed power and sovereignty.

Again, if the will determines itself, then either the will is active in determining its volitions, or it is not. If it be active in it, then the determination is an *act* of the will; and so there is one act of the will determining another. But if the will is not active in the determination, then how does it exercise any liberty in it? These gentlemen suppose that the thing wherein the will exercises liberty, is in its determining its own acts. But how can this be, if it ben't active in determining? Certainly the will, or the soul, can't exercise any liberty in that wherein it don't act, or wherein it don't exercise itself. So that if either part of this dilemma be taken, this scheme of liberty, consisting in self-determining power, is overthrown. If there be an act of the will in determining all its own free acts, then one free act of the will is determined by another; and so we have the absurdity of every free act, even the very first, determined by a foregoing free act. But if there be no act or exercise of the will in determining its own acts, then no liberty is exercised in determining them. From whence it follows, that no liberty consists in the will's power to determine its own acts: or, which is the same thing, that there is no such thing as liberty consisting in a self-determining power of the will.

If it should be said, that although it be true, if the soul determines its own volitions, it must be active in so doing, and the determination itself must be an act; yet there is no need of supposing this act to be prior to the volition determined; but the will or soul determines the act of the will *in willing;* it determines its own volition, *in* the very act of volition; it directs and limits the act of the will, causing it to be so and not otherwise, *in* exerting the act, without any preceding act to excite [1] that. If any should say after this manner, they must

1. [The 1754 ed. reads "exert." Corrected from the *printed* list of errata.]

mean one of these three things: either (1) that the determining act, though it be before the act determined in the order of nature, yet is not before it in the order of time. Or (2) that the determining act is not before the act determined, either in the order of time or nature, nor is truly distinct from it; but that the soul's determining the act of volition is the same thing with its exerting the act of volition: the mind's exerting such a particular act, is its causing and determining the act. Or (3) that volition has no cause, and is no effect; but comes into existence, with such a particular determination, without any ground or reason of its existence and determination. I shall consider these distinctly.

(1) If all that is meant, be, that the determining act is not before the act determined in order of time, it will not help the case at all, though it should be allowed. If it be before the determined act in the order of nature, being the cause or ground of its existence, this as much proves it to be distinct from it, and independent on it, as if it were before in the order of time. As the cause of the particular motion of a natural body in a certain direction, may have no distance as to time, yet can't be the same with the motion effected by it, but must be as distinct from it, as any other cause, that is before its effect in the order of time: as the architect is distinct from the house which he builds, or the father distinct from the son which he begets. And if the act of the will determining be distinct from the act determined, and before it in the order of nature, then we can go back from one to another, till we come to the first in the series, which has no act of the will before it in the order of nature, determining it; and consequently is an act not determined by the will, and so not a free act, in this notion of freedom. And this being the act which determines all the rest, none of them are free acts. As when there is a chain of many links, the first of which only is taken hold of and drawn by hand; all the rest may follow and be moved at the same instant, without any distance of time; but yet the motion of one link is before that of another in the order of nature; the last is moved by the next, and that by the next, and so till we come to the first; which not being moved by any other, but by something distinct from the whole chain, this as much proves that no part is moved by any self-moving power in the chain, as if the motion of one link followed that of another in the order of time.

(2) If any should say, that the determining act is not before the determined act, either in the order of time, or of nature, nor is dis-

tinct from it; but that the *exertion* of the act is the *determination* of the act; that for the soul to exert a particular volition, is for it to cause and determine that act of volition: I would on this observe, that the thing in question seems to be forgotten, or kept out of sight, in a darkness and unintelligibleness of speech; unless such an objector would mean to contradict himself. The very act of volition itself is doubtless a determination of mind; i.e. it is the mind's drawing up a conclusion, or coming to a choice between two things, or more, proposed to it. But determining among external *objects* of choice, is not the same with determining the *act* of choice itself, among various possible acts of choice.[2] The question is, what influences, directs, or determines the mind or will to come to such a conclusion or choice as it does? or what is the cause, ground or reason, why it concludes thus, and not otherwise? Now it must be answered, according to the Arminian notion of freedom, that the will influences, orders and determines itself thus to act. And if it does, I say, it must be by some antecedent act. To say, it is caused, influenced and determined by something, and yet not determined by anything antecedent, either in order of time or nature, is a contradiction. For that is what is meant by a thing's being prior in the order of nature, that it is some way the cause or reason of the thing, with respect to which it is said to be prior.

If the particular act or exertion of will, which comes into existence, be anything properly determined at all, then it has some cause of its existing, and of its existing in such a particular determinate manner, and not another; some cause, whose influence decides the matter: which cause is distinct from the effect, and prior to it. But to say, that the will or mind orders, influences and determines itself to exert such an act as it does, by the very exertion itself, is to make the exertion both cause and effect; or the exerting such an act, to be a cause of the exertion of such an act. For the question is, what is the cause and reason of the soul's exerting such an act? To which the answer is, the soul exerts such an act, and that is the cause of it. And so, by this, the exertion must be prior in the order of nature to itself, and distinct from itself.

(3) If the meaning be, that the soul's exertion of such a particular act of will, is a thing that comes to pass *of itself*, without any cause; and that there is absolutely no ground or reason of the soul's being determined to exert such a volition, and make such a choice, rather

2. [See Intro., Pt. 4, no. 4.]

than another; I say, if this be the meaning of Arminians, when they contend so earnestly for the will's determining its own acts, and for liberty of will consisting in self-determining power; they do nothing but confound themselves and others with words without a meaning. In the question, what determines the will? and in their answer, that the will determines itself, and in all the dispute about it, it seems to be taken for granted, that something determines the will; and the controversy on this head is not, whether anything at all determines it, or whether its determination has any cause or foundation at all: but where the foundation of it is, whether in the will itself, or some-where else. But if the thing intended be what is above mentioned, then all comes to this, that nothing at all determines the will; volition having absolutely no cause or foundation of its existence, either within, or without. There is a great noise made about self-determin-ing power, as the source of all free acts of the will: but when the matter comes to be explained, the meaning is, that no power at all is the source of these acts, neither self-determining power, nor any other, but they arise from nothing; no cause, no power, no influence, being at all concerned in the matter.

However, this very thing, even that the free acts of the will are events which come to pass without a cause, is certainly implied in the Arminian notion of liberty of will; though it be very inconsistent with many other things in their scheme, and repugnant to some things implied in their notion of liberty. Their opinion implies, that the particular determination of volition is without any cause; because they hold the free acts of the will to be *contingent* events; and con-tingence is essential to freedom in their notion of it. But certainly, those things which have a prior ground and reason of their particular existence, a cause which antecedently determines them to be, and determines them to be just as they are, don't happen contingently. If something foregoing, by a causal influence and connection, deter-mines and fixes precisely their coming to pass, and the manner of it, then it don't remain a contingent thing whether they shall come to pass or no.

And because it is a question, in many respects, very important in this controversy about the freedom of will, whether the free acts of the will are events which come to pass without a cause? I shall be particular in examining this point in the two following sections.

SECTION 3. WHETHER ANY EVENT WHATSOEVER, AND VOLITION IN PARTICULAR, CAN COME TO PASS WITHOUT A CAUSE OF ITS EXISTENCE

BEFORE I enter on any argument on this subject, I would explain how I would be understood, when I use the word "cause" in this discourse: since, for want of a better word, I shall have occasion to use it in a sense which is more extensive, than that in which it is sometimes used. The word is often used in so restrained a sense as to signify only that which has a positive efficiency or influence to produce a thing, or bring it to pass. But there are many things which have no such positive productive influence; which yet are causes in that respect, that they have truly the nature of a ground or reason why some things are, rather than others; or why they are as they are, rather than otherwise. Thus the absence of the sun in the night, is not the cause of the falling of the dew at that time, in the same manner as its beams are the cause of the ascending of the vapors in the daytime; and its withdrawment in the winter, is not in the same manner the cause of the freezing of the waters, as its approach in the spring is the cause of their thawing. But yet the withdrawment or absence of the sun is an antecedent, with which these effects in the night and winter are connected, and on which they depend; and is one thing that belongs to the ground and reason why they come to pass at that time, rather than at other times; though the absence of the sun is nothing positive, nor has any positive influence.

It may be further observed, that when I speak of connection of causes and effects, I have respect to moral causes, as well as those that are called natural in distinction from 'em. Moral causes may be causes in as proper a sense, as any causes whatsoever; may have as real an influence, and may as truly be the ground and reason of an event's coming to pass.

Therefore I sometimes use the word "cause," in this inquiry, to signify any antecedent, either natural or moral, positive or negative, on which an event, either a thing, or the manner and circumstance of a thing, so depends, that it is the ground and reason, either in whole, or in part, why it is, rather than not; or why it is as it is, rather than otherwise; or, in other words, any antecedent with which a consequent event is so connected, that it truly belongs to the reason why the proposition which affirms that event, is true; whether it has any positive influence, or not. And in an agreeableness to this, I sometimes use the word "effect" for the consequence of another thing, which is perhaps rather an occasion than a cause, most properly speaking.

I am the more careful thus to explain my meaning, that I may cut off occasion, from any that might seek occasion to cavil and object against some things which I may say concerning the dependence of all things which come to pass, on some cause, and their connection with their cause.

Having thus explained what I mean by cause, I assert, that nothing ever comes to pass without a cause. What is self-existent must be from eternity, and must be unchangeable: but as to all things that *begin to be,* they are not self-existent, and therefore must have some foundation of their existence without themselves. That whatsoever begins to be, which before was not, must have a cause why it then begins to exist, seems to be the first dictate of the common and natural sense which God hath implanted in the minds of all mankind, and the main foundation of all our reasonings about the existence of things, past, present, or to come.

And this dictate of common sense equally respects substances and modes, or things and the manner and circumstances of things. Thus, if we see a body which has hitherto been at rest, start out of a state of rest, and begin to move, we do as naturally and necessarily suppose there is some cause or reason of this new mode of existence, as of the existence of a body itself which had hitherto not existed. And so if a body, which had hitherto moved in a certain direction, should suddenly change the direction of its motion; or if it should put off its old figure, and take a new one; or change its color: the beginning of these new modes is a new event, and the mind of mankind necessarily supposes that there is some cause or reason of them.

If this grand principle of common sense be taken away, all arguing from effects to causes ceaseth, and so all knowledge of any existence, besides what we have by the most direct and immediate intuition. Particularly all our proof of the being of God ceases: we argue his being from our own being, and the being of other things, which we are sensible once were not, but have begun to be; and from the being of the world, with all its constituent parts, and the manner of their existence; all which we see plainly are not necessary in their own nature, and so not self-existent, and therefore must have a cause. But if things, not in themselves necessary, may begin to be without a cause, all this arguing is vain.

Indeed, I will not affirm, that there is in the nature of things no foundation for the knowledge of the being of God without any evidence of it from his works. I do suppose there is a great absurdity, in the nature of things simply considered, in supposing that there should be no God, or in denying being in general, and supposing an eternal, absolute, universal nothing: and therefore that here would be foundation of intuitive evidence that it cannot be, and that eternal infinite most perfect Being must be; if we had strength and comprehension of mind sufficient, to have a clear idea of general and universal being, or, which is the same thing, of the infinite, eternal, most perfect divine Nature and Essence. But then we should not properly come to the knowledge of the being of God by arguing; but our evidence would be intuitive: we should see it, as we see other things that are necessary in themselves, the contraries of which are in their own nature absurd and contradictory; as we see that twice two is four; and as we see that a circle has no angles. If we had as clear an idea of universal infinite entity, as we have of these other things, I suppose we should most intuitively see the absurdity of supposing such being not to be; should immediately see there is no room for the question, whether it is possible that being, in the most general abstracted notion of it, should not be. But we have not that strength and extent of mind, to know this certainly in this intuitive independent manner: but the way that mankind come to the knowledge of the being of God, is that which the Apostle speaks of (Rom. 1:20), "The invisible things of Him, from the creation of the world, are clearly seen; being understood by the things that are made; even his eternal power and Godhead." We first ascend, and prove a posteriori, or from effects, that there must be an eternal cause; and then secondly, prove by argumentation, not intuition, that this being must be necessarily existent; and then thirdly, from the proved necessity of his existence, we may descend, and prove many of his perfections a priori.

But if once this grand principle of common sense be given up, that what is not necessary in itself, must have a cause; and we begin to maintain, that things may come into existence, and begin to be, which heretofore have not been, of themselves, without any cause; all our means of ascending in our arguing from the creature to the Creator, and all our evidence of the being of God, is cut off at one blow. In this case, we can't prove that there is a God, either from the being of the world, and the creatures in it, or from the manner of their being, their order, beauty and use. For if things may come into existence without any cause at all, then they doubtless may without any cause answerable to the effect. Our minds do alike naturally suppose and determine both these things; namely, that what begins to be has a cause, and also that it has a cause proportionable and agreeable to the effect. The same principle which leads us to determine, that there cannot be anything coming to pass without a cause, leads us to determine that there cannot be more in the effect than in the cause.

Yea, if once it should be allowed, that things may come to pass without a cause, we should not only have no proof of the being of God, but we should be without evidence of the existence of anything whatsoever, but our own immediately present ideas and consciousness. For we have no way to prove anything else, but by arguing from effects to causes: from the ideas now immediately in view, we argue other things not immediately in view: from sensations now excited in us, we infer the existence of things without us, as the causes of these sensations: and from the existence of these things, we argue other things, which they depend on, as effects on causes. We infer the past existence of ourselves, or anything else, by memory; only as we argue, that the ideas, which are now in our minds, are the consequences of past ideas and sensations. We immediately perceive nothing else but the ideas which are this moment extant in our minds. We perceive or know other things only by means of these, as necessarily connected with others, and dependent on them. But if things may be without causes, all this necessary connection and dependence is dissolved, and so all means of our knowledge is gone. If there be no absurdity or difficulty in supposing one thing to start out of nonexistence, into being, of itself without a cause; then there is no absurdity or difficulty in supposing the same of millions of millions. For nothing, or no difficulty multiplied, still is nothing, or no difficulty: nothing multiplied by nothing don't increase the sum.

And indeed, according to the hypothesis I am opposing, of the acts of the will coming to pass without a cause, it is the case in fact, that millions of millions of events are continually coming into existence contingently, without any cause or reason why they do so, all over the world, every day and hour, through all ages. So it is in a constant succession, in every moral agent. This contingency, this efficient Nothing, this effectual No-Cause, is always ready at hand, to produce this sort of effects, as long as the agent exists, and as often as he has occasion.

If it were so, that things only of one kind, viz. acts of the will, seemed to come to pass of themselves; but those of this sort in general came into being thus; and it were an event that was continual, and that happened in a course, wherever were capable subjects of such events; this very thing would demonstrate that there was some cause of them, which made such a difference between this event and others, and that they did not really happen contingently. For contingence is blind, and does not pick and choose for a particular sort of events. Nothing has no choice. This No-Cause, which causes no existence, can't cause the existence which comes to pass, to be of one particular sort only, distinguished from all others. Thus, that only one sort of matter drops out of the heavens, even water, and that this comes so often, so constantly and plentifully, all over the world, in all ages, shows that there is some cause or reason of the falling of water out of the heavens; and that something besides mere contingence has a hand in the matter.

If we should suppose Nonentity to be about to bring forth; and things were coming into existence, without any cause or antecedent, on which the existence, or kind or manner of existence depends; or which could at all determine whether the things should be; stones, or stars, or beasts, or angels, or human bodies, or souls, or only some new motion or figure in natural bodies, or some new sensations in animals, or new ideas in the human understanding, or new volitions in the will; or anything else of all the infinite number of possibles; then certainly it would not be expected, although many millions of millions of things are coming into existence in this manner, all over the face of the earth, that they should all be only of one particular kind, and that it should be thus in all ages, and that this sort of existences should never fail to come to pass where there is room for them, or a subject capable of them, and that constantly, whenever there is occasion for them.

If any should imagine, there is something in the sort of event that renders it possible for it to come into existence without a cause; and should say, that the free acts of the will are existences of an exceeding different nature from other things; by reason of which they may come into existence without any previous ground or reason of it, though other things cannot; if they make this objection in good earnest, it would be an evidence of their strangely forgetting themselves: for they would be giving an account of some ground of the existence of a thing, when at the same time they would maintain there is no ground of its existence. Therefore I would observe, that the particular nature of existence, be it never so diverse from others, can lay no foundation for that thing's coming into existence without a cause; because to suppose this, would be to suppose the particular nature of existence to be a thing prior to the existence; and so a thing which makes way for existence, with such a circumstance, namely without a cause or reason of existence. But that which in any respect makes way for a thing's coming into being, or for any manner or circumstance of its first existence, must be prior to the existence. The distinguished nature of the effect, which is something belonging to the effect, can't have influence backward, to act before it is. The peculiar nature of that thing called volition, can do nothing, can have no influence, while it is not. And afterwards it is too late for its influence: for then the thing has made sure of existence already, without its help.

So that it is indeed as repugnant to reason, to suppose that an act of the will should come into existence without a cause, as to suppose the human soul, or an angel, or the globe of the earth, or the whole universe, should come into existence without a cause. And if once we allow, that such a sort of effect as a volition may come to pass without a cause, how do we know but that many other sorts of effects may do so too? 'Tis not the particular kind of effect that makes the absurdity of supposing it has being without a cause, but something which is common to all things that ever begin to be, viz. that they are not self-existent, or necessary in the nature of things.

SECTION 4. WHETHER VOLITION CAN ARISE WITHOUT A CAUSE, THROUGH THE ACTIVITY OF THE NATURE OF THE SOUL

THE AUTHOR [1] of the *Essay on the Freedom of the Will in God and the Creatures,* in answer to that objection against his doctrine of a self-determining power in the will (pp. 68, 69),[2] "that nothing is, or comes to pass, without a sufficient reason why it is, and why it is in this manner rather than another," allows that it is thus in corporeal things, "which are properly and philosophically speaking passive beings"; but denies that it is thus in "spirits, which are beings of an active nature, who have the spring of action within themselves, and can determine themselves." By which it is plainly supposed, that such event as an act of the will, may come to pass in a spirit, without a sufficient reason why it comes to pass, or why it is after this manner, rather than another; by reason of the activity of the nature of a spirit. But certainly this author, in this matter, must be very unwary and inadvertent. For,

1. The objection or difficulty proposed by this author, seems to be forgotten in his answer or solution. The very difficulty, as he himself proposes it, is this: how an event can "come to pass without a sufficient reason why it is, or why it is in this manner rather than another"? Instead of solving this difficulty, or answering this question with regard to volition, as he proposes, he forgets himself, and answers another question quite diverse, and wholly inconsistent with this, viz. what is a sufficient reason why it is, and why it is in this manner rather than another? And he assigns the active being's own determination as the cause, and a cause sufficient for the effect; and leaves all the difficulty unresolved, and the question unanswered, which yet returns, even, how the soul's own determination, which

1. [See Intro., Pt. 5, nos. 13, 14.]
2. [Isaac Watts, *An Essay on Freedom of Will in God and in Creatures,* (London, 1732) Sec. 6, *obj.* 2 and *ans.;* in *The Works of the Reverend and Learned Isaac Watts, D.D.,* ed. Jennings and Doddridge; 1st ed. 1753; 6 vols. London, 1811), *6, 265.*]

he speaks of, came to exist, and to be what it was without a cause? The activity of the soul may enable it to be the cause of effects; but it don't at all enable or help it to be the subject of effects which have no cause; which is the thing this author supposes concerning acts of the will. Activity of nature will no more enable a being to produce effects, and determine the manner of their existence, *within* itself, without a cause, than *out of* itself, in some other being. But if an active being should, through its activity, produce and determine an effect in some external object, how absurd would it be to say, that the effect was produced without a cause!

2. The question is not so much, how a spirit endowed with activity comes to act, as why it exerts such an act, and not another; or why it acts with such a particular determination? If activity of nature be the cause why a spirit (the soul of man for instance) acts, and don't lie still; yet that alone is not the cause why its action is thus and thus limited, directed and determined. Active nature is a *general* thing; 'tis an ability or tendency of nature to action, generally taken; which may be a cause why the soul acts as occasion or reason is given; but this alone can't be a sufficient cause why the soul exerts such a *particular* act, at such a time, rather than others. In order to this, there must be something besides a *general* tendency to action; there must also be a *particular* tendency to that individual action. If it should be asked, why the soul of man uses its activity in such a manner as it does; and it should be answered, that the soul uses its activity thus, rather than otherwise, because it has activity; would such an answer satisfy a rational man? Would it not rather be looked upon as a very impertinent one?

3. An active being can bring no effects to pass by his activity, but what are consequent upon his acting: he produces nothing by his activity, any other way than by the exercise of his activity, and so nothing but the fruits of its exercise: he brings nothing to pass by a dormant activity. But the exercise of his activity is action; and so his action, or exercise of his activity, must be prior to the effects of his activity. If an active being produces an effect in another being, about which his activity is conversant, the effect being the fruit of his activity, his activity must be first exercised or exerted, and the effect of it must follow. So it must be, with equal reason, if the active being is his own object, and his activity is conversant about himself, to produce and determine some effect in himself; still the exercise of his activity must go before the effect, which he brings to pass and deter-

mines by it. And therefore his activity can't be the cause of the determination of the first action, or exercise of activity itself, whence the
effects of activity arise; for that would imply a contradiction; it would
be to say, the first exercise of activity is before the first exercise of
activity, and is the cause of it.

4. That the soul, though an active substance, can't *diversify* its
own acts, but by first acting; or be a determining cause of *different*
acts, or any different effects, sometimes of one kind, and sometimes
of another, any other way than in consequence of its own diverse
acts, is manifest by this; that if so, then the *same* cause, the same
causal power, force or influence, *without variation in any respect,*
would produce *different* effects at different times. For the same substance of the soul before it acts, and the same active nature of the
soul before it is exerted (i.e. before in the order of nature) would be
the cause of different effects, viz. different volitions at different times.
But the substance of the soul before it acts, and its active nature before it is exerted, are the same without variation. For 'tis some act
that makes the first variation in the cause, as to any causal exertion,
force or influence. But if it be so, that the soul has no different
causality, or diverse causal force or influence, in producing these
diverse effects; then 'tis evident, that the soul has no influence, no
hand in the diversity of the effect; and that the difference of the effect
can't be owing to anything in the soul; or which is the same thing,
the soul don't determine the diversity of the effect; which is contrary
to the supposition. 'Tis true, the substance of the soul before it acts,
and before there is any difference in that respect, may be in a different
state and circumstances: but those whom I oppose, will not allow the
different circumstances of the soul to be the determining causes of
the acts of the will; as being contrary to their notion of self-determination and self-motion.

5. Let us suppose, as these divines do, that there are no acts of the
soul, strictly speaking, but free volitions; then it will follow, that
the soul is an active being in nothing further than it is a voluntary
or elective being; and whenever it produces effects actively, it produces effects voluntarily and electively. But to produce effects thus,
is the same thing as to produce effects in consequence of, and according to its own choice. And if so, then surely the soul don't by
its activity produce all its own acts of will or choice themselves:
for this, by the supposition, is to produce all its free acts of choice
voluntarily and electively, or in consequence of its own free acts of

choice, which brings the matter directly to the forementioned contradiction, of a free act of choice before the first free act of choice.
According to these gentlemen's own notion of action, if there arises
in the mind a volition without a free act of the will or choice to determine and produce it, the mind is not the active voluntary cause of
that volition; because it don't arise from, nor is regulated by choice
or design. And therefore it can't be, that the mind should be the
active, voluntary, determining cause of the first and leading volition
that relates to the affair. The mind's being a designing cause, only
enables it to produce effects in consequence of its design; it will not
enable it to be the designing cause of all its own designs. The mind's
being an elective cause, will only enable it to produce effects in consequence of its elections, and according to them; but can't enable it
to be the elective cause of all its own elections; because that supposes
an election before the first election. So the mind's being an active
cause enables it to produce effects in consequence of its own acts, but
can't enable it to be the determining cause of all its own acts; for
that is still in the same manner a contradiction; as it supposes a
determining act conversant about the first act, and prior to it, having
a causal influence on its existence, and manner of existence.

I can conceive of nothing else that can be meant by the soul's having power to cause and determine its own volitions, as a being to
whom God has given a power of action, but this; that God has given
power to the soul, sometimes at least, to excite volitions at its pleasure, or according as it chooses. And this certainly supposes, in all such
cases, a choice preceding all volitions which are thus caused, even the
very first of them. Which runs into the forementioned great absurdity.[3]

Therefore the activity of the nature of the soul affords no relief
from the difficulties which the notion of a self-determining power in
the will is attended with, nor will it help, in the least, its absurdities
and inconsistencies.

3. [JE's argument may possibly derive from Locke. See above, Intro., Pt. 4, no. 6.]

SECTION 5. SHEWING, THAT IF THE THINGS ASSERTED IN THESE EVASIONS SHOULD BE SUPPOSED TO BE TRUE, THEY ARE ALTOGETHER IMPERTINENT, AND CAN'T HELP THE CAUSE OF ARMINIAN LIBERTY; AND HOW (THIS BEING THE STATE OF THE CASE) ARMINIAN WRITERS ARE OBLIGED TO TALK INCONSISTENTLY

WHAT was last observed in the preceding section may shew, not only that the active nature of the soul can't be a reason why any act of the will is, or why it is in this manner, rather than another; but also that if it could be so, and it could be proved that volitions are contingent events, in that sense, that their being and manner of being is not fixed or determined by any cause, or anything antecedent; it would not at all serve the purpose of Arminians, to establish the freedom of the will, according to their notion of its freedom, as consisting in the will's determination of itself; which supposes every free act of the will to be determined by some act of the will going before to determine it; inasmuch as for the will to determine a thing, is the same as for the soul to determine a thing by *willing;* and there is no way that the will can determine an act of the will, than by *willing* that act of the will, or, which is the same thing, choosing it. So that here must be two acts of the will in the case, one going before another, one conversant about the other, and the latter the object of the former, and chosen by the former. If the will don't cause and determine the act by choice, it don't cause or determine it at all; for that which is not determined by choice, is not determined voluntarily or willingly: and to say, that the will determines something which the soul don't determine willingly, is as much as to say, that something is done by the will, which the soul don't do with its will.

So that if Arminian liberty of will, consisting in the will's determining its own acts, be maintained, the old absurdity and contradiction must be maintained, that every free act of will is caused and determined by a foregoing free act of will. Which don't consist with the free act's arising without any cause, and being so contingent, as not be fixed by anything foregoing. So that this evasion must be given up, as not at all relieving, and as that which, instead of support-ing this sort of liberty, directly destroys it.

And if it should be supposed, that the soul determines its own acts of will some other way, than by a foregoing act of will; still it will not help the cause of their liberty of will. If it determines them by an act of the understanding, or some other power, then *the will* don't determine *itself;* and so the self-determining power of the will is given up. And what liberty is there exercised, according to their own opinion of liberty, by the soul's being determined by something besides its own choice? The acts of the will, it is true, may be directed, and effectually determined and fixed; but it is not done by the soul's own will and pleasure: there is no exercise at all of choice or will in producing the effect: and if will and choice are not exercised in it, how is the liberty of the will exercised in it?

So that let Arminians turn which way they please with their no-tion of liberty, consisting in the will's determining its own acts, their notion destroys itself. If they hold every free act of will to be deter-mined by the soul's own free choice, or foregoing free act of will; foregoing, either in the order of time, or nature; it implies that gross contradiction, that the first free act belonging to the affair, is deter-mined by a free act which is before it. Or if they say that the free acts of the will are determined by some *other act* of the soul, and not an act of will or choice, this also destroys their notion of liberty, con-sisting in the acts of the will being determined by the will itself; or if they hold that the acts of the will are determined by *nothing at all* that is prior to them, but that they are contingent in that sense, that they are determined and fixed by no cause at all; this also destroys their notion of liberty, consisting in the will's determining its own acts.

This being the true state of the Arminian notion of liberty, it hence comes to pass, that the writers that defend it are forced into gross inconsistencies, in what they say upon this subject. To instance in Dr. Whitby; he in his "Discourse on the Freedom of the Will," [1] opposes the opinion of the Calvinists, who place man's liberty "only in a power of doing what he will," as that wherein they plainly agree

1. Daniel Whitby, *A Discourse concerning* [*the Five Points*], Dis. IV, ch. 4 (2d ed. London, 1735), pp. 350, 351, 352 [See above, Intro., Pt. 5, nos. 7, 8].

with Mr. Hobbes. And yet he himself mentions the very same notion of liberty, as the dictate of "the sense and common reason of
mankind, and a rule laid down by the light of nature"; viz. that
"liberty is a power of acting from ourselves, or *doing what we will.*" [2]
This is indeed, as he says, a thing agreeable to "the sense and common reason of mankind"; and therefore 'tis not so much to be won-
dered at, that he unawares acknowledges it against himself: for if
liberty don't consist in this, what else can be devised that it should
consist in? If it be said, as Dr. Whitby elsewhere [3] insists, that it don't
only consist in liberty of "doing what we will," but also a liberty of
willing without necessity; still the question returns, what does that
liberty of willing without necessity consist in, but in a power of willing *as we please,* without being impeded by a contrary necessity? or
in other words, a liberty for the soul in its willing to act *according
to its own choice?* Yea, this very thing the same author seems to allow,
and suppose again and again, in the use he makes of sayings of the
fathers, whom he quotes as his vouchers. Thus he cites these words
of Origen, which he produces as a testimony on his side: "The soul
acts by *her own choice,* and it is free for her to incline to whatever
part *she will.*" [4] And those words of Justin Martyr: "The doctrine of
the Christians is this, that nothing is done or suffered according to
fate, but that every man doth good or evil *according to his own free
choice.*" [5] And from Eusebius, these words: "If fate be established,
philosophy and piety are overthrown . . . all these things depending upon the necessity introduced by the stars, and not upon medita-
tion and exercise *proceeding from our own free choice.*" [6] And again,
the words of Macarius, "God, to preserve the liberty of man's will,
suffered their bodies to die, that it might be *in their choice* to turn to
good or evil . . . They who are acted by the Holy Spirit, are not
held under any necessity, but have liberty to turn themselves, and *do
what they will* in this life." [7]

2. Dis. IV, ch. 1; ibid., pp. 325 f.

3. [Dis. IV, ch. 3, ibid., and in the first part of the sentence just quoted: "That
only is voluntary which we lie under no Necessity to do or to forebear, and *what
we do being unwilling, we do out of Necessity, Liberty being a Power of Acting
from ourselves, or doing what we will*" (p. 326).]

4. Dis. IV, ch. 2; ibid., p. 342.

5. Dis. IV, ch. 4; ibid., p. 360.

6. Dis. IV, ch. 4; ibid., p. 363.

7. Dis. IV, ch. 5; ibid., pp. 369, 370. [Whitby quotes Macarius' saying that, had
the bodies of Christians been suddenly made immortal, *"the World beholding*

Thus, the Doctor in effect comes into that very notion of liberty, which the Calvinists have; which he at the same time condemns, as agreeing with the opinion of Mr. Hobbes, namely, the soul's acting by its own choice, men's doing good or evil according to their own free choice, their being in that exercise which proceeds from their own free choice, having it in their choice to turn to good or evil, and doing what they will. So that if men exercise this liberty in the acts of the will themselves, it must be in exerting acts of will as they will, or "according to their own free choice"; or exerting acts of will "that proceed from their choice." [8] And if it be so, then let everyone judge whether this don't suppose a free choice going before the free act of will, or whether an act of choice don't go before that act of the will which *proceeds from it*. And if it be thus with all free acts of the will, then let everyone judge, whether it won't follow that there is a free choice or will going before the first free act of the will exerted in the case. And then let everyone judge, whether this be not a contradiction. And finally, let everyone judge whether in the scheme of these writers there be any possibility of avoiding these absurdities.

If liberty consists, as Dr. Whitby himself says, in a man's "doing what he will"; and a man exercises this liberty, not only in external actions, but in the acts of the will themselves; then so far as liberty is exercised in the latter, it consists in *willing what he wills:* and if any say so, one of these two things must be meant, either (1) that a man has power to will, as he does will; because what he wills, he wills; and therefore has power to will what he has power to will. If this be their meaning, then all this mighty controversy about freedom of the will and self-determining power, comes wholly to nothing; all that is contended for being no more than this, that the mind of man does what it does, and is the subject of what it is the subject of, or that what is, is; wherein none has any controversy with them. Or (2) the meaning must be, that a man has power to will as he pleases or chooses to will: that is, he has power by one act of choice, to choose another; by an antecedent act of will to choose a consequent act; and therein to execute his own choice. And if this be their meaning, it is nothing but shuffling with those they dispute with, and baffling their own reason. For still the question returns, wherein lies man's liberty

---

. . . the Strangeness of the thing, would have been converted to Good . . . not by their own free Will, but by a kind of Necessity, and therefore God, to preserve the Liberty of Man's Will . . ."]

8. [See above, Intro., Pt. 5, no. 11.]

in that antecedent act of will which chose the consequent act? The answer according to the same principles must be, that his liberty in this also lies in his willing as he would, or as he chose, or agreeable to another act of choice preceding that. And so the question returns *in infinitum,* and the like answer must be made *in infinitum:* in order to support their opinion, there must be no beginning, but free acts of will must have been chosen by foregoing free acts of will, in the soul of every man, without beginning; and so before he had a being, from all eternity.[9]

9. [JE's argument may possibly derive from Locke. See above, Intro., Pt. 4, no. 6.]

SECTION 6. CONCERNING THE WILL'S DETERMINING IN THINGS WHICH ARE PERFECTLY INDIFFERENT, IN THE VIEW OF THE MIND

A GREAT ARGUMENT for self-determining power, is the supposed experience we universally have of an ability to determine our wills, in cases wherein no prevailing motive is presented: the will (as is supposed) has its choice to make between two or more things, that are perfectly equal in the view of the mind; and the will is apparently altogether indifferent; and yet we find no difficulty in coming to a choice; the will can instantly determine itself to one, by a sovereign power which it has over itself, without being moved by any preponderating inducement.

Thus the forementioned author of an *Essay on the Freedom of the Will, etc.* (pp. 25, 26, 27),[1] supposes,

> that there are many instances, wherein the will is determined neither by present uneasiness, nor by the greatest apparent good, nor by the last dictate of the understanding, nor by anything else, but merely by itself, as a sovereign self-determining power of the soul; and that the soul does not will this or that action, in some cases, by any other influence, but because it will. Thus (says he) I can turn my face to the south, or the north; I can point with my finger upward, or downward. And thus, in some cases, the will determines itself in a very sovereign manner, because it will, without a reason borrowed from the understanding: and hereby it discovers its own perfect power of choice, rising from within itself, and free from all influence or restraint of any kind.

And in pages 66, 70, and 73, 74,[2] this author very expressly supposes the will in many cases to be determined by "no motive at all, and acts altogether without motive, or ground of preference."—Here I would observe,

1. [Watts, *Essay*, Sec. 2; in *Works, 6,* 250.]
2. [Ibid., Sec. 6, *obj.* 2, 3; in *Works, 6,* 265–7.]

1. The very supposition which is here made, directly contradicts and overthrows itself. For the thing supposed, wherein this grand argument consists, is, that among several things the will actually chooses one before another, at the same time that it is perfectly indifferent; which is the very same thing as to say, the mind has a preference, at the same time that it has no preference. What is meant can't be, that the mind is indifferent before it comes to have a choice, or till it has a preference; or, which is the same thing, that the mind is indifferent until it comes to be not indifferent. For certainly this author did not suppose he had a controversy with any person in supposing this. And then it is nothing to his purpose, that the mind which chooses, was indifferent once; unless it chooses, remaining indifferent; for otherwise, it don't choose at all in that case of indifference, concerning which is all the question. Besides, it appears in fact, that the thing which this author supposes, is not that the will chooses one thing before another, concerning which it is indifferent *before* it chooses; but also is indifferent *when* it chooses; and that its being otherwise than indifferent is not till afterwards, in consequence of its choice; that the chosen thing's appearing preferable and more agreeable than another, arises from its choice already made. His words are (p. 30): [3]

> Where the objects which are proposed, appear equally fit or good, the will is left without a guide or director; and therefore must make its own choice, by its own determination; it being properly a self-determining power. And in such cases the will does as it were make a good to itself by its own choice, i.e. creates its own pleasure or delight in this self-chosen good. Even as a man by seizing upon a spot of unoccupied land, in an uninhabited country, makes it his own possession and property, and as such rejoices in it. Where things were indifferent before, the will finds nothing to make them more agreeable, considered merely in themselves; but the pleasure it feels *arising from its own choice,* and its perseverance therein. We love many things which we have chosen, *and purely because we chose them.*

This is as much as to say, that we first begin to prefer many things, now ceasing any longer to be indifferent with respect to them, purely because we have preferred and chosen them before. These things

3. [Ibid., Sec. 3, *prop.* 3; in *Works, 6,* 251.]

must needs be spoken inconsiderately by this author. Choice or preference can't be before itself, in the same instance, either in the order
of time or nature: it can't be the foundation of itself, or the fruit or
consequence of itself. The very act of choosing one thing rather than
another, is preferring that thing, and that is setting a higher value
on that thing. But that the mind sets an higher value on one thing
than another, is not, in the first place, the fruit of its setting a higher
value on that thing.

This author says (p. 36),[4] "The will may be perfectly indifferent,
and yet the will may determine itself to choose one or the other."
And again in the same page, "I am entirely indifferent to either; and
yet my will may determine itself to choose." And again, "Which I
shall choose must be determined by the mere act of my will." If the
choice is determined by a mere act of will, then the choice is determined by a mere act of choice. And concerning this matter, viz. that
the act of the will itself is determined by an act of choice, this writer
is express, in p. 72.[5] Speaking of the case, where there is no superior
fitness in objects presented, he has these words: "There it must act
by its own *choice,* and determine itself as it *pleases."* Where it is supposed that the very determination, which is the ground and spring of
the will's act, is an act of *choice* and *pleasure,* wherein one act is more
agreeable, and the mind better pleased in it than another; and this
preference, and superior *pleasedness* is the ground of all it does in
the case. And if so, the mind is not indifferent when it determines
itself, but *had rather* do one thing than another, had rather determine itself one way than another. And therefore the will don't act at
all in indifference; not so much as in the first step it takes, or the first
rise and beginning of its acting. If it be possible for the understanding to act in indifference, yet to be sure the will never does; because
the will's beginning to act is the very same thing as its beginning to
choose or prefer. And if in the very first act of the will, the mind
prefers something, then the idea of that thing preferred, does at that
time preponderate, or prevail in the mind; or, which is the same
thing, the idea of it has a prevailing influence on the will. So that this
wholly destroys the thing supposed, viz. that the mind can by a
sovereign power choose one of two or more things, which in the view
of the mind are, in every respect, perfectly equal, one of which does

4. [Ibid., Sec. 3, *prop.* 8; in *Works, 6,* 253.]
5. [Ibid., Sec. 6, *obj.* 3, *ans.* 2; in *Works, 6,* 267.]

not at all preponderate, nor has any prevailing influence on the mind above another.

So that this author, in his grand argument for the ability of the will to choose one of two, or more things, concerning which it is perfectly indifferent, does at the same time, in effect, deny the thing he supposes, and allows and asserts the point he endeavors to overthrow; even that the will, in choosing, is subject to no prevailing influence of the idea, or view of the thing chosen. And indeed it is impossible to offer this argument without overthrowing it; the thing supposed in it being inconsistent with itself, and that which denies itself. To suppose the will to act at all in a state of perfect indifference, either to determine itself, or to do anything else, is to assert that the mind chooses without choosing. To say that when it is indifferent, it can do as it pleases, is to say that it can follow its pleasure, when it has no pleasure to follow. And therefore if there be any difficulty in the instances of two cakes, or two eggs, etc. which are exactly alike, one as good as another; concerning which this author supposes the mind in fact has a *choice*,[6] and so in effect supposes that it has a *preference;* it as much concerned himself to solve the difficulty, as it does those whom he opposes. For if these instances prove anything to his purpose, they prove that a man chooses without choice. And yet this is not to his purpose; because if this is what he asserts, his own words are as much against him, and do as much contradict him, as the words of those he disputes against can do.

2. There is no great difficulty in shewing, in such instances as are alleged, not only *that it must needs be so,* that the mind must be influenced in its choice by something that has a preponderating influence upon it, but also *how it is so.* A little attention to our own experience, and a distinct consideration of the acts of our own minds in such cases, will be sufficient to clear up the matter.

Thus, supposing I have a chessboard before me; and because I am required by a superior, or desired by a friend, or to make some experiment concerning my own ability and liberty, or on some other consideration, I am determined to touch some one of the spots or squares on the board with my finger; not being limited or directed in the first proposal, or my own first purpose, which is general, to any one in particular; and there being nothing in the squares in themselves considered, that recommends any one of all the sixty-four, more than another: in this case, my mind determines to give itself up

6. [Ibid., Sec. 3, *prop.* 8; in *Works, 6,* 253–4.]

to what is vulgarly called accident,[7] by determining to touch that square which happens to be most in view, which my eye is especially upon at that moment, or which happens to be then most in my mind, or which I shall be directed to by some other suchlike accident. Here are several steps of the mind's proceeding (though all may be done as it were in a moment): the first step is its general determination that it will touch one of the squares. The next step is another *general* determination to give itself up to accident, in some certain way; as to touch that which shall be most in the eye or mind at that time, or to some other suchlike accident. The third and last step is a *particular* determination to touch a certain individual spot, even that square, which, by that sort of accident the mind has pitched upon, has actually offered itself beyond others. Now 'tis apparent that in none of these several steps does the mind proceed in absolute indifference, but in each of them is influenced by a preponderating inducement. So it is in the first step; the mind's general determination to touch one of the sixty-four spots: the mind is not absolutely indifferent whether it does so or no: it is induced to it, for the sake of making some experiment, or by the desire of a friend, or some other motive that prevails. So it is in the second step, the mind's determining to give itself up to accident, by touching that which shall be most in the eye, or the idea of which shall be most prevalent in the mind, etc. The mind is not absolutely indifferent whether it proceeds by this rule or no; but chooses it, because it appears at that time a convenient and requisite expedient in order to fulfill the general purpose aforesaid. And so it is in the third and last step, its determining to touch that individual spot which actually does prevail in the mind's view. The mind is not indifferent concerning this; but is influenced by a prevailing inducement and reason; which is, that this is a prosecution of the preceding determination, which appeared requisite, and was fixed before in the second step.

Accident will ever serve a man, without hindering him a moment, in such a case. It will always be so among a number of objects in view, one will prevail in the eye, or in idea beyond others. When we have our eyes open in the clear sunshine, many objects strike the eye at

7. I have elsewhere observed [p. 155] what that is which is vulgarly called "accident"; that it is nothing akin to the Arminian metaphysical notion of "contingence," something not connected with anything foregoing; but that it is something that comes to pass in the course of things, in some affair that men are concerned in, unforeseen, and not owing to their design.

once, and innumerable images may be at once painted in it by the
rays of light; but the attention of the mind is not equal to several of
them at once; or if it be, it don't continue so for any time. And so it
is with respect to the ideas of the mind in general: several ideas are
not in equal strength in the mind's view and notice at once; or at
least, don't remain so for any sensible continuance. There is nothing
in the world more constantly varying, than the ideas of the mind:
they don't remain precisely in the same state for the least perceivable
space of time: as is evident by this, that all perceivable time is judged
and perceived by the mind only by the succession or the successive
changes of its own ideas. Therefore while the views or perceptions of
the mind remain precisely in the same state, there is no perceivable
space or length of time, because no sensible succession at all.

As the acts of the will, in each step of the forementioned procedure,
don't come to pass without a particular cause, every act is owing to a
prevailing inducement; so the accident, as I have called it, or that
which happens in the unsearchable course of things, to which the
mind yields itself, and by which it is guided, is not anything that
comes to pass without a cause; and the mind in determining to be
guided by it, is not determined by something that has no cause; any
more than if it determined to be guided by a lot, or the casting of a
die. For though the die's falling in such a manner be accidental to
him that casts it, yet none will suppose that there is no cause why it
falls as it does. The involuntary changes in the succession of our
ideas, though the cause may not be observed, have as much a cause,
as the changeable motions of the motes that float in the air, or the
continual, infinitely various, successive changes of the unevennesses
on the surface of the water.

There are two things especially, which are probably the occasions
of confusion in the minds of them who insist upon it, that the will
acts in a proper indifference, and without being moved by any inducement, in its determinations in such cases as have been mentioned.

1. They seem to mistake the point in question, or at least not to
keep it distinctly in view. The question they dispute about, is,
whether the mind be indifferent about the *objects* presented, one of
which is to be taken, touched, pointed to, etc., as two eggs, two
cakes, which appear equally good. Whereas the question to be considered, is, whether the person be indifferent with respect to his own
actions; whether he don't, on some consideration or other, prefer

one act with respect to these objects before another. The mind in its determination and choice, in these cases, is not most immediately and directly conversant about the *objects presented;* but the *acts to be done* concerning these objects. The objects may appear equal, and the mind may never properly make any choice between them: but the next act of the will being about the external actions to be performed, taking, touching, etc., these may not appear equal, and one action may properly be chosen before another. In each step of the mind's progress, the determination is not about the objects, unless indirectly and improperly, but about the actions, which it chooses for other reasons than any preference of the objects, and for reasons not taken at all from the objects.

There is no necessity of supposing, that the mind does ever at all properly choose one of the objects before another; either before it has taken, or afterwards. Indeed the man chooses to *take* or *touch* one rather than another; but not because it chooses the *thing* taken, or touched; but from foreign considerations. The case may be so, that of two things offered, a man may, for certain reasons, choose and prefer the taking of that which he *undervalues,* and choose to neglect to take that which his mind *prefers.* In such a case, choosing the thing taken, and choosing to take, are diverse: and so they are in a case where the things presented are equal in the mind's esteem, and neither of them preferred. All that fact and experience make evident, is, that the mind chooses one action rather than another. And therefore the arguments which they bring, in order to be to their purpose, ought to be to prove that the mind chooses the action in perfect indifference, with respect to that *action;* and not to prove that the mind chooses the action in perfect indifference with respect to the *object;* which is very possible, and yet the will not act at all without prevalent inducement, and proper preponderation.[8]

2. Another reason of confusion and difficulty in this matter, seems to be, not distinguishing between a *general* indifference, or an indifference with respect to what is to be done in a more distant and general view of it, and a *particular* indifference, or an indifference with respect to the next immediate act, viewed with its particular and present circumstances. A man may be perfectly indifferent with respect to his own actions, in the former respect; and yet not in the latter. Thus, in the foregoing instance of touching one of the squares of a chessboard; when 'tis first proposed that I should touch one of them,

8. [See above, Intro., Pt. 4, no. 4.]

I may be perfectly indifferent which I touch; because as yet I view the matter remotely and generally, being but in the first step of the mind's progress in the affair. But yet, when I am actually come to the last step, and the very next thing to be determined is, which is to be touched, having already determined that I will touch that which happens to be most in my eye or mind, and my mind being now fixed on a particular one, the act of touching that, considered thus immediately, and in these particular present circumstances, is not what my mind is absolutely indifferent about.

SECTION 7. CONCERNING THE NOTION OF LIBERTY OF WILL CONSISTING IN INDIFFERENCE

WHAT has been said in the foregoing section, has a tendency in some measure to evince the absurdity of the opinion of such as place liberty in indifference, or in that equilibrium whereby the will is without all antecedent determination or bias, and left hitherto free from any prepossessing inclination to one side or the other; that the determination of the will to either side may be entirely from itself, and that it may be owing only to its own power, and that sovereignty which it has over itself, that it goes this way rather than that.[1]

But inasmuch as this has been of such long standing, and has been so generally received, and so much insisted on by Pelagians, semi-Pelagians, Jesuits, Socinians, Arminians, and others, it may deserve a more full consideration. And therefore I shall now proceed to a more particular and thorough inquiry into this notion.

Now lest some should suppose that I don't understand those that place liberty in indifference, or should charge me with misrepresenting their opinion, I would signify, that I am sensible, there are

1. Dr. Whitby, and some other Arminians, make a distinction of different kinds of freedom; one of God, and perfect spirits above; another of persons in a state of trial. The former Dr. Whitby allows to consist with necessity; the latter he holds to be without necessity; and this latter he supposes to be requisite to our being the subjects of praise or dispraise, rewards or punishments, precepts and prohibitions, promises and threats, exhortations and dehortations, and a covenant treaty. And to this freedom he supposes indifference to be requisite. In his *Discourse on the Five Points*, [Dis. IV, ch. 1] pp. 299, 300, he says: "It is a freedom (speaking of a freedom not only from coaction, but from necessity) requisite, as we conceive, to render us capable to trial or probation, and to render our actions worthy of praise or dispraise, and our persons of rewards or punishments." And in the next page, speaking of the same matter, he says, "Excellent to this purpose, are the words of Mr. Thorndike: 'We say not, that indifference is requisite to all freedom, but to the freedom of man alone in this state of travail and proficience; the ground of which is God's tender of a treaty, and conditions of peace and reconcilement to fallen man, together with those precepts and prohibitions, those promises and threats, those exhortations and dehortations, it is enforced with.' "

some, who when they talk of the liberty of the will as consisting in indifference, express themselves as though they would not be understood of the indifference of the inclination or tendency of the will, but of, I know not what, indifference of the soul's power of willing; or that the will, with respect to its power or ability to choose, is indifferent, can go either way indifferently, either to the right hand or left, either act or forbear to act, one as well as the other. Though this seems to be a refining only of some particular writers, and newly invented, and which will by no means consist with the manner of expression used by the defenders of liberty of indifference in general. And I wish such refiners would thoroughly consider, whether they distinctly know their own meaning, when they make a distinction between indifference of the soul as to its *power* or *ability* of willing or choosing, and the soul's indifference as to the preference or choice itself; and whether they don't deceive themselves in imagining that they have any distinct meaning at all. The indifference of the soul as to its ability or power to will, must be the same thing as the indifference of the state of the power or faculty of the will, or the indifference of the state which the soul itself, which has that power or faculty, hitherto remains in, as to the exercise of that power, in the choice it shall by and by make.

But not to insist any longer on the abstruseness and inexplicableness of this distinction; let what will be supposed concerning the meaning of them that make use of it, thus much must at least be intended by Arminians, when they talk of indifference as essential to liberty of will, if they intend anything, in any respect to their purpose, viz. that it is such an indifference as leaves the will not determined already; but free from actual possession, and vacant of predetermination, so far, that there may be room for the exercise of the *self-determining power* of the will; and that the will's freedom consists in, or depends upon this vacancy and opportunity that is left for the will itself to be the determiner of the act that is to be the free act.

And here I would observe in the first place, that to make out this scheme of liberty, the indifference must be *perfect* and *absolute;* there must be a perfect freedom from all antecedent preponderation or inclination. Because if the will be already inclined, before it exerts its own sovereign power on itself, then its inclination is not wholly owing to itself: if when two opposites are proposed to the soul for its choice, the proposal don't find the soul wholly in a state of indifference, then it is not found in a state of liberty for mere self-

determination. The least degree of antecedent bias must be inconsistent with their notion of liberty. For so long as prior inclination
possesses the will, and is not removed, it binds the will, so that it is
utterly impossible that the will should act otherwise than agreeably
to it. Surely the will can't act or choose contrary to a remaining prevailing inclination of the will. To suppose otherwise, would be the
same thing as to suppose, that the will is inclined contrary to its
present prevailing inclination, or contrary to what it is inclined to.
That which the will chooses and prefers, that, all things considered,
it preponderates and inclines to. It is equally impossible for the will
to choose contrary to its own remaining and present preponderating
inclination, as 'tis to prefer contrary to its own present preference, or
choose contrary to its own present choice. The will therefore, so long
as it is under the influence of an old preponderating inclination, is
not at liberty for a new free act, or any act that shall now be an act
of self-determination. The act which is a self-determined free act,
must be an act which the will determines in the possession and use
of such a liberty, as consists in a freedom from everything, which, if
it were there, would make it impossible that the will, at that time,
should be otherwise than that way to which it tends.

If anyone should say, there is no need that the indifference should
be perfect; but although a former inclination and preference still
remains, yet, if it ben't very strong and violent, possibly the strength
of the will may oppose and overcome it—

This is grossly absurd; for the strength of the will, let it be never so
great, does not at all enable it to act one way, and act the contrary
way,[2] both at the same time. It gives it no such sovereignty and command, as to cause itself to prefer and not to prefer at the same time,
or to choose contrary to its own present choice.

Therefore, if there be the least degree of antecedent pondera-
tion of the will, it must be perfectly abolished, before the will can
be at liberty to determine itself the contrary way. And if the will
determines itself the same way, it was not a free determination, because the will is not wholly at liberty in so doing: its determination
is not altogether from itself, but it was partly determined before, in
its prior inclination: and all the freedom the will exercises in the
case, is in an increase of inclination, which it gives itself, over and
above what it had by foregoing bias; so much is from itself, and so

2. [The 1754 ed. reads "and *not* the contrary way." Corrected from the *printed*
list of errata.]

much is from perfect indifference. For though the will had a previous tendency that way, yet as to that additional degree of inclination, it had no tendency. Therefore the previous tendency is of no consideration, with respect to the act wherein the will is free. So that it comes to the same thing which was said at first, that as to the act of the will, wherein the will is free, there must be *perfect* indifference, or equilibrium.

To illustrate this; if we should suppose a sovereign self-moving power in a natural body: but that the body is in motion already, by an antecedent bias; for instance, gravitation towards the center of the earth; and has one degree of motion already, by virtue of that previous tendency; but by its self-moving power it adds one degree more to its motion, and moves so much more swiftly towards the center of the earth than it would do by its gravity only: it is evident, that all that is owing to a self-moving power in this case, is the additional degree of motion; and that the other degree of motion which it had from gravity, is of no consideration in the case, don't help the effect of the free self-moving power in the least; the effect is just the same, as if the body had received from itself one degree of motion from a state of perfect rest. So if we should suppose a self-moving power given to the scale of a balance, which has a weight of one degree beyond the opposite scale; and we ascribe to it an ability to add to itself another degree of force the same way, by its self-moving power; this is just the same thing as to ascribe to it a power to give itself one degree of preponderation from a perfect equilibrium; and so much power as the scale has to give itself an overbalance from a perfect equipoise, so much self-moving self-preponderating power it has, and no more. So that its free power this way is always to be measured from perfect equilibrium.

I need say no more to prove, that, if indifference be essential to liberty, it must be perfect indifference; and that so far as the will is destitute of this, so far it is destitute of that freedom by which it is its own master, and in a capacity of being its own determiner, without being at all passive, or subject to the power and sway of something else, in its motions and determinations.

Having observed these things, let us now try whether this notion of the liberty of will consisting in indifference and equilibrium, and the will's self-determination in such a state, be not absurd and inconsistent.

And here I would lay down this as an axiom of undoubted truth;

that every free act is done *in* a state of freedom, and not only *after* such a state. If an act of the will be an act wherein the soul is free, it must be exerted in a *state* of freedom, and in the *time* of freedom. It will not suffice, that the act immediately follows a state of liberty; but liberty must yet continue, and coexist with the act; the soul remaining in possession of liberty. Because that is the notion of a free act of the soul, even an act wherein the soul uses or exercises liberty. But if the soul is not, in the very time of the act, in the possession of liberty, it can't at that time be in the use of it.

Now the question is, whether ever the soul of man puts forth any act of will, while it yet remains in a state of liberty, in that notion of a state of liberty, viz. as implying a state of indifference; or whether the soul ever exerts an act of choice or preference, while at that very time the will is in a perfect equilibrium, not inclining one way more than another. The very putting of the question is sufficient to show the absurdity of the affirmative answer: for how ridiculous would it be for anybody to insist, that the soul chooses one thing before another, when at the very same instant it is perfectly indifferent with respect to each! This is the same thing as to say, the soul prefers one thing to another, at the very same time that it has no preference. Choice and preference can no more be in a state of indifference, than motion can be in a state of rest, or than the preponderation of the scale of a balance can be in a state of equilibrium. Motion may be the next moment after rest; but can't coexist with it, in *any,* even the *least* part of it. So choice may be immediately after a state of indifference, but has no coexistence with it: even the very beginning of it is not in a state of indifference. And therefore if this be liberty, no act of the will, in any degree, is ever performed in a state of liberty, or in the time of liberty. Volition and liberty are so far from agreeing together, and being essential one to another, that they are contrary one to another, and one excludes and destroys the other, as much as motion and rest, light and darkness, or life and death. So that the will acts not at all, does not so much as begin to act in the time of such liberty: freedom is perfectly at an end, and has ceased to be, at the first moment of action; and therefore liberty can't reach the action, to affect, or qualify it, or give it a denomination, or any part of it, any more than if it had ceased to be twenty years before the action began. The moment that liberty ceases to be, it ceases to be a qualification of anything. If light and darkness succeed one another instantaneously, light qualifies nothing after it is gone out, to make anything lightsome or bright, any more at the first moment of perfect darkness, than months or years after. Life denominates nothing *vital* at the first moment of perfect death. So freedom, if it consists in, or implies indifference, can denominate nothing free, at the first moment of preference or preponderation. Therefore 'tis manifest, that no liberty which the soul is possessed of, or ever uses, in any of its acts of volition, consists in indifference; and that the opinion of such as suppose, that indifference belongs to the very essence of liberty, is to the highest degree absurd and contradictory.

If anyone should imagine, that this manner of arguing is nothing but trick and delusion; and to evade the reasoning, should say, that the thing wherein the will exercises its liberty, is not in the act of choice or preponderation itself, but in *determining* itself to a certain choice or preference; that the act of the will wherein it is free, and uses its own sovereignty, consists in its *causing* or determining the change or *transition* from a state of indifference to a certain preference, or determining to give a certain turn to the balance, which has hitherto been even; and that this act the will exerts in a state of liberty, or while the will yet remains in equilibrium, and perfect master of itself: I say, if anyone chooses to express his notion of liberty after this, or some such manner, let us see if he can make out his matters any better than before.

What is asserted is, that the will, while it yet remains in perfect equilibrium, without preference, determines to change itself from that state, and excite in itself a certain choice or preference. Now let us see whether this don't come to the same absurdity we had before. If it be so, that the will, while it yet remains perfectly indifferent, determines to put itself out of that state, and give itself a certain preponderation; then I would inquire, whether the soul don't determine this of choice; or whether the will's coming to a determination to do so, be not the same thing as the soul's coming to a choice to do so. If the soul don't determine this of choice, or in the exercise of choice, then it don't determine it voluntarily. And if the soul don't determine it voluntarily, or of its own will, then in what sense does its will determine it? And if the will don't determine it, then how is the liberty of the will exercised in the determination? What sort of liberty is exercised by the soul in those determinations, wherein there is no exercise of choice, which are not voluntary, and wherein the will is not concerned? But if it be allowed, that this determination is an act of choice, and it be insisted on, that the soul, while it yet remains in a state of perfect indifference, chooses to put itself out of that state, and to turn itself one way; then the soul is already come to a choice, and chooses that way. And so we have the very same absurdity which we had before. Here is the soul in a state of choice, and in a state of equilibrium, both at the same time: the soul already choosing one way, while it remains in a state of perfect indifference, and has no choice of one way more than the other. And indeed this manner of talking, though it may a little hide the absurdity, in the obscurity of expression, is more nonsensical, and increases the inconsistence. To say, the free act of the will, or the act which the will exerts in a state of freedom and indifference, does not imply preference in it, but is what the will does in order to causing or producing a preference, is as much as to say, the soul chooses (for to will and to choose are the same thing) without choice, and prefers without preference, in order to cause or produce the beginning of a preference, or the first choice. And that is, that the first choice is exerted without choice, in order to produce itself.

If any, to evade these things, should own, that a state of liberty, and a state of indifference are not the same, and that the former may be without the latter; but should say, that indifference is still essential to the freedom of an act of will, in some sort, namely, as 'tis necessary to go immediately before it; it being essential to the freedom of an act of will that it should directly and immediately arise out of a state of indifference: still this will not help the cause of Arminian liberty, or make it consistent with itself. For if the act springs immediately out of a state of indifference, then it does not arise from antecedent choice or preference. But if the act arises directly out of a state of indifference, without any intervening choice to choose and determine it, then the act not being determined by choice, is not determined by the will; the mind exercises no free choice in the affair, and free choice and free will have no hand in the determination of the act. Which is entirely inconsistent with their notion of the freedom of volition.

If any should suppose, that these difficulties and absurdities may be avoided, by saying, that the liberty of the mind consists in a power to suspend the act of the will, and so to keep it in a state of indifference, till there has been opportunity for consideration; and so shall say, that however indifference is not essential to liberty in such a manner, that the mind must make its choice in a state of indifference, which is an inconsistency, or that the act of will must spring immediately out of indifference; yet indifference may be essential to the liberty of acts of the will in this respect; viz. that liberty consists in a power of the mind to forbear or suspend the act of volition, and keep the mind in a state of indifference for the present, till there has been opportunity for proper deliberation: I say, if anyone imagines that this helps the matter, it is a great mistake: it reconciles no inconsistency, and relieves no difficulty which the affair is attended with.[3] For here the following things must be observed,

1. That this *suspending* of volition, if there be properly any such thing, is itself an act of volition. If the mind determines to suspend its act, it determines it voluntarily; it chooses, on some consideration, to suspend it. And this choice or determination, is an act of the will: and indeed it is supposed to be so in the very hypothesis; for 'tis supposed, that the liberty *of the will* consists in its power to do thus, and that its doing it is the very thing wherein *the will* exercises its liberty. But how can the will exercise liberty in it, if it ben't an act of the will? The liberty of the will is not exercised in anything but what the will does.

2. This determining to suspend acting is not only an act of the will, but 'tis supposed to be the only free act of the will; because it is said, that *this* is the thing wherein the liberty of the will consists. Now if this be so, then this is all the act of will that we have to consider in this controversy, about the liberty of will, and in our inquiries, wherein the liberty of man consists. And now the forementioned difficulties remain: the former question returns upon us; viz. wherein consists the freedom of the will *in those acts* wherein it is free? And if this act of determining a suspension be the only act in which the will is free, then wherein consists the will's freedom with respect to this act of suspension? And how is indifference essential to this act? The answer must be, according to what is supposed in the evasion under consideration, that the liberty of the will in this act of suspension, consists in a power to suspend even this act, till there has been opportunity for thorough deliberation. But this will be to plunge directly into the grossest nonsense: for 'tis the act of suspension itself that we are speaking of; and there is no room for a space of deliberation and suspension, in order to determine whether we will suspend or no. For that supposes, that even suspension itself may be deferred: which is absurd; for the very deferring the determination of suspension, to consider whether we will suspend or no, will

3. [See above, Intro., Pt. 4, no. 5.]

be actually suspending. For during the space of suspension, to consider whether to suspend, the act is *ipso facto* suspended. There is no medium between suspending to act, and immediately acting; and therefore no possibility of avoiding either the one or the other one moment; and so no room for deliberation before we do either of them.

And besides, this is attended with ridiculous absurdity another way: for now it is come to that, that liberty consists wholly in the mind's having power to suspend its determination whether to suspend or no; that there may be time for consideration, whether it be best to suspend. And if liberty consists in this only, then this is the liberty under consideration: we have to inquire now, how liberty with respect to this act of suspending a determination of suspension, consists in indifference, or how indifference is essential to it. The answer, according to the hypothesis we are upon, must be, that it consists in a power of suspending even this last mentioned act, to have time to consider whether to suspend that. And then the same difficulties and inquiries return over again with respect to that; and so on forever. Which, if it would shew anything, would shew only that there is no such thing as a free act. It drives the exercise of freedom back *in infinitum;* and that is to drive it out of the world.

And besides all this, there is a delusion, and a latent gross contradiction in the affair another way; inasmuch as in explaining how, or in what respect the will is free with regard to a particular act of volition, 'tis said, that its liberty consists in a power to determine to suspend *that act,* which places liberty not in that act of volition which the inquiry is about, but altogether in another antecedent act. Which contradicts the thing supposed in both the question and answer. The question is, wherein consists the mind's liberty *in any particular act* of volition? And the answer, in pretending to shew wherein lies the mind's liberty *in that act,* in effect says, it don't lie in that act at all, but in another, viz. a volition *to suspend that act.* And therefore the answer is both contradictory, and altogether impertinent and beside the purpose. For it don't shew wherein the liberty of the will consists in the act in question; instead of that, it supposes it don't consist in that act at all, but in another distinct from it, even a volition to suspend that act, and take time to consider of it. And no account is pretended to be given wherein the mind is free with respect to that act, wherein this answer supposes the liberty of the mind indeed consists, viz. the act of suspension, or of determining the suspension.

On the whole, 'tis exceeding manifest, that the liberty of the mind does not consist in indifference, and that indifference is not essential or necessary to it, or at all belonging to it, as the Arminians suppose; that opinion being full of nothing but absurity and self-contradiction.

SECTION 8. CONCERNING THE SUPPOSED LIBERTY OF THE WILL, AS OPPOSITE TO ALL NECESSITY

'TIS A THING chiefly insisted on by Arminians, in this controversy, as a thing most important and essential in human liberty, that volitions, or the acts of the will, are *contingent* events; understanding contingence as opposite, not only to constraint, but to all necessity. Therefore I would particularly consider this matter. And

1. I would inquire, whether there is, or can be any such thing, as a volition which is contingent in such a sense, as not only to come to pass without any necessity of constraint or coaction,[1] but also without a *necessity of consequence*,[2] or an infallible connection with anything foregoing.

2. Whether, if it were so, this would at all help the cause of liberty.

I. I would consider whether volition is a thing that e'er does, or can come to pass, in this manner, contingently.

And here it must be remembered, that it has been already shown, that nothing can ever come to pass without a cause, or reason why it exists in this manner rather than another; and the evidence of this has been particularly applied to the acts of the will. Now if this be so, it will demonstrably follow, that the acts of the will are never contingent, or without necessity, in the sense spoken of; inasmuch as those things which have a cause, or reason of their existence, must be connected with their cause. This appears by the following considerations.

1. For an event to have a cause and ground of its existence, and yet not to be connected with its cause, is an inconsistence. For if the event ben't connected with the cause, it is not dependent on the cause; its existence is as it were loose from its influence, and may at-

1. [JE uses the word "coaction" to mean external compulsion. See above, Intro., Pt. 3. Whitby explains the meaning of the term then current "by the Example of a Dog tied to a Cart's Tail; he may follow without being drawn, but if he doth not, he must follow by being drawn" (Dis. IV, ch. 4, no. 2; p. 355).]
2. [See JE's discussion of three forms of "philosophical necessity," Pt. I, Sec. 3.]

tend it, or may not; it being a mere contingence, whether it follows or attends the influence of the cause, or not: and that is the same thing as not to be dependent on it. And to say, the event is not dependent on its cause, is absurd: 'tis the same thing as to say, it is not its cause, nor the event the effect of it: for dependence on the influence of a cause, is the very notion of an effect. If there be no such relation between one thing and another, consisting in the connection and dependence of one thing on the influence of another, then it is certain there is no such relation between them as is signified by the terms "cause" and "effect." So far as an event is dependent on a cause, and connected with it, so much causality is there in the case, and no more. The cause does, or brings to pass no more in any event, than is dependent on it. If we say, the connection and dependence is not total, but partial, and that the effect, though it has some connection and dependence, yet is not entirely dependent on it; that is the same thing as to say, that not all that is in the event is an effect of that cause, but that only part of it arises from thence, and part some other way.

2. If there are some events which are not necessarily connected with their causes, then it will follow, that there are some things which come to pass without any cause, contrary to the supposition. For if there be any event which was not necessarily connected with the influence of the cause under such circumstances, then it was contingent whether it would attend or follow the influence of the cause, or no; it might have followed, and it might not, when the cause was the same, its influence the same, and under the same circumstances. And if so, why did it follow, rather than not follow? There is no cause or reason of this. Therefore here is something without any cause or reason why it is, viz. the following of the effect on the influence of the cause, with which it was not necessarily connected. If there be [not] [3] a necessary connection of the effect on anything antecedent, then we may suppose that sometimes the event will follow the cause, and sometimes not, when the cause is the same, and in every respect in the same state and circumstances. And what can be the cause and reason of this strange phenomenon, even this diversity, that in one instance, the effect should follow, in another not? 'Tis evident by the supposition, that this is wholly without any cause or ground. Here is something in the present manner of the existence of things, and state of the world, that is absolutely without a cause. Which is contrary to the supposition, and contrary to what has been before demonstrated.

3. [Here I follow JE, Jr., and correct the text.]

3. To suppose there are some events which have a cause and ground of their existence, that yet are not necessarily connected with their cause, is to suppose that they have a cause which is not their cause. Thus, if the effect be not necessarily connected with the cause, with its influence, and influential circumstances; then, as I observed before, 'tis a thing possible and supposable, that the cause may sometimes exert the same influence, under the same circumstances, and yet the effect not follow. And if this actually happens in any instance, this instance is a proof, in fact, that the influence of the cause is not sufficient to produce the effect. For if it had been sufficient, it would have done it. And yet, by the supposition, in another instance, the same cause, with perfectly the same influence, and when all circumstances which have any influence, are the same, it *was followed* with the effect. By which it is manifest, that the effect in this last instance was not owing to the influence of the cause, but must come to pass some other way. For it was proved before, that the influence of the cause was not sufficient to produce the effect. And if it was not sufficient to produce it, then the production of it could not be owing to that influence, but must be owing to something else, or owing to nothing. And if the effect be not owing to the influence of the cause, then it is not the cause. Which brings us to the contradiction, of a cause, and no cause, that which is the ground and reason of the existence of a thing, and at the same time is not the ground and reason of its existence, nor is sufficient to be so.

If the matter be not already so plain as to render any further reasoning upon it impertinent, I would say, that that which seems to be the cause in the supposed case, can be no cause; its power and influence having, on a full trial, proved insufficient to produce such an effect: and if it be not sufficient to produce it, then it don't produce it. To say otherwise, is to say, there is power to do that which there is not power to do. If there be in a cause sufficient power exerted, and in circumstances sufficient to produce an effect, and so the effect be actually produced at *one time;* these things all concurring, will produce the effect at *all times.* And so we may turn it the other way; that which proves not sufficient at one time, cannot be sufficient at another, with precisely the same influential circumstances. And therefore if the effect follows, it is not owing to that cause; unless the different time be a circumstance which has influence: but that is contrary to the supposition; for 'tis supposed that all circumstances that have influence, are the same. And besides, this would be to suppose the time to be the cause; which is contrary to the supposition of the other thing's being the cause. But if merely diversity of time has no influence, then 'tis evident that it is as much of an absurdity to say, the cause was sufficient to produce the effect at one time, and not at another; as to say, that it is sufficient to produce the effect at a certain time, and yet not sufficient to produce the same effect at that same time.

On the whole, it is clearly manifest, that every effect has a necessary connection with its cause, or with that which is the true ground and reason of its existence. And therefore if there be no event without a cause, as was proved before, then no event whatsoever is contingent in the manner that Arminians suppose the free acts of the will to be contingent.

SECTION 9. OF THE CONNECTION OF THE ACTS OF THE WILL WITH THE DICTATES OF THE UNDERSTANDING

IT IS MANIFEST, that the acts of the will are none of them contingent in such a sense as to be without all necessity, or so as not to be necessary with a necessity of consequence and connection; because every act of the will is some way connected with the understanding, and is as the greatest apparent good is, in the manner which has already been explained; namely, that the soul always wills or chooses that which, in the present view of the mind, considered in the whole of that view, and all that belongs to it, appears most agreeable. Because, as was observed before, nothing is more evident than that, when men act voluntarily, and do what they please, then they do what appears most agreeable to them; and to say otherwise, would be as much as to affirm, that men don't choose what appears to suit them best, or what seems most pleasing to them; or that they don't choose what they prefer. Which brings the matter to a contradiction.

As 'tis very evident in itself, that the acts of the will have some connection with the dictates or views of the understanding, so this is allowed by some of the chief of the Arminian writers: particularly by Dr. Whitby and Dr. Samuel Clarke. Dr. Turnbull, though a great enemy to the doctrine of necessity, allows the same thing. In his *Christian Philosophy* (p. 196) he with much approbation cites another philosopher, as of the same mind, in these words:

> No man (says an excellent philosopher) sets himself about anything, but upon some view or other, which serves him for a reason for what he does; and whatsoever faculties he employs, the understanding, with such light as it has, well or ill informed, constantly leads; and by that light, true or false, all her operative powers are directed. The will itself, how absolute and incontrollable soever it may be thought, never fails in its obedience to the dictates of the understanding. Temples have their sacred images; and we

see what influence they have always had over a great part of mankind; but in truth, the ideas and images in men's minds are the invisible powers that constantly govern them; and to these they all pay universally a ready submission.[1]

But whether this be in a just consistence with themselves, and their own notions of liberty, I desire may now be impartially considered.

Dr. Whitby plainly supposes, that the acts and determinations of the will always follow the understanding's apprehension or view of the greatest good to be obtained, or evil to be avoided; or in other words, that the determinations of the will constantly and infallibly follow these two things in the understanding: 1. The degree of good to be obtained, and evil to be avoided, proposed to the understanding, and apprehended, viewed, and taken notice of by it. 2. The degree of the understanding's view, notice or apprehension of that good or evil; which is increased by attention and consideration. That this is an opinion he is exceeding peremptory in (as he is in every opinion which he maintains in his controversy with the Calvinists), with disdain of the contrary opinion, as absurd and self-contradictory, will appear by the following words of his, in his *Discourse on the Five Points.*

> Now, 'tis certain, that what naturally makes the understanding to perceive, is evidence proposed, and apprehended, considered or adverted to: for nothing else can be requisite to make us come to the knowledge of the truth. . . . Again, what makes the will choose, is something approved by the understanding; and consequently appearing to the soul as good. And whatsoever it refuseth,

1. [George Turnbull, *The Principles of Moral and Christian Philosophy* (2 vols. London, 1740), 2 (containing *Christian Philosophy*), 196. Turnbull goes on to remark following the quotation that " 'tis obvious from what hath been said, that nothing can be more false than to assert that men are not accountable for their understanding; for if men are not accountable for their understanding, they cannot be accountable for their actions: if it is not in their power to have sufficient light to guide them, they cannot have it in their power to direct themselves aright. . . . It is by repeated acts that reason can alone acquire or preserve its rightful power and authority of governing. This is the consequence of the law of habits, which renders us capable of improvement to perfection. So that without such a law man would not be a free agent" (pp. 195, 197). JE gives a more adequate account of Turnbull's philosophy in citations to his works that are to be found near the end of the present *Inquiry*.]

is something represented by the understanding, and so appearing to the will, as evil. Whence all that God requires of us is, and can be only this; to refuse the evil, and choose the good. Wherefore, to say that evidence proposed, apprehended and considered, is not sufficient to make the understanding approve; or that the greatest good proposed, the greatest evil threatened, when equally believed and reflected on, is not sufficient to engage the will to choose the good and refuse the evil, is in effect to say, *that which alone doth move the will to choose or to refuse,* is not sufficient to engage it so to do; which being contradictory to itself, must of necessity be false. Be it then so, that we naturally have an aversation to the truths proposed to us in the gospel; that only can make us indisposed to attend to them, but cannot hinder our conviction, when we do apprehend them, and attend to them. . . . Be it, that there is in us also a renitency to the good we are to choose; that only can indispose us to believe it is, and to approve it as our chiefest good. Be it, that we are prone to the evil that we should decline; that only can render it the more difficult for us to believe it is the worst of evils. But yet, *what we do really believe to be our chiefest good, will still be chosen; and what we apprehend to be the worst of evils, will, whilst we do continue under that conviction, be refused by us.* It therefore can be only requisite, in order to these ends, that the good Spirit should so illuminate our understandings, that we attending to, and considering what lies before us, should apprehend, and be convinced of our duty; and that the blessings of the gospel should be so propounded to us, as that we may discern them to be our chiefest good; and the miseries it threateneth, so as we may be convinced they are the worst of evils; that we may choose the one, and refuse the other.[2]

Here let it be observed, how plainly and peremptorily it is asserted, that the greatest good proposed, and the greatest evil threatened, when equally believed and reflected on, is sufficient to engage the will to choose the good, and refuse the evil, and is that alone which doth move the will to choose or to refuse; and that it is contradictory to itself, to suppose otherwise; and therefore must of necessity be false; and then what we do really believe to be our chiefest good will still be chosen, and what we apprehend to be the worst of evils, will, whilst we continue under that conviction, be refused by

2. Whitby, *Discourse on the Five Points,* pp. 211, 212, 213 (Dis. III, ch. 1).

us. Nothing could have been said more to the purpose, fully to signify and declare, that the determinations of the will must evermore follow the illumination, conviction and notice of the understanding, with regard to the greatest good and evil proposed, reckoning both the degree of good and evil understood, and the degree of understanding, notice and conviction of that proposed good and evil; and that it is thus necessarily, and can be otherwise in no instance: because it is asserted, that it implies a contradiction, to suppose it ever to be otherwise.

I am sensible, the Doctor's aim in these assertions is against the Calvinists; to shew, in opposition to them, that there is no need of any physical operation of the Spirit of God on the will, to change and determine that to a good choice, but that God's operation and assistance is only moral, suggesting ideas to the understanding; which he supposes to be enough, if those ideas are attended to, infallibly to obtain the end. But whatever his design was, nothing can more directly and fully prove, that every determination of the will, in choosing and refusing, is necessary; directly contrary to his own notion of the liberty of the will. For if the determination of the will, evermore, in this manner, follows the light, conviction and view of the understanding, concerning the greatest good and evil, and this be that alone which moves the will, and it be a contradiction to suppose otherwise; then it is *necessarily* so, the will necessarily follows this light or view of the understanding, not only in some of its acts, but in every act of choosing and refusing. So that the will don't determine itself in any one of its own acts; but all its acts, every act of choice and refusal, depends on, and is necessarily connected with some antecedent cause; which cause is not the will itself, nor any act of its own, nor anything pertaining to that faculty, but something belonging to another faculty, whose acts go before the will, in all its acts, and govern and determine them every one.

Here, if it should be replied, that although it be true, that according to the Doctor, the final determination of the will always depends upon, and is infallibly connected with the understanding's conviction, and notice of the greatest good; yet the acts of the will are not necessary; because that conviction and notice of the understanding is first dependent on a preceding act of the will, in determining to attend to, and take notice of the evidence exhibited; by which means the mind obtains that degree of conviction which is sufficient and effectual to determine the consequent and ultimate choice of the will; and that the will with regard to that preceding act, whereby it determines whether to attend or no, is not necessary; and that in this, the liberty of the will consists, that when God holds forth sufficient objective light, the will is at liberty whether to command the attention of the mind to it—

Nothing can be more weak and inconsiderate than such a reply as this. For that preceding act of the will, in determining to attend and consider, still is an act of the will (it is so to be sure, if the liberty of the will consists in it, as is supposed); and if it be an act of the will, it is an act of choice or refusal. And therefore, if what the Doctor asserts be true, it is determined by some antecedent light in the understanding concerning the greatest apparent good or evil. For he asserts, it is that light "which alone doth move the will to choose or refuse." And therefore the will must be moved by that in choosing to attend to the objective light offered, in order to another consequent act of choice: so that this act is no less necessary than the other. And if we suppose another act of the will, still preceding both these mentioned, to determine both, still that also must be an act of the will, and an act of choice; and so must, by the same principles, be infallibly determined by some certain degree of light in the understanding concerning the greatest good. And let us suppose as many acts of the will, one preceding another, as we please, yet they are everyone of them necessarily determined by a certain degree of light in the understanding, concerning the greatest and most eligible good in that case; and so, not one of them free according to Dr. Whitby's notion of freedom. And if it be said, the reason why men don't attend to light held forth, is because of ill habits contracted by evil acts committed before, whereby their minds are indisposed to attend to, and consider of the truth held forth to them by God, the difficulty is not at all avoided: still the question returns, what determined the will in those preceding evil acts? It must, by Dr. Whitby's principles, still be the view of the understanding concerning the greatest good and evil. If this view of the understanding be "that alone which doth move the will to choose or refuse," as the Doctor asserts, then every act of choice or refusal, from a man's first existence, is moved and determined by this view; and this view of the understanding exciting and governing the act, must be before the act: and therefore the will is necessarily determined, in everyone of its acts, from a man's first existence, by a cause beside the will, and a cause that don't proceed from, or depend on any act of the will at all. Which at once utterly abolishes the Doctor's whole scheme of liberty of will; and he, at one stroke, has cut the sinews of all his arguments from the goodness, righteousness, faithfulness and sincerity of God, in his commands, promises, threatenings, calls, invitations, expostulations; which he makes use of, under the heads of reprobation, election, universal redemption, sufficient and effectual grace, and the freedom of the will of man; [3] and has enervated and made vain all those exclamations against the doctrine of the Calvinists, as charging God with manifest unrighteousness, unfaithfulness, hypocrisy, fallaciousness, and cruelty; which he has over, and over, and over again, numberless times in his book.

Dr. Samuel Clarke, in his *Demonstration of the Being and Attributes of God,*[4] to evade the argument to prove the necessity of volition, from its necessary connection with the last dictate of the understanding, supposes the latter *not to be diverse from* the act of the will itself. But if it be so, it will not alter the case as to the evidence of the necessity of the act of the will. If the dictate of the understanding be the very same with the determination of the will or choice, as Dr. Clarke supposes, then this determination is no *fruit* or *effect* of choice: and if so, no liberty of choice has any hand in it: as to volition or choice, it is necessary; that is, choice can't prevent it. If the last dictate of the understanding be the same with the determination of volition itself, then the existence of that determination must be necessary as to volition; inasmuch as volition can have no opportunity to determine whether it shall exist or no, it having existence already before volition has opportunity to determine anything. It is itself the very rise and existence of volition. But a thing, after it exists, has no opportunity to determine as to its own existence; it is too late for that.

If liberty consists in that which Arminians suppose, viz. in the will's determining its own acts, having free opportunity, and being without all necessity; this is the same as to say, that liberty consists in the soul's having power and opportunity to have what determinations of the will it pleases or chooses. And if the determinations of the will, and the last dictates of the understanding be the same thing, then liberty consists in the mind's having power to have what dictates of the understanding it pleases, having opportunity to choose its own dictates of understanding. But this is absurd; for it is to make the

3. [See Intro., Pt. 5, no. 8.]
4. Sixth ed. (London, 1725), p. 93.

determination of choice prior to the dictate of understanding, and the ground of it; which can't consist with the dictate of understanding's being the determination of choice itself.

Here is no way to do in this case, but only to recur to the old absurdity, of one determination before another, and the cause of it; and another before that, determining that; and so on *in infinitum*. If the last dictate of the understanding be the determination of the will itself, and the soul be free with regard to that dictate, in the Arminian notion of freedom; then the soul, before that dictate of its understanding exists, voluntarily and according to its own choice determines, in every case, what that dictate of the understanding shall be; otherwise that dictate, as to the will, is necessary; and the acts determined by it, must also be necessary. So that here is a determination of the mind prior to that dictate of the understanding, an act of choice going before it, choosing and determining what that dictate of the understanding shall be: and this preceding act of choice, being a free act of will, must also be the same with another last dictate of the understanding: and if the mind also be free in that dictate of understanding, that must be determined still by another; and so on forever.

Besides, if the dictate of the understanding, and determination of the will be the same, this confounds the understanding and will, and makes them the same. Whether they be the same or no, I will not now dispute; but only would observe, that if it be so, and the Arminian notion of [liberty be just, then all] [5] liberty consists in a self-determining power in the understanding, free of all necessity; being independent, undetermined by anything prior to its own acts and determinations; and the more the understanding is thus independent, and sovereign over its own determinations, the more free. By this therefore the freedom of the soul, as a moral agent, must consist in the independence of the understanding on any evidence or appearance of things, or anything whatsoever that stands forth to the view of the mind, prior to the understanding's determination. And what a sort of liberty is this! consisting in an ability, freedom and easiness of judging, either according to evidence, or against it; having a sovereign command over itself at all times, to judge, either agreeably or disagreeably to what is plainly exhibited to its own view. Certainly, 'tis no liberty that renders persons the proper subjects of persuasive reasoning, arguments, expostulations, and suchlike moral

5. [Corrected from the *printed* list of errata.]

means and inducements. The use of which with mankind, is a main argument of the Arminians, to defend their notion of liberty without all necessity. For according to this, the more free men are, the less they are under the government of such means, less subject to the power of evidence and reason, and more independent on their influence, in their determinations.

And whether the understanding and will are the same or no, as Dr. Clarke seems to suppose, yet in order to maintain the Arminian notion of liberty without necessity, the free will is not determined by the understanding, nor necessarily connected with the understanding; and the further from such connection, the greater the freedom. And when the liberty is full and complete, the determinations of the will have no connection at all with the dictates of the understanding. And if so, in vain are all applications to the understanding, in order to induce to any free virtuous act; and so in vain are all instructions, counsels, invitations, expostulations, and all arguments and persuasives whatsoever: for these are but applications to the understanding, and a clear and lively exhibition of the objects of choice to the mind's view. But if, after all, the will must be self-determined, and independent on the understanding, to what purpose are things thus represented to the understanding, in order to determine the choice?

SECTION 10. VOLITION NECESSARILY CONNECTED WITH THE INFLUENCE OF MOTIVES; WITH PARTICULAR OBSERVATIONS ON THE GREAT INCONSISTENCE OF MR. CHUBB'S ASSERTIONS AND REASONINGS, ABOUT THE FREEDOM OF THE WILL

THAT every act of the will has some cause, and consequently (by what has been already proved) has a necessary connection with its cause, and so is necessary by a necessity of connection and consequence, is evident by this, that every act of the will whatsoever, is excited by some motive: which is manifest, because, if the will or mind, in willing and choosing after the manner that it does, is excited so to do by no motive or inducement, then it has no end which it proposes to itself, or pursues in so doing; it aims at nothing, and seeks nothing. And if it seeks nothing, then it don't go after anything, or exert any inclination or preference towards anything. Which brings the matter to a contradiction; because for the mind to will something, and for it to go after something by an act of preference and inclination, are the same thing.

But if every act of the will is excited by a motive, then that motive is the cause of the act of the will. If the acts of the will are excited by motives, then motives are the causes of their being excited; or, which is the same thing, the cause of their being put forth into act and existence. And if so, the existence of the acts of the will is properly the effect of their motives. Motives do nothing as motives or inducements, but by their influence; and so much as is done by their influence, is the effect of them. For that is the notion of an effect, something that is brought to pass by the influence of another thing.

And if volitions are properly the effects of their motives, then they are necessarily connected with their motives. Every effect and event being, as was proved before, necessarily connected with that which is the proper ground and reason of its existence. Thus it is manifest, that volition is necessary, and is not from any self-determining power in the will: the volition which is caused by previous motive and inducement, is not caused by the will exercising a sovereign power over itself, to determine, cause and excite volitions in itself. This is not consistent with the will's acting in a state of indifference and equilibrium, to determine itself to a preference; for the way in which motives operate, is by biasing the will, and giving it a certain inclination or preponderation one way.

Here it may be proper to observe, that Mr. Chubb, in his collection of *Tracts on Various Subjects*,[1] has advanced a scheme of liberty, which is greatly divided against itself, and thoroughly subversive of itself; and that many ways.

I. He is abundant in asserting, that the will, in all its acts, is influenced by motive and excitement; and that this is the previous ground and reason of all its acts, and that it is never otherwise in any instance. He says (p. 262), "No action can take place without some motive to excite it." And in p. 263: "Volition cannot take place without some previous reason or motive to induce it." And in p. 310: "Action would not take place without some reason or motive to induce it; it being absurd to suppose, that the active faculty would be exerted without some previous reason to dispose the mind to action."[2] So also p. 257. And he speaks of these things as what we may be absolutely certain of, and which are the foundation, the only foundation we have of a certainty of the moral perfections of God (pp. 252, 253, 254, 255, 261, 262, 263, 264).

And yet at the same time, by his scheme, the influence of motives upon us to excite to action, and to be actually a ground of volition, is *consequent* on the volition or choice of the mind. For he very greatly insists upon it, that in all free actions, before the mind is the subject of those volitions which motives excite, it chooses to be so. It chooses whether it will comply with the motive, which presents itself in view, or not; and when various motives are presented, it chooses which it will yield to, and which it will reject. So p. 256: "Every man has power to act, or to refrain from acting agreeably with, or contrary to, any motive that presents." P. 257: "Every man is at liberty to act, or refrain from acting agreeably with, or contrary to, what each of these motives, considered singly, would excite him to. . . . Man has power, and is as much at liberty to reject the mo-

1. [Thomas Chubb, *A Collection of Tracts on Various Subjects*, London, 1730. See above, Intro., Pt. 5, no. 2. For a key to JE's page citations of Chubb's treatises, see above, p. 73 n.]

2. [See above, Intro., Pt. 5, no. 3.]

tive that does prevail, as he has power, and is at liberty to reject those motives that do not." And so pp. 310, 311: "In order to constitute a moral agent, it is necessary, that he should have power to act, or to refrain from acting, upon such moral motives as he pleases." And to the like purpose in many other places. According to these things, the will acts first, and chooses or refuses to comply with the motive that is presented, before it falls under its prevailing influence: and 'tis first determined by the mind's pleasure or choice, what motives it will be induced by, before it is induced by them.

Now, how can these things hang together? How can the mind first act, and by its act of volition and choice determine what motives shall be the ground and reason of its volition and choice? For this supposes, the choice is already made, before the motive has its effect; and that the volition is already exerted, before the motive prevails, so as actually to be the ground of the volition; and makes the prevailing of the motive, the consequence of the volition, which yet it is the ground of. If the mind has already chosen to comply with a motive, and to yield to its excitement, it don't need to yield to it after this: for the thing is effected already, that the motive would excite to, and the will is beforehand with the excitement; and the excitement comes in too late, and is needless and in vain afterwards. If the mind has already chosen to yield to a motive which invites to a thing, that implies and in fact is a choosing the thing invited to; and the very act of choice is before the influence of the motive which induces, and is the ground of the choice; the son is beforehand with the father that begets him: the choice is supposed to be the ground of that influence of the motive, which very influence is supposed to be the ground of the choice. And so *vice versa,* the choice is supposed to be the consequence of the influence of the motive, which influence of the motive is the consequence of that very choice.

And besides, if the will acts first towards the motive before it falls under its influence, and the prevailing of the motive upon it to induce it to act and choose, be the fruit and consequence of its act and choice, then how is the motive "a *previous* ground and reason of the act and choice," so that "in the nature of the things, volition cannot take place without some *previous* reason and motive to induce it"; and that this act is consequent upon, and follows the motive? Which things Mr. Chubb often asserts, as of certain and undoubted truth. So that the very same motive is both *previous* and *consequent,* both before and after, both the ground and fruit of the very same thing!

II. Agreeable to the forementioned inconsistent notion of the will's first acting towards the motive, choosing whether it will comply with it, in order to its becoming a ground of the will's acting, before any act of volition can take place, Mr. Chubb frequently calls motives and excitements to the action of the will, "the passive ground or reason of that action." [3] Which is a remarkable phrase; than which I presume there is none more unintelligible, and void of distinct and consistent meaning, in all the writings of Duns Scotus, or Thomas Aquinas. When he represents the motive to action or volition as passive, he must mean—passive in that affair, or passive with respect to that action which he speaks of; otherwise it is nothing to his purpose, or relating to the design of his argument: he must mean (if that can be called a meaning) that the motive to volition is first acted *upon* or *towards* by the volition, choosing to yield to it, making it a ground of action, or determining to fetch its influence from thence; and so to make it a previous ground of its own excitation and existence. Which is the same absurdity, as if one should say, that the soul of man, or any other thing should, previous to its existing, choose what cause it would come into existence by, and should act upon its cause, to fetch influence from thence, to bring it into being; and so its cause should be a passive ground of its existence!

Mr. Chubb does very plainly suppose motive or excitement to be the ground of the being of volition. He speaks of it as the ground or reason of the *exertion* of an act of the will (pp. 391 and 392); [4] and expressly says, that "volition cannot *take place* without some previous ground or motive to induce it" (p. 263). [5] And he speaks of the act as *from* the motive, and *from the influence* of the motive (p. 352); and from the influence that the motive has on the man, for the *production* of an action (p. 317). Certainly, there is no need of multiplying words about this; 'tis easily judged, whether motive can be the ground of volition's being exerted and taking place, so that the very production of it is from the influence of the motive, and yet the motive, before it becomes the ground of the volition, is passive, or acted upon by the volition. But this I will say, that a man who in-

3. [*Tracts,* pp. 257, 258, 263, 264.]

4. [See above, Intro., Pt. 5, no. 4, esp. p. 77.]

5. [JE's reference here to p. 363 is in error. So also is the immediately following reference to p. 352, which, however, has not been changed because it is impossible to determine the exact location JE had in mind for a view Chubb expresses many times.]

sists so much on clearness of meaning in others, and is so much in blaming their confusion and inconsistence, ought, if he was able, to have explained his meaning in this phrase of "passive ground of action," so as to show it not to be confused and inconsistent.

If any should suppose, that Mr. Chubb, when he speaks of motive as a "passive ground of action," don't mean passive with regard to that volition which it is the ground of, but some other antecedent volition (though his purpose and argument, and whole discourse, will by no means allow of such a supposition) yet it would not help the matter in the least. For (1) if we suppose there to be an act of volition or choice, by which the soul chooses to yield to the invitation of a motive to another volition, by which the soul chooses something else; both these supposed volitions are in effect the very same. A volition, or choosing to yield to the force of a motive inviting to choose something, comes to just the same thing as choosing the thing which the motive invites to, as I observed before. So that here can be no room to help the matter, by a distinction of two volitions. (2) If the motive be passive with respect, not to the same volition that the motive excites to, but one truly distinct and prior; yet, by Mr. Chubb, that prior volition can't take place, without a motive or excitement, as a "previous ground" of its existence. For he insists, that "it is absurd to suppose any volition should take place without some previous motive to induce it." So that at last it comes to just the same absurdity: for if *every* volition must have a previous motive, then the very *first* in the whole series must be excited by a previous motive; and yet the motive to that first volition is passive; but can't be passive with regard to another antecedent volition, because, by the supposition, it is the very first: therefore if it be passive with respect to any volition, it must be so with regard to that very volition that it is the ground of, and that is excited by it.

III. Though Mr. Chubb asserts, as above, that every volition has some motive, and that, "in the nature of the thing, no volition can take place without some motive to induce it"; yet he asserts, that volition does not always follow the strongest motive; or in other words, is not governed by any superior strength of the motive that is followed, beyond motives to the contrary, previous to the volition itself. His own words, p. 258, are as follows: "Though with regard to physical causes, that which is strongest always prevails, yet it is otherwise with regard to moral causes. Of these, sometimes the stronger, sometimes the weaker, prevails. And the ground of this difference is evident, namely, that what we call moral causes, strictly speaking, are no causes at all, but barely passive reasons of, or excitements to the action, or to the refraining from acting: which excitements we have power, or are at liberty to comply with or reject, as I have shewed above." And so throughout the paragraph, he, in a variety of phrases, insists, that the will is not always determined by the strongest motive, unless by strongest we preposterously mean actually prevailing in the event; [6] which is not in the motive, but in the will; but that the will is not always determined by the motive which is strongest, by any strength previous to the volition itself. And he elsewhere does abundantly assert, that the will is determined by no superior strength or advantage that motives have, from any constitution or state of things, or any circumstances whatsoever, previous to the actual determination of the will. And indeed his whole discourse on human liberty implies it, his whole scheme is founded upon it.

But these things cannot stand together. There is such a thing as a diversity of strength in motives to choice, previous to the choice itself. Mr. Chubb himself supposes, that they do "previously invite," "induce," "excite" and "dispose the mind to action." This implies, that they have something in themselves that is *inviting,* some tendency to *induce* and *dispose* to volition, previous to volition itself. And if they have in themselves this nature and tendency, doubtless they have it in certain limited degrees, which are capable of diversity; and some have it in greater degrees, others in less; and they that have most of this tendency, considered with all their nature and circumstances, previous to volition, they are the strongest motives; and those that have least, are the weakest motives.

Now if volition sometimes don't follow the motive which is strongest, or has most previous tendency or advantage, all things considered, to induce or excite it, but follows the weakest, or that which as it stands previously in the mind's view, has least tendency to induce it; herein the will apparently acts wholly without motive, without any previous reason to dispose the mind to it, contrary to what the same author supposes. The act wherein the will must proceed without previous motive to induce it, is the act of preferring the weakest motive. For how absurd is it to say, the mind sees previous reason in the motive, to prefer that motive before the other; and at the same time to suppose, that there is nothing in the motive, in its nature,

6. [I.e. unless by the motive prevailing because it was strongest, we mean to say "that it prevailed, because it *did prevail*" (Chubb, p. 258).]

state, or any circumstances of it whatsoever, as it stands in the previous view of the mind, that gives it any preference; but on the contrary, the other motive that stands in competition with it, in all these respects, has most belonging to it, that is inviting and moving, and has most of a tendency to choice and preference? This is certainly as much as to say, there is previous ground and reason in the motive for the act of preference, and yet no previous reason for it. By the supposition, as to all that is in the two rival motives which tends to preference, previous to the act of preference, it is not in that which is preferred, but wholly in the other: because appearing superior strength, and all appearing preferableness is in that; and yet Mr. Chubb supposes, that the act of preference is from "previous ground and reason" in the motive which is preferred. But are these things consistent? Can there be previous ground in a thing for an event that takes place, and yet no previous tendency in it to that event? If one thing follows another, without any previous tendency to its following, then I should think it very plain, that it follows it without any manner of previous reason why it should follow.[7]

Yea, in this case, Mr. Chubb supposes, that the event follows an antecedent or a previous thing, as the ground of its existence, not only that has *no tendency* to it, but *a contrary tendency*. The event is the preference which the mind gives to that motive which is weaker, as it stands in the previous view of the mind; the immediate antecedent is the view the mind has of the two rival motives conjunctly; in which previous view of the mind, all the preferableness, or previous tendency to preference, is supposed to be on the other side, or in the contrary motive; and all the unworthiness of preference, and so previous tendency to comparative neglect, rejection or undervaluing, is on that side which is preferred: and yet in this view of the mind is supposed to be the "previous ground or reason" of this act of preference, "exciting it, and disposing the mind to it." Which, I leave the reader to judge, whether it be absurd or not. If it be not, then it is not absurd to say, that the previous tendency of an antecedent to a consequent, is the ground and reason why that consequent does not follow; and the want of a previous tendency to an event, yea, a tendency to the contrary, is the true ground and reason why that event does follow.

An act of choice or preference is a comparative act, wherein the mind acts with reference to two or more things that are compared,

7. [See above, Intro., Pt. 5, nos. 3, 4.]

and stand in competition in the mind's view. If the mind, in this comparative act, prefers that which appears inferior in the comparison, then the mind herein acts absolutely without motive, or inducement, or any temptation whatsoever. Thus,[8] if a hungry man has the offer of two sorts of food, both which he finds an appetite to, but has a stronger appetite to one than the other; and there be no circumstances or excitements whatsoever in the case to induce him to take either one or the other, but merely his appetite: if in the choice he makes between them, he chooses that which he has least appetite to, and refuses that to which he has the strongest appetite, this is a choice made absolutely without previous motive, excitement, reason or temptation, as much as if he were perfectly without all appetite to either: because his volition in this case is a comparative act, attending and following a comparative view of the food which he chooses, viewing it as related to, and compared with the other sort of food, in which view his preference has absolutely no previous ground, yea, is against all previous ground and motive. And if there be any principle in man from whence an act of choice may arise after this manner, from the same principle volition may arise wholly without motive on either side. If the mind in its volition can go beyond motive, then it can go without motive: for when it is beyond the motive, it is out of the reach of the motive, out of the limits of its influence, and so without motive. If volition goes beyond the strength and tendency of motive, and especially if it goes against its tendency, this demonstrates the independence of volition on [9] motive. And if so, no reason can be given for what Mr. Chubb so often asserts, even that "in the nature of things volition cannot take place without a motive to induce it."

If the most High should endow a balance with agency or activity of nature, in such a manner, that when unequal weights are put into the scales, its agency could enable it to cause that scale to descend which has the least weight, and so to raise the greater weight; this would clearly demonstrate, that the motion of the balance does not depend on weights in the scales, at least as much, as if the balance should move itself, when there is no weight in either scale. And the activity of the balance which is sufficient to move itself against the

---

8. [The 1754 ed. reads "Then." Corrected from the *printed* list of errata.]

9. [The 1754 ed. reads "or." JE means that if this hypothesis were true, it would prove that volition is independent *of* motive; or, as he says, *not* dependent *on* motive. Text corrected from the *printed* list of errata.]

greater weight, must certainly be more than sufficient to move it when there is no weight at all.

Mr. Chubb supposes, that the will can't stir at all without some motive; and also supposes, that if there be a motive to one thing, and none to the contrary, volition will infallibly follow that motive. This is virtually to suppose an entire dependence of the will on motives: if it were not wholly dependent on them, it could surely help itself a little without them, or help itself a little against a motive, without help from the strength and weight of a contrary motive. And yet his supposing that the will, when it has before it various opposite motives, can use them as it pleases, and choose its own influence from them, and neglect the strongest, and follow the weakest, supposes it to be wholly independent on motives.

It further appears, on Mr. Chubb's supposition, that volition must be without any previous ground in any motive, thus: if it be as he supposes, that the will is not determined by any previous superior strength of the motive, but determines and chooses its own motive, then, when the rival motives are exactly equal in strength and tendency to induce, in all respects, it may follow either; and may in such a case, sometimes follow one, sometimes the other. And if so, this diversity which appears between the acts of the will, is plainly without previous ground in either of the motives; for all that is previously in the motives, is supposed precisely and perfectly the same, without any diversity whatsoever. Now perfect identity, as to all that is previous in the antecedent, can't be the ground and reason of diversity in the consequent. Perfect identity in the ground can't be a reason why it is not followed with the same consequence. And therefore the source of this diversity of consequence must be sought for elsewhere.

And lastly, it may be observed, that however Mr. Chubb does much insist that no volition can take place without some motive to induce it, which previously disposes the mind to it; yet, as he also insists that the mind without reference to any previous superior strength of motives, picks and chooses for its motive to follow; he himself herein plainly supposes, that with regard to the mind's preference of one motive before another, it is not the motive that disposes the will, but the will disposes itself to follow the motive.[1]

IV. Mr. Chubb supposes necessity to be utterly inconsistent with *agency;* and that to suppose a being to be an agent in that which is

1. [See above, Intro., Pt. 5, no. 5.]

necessary, is a plain contradiction (p. 311). And throughout his discourses on the subject of liberty, he supposes, that necessity cannot consist with agency or freedom; and that to suppose otherwise, is to make liberty and necessity, action and passion, the same thing. And so he seems to suppose, that there is no action strictly speaking, but volition; and that as to the effects of volition in body or mind, in themselves considered, being necessary, they are said to be free, only as they are the effects of an act that is not necessary.[2]

And yet, according to him, volition itself is the *effect of volition;* yea, every act of free volition: and therefore every act of free volition must, by what has now been observed from him, be necessary. That every act of free volition is itself the effect of volition, is abundantly supposed by him. In p. 341, he says, "If a man is such a creature as I have above proved him to be, that is, if he has in him a power or liberty of doing either good or evil, and either of these is the subject of his own free choice, so that he might, *if he had pleased,* have *chosen* and done the contrary." Here he supposes, all that is good or evil in man is the effect of his choice; and so that his good or evil choice itself is the effect of his pleasure or choice, in these words, "he might if he had *pleased,* have *chosen* the contrary." So in p. 386: [3] "Though it be highly reasonable, that a man should always choose the greater good . . . yet he may, if he *please, choose* otherwise." Which is the same thing as if he had said, he may, if he *chooses, choose* otherwise. And then he goes on, "that is, he may, *if he pleases, choose* what is good for himself, etc." And again in the same page, "The will is not confined by the understanding to any particular sort of good, whether greater or less; but is at liberty to *choose* what kind of good *it pleases.*" If there be any meaning in these last words, the meaning must be this, that *the will is at liberty to choose what kind of good it chooses to choose;* supposing the act of choice itself determined by an antecedent choice. The liberty Mr. Chubb speaks of, is not only a man's having power to move his body agreeably to an antecedent act of choice, but to use or exert the faculties of his soul. Thus, in p. 379, speaking of the faculties of his mind, he says, "Man has power, and is at liberty to neglect these faculties, to use them aright, or to abuse

2. [They are thus said to be moral *actions*—"As to the word *free,* which is commonly added in this case, this term is wholly superfluous; because every agent is free . . . so far as he is an agent; a necessary agent being a plain contradiction" (Chubb, p. 311).]

3. [Corrected page reference.]

them, *as he pleases.*" And that he supposes an act of choice, or exercise of pleasure, properly distinct from, and antecedent to those acts thus chosen, directing, commanding and producing the chosen acts, and even the acts of choice themselves, is very plain in p. 283, "He can *command his actions;* and herein consists his liberty; he can give or deny himself that pleasure *as he pleases.*" And p. 377: "If the actions of men . . . are not the *produce of a free choice,* or election, but spring from a necessity of nature . . . he cannot in reason be the object of reward or punishment on their account. Whereas, if action in man, whether good or evil, is *the produce of will or free choice;* so that a man in either case, had it in his power, and was at liberty to have *chosen* the contrary, he is the proper object of reward or punishment, according as he *chooses* to behave himself." Here in these last words, he speaks of liberty of *choosing, according as he chooses.* So that the behavior which he speaks of as subject to his choice, is his *choosing* itself, as well as his external conduct consequent upon it. And therefore 'tis evident, he means not only external actions, but the acts of choice themselves, when he speaks of "all free actions, as the *produce* of free choice." And this is abundantly evident in what he says in pp. 372, and 373.

Now these things imply a twofold great absurdity and inconsistence.

1. To suppose, as Mr. Chubb plainly does, that every free act of choice is "commanded by," and is the "produce of free choice," is to suppose the first free act of choice belonging to the case, yea, the first free act of choice that ever man exerted, to be "the produce" of an antecedent act of choice. But I hope I need not labor at all to convince my readers, that 'tis an absurdity to say, the very *first* act is the produce of another act that went *before* it.

2. If it were both possible and real, as Mr. Chubb insists, that every free act of choice were the produce or the effect of a free act of choice; yet even then, according to his principles, no one act of choice would be free, but everyone necessary; because, every act of choice being the effect of a foregoing act, every act would be necessarily connected with that foregoing cause. For Mr. Chubb himself says (p. 389), "When the self-moving power is exerted, it becomes the necessary cause of its effects." [4] So that his notion of a free act, that is rewardable or punishable, is a heap of contradictions. It is a free act, and yet, by his own notion of freedom, is necessary; and there-

4. [See above, Intro., Pt. 5, no. 6.]

fore by him it is a contradiction, to suppose it to be free. According to him, every free act is the produce of a free act; so that there must be an infinite number of free acts in succession, without any beginning, in an agent that has a beginning. And therefore here is an infinite number of free acts, everyone of them free; and yet not any one of them free, but every act in the whole infinite chain a necessary effect. All the acts are rewardable or punishable, and yet the agent cannot, in reason, be the object of reward or punishment, on account of any one of these actions. He is active in them all, and passive in none; yet active in none, but passive in all, etc.

V. Mr. Chubb does most strenuously deny, that motives are "causes" of the acts of the will; or that the moving principle in man is "moved," or "caused to be exerted" by motives. His words (p. 388) are, "If the moving principle in man is *moved,* or *caused to be exerted,* by something external to man, which all motives are, then it would not be a self-moving principle, seeing it would be moved by a principle external to itself. And to say, that a self-moving principle is *moved,* or *caused to be exerted,* by a cause external to itself, is absurd and a contradiction, etc." And in the next page, 'tis particularly and largely insisted, that motives are causes in no case, that "they are merely passive in the production of action, and have no causality in the production of it . . . no causality, to be the cause of the exertion of the will."

Now I desire it may be considered, how this can possibly consist with what he says in other places. Let it be noted here,

1. Mr. Chubb abundantly speaks of motives as "excitements of the acts of the will"; and says, that "motives do excite volition, and induce it," and that they are necessary to this end; that "in the reason and nature of things, volition cannot take place without motives to excite it." But now if motives *excite* the will, they *move* it; and yet he says, 'tis absurd to say, the will is moved by motives. And again (if language is of any significance at all) if motives excite volition, then they are the cause of its being excited; and to cause volition to be excited, is to cause it to be put forth or exerted. Yea, Mr. Chubb says himself (p. 317), motive is necessary to the "exertion" of the active faculty. To excite, is positively to *do* something; and certainly that which does something, is the cause of the thing *done* by it. To create, is to cause to be created; to make, is to cause to be made; to kill, is to cause to be killed; to quicken, is to cause to be quickened;

and *to excite,* is *to cause to be excited.*[5] To excite, is to be a cause, in the most proper sense, not merely a negative occasion, but a ground of existence by positive influence. The notion of exciting, is exerting influence to cause the effect to arise or come forth into existence.

2. Mr. Chubb himself (p. 317) speaks of motives as the ground and reason of action by "influence," and by "prevailing influence." Now, what can be meant by a cause, but something that is the ground and reason of a thing by its influence, an influence that is *prevalent* and so effectual?

3. This author not only speaks of motives as the ground and reason of action, by prevailing influence; but expressly of their "influence as prevailing *for the production* of an action," in the same p. 317: which makes the inconsistency still more palpable and notorious. The *production* of an effect is certainly the *causing* of an effect; and productive influence is causal influence, if anything is; and that which has this influence prevalently, so as thereby to become the ground of another thing, is a cause of that thing, if there be any such thing as a cause. This influence, Mr. Chubb says, motives have to produce an action; and yet he says, 'tis absurd and a contradiction, to say they are causes.

4. In the same page, he once and again speaks of motives as "disposing" the agent to action, "by their influence." His words are these:

> As motive, which takes place in the understanding, and is the product of intelligence, is *necessary* to action, that is, to the *exertion* of the active faculty, because that faculty would not be exerted without some *previous reason* to *dispose* the mind to action; so from hence it plainly appears, that when a man is said to be *disposed* to one action rather than another, this properly signifies the *prevailing influence* that one motive has upon a man *for the production* of an action, or for the being at rest, before all other motives, for the production of the contrary. For as motive is the ground and reason of any action, so the motive that prevails, *disposes* the agent to the performance of that action.[6]

Now, if motives dispose the mind to action, then they *cause* the mind to be disposed; and to cause the mind to be disposed, is to cause it to be willing; and to cause it to be willing, is to cause it to will;

5. [See above, Intro., Pt. 5, no. 3.]
6. [See above, Intro., Pt. 5, no. 6, esp. p. 81.]

and that is the same thing as to be the cause of an act of the will. And yet this same Mr. Chubb holds it to be absurd, to suppose motive to be a cause of the act of the will.

And if we compare these things together, we have here again a whole heap of inconsistencies. "Motives are the previous ground and reason" of the acts of the will; yea, the "necessary" ground and reason of "their exertion, without which they will not be exerted, and cannot in the nature of things take place"; and they do "excite" these acts of the will, and do this by a "prevailing influence"; yea, "an influence which prevails for the production of the act" of the will, and for "the disposing of the mind to it": and yet 'tis "absurd," to suppose "motive to be a cause" of an act of the will, or that "a principle of will is moved or caused to be exerted by it," or that it has "any causality in the production of it, or any causality to be the cause of the exertion of the will."

A due consideration of these things which Mr. Chubb has advanced, the strange inconsistencies which the notion of liberty consisting in the will's power of self-determination void of all necessity, united with that dictate of common sense, that there can be no volition without a motive, drove him into, may be sufficient to convince us, that it is utterly impossible ever to make that notion of liberty consistent with the influence of motives in volition. And as it is in a manner self-evident, that there can be no act of will, choice or preference of the mind, without some motive or inducement, something in the mind's view, which it aims at, seeks, inclines to, and goes after; so 'tis most manifest, there is no such liberty in the universe as Arminians insist on; nor any such thing possible, or conceivable.

THAT the acts of the wills of moral agents are not contingent events, in that sense, as to be without all necessity, appears by God's certain foreknowledge of such events.

In handling this argument, I would in the first place prove, that God has a certain foreknowledge of the voluntary acts of moral agents; and secondly, show the consequence, or how it follows from hence, that the volitions of moral agents are not contingent, so as to be without necessity of connection and consequence.

First, I am to prove, that God has an absolute and certain foreknowledge of the free actions of moral agents.

One would think, it should be wholly needless to enter on such an argument with any that profess themselves Christians: but so it is; God's certain foreknowledge of the free acts of moral agents, is denied by some that pretend to believe the Scriptures to be the Word of God; and especially of late. I therefore shall consider the evidence of such a prescience in the most High, as fully as the designed limits of this essay will admit of; supposing myself herein to have to do with such as own the truth of the Bible.

Arg. I. My first argument shall be taken from God's prediction of such events. Here I would in the first place lay down these two things as axioms.

(1) If God don't foreknow, he can't foretell such events; that is, he can't peremptorily and certainly foretell them. If God has no more than an uncertain guess concerning events of this kind, then he can declare no more than an uncertain guess. Positively to foretell, is to profess to foreknow, or to declare positive foreknowledge.

(2) If God don't certainly foreknow the future volitions of moral agents, then neither can he certainly foreknow those events which are consequent and dependent on these volitions. The existence of the one depending on the existence of the other, the knowledge of

the existence of the one depends on the knowledge of the existence of the other; and the one can't be more certain than the other.

Therefore, how many, how great, and how extensive soever the consequences of the volitions of moral agents may be; though they should extend to an alteration of the state of things through the universe, and should be continued in a series of successive events to all eternity, and should in the progress of things branch forth into an infinite number of series, each of them going on in an endless line or chain of events; God must be as ignorant of all these consequences, as he is of the volition whence they first take their rise: all these events, and the whole state of things depending on them, how important, extensive and vast soever, must be hid from him.

These positions being such as I suppose none will deny, I now proceed to observe the following things.

1. Men's moral conduct and qualities, their virtues and vices, their wickedness and good practice, things rewardable and punishable, have often been foretold by God. Pharaoh's moral conduct, in refusing to obey God's command, in letting his people go, was foretold. God says to Moses (Ex. 3:19), "I am sure, that the king of Egypt will not let you go." Here God professes not only to guess at, but to know Pharaoh's future disobedience. In ch. 7:4, God says, "But Pharaoh shall not hearken unto you; that I may lay mine hand upon Egypt," etc. And ch. 9:30: Moses says to Pharaoh, "As for thee, and thy servants, I know that ye will not fear the Lord." See also ch. 9:9. The moral conduct of Josiah, by name, in his zealously exerting himself in opposition to idolatry, in particular acts of his, was foretold above three hundred years before he was born, and the prophecy sealed by a miracle, and renewed and confirmed by the words of a second prophet, as what surely would not fail (I Kgs. 13:1–6, 32). This prophecy was also in effect a prediction of the moral conduct of the people, in upholding their schismatical and idolatrous worship till that time, and the idolatry of those priests of the high places, which it is foretold Josiah should offer upon that altar of Bethel. Micaiah foretold the foolish and sinful conduct of Ahab, in refusing to hearken to the word of the Lord by him, and choosing rather to hearken to the false prophets, in going to Ramoth-Gilead to his ruin (I Kgs. 21:20–22). The moral conduct of Hazael was foretold, in that cruelty he should be guilty of; on which Hazael says, "What, is thy servant a dog, that he should do this thing!" [II Kgs. 8:13.] The prophet speaks of the event as what he knew, and not what he con-

jectured. II Kgs. 8:12: "I know the evil thou wilt do unto the children of Israel: thou wilt dash their children, and rip up their women with child." The moral conduct of Cyrus is foretold, long before he had a being, in his mercy to God's people, and regard to the true God, in turning the captivity of the Jews, and promoting the building of the Temple (Is. 44:28 and 45:13; compare II Chron. 36:22, 23 and Ezra 1:1–4). How many instances of the moral conduct of the kings of the north and south, particular instances of the wicked behavior of the kings of Syria and Egypt, are foretold in the eleventh chapter of Daniel? Their corruption, violence, robbery, treachery, and lies. And particularly, how much is foretold of the horrid wickedness of Antiochus Epiphanes, called there a "vile person," instead of "Epiphanes," or illustrious. In that chapter, and also in 8:9–14, 23, to the end, are foretold his flattery, deceit and lies, his having "his heart set to do mischief," and set "against the holy Covenant," his "destroying and treading under foot the holy people," in a marvelous manner, his "having indignation against the holy Covenant, setting his heart against it," and "conspiring against it," his "polluting the sanctuary of strength, treading it under foot, taking away the daily sacrifice, and placing the abomination that maketh desolate"; his great pride, "magnifying himself against God," and "uttering marvellous blasphemies against Him," till God in "indignation should destroy him." Withal the moral conduct of the Jews, on occasion of his persecution, is predicted. 'Tis foretold, that "he should corrupt many by flatteries" (11:32–34). But that others should behave with a glorious constancy and fortitude, in opposition to him (ver. 32). And that some good men should fall, and repent (ver. 35). Christ foretold Peter's sin, in denying his Lord, with its circumstances, in a peremptory manner. And so, that great sin of Judas, in betraying his master, and its dreadful and eternal punishment in hell, was foretold in the like positive manner (Matt. 26:21–25 and parallel places in the other Evangelists).

2. Many events have been foretold by God, which were consequent and dependent on the moral conduct of particular persons, and were accomplished, either by their virtuous or vicious actions. Thus, the children of Israel's going down into Egypt to dwell there, was foretold to Abraham (Gen. 15), which was brought about by the wickedness of Joseph's brethren in selling him, and the wickedness of Joseph's mistress, and his own signal virtue in resisting her temptation. The accomplishment of the thing prefigured in Joseph's dream, de-

pended on the same moral conduct. Jotham's parable and prophecy
(Judg. 9:15–20), was accomplished by the wicked conduct of Abime-
lech, and the men of Shechem. The prophecies against the house of
Eli (I Sam. 2, 3) were accomplished by the wickedness of Doeg the
Edomite, in accusing the priests; and the great impiety, and extreme
cruelty of Saul in destroying the priests at Nob (I Sam. 22). Nathan's
prophecy against David (II Sam. 12:11, 12) was fulfilled by the horrible wickedness of Absalom, in rebelling against his father, seeking
his life, and lying with his concubines in the sight of the sun. The
prophecy against Solomon (I Kgs. 11:11–13) was fulfilled by Jeroboam's rebellion and usurpation, which are spoken of as his wickedness (II Chron. 13:5, 6; compare ver. 18). The prophecy against
Jeroboam's family (I Kgs. 14) was fulfilled by the conspiracy, treason,
and cruel murders of Baasha (I Kgs. 15:27, etc.). The predictions
of the prophet Jehu against the house of Baasha (I Kgs. 16 at the beginning) were fulfilled by the treason and parricide of Zimri (I Kgs.
16:9–13, 20).

3. How often has God foretold the future moral conduct of nations and peoples, of numbers, bodies, and successions of men; with
God's judicial proceedings, and many other events consequent and
dependent on their virtues and vices; which could not be foreknown,
if the volitions of men, wherein they acted as moral agents, had not
been foreseen? The future cruelty of the Egyptians in oppressing
Israel, and God's judging and punishing them for it, was foretold
long before it came to pass (Gen. 15:13, 14). The continuance of the
iniquity of the Amorites, and the increase of it until it "should be
full," and they ripe for destruction, was foretold above four hundred
years beforehand (Gen. 15:16; Acts 7:6, 7). The prophecies of the
destruction of Jerusalem, and the land of Judah, were absolute
(II Kgs. 20:17–19; ch. 22:15 to the end). It was foretold in Hezekiah's time, and was abundantly insisted on in the book of the
prophet Isaiah, who wrote nothing after Hezekiah's days. It was
foretold in Josiah's time, in the beginning of a great reformation
(II Kgs. 22). And it is manifest by innumerable things in the predictions of the prophets, relating to this event, its time, its circumstances, its continuance and end; the return from the captivity, the
restoration of the Temple, city and land, and many circumstances,
and consequences of that; I say, these shew plainly, that the
prophecies of this great event were *absolute*. And yet this event was

connected with, and dependent on two things in men's moral conduct: first, the injurious rapine and violence of the king of Babylon
and his people, as the efficient cause; which God often speaks of as
what he highly resented, and would severely punish; and secondly,
the final obstinacy of the Jews. That great event is often spoken of as
suspended on this (Jer. 4:1; 5:1; 7:1–7; 11:1–6; 17:24 to the end;
25:1–7; 26:1–8, 13; and 38:17, 18). Therefore this destruction and
captivity could not be foreknown, unless such a moral conduct of the
Chaldeans and Jews had been foreknown. And then it was foretold,
that the people "should be finally obstinate," to the destruction and
utter desolation of the city and land (Is. 6:9–11; Jer. 1:18, 19;
7:27–29; Ezek. 3:7; and 24:13, 14).

The final obstinacy of those Jews who were left in the land of
Israel, and who afterwards went down into Egypt, in their idolatry
and rejection of the true God, was foretold by God, and the prediction confirmed with an oath (Jer. 44:26, 27). And God tells the people
(Is. 48:3, 4–8) that he had predicted those things which should be
consequent on their treachery and obstinacy, because he knew they
would be obstinate; and that he had declared these things beforehand,
for their conviction of his being the only true God, etc.

The destruction of Babylon, with many of the circumstances of
it, was foretold, as the judgment of God for the exceeding pride and
haughtiness of the heads of that monarchy, Nebuchadnezzar, and his
successors, and their wickedly destroying other nations, and particularly for their exalting themselves against the true God and his
people, before any of these monarchs had a being (Is. chs. 13, 14, 47;
compare Hab. 2:5 to the end, and Jer. 50 and 51). That Babylon's
destruction was to be a recompense, according to the works of their
own hands, appears by Jer. 25:14. The immorality which the people
of Babylon, and particularly her princes and great men, were guilty
of, that very night that the city was destroyed, their reveling and
drunkenness at Belshazzar's idolatrous feast, was foretold (Jer. 51:39,
57).

The return of the Jews from the Babylonish captivity is often very
particularly foretold, with many circumstances, and the promises of
it are very peremptory (Jer. 31:35–40; and 32:6–15, 41–44; and
33:24–26). And the very time of their return was prefixed (Jer.
25:11, 12; and 29:10, 11; II Chron. 36:21; Ezek. 4:5, 6; and Dan.
9:2). And yet the prophecies represent their return as consequent on

their repentance. And their repentance itself is very expressly and particularly foretold (Jer. 29:12, 13, 14; 31:8, 9, 18–31; 33:8; 50:4, 5; Ezek. 6:8, 9, 10; 7:16; 14:22, 23; and 20:43, 44).

It was foretold under the Old Testament, that the Messiah should suffer greatly through the malice and cruelty of men; as is largely and fully set forth (Ps. 22, applied to Christ in the New Testament, Matt. 27:35, 43; Luke 23:34; John 19:24; Heb. 2:12). And likewise in Ps. 69, which, it is also evident by the New Testament, is spoken of Christ (John 15:25; 7:5, etc.; and 2:17; Rom. 15:3; Matt. 27:34, 48; Mark 15:23; John 19:29). The same thing is also foretold, Is. 53 and 50:6; and Mic. 5:1. This cruelty of men was their sin, and what they acted as moral agents. It was foretold, that there should be an union of heathen and Jewish rulers against Christ (Ps. 2:1, 2, compared with Acts 4:25–28). It was foretold, that the Jews should generally reject and despise the Messiah (Is. 49:5, 6, 7 and 53:1–3; Ps. 22:6, 7 and 69:4, 8, 19, 20). And it was foretold, that the body of that nation should be rejected in the Messiah's days, from being God's people, for their obstinacy in sin (Is. 49:4–7 and 8:14, 15, 16, compared with Rom. 10:19; and Is. 65 at the beginning, compared with Rom. 10:20, 21). It was foretold, that Christ should be rejected by the chief priests and rulers among the Jews (Ps. 118:22, compared with Matt. 21:42; Acts 4:11; I Pet. 2:4, 7).

Christ himself foretold his being delivered into the hands of the elders, chief priests and scribes, and his being cruelly treated by them, and condemned to death; and that he by them should be delivered to the Gentiles; and that he should be mocked, and scourged, and crucified (Matt. 16:21 and 20:17–19; Luke 9:22; John 8:28), and that the people should be concerned in and consenting to his death (Luke 20:13–18), especially the inhabitants of Jerusalem (Luke 13:33–35). He foretold, that the disciples should all be offended because of him that night that he was betrayed, and should forsake him (Matt. 26:31; John 16:32). He foretold that he should be rejected of that generation, even the body of the people, and that they should continue obstinate, to their ruin (Matt. 12:45; 21:33–42; and 22:1–7; Luke 13:25–35; 17:25; 19:14, 27, 41–44; 20:13–18; and 23:34–39).

As it was foretold in both Old Testament and New, that the Jews should reject the Messiah, so it was foretold that the Gentiles should receive him, and so be admitted to the privileges of God's people; in places too many to be now particularly mentioned. It was foretold in the Old Testament, that the Jews should envy the Gentiles on this account (Deut. 32:21 compared with Rom. 10:19). Christ himself often foretold, that the Gentiles would embrace the true religion, and become his followers and people (Matt. 8:10, 11, 12; 21:41–43; and 22:8–10; Luke 13:28; 14:16–24; and 20:16; John 10:16). He also foretold the Jews' envy of the Gentiles on this occasion (Matt. 20:12–16; Luke 15:26 to the end). He foretold, that they should continue in this opposition and envy, and should manifest it in cruel persecutions of his followers, to their utter destruction (Matt. 21:33–42; 22:6; and 23:34–39; Luke 11:49–51). The Jews' obstinacy is also foretold (Acts 22:18). Christ often foretold the great persecutions his followers should meet with, both from Jews and Gentiles (Matt. 10:16–18, 21, 22, 34–36; and 24:9; Mark 13:9; Luke 10:3; 12:11, 49–53; and 21:12, 16, 17; John 15:18–21; and 16:1–4, 20–22, 33). He foretold the martyrdom of particular persons (Matt. 20:23; John 13:36; and 21:18, 19, 22). He foretold the great success of the gospel in the city of Samaria, as near approaching; which afterwards was fulfilled by the preaching of Philip (John 4:35–38). He foretold the rising of many deceivers, after his departure (Matt. 24:4, 5, 11), and the apostasy of many of his professed followers (Matt. 24:10–12).

The persecutions, which the Apostle Paul was to meet with in the world, were foretold (Acts 9:16–20:23; and 21:11). The Apostle says to the Christian Ephesians (Acts 20:29, 30), "I know, that after my departure shall grievous wolves enter in among you, not sparing the flock: also of your own selves shall men arise, speaking perverse things, to draw away disciples after them." The Apostle says, he *knew* this; but he did not know it, if God did not know the future actions of moral agents.

4. Unless God foreknows the future acts of moral agents, all the prophecies we have in Scripture concerning the great Antichristian apostasy; the rise, reign, wicked qualities and deeds of the Man of Sin, and his instruments and adherents; the extent and long continuance of his dominion, his influence on the minds of princes and others, to corrupt them, and draw them away to idolatry, and other foul vices; his great and cruel persecutions; the behavior of the saints under these great temptations, etc.: I say, unless the volitions of moral agents are foreseen, all these prophecies are uttered without knowing the things foretold.

The predictions relating to this great apostasy are all of a moral nature, relating to men's virtues and vices, and their exercises, fruits and consequences, and events depending on them; and are very particular; and most of them often repeated, with many precise characteristics, descriptions, and limitations of qualities, conduct, influence, effects, extent, duration, periods, circumstances, final issue, etc. which it would be very long to mention particularly. And to suppose, all these are predicted by God without any certain knowledge of the future moral behavior of free agents, would be to the utmost degree absurd.

5. Unless God foreknows the future acts of men's wills, and their behavior as moral agents, all those great things which are foretold in both Old Testament and New concerning the erection, establishment, and universal extent of the kingdom of the Messiah, were predicted and promised while God was in ignorance whether any of these things would come to pass or no, and did but guess at them. For that kingdom is not of this world, it don't consist in things external, but is within men, and consists in the dominion of virtue in their hearts, in righteousness, and peace, and joy in the Holy Ghost; and in these things made manifest in practice, to the praise and glory of God. The Messiah came to save men from their sins, and deliver them from their spiritual enemies; that they might serve him in righteousness and holiness before him: he gave himself for us, that he might redeem us from all iniquity, and purify unto himself a peculiar people, zealous of good works. And therefore his success consists in gaining men's hearts to virtue, in their being made God's willing people in the day of his power. His conquest of his enemies consists in his victory over men's corruptions and vices. And such success, such victory, and such a reign and dominion is often expressly foretold: that his kingdom shall fill the earth; that all people, nations and languages should serve and obey him; and so, that all nations should go up to the mountain of the house of the Lord, that he might teach them his ways, and that they might walk in his paths: and that all men should be drawn to Christ, and the earth be full of the knowledge of the Lord (by which, in the style of Scripture, is meant true virtue and religion) as the waters cover the seas; that God's law should be put into men's inward parts, and written in their hearts; and that God's people should be all righteous, etc., etc.

A very great part of the prophecies of the Old Testament is taken up in such predictions as these. And here I would observe, that the prophecies of the universal prevalence of the kingdom of the Messiah, and true religion of Jesus Christ, are delivered in the most peremptory manner, and confirmed by the oath of God. Is. 45:22 to the end: "Look to me, and be ye saved, all the ends of the earth; for I am God, and there is none else. I have *sworn* by myself, the word is gone out of my mouth in righteousness, and shall not return, that unto me every knee shall bow; and every tongue shall swear. *Surely,* shall one say, in the Lord have I righteousness and strength: even to him shall men come," etc. But here this peremptory declaration, and great oath of the most High, are delivered with such mighty solemnity, to things which God did not know, if he did not certainly foresee the volitions of moral agents.

And all the predictions of Christ and his apostles, to the like purpose, must be without knowledge: as those of our Saviour comparing the kingdom of God to a grain of mustard seed, growing exceeding great, from a small beginning; and to leaven, hid in three measures of meal, till the whole was leavened, etc. And the prophecies in the Epistles concerning the restoration of the nation of the Jews to the true church of God, and the bringing in the fulness of the Gentiles; and the prophecies in all the Revelation concerning the glorious change in the moral state of the world of mankind, attending the destruction of Antichrist, the kingdoms of the world becoming the kingdoms of our Lord and of his Christ; and its being granted to the Church to be arrayed in that fine linen, white and clean, which is the righteousness of saints, etc.

Corol. 1. Hence that great promise and oath of God to Abraham, Isaac and Jacob, so much celebrated in Scripture, both in the Old Testament and New, namely, that in their seed all the nations and families of the earth should be blessed, must be made on uncertainties, if God don't certainly foreknow the volitions of moral agents. For the fulfillment of this promise consists in that success of Christ in the work of redemption, and that setting up of his spiritual kingdom over the nations of the world, which has been spoken of. Men are blessed in Christ no otherwise than as they are brought to acknowledge him, trust in him, love and serve him, as is represented and predicted in Ps. 72:11: "All kings shall fall down before him; all nations shall serve him." With ver. 17: "Men shall be blessed in him; all nations shall call him Blessed." This oath to Jacob and Abraham is fulfilled in subduing men's iniquities; as is implied in that of the prophet Micah (Mic. 7:19, 20).

Corol. 2. Hence also it appears, that first gospel promise that ever was made to mankind, that great prediction of the salvation of the

Messiah, and his victory over Satan, made to our first parents (Gen.
3:15), if there be no certain prescience of the volitions of moral
agents, must have no better foundation than conjecture. For Christ's
victory over Satan consists in men's being saved from sin, and in the
victory of virtue and holiness, over that vice and wickedness, which
Satan by his temptation has introduced, and wherein his kingdom
consists.

6. If it be so, that God has not a prescience of the future actions of
moral agents, it will follow, that the prophecies of Scripture in general are without foreknowledge. For Scripture prophecies, almost all
of them, if not universally without any exception, are either predictions of the actings and behaviors of moral agents, or of events depending on them, or some way connected with them; judicial dispensations, judgments on men for their wickedness, or rewards of
virtue and righteousness, remarkable manifestations of favor to the
righteous, or manifestations of sovereign mercy to sinners, forgiving
their iniquities, and magnifying the riches of divine grace; or dispensations of providence, in some respect or other, relating to the
conduct of the subjects of God's moral government, wisely adapted
thereto; either providing for what should be in a future state of
things, through the volitions and voluntary actions of moral agents,
or consequent upon them, and regulated and ordered according to
them. So that all events that are foretold, are either moral events, or
other events which are connected with, and accommodated to moral
events.

That the predictions of Scripture in general must be without
knowledge, if God don't foresee the volitions of men, will further
appear, if it be considered, that almost all events belonging to the
future state of the world of mankind, the changes and revolutions
which come to pass in empires, kingdoms, and nations, and all societies, depend innumerable ways on the acts of men's wills; yea, on
an innumerable multitude of millions of millions of volitions of
mankind. Such is the state and course of things in the world of mankind, that one single event, which appears in itself exceeding inconsiderable, may in the progress and series of things, occasion a succession of the greatest and most important and extensive events; causing the state of mankind to be vastly different from what it would
otherwise have been, for all succeeding generations.

For instance, the coming into existence of those particular men,
who have been the great conquerors of the world, which under God

have had the main hand in all the consequent state of the world, in all after ages; such as Nebuchadnezzar, Cyrus, Alexander, Pompey, Julius Caesar, etc.; undoubtedly depended on many millions of acts of the will, which followed, and were occasioned one by another, in their parents. And perhaps most of these volitions depended on millions of volitions of hundreds and thousands of others, their contemporaries of the same generation; and most of these on millions of millions of volitions of others in preceding generations. As we go back, still the number of volitions, which were some way the occasion of the event, multiply as the branches of a river, till they come at last, as it were, to an infinite number. This will not seem strange, to anyone who well considers the matter; if we recollect what philosophers tell us of the innumerable multitudes of those things which are as it were the *principia,* or *stamina vitae,* concerned in generation; the *animalcula* in *semine masculo,* and the *ova* in the womb of the female; the impregnation, or animating of one of these in distinction from all the rest, must depend on things infinitely minute, relating to the time and circumstances of the act of the parents, the state of their bodies, etc. which must depend on innumerable foregoing circumstances and occurrences; which must depend, infinite ways, on foregoing acts of their wills; which are occasioned by innumerable things that happen in the course of their lives, in which their own, and their neighbor's behavior, must have a hand, an infinite number of ways. And as the volitions of others must be so many ways concerned in the conception and birth of such men; so, no less, in their preservation, and circumstances of life, their particular determinations and actions, on which the great revolutions they were the occasions of, depended. As for instance, when the conspirators in Persia, against the Magi, were consulting about a succession to the empire, it came into the mind of one of them, to propose, that he whose horse neighed first, when they came together the next morning, should be king. Now such a thing's coming into his mind, might depend on innumerable incidents, wherein the volitions of mankind had been concerned. But in consequence of this accident, Darius, the son of Histaspes, was king. And if this had not been, probably his successor would not have been the same, and all the circumstances of the Persian empire might have been far otherwise. And then perhaps Alexander might never have conquered that empire. And then probably the circumstances of the world in all succeeding ages, might have been vastly otherwise. I might further instance in many other

occurrences; such as those on which depended Alexander's preservation, in the many critical junctures of his life, wherein a small trifle
would have turned the scale against him; and the preservation and
success of the Roman people, in the infancy of their kingdom and
commonwealth, and afterwards; which all the succeeding changes in
their state, and the mighty revolutions that afterwards came to pass
in the habitable world, depended upon. But these hints may be sufficient for every discerning considerate person, to convince him, that
the whole state of the world of mankind, in all ages, and the very
being of every person who has ever lived in it, in every age, since the
times of the ancient prophets, has depended on more volitions, or acts
of the wills of men, than there are sands on the seashore.

And therefore, unless God does most exactly and perfectly foresee
the future acts of men's wills, all the predictions which he ever uttered
concerning David, Hezekiah, Josiah, Nebuchadnezzar, Cyrus, Alexander; concerning the four monarchies, and the revolutions in them;
and concerning all the wars, commotions, victories, prosperities and
calamities, of any of the kingdoms, nations, or communities of the
world, have all been without knowledge.

So that, according to this notion of God's not foreseeing the volitions and free actions of men, God could foresee nothing pertaining
to the state of the world of mankind in future ages; not so much as the
being of one person that should live in it; and could foreknow no
events, but only such as he would bring to pass himself by the extraordinary interposition of his immediate power; or things which should
come to pass in the natural material world, by the laws of motion, and
course of nature, wherein that is independent on the actions or works
of mankind: that is, as he might, like a very able mathematician and
astronomer, with great exactness calculate the revolutions of the
heavenly bodies, and the greater wheels of the machine of the external creation.

And if we closely consider the matter, there will appear reason to
convince us, that he could not with any absolute certainty foresee
even these. As to the first, namely things done by the immediate and
extraordinary interposition of God's power, these can't be foreseen,
unless it can be foreseen when there shall be occasion for such extraordinary interposition. And that can't be foreseen, unless the state
of the moral world can be foreseen. For whenever God thus interposes, it is with regard to the state of the moral world, requiring such
divine interposition. Thus God could not certainly foresee the uni-

versal deluge, the calling of Abraham, the destruction of Sodom and Gomorrah, the plagues on Egypt, and Israel's redemption out of it, the expelling the seven nations of Canaan, and the bringing Israel into that land; for these all are represented as connected with things belonging to the state of the moral world. Nor can God foreknow the most proper and convenient time of the day of judgment, and general conflagration; for that chiefly depends on the course and state of things in the moral world.

Nor, secondly, can we on this supposition reasonably think, that God can certainly foresee what things shall come to pass, in the course of things, in the natural and material world, even those which in an ordinary state of things might be calculated by a good astronomer. For the moral world is the end of the natural world; and the course of things in the latter, is undoubtedly subordinate to God's designs with respect to the former.[1] Therefore he has seen cause, from regard to the state of things in the moral world, extraordinarily to interpose, to interrupt and lay an arrest on the course of things in the natural world; and even in the greater wheels of its motion; even so as to stop the sun in its course. And unless he can foresee the volitions of men, and so know something of the future state of the moral world, he can't know but that he may still have as great occasion to interpose in this manner, as ever he had: nor can he foresee how, or when, he shall have occasion thus to interpose.

Corol. 1. It appears from the things which have been observed, that unless God foresees the volitions of moral agents, that cannot be true which is observed by the Apostle James, Acts 15:18: "Known unto God are all his works from the beginning of the world."

Corol. 2. It appears from what has been observed, that unless God foreknows the volitions of moral agents, all the prophecies of Scripture have no better foundation than mere conjecture; and that, in most instances, a conjecture which must have the utmost uncertainty; depending on an innumerable, and as it were infinite, multitude of volitions, which are all, even to God, uncertain events: however, these prophecies are delivered as absolute predictions, and very many of them in the most positive manner, with asseverations; and some of them with the most solemn oaths.

Corol. 3. It also follows from what has been observed, that if this notion of God's ignorance of future volitions be true, in vain did

1. [The 1754 ed. reverses the sequence of the words "former" and "latter." I follow JE, Jr., in making this correction.]

Christ say (after uttering many great and important predictions, concerning God's moral kingdom, and things depending on men's moral actions, Matt. 24:35): "Heaven and earth shall pass away; but my words shall not pass away."

Corol. 4. From the same notion of God's ignorance, it would follow, that in vain has God himself often spoken of the predictions of his Word, as evidences of his foreknowledge; and so as evidences of that which is his prerogative as God, and his peculiar glory, greatly distinguishing him from all other beings; as in Is. 41:22–26; 43:9, 10; 44:8; 45:21; 46:10; and 48:14.

Arg. II. If God don't foreknow the volitions of moral agents, then he did not foreknow the *fall* of man, nor of angels, and so could not foreknow the great things which are *consequent* on these events; such as his sending his Son into the world to die for sinners, and all things pertaining to the great work of redemption; all the things which were done for four thousand years before Christ came, to prepare the way for it; and the incarnation, life, death, resurrection and ascension of Christ; and the setting him at the head of the universe, as king of heaven and earth, angels and men; and the setting up his church and kingdom in this world, and appointing him the judge of the world; and all that Satan should do in the world in opposition to the kingdom of Christ: and the great transactions of the day of judgment, that men and devils shall be the subjects of, and angels concerned in; they are all what God was ignorant of before the fall. And if so, the following scriptures, and others like them, must be without any meaning, or contrary to truth: Eph. 1:4: "According as he hath chosen us in him before the foundation of the world." I Pet. 1:20: "Who verily was foreordained before the foundation of the world." II Tim. 1:9: "Who hath saved us, and called us with an holy calling; not according to our works, but according to his own purpose, and grace, which was given us in Christ Jesus before the world began." So, Eph. 3:11 (speaking of the wisdom of God in the work of redemption): "According to the eternal purpose which he purposed in Christ Jesus." Titus 1:2: "In hope of eternal life, which God, that cannot lie, promised before the world began." Rom. 8:29: "Whom he did foreknow, them he also did predestinate," etc. I Pet. 1:2: "Elect, according to the foreknowledge of God the Father."

If God did not foreknow the fall of man, nor the redemption by Jesus Christ, nor the volitions of man since the fall; then he did not foreknow the saints in any sense; neither as particular persons, nor as societies or nations; either by election, or mere foresight of their virtue or good works; or any foresight of anything about them relating to their salvation; or any benefit they have by Christ, or any manner of concern of theirs with a Redeemer.

Arg. III. On the supposition of God's ignorance of the future volitions of free agents, it will follow, that God must in many cases truly repent what he has done, so as properly to wish he had done otherwise: by reason that the event of things, in those affairs which are most important, viz. the affairs of his moral kingdom, being uncertain and contingent, often happens quite otherwise than he was aware beforehand. And there would be reason to understand that, in the most literal sense, in Gen. 6:6: "It repented the Lord, that he had made man on the earth, and it grieved him at his heart." And that, I Sam. 15:11, contrary to that, Num. 23:19: "God is not the son of man, that he should repent." And, I Sam. 15:15, 29: "Also the Strength of Israel will not lie, nor repent: for he is not a man that he should repent." Yea, from this notion it would follow, that God is liable to repent and be grieved at his heart, in a literal sense, continually; and is always exposed to an infinite number of real disappointments, in his governing the world; and to manifold, constant, great perplexity and vexation: but this is not very consistent with his title of "God over all, blessed for evermore"; which represents him as possessed of perfect, constant and uninterrupted tranquillity and felicity, as God over the universe, and in his management of the affairs of the world, as supreme and universal ruler. See Rom. 1:25; 9:5; II Cor. 11:31; I Tim. 6:15.

Arg. IV. It will also follow from this notion, that as God is liable to be continually repenting what he has done; so he must be exposed to be constantly changing his mind and intentions, as to his future conduct; altering his measures, relinquishing his old designs, and forming new schemes and projections. For his purposes, even as to the main parts of his scheme, namely, such as belong to the state of his moral kingdom, must be always liable to be broken, through want of foresight; and he must be continually putting his system to rights, as it gets out of order, through the contingence of the actions of moral agents: he must be a being, who, instead of being absolutely immutable, must necessarily be the subject of infinitely the most numerous acts of repentance, and changes of intention, of any being whatsoever; for this plain reason, that his vastly extensive charge comprehends an infinitely greater number of those things which are to him

contingent and uncertain. In such a situation, he must have little else
to do, but to mend broken links as well as he can, and be rectifying
his disjointed frame and disordered movements, in the best manner
the case will allow. The supreme Lord of all things must needs be
under great and miserable disadvantages, in governing the world
which he has made, and has the care of, through his being utterly
unable to find out things of chief importance, which hereafter shall
befall his system; which if he did but know, he might make season-
able provision for. In many cases, there may be very great necessity
that he should make provision, in the manner of his ordering and
disposing things, for some great events which are to happen, of vast
and extensive influence, and endless consequence to the universe;
which he may see afterwards, when it is too late, and may wish in
vain that he had known beforehand, that he might have ordered his
affairs accordingly. And it is in the power of man, on these principles,
by his devices, purposes and actions, thus to disappoint God, break
his measures, make him continually to change his mind, subject him
to vexation, and bring him into confusion.

But how do these things consist with reason, or with the Word of
God? Which represents, that all God's works, all that he has ever to
do, the whole scheme and series of his operations, are from the beginning perfectly in his view; and declares, that whatever "devices"
and designs "are in the hearts of men, the counsel of the Lord is that
which shall stand," and "the thoughts of his heart to all generations"
(Prov. 19:21; Ps. 33:10, 11). "And that which the Lord of Hosts hath
purposed, none shall disannul" (Is. 14:27). And that he cannot be
frustrated "in one design or thought" (Job 42:2). "And that what
God doth, it shall be forever, that nothing can be put to it, or taken
from it" (Eccles. 3:14). The stability and perpetuity of God's counsels are expressly spoken of as connected with the foreknowledge of
God (Is. 46:10), "Declaring the end from the beginning, and from
ancient times the things that are not yet done; saying, my counsel
shall stand, and I will do all my pleasure." And how are these things
consistent with what the Scripture says of God's immutability, which
represents him as "without variableness, or shadow of turning"; and
speaks of him most particularly as unchangeable with regard to his
purposes. Mal. 3:6: "I am the Lord; I change not; therefore ye sons
of Jacob are not consumed." Ex. 3:14: "I am that I am." Job 23:13,
14: "He is in one mind; and who can turn him? And what his soul

desireth, even that he doth: for he performeth the thing that is appointed for me."

Arg. V. If this notion of God's ignorance of the future volitions of moral agents be thoroughly considered in its consequences, it will appear to follow from it, that God, after he had made the world, was liable to be *wholly frustrated of his end* in the creation of it; and so has been in like manner liable to be frustrated of his end in all the great works he hath wrought. 'Tis manifest, the moral world is the end of the natural: the rest of the creation is but an house which God hath built, with furniture, for moral agents: and the good or bad state of the moral world depends on the improvement they make of their moral [2] agency, and so depends on their volitions. And therefore, if these can't be foreseen by God, because they are contingent, and subject to no kind of necessity, then the affairs of the moral world are liable to go wrong, to any assignable degree; yea, liable to be utterly ruined. As on this scheme, it may well be supposed to be literally said, when mankind, by the abuse of their moral agency, became very corrupt before the flood, "that the Lord repented that he had made man on the earth, and it grieved him at his heart" [Gen. 6:6]; so, when he made the universe, he did not know but that he might be so disappointed in it, that it might grieve him at his heart that he had made it. It actually proved, that all mankind became sinful, and a very great part of the angels apostatized: and how could God know beforehand, that all of them would not? And how could God know but that all mankind, notwithstanding means used to reclaim them, being still left to the freedom of their own will, would continue in their apostasy, and grow worse and worse, as they of the old world before the flood did?

According to the scheme I am endeavoring to confute, neither the fall of men nor angels, could be foreseen, and God must be greatly disappointed in these events; and so the grand scheme and contrivance for our redemption, and destroying the works of the devil, by the Messiah, and all the great things God has done in the prosecution of these designs, must be only the fruits of his own disappointment, and contrivances of his to mend and patch up, as well as he could, his system, which originally was all very good, and perfectly beautiful; but was marred, broken and confounded by the free will

2. [The 1754 ed. reads "natural." Correction made from the *printed* list of errata.]

of angels and men. And still he must be liable to be totally disappointed a second time: he could not know, that he should have his desired success, in the incarnation, life, death, resurrection and exaltation of his only begotten Son, and other great works accomplished to restore the state of things: he could not know after all, whether there would actually be any tolerable measure of restoration; for this depended on the free will of man. There has been a general great apostasy of almost all the Christian world, to that which was worse than heathenism; which continued for many ages. And how could God, without foreseeing men's volitions, know whether ever Christendom would return from this apostasy? And which way could he tell beforehand how soon it would begin? The Apostle says, it began to work in his time; and how could it be known how far it would proceed in that age? Yea, how could it be known that the gospel, which was not effectual for the reformation of the Jews, would ever be effectual for the turning of the heathen nations from their heathen apostasy, which they had been confirmed in for so many ages?

'Tis represented often in Scripture, that God who made the world for himself, and created it for his pleasure, would infallibly obtain his end in the creation, and in all his works; that as all things are *of* him, so they would all be *to* him; and that in the final issue of things, it would appear that he is the first, and the last. Rev. 21:6: "And he said unto me, it is done. I am Alpha and Omega, the beginning and the end, the first and the last." But these things are not consistent with God's being so liable to be disappointed in all his works, nor indeed with his failing of his end in anything that he has undertaken, or done.

SECTION 12. GOD'S CERTAIN FOREKNOWLEDGE OF THE FUTURE VOLITIONS OF MORAL AGENTS, INCONSISTENT WITH SUCH A CONTINGENCE OF THOSE VOLITIONS, AS IS WITHOUT ALL NECESSITY

HAVING proved, that God has a certain and infallible prescience of the acts of the will of moral agents, I come now, in the second place, to shew the consequence; to shew how it follows from hence, that these events are *necessary*, with a necessity of connection or consequence.

The chief Arminian divines, so far as I have had opportunity to observe, deny this consequence; and affirm, that if such foreknowledge be allowed, 'tis no evidence of any necessity of the event foreknown. Now I desire, that this matter may be particularly and thoroughly inquired into. I cannot but think, that on particular and full consideration, it may be perfectly determined, whether it be indeed so, or not.

In order to a proper consideration of this matter, I would observe the following things.

I. 'Tis very evident, with regard to a thing whose existence is infallibly and indissolubly connected with something which already hath, or has had existence, the existence of that thing is necessary. Here may be noted,

1. I observed before, in explaining the nature of necessity, that in things which are past, their past existence is now necessary: having already made sure of existence, 'tis too late for any possibility of alteration in that respect: 'tis now impossible, that it should be otherwise than true, that that thing has existed.

2. If there be any such thing as a divine foreknowledge of the volitions of free agents, that foreknowledge, by the supposition, is a thing which already *has*, and long ago *had* existence; and so, now its existence is necessary; it is now utterly impossible to be otherwise, than that this foreknowledge should be, or should have been.

3. 'Tis also very manifest, that those things which are indissolubly connected with other things that are necessary, are themselves necessary. As that proposition whose truth is necessarily connected with another proposition, which is necessarily true, is itself necessarily true. To say otherwise, would be a contradiction; it would be in effect to say, that the connection was indissoluble, and yet was not so, but might be broken. If that, whose existence is indissolubly connected with something whose existence is now necessary, is itself not necessary, then it may *possibly not exist,* notwithstanding that indissoluble connection of its existence. Whether the absurdity ben't glaring, let the reader judge.

4. 'Tis no less evident, that if there be a full, certain and infallible foreknowledge of the future existence of the volitions of moral agents, then there is a certain infallible and indissoluble connection between those events and that foreknowledge; and that therefore, by the preceding observations, those events are necessary events; being infallibly and indissolubly connected with that whose existence already is, and so is now necessary, and can't but have been.

To say, the foreknowledge is certain and infallible, and yet the connection of the event with that foreknowledge is not indissoluble, but dissoluble and fallible, is very absurd. To affirm it, would be the same thing as to affirm, that there is no necessary connection between a proposition's being infallibly known to be true, and its being true indeed. So that it is perfectly demonstrable, that if there be any infallible knowledge of future volitions, the event is *necessary;* or, in other words, that it is *impossible* but the event should come to pass. For if it ben't impossible but that it may be otherwise, then it is not impossible but that the proposition which affirms its future coming to pass, may not now be true. But how absurd is that, on the supposition that there is now an infallible knowledge (i.e. knowledge which it is impossible should fail) that it is true. There is this absurdity in it, that it is not impossible but that there now should be no truth in that proposition, which is now infallibly known to be true.

II. That no future event can be certainly foreknown, whose existence is contingent, and without all necessity, may be proved thus; 'tis impossible for a thing to be certainly known to any intellect without *evidence.* To suppose otherwise, implies a contradiction: because for a thing to be certainly known to any understanding, is for it to be *evident* to that understanding: and for a thing to be evident to any understanding, is the same thing, as for that understanding to *see evidence* of it: but no understanding, created or increated, can see evidence where there is none: for that is the same thing, as to see that to be, which is not. And therefore, if there be any truth which is absolutely without evidence, that truth is absolutely unknowable, insomuch that it implies a contradiction to suppose that it is known.

But if there be any future event, whose existence is contingent, without all necessity, the future existence of that event is absolutely *without evidence.* If there be any evidence of it, it must be one of these two sorts, either *self-evidence,* or *proof;* for there can be no other sort of evidence but one of these two; an evident thing must be either evident *in itself,* or evident *in something else;* that is, evident by connection with something else. But a future thing, whose existence is without all necessity, can have neither of these sorts of evidence. It can't be self-evident: for if it be, it may be now known by what is now to be seen in the thing itself; either its present existence, or the necessity of its nature: but both these are contrary to the supposition. It is supposed, both that the thing has no present existence to be seen; and also that it is not of such a nature as to be necessarily existent for the future: so that its future existence is not self-evident. And secondly, neither is there any proof, or evidence in anything else, or evidence of connection with something else that is evident; for this also is contrary to the supposition. 'Tis supposed, that there is now nothing existent, with which the future existence of the *contingent* event is connected. For such a connection destroys its contingence, and supposes necessity. Thus 'tis demonstrated, that there is in the nature of things absolutely no evidence at all of the future existence of that event, which is contingent, without all necessity (if any such event there be); neither self-evidence nor proof. And therefore the thing in reality is not evident; and so can't be seen to be evident, or, which is the same thing, can't be known.

Let us consider this in an example. Suppose that five thousand seven hundred and sixty years ago, there was no other being but the divine Being; and then this world, or some particular body or spirit, all at once starts out of nothing into being, and takes on itself a particular nature and form; all in *absolute contingence,* without any concern of God, or any other cause, in the matter; without any manner of ground or reason of its existence; or any dependence upon, or connection at all with anything foregoing: I say, that if this be supposed, there was no evidence of that event beforehand. There was no evidence of it to be seen *in the thing itself;* for the thing itself, as yet, was not. And there was no evidence of it to be seen *in anything else;* for evidence in something else, is *connection with* something else: but such connection is contrary to the supposition. There was no evidence before, that this thing *would happen;* for by the supposition, there was no reason why it *should happen,* rather than something else, or rather than nothing. And if so, then all things before were exactly equal, and the same, with respect to that and other possible things; there was no preponderation, no superior weight or value; and therefore nothing that could be of any weight or value to determine any understanding. The thing was absolutely without evidence, and absolutely unknowable. An increase of understanding, or of the capacity of discerning, has no tendency, and makes no advance, to a discerning any signs or evidences of it, let it be increased never so much; yea, if it be increased infinitely. The increase of the strength of sight may have a tendency to enable to discern the evidence which is far off, and very much hid, and deeply involved in clouds and darkness; but it has no tendency to enable to discern evidence where there is none. If the sight be infinitely strong, and the capacity of discerning infinitely great, it will enable [a being] to see all that there is, and to see it perfectly, and with ease; yet it has no tendency at all to enable a being to discern that evidence which is not; but on the contrary, it has a tendency to enable to discern with great certainty that there is none.

III. To suppose the future volitions of moral agents not to be necessary events; or, which is the same thing, events which it is not impossible but that they may not come to pass; and yet to suppose that God certainly foreknows them, and knows all things; is to suppose God's knowledge to be inconsistent with itself. For to say, that God certainly, and without all conjecture, knows that a thing will infallibly be, which at the same time he knows to be so contingent, that it may possibly not be, is to suppose his knowledge inconsistent with itself; or that one thing that he knows is utterly inconsistent with another thing that he knows. 'Tis the same thing as to say, he now knows a proposition to be of certain infallible truth, which he knows to be of contingent uncertain truth. If a future volition is so without all necessity, that there is nothing hinders but that it may not be, then the proposition which asserts its future existence, is so uncertain, that there is nothing hinders but that the truth of it may entirely fail. And if God knows all things, he knows this proposition to be thus uncertain. And that is inconsistent with his knowing that it is infallibly true; and so inconsistent with his infallibly knowing that it is true. If the thing be indeed contingent, God views it so, and judges it to be contingent, if he views things as they are. If the event be not necessary, then it is possible it may never be: and if it be possible it may never be, God knows it may possibly never be; and that is to know that the proposition which affirms its existence, may possibly not be true; and that is to know that the truth of it is uncertain; which surely is inconsistent with his knowing it as a certain truth. If volitions are in themselves contingent events, without all necessity, then 'tis no argument of perfection of knowledge in any being to determine peremptorily that they will be; but on the contrary, an argument of ignorance and mistake: because it would argue, that he supposes that proposition to be certain, which in its own nature, and all things considered, is uncertain and contingent. To say in such a case, that God may have ways of knowing contingent events which we can't conceive of, is ridiculous; as much so, as to say, that God may know contradictions to be true, for ought we know, or that he may know a thing to be certain, and at the same time know it not to be certain, though we can't conceive how; because he has ways of knowing, which we can't comprehend.

Corol. 1. From what has been observed it is evident, that the absolute *decrees* of God are no more inconsistent with human liberty, on account of any necessity of the event which follows from such decrees, than the absolute *foreknowledge* of God. Because the connection between the event and certain foreknowledge, is as infallible and indissoluble, as between the event and an absolute decree. That is, 'tis no more impossible that the event and decree should not agree together, than that the event and absolute knowledge should disagree. The connection between the event and foreknowledge is absolutely perfect, by the supposition: because it is supposed, that the certainty and infallibility of the knowledge is absolutely perfect. And it being so, the certainty can't be increased; and therefore the connection between the knowledge and thing known, can't be increased; so that if a decree be added to the foreknowledge, it don't at all increase the connection, or make it more infallible and indissoluble. If it were not so, the certainty of knowledge might be increased by the addition of a decree; which is contrary to the supposition, which is, that the knowledge is absolutely perfect, or perfect to the highest possible degree.

There is as much of an impossibility but that the things which are infallibly foreknown, should be, or (which is the same thing) as great a necessity of their future existence, as if the event were already written down, and was known and read by all mankind, through all preceding ages, and there were the most indissoluble and perfect connection possible, between the writing, and the thing written. In such a case, it would be as impossible the event should fail of existence, as if it had existed already; and a decree can't make an event surer or more necessary than this.

And therefore, if there be any such foreknowledge, as it has been proved there is, then necessity of connection and consequence, is not at all inconsistent with any liberty which man, or any other creature enjoys. And from hence it may be inferred, that absolute decrees of God, which don't at all increase the necessity, are not at all inconsistent with the liberty which man enjoys, on any such account, as that they make the event decreed necessary, and render it utterly impossible but that it should come to pass. Therefore if absolute decrees are inconsistent with man's liberty as a moral agent, or his liberty in a state of probation, or any liberty whatsoever that he enjoys, it is not on account of any necessity which absolute decrees infer.

Dr. Whitby supposes, there is a great difference between God's foreknowledge, and his decrees, with regard to necessity of future events. In his *Discourse on the Five Points,* p. 474, etc.[1] he says, "God's prescience has no influence at all on our actions. . . . Should God (says he) by immediate revelation, give me the knowledge of the event of any man's state or actions, would my knowledge of them have any influence upon his actions? Surely none at all. . . . Our knowledge doth not affect the things we know, to make them more certain, or more future, than they would be without it. Now foreknowledge in God is knowledge. As therefore knowledge has no influence on things that are, so neither has foreknowledge on things that shall be. And consequently, the foreknowledge of any action that would be otherwise free, cannot alter or diminish that freedom. Whereas God's decree of election is powerful and active, and comprehends the preparation and exhibition of such means, as shall unfrustrably produce the end. . . . Hence God's prescience renders no actions necessary." And to this purpose (p. 473), he cites Origen, where he says, "God's prescience is not the cause of things future, but

1. [Whitby, *Discourse on the Five Points,* Dis. VI, ch. 1; pp. 474–5.]

their being future is the cause of God's prescience that they will be": and Le Blanc, where he says, "This is the truest resolution of this difficulty, that prescience is not the cause that things are future; but their being future is the cause they are foreseen." In like manner Dr. Clarke, in his *Demonstration of the Being and Attributes of God* (pp. 95–99). And the author of *The Freedom of Will, in God and the Creature,* speaking to the like purpose with Dr. Whitby, represents "foreknowledge as having no more influence on things known, to make them necessary," than "after-knowledge," or to that purpose.[2]

To all which I would say; that what is said about knowledge, its not having influence on the thing known to make it necessary, is nothing to the purpose, nor does it in the least affect the foregoing reasoning. Whether prescience be the thing that *makes* the event necessary or no, it alters not the case. Infallible foreknowledge may *prove* the necessity of the event foreknown, and yet not be the thing which *causes* the necessity. If the foreknowledge be absolute, this *proves* the event known to be necessary, or proves that 'tis impossible but that the event should be, by some means or other, either by a decree, or some other way, if there be any other way: because, as was said before, 'tis absurd to say, that a proposition is known to be certainly and infallibly true, which yet may possibly prove not true.

The whole of the seeming force of this evasion lies in this; that, inasmuch as certain foreknowledge don't *cause* an event to be necessary, as a decree does; therefore it don't *prove* it to be necessary, as a decree does. But there is no force in this arguing: for it is built wholly on this supposition, that nothing can prove, or be an evidence of a thing's being necessary, but that which has a causal influence to make it so. But this can never be maintained. If certain foreknowledge of the future existing of an event, be not the thing which first *makes* it impossible that it should fail of existence; yet it may, and certainly does *demonstrate,* that it is impossible it should fail of it, however that impossibility comes. If foreknowledge be not the cause, but the effect of this impossibility, it may prove that there is such

2. [Neither this statement nor one remotely resembling it is to be found in Watts' treatise. Turnbull, *Principles,* 2, 135–8, takes the same position as the authors JE quotes at this point; and he comes as close as any to saying what JE attributes to Watts when he writes that "knowledge of no kind, neither knowledge of present, past, nor to come, can have any productive efficiency" (p. 135), and suchlike statements.]

an impossibility, as much as if it were the cause. It is as strong arguing from the effect to the cause, as from the cause to the effect. 'Tis enough, that an existence which is infallibly foreknown, cannot fail, whether that impossibility arises from the foreknowledge, or is prior to it. 'Tis as evident, as 'tis possible anything should be, that it is impossible a thing which is infallibly known to be true, should prove not to be true: therefore there is a necessity that it should [not] be otherwise; [3] whether the knowledge be the cause of this necessity, or the necessity the cause of the knowledge.

All certain knowledge, whether it be foreknowledge or after-knowledge, or concomitant knowledge, proves the thing known now to be necessary, by some means or other; or proves that it is impossible it should now be otherwise than true. I freely allow, that foreknowledge don't prove a thing to be necessary any more than after-knowledge: but then after-knowledge which is certain and infallible, proves that 'tis now become impossible but that the proposition known should be true. Certain after-knowledge proves that it is now, in the time of the knowledge, by some means or other, become impossible but that the proposition which predicates *past* existence on the event, should be true. And so does certain foreknowledge prove, that now, in the time of the knowledge, it is by some means or other, become impossible but that the proposition which predicates *future* existence on the event, should be true. The necessity of the truth of the propositions, consisting in the present impossibity of the nonexistence of the event affirmed, in both cases, is the immediate ground of the certainty of the knowledge; there can be no certainty of knowledge without it.

There must be a certainty in things themselves, before they are certainly known, or (which is the same thing) known to be certain. For certainty of knowledge is nothing else but knowing or discerning the certainty there is in the things themselves which are known. Therefore there must be a certainty in things to be a ground of certainty of knowledge, and to render things capable of being known to be certain. And this is nothing but the necessity of the truth known, or its being impossible but that it should be true; or, in other

3. [This slight correction of the text is needed to restore JE's meaning. The Worcester edition reads, "Therefore there is a *Necessity* connected with such knowledge"; and here for once the Dwight edition sticks closer to the original by repeating the error, which must simply have been a slip on JE's part, or his printer's.]

words, the firm and infallible connection between the subject and predicate of the proposition that contains that truth. All certainty of knowledge consists in the view of the firmness of that connection. So God's certain foreknowledge of the future existence of any event, is his view of the firm and indissoluble connection of the subject and predicate of the proposition that affirms its future existence. The subject is that possible event; the predicate is its future existing: but if future existence be firmly and indissolubly connected with that event, then the future existence of that event is necessary. If God certainly knows the future existence of an event which is wholly contingent, and may possibly never be, then he sees a firm connection between a subject and predicate that are not firmly connected; which is a contradiction.

I allow what Dr. Whitby says to be true, "that mere knowledge don't affect the thing known, to make it more certain or more future." But yet, I say, it supposes and proves the thing to be *already*, both future, and certain; i.e. necessarily future. Knowledge of futurity, supposes futurity; and a *certain knowledge* of futurity, supposes *certain futurity*, antecedent to that certain knowledge. But there is no other certain futurity of a thing, antecedent to certainty of knowledge, than a prior impossibility but that the thing should prove true; or (which is the same thing) the necessity of the event.

I would observe one thing further concerning this matter, and it is this; that if it be as those forementioned writers suppose, that God's foreknowledge is not the cause, but the effect of the existence of the event foreknown; this is so far from shewing that this foreknowledge don't infer the necessity of the existence of that event, that it rather shews the contrary the more plainly. Because it shews the existence of the event to be so settled and firm, that it is as if it had already been; inasmuch as *in effect* it actually exists already; its future existence has already had actual influence and efficiency, and has *produced an effect*, viz. prescience: the effect exists already; and as the effect supposes the cause, is connected with the cause, and depends entirely upon it, therefore it is as if the future event, which is the cause, had existed already. The effect is firm as possible, it having already the possession of existence, and has made sure of it. But the effect can't be more firm and stable than its cause, ground and reason. The building can't be firmer than the foundation.

To illustrate this matter, let us suppose the appearances and images of things in a glass; for instance, a reflecting telescope, to be the real effects of heavenly bodies (at a distance, and out of sight) which they resemble: if it be so, then, as these images in the telescope have had a past actual existence, and it is become utterly impossible now that it should be otherwise than that they have existed; so they being the true effects of the heavenly bodies they resemble, this proves the existing of those heavenly bodies to be as real, infallible, firm and necessary, as the existing of these effects; the one being connected with, and wholly depending on the other. Now let us suppose future existences some way or other to have influence back, to produce effects beforehand, and cause exact and perfect images of themselves in a glass, a thousand years before they exist, yea, in all preceding ages; but yet that these images are real effects of these future existences, perfectly dependent on, and connected with their cause; these effects and images, having already had actual existence, rendering that matter of their existing perfectly firm and stable, and utterly impossible to be otherwise; this proves in like manner as in the other instance, that the existence of the things which are their causes, is also equally sure, firm and necessary; and that it is alike impossible but that they should be, as if they had been already, as their effects have. And if instead of images in a glass, we suppose the antecedent effects to be perfect ideas of them in the divine mind, which have existed there from all eternity, which are as properly effects, as truly and properly connected with their cause, the case is not altered.

Another thing which has been said by some Arminians, to take off the force of what is urged from God's prescience, against the contingence of the volitions of moral agents, is to this purpose; "that when we talk of foreknowledge in God, there is no strict propriety in our so speaking; and that although it be true, that there is in God the most perfect knowledge of all events from eternity to eternity, yet there is no such thing as *before* and *after* in God, but he sees all things by one perfect unchangeable view, without any succession." To this I answer,

1. It has been already shewn, that all certain knowledge proves the necessity of the truth known; whether it be before, after, or at the same time. Though it be true, that there is no succession in God's knowledge, and the manner of his knowledge is to us inconceivable, yet thus much we know concerning it, that there is no event, past, present, or to come, that God is ever uncertain of; he never is, never was, and never will be without infallible knowledge of it; he always sees the existence of it to be certain and infallible. And as he always

sees things just as they are in truth; hence there never is in reality anything contingent in such a sense, as that possibly it may happen never to exist. If, strictly speaking, there is no foreknowledge in God, 'tis because those things which are future to us, are as present to God, as if they already had existence: and that is as much as to say, that future events are always in God's view as evident, clear, sure and necessary, as if they already were. If there never is a time wherein the existence of the event is not present with God, then there never is a time wherein it is not as much impossible for it to fail of existence, as if its existence were present, and were already come to pass.

God's viewing things so perfectly and unchangeably as that there is no succession in his ideas or judgment, don't hinder but that there is properly now, in the mind of God, a certain and perfect knowledge of the moral actions of men, which to us are an hundred years hence: yea, the objection supposes this; and therefore it certainly don't hinder but that, by the foregoing arguments, it is now impossible these moral actions should not come to pass.

We know, that God knows the future voluntary actions of men in such a sense beforehand, as that he is able particularly to declare, and foretell them, and write them, or cause them to be written down in a Book, as he often has done; and that therefore the necessary connection which there is between God's knowledge and the event known, does as much prove the event to be necessary beforehand, as if the divine knowledge were in the same sense before the event, as the prediction or writing is. If the knowledge be infallible, then the expression of it in the written prediction is infallible; that is, there is an infallible connection between that written prediction and the event. And if so, then it is impossible it should ever be otherwise, than that that prediction and the event should agree: and this is the same thing as to say, 'tis impossible but that the event should come to pass: and this is the same as to say, that its coming to pass is necessary. So that it is manifest, that there being no proper succession in God's mind, makes no alteration as to the necessity of the existence of the events which God knows. Yea,

2. This is so far from weakening the proof, which has been given of the impossibility of the not coming to pass of future events known, as that it establishes that wherein the strength of the foregoing arguments consists, and shews the clearness of the evidence. For,

(1) The very reason why God's knowledge is without succession, is, because it is absolutely perfect, to the highest possible degree of

clearness and certainty: all things, whether past, present or to come, being viewed with equal evidence and fullness; future things being seen with as much clearness, as if they were present; the view is always in absolute perfection; and absolute constant perfection admits of no alteration, and so no succession; the actual existence of the thing known, don't at all increase, or add to the clearness or certainty of the thing known: God calls the things that are not, as though they were; they are all one to him as if they had already existed. But herein consists the strength of the demonstration before given, of the impossibility of the not existing of those things whose existence God knows; that it is as impossible they should fail of existence, as if they existed already. This objection, instead of weakening this argument, sets it in the clearest and strongest light; for it supposes it to be so indeed, that the existence of future events is in God's view so much as if it already had been, that when they come actually to exist, it makes not the least alteration or variation in his view or knowledge of them.

(2) The objection is founded on the *immutability* of God's knowledge: for 'tis the immutability of knowledge makes his knowledge to be without succession. But this most directly and plainly demonstrates the thing I insist on, viz. that 'tis utterly impossible the known events should fail of existence. For if that were possible, then it would be possible for there to be a change in God's knowledge and view of things. For if the known event should fail of existence, and not come into being, as God expected, then God would see it, and so would change his mind, and see his former mistake; and thus there would be change and succession in his knowledge. But as God is immutable, and so it is utterly and infinitely impossible that his view should be changed; so 'tis, for the same reason, just so impossible that the foreknown event should not exist: and that is to be impossible in the highest degree: and therefore the contrary is necessary. Nothing is more impossible than that the immutable God should be changed, by the succession of time; who comprehends all things, from eternity to eternity, in one, most perfect, and unalterable view; so that his whole eternal duration is *vitae interminabilis, tota, simul,* and *perfecta possessio.*

On the whole, I need not fear to say, that there is no geometrical theorem or proposition whatsoever, more capable of strict demonstration, than that God's certain prescience of the volitions of moral agents is inconsistent with such a contingence of these events, as is without all necessity; and so is inconsistent with the Arminian notion of liberty.

Corol. 2. Hence the doctrine of the Calvinists, concerning the absolute decrees of God, does not at all infer any more fatality in things, than will demonstrably follow from the doctrine of most Arminian divines, who acknowledge God's omniscience, and universal prescience. Therefore all objections they make against the doctrine of the Calvinists, as implying Hobbes' doctrine of necessity, or the Stoical doctrine of fate, lie no more against the doctrine of Calvinists, than their own doctrine: and therefore it don't become those divines, to raise such an outcry against the Calvinists, on this account.

Corol. 3. Hence all arguing from necessity, against the doctrine of the inability of unregenerate men to perform the conditions of salvation, and the commands of God requiring spiritual duties, and against the Calvinistic doctrine of efficacious grace; I say, all arguings of Arminians (such of 'em as own God's omniscience) against these things, on this ground, that these doctrines, though they don't suppose men to be under any constraint or coaction, yet suppose 'em under necessity, with respect to their moral actions, and those things which are required of 'em in order to their acceptance with God; and their arguing against the necessity of men's volitions, taken from the reasonableness of God's commands, promises, and threatenings, and the sincerity of his counsels and invitations; and all objections against any doctrines of the Calvinists as being inconsistent with human liberty, because they infer necessity; I say, all these arguments and objections must fall to the ground, and be justly esteemed vain and frivolous, as coming from them; being maintained in an inconsistence with themselves, and in like manner leveled against their own doctrine, as against the doctrine of the Calvinists.

SECTION 13. WHETHER WE SUPPOSE THE VOLITIONS
OF MORAL AGENTS TO BE CONNECTED
WITH ANYTHING ANTECEDENT, OR NOT,
YET THEY MUST BE NECESSARY IN SUCH
A SENSE AS TO OVERTHROW
ARMINIAN LIBERTY

EVERY act of the will has a cause, or it has not. If it has a cause, then, according to what has already been demonstrated, it is not contingent, but necessary; the effect being necessarily dependent and consequent on its cause; and that, let the cause be what it will. If the cause is the will itself, by antecedent acts choosing and determining; still the *determined* and *caused* act must be a necessary effect. The act that is the determined effect of the foregoing act which is its cause, can't prevent the efficiency of its cause; but must be wholly subject to its determination and command, as much as the motions of the hands and feet: the consequent commanded acts of the will are as passive and as necessary, with respect to the antecedent determining acts, as the parts of the body are to the volitions which determine and command them. And therefore, if all the free acts of the will are thus, if they are all determined effects, determined by the will itself, that is, determined by antecedent choice, then they are all necessary; they are all subject to, and decisively fixed by the foregoing act, which is their cause: yea, even the determining act itself; for that must be determined and fixed by another act, preceding that, if it be a free and voluntary act; and so must be necessary. So that by this all the free acts of the will are necessary, and can't be free unless they are necessary: because they can't be free, according to the Arminian notion of freedom, unless they are determined by the will; which is to be determined by antecedent choice; which being their cause, proves 'em necessary. And yet they say, necessity is utterly inconsistent with liberty. So that, by their scheme, the acts of the will can't be free unless they are necessary, and yet cannot be free if they be necessary! [1]

But if the other part of the dilemma be taken, and it be affirmed that the free acts of the will have no cause, and are connected with nothing whatsoever that goes before them and determines them, in order to maintain their proper and absolute contingence, and this should be allowed to be possible; still it will not serve their turn. For if the volition comes to pass by perfect contingence, and without any cause at all, then it is certain, no act of the will, no prior act of the soul was the cause, no determination or choice of the soul, had any hand in it. The will, or the soul, was indeed the subject of what happened to it accidentally, but was not the cause. The will is not active in causing or determining, but purely the passive subject; at least according to their notion of action and passion. In this case, contingence does as much to prevent the determination of the will, as a proper cause; and as to the will, it was necessary, and could be no otherwise. For to suppose that it could have been otherwise, if the will or soul had pleased, is to suppose that the act is dependent on some prior act of choice or pleasure; contrary to what now is supposed: it is to suppose that it might have been otherwise, if its cause had made it or ordered it otherwise. But this don't agree to its having no cause or orderer at all. That must be necessary as to the soul, which is dependent on no free act of the soul: but that which is without a cause, is dependent on no free act of the soul: because, by the supposition, it is dependent on nothing, and is connected with nothing. In such a case, the soul is necessarily subjected to what accident brings to pass, from time to time, as much as the earth, that is inactive, is necessarily subjected to what falls upon it. But this don't consist with the Arminian notion of liberty, which is the will's power of determining itself in its own acts, and being wholly active in it, without passiveness, and without being subject to necessity. Thus, contingence belongs to the Arminian notion of liberty, and yet is inconsistent with it.

I would here observe, that the author of the *Essay on the Freedom of Will, in God and the Creature* (pp. 76, 77) [2] says as follows, "The word 'chance' always means something done without design. Chance and design stand in direct opposition to each other: and chance can never be properly applied to the acts of the will, which is the spring

1. [The 1754 ed. reads "be *not* necessary." Correction made from the *printed* list of errata.]

2. [Watts, *Essay*, Sec. 6, *ans.* to *obj.* 5; in *Works, 6,* 268.]

of all design, and which designs to choose whatsoever it doth choose, whether there be any superior fitness in the thing which it chooses, or no; and it designs to determine itself to one thing, where two things perfectly equal are proposed, merely because it will." But herein appears a very great inadvertence in this author. For if "the will be the spring of all design," as he says, then certainly it is not always the *effect* of design; and the acts of the will themselves must sometimes come to pass when they don't *spring from* design; and consequently come to pass by chance, according to his own definition of chance. And if "the will designs to choose whatsoever it does choose, and designs to determine itself," as he says, then it designs to determine all its designs. Which carries us back from one design to a foregoing design determining that, and to another determining that; and so on *in infinitum*. The very first design must be the effect of foregoing design, or else it must be by chance, in his notion of it.

Here another alternative may be proposed, relating to the connection of the acts of the will with something foregoing that is their cause, not much unlike to the other; which is this: either human liberty is such that it may well stand with volitions being necessarily connected with the views of the understanding, and so is consistent with necessity; or it is inconsistent with, and contrary to such a connection and necessity. The former is directly subversive of the Arminian notion of liberty, consisting in freedom from all necessity. And if the latter be chosen, and it be said, that liberty is inconsistent with any such necessary connection of volition with foregoing views of the understanding, it consisting in freedom from any such necessity of the will as that would imply; then the liberty of the soul consists (in part at least) in the freedom from restraint, limitation and government, in its actings, by the understanding, and in liberty and liableness to act contrary to the understanding's views and dictates: and consequently the more the soul has of this disengagedness, in its acting, the more liberty. Now let it be considered what this brings the noble principle of human liberty to, particularly when it is possessed and enjoyed in its perfection, viz. a full and perfect freedom and liableness to act altogether at random, without the least connection with, or restraint or government by, any dictate of reason, or anything whatsoever apprehended, considered or viewed by the understanding; as being inconsistent with the full and perfect sovereignty of the will over its own determinations. The notion mankind have conceived of liberty, is some dignity or privilege, something worth claiming. But what dignity or privilege is there, in being given up to such a wild contingence as this, to be perfectly and constantly liable to act unintelligently and unreasonably, and as much without the guidance of understanding, as if we had none, or were as destitute of perception as the smoke that is driven by the wind!

PART THREE

Wherein Is Inquired, Whether Any Such Liberty of Will as Arminians Hold, Be Necessary to Moral Agency, Virtue and Vice, Praise, and Dispraise, etc.

SECTION 1. GOD'S MORAL EXCELLENCY NECESSARY, YET VIRTUOUS AND PRAISEWORTHY

Having considered the first thing that was proposed to be inquired into, relating to that freedom of will which Arminians maintain; namely, whether any such thing does, ever did, or ever can exist, or be conceived of; I come now to the second thing proposed to be the subject of inquiry, viz. whether any such kind of liberty be requisite to moral agency, virtue and vice, praise and blame, reward and punishment, etc.

I shall begin with some consideration of the virtue and agency of the supreme moral Agent, and fountain of all agency and virtue.

Dr. Whitby, in his *Discourse on the Five Points* (p. 14),[1] says, "If all human actions are necessary, virtue and vice must be empty names; we being capable of nothing that is blameworthy, or deserveth praise; for who can blame a person for doing only what he could not help, or judge that he deserveth praise only for what he could not avoid?" To the like purpose he speaks in places innumerable; especially in his discourse on the freedom of the will; constantly maintaining, that a "freedom not only from coaction, but [from] necessity," is absolutely requisite, in order to actions being either worthy of blame, or deserving of praise.[2] And to this agrees, as is well known, the current doctrine of Arminian writers; who in general hold, that there is no virtue or vice, reward or punishment, nothing to be commended or blamed, without this freedom. And yet Dr. Whitby, p. 300, allows, that God is without this freedom;[3] and Arminians, so far as I have had opportunity to observe, generally acknowledge, that God is

1. [Whitby, *Discourse on the Five Points,* Dis. I, ch. 1; p. 14.]
2. [Ibid., Dis. I, ch. 1; p. 328.]
3. [Because God and the "confirmed" angels, as well as devils and damned spirits, are "in no state of trial." Consequently, the former are not "rewardable," and the latter will be punished on judgment day only for what they did during their state of trial.]

necessarily holy, and his will necessarily determined to that which is good.

So that, putting these things together, the infinitely holy God, who always used to be esteemed by God's people, not only virtuous, but a being in whom is all possible virtue, and every virtue in the most absolute purity and perfection, and in infinitely greater brightness and amiableness than in any creature; the most perfect pattern of virtue, and the fountain from whom all others' virtue is but as beams from the sun; and who has been supposed to be, on the account of his virtue and holiness, infinitely more worthy to be esteemed, loved, honored, admired, commended, extolled and praised, than any creature; and he who is thus everywhere represented in Scripture; I say, this being, according to this notion of Dr. Whitby, and other Arminians, has no virtue at all; virtue, when ascribed to him, is but "an empty name"; and he is deserving of no commendation or praise; because he is under necessity, he can't avoid being holy and good as he is; therefore no thanks to him for it. It seems, the holiness, justice, faithfulness, etc. of the most High, must not be accounted to be of the nature of that which is virtuous and praiseworthy. They will not deny, that these things in God are good; but then we must understand them, that they are no more virtuous, or of the nature of anything commendable, than the good that is in any other being that is not a moral agent; as the brightness of the sun, and the fertility of the earth are good, but not virtuous, because these properties are necessary to these bodies, and not the fruit of self-determining power.[4]

There needs no other confutation of this notion of God's not being virtuous or praiseworthy, to Christians acquainted with the Bible, but only stating and particularly representing of it. To bring texts of Scripture, wherein God is represented as in every respect, in the highest manner virtuous, and supremely praiseworthy, would be endless, and is altogether needless to such as have been brought up under the light of the gospel.

It were to be wished, that Dr. Whitby, and other divines of the same sort, had explained themselves, when they have asserted that that which is necessary, is "not deserving of praise"; at the same time that they have owned God's perfection to be necessary, and so in effect represented God as not deserving praise. Certainly, if their words have any meaning at all, by "praise," they must mean the exercise or testimony of some sort of esteem, respect, or honorable re-

4. [See above, Intro., Pt. 5, no. 10.]

gard. And will they then say, that men are worthy of that esteem, respect, and honor for their virtue, small and imperfect as it is, which yet God is not worthy of, for his infinite righteousness, holiness, and goodness? If so, it must be because of some sort of peculiar excellency in the virtuous man, which is his prerogative, wherein he really has the preference; some dignity, that is entirely distinguished from any excellency, amiableness or honorableness in God; not in imperfection and dependence, but in pre-eminence; which therefore he don't receive from God, nor is God the fountain or pattern of it; nor can God, in that respect, stand in competition with him, as the object of honor and regard; but man may claim a peculiar esteem, commendation and glory, that God can have no pretension to. Yea, God has no right, by virtue of his necessary holiness, to intermeddle with that grateful respect and praise, due to the virtuous man, who chooses virtue, in the exercise of a freedom *ad utrumque;* [5] any more than a precious stone, which can't avoid being hard and beautiful.

And if it be so, let it be explained what that peculiar respect is, that is due to the virtuous man, which differs in nature and kind, in some way of pre-eminence, from all that is due to God. What is the name or description of that peculiar affection? Is it esteem, love, admiration, honor, praise, or gratitude? The Scripture everywhere represents God as the highest object of all these: there we read of the "soul's magnifying the Lord," or "loving him with all the heart, with all the soul, with all the mind, and with all the strength"; admiring him, and his righteous acts, or greatly regarding them as marvellous and wonderful; honoring, glorifying, exalting, extolling, blessing, thanking, and praising him; "giving unto him all the glory" of the good which is done or received, rather than unto men; "that no flesh should glory in his presence"; but that he should be regarded as the being to whom all glory is due. What then is that respect? What passion, affection, or exercise is it, that Arminians call "praise," diverse from all these things, which men are worthy of for their virtue, and which God is not worthy of, in any degree?

If that necessity which attends God's moral perfections and actions, be as inconsistent with a being worthy of praise, as a necessity of coaction; as is plainly implied in or inferred from Dr. Whitby's discourse; then why should we thank God for his goodness, any more than if he were forced to be good, or any more than we should thank

5. [Freedom to choose either of two things, or to act in either way or direction or on either side.]

one of our fellow creatures who did us good, not freely, and of good will, or from any kindness of heart, but from mere compulsion, or extrinsical necessity? Arminians suppose, that God is necessarily a good and gracious being: for this they make the ground of some of their main arguments against many doctrines maintained by Calvinists: they say, these are "certainly" false, and it is "impossible" they should be true, because they are not consistent with the goodness of God. This supposes, that it is *impossible* but that God should be good: for if it be possible that he should be otherwise, then that impossibility of the truth of these doctrines ceases, according to their own argument.

That virtue in God is not, in the most proper sense, *rewardable,* is not for want of merit in his moral perfections and actions, sufficient to deserve rewards from his creatures; but because he is infinitely above all capacity of receiving any reward or benefit from the creature: he is already infinitely and unchangeably happy, and we can't be profitable unto him. But still he is worthy of our supreme benevolence for his virtue; and would be worthy of our beneficence, which is the fruit and expression of benevolence, if our goodness could extend to him. If God deserves to be thanked and praised for his goodness, he would for the same reason, deserve that we should also requite his kindness, if that were possible. "What shall I render to the Lord for all his benefits?" [Ps. 116:12] is the natural language of thankfulness: and so far as in us lies, it is our duty to recompense God's goodness, and *render again according to benefits received.* And that we might have opportunity for so natural an expression of our gratitude to God, as beneficence, notwithstanding his being infinitely above our reach; he has appointed others to be his receivers, and to stand in his stead, as the objects of our beneficence; such are especially our indigent brethren.

SECTION 2. THE ACTS OF THE WILL OF THE HUMAN SOUL OF JESUS CHRIST NECESSARILY HOLY, YET TRULY VIRTUOUS, PRAISEWORTHY, REWARDABLE, ETC.

I HAVE already considered how Dr. Whitby insists upon it, that a freedom, not only from coaction, but necessity, is "requisite to either virtue or vice, praise or dispraise, reward or punishment." He also insists on the same freedom as absolutely requisite to a person's being the subject of a law, of precepts or prohibitions; in the book before mentioned (pp. 301, 314, 328, 339, 340, 341, 342, 347, 361, 373, 410). And of promises and threatenings (pp. 298, 301, 305, 311, 339, 340, 363). And as requisite to a state of trial (p. 297, etc.).

Now therefore, with an eye to these things, I would inquire into the moral conduct and practice of our Lord Jesus Christ, which he exhibited in his human nature here, in his state of humiliation. And first, I would show, that his holy behavior was necessary; or that it was impossible it should be otherwise, than that he should behave himself holily, and that he should be perfectly holy in each individual act of his life. And secondly, that his holy behavior was properly of the nature of virtue, and was worthy of praise; and that he was the subject of law, precepts or commands, promises and rewards; and that he was in a state of trial.

I. It was impossible, that the acts of the will of the human soul of Christ should, in any instance, degree or circumstance, be otherwise than holy, and agreeable to God's nature and will. The following things make this evident.

1. God had promised so effectually to preserve and uphold him by his Spirit, under all his temptations, that he should not fail of reaching the end for which he came into the world; which he would have failed of, had he fallen into sin. We have such a promise (Is. 42:1, 2, 3, 4), "Behold my servant, whom I uphold; mine elect, in whom my soul delighteth: I have put my Spirit upon him: he shall bring forth judgment to the Gentiles: he shall not cry, nor lift up,

nor cause his voice to be heard in the street . . . He shall bring
forth judgment unto truth. He shall not fail, nor be discouraged, till
he have set judgment in the earth; and the isles shall wait for his
law." This promise of Christ's having God's Spirit put upon him, and
his not crying and lifting up his voice, etc. relates to the time of
Christ's appearance on earth; as is manifest from the nature of the
promise, and also the application of it in the New Testament (Matt.
12:18). And the words imply a promise of his being so upheld by
God's Spirit, that he should be preserved from sin; particularly from
pride and vainglory, and from being overcome by any of the temptations he should be under to affect the glory of this world; the pomp
of an earthly prince, or the applause and praise of men: and that he
should be so upheld, that he should by no means fail of obtaining
the end of his coming into the world, of bringing forth judgment
unto victory, and establishing his kingdom of grace in the earth. And
in the following verses, this promise is confirmed, with the greatest
imaginable solemnity: "Thus saith the Lord, he that created the
heavens, and stretched them out; he that spread forth the earth, and
that which cometh out of it; he that giveth breath unto the people
upon it, and spirit to them that walk therein: I the Lord have called
thee in righteousness, and will hold thine hand; and will keep thee,
and give thee for a covenant of the people, for a light of the Gentiles,
to open the blind eyes, to bring out the prisoners from the prison,
and them that sit in darkness out of the prison-house. I am Jehovah,
that is my name," etc. [Is. 42:5–8].

Very parallel with these promises is that (Is. 49:7, 8, 9) which also
has an apparent respect to the time of Christ's humiliation on earth:
"Thus saith the Lord, the Redeemer of Israel, and his holy One, to
him whom man despiseth, to him whom the nation abhorreth, to a
servant of rulers; kings shall see and arise, princes also shall worship; because of the Lord that is faithful, and the holy One of Israel,
and he shall choose thee. Thus saith the Lord, in an acceptable time
have I heard thee; in a day of salvation have I helped thee; and I will
preserve thee, and give thee for a covenant of the people, to establish
the earth," etc.

And in Is. 50:5–9, we have the Messiah expressing his assurance,
that God would help him, by so opening his ear, or inclining his
heart to God's commandments, that he should not be rebellious, but
should persevere, and not apostatize, or turn his back: that through
God's help, he should be immovable, in a way of obedience, under

the great trials of reproach and suffering he should meet with; setting his face like a flint: so that he knew he should not be ashamed, or frustrated in his design; and finally should be approved and justified, as having done his work faithfully: "The Lord hath opened mine ear; so that I was not rebellious, neither turned away my back: I gave my back to the smiters, and my cheeks to them that plucked off the hair; I hid not my face from shame and spitting. For the Lord God will help me; therefore shall I not be confounded: therefore have I set my face as a flint, and I know that I shall not be ashamed. He is near that justifieth me: who will contend with me? Let us stand together. Who is mine adversary? Let him come near to me. Behold the Lord God will help me: who is he that shall condemn me? Lo, they shall all wax old as a garment, the moth shall eat them up."

2. The same thing is evident from all the promises which God made to the Messiah, of his future glory, kingdom and success, in his office and character of a mediator: which glory could not have been obtained, if his holiness had failed, and he had been guilty of sin. God's absolute promise of any things makes the things promised *necessary,* and their failing to take place absolutely *impossible:* and in like manner it makes those things necessary, on which the thing promised depends, and without which it can't take effect. Therefore it appears, that it was utterly impossible that Christ's holiness should fail, from such absolute promises as those (Ps. 110:4), "The Lord hath sworn, and will not repent, thou art a priest forever, after the order of Melchizedek." And from every other promise in that psalm, contained in each verse of it. And Ps. 2:6, 7, "I will declare the decree: the Lord hath said unto me, thou art my Son, this day have I begotten thee: ask of me, and I will give thee the heathen for thine inheritance," etc. Ps. 45:3, 4, etc.: "Gird thy sword on thy thigh, O most mighty, with thy glory and thy majesty; and in thy majesty ride prosperously." And so everything that is said from thence to the end of the psalm. And those promises, Is. 52:13, 14, 15; and 53:10, 11, 12. And all those promises which God makes to the Messiah, of success, dominion and glory in the character of redeemer, in Is. ch. 49.

3. It was often promised to the church of God of old, for their comfort, that God would give them a righteous, sinless Saviour. Jer. 23:5, 6: "Behold, the days come, saith the Lord, that I will raise up unto David a righteous branch; and a king shall reign and prosper, and shall execute judgment and justice in the earth. In his days shall Judah be saved, and Israel shall dwell safely. And this is the name

whereby he shall be called, the Lord our Righteousness." So, Jer. 33:15: "I will cause the branch of righteousness to grow up unto David; and he shall execute judgment and righteousness in the land." Is. 9:6, 7: "For unto us a child is born . . . upon the throne of David and of his kingdom, to order it, and to establish it with judgment and justice, from henceforth, even forever: the zeal of the Lord of hosts will do this." Ch. 11, at the beginning: "There shall come forth a rod out of the stem of Jesse, and a branch shall grow out of his roots; and the Spirit of the Lord shall rest upon him . . . the spirit of knowledge, and of the fear of the Lord . . . with righteousness shall he judge the poor, and reprove with equity . . . righteousness shall be the girdle of his loins, and faithfulness the girdle of his reins." Ch. 52:13: "My servant shall deal prudently." Ch. 53:9: "Because he had done no violence, neither was guile found in his mouth." If it be impossible, that these promises should fail, and it be easier for heaven and earth to pass away, than for one jot or tittle of these promises of God to pass away, then it was impossible that Christ should commit any sin. Christ himself signified, that it was impossible but that the things which were spoken concerning him should be fulfilled. Luke 24:44: "That all things must be fulfilled, which were written in the law of Moses, and in the prophets, and in the Psalms concerning me." Matt. 26:54: "But how then shall the Scripture be fulfilled, that thus it must be?" Mark 14:49: "But the Scriptures must be fulfilled." And so the Apostle, Acts 1:16, 17: "This Scripture must needs have been fulfilled."

4. All the promises which were made to the church of old, of the Messiah as a future Saviour, from that made to our first parents in paradise, to that which was delivered by the prophet Malachi, show it to be impossible that Christ should not have persevered in perfect holiness. The ancient predictions given to God's church, of the Messiah as a Saviour, were of the nature of promises; as is evident by the predictions themselves, and the manner of delivering them. But they are expressly, and very often called promises in the New Testament; as in Luke 1:54, 55, 72, 73; Acts 13:32, 33; Rom. 1:1, 2, 3; and ch. 15:8; Heb. 6:13, etc. These promises were often made with great solemnity, and confirmed with an oath; as in Gen. 22:16, 17, "By myself have I sworn, saith the Lord, that in blessing, I will bless thee, and in multiplying, I will multiply thy seed, as the stars of heaven, and as the sand which is upon the seashore: . . . and in thy seed shall all the nations of the earth be blessed." Compare Luke 1:72, 73

and Gal. 3:8, 15, 16. The Apostle in Heb. 6:17, 18 speaking of this promise to Abraham, says, "Wherein God willing more abundantly to shew to the heirs of promise the immutability of his counsel, confirmed it by an oath; that by two *immutable* things, in which it was *impossible* for God to lie, we [1] might have strong consolation." In which words, the *necessity* of the accomplishment, or (which is the same thing) the *impossibility* of the contrary, is fully declared. So God confirmed the promise of the great salvation of the Messiah, made to David, by an oath (Ps. 89:3, 4), "I have made a covenant with my chosen, I have sworn unto David my servant; thy seed will I establish forever, and build up thy throne to all generations." There is nothing that is so abundantly set forth in Scripture, as sure and irrefragable, as this promise and oath to David. See Ps. 89:34, 35, 36; II Sam. 23:5; Is. 55:3; Acts 2:29, 30; and 13:34. The Scripture expressly speaks of it as utterly impossible that this promise and oath to David, concerning the everlasting dominion of the Messiah of his seed, should fail. Jer. 33:15, etc.: "In those days, and at that time, I will cause the branch of righteousness to grow up unto David. . . . For thus saith the Lord, David shall never want a man to sit upon the throne of the house of Israel." Ver. 20, 21: "If you can break my covenant of the day, and my covenant of the night, and that there should not be day and night in their season; then may also my covenant be broken with David my servant, that he should not have a son to reign upon his throne." So in ver. 25, 26. Thus abundant is the Scripture in representing how impossible it was, that the promises made of old concerning the great salvation and kingdom of the Messiah should fail: which implies, that it was impossible that this Messiah, the second Adam, the promised seed of Abraham, and of David, should fall from his integrity, as the first Adam did.

5. All the promises that were made to the church of God under the Old Testament, of the great enlargement of the church, and advancement of her glory, in the days of the gospel, after the coming of the Messiah; the increase of her light, liberty, holiness, joy, triumph over her enemies, etc. of which so great a part of the Old Testament consists; which are repeated so often, are so variously exhibited, so frequently introduced with great pomp and solemnity, and are so abundantly sealed with typical and symbolical representations; I say, all these promises imply, that the Messiah should perfect the work of redemption; and this implies, that he should persevere in the work

1. [The 1754 ed. reads "he."]

which the Father had appointed him, being in all things conformed to his will. These promises were often confirmed by an oath (see Is. 54:9 with the context; ch. 62:8). And it is represented as utterly impossible that these promises should fail (Is. 49:15 with the context; ch. 54:10 with the context; ch. 51:4–8; ch. 40:8 with the context). And therefore it was impossible, that the Messiah should fail, or commit sin.

6. It was *impossible,* that the Messiah should fail of persevering in integrity and holiness, as the first Adam did, because this would have been inconsistent with the promises which God made to the blessed Virgin, his mother, and to her husband; implying, that "he should save his people from their sins," that "God would give him the throne of his father David," that "he should reign over the house of Jacob forever"; and that "of his kingdom there should be no end" [Matt. 1:21; Luke 1:32, 33]. These promises were sure, and it was impossible they should fail. And therefore the Virgin Mary, in trusting fully to them, acted reasonably, having an immovable foundation of her faith; as Elizabeth observes, [Luke 1:] ver. 45, "And blessed is she that believeth; for there shall be a performance of those things which were told her from the Lord."

7. That it should have been possible that Christ should sin, and so fail in the work of our redemption, does not consist with the eternal purpose and decree of God, revealed in the Scriptures, that he would provide salvation for fallen man in and by Jesus Christ, and that salvation should be offered to sinners through the preaching of the gospel. Such an absolute decree as this Arminians don't deny. Thus much at least (out of all controversy) is implied in such Scriptures, as I Cor. 2:7; Eph. 1:4, 5 and ch. 3:9, 10, 11; I Pet. 1:19, 20. Such an absolute decree as this, Arminians allow to be signified in these texts. And the Arminians' election of nations and societies, and general election of the Christian church, and conditional election of particular persons, imply this. God could not decree before the foundation of the world, to save all that should believe in, and obey Christ, unless he had absolutely decreed that salvation should be provided, and effectually wrought out by Christ. And since (as the Arminians themselves strenuously maintain) a decree of God infers necessity; hence it became necessary that Christ should persevere, and actually work out salvation for us, and that he should not fail by the commission of sin.

8. That it should have been possible for Christ's holiness to fail,

is not consistent with what God promised to his Son before all ages. For, that salvation should be offered to men through Christ, and be- stowed on all his faithful followers, is what is at least implied in that certain and infallible promise spoken of by the Apostle (Titus 1:2), "In hope of eternal life; which God, that cannot lie, promised before the world began." This don't seem to be controverted by Arminians.[2]

9. That it should be possible for Christ to fail of doing his Father's will, is inconsistent with the promise made to the Father by the Son, by the *Logos* that was with the Father from the beginning, before he took the human nature: as may be seen in Ps. 40:6, 7, 8 (compared with the Apostle's interpretation, Heb. 10:5–9), "Sacrifice and offer- ing thou didst not desire: mine ears hast thou opened (or bored); burnt-offering and sin-offering thou hast not required. Then said I, Lo, I come: in the Volume of the Book it is written of me, I delight to do thy will, O my God, and thy law is within my heart." Where is a manifest allusion to the covenant which the willing servant, who loved his master's service, made with his master, to be his servant forever, on the day wherein he had his ear bored; which covenant was probably inserted in the public records, called the "Volume of the Book," by the judges, who were called to take cognizance of the transaction (Ex. 21). If the *Logos,* who was with the Father, before the world, and who made the world, thus engaged in covenant to do the will of the Father in the human nature, and the promise, was as it were recorded, that it might be made sure, doubtless it was *im- possible* that it should fail; and so it was *impossible* that Christ should fail of doing the will of the Father in the human nature.

10. If it was possible for Christ to have failed of doing the will of his Father, and so to have failed of effectually working out redemption for sinners, then the salvation of all the saints, who were saved from the beginning of the world, to the death of Christ, was not built on a firm foundation. The Messiah, and the redemption which he was to work out by his obedience unto death, was the foundation of the salvation of all the posterity of fallen man, that ever were saved. Therefore, if when the Old Testament saints had the pardon of their sins, and the favor of God promised them, and salvation bestowed

2. See Dr. Whitby *Discourse on the Five Points,* Dis. I, ch. 3; pp. 48 ff. [where, concerning the terms "foreknowledge," "purpose," and "fore-appointment," Whitby asserts "that none of them relate to particular or individual Persons (save only when they are used of our Blessed Lord and his Sufferings for us) but only to Churches and Nations in general" (p. 48)].

upon them, still it was possible that the Messiah, when he came, might commit sin, then all this was on a foundation that was not firm and stable, but liable to fail; something which it was possible might never be. God did as it were trust to what his Son had engaged and promised to do in future time; and depended so much upon it, that he proceeded actually to save men on the account of it, as though it had been already done. But this trust and dependence of God, on the supposition of Christ's being liable to fail of doing his will, was leaning on a staff that was weak, and might possibly break. The saints of old trusted on the promises of a future redemption to be wrought out and completed by the Messiah, and built their comfort upon it: Abraham saw Christ's day and rejoiced; and he and the other patriarchs died in the faith of the promise of it (Heb. 11:13). But on this supposition, their faith and their comfort, and their salvation, was built on a movable fallible foundation; Christ was not to them a tried stone, a sure foundation; as in Is. 28:16. David entirely rested on the covenant of God with him, concerning the future glorious dominion and salvation of the Messiah, of his seed; says, it was "all his salvation, and all his desire"; and comforts himself that this covenant was an "everlasting covenant, ordered in all things and sure" (II Sam. 23:5). But if Christ's virtue might fail, he was mistaken: his great comfort was not built so sure, as he thought it was, being founded entirely on the determinations of the free will of Christ's human soul; which was subject to no necessity, and might be determined either one way or the other. Also the dependence of those who looked for redemption in Jerusalem, and waited for the consolation of Israel (Luke 2:25 and 38), and the confidence of the disciples of Jesus, who forsook all and followed him, that they might enjoy the benefits of his future kingdom, was built on a sandy foundation.

11. The man Christ Jesus, before he had finished his course of obedience, and while in the midst of temptations and trials, was abundant in positively predicting his own future glory in his kingdom, and the enlargement of his church, the salvation of the Gentiles through him, etc. and in promises of blessings he would bestow on his true disciples in his future kingdom; on which promises he required the full dependence of his disciples (John 14). But the disciples would have had no ground for such dependence, if Christ had been liable to fail in his work: and Christ himself would have been guilty of presumption, in so abounding in peremptory promises of great things, which depended on a mere contingence; viz. the

determinations of his free will, consisting in a freedom *ad utrumque,* to either sin or holiness, standing in indifference, and incident, in thousands of future instances, to go either one way or the other.

Thus it is evident, that it was *impossible* that the acts of the will of the human soul of Christ should be otherwise than holy, and conformed to the will of the Father; or, in other words, they were necessarily so conformed.

I have been the longer in the proof of this matter, it being a thing denied by some of the greatest Arminians, by Episcopius [3] in particular; and because I look upon it as a point clearly and absolutely determining the controversy between Calvinists and Arminians, concerning the necessity of such a freedom of will as is insisted on by the latter, in order to moral agency, virtue, command or prohibition, promise or threatening, reward or punishment, praise or dispraise, merit or demerit. I now therefore proceed,

II. To consider whether Christ, in his holy behavior on earth, was not thus a moral agent, subject to commands, promises, etc.:

Dr. Whitby very often speaks of what he calls a freedom *ad utrumlibet,* [4] without necessity, as requisite to law and commands; and speaks of necessity as entirely inconsistent with injunctions and prohibitions. But yet we read of Christ's being the subject of the commands of his Father (John 10:18; and 15:10). And Christ tells us, that everything that he said, or did, was in compliance with commandments he had received of the Father (John 12:49, 50; and 14:31). And we often read of Christ's obedience to his Father's commands (Rom. 5:19; Phil. 2:8; Heb. 5:8).

The forementioned writer represents promises offered as motives to persons to do their duty, or a being moved and induced by promises, as utterly inconsistent with a state wherein persons have not a liberty *ad utrumlibet,* but are necessarily determined to one. (See particularly, pp. 298 and 311). But the thing which this writer asserts, is demonstrably false, if the Christian religion be true. If there be any truth in Christianity or the holy Scriptures, the man Christ Jesus

3. [Simon Episcopius (1583–1643), Dutch theologian, who studied under Arminius and Gomarus at Leyden and succeeded Gomarus as professor there, was one of the leaders of the Remonstrants before the Synod of Dort (1618–19), Banished for a time, he later returned to Holland and headed the newly founded Remonstrant seminary in Amsterdam.]

4. [Freedom to choose either of two things, or to act in either way or direction, *whichever one pleases.*]

had his will infallibly, unalterably and unfrustrably determined to good, and that alone; but yet he had promises of glorious rewards made to him, on condition of his persevering in, and perfecting the work which God had appointed him (Is. 53:10, 11, 12; Ps. 2 and 110; Is. 49:7, 8, 9). In Luke 22:28, 29, Christ says to his disciples, "Ye are they which have continued with me in my temptations; and I appoint unto you a kingdom, as my Father hath appointed unto me." The word most properly signifies to appoint by covenant, or promise. The plain meaning of Christ's words is this: "As you have partook of my temptations and trials, and have been steadfast, and have overcome; I promise to make you partakers of my reward, and to give you a kingdom; as the Father has promised me a kingdom for continuing steadfast, and overcoming in those trials." And the words are well explained by those in Rev. 3:21, "To him that overcometh, will I grant to sit with me in my throne; even as I also overcame, and am set down with my Father in his throne." And Christ had not only promises of glorious success and rewards made to his obedience and sufferings, but the Scriptures plainly represent him as using these promises for motives and inducements to obey and suffer; and particularly that promise of a kingdom which the Father had appointed him, or sitting with the Father on his throne; as in Heb. 12:1, 2, "Let us lay aside every weight, and the sin which doth easily beset us, and let us run with patience the race that is set before us, looking unto Jesus, the author and finisher of our faith; who for the joy that was set before him, endured the cross, despising the shame, and is set down on the right hand of the throne of God."

And how strange would it be to hear any Christian assert, that the holy and excellent temper and behavior of Jesus Christ, and that obedience which he performed under such great trials, was not virtuous or praiseworthy; because his will was not free *ad utrumque,* to either holiness or sin, but was unalterably determined to one; that upon this account, there is no virtue at all, in all Christ's humility, meekness, patience, charity, forgiveness of enemies, contempt of the world, heavenly-mindedness, submission to the will of God, perfect obedience to his commands (though he was obedient unto death, even the death of the cross), his great compassion to the afflicted, his unparalleled love to mankind, his faithfulness to God and man, under such great trials; his praying for his enemies, even when nailing him to the cross; that "virtue," when applied to these things, "is but an empty name"; that there was no merit in any of these things; that is, that Christ was "worthy" of nothing at all on the account of them, worthy of no reward, no praise, no honor or respect from God or man; because his will was not indifferent, and free either to these things, or the contrary; but under such a strong inclination or bias to the things that were excellent, as made it *impossible* that he should choose the contrary; that upon this account (to use Dr. Whitby's language) "it would be sensibly unreasonable" that the human nature should be rewarded for any of these things! [5]

According to this doctrine, that Creature who is evidently set forth in Scripture as the "first born of every creature," as having "in all things the preëminence" [Col. 1:15, 18], and as the highest of all creatures in virtue, honor, and worthiness of esteem, praise and glory, on the account of his virtue, is less worthy of reward or praise, than the very least of saints; yea, no more worthy than a clock or mere machine, that is purely passive, and moved by natural necessity.

If we judge by scriptural representations of things, we have reason to suppose, that Christ took on him our nature, and dwelt with us in this world, in a suffering state, not only to satisfy for our sins; but that he, being in our nature and circumstances, and under our trials, might be our most fit and proper example, leader and captain, in the exercise of glorious and victorious virtue, and might be a visible instance of the glorious end and reward of it; that we might see in him the beauty, amiableness, and true honor and glory, and exceeding benefit of that virtue, which it is proper for us human beings to practice; and might thereby learn, and be animated, to seek the like glory and honor, and to obtain the like glorious reward. See Heb. 2:9–14, with 5:8, 9 and 12:1, 2, 3; John 15:10; Rom. 8:17; II Tim. 2:11, 12; I Pet. 2:19, 20; and 4:13. But if there was nothing of any virtue or merit, or worthiness of any reward, glory, praise or commendation at all, in all that he did, because it was all necessary, and he could not help it; then how is here anything so proper to animate and incite us, frce creatures, by patient continuance in well doing, to seek for honor, glory, and virtue?

God speaks of himself as peculiarly well pleased with the righteousness of this servant of his (Is. 42:21), "The Lord is well pleased for his righteousness sake." The sacrifices of old are spoken of as a sweet savor to God, but the obedience of Christ as far more acceptable than

5. [*Discourse on the Five Points,* Dis. I, ch. 1, no. 3; p. 15.]

they. Ps. 40:6, 7, 8: "Sacrifice and offering thou didst not desire: mine ear hast thou opened [as thy servant performing willing obedience]; [6] burnt-offering and sin-offering hast thou not required: then said I, Lo, I come [as a servant that cheerfully answers the calls of his master]: [6] I delight to do thy will, O my God, and thy law is within mine heart." Matt. 17:5: "This is my beloved Son, in whom I am well pleased." And Christ tells us expressly, that the Father loves him for that wonderful instance of his obedience, his voluntarily yielding himself to death, in compliance with the Father's command. John 10:17, 18: "Therefore doth my Father love me, because I lay down my life: . . . no man taketh it from me; but I lay it down of myself. . . . This commandment received I of my Father."

And if there was no merit in Christ's obedience unto death, if it was not worthy of praise, and of the most glorious rewards, the heavenly hosts were exceedingly mistaken, by the account that is given of them, in Rev. 5:8–12, "The four beasts and the four and twenty elders fell down before the Lamb, having everyone of them harps, and golden vials full of odors . . . and they sung a new song, saying, thou art *worthy* to take the book, and to open the seals thereof; for thou wast slain . . . and I beheld, and I heard the voice of many angels round about the throne, and the beasts, and the elders, and the number of them was ten thousand times ten thousand, and thousands of thousands, saying with a loud voice, *worthy* is the Lamb that was slain, to receive power, and riches, and wisdom, and strength, and honor, and glory, and blessing."

Christ speaks of the eternal life which he was to receive, as the reward of his obedience to the Father's commandments. John 12:49, 50: "I have not spoken of myself; but the Father which sent me, he gave me a commandment what I should say, and what I should speak: and I know that his commandment is life everlasting: whatsoever I speak therefore, even as the Father said unto me, so I speak." God promises to divide him a portion with the great etc. for his being his righteous servant, for his glorious virtue under such great trials and sufferings. Is. 53:11, 12: "He shall see of the travail of his soul and be satisfied: by his knowledge shall my righteous servant justify many; for he shall bear their iniquities. Therefore will I divide him a portion with the great, and he shall divide the spoil with the strong, because he hath poured out his soul unto death." The Scriptures rep-

6. [JE's brackets.]

resent God as rewarding him far above all his other servants. Phil.
2:7, 8, 9: "He took on him the form of a servant, and was made in
the likeness of men: and being found in fashion as a man, he humbled
himself, and became obedient unto death, even the death of the
cross: wherefore God also hath highly exalted him, and given him a
Name above every name." Ps. 45:7: "Thou lovest righteousness, and
hatest wickedness; therefore God, thy God, hath anointed thee with
the oil of gladness above thy fellows."

There is no room to pretend, that the glorious benefits bestowed
in consequence of Christ's obedience, are not properly of the nature
of a reward. What is a reward, in the most proper sense, but a benefit bestowed in consequence of something morally excellent in quality
or behavior, in testimony of well-pleasedness in that moral excellency,
and respect and favor on that account? If we consider the nature of
a reward most strictly, and make the utmost of it, and add to the
things contained in this description, proper merit or worthiness, and
the bestowment of the benefit in consequence of a promise; still it
will be found, there is nothing belonging to it, but that the Scripture
is most express as to its belonging to the glory bestowed on Christ,
after his sufferings; as appears from what has been already observed:
there was a glorious benefit bestowed in consequence of something
morally excellent, being called "righteousness" and "obedience";
there was great favor, love and well-pleasedness, for this righteousness
and obedience, in the bestower; there was proper merit, or worthiness of the benefit, in the obedience; it was bestowed in fulfillment
of promises, made to that obedience; and was bestowed *therefore,* or
because he had performed that obedience.

I may add to all these things, that Jesus Christ, while here in the
flesh, was manifestly in a state of trial. The last Adam, as Christ is
called (I Cor. 15:45; Rom. 5:14), taking on him the human nature,
and so the form of a servant, and being under the law, to stand and
act for us, was put into a state of trial, as the first Adam was. Dr.
Whitby mentions these three things as evidences of persons being in
a state of trial (*on the Five Points,* pp. 298, 299): namely, their afflictions being spoken of as their trials or temptations, their being the
subjects of promises, and their being exposed to Satan's temptations.
But Christ was apparently the subject of each of these. Concerning
promises made to him, I have spoken already. The difficulties and
afflictions he met with in the course of his obedience, are called his

temptations or trials (Luke 22:28), "Ye are they which have continued with me in my temptations," or trials.[7] Heb. 2:18: "For in that he himself hath suffered, being tempted [or tried] [8] he is able to succor them that are tempted." And ch. 4:15, "We have not an High Priest, which cannot be touched with the feeling of our infirmities; but was in all points tempted like as we are, yet without sin." And as to his being tempted by Satan, it is what none will dispute.

7. [The Revised Standard Version (1946) uses JE's word in translating this verse: "You are those who have continued with me in my trials."]
8. [JE's brackets.]

SECTION 3. THE CASE OF SUCH AS ARE GIVEN UP OF GOD TO SIN, AND OF FALLEN MAN IN GENERAL, PROVES MORAL NECESSITY AND INABILITY TO BE CONSISTENT WITH BLAMEWORTHINESS

D R. WHITBY asserts freedom, not only from coaction, but necessity, to be essential to anything deserving the name of "sin," and to an action's being culpable: in these words (*Discourse on Five Points*, edit. 3, p. 348),[1] "If they be thus necessitated, then neither their sins of omission or commission could deserve that name; it being essential to the nature of sin, according to St. Austin's[2] definition, that it be an action, *a quo liberum est abstinere*. Three things seem plainly necessary to make an action or omission culpable: 1. That it be in our power to perform or forbear it: for, as Origen, and all the fathers say, no man is blameworthy for not doing what he could not do." And elsewhere the Doctor insists, that when any do evil of necessity, what they do is no vice, that they are guilty of no fault,[3] are worthy of no blame, dispraise,[4] or dishonor,[5] but are unblamable.[6]

1. [*Discourse on the Five Points*, Dis. IV, ch. 3, no. 4. At this point JE begins to refer to the 3d ed. of Whitby's work. The pagination, however, is the same as the 2d ed. he used before, and the notation of a different edition may be a mistake.]

2. ["St. Austin," to whom is attributed the internal Latin quotation, almost certainly means St. Augustine of Hippo, even though Whitby cites Eusebius' *Praeparatio evangelica* as his source for it. Eusebius' dates were A.D. 275–339, while Augustine was not born until 354. Yet "Austin" was a syncopated form of his name frequently used in the eighteenth century, and nearby references (e.g. p. 340) which Whitby draws directly from such works as *De gratia et libero arbitrio* make it plain that it was St. Augustine he meant to range on the side of free will.]

3. *Discourse on the Five Points*, Dis. IV, ch. 3, no. 3; p. 347. Ibid., ch. 4, no. 3; pp. 360 f. Ibid., ch. 5, no. 2; p. 377.

4. Ibid., Dis. IV, ch. 1, no. 3; p. 303. Ibid., no. 8; p. 326. Ibid., ch. 2; p. 329. And many other places.

5. Ibid., Dis. IV, ch. 5, no. 2; p. 371.

6. Ibid., Dis. IV, ch. 1, no. 3; p. 304. Ibid., ch. 4, no. 3; p. 361.

If these things are true, in Dr. Whitby's sense of necessity, they will prove all such to be blameless, who are given up of God to sin, in what they commit after they are thus given up. That there is such a thing as men's being judicially given up to sin, is certain, if the Scripture rightly informs us; such a thing being often there spoken of: as in Ps. 81:12, "So I gave them up to their own hearts' lust, and they walked in their own counsels." Acts 7:42: "Then God turned, and gave them up to worship the host of heaven." Rom. 1:24: "Wherefore, God also gave them up to uncleanness, through the lusts of their own hearts, to dishonor their own bodies between themselves." Ver. 26: "For this cause God gave them up to vile affections." Ver. 28: "And even as they did not like to retain God in their knowledge, God gave them over to a reprobate mind, to do those things that are not convenient."

'Tis needless to stand particularly to inquire, what God's "giving men up to their own hearts' lusts" signifies: it is sufficient to observe, that hereby is certainly meant God's so ordering or disposing things, in some respect or other, either by doing or forebearing to do, as that the consequence should be men's continuing in their sins. So much as men are given up *to,* so much is the consequence of their being given up; whether that be less or more. If God don't order things so, by action or permission, that sin will be the consequence, then the event proves that they are not given up to that consequence. If good be the consequence, instead of evil, then God's mercy is to be acknowledged in that good; which mercy must be contrary to God's judgment in giving up to evil. If the event must prove that they are given up to evil as the consequence, then the persons who are the subjects of this judgment, must be the subjects of such an event, and so the event is necessary.

If not only *coaction,* but *all necessity,* will prove men blameless, then Judas was blameless, after Christ had given him over, and had already declared his certain damnation, and that he should *verily* betray him. He was guilty of no sin in betraying his master, on this supposition; though his so doing is spoken of by Christ as the most aggravated sin, more heinous than the sin of Pilate in crucifying him. And the Jews in Egypt, in Jeremiah's time, were guilty of no sin, in their not worshipping the true God, after God had "sworn by his great Name, that his name should be no more named in the mouth of any man of Judah, in all the land of Egypt" (Jer. 44:26).

Dr. Whitby (*Discourse on Five Points*, pp. 302, 303) [7] denies, that men, in this world, are ever so given up by God to sin, that their wills should be necessarily determined to evil; though he owns, that hereby it may become "exceeding difficult" for men to do good, having a strong bent, and powerful inclination to what is evil. But if we should allow the case to be just as he represents, the judgment of giving up to sin will no better agree with his notions of that liberty, which is essential to praise or blame, than if we should suppose it to render the avoiding of sin *impossible*. For if an impossibility of avoiding sin wholly excuses a man; then, for the same reason, its being difficult to avoid it excuses him in part; and this just in proportion to the degree of difficulty. If the influence of *moral* impossibility or inability be the same, to excuse persons in not doing, or not avoiding anything, as that of *natural* inability (which is supposed), then undoubtedly, in like manner, *moral difficulty* has the same influence to excuse with *natural difficulty*. But all allow, that natural impossibility wholly excuses, and also that natural difficulty excuses in part, and makes the act or omission less blamable, in proportion to the difficulty. All natural difficulty, according to the plainest dictates of the light of nature, excuses in some degree, so that the neglect is not so blamable, as if there had been no difficulty in the case: and so the greater the difficulty is, still the more excusable, in proportion to the increase of the difficulty. And as natural impossibility wholly excuses and excludes all blame, so the nearer the difficulty approaches to impossibility, still the nearer a person is to blamelessness, in proportion to that approach. And if the case of moral impossibility or necessity, be just the same with natural necessity or coaction, as to influence to excuse a neglect, then also, for the same reason, the case of natural difficulty don't differ in influence, to excuse a neglect, from moral difficulty, arising from a strong bias or bent to evil, such as Dr. Whitby owns in the case of those that are given up to their own hearts' lusts. So that the fault of such persons must be lessened, in proportion to the difficulty, and approach to impossibility. If ten degrees of moral difficulty make the action quite impossible, and so wholly excuse, then if there be nine degrees of difficulty, the person is in great part excused, and in nine degrees in ten, less blameworthy, than if there had been no difficulty at all; and he has but one degree of blameworthiness. The reason is plain, on Arminian principles; viz.

7. Ibid., Dis. IV, ch. 1, no. 3.

because as difficulty, by antecedent bent and bias on the will, is increased, liberty of indifference, and self-determination in the will, is diminished: so much hindrance and impediment is there, in the way of the will's acting freely, by mere self-determination. And if ten degrees of such hindrance take away all such liberty, then nine degrees take away nine parts in ten, and leave but one degree of liberty. And therefore there is but one degree of blamableness, *caeteris paribus,* in the neglect; the man being no further blamable in what he does, or neglects, than he has liberty in that affair: for blame or praise (say they) arises wholly from a good use or abuse of liberty.

From all which it follows, that a strong bent and bias one way, and difficulty of going the contrary, never causes a person to be at all more exposed to sin, or anything blamable: because as the difficulty is increased, so much the less is required and expected. Though in one respect, exposedness to sin or fault is increased, viz. by an increase of exposedness to the evil action or omission; yet it is diminished in another respect, to balance it; namely, as the sinfulness or blamableness of the action or omission is diminished in the same proportion. So that, on the whole, the affair, as to exposedness to guilt or blame, is left just as it was.

To illustrate this, let us suppose a scale of a balance to be intelligent, and a free agent, and indued with a self-moving power, by virtue of which it could act and produce effects to a certain degree; ex. gr.[8] to move itself up or down with a force equal to a weight of ten pounds; and that it might therefore be required of it, in ordinary circumstances, to move itself down with that force; for which it has power and full liberty, and therefore would be blameworthy if it failed of it. But then let us suppose a weight of ten pounds to be put in the opposite scale, which in force entirely counterbalances its self-moving power, and so renders it impossible for it to move down at all; and therefore wholly excuses it from any such motion. But if we suppose there to be only nine pounds in the opposite scale, this renders its motion not impossible, but yet more difficult; so that it can now only move down with the force of one pound: but however, this is all that is required of it under these circumstances; it is wholly excused from nine parts of its motion: and if the scale, under these circumstances, neglects to move, and remains at rest, all that it will be blamed for, will be its neglect of that one tenth part of its motion;

8. ["*ex gratia*" (from grace), or as we put it in this less religious age, "e.g." (for example).]

which it had as much liberty and advantage for, as in usual circumstances, it has for the greater motion, which in such a case would be required. So that this new difficulty, don't at all increase its exposedness to anything blameworthy.

And thus the very supposition of difficulty in the way of a man's duty, or proclivity to sin, through a being given up to hardness of heart, or indeed by any other means whatsoever, is an inconsistence, according to Dr. Whitby's notions of liberty, virtue and vice, blame and praise. The avoiding sin and blame, and the doing what is virtuous and praiseworthy, must be always equally easy.

Dr. Whitby's notions of liberty, obligation, virtue, sin, etc. lead him into another great inconsistence. He abundantly insists, that necessity is inconsistent with the nature of sin or fault. He says in the forementioned treatise (p. 14), "Who can blame a person for doing what he could not help?" And (p. 15), "It being sensibly unjust, to punish any man for doing that which it was never in his power to avoid." [9] And in p. 341 to confirm his opinion, he quotes one of the fathers, saying, "Why doth God command, if man hath not free will and power to obey?" And again in the same and the next page, "Who will not cry out, that it is folly to command him, that hath not liberty to do what is commanded; and that it is unjust to condemn him, that has it not in his power to do what is required?" [1] And in p. 373, he cites another saying, "A law is given to him that can turn to both parts; i.e. obey or transgress it: but no law can be against him who is bound by nature." [2]

And yet the same Dr. Whitby asserts, that fallen man is not able to perform perfect obedience. In p. 165 he has these words, "The nature of Adam had power to continue innocent, and without sin; whereas it is certain, our nature never had so." [3] But if we han't power to continue innocent and without sin, then sin is consistent with necessity, and we may be sinful in that which we have not power to avoid; and those things can't be true, which he asserts elsewhere, namely, "That if we be necessitated, neither sins of omission nor commission, would deserve that name" (p. 348). [4] If we have it not in our power to be innocent, then we have it not in our power to be

---

9. [*Discourse on the Five Points*, Dis. I, ch. 1, no. 3.]
1. [Ibid., Dis. IV, ch. 2, no. 4.]
2. [Ibid., Dis. IV, ch. 5, no. 2.]
3. [Ibid., Dis. II, ch. 6, no. 7. See above, Intro., Pt. 5, no. 9.]
4. [Ibid., Dis. IV, ch. 3, no. 3.]

blameless: and if so, we are under a necessity of being blameworthy. And how does this consist with what he so often asserts, that necessity is inconsistent with blame or praise? If we have it not in our power to perform perfect obedience to all the commands of God, then we are under a necessity of breaking some commands, in some degree; having no power to perform so much as is commanded. And if so, why does he cry out of the unreasonableness and folly of commanding beyond what men have power to do?

And Arminians in general are very inconsistent with themselves in what they say of the inability of fallen man in this respect. They strenuously maintain, that it would be unjust in God, to require anything of us beyond our present power and ability to perform; and also hold, that we are now unable to perform perfect obedience, and that Christ died to satisfy for the imperfections of our obedience, and has made way that our imperfect obedience might be accepted instead of perfect: wherein they seem insensibly to run themselves into the grossest inconsistence. For (as I have observed elsewhere), "They hold that God in mercy to mankind has abolished that rigorous constitution or law, that they were under originally; and instead of it, has introduced a more mild constitution, and put us under a new law, which requires no more than imperfect sincere obedience, in compliance with our poor infirm impotent circumstances since the fall." [5]

Now, how can these things be made consistent? I would ask what law these imperfections of our obedience are a breach of? If they are a breach of no law that we were ever under, then they are not sins. And if they be not sins, what need of Christ's dying to satisfy for them? But if they are sins, and the breach of some law, what law is it? They can't be a breach of their new law; for that requires no other than imperfect obedience, or obedience with imperfections: and therefore to have obedience attended with imperfections, is no breach of it; for 'tis as much as it requires. And they can't be a breach of their old law; for that, they say, is entirely abolished, and we never were under it. They say, it would not be just in God to require of us perfect obedience, because it would not be just to require more than we can perform, or to punish us for failing of it. And therefore, by their own scheme, the imperfections of our obedience don't deserve

5. ["Justification by Faith Alone," a sermon in a series presumably delivered in 1734 and published in 1738. *Sermons on Various Important Subjects,* in Worcester ed., *7, 33.*]

to be punished. What need therefore of Christ's dying, to satisfy for them? What need of his suffering, to satisfy for that which is no fault, and in its own nature deserves no suffering? What need of Christ's dying, to purchase, that our *imperfect* obedience should be accepted, when according to their scheme, it would be unjust in itself, that any other obedience than *imperfect* should be required? What need of Christ's dying to make way for God's accepting such an obedience, as it would be unjust in him not to accept? Is there any need of Christ's dying, to prevail with God not to do unrighteously? If it be said, that Christ died to satisfy that old law for us, that so we might not be under it, but that there might be room for our being under a more mild law; still I would inquire, what need of Christ's dying that we might not be under a law, which (by their principles) it would be in itself unjust that we should be under, whether Christ had died or no, because in our present state we are not able to keep it?

So the Arminians are inconsistent with themselves, not only in what they say of the need of Christ's satisfaction to atone for those imperfections which we cannot avoid, but also in what they say of the grace of God, granted to enable men to perform the sincere obedience of the new law. "I grant (says Dr. Stebbing) [6] indeed, that by reason of original sin, we are utterly disabled for the performance of the condition, without new grace from God. But I say then, that he gives such grace to all of us, by which the performance of the condition is truly possible: and upon this ground he may, and doth most righteously require it." If Dr. Stebbing intends to speak properly, by "grace" he must mean, that assistance which is of grace, or of free favor and kindness. But yet in the same place he speaks of it as very "unreasonable, unjust and cruel," for God to require that, as the condition of pardon, that is become impossible by original sin. If it be so, what *grace* is there in giving assistance and ability to perform the condition of pardon? Or why is that called by the name of grace, that is an absolute debt, which God is bound to bestow, and which it would be unjust and cruel in him to withhold, seeing he requires that, *as the condition of pardon,* which we cannot perform without it?

6. Henry Stebbing, *A Treatise Concerning the Operations of the Holy Spirit, Being the Substance of the late Reverend and Learned Dr. William Clagett's Discourse upon That Subject, with Large Additions,* 1719. [The quotation appears to be the words of Dr. William Clagett, in his book against Dr. Owen, here abstracted by Stebbing.]

SECTION 4. COMMAND, AND OBLIGATION TO OBEDIENCE, CONSISTENT WITH MORAL INABILITY TO OBEY

IT BEING so much insisted on by Arminian writers, that necessity is inconsistent with law or command, and particularly, that it is absurd to suppose God by his command should require that of men which they are unable to do; not allowing in this case for any difference that there is between natural and moral inability; I would therefore now particularly consider this matter.

And for the greater clearness, I would distinctly lay down the following things.

I. The will itself, and not only those actions which are the effects of the will, is the proper object of precept or command. That is, such or such a state or acts of men's wills, is in many cases, properly required of them by command; and not only those alterations in the state of their bodies or minds that are the consequences of volition. This is most manifest; for 'tis the soul only, that is properly and directly the subject of precepts or commands; that only being capable of receiving or perceiving commands. The motions or state of the body are matter of command, only as they are subject to the soul, and connected with its acts. But now the soul has no other faculty whereby it can, in the most direct and proper sense, consent, yield to, or comply with any command, but the faculty of the will; and 'tis by this faculty only, that the soul can directly disobey, or refuse compliance: for the very notions of "consenting," "yielding," "accepting," "complying," "refusing," "rejecting," etc. are, according to the meaning of the terms, nothing but certain acts of the will. Obedience, in the primary nature of it, is the submitting and yielding of the will of one to the will of another. Disobedience is the not consenting, not complying of the will of the commanded to the manifested will of the commander. Other acts that are not the acts of the will, as certain motions of the body and alterations in the soul, are obedience or disobedience only indirectly, as they are connected with the state or actions of the will, according to an established law of nature. So that 'tis manifest, the will itself may be required: and the being of a good will is the most proper, direct and immediate subject of command; and if this can't be prescribed or required by command or precept, nothing can; for other things can be required no otherwise than as they depend upon, and are the fruits of a good will.

Corol. 1. If there be several acts of the will, or a series of acts, one following another, and one the effect of another, the *first and determining act* is properly the subject of command, and not only the consequent acts, which are dependent upon it. Yea, 'tis this more especially which is that which command or precept has a proper respect to; because 'tis this act that determines the whole affair: in this act the obedience or disobedience lies, in a peculiar manner; the consequent acts being all subject to it, and governed and determined by it. This determining governing act must be the proper subject of precept, or none.

Corol. 2. It also follows from what has been observed, that if there be any sort of act, or exertion of the soul, prior to all free acts of the will or acts of choice in the case, directing and determining what the acts of the will shall be; that act or exertion of the soul can't properly be subject to any command or precept, in any respect whatsoever, either directly or indirectly, immediately or remotely. Such acts can't be subject to commands *directly,* because they are no acts of the will; being by the supposition prior to all acts of the will, determining and giving rise to all its acts: they not being acts of the will, there can be in them no consent to, or compliance with any command. Neither can they be subject to command or precept *indirectly* or *remotely;* for they are not so much as the effects or consequences of the will, being prior to all its acts. So that if there be any obedience in that original act of the soul, determining all volitions, it is an act of obedience wherein the will has no concern at all; it preceding every act of will. And therefore, if the soul either obeys or disobeys in this act, it is wholly involuntarily; there is no willing obedience or rebellion, no compliance or opposition of the will in the affair: and what sort of obedience or rebellion is this!

And thus the Arminian notion of the freedom of the will consisting in the soul's determining its own acts of will, instead of being essential to moral agency, and to men's being the subjects of moral government, is utterly inconsistent with it. For if the soul determines *all* its acts of will, it is therein subject to no command or moral government, as has been now observed; because its original determining act is no act of will or choice, it being prior, by the supposition, to *every act* of will. And the soul can't be the subject of command in the act of the will itself, which depends on the foregoing determining act, and is determined by it; inasmuch as this is necessary, being the necessary consequence and effect of that prior determining act, which is not voluntary. Nor can the man be the subject of command or government in his external actions; because these are all necessary, being the necessary effects of the acts of the will themselves. So that mankind, according to this scheme, are subjects of command or moral government in nothing at all; and all their moral agency is entirely excluded, and no room left for virtue or vice in the world.

So that 'tis the Arminian scheme, and not the scheme of the Calvinists, that is utterly inconsistent with moral government, and with all use of laws, precepts, prohibitions, promises, or threatenings. Neither is there any way whatsoever to make their principles consist with these things. For if it be said, that there is no prior determining act of the soul, preceding the acts of the will, but that volitions are events that come to pass by pure accident, without any determining cause, this is most palpably inconsistent with all use of laws and precepts; for nothing is more plain than that laws can be of no use to direct and regulate perfect accident; which by the supposition of its being pure accident, is in no case regulated by anything preceding; but happens this way or that perfectly by chance, without any cause or rule. The perfect uselessness of laws and precepts also follows from the Arminian notion of indifference, as essential to that liberty which is requisite to virtue or vice. For the end of laws is to *bind to one side;* and the end of commands is to turn the will one way: and therefore they are of no use unless they turn or bias the will that way. But if liberty consists in indifference, then their biasing the will one way only, destroys liberty; as it puts the will out of equilibrium. So that the will, having a bias, through the influence of binding law, laid upon it, is not wholly left to itself, to determine itself which way it will, without influence from without.

II. Having shown that the will itself, especially in those acts which are original, leading and determining in any case, is the proper subject of precept and command, and not only those alterations in the body, etc. which are the effects of the will; I now proceed in the second place, to observe that the very opposition or defect of the will itself, in that act which is its *original and determining act* in the case,

I say the will's opposition *in this act* to a thing proposed or com-manded, or its failing of compliance, implies a moral inability to that thing: or in other words, whenever a command requires a cer-tain state or act of the will, and the person commanded, notwithstand-ing the command and the circumstances under which it is exhibited, still finds his will opposite or wanting, in *that,* belonging to its state or acts, *which is original and determining in the affair,* that man is morally unable to obey that command.

This is manifest from what was observed in the first part, concern-ing the nature of *moral* inability, as distinguished from *natural:* where it was observed, that a man may then be said to be morally unable to do a thing, when he is under the influence or prevalence of a contrary inclination, or has a want of inclination, under such cir-cumstances and views. 'Tis also evident from what has been before proved, that the will is always, and in every individual act, neces-sarily determined by the strongest motive; and so is always unable to go against the motive, which all things considered, has now the greatest strength and advantage to move the will. But not further to insist on these things, the truth of the position now laid down, viz. that when the will is opposite *to,* or failing of a compliance with a thing *in its original determining inclination or act,* it is not able to comply, appears by the consideration of these two things.

1. The will in the time of that diverse or opposite leading act or inclination, and when actually under the influence of it, is not able to exert itself to the contrary, to make an alteration, in order to a compliance. The inclination is unable to change itself; and that for this plain reason, that it is unable to incline to change itself. Present choice can't at present choose to be otherwise: for that would be *at present* to choose something diverse from what is *at present* chosen. If the will, all things now considered, inclines or chooses to go that way, then it can't choose, all things now considered, to go the other way, and so can't choose to be made to go the other way. To suppose that the mind is now sincerely inclined to change itself to a different inclination, is to suppose the mind is now truly inclined otherwise than it is now inclined. The will may oppose some future remote act that it is exposed to, but not its own present act.

2. As it is impossible that the will should comply with the thing commanded with respect to its *leading act,* by any act of its own, in the time of that diverse or opposite *leading and original act,* or after it is actually come under the influence of that *determining*

choice or inclination; so 'tis impossible it should be determined to a compliance by any foregoing act; for by the very supposition, there is no foregoing act; the opposite or noncomplying act being that act which is *original* and *determining* in the case. Therefore it must be so, that if this *first determining act* be found noncomplying, on the proposal of the command, the mind is morally unable to obey. For to suppose it to be able to obey, is to suppose it to be able to determine and cause its *first determining act* to be otherwise, and that it has power better to govern and regulate its *first governing and regulating act,* which is absurd; for it is to suppose a prior act of the will, determining its first determining act; that is, an act prior to the first, and leading and governing the original and governing act of all; which is a contradiction.

Here if it should be said, that although the mind has not any ability to will contrary to what it does will, in the original and leading act of the will, because there is supposed to be no prior act to determine and order it otherwise, and the will can't immediately change itself, because it can't at present incline to a change; yet the mind has an ability for the present to *forbear* to proceed to action, and take time for deliberation; which may be an occasion of the change of the inclination—

I answer, (1) In this objection that seems to be forgotten which was observed before, viz. that the determining to take the matter into consideration, is itself an act of the will: and if this be all the act wherein the mind exercises ability and freedom, then this, by the supposition, must be all that can be commanded or required by precept. And if this act be the commanded act, then all that has been observed concerning the commanded act of the will remains true, that the very want of it is a moral inability to exert it, etc. (2) We are speaking concerning the first and leading act of the will in the case, or about the affair; and if a determining to deliberate, or on the contrary, to proceed immediately without deliberating, be the first and leading act; or whether it be or no, if there be another act before it, which determines that; or whatever be the original and leading act; still the foregoing proof stands good, that the non-compliance of the leading act implies moral inability to comply.

If it should be objected, that these things make all moral inability equal, and suppose men morally unable to will otherwise than they actually do will, in all cases, and equally so, in every instance—

In answer to this objection, I desire two things may be observed.

First, that if by being *equally* unable, be meant as *really* unable; then so far as the inability is merely moral, 'tis true, the will, in every instance, acts by moral necessity, and is morally unable to act otherwise, as truly and properly in one case as another; as, I humbly conceive, has been perfectly and abundantly demonstrated by what has been said in the preceding part of this essay. But yet, in some respect, the inability may be said to be greater in some instances than others: though the man may be truly unable (if moral inability can truly be called inability), yet he may be further from being able to do some things than others. As it is in things which men are naturally unable to do. A person whose strength is no more than sufficient to lift the weight of one hundred pounds, is as truly and really unable to lift one hundred and one pounds, as ten thousand pounds; but yet he is further from being able to lift the latter weight than the former; and so, according to common use of speech, has a greater inability for it. So it is in moral inability. A man is truly morally unable to choose contrary to a present inclination, which in the least degree prevails; or contrary to that motive, which, all things considered, has strength and advantage now to move the will, in the least degree, superior to all other motives in view: but yet he is further from ability to resist a very strong habit, and a violent and deeply rooted inclination, or a motive vastly exceeding all others in strength. And again, the inability may in some respects be called greater, in some instances than others, as it may be *more general* and *extensive to all acts of that kind.* So men may be said to be unable in a different sense, and to be further from moral ability, who have that moral inability which is *general* and *habitual,* than they who have only that inability which is *occasional* and *particular.*[1] Thus in cases of natural inability; he that is born blind may be said to be unable to see, in a different manner, and is in some respects further from being able to see, than he whose sight is hindered by a transient cloud or mist.

And besides, that which was observed in the first part of this discourse concerning the inability which attends a *strong and settled habit,* should be here remembered; viz. that fixed habit is attended with this peculiar moral inability, by which it is distinguished from *occasional volition,* namely, that endeavors to avoid future volitions of that kind, which are agreeable to such a habit, much more frequently and commonly prove vain and insufficient. For though it is

1. See this distinction of moral inability explained in Pt. I, Sec. 4.

impossible there should be any true sincere desires and endeavors against a present volition or choice, yet there may be against volitions of that kind, when viewed at a distance. A person may desire and use means to prevent future exercises of a certain inclination; and in order to it, may wish the habit might be removed; but his desires and endeavors may be ineffectual. The man may be said in some sense to be unable; yea, even as the word "unable" is a *relative term,* and has relation to ineffectual endeavors; yet not with regard to present, but remote endeavors.

Secondly, it must be borne in mind, according to what was observed before, that indeed no inability whatsoever which is merely moral, is properly called by the name of "inability"; and that in the strictest propriety of speech, a man may be said to have a thing in his power, if he has it at his election; and he can't be said to be unable to do a thing, when he can if he now pleases, or whenever he has a proper, direct and immediate desire for it. As to those desires and endeavors that may be against the exercises of a strong habit, with regard to which men may be said to be unable to avoid those exercises, they are remote desires and endeavors in two respects. First, as to *time;* they are never against present volitions, but only against volitions of such a kind, when viewed at a distance. Secondly, as to their *nature;* these opposite desires are not directly and properly against the habit and inclination itself, or the volitions in which it is exercised; for these, in themselves considered, are agreeable; but against something else, that attends them, or is their consequence; the opposition of the mind is leveled entirely against this; the inclination or volitions themselves are not at all opposed directly, and for their own sake; but only indirectly, and remotely on the account of something alien and foreign.

III. Though the opposition of the will itself, or the very want of will to a thing commanded, implies a moral inability to that thing; yet, if it be as has been already shown, that the being of a good state or act of will, is a thing most properly required by command; then, in some cases such a state or act of will may properly be required, which at present is not, and which may also be wanting after it is commanded. And therefore those things may properly be commanded, which men have a moral inability for.

Such a state or act of the will, may be required by command, as does not already exist. For if that volition only may be commanded to be which already is, there could be no use of precept; commands in all cases would be perfectly vain and impertinent. And not only may such a will be required as is wanting before the command is given, but also such as may possibly be wanting afterwards; such as the exhibition of the command may not be effectual to produce or excite. Otherwise, no such thing as disobedience to a proper and rightful command is possible in any case; and there is no case supposable or possible, wherein there can be an inexcusable or faulty disobedience. Which Arminians cannot affirm, consistently with their principles: for this makes obedience to just and proper commands always *necessary*, and disobedience impossible. And so the Arminian would overthrow himself, yielding the very point we are upon, which he so strenuously denies, viz. that law and command are consistent with necessity.

If merely that inability will excuse disobedience, which is implied in the opposition or defect of inclination, remaining after the command is exhibited, then wickedness always carries that in it which excuses it. 'Tis evermore so, that by how much the more wickedness there is in a man's heart, by so much is his inclination to evil the stronger, and by so much the more therefore has he of moral inability to the good required. His moral inability, consisting in the strength of his evil inclination, is the very thing wherein his wickedness consists; and yet according to Arminian principles, it must be a thing inconsistent with wickedness; and by how much the more he has of it, by so much is he the further from wickedness.

Therefore, on the whole, it is manifest, that moral inability alone (which consists in disinclination) never renders anything improperly the subject matter of precept or command, and never can excuse any person in disobedience, or want of conformity to a command.

Natural inability, arising from the want of natural capacity, or external hindrance (which alone is properly called inability) without doubt wholly excuses, or makes a thing improperly the matter of command. If men are excused from doing or acting any good thing, supposed to be commanded, it must be through some defect or obstacle that is not in the will itself, but extrinsic to it; either in the capacity of understanding, or body, or outward circumstances.

Here two or three things may be observed,

1. As to spiritual duties or acts, or any good thing in the state of immanent acts of the will itself, or of the affections (which are only certain modes of the exercise of the will) if persons are justly excused, it must be through want of capacity in the natural faculty of

understanding. Thus the same spiritual duties, or holy affections and exercises of heart, can't be required of men, as may be of angels; the capacity of understanding being so much inferior. So men can't be required to love those amiable persons whom they have had no opportunity to see, or hear of, or come to the knowledge of, in any way agreeable to the natural state and capacity of the human understanding. But the insufficiency of motives will not excuse; unless their being insufficient arises not from the moral state of the will or inclination itself, but from the state of the natural understanding. The great kindness and generosity of another may be a motive insufficient to excite gratitude in the person that receives the kindness, through his vile and ungrateful temper: in this case, the insufficiency of the motive arises from the state of the will or inclination of heart, and don't at all excuse. But if this generosity is not sufficient to excite gratitude, being unknown, there being no means of information adequate to the state and measure of the person's faculties, this insufficiency is attended with a natural inability, which entirely excuses.

2. As to such motions of body, or exercises and alterations of mind, which don't consist in the immanent acts or state of the will itself, but are supposed to be required as effects of the will; I say, in such supposed effects of the will, in cases wherein there is no want of a capacity of understanding; that inability, and that only excuses, which consists in want of connection between them and the will. If the will fully complies, and the proposed effect don't prove, according to the laws of nature, to be connected with his volition, the man is perfectly excused; he has a natural inability to the thing required. For the will itself, as has been observed, is all that can be directly and immediately required by command; and other things only indirectly, as connected with the will. If therefore there be a full compliance of will, the person has done his duty; and if other things don't prove to be connected with his volition, that is not owing to him.

3. Both these kinds of natural inability that have been mentioned, and so all inability that excuses, may be resolved into one thing; namely, want of natural capacity or strength; either capacity of understanding, or external strength. For when there are external defects and obstacles, they would be no obstacles, were it not for the inperfection and limitations of understanding and strength.

Corol. If things for which men have a moral inability, may properly be the matter of precept or command, then they may also of invitation and counsel. Commands, and invitations come very much to the same thing; the difference is only circumstantial: commands are as much a manifestation of the will of him that speaks, as invitations, and as much testimonies of expectation of compliance. The difference between them lies in nothing that touches the affair in hand. The main difference between command and invitation consists in the enforcement of the will of him who commands or invites. In the latter it is his *kindness,* the goodness which his will arises from: in the former it is his *authority.* But whatever be the ground of the will of him that speaks, or the enforcement of what he says, yet seeing neither his will nor expectation is any more testified in the one case than the other; therefore a person's being known to be morally unable to do the thing to which he is directed *by invitation,* is no more an evidence of insincerity in him that directs, in manifesting either a will, or expectation which he has not, than his being known to be morally unable to do what he is directed to *by command.* So that all this grand objection of Arminians against the inability of fallen men to exert faith in Christ, or to perform other spiritual gospel duties, from the sincerity of God's counsels and invitations, must be without force.

SECTION 5. THAT SINCERITY OF DESIRES AND ENDEAVORS, WHICH IS SUPPOSED TO EXCUSE IN THE NONPERFORMANCE OF THINGS IN THEMSELVES GOOD, PARTICULARLY CONSIDERED

'TIS WHAT is much insisted on by many, that some men, though they are not able to perform spiritual duties, such as repentance of sin, love to God, a cordial acceptance of Christ as exhibited and offered in the gospel, etc. yet they may sincerely desire and endeavor these things; and therefore must be excused; it being unreasonable to blame 'em for the omission of those things which they sincerely desire and endeavor to do, but can't do.

Concerning this matter, the following things may be observed.

1. What is here supposed, is a great mistake, and gross absurdity; even that men may sincerely choose and desire those spiritual duties of love, acceptance, choice, rejection, etc. consisting in the exercise of the will itself, or in the disposition and inclination of the heart; and yet not be able to perform or exert them. This is absurd, because 'tis absurd to suppose that a man should directly, properly and sincerely incline to have an inclination, which at the same time is contrary to his inclination: for that is to suppose him not to be inclined to that which he is inclined to. If a man, in the state and acts of his will and inclination, does properly and directly fall in with those duties, he therein performs 'em: for the duties themselves consist in that very thing; they consist in the state and acts of the will being so formed and directed. If the soul properly and sincerely falls in with a certain proposed act of will or choice, the soul therein makes that choice its own. Even as when a moving body falls in with a proposed direction of its motion, that is the same thing as to move in that direction.

2. That which is called a "desire" and "willingness" for those inward duties, in such as don't perform them, has respect to these duties only indirectly and remotely, and is improperly represented as a will-

ingness for them; not only because (as was observed before) it respects those good volitions only in a distant view, and with respect to future time; but also because evermore, not these things themselves, but something else, that is alien and foreign, is the object that terminates these volitions and desires.

A drunkard, who continues in his drunkenness, being under the power of a love, and violent appetite to strong drink, and without any love to virtue; but being also extremely covetous and close, and very much exercised and grieved at the diminution of his estate, and prospect of poverty, may in a sort "desire" the virtue of temperance: and though his present will is to gratify his extravagant appetite, yet he may wish he had a heart to forbear future acts of intemperance, and forsake his excesses, through an unwillingness to part with his money: but still he goes on with his drunkenness; his wishes and endeavors are insufficient and ineffectual: such a man has no proper, direct, sincere willingness to forsake this vice, and the vicious deeds which belong to it: for he acts voluntarily in continuing to drink to excess: his desire is very improperly called a willingness to be temperate; it is no true desire of that virtue; for it is not that virtue that terminates his wishes; nor have they any direct respect at all to it. 'Tis only *the saving his money,* and avoiding poverty, that terminates, and exhausts the whole strength of his desire. The virtue of temperance is regarded only very indirectly and improperly, even as a necessary means of gratifying the vice of covetousness.

So, a man of an exceeding corrupt and wicked heart, who has no love to God and Jesus Christ, but on the contrary, being very profanely and carnally inclined, has the greatest distaste of the things of religion, and enmity against 'em; yet being of a family, that from one generation to another, have most of 'em died in youth of an hereditary consumption; and so having little hope of living long; and having been instructed in the necessity of a supreme love to Christ, and gratitude for his death and sufferings, in order to his salvation from eternal misery; if under these circumstances he should, through fear of eternal torments, wish he had such a disposition: but his profane and carnal heart remaining, he continues still in his habitual distaste of, and enmity to God and religion, and wholly without any exercise of that love and gratitude (as doubtless the very devils themselves, notwithstanding all the devilishness of their temper, would wish for a holy heart, if by that means they could get out of hell): in this case, there is no sincere willingness to love Christ and choose him as his chief good: these holy dispositions and exercises are not at all the direct object of the will: they truly share no part of the inclination or desire of the soul; but all is terminated on deliverance from torment: and these graces and pious volitions, notwithstanding this forced consent, are looked upon [as] undesirable; as when a sick man desires a dose he greatly abhors, to save his life.—From these things it appears:

3. That this indirect willingness which has been spoken of, is not that exercise of the will which the command requires; but is entirely a different one; being a volition of a different nature, and terminated altogether on different objects; wholly falling short of that virtue of will, which the command has respect to.

4. This other volition, which has only some indirect concern with the duty required, can't excuse for the want of that good will itself, which is commanded; being not the thing which answers and fulfills the command, and being wholly destitute of the virtue which the command seeks.

Further to illustrate this matter: If a child has a most excellent father, that has ever treated him with fatherly kindness and tenderness, and has every way in the highest degree merited his love and dutiful regard, being withal very wealthy; but the son is of so vile a disposition, that he inveterately hates his father; and yet, apprehending that his hatred of him is like to prove his ruin, by bringing him finally to poverty and abject circumstances, through his father's disinheriting him, or otherwise; which is exceeding cross to his avarice and ambition; he therefore wishes it were otherwise: but yet remaining under the invincible power of his vile and malignant disposition, he continues still in his settled hatred of his father. Now if such a son's indirect willingness to have love and honor towards his father, at all acquits or excuses before God, for his failing of actually exercising these dispositions towards him which God requires, it must be on one of these two accounts. (1) Either that it answers and fulfills the command. But this it does not, by the supposition; because the thing commanded is love and honor to his worthy parent. If the command be proper and just, as is supposed, then it obliges to the thing commanded; and so nothing else but that can answer the obligation. Or (2) it must be at least because there is that virtue or goodness in his indirect willingness, that is equivalent to the virtue required; and so balances or countervails it, and makes up for the want of it. But that also is contrary to the supposition. The willingness the son has merely from a regard to money and honor, has no goodness in it, to countervail the want of the pious filial respect required.

Sincerity and reality, in that indirect willingness which has been spoken of, don't make it the better. That which is real and hearty is often called sincere; whether it be in virtue or vice. Some persons are sincerely *bad;* others are sincerely *good;* and others may be sincere and hearty in things which are in their own nature *indifferent;* as a man may be sincerely desirous of eating when he is hungry. But a being sincere, hearty and in good earnest, is no virtue, unless it be in a thing that is virtuous. A man may be sincere and hearty in joining a crew of pirates, or a gang of robbers. When the devils cried out, and besought Christ not to torment them, it was no mere pretence; they were very hearty in their desires not to be tormented: but this did not make their will or desires virtuous. And if men have sincere desires, which are in their kind and nature no better, it can be no excuse for the want of any required virtue.

And as a man's being sincere in such an indirect desire or *willingness* to do his duty, as has been mentioned, can't excuse for the want of performance; so it is with *endeavors* arising from such a willingness. The endeavors can have no more goodness in 'em, than the will which they are the effect and expression of. And therefore, however sincere and real, and however great a person's endeavors are; yea, though they should be to the utmost of his ability; unless the will which they proceed from be truly good and virtuous, they can be of no avail, influence or weight to any purpose whatsoever, in a moral sense or respect. That which is not truly virtuous in God's sight, is looked upon by him as good for nothing: and so can be of no value, weight or influence in his account, to recommend, satisfy, excuse or make up for any moral defect. For nothing can counterbalance evil, but good. If evil be in one scale, and we put a great deal into the other, sincere and earnest desires, and many and great endeavors; yet if there be no real goodness in all, there is no weight in it; and so it does nothing towards balancing the real weight which is in the opposite scale. 'Tis only like the substracting a thousand noughts from before a real number, which leaves the sum just as it was.

Indeed such endeavors may have a *negatively* good influence. Those things which have no positive virtue, have no positive moral influence; yet they may be an occasion of persons avoiding some positive evils. As if a man were in the water with a neighbor that he had ill will to, who could not swim, holding him by his hand; which

neighbor was much in debt to him; and should be tempted to let him
sink and drown; but should refuse to comply with the temptation;
not from love to his neighbor, but from the love of money, and because by his drowning he should lose his debt; that which he does in
preserving his neighbor from drowning, is nothing good in the sight
of God: yet hereby he avoids the greater guilt that would have been
contracted, if he had designedly let his neighbor sink and perish. But
when Arminians in their disputes with Calvinists insist so much on
sincere desires and endeavors, as what must excuse men, must be
accepted of God, etc. 'tis manifest they have respect to some positive
moral weight or influence of those desires and endeavors. Accepting,
justifying, or excusing on the account of sincere honest endeavors
(as they are called) and men's doing what they can, etc. has relation
to some moral value, something that is accepted as good, and as such,
countervailing some defect.

But there is a great and unknown deceit, arising from the ambiguity of the phrase, "sincere endeavors." Indeed there is a vast
indistinctness and unfixedness in most, or at least very many of the
terms used to express things pertaining to moral and spiritual matters. Whence arise innumerable mistakes, strong prejudices, inex-
tricable confusion, and endless controversy.

The word "sincere" is most commonly used to signify something
that is good: men are habituated to understand by it the same as
"honest" and "upright"; which terms excite an idea of something
good in the strictest and highest sense; good in the sight of him who
sees not only the outward appearance, but the heart. And therefore
men think that if a person be sincere, he will certainly be accepted.
If it be said that anyone is sincere in his endeavors, this suggests to
men's minds as much, as that his heart and will is good, that there is
no defect of duty, as to virtuous inclination; he honestly and up-
rightly desires and endeavors to do as he is required; and this leads
'em to suppose that it would be very hard and unreasonable to
punish him, only because he is unsuccessful in his endeavors, the
thing endeavored being beyond his power.—Whereas it ought to be
observed, that the word "sincere" has these different significations:

1. "Sincerity," as the word is sometimes used, signifies no more
then *reality of will and endeavor,* with respect to anything that is
professed or pretended; without any consideration of the nature of
the principle or aim, whence this real will and true endeavor arises.
If a man has some real desire to obtain a thing, either direct or in-

direct, or does really endeavor after a thing, he is said sincerely to desire or endeavor it; without any consideration of the goodness or virtuousness of the principle he acts from, or any excellency or worthiness of the end he acts for. Thus a man that is kind to his neighbor's wife, who is sick and languishing, and very helpful in her case, makes a shew of desiring and endeavoring her restoration to health and vigor; and not only makes such a shew, but there is a reality in his pretense, he does heartily and earnestly desire to have her health restored, and uses his true and utmost endeavors for it; he is said sincerely to desire and endeavor it, because he does so truly or really; though perhaps the principle he acts from, is no other than a vile and scandalous passion; having lived in adultery with her, he earnestly desires to have her health and vigor restored, that he may return to his criminal pleasures with her. Or,

2. By "sincerity" is meant, not merely a *reality* of will and endeavor of some sort or other, and from some consideration or other, but a *virtuous sincerity*. That is, that in the performance of those particular acts that are the matter of virtue or duty, there be not only the matter, but the form and essence of virtue, consisting in the aim that governs the act, and the principle exercised in it. There is not only the reality of the act, that is as it were the *body* of the duty; but also the *soul,* which should properly belong to such a body. In this sense, a man is said to be sincere, when he acts with a *pure intention;* not from sinister views, or by-ends: he not only in reality desires and seeks the thing to be done, or qualification to be obtained, for some end or other; but he wills the thing directly and properly, as neither forced nor bribed; the virtue of the thing is properly the object of the will.

In the former sense, a man is said to be sincere, in opposition to a mere pretense, and shew of the *particular thing* to be done or exhibited, without any real desire or endeavor at all. In the latter sense, a man is said to be sincere, in opposition to that shew of *virtue* there is in merely doing the matter of duty, without the reality of the virtue itself in the soul, and the essence of it, which there is a shew of. A man may be sincere in the former sense, and yet in the latter be in the sight of God, who searches the heart, a vile hypocrite.

In the latter kind of sincerity, only, is there anything truly valuable or acceptable in the sight of God. And this is the thing which in Scripture is called sincerity, uprightness, integrity, truth in the inward parts, and a being of a perfect heart. And if there be such a

sincerity, and such a degree of it as there ought to be, and there be anything further that the man is not able to perform, or which don't prove to be connected with his sincere desires and endeavors, the man is wholly excused and acquitted in the sight of God; his will shall surely be accepted for his deed: and such a sincere will and endeavor is all that in strictness is required of him, by any command of God. But as to the other kind of sincerity of desires and endeavors, it having no virtue in it (as was observed before), can be of no avail before God, in any case, to recommend, satisfy, or excuse, and has no positive moral weight or influence whatsoever.

Corol. 1. Hence it may be inferred, that nothing in the reason and nature of things appears, from the consideration of any moral weight of that former kind of sincerity, which has been spoken of, at all obliging us to believe, or leading us to suppose, that God has made any positive promises of salvation, or grace, or any saving assistance, or any spiritual benefit whatsoever, to any desires, prayers, endeavors, striving, or obedience of those, who hitherto have no true virtue or holiness in their hearts; though we should suppose all the sincerity, and the utmost degree of endeavor, that is possible to be in a person without holiness.

Some object against God's requiring, as the condition of salvation, those holy exercises, which are the result of a supernatural renovation; such as a supreme respect to Christ, love to God, loving holiness for its own sake, etc. that these inward dispositions and exercises are above men's power, as they are by nature; and therefore that we may conclude, that when men are brought to be sincere in their endeavors, and do as well as they can, they are accepted; and that this must be all that God requires in order to men's being received as the objects of his favor, and must be what God has appointed as the condition of salvation. Concerning which I would observe, that in such a manner of speaking of men's being accepted, because they are sincere, and do as well as they can, there is evidently a supposition of some virtue, some degree of that which is truly good; though it don't go so far as were to be wished. For if men "do what they can," unless their so doing be from some good principle, disposition, or exercise of heart, some virtuous inclination or act of the will; their so doing what they can, is in some respects not a whit better than if they did nothing at all. In such a case, there is no more positive moral goodness in a man's doing what he can, than in a windmill's doing what it can; because the action does no more proceed from virtue; and there is nothing in such sincerity of endeavor, or doing what we can, that should render it any more a proper or fit recommendation to positive favor and acceptance, or the condition of any reward or actual benefit, than doing nothing; for both the one and the other are alike nothing, as to any true moral weight or value.

Corol. 2. Hence also it follows, there is nothing that appears in the reason and nature of things, which can justly lead us to determine, that God will certainly give the necessary means of salvation, or some way or other bestow true holiness and eternal life on those heathen, who are sincere (in the sense above explained) in their endeavors to find out the will of the deity, and to please him, according to their light, that they may escape his future displeasure and wrath, and obtain happiness in their future state, through his favor.

SECTION 6. LIBERTY OF INDIFFERENCE, NOT ONLY NOT NECESSARY TO VIRTUE, BUT UTTERLY INCONSISTENT WITH IT; AND ALL, EITHER VIRTUOUS OR VICIOUS HABITS OR INCLINATIONS, INCONSISTENT WITH ARMINIAN NOTIONS OF LIBERTY AND MORAL AGENCY

TO SUPPOSE such a freedom of will, as Arminians talk of, to be requisite to virtue and vice, is many ways contrary to common sense.

If indifference belongs to liberty of will, as Arminians suppose, and it be essential to a virtuous action that it be performed in a state of liberty, as they also suppose; it will follow, that it is essential to a virtuous action that it be performed in a state of indifference: and if it be performed in a *state* of indifference, then doubtless it must be performed in the *time* of indifference. And so it will follow, that in order to the virtuousness of an act, the heart must be indifferent in the time of the performance of that act, and the more indifferent and cold the heart is with relation to the act which is performed, so much the better; because the act is performed with so much the greater liberty. But is this agreeable to the light of nature? Is it agreeable to the notions which mankind, in all ages, have of virtue, that it lies in that which is contrary to indifference, even in the tendency and inclination of the heart to virtuous action; and that the stronger the inclination, and so the further from indifference, the more virtuous the *heart*, and so much the more praiseworthy the *act* which proceeds from it?

If we should suppose (contrary to what has been before demonstrated) that there may be an act of will in a state of indifference; for instance, this act, viz. the will's determining to put itself out of a state of indifference, and give itself a preponderation one way, then it would follow, on Arminian principles, that this act or determination of the will is that alone wherein virtue consists, because this only is performed while the mind remains in a state of indifference, and so in a state of liberty: for when once the mind is put out of its equilibrium, it is no longer in such a state; and therefore all the acts which follow afterwards, proceeding from bias, can have the nature neither of virtue nor vice. Or if the thing which the will can do, while yet in a state of indifference, and so of liberty, be only to suspend acting, and determine to take the matter into consideration, then this determination is that alone wherein virtue consists, and not proceeding to action after the scale is turned by consideration. So that it will follow from these principles, all that is done after the mind, by any means, is once out of its equilibrium and already possessed by an inclination, and arising from that inclination, has nothing of the nature of virtue or vice, and is worthy of neither blame nor praise. But how plainly contrary is this to the universal sense of mankind, and to the notion they have of sincerely virtuous actions? Which is, that they are actions which proceed from a heart *well disposed* and *inclined;* and the *stronger,* and the more *fixed* and *determined* the good disposition of the heart, the greater the sincerity of virtue, and so the more of the truth and reality of it. But if there be any acts which are done in a state of equilibrium, or spring immediately from perfect indifference and coldness of heart, they cannot arise from any good principle or disposition in the heart; and consequently, according to common sense, have no sincere goodness in 'em, having no virtue of heart in 'em. To have a virtuous heart, is to have a heart that favors virtue, and is friendly to it, and not one perfectly cold and indifferent about it.

And besides the actions that are done in a state of indifference, or that arise immediately out of such a state, can't be virtuous, because, by the supposition, they are not determined by any preceding choice. For if there be preceding choice, then choice intervenes between the act and the state of indifference; which is contrary to the supposition of the acts arising immediately out of indifference. But those acts which are not determined by preceding choice, can't be virtuous or vicious by Arminian principles, because they are not determined by the will. So that neither one way, nor the other, can any actions be virtuous or vicious according to Arminian principles. If the action *be determined* by a preceding act of choice it can't be virtuous; because the action is not done in a state of indifference, nor does immediately arise from such a state; and so is not done in a state of liberty. If the action be *not determined* by a preceding act of choice, then it can't be virtuous; because then the will is not self-determined in it.

So that 'tis made certain, that neither virtue nor vice can ever find any place in the universe.

Moreover, that it is necessary to a virtuous action that it be performed in a state of indifference, under a notion of that's being a state of liberty, is contrary to common sense; as 'tis a dictate of common sense, that indifference itself, in many cases, is vicious, and so to a high degree. As if when I see my neighbor or near friend, and one who has in the highest degree merited of me, in extreme distress, and ready to perish, I find an indifference in my heart with respect to anything proposed to be done, which I can easily do, for his relief. So if it should be proposed to me, to blaspheme God, or kill my father, or to do numberless other things which might be mentioned; the being indifferent, for a moment, would be highly vicious and vile.

And it may be further observed, that to suppose this liberty of indifference is essential to virtue and vice, destroys the great difference of degrees of the guilt of different crimes, and takes away the heinousness of the most flagitious horrid iniquities; such as adultery, bestiality, murder, perjury, blasphemy, etc. For according to these principles, there is no harm at all in having the mind in a state of perfect indifference with respect to these crimes; nay, 'tis absolutely necessary in order to any virtue in avoiding them, or vice in doing them. But for the mind to be in a state of indifference with respect to 'em, is to be next door to doing them: it is then infinitely near to choosing, and so committing the fact: for equilibrium is the next step to a degree of preponderation; and one, even the least degree of preponderation (all things considered) is choice. And not only so, but for the will to be in a state of perfect equilibrium with respect to such crimes, is for the mind to be in such a state, as to be full as likely to choose 'em as to refuse 'em, to do 'em as to omit 'em. And if our minds must be in such a state wherein it is as near to choosing as refusing, and wherein it must of necessity, according to the nature of things, be as likely to commit 'em, as to refrain from 'em; where is the exceeding heinousness of choosing and committing them? If there be no harm in often being in such a state, wherein the probability of doing and forbearing are exactly equal, there being an equilibrium, and no more tendency to one than the other; then according to the nature and laws of such a contingence, it may be expected, as an *inevitable* consequence of such a disposition of things, that we should choose 'em as often as reject 'em: that it should generally so fall out is necessary, as equality in the effect is the natural consequence of the equal tendency of the cause, or of the antecedent state of things from which the effect arises: why then should we be so exceedingly to blame, if it does so fall out?

'Tis many ways apparent, that the Arminian scheme of liberty is utterly inconsistent with the being of any such things as either virtuous or vicious habits or dispositions. If liberty of *indifference* be essential to moral agency, then there can be no virtue in any habitual inclinations of the heart; which are contrary to indifference, and imply in their nature the very destruction and exclusion of it. They suppose nothing can be virtuous, in which no liberty is exercised; but how absurd is it to talk of exercising indifference under bias and preponderation!

And if *self-determining power* in the will be necessary to moral agency, praise, blame, etc. then nothing done by the will can be any further praise or blameworthy, than so far as the will is moved, swayed and determined by itself, and the scales turned by the sovereign power the will has over itself. And therefore the will must not be put out of its balance already, the preponderation must not be determined and effected beforehand; and so the self-determining act anticipated. Thus it appears another way, that habitual bias is inconsistent with that liberty which Arminians suppose to be necessary to virtue or vice; and so it follows, that habitual bias itself cannot be either virtuous or vicious.

The same thing follows from their doctrine concerning the inconsistence of necessity with liberty, praise, dispraise, etc. None will deny, that bias and inclination may be so strong as to be invincible, and leave no possibility of the will's determining contrary to it; and so be attended with necessity. This Dr. Whitby allows concerning the will of God, angels and glorified saints, with respect to good; and the will of devils with respect to evil.[1] Therefore if necessity be inconsistent with liberty; then when fixed inclination is to such a degree of strength, it utterly excludes all virtue, vice, praise or blame. And if so, then the nearer habits are to this strength, the more do they impede liberty, and so diminish praise and blame. If very strong habits destroy liberty, the lesser ones proportionably hinder it, according to their degree of strength. And therefore it will follow, that

1. [See above, n. 3 to Sec. 1 of this part, and the Intro., Pt. 5, no. 10.]

then is the act most virtuous or vicious, when performed without any inclination or habitual bias at all; because it is then performed with most liberty.

Every prepossessing fixed bias on the mind brings a degree of moral inability for the contrary; because so far as the mind is biased and prepossessed, so much hindrance is there of the contrary. And therefore if moral inability be inconsistent with moral agency, or the nature of virtue and vice, then so far as there is any such thing as evil disposition of heart, or habitual depravity of inclination; whether covetousness, pride, malice, cruelty, or whatever else; so much the more excusable persons are; so much the less have their evil acts of this kind, the nature of vice. And on the contrary, whatever excellent dispositions and inclinations they have, so much are they the less virtuous.

'Tis evident, that no habitual disposition of heart, whether it be to a greater or lesser degree, can be in *any degree* virtuous or vicious; or the actions which proceed from them *at all* praise or blameworthy. Because, though we should suppose the habit not to be of such strength as wholly to take away all moral ability and self-determining power; or hinder but that, although the act be partly from bias, yet it may be in part from self-determination; yet in this case, all that is from antecedent bias must be set aside, as of no consideration; and in estimating the degree of virtue or vice, no more must be considered than what arises from self-determining power, without any influence of that bias, because liberty is exercised in no more: so that all that is the exercise of habitual inclination, is thrown away, as not belonging to the morality of the action. By which it appears, that no exercise of these habits, let 'em be stronger or weaker, can ever have anything of the nature of either virtue or vice.

Here if anyone should say, that notwithstanding all these things, there may be the nature of virtue and vice in habits of the mind; because these habits may be the effects of those acts wherein the mind exercised liberty; that however the forementioned reasons will prove that no habits which are natural, or that any are born or created with,[2] can be either virtuous or vicious; yet they will not prove this of habits, which have been acquired and established by repeated free acts—

To such an objector I would say, that this evasion will not at all help the matter. For if freedom of will be essential to the very *nature*

2. [The 1754 ed. reads "with *us*." Text corrected from the *printed* list of errata.]

of virtue and vice, then there is no virtue or vice but only in that very thing, wherein this liberty is exercised. If a man in one or more thing that he does, exercises liberty, and then by those acts is brought into such circumstances, that his liberty ceases, and there follows a long series of acts or events that come to pass necessarily; those consequent acts are not virtuous or vicious, rewardable or punishable; but only the free acts that established this necessity; for in them alone was the man free. The following effects that are necessary, have no more of the nature of virtue or vice, than health or sickness of body have properly the nature of virtue or vice, being the effects of a course of free acts of temperance or intemperance; or than the good qualities of a clock are of the nature of virtue, which are the effects of free acts of the artificer; or the goodness and sweetness of the fruits of a garden are moral virtues, being the effects of the free and faithful acts of the gardener. If liberty be absolutely requisite to the morality of actions, and necessity wholly inconsistent with it, as Arminians greatly insist; then no *necessary effects* whatsoever, let the cause be never so good or bad, can be virtuous or vicious; but the virtue or vice must be only in the *free cause*. Agreeably to this, Dr. Whitby supposes, the necessity that attends the good and evil habits of the saints in heaven, and damned in hell, which are the consequence of their free acts in their state of probation, [shews they] [3] are not rewardable or punishable.

On the whole, it appears, that if the notions of Arminians concerning liberty and moral agency be true, it will follow that there is no virtue in any such habits or qualities as humility, meekness, patience, mercy, gratitude, generosity, heavenly-mindedness; nothing at all praiseworthy in loving Christ above father and mother, wife and children, or our own lives; or in delight in holiness, hungering and thirsting after righteousness, love to enemies, universal benevolence to mankind: and on the other hand, there is nothing at all vicious, or worthy of dispraise, in the most sordid, beastly, malignant, devilish dispositions; in being ungrateful, profane, habitually hating God, and things sacred and holy; or in being most treacherous, envious and cruel towards men. For all these things are dispositions and inclinations of the heart. And in short, there is no such thing as any virtuous or vicious *quality of mind;* no such thing as inherent virtue and holiness, or vice and sin: and the stronger those habits or dispositions are, which used to be called virtuous and vicious, the

3. [Insertion made from the *printed* list of errata.]

further they are from being so indeed; the more violent men's lusts are, the more fixed their pride, envy, ingratitude and maliciousness, still the further are they from being blameworthy. If there be a man that by his own repeated acts, or by any other means, is come to be of the most hellish disposition, desperately inclined to treat his neighbors with injuriousness, contempt and malignity; the further they should be from any disposition to be angry with him, or in the least to blame him. So on the other hand, if there be a person, who is of a most excellent spirit, strongly inclining him to the most amiable actions, admirably meek, benevolent, etc. so much is he further from anything rewardable or commendable. On which principles, the man Jesus Christ was very far from being praiseworthy for those acts of holiness and kindness which he performed, these propensities being so strong in his heart. And above all, the infinitely holy and gracious God, is infinitely remote from anything commendable, his good inclinations being infinitely strong, and he therefore at the utmost possible distance from being at liberty. And in all cases, the stronger the inclinations of any are to virtue, and the more they love it, the less virtuous they are; and the more they love wickedness, the less vicious. Whether these things are agreeable to Scripture, let every Christian, and every man who has read the Bible, judge: and whether they are agreeable to common sense, let everyone judge, that have human understanding in exercise.

And if we pursue these principles, we shall find that virtue and vice are wholly excluded out of the world; and that there never was, nor ever can be any such thing as one or the other; either in God, angels or men. No propensity, disposition or habit can be virtuous or vicious, as has been shewn; because they, so far as they take place, destroy the freedom of the will, the foundation of all moral agency, and exclude all capacity of either virtue or vice. And if habits and dispositions themselves be not virtuous nor vicious, neither can the exercise of these dispositions be so: for the exercise of *bias* is not the exercise of *free self-determining will,* and so there is no exercise of liberty in it. Consequently no man is virtuous or vicious, either in being well or ill disposed, nor in acting from a good or bad disposition. And whether this bias or disposition be habitual or not, if it exists but a moment before the act of will, which is the effect of it, it alters not the case, as to the necessity of the effect. Or if there be no previous disposition at all, either habitual or occasional, that determines the act, then it is not choice that determines it: it is therefore a contingence, that happens to the man, arising from nothing in him; and is necessary, as to any inclination or choice of his; and therefore can't make him either the better or worse, any more than a tree is better than other trees, because it oftener happens to be lit upon by a swan or nightingale; or a rock more vicious than other rocks, because rattlesnakes have happened oftener to crawl over it. So that there is no virtue nor vice in good or bad dispositions, either fixed or transient; nor any virtue or vice in acting from any good or bad previous inclination; nor yet any virtue or vice in acting wholly without any previous inclination. Where then shall we find room for virtue or vice?

SECTION 7. ARMINIAN NOTIONS OF MORAL AGENCY INCONSISTENT WITH ALL INFLUENCE OF MOTIVE AND INDUCEMENT, IN EITHER VIRTUOUS OR VICIOUS ACTIONS

As ARMINIAN notions of that liberty, which is essential to virtue or vice, are inconsistent with common sense, in their being inconsistent with all virtuous or vicious habits and dispositions; so they are no less so in their inconsistency with all influence of motives in moral actions.

'Tis equally against those notions of liberty of will, whether there be, previous to the act of choice, a preponderancy of the inclination, or a preponderancy of those circumstances, which have a tendency to move the inclination. And indeed it comes to just the same thing: to say, the circumstances of the mind are such as tend to sway and turn its inclination one way, is the same thing as to say, the inclination of the mind, as under such circumstances, tends that way.

Or if any think it most proper to say, that motives do alter the inclination, and give a new bias to the mind; it will not alter the case, as to the present argument. For if motives operate by giving the mind an inclination, then they operate by destroying the mind's indifference, and laying it under a bias. But to do this, is to destroy the Arminian freedom: it is not to leave the will to its own self-determination, but to bring it into subjection to the power of something extrinsic, which operates upon it, sways and determines it, previous to its own determination. So that what is done from motive, can't be either virtuous or vicious. And besides, if the acts of the will are excited by motives, those motives are the *causes* of those acts of the will: which makes the acts of the will necessary; as effects necessarily follow the efficiency of the cause. And if the influence and power of the motive causes the volition, then the influence of the motive determines volition, and volition don't determine itself; and so is not free, in the sense of Arminians (as has been largely shewn already), and consequently can be neither virtuous nor vicious.

The supposition, which has already been taken notice of as an insufficient evasion in other cases, would be in like manner impertinently alleged in this case; namely, the supposition that liberty consists in a power of suspending action for the present, in order to deliberation. If it should be said, though it be true, that the will is under a necessity of finally following the strongest motive, yet it may for the present forbear to act upon the motive presented, till there has been opportunity thoroughly to consider it, and compare its real weight with the merit of other motives. I answer, as follows:

Here again it must be remembered, that if determining thus to suspend and consider, be that act of the will wherein alone liberty is exercised, then in this all virtue and vice must consist; and the acts that follow this consideration, and are the effects of it, being necessary, are no more virtuous or vicious than some good or bad events which happen when they are fast asleep, and are the consequences of what they did when they were awake. Therefore I would here observe two things.

1. To suppose that all virtue and vice, in every case, consists in determining whether to take time for consideration, or not, is not agreeable to common sense. For according to such a supposition, the most horrid crimes, adultery, murder, buggery,[1] blasphemy, etc. do not at all consist in the horrid nature of the things themselves, but only in the neglect of thorough consideration before they were perpetrated: which brings their viciousness to a small matter, and makes all crimes equal. If it be said, that neglect of consideration, when such heinous evils are proposed to choice, is worse than in other cases: I answer, this is inconsistent, as it supposes the very thing to be, which at the same time is supposed not to be; it supposes all moral evil, all viciousness and heinousness, does not consist merely in the want of consideration. It supposes some crimes *in themselves,*

1. [I.e. sodomy. The word "buggery" in eighteenth-century usage was derived from the word "Bulgarian," in the following way: The Paulician heresy emerged in Bulgaria during the late middle ages and spread westward, where it led to a revival of Manicheism with its dualistic disparagement of the body and of progeny. Heretics were indiscriminately termed "Bulgarians" ("Bulgari" or "Boulgres"), which was corrupted to "Bugari" and "Bougres." The sexual antinomianism of the "Bugari" became notorious in the popular mind, and the word came to signify that class of heretic whose religious views were believed to encourage or condone sodomy. Finally, "bougrerie" came to denote sodomy no matter what system of religion a man held. Derrick Sherwin Bailey, *Homosexuality and the Western Christian Tradition* (New York, 1955), pp. 135–44.]

in their *own nature,* to be more heinous than others, antecedent to consideration or inconsideration, which lays the person under a previous obligation to consider in some cases more than others.

2. If it were so, that all virtue and vice, in every case, consisted only in the act of the will, whereby it determines whether to consider or no, it would not alter the case in the least, as to the present argument. For still in this act of the will on this determination, it is induced by some motive, and necessarily follows the strongest motive; and so is necessary, even in that act wherein alone it is either virtuous or vicious.

One thing more I would observe, concerning the inconsistence of Arminian notions of moral agency with the influence of motives. I suppose none will deny, that 'tis possible for motives to be set before the mind so powerful, and exhibited in so strong a light, and under so advantageous circumstances, as to be invincible; and such as the mind cannot but yield to. In this case, Arminians will doubtless say, liberty is destroyed. And if so, then if motives are exhibited with half so much power, they hinder liberty in proportion to their strength, and go half way towards destroying it. If a thousand degrees of motive abolish all liberty, then five hundred take it half away. If one degree of the influence of motive don't at all infringe or diminish liberty, then no more do two degrees; for nothing doubled, is still nothing. And if two degrees don't diminish the will's liberty, no more do four, eight, sixteen, or six thousand. For nothing multiplied never so much, comes to but nothing. If there be nothing in the nature of motive or moral suasion, that is at all opposite to liberty, then the greatest degree of it can't hurt liberty. But if there be anything in the nature of the thing, that is against liberty, then the least degree of it hurts it in some degree; and consequently hurts and diminishes virtue. If invincible motives to that action which is good, take away all the freedom of the act, and so all the virtue of it; then the more forcible the motives are, so much the worse, so much the less virtue; and the weaker the motives are, the better for the cause of virtue; and none is best of all.

Now let it be considered, whether these things are agreeable to common sense. If it should be allowed, that there are some instances wherein the soul chooses without any motive, what virtue can there be in such a choice? I am sure, there is no prudence or wisdom in it. Such a choice is made for no good end; for it is for no end at all. If it were for any end, the view of the end would be the motive exciting to the act; and if the act be for no good end, and so from no good aim, then there is no good intention in it: and therefore, according to all our natural notions of virtue, no more virtue in it than in the motion of the smoke, which is driven to and fro by the wind, without any aim or end in the thing moved, and which knows not whither, nor why and wherefore, it is moved.

Corol. 1. By these things it appears, that the argument against the Calvinists, taken from the use of counsels, exhortations, invitations, expostulations, etc. so much insisted on by Arminians, is truly against themselves. For these things can operate no other way to any good effect, than as in them is exhibited motive and inducement, tending to excite and determine the acts of the will. But it follows on their principles, that the acts of will excited by such causes, can't be virtuous; because so far as they are from these, they are not from the will's self-determining power. Hence it will follow, that it is not worth the while to offer any arguments to persuade men to any virtuous volition or voluntary action; 'tis in vain to set before them the wisdom and amiableness of ways of virtue, or the odiousness and folly of ways of vice. This notion of liberty and moral agency frustrates all endeavors to draw men to virtue by instruction, or persuasion, precept, or example: for though these things may induce men to what is *materially* virtuous, yet at the same time they take away the *form* of virtue, because they destroy liberty; as they, by their own power, put the will out of its equilibrium, determine and turn the scale, and take the work of self-determining power out of its hands. And the clearer the instructions are that are given, the more powerful the arguments that are used, and the more moving the persuasions or examples, the more likely they are to frustrate their own design; because they have so much the greater tendency to put the will out of its balance, to hinder its freedom of self-determination; and so to exclude the very form of virtue, and the essence of whatsoever is praiseworthy.

So it clearly follows from these principles, that God has no hand in any man's virtue, nor does at all promote it, either by a physical or moral influence; that none of the moral methods he uses with men to promote virtue in the world, have tendency to the attainment of that end; that all the instructions which he has given to men, from the beginning of the world to this day, by prophets, or apostles, or by his son Jesus Christ; that all his counsels, invitations, promises, threatenings, warnings and expostulations; that all means he has used with men, in ordinances, or providences; yea, all influences of his Spirit, ordinary and extraordinary, have had no tendency at all to excite any one virtuous act of the mind, or to promote anything morally good and commendable, in any respect. For there is no way that these or any other means can promote virtue, but one of these three. Either (1) by a physical operation on the heart. But all effects that are wrought in men in this way, have no virtue in them, by the concurring voice of all Arminians. Or (2) morally, by exhibiting motives to the understanding, to excite good acts in the will. But it has been demonstrated, that volitions which are excited by motives, are necessary, and not excited by a self-moving power; and therefore, by their principles, there is no virtue in them. Or (3) by merely giving the will an opportunity to determine itself concerning the objects proposed, either to choose or reject, by its own uncaused, unmoved, uninfluenced self-determination. And if this be all, then all those means do no more to promote virtue, than vice: for they do nothing but give the will opportunity to determine itself *either* way, either to good or bad, without laying it under any bias to either: and so there is really as much of an opportunity given to determine in favor of evil, as of good.

Thus that horrid blasphemous consequence will certainly follow from the Arminian doctrine, which they charge on others; namely, that God acts an inconsistent part in using so many counsels, warnings, invitations, entreaties, etc. with sinners, to induce 'em to forsake sin, and turn to the ways of virtue; and that all are insincere and fallacious. It will follow from their doctrine, that God does these things when he knows at the same time, that they have no manner of tendency to promote the effect he seems to aim at; yea, knows that if they have any influence, this very influence will be inconsistent with such an effect, and will prevent it. But what an imputation of insincerity would this fix on Him who is infinitely holy and true! So that theirs is the doctrine which if pursued in its consequences, does horribly reflect on the most High, and fix on him the charge of hypocrisy; and not the doctrine of the Calvinist; according to their frequent, and vehement exclamations and invectives.

Corol. 2. From what has been observed in this section, it again appears, that Arminian principles and notions, when fairly examined, and pursued in their demonstrable consequences, do evidently shut all virtue out of the world, and make it impossible that there should ever be any such thing, in any case; or that any such thing should ever be conceived of. For by these principles, the very notion of virtue or vice implies absurdity and contradiction. For it is absurd in itself, and contrary to common sense, to suppose a virtuous act of mind without any good intention or aim; and by their principles, it is absurd to suppose a virtuous act with a good intention or aim; for to act for an end, is to act from a motive. So that if we rely on these principles, there can be no virtuous act with a good design and end; and 'tis self-evident, there can be none without: consequently there can be no virtuous act at all.

Corol. 3. 'Tis manifest, that Arminian notions of moral agency, and *the being* of a faculty of will, cannot consist together; and that if there be any such thing as, either a virtuous, or vicious act, it can't be an act of will; no will can be at all concerned in it. For that act which is performed without inclination, without motive, without end, must be performed without any concern of the will. To suppose an act of the will without these, implies a contradiction. If the soul in its act has no motive or end; then in that act (as was observed before) it seeks nothing, goes after nothing, exerts no inclination to anything; and this implies, that in that act it desires nothing, and chooses nothing; so that there is no act of choice in the case: and that is as much as to say, there is no act of will in the case. Which very effectually shuts out all vicious and virtuous acts out of the universe; inasmuch as, according to this, there can be no vicious or virtuous act wherein the will is concerned; and according to the plainest dictates of reason, and the light of nature, and also the principles of Arminians themselves, there can be no virtuous or vicious act wherein the will is not concerned. And therefore there is no room for any virtuous or vicious acts at all.

Corol. 4. If none of the moral actions of intelligent beings are influenced by either previous inclination or motive, another strange thing will follow; and this is, that God not only can't foreknow any of the future moral actions of his creatures, but he can make no conjecture, can give no probable guess concerning them. For, all conjecture in things of this nature, must depend on some discerning or apprehension of these two things, *previous disposition,* and *motive;* which, as has been observed, Arminian notions of moral agency, in their real consequence, altogether exclude.

PART FOUR

Wherein the Chief Grounds of the Reasonings of Arminians, in Support and Defense of the Forementioned Notions of Liberty, Moral Agency, etc. and Against the Opposite Doctrine, Are Considered

SECTION 1. THE ESSENCE OF THE VIRTUE AND VICE OF DISPOSITIONS OF THE HEART, AND ACTS OF THE WILL, LIES NOT IN THEIR CAUSE, BUT THEIR NATURE

ONE main foundation of the reasons, which are brought to establish the forementioned notions of liberty, virtue, vice, etc. is a supposition, that the virtuousness of the dispositions or acts of the will consists not in the nature of these dispositions or acts, but wholly in the origin or cause of them: so that if the disposition of the mind or act of the will be never so good, yet if the cause of the disposition or act be not our virtue, there is nothing virtuous or praiseworthy in it; and on the contrary, if the will in its inclination or acts be never so bad, yet unless it arises from something that is our vice or fault, there is nothing vicious or blameworthy in it. Hence their grand objection and pretended demonstration, or self-evidence, against any virtue and commendableness, or vice and blameworthiness, of those habits or acts of the will, which are not from some virtuous or vicious determination of the will itself.

Now, if this matter be well considered, it will appear to be altogether a mistake, yea, a gross absurdity; and that it is most certain, that if there be any such things, as a virtuous, or vicious disposition, or volition of mind, the virtuousness or viciousness of them consists not in the origin or cause of these things, but in the nature of them.

If the essence of virtuousness or commendableness, and of viciousness or fault, don't lie in the nature of the dispositions or acts of mind, which are said to be our virtue or our fault, but in their cause, then it is certain it lies nowhere at all. Thus, for instance, if the vice of a *vicious* act of will, lies not in the nature of the act, but the cause; so that its being of a bad nature will not make it at all our fault, unless it arises from some faulty determination of ours as its cause, or something in us that is our fault; then for the same reason, neither can the viciousness of that cause lie in the nature of the thing itself, but in *its* cause: that evil determination of ours is not our fault,

337

merely because it is of a bad nature, unless it arises from some cause in us that is our fault. And when we are come to this higher cause, still the reason of the thing holds good; though this cause be of a bad nature, yet we are not at all to blame on that account, unless it arises from something faulty in us. Nor yet can blameworthiness lie in the nature of *this cause,* but in the cause of *that.* And thus we must drive faultiness back from step to step, from a lower cause to a higher, *in infinitum:* and that is thoroughly to banish it from the world, and to allow it no possibility of existence anywhere in the universality of things. On these principles, vice or moral evil can't consist in anything that is an *effect;* because *fault* don't consist in the nature of things, but in their cause; as well as because effects are necessary, being unavoidably connected with their cause: therefore the cause only is to blame. And so it follows, that faultiness can lie *only in that cause,* which is a *cause only,* and no effect of anything. Nor yet can it lie in this; for then it must lie in the nature of the thing itself; not in its being from any determination of ours, nor anything faulty in us which is the cause, nor indeed from any cause at all, for by the supposition, it is no effect, and *has no cause.* And thus, he that will maintain, it is not the nature of habits or acts of will that makes them virtuous or faulty, but the cause, must immediately run himself out of his own assertion; and in maintaining it, will insensibly contradict and deny it.

This is certain, that if effects are vicious and faulty, not from their nature, or from anything inherent in them, but because they are from a bad cause, it must be on account of the *badness* of the cause; and so on account of the *nature* of the cause: a bad effect in the will must be bad, because the cause is *bad,* or *of an evil nature,* or *has badness* as a quality inherent in it: and a *good* effect in the will must be *good,* by reason of the *goodness* of the cause, or its being *of a good kind and nature.* And if this be what is meant, the very supposition of fault and praise lying not in the nature of the thing, but the cause, contradicts itself, and does at last [1] resolve the essence of virtue and vice into the nature of things, and supposes it originally to consist in that. And if a caviller has a mind to run from the absurdity, by saying, "No, the fault of the thing which is the cause, lies not in this, that the cause itself is *of an evil nature,* but that the cause is evil in that sense, that it is from another bad cause." Still the absurdity will follow him; for if so, then the cause before charged is at once

1. [The 1754 ed. reads "at least." I follow JE, Jr., in making this correction.]

acquitted, and all the blame must be laid to the higher cause, and must consist in that's being *evil*, or *of an evil nature*. So now we are come again to lay the blame of the thing blameworthy, to the nature of the thing, and not to the cause. And if any is so foolish as to go higher still, and ascend from step to step, till he is come to that which is the first cause concerned in the whole affair, and will say, all the blame lies in that; then at last he must be forced to own, that the faultiness of the thing which he supposes alone blameworthy, lies wholly *in the nature* of the thing, and not in the original or cause of it; for the supposition is, that it has no original, it is determined by no act of ours, is caused by nothing faulty in us, being absolutely *without any cause*. And so the race is at an end, but the evader is taken in his flight.

'Tis agreeable to the natural notions of mankind, that moral evil, with its desert of dislike and abhorrence, and all its other ill-deservings, consists in a certain *deformity* in the *nature* of certain dispositions of the heart, and acts of the will; and not in the deformity of *something else,* diverse from the very thing itself, which deserves abhorrence, supposed to be the cause of it. Which would be absurd, because that would be to suppose, a thing that is innocent and not evil, is truly evil and faulty, because another thing is evil. It implies a contradiction; for it would be to suppose, the very thing which is morally evil and blameworthy, is innocent and not blameworthy; but that something else, which is its cause, is only to blame. To say, that vice don't consist in the thing which is vicious, but in its cause, is the same as to say, that vice don't consist in vice, but in that which produces it.

'Tis true, a cause may be to blame, for being the cause of vice: it may be wickedness in the cause, that it produces wickedness. But it would imply a contradiction, to suppose that these two are the same individual wickedness. The wicked act of the cause in producing wickedness, is one wickedness; and the wickedness produced, if there be any produced, is another. And therefore the wickedness of the latter don't lie in the former, but is distinct from it; and the wickedness of both lies in the *evil nature* of the things which are wicked.

The thing which makes sin hateful, is that by which it deserves punishment; which is but the expression of hatred. And that which renders virtue lovely, is the same with that, on the account of which, it is fit to receive praise and reward; which are but the expressions of esteem and love. But that which makes vice hateful, is its hateful nature; and that which renders virtue lovely, is its amiable nature. 'Tis a certain beauty or deformity that are *inherent* in that good or evil will, which is the *soul* of virtue and vice (and not in the *occasion* of it) which is their worthiness of esteem or disesteem, praise or dispraise, according to the common sense of mankind. If the cause or occasion of the rise of an hateful disposition or act of will, be also hateful; suppose another antecedent evil will; that is entirely another sin, and deserves punishment by itself, under a distinct consideration. There is worthiness of dispraise in the nature of an evil volition, and not wholly in some foregoing act which is its cause; otherwise the evil volition which is the effect, is no moral evil, any more than sickness, or some other natural calamity, which arises from a cause morally evil.

Thus for instance, ingratitude is hateful and worthy of dispraise, according to common sense; not because something as bad, or worse than ingratitude, was the cause that produced it; but because it is hateful in itself, by its own inherent deformity. So the love of virtue is amiable, and worthy of praise, not merely because something else went before this love of virtue in our minds, which caused it to take place there; for instance our own choice; we chose to love virtue, and by some method or other wrought ourselves into the love of it; but because of the amiableness and condecency of such a disposition and inclination of heart. If that *was* the case, that we *did* choose to love virtue, and so produced that love in ourselves, this choice itself could be no otherwise amiable or praiseworthy, than as love to virtue, or some other amiable inclination, was exercised and implied in it. If that choice was amiable at all, it must be so on account of some amiable quality in the nature of the choice. If we chose to love virtue, not in love to virtue, or anything that was good, and exercised no sort of good disposition in the choice, the choice itself was not virtuous, nor worthy of any praise, according to common sense, because the choice was not of a *good nature.*

It may not be improper here to take notice of something said by an author, that has lately made a mighty noise in America. "A necessary holiness (says he) [2] is no holiness. . . . Adam could not be orig-

2. John Taylor: *The Scripture-Doctrine of Original Sin Proposed to Free and Candid Examination,* 3d ed. Belfast, John Hay, 1746) p. 180. [The context is a discussion of whether the "image of God" in which Adam was created should be interpreted as his natural and rational faculties or as the righteous exercise of these powers. "Righteousness is the right Use and Application of our Powers,"

inally created in righteousness and true holiness, because he must *choose* to be righteous, *before* he could be righteous. And therefore he must exist, he must be created, yea, he must exercise thought and reflection, before he was righteous." There is much more to the same effect in that place, and also in pp. 437, 438, 439, 440. If these things are so, it will certainly follow, that the first choosing to be righteous is no righteous choice; there is no righteousness or holiness in it; because no choosing to be righteous goes before it. For he plainly speaks of *choosing to be righteous,* as *what must go before righteousness:* and that which follows the choice, being the effect of the choice, can't be righteousness or holiness: for an effect is a thing necessary, and can't prevent the influence or efficacy of its cause; and therefore is unavoidably dependent upon the cause: and he says, "a necessary holiness is no holiness." So that neither can a choice of righteousness be righteousness or holiness, nor can anything that is consequent on that choice, and the effect of it, be righteousness or holiness; nor can anything that is without choice, be righteousness or holiness. So that by his scheme, all righteousness and holiness is at once shut out of the world, and no door left open, by which it can ever possibly enter into the world.

I suppose, the way that men came to entertain this absurd inconsistent notion, with respect to *internal inclinations and volitions* themselves (or notions that imply it), viz. that the essence of their moral good or evil lies not in their nature, but their cause; was, that it is indeed a very plain dictate of common sense, that it is so with respect to all *outward actions,* and sensible motions of the body; that the moral good or evil of 'em don't lie at all in the motions themselves; which taken by themselves, are nothing of a moral nature; and the essence of all the moral good or evil that concerns them, lies in those internal dispositions and volitions which are the cause of them. Now being always used to determine this, without hesitation or dispute, concerning *external actions;* which are the things that in the common use of language are signified by such phrases, as men's "actions," or their "doings"; hence when they came to speak of volitions, and *internal exercises* of their inclinations, under the same denomination of their "actions," or what they "do," they unwarily

writes Taylor; "consequently our Powers must not only exist, but also be used and applied before we can be righteous." Therefore, *"Original Righteousness is just as far from Truth as Original Sin.* And to talk of our *wanting that Righteousness in which Adam was created,* is to talk of nothing we want" (pp. 180–1).]

determined the case must also be the same with these, as with external actions; not considering the vast difference in the nature of the case.

If any shall still object and say, why is it not necessary that the cause should be considered, in order to determine whether anything be worthy of blame or praise? Is it agreeable to reason and common sense, that a man is to be praised or blamed for that which he is not the cause or author of, and has no hand in?

I answer, such phrases as "being the cause," "being the author," "having a hand," and the like are ambiguous. They are most vulgarly understood for being the designing voluntary cause, or cause by antecedent choice: and it is most certain that men are not in this sense the causes or authors of the first act of their wills, in any case; as certain as anything is, or ever can be; for nothing can be more certain, than that a thing is not before it is, nor a thing of the same kind before the first thing of that kind; and so no choice before the first choice. As the phrase, "being the author," may be understood, not of being the producer by an antecedent act of will; but as a person may be said to be the author of the act of will itself, by his being the immediate agent, or the being that *is acting,* or *in exercise* in that act; if the phrase of "being the author," is used to signify this, then doubtless common sense requires men's being the authors of their own acts of will, in order to their being esteemed worthy of praise or dispraise on account of them. And common sense teaches, that they must be the authors of *external* actions, in the former sense, namely, their being the causes of 'em by an act of will or choice, in order to their being justly blamed or praised: but it teaches no such thing with respect to the acts of the will themselves. But this may appear more manifest by the things which will be observed in the following section.

SECTION 2. THE FALSENESS AND INCONSISTENCE OF THAT METAPHYSICAL NOTION OF ACTION, AND AGENCY, WHICH SEEMS TO BE GENERALLY ENTERTAINED BY THE DEFENDERS OF THE ARMINIAN DOCTRINE CONCERNING LIBERTY, MORAL AGENCY, ETC.

ONE thing that is made very much a ground of argument and supposed demonstration by Arminians, in defense of the forementioned principles, concerning moral agency, virtue, vice, etc. is their *metaphysical notion of agency and action*. They say, unless the soul has a self-determining power, it has no power of "action"; if its volitions be not caused by itself, but are excited and determined by some extrinsic cause, they can't be the soul's own "acts"; and that the soul can't be "active," but must be wholly "passive," in those effects which it is the subject of necessarily, and not from its own free determination.

Mr. Chubb lays the foundation of his scheme of liberty, and of his arguments to support it, very much in this position, that man is an agent, and capable of action. Which doubtless is true: but *self-determination* belongs to his notion of "action," and is the very essence of it. Whence he infers that it is impossible for a man to act and be acted upon, in the same thing, at the same time; and that nothing that is an action, can be the effect of the action of another: and he insists, that a "necessary agent," or an agent that is necessarily determined to act, is a "plain contradiction." [1]

But those are a precarious sort of demonstrations, which men build on the meaning that they arbitrarily affix to a word; especially when that meaning is abstruse, inconsistent, and entirely diverse from the original sense of the word in common speech.

That the meaning of the word "action," as Mr. Chubb and many others use it, is utterly unintelligible and inconsistent, is manifest,

1. [*Tracts,* p. 311, and see above, p. 234, n. 2.]

because it belongs to their notion of an action, that 'tis something wherein is no passion or passiveness; that is (according to their sense of passiveness) it is under the power, influence or action of no cause. And this implies, that action has no cause, and is no effect: for to be an effect implies *passiveness,* or the being subject to the power and action of its cause. And yet they hold, that the mind's *action* is the effect of its own determination, yea, the mind's free and voluntary determination; which is the same with free choice. So that action is the effect of something preceding, even a preceding act of choice: and consequently, in this effect the mind is passive, subject to the power and action of the preceding cause, which is the foregoing choice, and therefore can't be active. So that here we have this contradiction, that action is always the effect of foregoing choice; and therefore can't be action; because it is *passive* to the power of that preceding causal choice; and the mind can't be active and passive in the same thing, at the same time. Again, they say, necessity is utterly inconsistent with action, and a necessary action is a contradiction; and so their notion of action implies contingence, and excludes all necessity. And therefore their notion of action implies, that it has no necessary dependence or connection with anything foregoing; for such a dependence or connection excludes contingence, and implies necessity. And yet their notion of action implies necessity, and supposes that it is necessary, and can't be contingent. For they suppose, that whatever is properly called action, must be determined by the will and free choice; and this is as much as to say, that it must be necessary, being dependent upon, and determined by something foregoing; namely, a foregoing act of choice. Again, it belongs to their notion of action, of that which is a proper and mere act, that it is the beginning of motion, or of exertion of power; but yet it is implied in their notion of action, that it is not the beginning of motion or exertion of power, but is consequent and dependent on a preceding exertion of power, viz. the power of will and choice: for they say there is no proper action but what is freely *chosen;* or, which is the same thing, determined by a foregoing act of free choice. But if any of them shall see cause to deny this, and say they hold no such thing as that every action is chosen, or determined by a foregoing choice; but that the very first exertion of will only, undetermined by any preceding act, is properly called action; then I say, such a man's notion of action implies necessity; for what the mind is the subject of without the determination of its own previous choice, it is the subject of necessarily, as to any hand that free choice has in the affair; and without any ability the mind has to prevent it, by any will or election of its own: because by the supposition it precludes all previous acts of the will or choice in the case, which might prevent it. So that it is again, in this other way, implied in their notion of act, that it is both necessary and not necessary. Again, it belongs to their notion of an "act," that it is no effect of a predetermining bias or preponderation, but springs immediately out of indifference; and this implies that it can't be from foregoing choice, which is foregoing preponderation: if it be not habitual, but occasional, yet if it causes the act, it is truly previous, efficacious and determining. And yet, at the same time, 'tis essential to their notion of an act, that it is what the agent is the author of freely and voluntarily, and that is, by previous choice and design.

So that according to their notion of an act, considered with regard to its consequences, these following things are all essential to it; viz. that it should be necessary, and not necessary; that it should be from a cause, and no cause; that it should be the fruit of choice and design, and not the fruit of choice and design; that it should be the beginning of motion or exertion, and yet consequent on previous exertion; that it should be before it is; that it should spring immediately out of indifference and equilibrium, and yet be the effect of preponderation; that it should be self-originated, and also have its original from something else; that it is what the mind causes itself, of its own will, and can produce or prevent, according to its choice or pleasure, and yet what the mind has no power to prevent, it precluding all previous choice in the affair.

So that an act, according to their metaphysical notion of it, is something of which there is no idea; 'tis nothing but a confusion of the mind, excited by words without any distinct meaning, and is an absolute nonentity; and that in two respects: (1) there is nothing in the world that ever was, is, or can be, to answer the things which must belong to its description, according to what they suppose to be essential to it. And (2) there neither is, nor ever was, nor can be, any notion or idea to answer the word, as they use and explain it. For if we should suppose any such notion, it would many ways destroy itself. But 'tis impossible, any idea or notion should subsist in the mind, whose very nature and essence, which constitutes it, destroys it. If some learned philosopher, who had been abroad, in giving an account of the curious observations he had made in his travels, should say, he "had been in Tierra del Fuego, and there had seen an animal, which he calls by a certain name, that begat and brought forth itself, and yet had a sire and a dam distinct from itself; that it had an appetite, and was hungry before it had being; that his master, who led him, and governed him at his pleasure, was always governed by him, and driven by him as he pleased; that when he moved, he always took a step before the first step; that he went with his head first, and yet always went tail foremost; and this, though he had neither head nor tail": it would be no impudence at all, to tell such a traveler, though a learned man, that he himself had no notion or idea of such an animal as he gave an account of, and never had, nor ever would have.

As the forementioned notion of action is very inconsistent, so it is wholly diverse from the original meaning of the word. The more usual signification of it in vulgar speech, seems to be some motion or exertion of power, that is voluntary, or that is the *effect* of the will; and is used in the same sense as "doing": and most commonly 'tis used to signify *outward* actions. So thinking is often distinguished from acting; and desiring and willing, from doing.

Besides this more usual and proper signification of the word "action," there are other ways in which the word is used that are less proper, which yet have place in common speech. Oftentimes 'tis used to signify some motion or alteration in inanimate things, with relation to some object and effect. So the spring of a watch is said to act upon the chain and wheels; the sunbeams, to act upon plants and trees; and the fire, to act upon wood. Sometimes the word is used to signify motions, alterations, and exertions of power, which are seen in corporeal things, *considered absolutely;* especially when these motions seem to arise from some internal cause which is *hidden;* so that they have a greater resemblance of those motions of our bodies, which are the effects of internal volition, or invisible exertions of will. So the fermentation of liquor, the operations of the loadstone, and of electrical bodies, are called the action of these things. And sometimes the word "action" is used to signify the exercise of thought, or of will and inclination: so meditating, loving, hating, inclining, disinclining, choosing and refusing, may be sometimes called acting; though more rarely (unless it be by philosophers and metaphysicians) than in any of the other senses.

But the word is never used in vulgar speech in that sense which Arminian divines use it in, namely, for the self-determinate exercise of the will, or an exertion of the soul that arises without any necessary connection with anything foregoing. If a man does something voluntarily, or as the effect of his choice, then in the most proper sense, and as the word is most originally and commonly used, he is said to act: but whether that choice or volition be self-determined, or no, whether it be connected with foregoing habitual bias, whether it be the certain effect of the strongest motive, or some extrinsic cause, never comes into consideration in the meaning of the word.

And if the word "action" is arbitrarily used by some men otherwise, to suit some scheme of metaphysics or morality, no argument can reasonably be founded on such a use of this term, to prove anything but their own pleasure. For divines and philosophers strenuously to urge such arguments, as though they were sufficient to support and demonstrate a whole scheme of moral philosophy and divinity, is certainly to erect a mighty edifice on the sand, or rather on a shadow. And though it may now perhaps, through custom, have become natural for 'em to use the word in this sense (if that may be called a sense or meaning, which is so inconsistent with itself) yet this don't prove that it is agreeable to the natural notions men have of things, or that there can be anything in the creation that should answer such a meaning. And though they appeal to experience, yet the truth is, that men are so far from experiencing any such thing, that it is impossible for 'em to have any conception of it.

If it should be objected, that "action" and "passion" are doubtless words of a contrary signification; but to suppose that the agent, in its action, is under the power and influence of something extrinsic, is to confound action and passion, and make 'em the same thing—

I answer, that action and passion are doubtless, as they are sometimes used, words of opposite signification; but not as signifying opposite *existences,* but only opposite *relations.* The words "cause" and "effect" are terms of opposite signification; but nevertheless, if I assert that the same thing may at the same time, in different respects and relations, be both cause and effect, this will not prove that I confound the terms. The soul may be both active and passive in the same thing in different respects, active with relation to one thing, and passive with relation to another. The word "passion" when set in opposition to *action* or rather *activeness,* is merely a relative term: it signifies no effect or cause, nor any proper existence; but is the same with *passiveness,* or a being passive, or a being acted upon by something. Which is a mere relation of a thing to some power or force exerted by some cause, producing some effect in it, or upon it. And "action," when set properly in opposition to *passion,* or *passiveness,* is no real existence; it is not the same with "an action," but is a mere relation: 'tis the *activeness* of something on another thing, being the opposite relation to the other, viz. a relation of power, or force exerted by some cause, towards another thing, which is the subject of the effect of that power. Indeed the word "action" is frequently used to signify something not merely relative, but more absolute, and a real existence; as when we say "an action"; when the word is not used transitively, but absolutely, for some motion or exercise of body or mind, without any relation to any object or effect: and as used thus, it is not properly the opposite of "passion"; which ordinarily signifies nothing absolute, but merely the *relation* of *being acted upon.* And therefore if the word "action" be used in the like relative sense, then action and passion are only two contrary relations. And 'tis no absurdity to suppose, that contrary relations may belong to the same thing, at the same time, with respect to different things. So to suppose, that there are acts of the soul by which a man voluntarily moves, and acts upon objects, and produces effects, which yet themselves are effects of something else, and wherein the soul itself is the object of something acting upon, and influencing that, don't at all confound "action" and "passion." The words may nevertheless be properly of opposite signification: there may be as true and real a difference between *acting* and being *caused to act,* though we should suppose the soul to be both in the same volition, as there is between *living,* and *being quickened,* or *made to live.* 'Tis no more a contradiction, to suppose that action may be the effect of some other cause, besides the agent, or being that acts, than to suppose that life may be the effect of some other cause, besides the liver, or the being that lives, in whom life is caused to be.

The thing which has led men into this inconsistent notion of action, when applied to volition, as though it were essential to this internal action, that the agent should be self-determined in it, and that the will should be the cause of it, was probably this; that according to the sense of mankind, and the common use of language it is so, with respect to men's external actions; which are what originally, and according to the vulgar use and most proper sense of the word, are called "actions." Men in these are self-directed, self-determined, and their wills are the cause of the motions of their bodies, and the external things that are done; so that unless men do 'em voluntarily, and of choice, and the action be determined by their antecedent volition, it is no action or doing of theirs. Hence some metaphysicians have been led unwarily, but exceeding absurdly, to suppose the same concerning volition itself, that that also must be determined by the will; which is to be determined by antecedent volition, as the motion of the body is; not considering the contradiction it implies.

But 'tis very evident, that in the metaphysical distinction between action and passion (though long since become common and the general vogue), due care has not been taken to conform language to the nature of things, or to any distinct clear ideas. As it is in innumerable other philosophical, metaphysical terms, used in these disputes; which has occasioned inexpressible difficulty, contention, error and confusion.

And thus probably it came to be thought, that necessity was inconsistent with action, as these terms are applied to volition. First, these terms "action" and "necessity" are changed from their original meaning, as signifying external voluntary action, and constraint (in which meaning they are evidently inconsistent), to signify quite other things, viz. volition itself, and certainty of existence. And when the change of signification is made, care is not taken to make proper allowances and abatements for the difference of sense; but still the same things are unwarily attributed to "action" and "necessity," in the new meaning of the words, which plainly belonged to 'em in their first sense; and on this ground, maxims are established without any real foundation, as though they were the most certain truths, and the most evident dictates of reason.

But however strenuously it is maintained, that what is necessary can't be properly called action, and that a necessary action is a contradiction, yet 'tis probable there are few Arminian divines, who if thoroughly tried, would stand to these principles. They will allow, that God is in the highest sense an active being, and the highest fountain of life and action; and they would not probably deny, that those that are called God's acts of righteousness, holiness and faithfulness, are truly and properly God's *acts,* and God is really a holy *agent* in them: and yet I trust, they will not deny, that God necessarily acts justly and faithfully, and that it is impossible for him to act unrighteously and unholily.

SECTION 3. THE REASONS WHY SOME THINK IT CONTRARY TO COMMON SENSE, TO SUPPOSE THOSE THINGS WHICH ARE NECESSARY, TO BE WORTHY OF EITHER PRAISE OR BLAME

'TIS abundantly affirmed and urged by Arminian writers, that it is contrary to common sense, and the natural notions and apprehensions of mankind, to suppose otherwise than that necessity (making no distinction between natural and moral necessity) is inconsistent with virtue and vice, praise and blame, reward and punishment. And their arguments from hence have been greatly triumphed in; and have been not a little perplexing to many who have been friendly to the truth, as clearly revealed in the holy Scriptures: it has seemed to them indeed difficult, to reconcile Calvinistic doctrines with the notions men commonly have of justice and equity. And the true reasons of it seem to be these that follow.

I. 'Tis indeed a very plain dictate of common sense, that natural necessity is wholly inconsistent with just praise or blame. If men do things which in themselves are very good, fit to be brought to pass, and very happy effects, properly against their wills, and can't help it; or do them from a necessity that is without their wills, or with which their wills have no concern or connection; then 'tis a plain dictate of common sense, that it's none of their virtue, nor any moral good in them; and that they are not worthy to be rewarded or praised; or at all esteemed, honored or loved on that account. And on the other hand, that if from like necessity they do those things which in themselves are very unhappy and pernicious, and do them because they can't help it; the necessity is such, that it is all one whether they will them, or no; and the reason why they are done, is from necessity only, and not from their wills; 'tis a very plain dictate of common sense that they are not at all to blame; there is no vice, fault, or moral evil at all in the effect done; nor are they who are thus necessitated, in any wise worthy to be punished, hated, or in the least disrespected, on that account.

In like manner, if things in themselves good and desirable are absolutely impossible, with a natural impossibility, the universal reason of mankind teaches, that this *wholly* and *perfectly* excuses persons in their not doing them.

And 'tis also a plain dictate of common sense, that if the doing things in themselves good, or avoiding things in themselves evil, is not *absolutely impossible,* with such a natural impossibility, but very *difficult,* with a natural difficulty; that is, a difficulty prior *to,* and not at all consisting *in* will and inclination itself, and which would remain the same, let the inclination be what it will; then a person's neglect or omission is excused *in some measure,* though not wholly; his sin is less aggravated, than if the thing to be done were easy. And if instead of difficulty and hindrance, there be a contrary natural propensity in the state of things, to the thing to be done, or effect to be brought to pass, abstracted from any consideration of the inclination of the heart; though the propensity be not so great as to amount to a natural necessity; yet being some approach to it, so that the doing the good thing be very much from this natural tendency in the state of things, and but little from a good inclination; then it is a dictate of common sense, that there is so much the less virtue in what is done; and so it is less praiseworthy and rewardable. The reason is easy, viz. because such a natural propensity or tendency is an approach to natural necessity; and the greater the propensity, still so much the nearer is the approach to necessity. And therefore as natural necessity takes away or shuts out *all* virtue, so this propensity approaches to an abolition of virtue; that is, it *diminishes* it. And on the other hand, natural difficulty in the state of things is an approach to natural impossibility. And as the latter, when it is complete and absolute, *wholly* takes away blame; so such difficulty takes away *some* blame, or diminishes blame; and makes the thing done to be less worthy of punishment.

II. Men in their first use of such phrases as these, "must," "can't," "can't help it," "can't avoid it," "necessary," "unable," "impossible," "unavoidable," "irresistible," etc. use them to signify a necessity of constraint or restraint, a natural necessity or impossibility; or some necessity that the will has nothing to do in; which may be, whether men will or no; and which may be supposed to be just the same, let men's inclinations and desires be what they will. Such kind of terms in their original use, I suppose among all nations, are relative; carrying in their signification (as was before observed) a reference or respect to some contrary will, desire or endeavor, which, it is supposed, is, or may be in the case. All men find, and begin to find in early childhood, that there are innumerable things that can't be done, which they desire to do; and innumerable things which they are averse to, that must be, they can't avoid them, they will be, whether they choose them or no. 'Tis to express this necessity, which men so soon and so often find, and which so greatly and so early affects them in innumerable cases, that such terms and phrases are first formed; and 'tis to signify such a necessity, that they are first used, and that they are most constantly used, in the common affairs of life; and not to signify any such metaphysical, speculative and abstract notion, as that connection in the nature or course of things, which is between the subject and predicate of a proposition, and which is the foundation of the certain truth of that proposition; to signify which, they who employ themselves in philosophical inquiries into the first origin and metaphysical relations and dependences of things, have borrowed these terms, for want of others. But we grow up from our cradles in a use of such terms and phrases, entirely different from this, and carrying a sense exceeding diverse from that in which they are commonly used in the controversy between Arminians and Calvinists. And it being, as was said before, a dictate of the universal sense of mankind, evident to us as soon as we begin to think, that the necessity signified by these terms, in the sense in which we first learn them, does excuse persons, and free them from all fault or blame; hence our ideas of excusableness or faultlessness is tied to these terms and phrases by a strong habit, which is begun in childhood as soon as we begin to speak, and grows up with us, and is strengthened by constant use and custom, the connection growing stronger and stronger.

The habitual connection which is in men's minds between blamelessness and those forementioned terms, "must," "cannot," "unable," "necessary," "impossible," "unavoidable," etc. becomes very strong; because as soon as ever men begin to use reason and speech, they have occasion to excuse themselves, from the natural necessity signified by these terms, in numerous instances. "I can't do it." "I could not help it." And all mankind have constant and daily occasion to use such phrases in this sense, to excuse themselves and others in almost all the concerns of life, with respect to disappointments, and things that happen which concern and affect us and others, that are hurtful, or disagreeable to us or them, or things desirable that we or others fail of.

That a being accustomed to an union of different ideas, from early childhood, makes the habitual connection exceeding strong, as though such connection were owing to *nature,* is manifest in innumerable instances. It is altogether by such an habitual connection of ideas, that men judge of the bigness or distance of the objects of sight from their appearance. Thus 'tis owing to such a connection early established, and growing up with a person, that he judges a mountain, which he sees at ten miles distance, to be bigger than his nose, or further off than the end of it. Having been used so long to join a considerable distance and magnitude with such an appearance, men imagine it is by a dictate of natural sense: whereas it would be quite otherwise with one that had his eyes newly opened, who had been born blind: he would have the same visible appearance, but natural sense would dictate no such thing concerning the magnitude or distance of what appeared.

III. When men, after they had been so habituated to connect ideas of innocency or blamelessness with such terms, that the union seems to be the effect of mere nature, come to hear the same terms used, and learn to use them themselves in the forementioned new and metaphysical sense, to signify quite another sort of necessity, which has no such kind of relation to a contrary supposable will and endeavor; the notion of plain and manifest blamelessness, by this means, is by a strong prejudice, insensibly and unwarily transferred to a case to which it by no means belongs: the change of the use of the terms, to a signification which is very diverse, not being taken notice of, or adverted to. And there are several reasons why it is not.

1. The terms, as used by philosophers, are not very distinct and clear in their meaning: few use them in a fixed determined sense. On the contrary, their meaning is very vague and confused. Which is what commonly happens to the words used to signify things intellectual and moral, and to express what Mr. Locke calls "mixed modes." [1] If men had a clear and distinct understanding of what is

---

1. [*Essay,* Bk. II, ch. 22; *1,* 381–9. Locke devised the expression "mixed modes" for complex ideas consisting of "several combinations of simple ideas of *different* kinds," in distinction from "simple modes," or the combination of "simple ideas of the *same* kind." Mixed modes also differ from complex ideas, such as substance, in that they are "not looked upon to be characteristical marks of any real beings that have a steady existence" (no. 1, p. 381). They are, therefore, general terms or

intended by these metaphysical terms, they would be able more easily to compare them with their original and common sense; and so would not be so easily cheated by them. The minds of men are so easily led into delusion by no sort of terms in the world, as by words of this sort.

2. The change of the signification of the terms is the more insensible, because the things signified, though indeed very different, yet do in some generals agree. In "necessity," that which is *vulgarly* so called, there is a strong connection between the thing said to be necessary, and something antecedent to it, in the order of nature; so there is also in "philosophical necessity." And though in both kinds of necessity, the connection can't be called by that name, with relation to an opposite will or endeavor, to which it is *superior;* which is the case in vulgar necessity; yet in both, the connection is *prior* to will and endeavor, and so in some respect *superior.* In both kinds of necessity there is a foundation for some certainty of the proposition that affirms the event. The terms used being the same, and the things signified agreeing in these and some other general circumstances, and the expressions as used by philosophers being not well defined, and so of obscure and loose signification; hence persons are not aware of the great difference; and the notions of innocence or faultlessness, which were so strongly associated with them, and were strictly united in their minds, ever since they can remember, remain united with them still, as if the union were altogether natural and necessary; and they that go about to make a separation, seem to them to do great violence even to nature itself.

IV. Another reason why it appears difficult to reconcile it with reason, that men should be blamed for that which is necessary with a moral necessity (which as was observed before is a species of philosophical necessity) is, that for want of due consideration, men inwardly entertain that apprehension, that this necessity may be against men's wills and sincere endeavors. They go away with that notion, that men may truly will and wish and strive that it may be otherwise; but that invincible necessity stands in the way. And many think thus

notions (no. 2, p. 382), such as "obligation," "drunkenness," "hypocrisy," etc. The mind exercises its most *active* power in making these notions, with a view to improving the benefit of language (as JE does in using philosophical "necessity" as a term of art). In Locke's *Essay,* the chapter on mixed modes follows immediately upon the chapter "Of Power," which, according to Locke, is a "simple idea" (no. 10, p. 387).]

concerning themselves: some that are wicked men think they wish that they were good, that they loved God and holiness; but yet don't find that their wishes produce the effect. The reasons why men think thus, are as follows: (1) They find what may be called an *indirect willingness* to have a better will, in the manner before observed. For it is impossible, and a contradiction to suppose the will to be directly and properly against itself. And they don't consider, that this indirect willingness is entirely a different thing from properly willing the thing that is the duty and virtue required; and that there is no virtue in that sort of willingness which they have. They don't consider, that the volitions which a wicked man may have that he loved God, are no acts of the will at all against the moral evil of not loving God; but only some disagreeable consequences. But the making the requisite distinction requires more care of reflection and thought than most men are used to. And men through a prejudice in their own favor, are disposed to think well of their own desires and dispositions, and to account 'em good and virtuous, though their respect to virtue be only *indirect* and *remote,* and 'tis nothing at all that is virtuous that truly excites or terminates their inclinations. (2) Another thing that insensibly leads and beguiles men into a supposition that this moral necessity or impossibility is, or may be against men's wills, and true endeavors, is the derivation and formation of the terms themselves, that are often used to express it, which is such as seems directly to point to, and hold this forth. Such words, for instance, as "unable," "unavoidable," "impossible," "irresistible"; which carry a plain reference to a supposable power exerted, endeavors used, resistance made, in opposition to the necessity: and the persons that hear them, not considering nor suspecting but that they are used in their proper sense: that sense being therefore understood, there does naturally, and as it were necessarily arise in their minds a supposition that it may be so indeed, that true desires and endeavors may take place, but that invincible necessity stands in the way, and renders 'em vain and to no effect.

V. Another thing which makes persons more ready to suppose it to be contrary to reason, that men should be exposed to the punishments threatened to sin, for doing those things which are morally necessary, or not doing those things morally impossible, is, that imagination strengthens the argument, and adds greatly to the power and influence of the seeming reasons against it, from the greatness of that punishment. To allow that they may be justly exposed to a small punishment, would not be so difficult. Whereas, if there were any good reason in the case, if it were truly a dictate of reason that such necessity was inconsistent with faultiness, or just punishment, the demonstration would be equally certain with respect to a small punishment, or any punishment at all, as a very great one: but it is not equally easy to the imagination. They that argue against the justice of damning men for those things that are thus necessary, seem to make their argument the stronger, by setting forth the greatness of the punishment in strong expressions: "That a man should be cast into eternal burnings, that he should be made to fry in hell to all eternity, for those things which he had no power to avoid, and was under a fatal, unfrustrable, invincible necessity of doing."

SECTION 4. IT IS AGREEABLE TO COMMON SENSE, AND THE NATURAL NOTIONS OF MANKIND, TO SUPPOSE MORAL NECESSITY TO BE CONSISTENT WITH PRAISE AND BLAME, REWARD AND PUNISHMENT

WHETHER the reasons that have been given, why it appears difficult to some persons to reconcile with common sense the praising or blaming, rewarding or punishing those things which are morally necessary, are thought satisfactory, or not; yet it most evidently appears by the following things, that if this matter be rightly understood, setting aside all delusion arising from the impropriety and ambiguity of terms, this is not at all inconsistent with the natural apprehensions of mankind, and that sense of things which is found everywhere in the common people, who are furthest from having their thoughts perverted from their natural channel, by metaphysical and philosophical subtleties; but on the contrary, altogether agreeable *to,* and the very voice and dictate *of* this natural and vulgar sense.

I. This will appear if we consider what the vulgar notion of blameworthiness is. The idea which the common people through all ages and nations have of faultiness, I suppose to be plainly this; a person's being or doing wrong, with his own will and pleasure; containing these two things: 1. His doing wrong, when he does as he pleases. 2. His pleasure's being wrong. Or in other words, perhaps more intelligibly expressing their notion; a person's having his heart wrong, and doing wrong from his heart. And this is the sum total of the matter.

The common people don't ascend up in their reflections and abstractions, to the metaphysical sources, relations and dependences of things, in order to form their notion of faultiness or blameworthiness. They don't wait till they have decided by their refinings, what first determines the will; whether it be determined by something extrinsic, or intrinsic; whether volition determines volition, or whether the understanding determines the will; whether there be

357

any such thing as metaphysicians mean by contingence (if they have any meaning); whether there be a sort of a strange unaccountable sovereignty in the will, in the exercise of which, by its own sovereign acts, it brings to pass all its own sovereign acts. They don't take any part of their notion of fault or blame from the resolution of any such questions. If this were the case, there are multitudes, yea, the far greater part of mankind, nine hundred and ninety-nine out of a thousand would live and die without having any such notion as that of fault ever entering into their heads, or without so much as once having any conception that anybody was to be either blamed or commended for anything. To be sure, it would be a long time before men came to have such notions. Whereas 'tis manifest, they are some of the first notions that appear in children; who discover as soon as they can think, or speak, or act at all as rational creatures, a sense of desert. And certainly, in forming their notion of it, they make no use of metaphysics. All the ground they go upon consists in these two things; *experience,* and a *natural sensation* of a certain fitness or agreeableness which there is in uniting such moral evil as is above described, viz. *a being or doing wrong with the will,* and resentment in others, and pain inflicted on the person in whom this moral evil is. Which *natural sense* is what we call by the name of "conscience."

'Tis true, the common people and children, in their notion of a faulty act or deed of any person, do suppose that it is the person's *own act* and deed. But this is all that belongs to what they understand by a thing's being a person's *own deed* or action; even that it is something done by him of choice. That some exercise or motion should begin of itself, don't belong to their notion of an action, or doing. If so, it would belong to their notion of it, that it is something which is the cause of its own beginning: and that is as much as to say, that it is before it begins to be. Nor is their notion of an action some motion or exercise that begins accidentally, without any cause or reason; for that is contrary to one of the prime dictates of common sense, namely, that everything that begins to be, has some cause or reason why it is.

The common people, in their notion of a faulty or praiseworthy deed or work done by anyone, do suppose that the man does it in the exercise of *liberty.* But then their notion of liberty is only a person's having opportunity of doing as he pleases. They have no notion of liberty consisting in the will's first acting, and so causing its own acts; and determining, and so causing its own determinations; or choosing, and so causing its own choice. Such a notion of liberty is what none have, but those that have darkened their own minds with confused metaphysical speculation, and abstruse and ambiguous terms. If a man is not restrained from acting as his will determines, or constrained to act otherwise; then he has liberty, according to common notions of liberty, without taking into the idea that grand contradiction of all the determinations of a man's free will being the effects of the determinations of his free will. Nor have men commonly any notion of freedom consisting in indifference. For if so, then it would be agreeable to their notion, that the greater indifference men act with, the more freedom they act with; whereas the reverse is true. He that in acting, proceeds with the fullest inclination, does what he does with the greatest freedom, according to common sense. And so far is it from being agreeable to common sense, that such liberty as consists in indifference is requisite to praise or blame, that on the contrary, the dictate of every man's natural sense through the world is, that the further he is from being indifferent in his acting good or evil, and the more he does either with full and strong inclination, the more is he esteemed or abhorred, commended or condemned.

II. If it were inconsistent with the common sense of mankind, that men should be either to be blamed or commended in any volitions they have or fail of, in case of moral necessity or impossibility; then it would surely also be agreeable to the same sense and reason of mankind, that the nearer the case approaches to such a moral necessity or impossibility, either through a strong antecedent moral propensity on the one hand,[1] or a great antecedent opposition and difficulty on the other, the nearer does it approach to a being neither blamable nor commendable; so that acts exerted with such preceding propensity would be worthy of proportionably less praise; and when omitted, the act being attended with such difficulty, the omission would be worthy of the less blame. It is so, as was observed before, with natural necessity and impossibility, propensity and difficulty: as 'tis a plain dictate of the sense of all mankind, that natural necessity and impossibility takes away *all* blame and praise; and therefore, that the nearer the approach is to these through previous propensity or difficulty, so praise and blame are proportionably *diminished*. And if it were as much a dictate of common sense, that moral

1. 'Tis here argued, on supposition that not all propensity implies moral necessity, but only some very high degrees; which none will deny.

necessity of doing, or impossibility of avoiding, takes away *all* praise and blame, as that natural necessity or impossibility does this; then, by a perfect parity of reason, it would be as much the dictate of common sense, that an *approach* to moral necessity of doing, or impossibility of avoiding, *diminishes* praise and blame, as that an approach to natural necessity and impossibility does so. 'Tis equally the voice of common sense, that persons are *excusable in part,* in neglecting things difficult against their wills, as that they are *excusable wholly* in neglecting things impossible against their wills. And if it made no difference, whether the impossibility were natural and against the will, or moral, lying in the will, with regard to excusableness; so neither would it make any difference, whether the difficulty, or approach to necessity be natural against the will, or moral, lying in the propensity of the will.

But 'tis apparent, that the reverse of these things is true. If there be an approach to a moral necessity in a man's exertion of good acts of will, they being the exercise of a strong propensity to good, and a very powerful love to virtue; 'tis so far from being the dictate of common sense, that he is less virtuous, and the less to be esteemed, loved and praised; that 'tis agreeable to the natural notions of all mankind that he is so much the better man, worthy of greater respect, and higher commendation. And the stronger the inclination is, and the nearer it approaches to necessity in that respect, or to impossibility of neglecting the virtuous act, or of doing a vicious one; still the more virtuous, and worthy of higher commendation. And on the other hand, if a man exerts evil acts of mind; as for instance, acts of pride or malice, from a rooted and strong habit or principle of haughtiness and maliciousness, and a violent propensity of heart to such acts; according to the natural sense of all men, he is so far from being the less hateful and blamable on that account, that he is so much the more worthy to be detested and condemned by all that observe him.

Moreover, 'tis manifest that it is no part of the notion which mankind commonly have of a blamable or praiseworthy act of the will, that it is an act which is not determined by an antecedent bias or motive, but by the sovereign power of the will itself; because if so, the greater hand such causes have in determining any acts of the will, so much the less virtuous or vicious would they be accounted; and the less hand, the more virtuous or vicious. Whereas the reverse is true: men don't think a good act to be the less praiseworthy, for the agent's being much determined in it by a good inclination or a good motive; but the more. And if good inclination or motive has but little influence in determining the agent, they don't think his act so much the more virtuous, but the less. And so concerning evil acts, which are determined by evil motives or inclinations.

Yea, if it be supposed that good or evil dispositions are implanted in the hearts of men by nature itself (which, it is certain, is vulgarly supposed in innumerable cases) yet it is not commonly supposed that men are worthy of no praise or dispraise for such dispositions; although what is natural is undoubtedly necessary, nature being prior to all acts of the will whatsoever. Thus for instance, if a man appears to be of a very haughty or malicious disposition, and is supposed to be so by his natural temper, 'tis no vulgar notion, no dictate of the common sense and apprehension of men, that such dispositions are no vices or moral evils, or that such persons are not worthy of disesteem, odium and dishonor; or that the proud or malicious acts which flow from such natural dispositions, are worthy of no resentment. Yea, such vile natural dispositions, and the strength of 'em, will commonly be mentioned rather as an aggravation of the wicked acts that come from such a fountain, than an extenuation of 'em. Its being natural for men to act thus, is often observed by men in the height of their indignation: they will say, " 'Tis his very nature: he is of a vile natural temper; 'tis as natural to him to act so, as it is to breathe; he can't help serving the devil," etc. But it is not thus with regard to hurtful mischievous things that any are the subjects or occasions of by *natural necessity,* against their inclinations. In such a case, the necessity, by the common voice of mankind, will be spoken of as a full excuse. Thus 'tis very plain, that common sense makes a vast difference between these two kinds of necessity, as to the judgment it makes of their influence on the moral quality and desert of men's actions.

And these dictates of men's minds are so natural and necessary, that it may be very much doubted whether the Arminians themselves have ever got rid of 'em; yea, their greatest doctors, that have gone furthest in defense of their metaphysical notions of liberty, and have brought their arguments to their greatest strength, and as they suppose to a demonstration, against the consistence of virtue and vice with any necessity: 'tis to be questioned, whether there is so much as one of them, but that if he suffered very much from the injurious acts of a man under the power of an invincible haughtiness and malignancy of temper, would not, from the forementioned natural sense of mind, resent it far otherwise, than if as great sufferings came upon him from the wind that blows, and fire that burns by natural necessity; and otherwise than he would, if he suffered as much from the conduct of a man perfectly delirious; yea, though he first brought his distraction upon him some way by his own fault.

Some seem to disdain the distinction that we make between *natural* and *moral* necessity, as though it were altogether impertinent in this controversy: "That which is necessary (say they) is necessary; it is that which must be, and can't be prevented. And that which is impossible, is impossible, and can't be done: and therefore none can be to blame for not doing it." And such comparisons are made use of, as the commanding of a man to walk who has lost his legs, and condemning and punishing him for not obeying; inviting and calling upon a man, who is shut up in a strong prison, to come forth, etc. But in these things Arminians are very unreasonable. Let common sense determine whether there be not a great difference between those two cases; the one, that of a man who has offended his prince, and is cast into prison; and after he has lain there a while, the king comes to him, calls him to come forth to him; and tells him that if he will do so, and will fall down before him, and humbly beg his pardon, he shall be forgiven, and set at liberty, and also be greatly enriched, and advanced to honor: the prisoner heartily repents of the folly and wickedness of his offense against his prince, is thoroughly disposed to abase himself, and accept of the king's offer; but is confined by strong walls, with gates of brass, and bars of iron. The other case is, that of a man who is of a very unreasonable spirit, of a haughty, ungrateful, willful disposition; and moreover, has been brought up in traitorous principles; and has his heart possessed with an extreme and inveterate enmity to his lawful sovereign; and for his rebellion is cast into prison, and lies long there, loaden with heavy chains, and in miserable circumstances. At length the compassionate prince comes to the prison, orders his chains to be knocked off, and his prison doors to be set wide open; calls to him, and tells him, if he will come forth to him, and fall down before him, acknowledge that he has treated him unworthily, and ask his forgiveness; he shall be forgiven, set at liberty, and set in a place of great dignity and profit in his court. But he is so stout and stomachful, and full of haughty malignity, that he can't be willing to accept the offer: his rooted strong pride and malice have perfect power over him, and as it were bind him, by binding his heart: the opposition of his heart has the mastery over him, having an influence on his mind far superior to the king's grace and condescension, and to all his kind offers and promises. Now, is it agreeable to common sense, to assert and stand to it, that there is no difference between these two cases, as to any worthiness of blame in the prisoners; because, forsooth, there is a necessity in both, and the required act in each case is impossible? 'Tis true, a man's evil dispositions may be as strong and immovable as the bars of a castle. But who can't see, that when a man, in the latter case, is said to be "unable" to obey the command, the expression is used improperly, and not in the sense it has originally and in common speech? And that it may properly be said to be in the rebel's power to come out of prison, seeing he can easily do it if he pleases; though by reason of his vile temper of heart which is fixed and rooted, 'tis impossible that it should please him?

Upon the whole, I presume there is no person of good understanding, who impartially considers the things which have been observed, but will allow that 'tis not evident from the dictates of the common sense, or natural notions of mankind, that moral necessity is inconsistent with praise and blame. And therefore, if the Arminians would prove any such inconsistency, it must be by some philosophical and metaphysical arguments, and not common sense.

There is a grand illusion in the pretended demonstration of Arminians from common sense. The main strength of all these demonstrations, lies in that prejudice that arises through the insensible change of the use and meaning of such terms as "liberty," "able," "unable," "necessary," "impossible," "unavoidable," "invincible," "action," etc. from their original and vulgar sense, to a metaphysical sense entirely diverse; and the strong connection of the ideas of blamelessness, etc. with some of these terms, by an habit contracted and established, while these terms were used in their first meaning. This prejudice and delusion is the foundation of all those positions they lay down as maxims, by which most of the scriptures, which they allege in this controversy, are interpreted, and on which all their pompous demonstrations from Scripture and reason depend. From this secret delusion and prejudice they have almost all their advantages: 'tis the strength of their bulwarks, and the edge of their weapons. And this is the main ground of all the right they have to treat their neighbors in so assuming a manner, and to insult others, perhaps as wise and good as themselves, as weak bigots, men that dwell in the dark caves of superstition, perversely set, obstinately shutting their eyes against the noonday light, enemies to common sense, maintaining the first-born of absurdities, etc. But perhaps an impartial consideration of the things which have been observed in the preceding parts of this inquiry, may enable the lovers of truth better to judge, whose doctrine is indeed absurd, abstruse, self-contradictory, and inconsistent with common sense, and many ways repugnant to the universal dictates of the reason of mankind.

Corol. From things which have been observed, it will follow, that it is agreeable to common sense to suppose, that the glorified saints have not their freedom at all diminished, in any respect; and that God himself has the highest possible freedom, according to the true and proper meaning of the term; and that he is in the highest possible respect an agent, and active in the exercise of his infinite holiness; though he acts therein in the highest degree necessarily: and his actions of this kind are in the highest, most absolutely perfect manner virtuous and praiseworthy; and are so, for that very reason, because they are most perfectly necessary.

SECTION 5. CONCERNING THOSE OBJECTIONS, THAT
            THIS SCHEME OF NECESSITY RENDERS
            ALL MEANS AND ENDEAVORS FOR THE
            AVOIDING OF SIN, OR THE OBTAINING
            VIRTUE AND HOLINESS, VAIN, AND TO
            NO PURPOSE; AND THAT IT MAKES MEN
            NO MORE THAN MERE MACHINES IN
            AFFAIRS OF MORALITY AND RELIGION

ARMINIANS say, if it be so, that sin and virtue come to pass by a necessity consisting in a sure connection of causes and effects, antecedents and consequents, it can never be worth the while to use any means or endeavors to obtain the one, and avoid the other; seeing no endeavors can alter the futurity of the event, which is become necessary by a connection already established.

But I desire, that this matter may be fully considered; and that it may be examined with a thorough strictness, whether it will follow that endeavors and means, in order to avoid or obtain any future thing, must be more in vain, on the supposition of such a connection of antecedents and consequents, than if the contrary be supposed.

For endeavors to be in vain, is for 'em not to be successful; that is to say, for 'em not eventually to be the means of the thing aimed at, which can't be, but in one of these two ways; either, first, that although the means are used, yet the event aimed at don't follow: or, secondly, if the event does follow, it is not because of the means, or from any connection or dependence of the event on the means, the event would have come to pass, as well without the means, as with them. If either of these two things are the case, then the means are not properly successful, and are truly in vain. The successfulness or unsuccessfulness of means, in order to an effect, or their being in vain or not in vain, consists in those means being connected, or not connected, with the effect, in such a manner as this, viz. that the effect is *with* the means, and not *without* them; or, that the being of the effect is, on the one hand, connected with the means, and the want of the effect, on the other hand, is connected with the want of the means. If there be such a connection as this between means and end, the means are not in vain: the more there is of such a connection, the further they are from being in vain; and the less of such a connection, the more are they in vain.

Now therefore the question to be answered (in order to determine, whether it follows from this doctrine of the necessary connection between foregoing things and consequent ones, that means used in order to any effect, are more in vain than they would be otherwise) is, whether it follows from it, that there is less of the forementioned connection between means and effect; that is, whether on the supposition of there being a real and true connection between antecedent things and consequent ones, there must be less of a connection between means and effect, than on the supposition of there being no fixed connection between antecedent things and consequent ones: and the very stating of this question is sufficient to answer it. It must appear to everyone that will open his eyes, that this question can't be affirmed, without the grossest absurdity and inconsistence. Means are foregoing things, and effects are following things: and if there were no connection between foregoing things, and following ones, there could be no connection between means and end; and so all means would be wholly vain and fruitless. For 'tis by virtue of some connection only, that they become successful: 'tis some connection observed, or revealed, or otherwise known, between antecedent things and following ones, that is what directs in the choice of means. And if there were no such thing as an established connection, there could be no choice, as to means; one thing would have no more tendency to an effect, than another; there would be no such thing as tendency in the case. All those things which are successful means of other things, do therein prove connected antecedents of them: and therefore to assert, that a fixed connection between antecedents and consequents makes means vain and useless, or stands in the way to hinder the connection between means and end, is just so ridiculous, as to say, that a connection between antecedents and consequents stands in the way to hinder a connection between antecedents and consequents.

Nor can any supposed connection of the succession or train of antecedents and consequents, from the very beginning of all things, the connection being made already sure and necessary, either by established laws of nature, or by these together with a decree of sovereign immediate interpositions of divine power, on such and such occasions, or any other way (if any other there be); I say, no such necessary connection of a series of antecedents and consequents can in the least tend to hinder, but that the means we use may belong to the series; and so may be some of those antecedents which are connected with the consequents we aim at, in the established course of things. Endeavors which we use, are things that exist; and therefore they belong to the general chain of events; all the parts of which chain are supposed to be connected: and so endeavors are supposed to be connected with some effects, or some consequent things, or other. And certainly this don't hinder but that the events they are connected with, may be those which we aim at, and which we choose, because we judge 'em most likely to have a connection with those events, from the established order and course of things which we observe, or from something in divine revelation.

Let us suppose a real and sure connection between a man's having his eyes open in the clear daylight, with good organs of sight, and seeing; so that seeing is connected with his opening his eyes, and not seeing with his not opening his eyes; and also the like connection between such a man's attempting to open his eyes, and his actually doing it: the supposed established connection between these antecedents and consequents, let the connection be never so sure and necessary, certainly don't prove that it is in vain, for a man in such circumstances to attempt to open his eyes, in order to seeing: his aiming at that event, and the use of the means, being the effect of his will, don't break the connection, or hinder the success.

So that the objection we are upon, don't lie against the doctrine of the necessity of events by a certainty of connection and consequence: on the contrary, it is truly forcible against the Arminian doctrine of contingence and self-determination; which is inconsistent with such a connection. If there be no connection between those events wherein virtue and vice consist, and anything antecedent; then there is no connection between these events and any means or endeavors used in order to them: and if so, then those means must be in vain. The less there is of connection between foregoing things and following ones, so much the less there is between means and end, endeavors and success; and in the same proportion are means and endeavors ineffectual and in vain.

It will follow from Arminian principles, that there is no degree of connection between virtue or vice, and any foregoing event or thing: or in other words, that the determination of the existence of virtue or vice don't in the least depend on the influence of anything that comes to pass antecedently, from which the determination of its existence is, as its cause, means, or ground; because, so far as it is so, it is not from self-determination: and therefore, so far there is nothing of the nature of virtue or vice. And so it follows, that virtue and vice are not at all, in any degree, dependent upon, or connected with any foregoing event or existence, as its cause, ground, or means. And if so, then all foregoing means must be totally in vain.

Hence it follows, that there cannot, in any consistence with the Arminian scheme, be any reasonable ground of so much as a conjecture concerning the consequence of any means and endeavors, in order to escaping vice or obtaining virtue, or any choice or preference of means, as having a greater probability of success by some than others; either from any natural connection or dependence of the end on the means, or through any divine constitution, or revealed way of God's bestowing or bringing to pass these things, in consequence of any means, endeavors, prayers or deeds. Conjecture in this latter case depends on a supposition that God himself is the giver, or determining cause of the events sought: but if they depend on self-determination, then God is not the determining or disposing author of them: and if these things are not of his disposal, then no conjecture can be made from any revelation he has given concerning any way or method of his disposal of them.

Yea, on these principles, it will not only follow that men can't have any reasonable ground of judgment or conjecture, that their means and endeavors to obtain virtue or avoid vice, will be successful, but they may be sure they will not; they may be certain, that they will be in vain; and that if ever the thing which they seek comes to pass, it will not be at all owing to the means they use. For means and endeavors can have no effect at all, in order to obtain the end, but in one of these two ways; either (1) through a natural tendency and influence, to prepare and dispose the mind more to virtuous acts, either by causing the disposition of the heart to be more in favor of such acts, or by bringing the mind more into the view of powerful motives and inducements: or (2) by putting persons more in the way of God's bestowment of the benefit. But neither of these can be the case. Not the latter; for as has been just now observed, it don't consist with the Arminian notion of self-determination, which they suppose essential to virtue, that God should be the bestower, or (which

is the same thing) the determining, disposing author of virtue. Not
the former; for natural influence and tendency supposes causality
and connection; and that supposes necessity of event, which is inconsistent with Arminian liberty. A tendency of means, by biasing the
heart in favor of virtue, or by bringing the will under the influence
and power of motives in its determinations, are both inconsistent
with Arminian liberty of will, consisting in indifference, and sovereign self-determination, as has been largely demonstrated.

But for the more full removal of this prejudice against that doctrine of necessity which has been maintained, as though it tended to
encourage a total neglect of all endeavors as vain; the following things
may be considered.

The question is not, whether men may not thus improve this doctrine: we know that many true and wholesome doctrines are abused:
but, whether the doctrine gives any just occasion for such an improvement; or whether, on the supposition of the truth of the doctrine,
such a use of it would not be unreasonable? If any shall affirm, that
it would not, but that the very nature of the doctrine is such as gives
just occasion for it, it must be on this supposition; namely, that such
an invariable necessity of all things already settled, must render the
interposition of all means, endeavors, conclusions or actions of ours,
in order to the obtaining any future end whatsoever, perfectly insignificant; because they can't in the least alter or vary the course and
series of things, in any event or circumstance; all being already fixed
unalterably by necessity: and that therefore 'tis folly, for men to use
any means for *any* end; but their wisdom, to save themselves the
trouble of endeavors, and take their ease. No person can draw such
an inference from this doctrine, and come to such a conclusion, without contradicting himself, and going counter to the very principles he
pretends to act upon: for he comes to a conclusion, and takes a course,
in order to an end, even *his ease,* or the saving himself from trouble;
he seeks something future, and uses means in order to a future thing,
even in his drawing up that conclusion, that he will seek nothing, and
use no means in order to anything future; he seeks his future ease,
and the benefit and comfort of indolence. If prior necessity that determines all things, makes vain all actions or conclusions of ours, in
order to anything future; then it makes vain all conclusions and
conduct of ours, in order to our future ease. The measure of our
ease, with the time, manner and every circumstance of it, is already
fixed, by all-determining necessity, as much as anything else. If he

says within himself, "What future happiness or misery I shall have, is already in effect determined by the necessary course and connection of things; therefore I will save myself the trouble of labor and diligence, which can't add to my determined degree of happiness, or diminish my misery; but will take my ease, and will enjoy the comfort of sloth and negligence." Such a man contradicts himself: he says, the measure of his future happiness and misery is already fixed, and he won't try to diminish the one, nor add to the other: but yet in his very conclusion, he contradicts this; for he takes up this conclusion, *to add to his future happiness,* by the ease and comfort of his negligence; and to diminish his future trouble and misery, by saving himself the trouble of using means and taking pains.

Therefore persons can't reasonably make this improvement of the doctrine of necessity, that they will go into a voluntary negligence of means for their own happiness. For the principles they must go upon, in order to this, are inconsistent with their making any improvement at all of the doctrine: for to make some improvement of it, is to be influenced by it, to come to some voluntary conclusion, in regard to their own conduct, with some view or aim: but this, as has been shown, is inconsistent with the principles they pretend to act upon. In short, the principles are such as cannot be acted upon at all, or in any respect, consistently. And therefore in every pretence of acting upon them, or making any improvement at all of them, there is a self-contradiction.

As to that objection against the doctrine which I have endeavored to prove, that it makes men no more than mere machines; I would say, that notwithstanding this doctrine, man is entirely, perfectly and unspeakably different from a mere machine, in that he has reason and understanding, and has a faculty of will, and so is capable of volition and choice; and in that, his will is guided by the dictates or views of his understanding; and in that his external actions and behavior, and in many respect also his thoughts, and the exercises of his mind, are subject to his will; so that he has liberty to act according to his choice, and do what he pleases; and by means of these things, is capable of moral habits and moral acts, such inclinations and actions as according to the common sense of mankind, are worthy of praise, esteem, love and reward; or on the contrary, of disesteem, detestation, indignation and punishment.

In these things is all the difference from mere machines, as to liberty and agency, that would be any perfection, dignity or privilege, in any respect: all the difference that can be desired, and all that can be conceived of; and indeed all that the pretensions of the Arminians themselves come to, as they are forced often to explain themselves (though their explications overthrow and abolish the things asserted, and pretended to be explained). For they are forced to explain a self-determining power of will, by a power in the soul, to determine as it chooses or wills; which comes to no more than this, that a man has a power of choosing, and in many instances, can do as he chooses. Which is quite a different thing from that contradiction, his having power of choosing his first act of choice in the case.

Or if their scheme makes any other difference than this, between men and machines, it is for the worse: it is so far from supposing men to have a dignity and privilege above machines, that it makes the manner of their being determined still more unhappy. Whereas machines are guided by an understanding cause, by the skillful hand of the workman or owner; the will of man is left to the guidance of nothing, but absolute blind contingence.

SECTION 6. CONCERNING THAT OBJECTION AGAINST THE DOCTRINE WHICH HAS BEEN MAINTAINED, THAT IT AGREES WITH THE STOICAL DOCTRINE OF FATE, AND THE OPINIONS OF MR. HOBBES

WHEN Calvinists oppose the Arminian notion of the freedom of will, and contingence of volition, and insist that there are no acts of the will, nor any other events whatsoever, but what are attended with some kind of necessity; their opposers cry out of them, as agreeing with the ancient Stoics in their doctrine of fate, and with Mr. Hobbes in his opinion of necessity.

It would not be worth while, to take notice of so impertinent an objection, had it not been urged by some of the chief Arminian writers. There were many important truths maintained by the ancient Greek and Roman philosophers, and especially the Stoics, that are never the worse for being held by them. The Stoic philosophers, by the general agreement of Christian divines, and even Arminian divines, were the greatest, wisest and most virtuous of all the heathen philosophers; and in their doctrine and practice came the nearest to Christianity of any of their sects. How frequently are the sayings of these philosophers, in many of the writings and sermons, even of Arminian divines, produced, not as arguments of the falseness of the doctrines which they delivered, but as a confirmation of some of the greatest truths of the Christian religion, relating to the unity and perfections of the Godhead, a future state, the duty and happiness of mankind, etc. as observing how the light of nature and reason in the wisest and best of the heathen, harmonized with, and confirms the gospel of Jesus Christ.

And it is very remarkable concerning Dr. Whitby, that although he alleges the agreement of the Stoics with us, wherein he supposes they maintained the like doctrine with us, as an argument against the truth of our doctrine; yet this very Dr. Whitby alleges the agreement of the Stoics with the Arminians, wherein he supposes they taught the same doctrine with them, as an argument for the truth of their doctrine.[1] So that when the Stoics agree with *them,* this (it seems) is a confirmation of their doctrine, and a confutation of ours, as shewing that our opinions are contrary to the natural sense and common reason of mankind: nevertheless, when the Stoics agree with *us,* it argues no such thing in our favor; but on the contrary, is a great argument against us, and shews our doctrine to be heathenish.

It is observed by some Calvinistic writers, that the Arminians symbolize with the Stoics, in some of those doctrines wherein they are opposed by the Calvinists; particularly in their denying an original, innate, total corruption and depravity of heart; and in what they held of man's ability to make himself truly virtuous and conformed to God; and in some other doctrines.

It may be further observed, 'tis certainly no better objection against our doctrine, that it agrees in some respects with the doctrine of the ancient Stoic philosophers, than it is against theirs, wherein they differ from us, that it agrees in some respects with the opinion of the very worst of the heathen philosophers, the followers of Epicurus, that father of atheism and licentiousness, and with the doctrine of the Sadducees and Jesuits.

I am not much concerned to know precisely what the ancient Stoic philosophers held concerning fate, in order to determine what is truth; as though it were a sure way to be in the right, to take good heed to differ from them. It seems that they differed among themselves; and probably the doctrine of fate, as maintained by most of 'em, was in some respects erroneous. But whatever their doctrine was, if any of 'em held such a fate, as is repugnant to any liberty consisting in our doing as we please, I utterly deny such a fate. If they held any such fate, as is not consistent with the common and universal notions that mankind have of liberty, activity, moral agency, virtue and vice; I disclaim any such thing, and think I have demonstrated that the scheme I maintain is no such scheme. If the Stoics by fate meant anything of such a nature, as can be supposed to stand in the way of the advantage and benefit of the use of means and endeavors, or makes it less worth the while for men to desire, and seek after anything wherein their virtue and happiness consists; I hold no doctrine that is clogged with any such inconvenience, any more than any other scheme whatsoever; and by no means so much as the Arminian

1. *Discourse on the Five Points,* Dis. IV, ch. 1, no. 8; pp. 325, 326, 327. [See above, Intro., Pt. 5, no. 12.]

scheme of contingence; as has been shewn. If they held any such doctrine of universal fatality, as is inconsistent with any kind of liberty, that is or can be any perfection, dignity, privilege or benefit, or anything desirable, in any respect, for any intelligent creature, or indeed with any liberty that is possible or conceivable; I embrace no such doctrine. If they held any such doctrine of fate as is inconsistent with the world's being in all things subject to the disposal of an intelligent wise agent, that presides, not as the soul of the world, but as the sovereign Lord of the universe, governing all things by proper will, choice and design, in the exercise of the most perfect liberty conceivable, without subjection to any constraint, or being properly under the power or influence of anything before, above or without himself; I wholly renounce any such doctrine.

As to Mr. Hobbes' maintaining the same doctrine concerning necessity; I confess, it happens I never read Mr. Hobbes. Let his opinion be what it will, we need not reject all truth which is demonstrated by clear evidence, merely because it was once held by some bad man. This great truth, that Jesus is the Son of God, was not spoiled because it was once and again proclaimed with a loud voice by the devil. If truth is so defiled because it is spoken by the mouth, or written by the pen of some ill-minded mischievous man, that it must never be received, we shall never know when we hold any of the most precious and evident truths by a sure tenure. And if Mr. Hobbes has made a bad use of this truth, that is to be lamented: but the truth is not to be thought worthy of rejection on that account. 'Tis common for the corruptions of the hearts of evil men, to abuse the best things to vile purposes.

I might also take notice of its having been observed, that the Arminians agree with Mr. Hobbes [2] in many more things than the Calvinists. As, in what he is said to hold concerning original sin, in denying the necessity of supernatural illumination, in denying infused grace, in denying the doctrine of justification by faith alone; and other things.

2. Dr. Gill, in his answer to Dr. Whitby [John Gill, *The Cause of God and Truth, Being a Confutation of the Arguments from Reason Used by the Arminians; and Particularly by Dr. Whitby, in His Discourse on the Five Points,* ch. 5, sec. 11, nos. 6 f. (London, 1737), Pt. III, pp. 183 ff.].

SECTION 7. CONCERNING THE NECESSITY OF THE DIVINE WILL

SOME may possibly object against what has been supposed of the absurdity and inconsistence of a self-determining power in the will, and the impossibility of its being otherwise, than that the will should be determined in every case by some motive, and by a motive which (as it stands in the view of the understanding) is of superior strength to any appearing on the other side; that if these things are true, it will follow, that not only the will of created minds, but the will of *God himself* is necessary in all its determinations. Concerning which says the author of the *Essay on the Freedom of Will in God and in the Creature* (p. 85, 86),[1]

> What strange doctrine is this, contrary to all our ideas of the dominion of God? Does it not destroy the glory of his liberty of choice, and take away from the creator and governor and bene-factor of the world, that most free and sovereign agent, all the glory of this sort of freedom? Does it not seem to make him a kind of mechanical medium of fate, and introduce Mr. Hobbes's doctrine of fatality and necessity, into all things that God hath to do with? Does it not seem to represent the blessed God, as a being of vast understanding, as well as power and efficiency, but still to leave him without a will to choose among all the objects within his view? In short, it seems to make the blessed God a sort of almighty minister of fate, under its universal and supreme influence; as it was the professed sentiment of some of the an-cients, that fate was above the gods.

This is declaiming, rather than arguing; and an application to men's imaginations and prejudices, rather than to mere reason. But I would calmly endeavor to consider whether there be any reason in this frightful representation. But before I enter upon a particular

1. [Watts, *Essay*, Sec. 7, *dif.* 1; in *Works, 6, 272.*]

consideration of the matter, I would observe this: that 'tis reasonable to suppose, it should be much more difficult to express or conceive things according to exact metaphysical truth, relating to the nature and manner of the existence of things in the divine understanding and will, and the operation of these faculties (if I may so call them) of the divine mind, than in the human mind; which is infinitely more within our view, and nearer to a proportion to the measure of our comprehension, and more commensurate to the use and import of human speech. Language is indeed very deficient, in regard of terms to express precise truth concerning our own minds, and their faculties and operations. Words were first formed to express external things; and those that are applied to express things internal and spiritual, are almost all borrowed, and used in a sort of figurative sense. Whence they are most of 'em attended with a great deal of ambiguity and unfixedness in their signification, occasioning innumerable doubts, difficulties and confusions in inquiries and controversies about things of this nature. But language is much less adapted to express things in the mind of the incomprehensible Deity, precisely as they are.

We find a great deal of difficulty in conceiving exactly of the nature of our own souls. And notwithstanding all the progress which has been made in past and present ages, in this kind of knowledge, whereby our metaphysics, as it relates to these things, is brought to greater perfection than once it was; yet here is still work enough left for future inquiries and researches, and room for progress still to be made, for many ages and generations. But we had need to be infinitely able metaphysicians, to conceive with clearness, according to strict, proper and perfect truth, concerning the nature of the divine essence, and the modes of the action and operation of the powers of the divine mind.

And it may be noted particularly, that though we are obliged to conceive of some things in God as consequent and dependent on others, and of some things pertaining to the divine nature and will as the foundation of others, and so before others in the order of nature: as, we must conceive of the knowledge and holiness of God as prior in the order of nature to his happiness; the perfection of his understanding, as the foundation of his wise purposes and decrees; the holiness of his nature, as the cause and reason of his holy determinations. And yet when we speak of cause and effect, antecedent and consequent, fundamental and dependent, determining and de-

termined, in the first Being, who is self-existent, independent, of perfect and absolute simplicity and immutability, and the first cause of
all things; doubtless there must be less propriety in such representations, than when we speak of derived dependent beings, who are
compounded, and liable to perpetual mutation and succession.

Having premised this, I proceed to observe concerning the forementioned author's exclamation, about the *necessary* determination
of God's will, in all things, by what he sees to be *fittest* and *best*.

That all the seeming force of such objections and exclamations
must arise from an imagination, that there is some sort of privilege
or dignity in being without such a moral necessity, as will make it
impossible to do any other, than always choose what is wisest and
best; as though there were some disadvantage, meanness and subjection, in such a necessity; a thing by which the will was confined, kept
under, and held in servitude by something, which, as it were, maintained a strong and invincible power and dominion over it, by bonds
that held him fast, and that he could by no means deliver himself
from. Whereas, this must be all mere imagination and delusion. 'Tis
no disadvantage or dishonor to a being, necessarily to act in the most
excellent and happy manner, from the necessary perfection of his
own nature. This argues no imperfection, inferiority or dependence,
nor any want of dignity, privilege or ascendancy.[2] 'Tis not incon-

2. "It might have been objected with much more plausibleness, that the supreme cause cannot be free, because he must needs do always what is best in the
whole. But this would not at all serve Spinoza's purpose: for this is a necessity,
not of nature and fate, but of fitness and wisdom; a necessity consistent with the
greatest freedom, and most perfect choice. For the only foundation of this necessity is such an unalterable rectitude of will, and perfection of wisdom, as makes
it impossible for a wise being to act foolishly." Samuel Clarke, *Demonstration of
the Being and Attributes of God* (6th ed. London, 1725), p. 64.

"Though God is a most perfectly free agent, yet he cannot but do always what
is best and wisest in the whole. The reason is evident; because perfect wisdom and
goodness are as steady and certain principles of action, as necessity itself; and an
infinitely wise and good being, indued with the most perfect liberty, can no more
choose to act in contradiction to wisdom and goodness, than a necessary agent
can act contrary to the necessity by which it is acted; it being as great an absurdity
and impossibility in choice, for infinite wisdom to choose to act unwisely, or
infinite goodness to choose what is not good, as it would be in nature, for absolute necessity to fail of producing its necessary effect. There was indeed no necessity in nature, that God should at first create such beings as he has created, or
indeed any being at all; because he is in himself infinitely happy and all-sufficient.
There was also no necessity in nature, that he should preserve and continue things
in being, after they were created; because he would be self-sufficient without their

sistent with the absolute, and most perfect sovereignty of God. The sovereignty of God is his ability and authority to do whatever pleases him; whereby "he doth according to his will in the armies of heaven, and amongst the inhabitants of the earth, and none can stay his hand, or say unto him, what dost thou?" [Dan. 4:35]. The following things belong to the *sovereignty* of God; viz. (1) supreme, universal, and

---

continuance, as he was before their creation. But it was fit and wise and good, that infinite wisdom should manifest, and infinite goodness communicate itself; and therefore it was necessary, in the sense of necessity I am now speaking of, that things should be made *at such a time,* and continued *so long,* and indeed with various perfections in such degrees, as infinite wisdom and goodness saw it wisest and best that they should." Ibid., pp. 112 f.

" 'Tis not a fault, but a perfection of our nature, to desire, will and act, according to the last result of a fair examination" [See above, Intro., Pt. 4, no. 5].

"This is so far from being a restraint or diminution of freedom, that it is the very improvement and benefit of it: 'tis not an abridgment, 'tis the end and use of our liberty; and the further we are removed from such a determination, the nearer we are to misery and slavery. A perfect indifference in the mind, not determinable by its last judgment of the good or evil that is thought to attend its choice, would be so far from being an advantage and excellency of any intellectual nature, that it would be as great an imperfection as the want of indifference to act, or not to act, till determined by the will, would be an imperfection on the other side. . . . 'Tis as much a perfection, that desire or the power of preferring should be determined by good, as that the power of acting should be determined by the will: and the certainer such determination is, the greater the perfection. Nay, were we determined by anything but the last result of our own minds, judging of the good or evil of any action, we were not free. The very end of our freedom being, that we might attain the good we choose; and therefore every man is brought under a necessity by his constitution, as an intelligent being, to be determined in willing by his own thought and judgment, what is best for him to do; also he would be under the determination of some other than himself, which is want of liberty. And to deny that a man's will, in every determination, follows his own judgment, is to say, that a man wills and acts for an end that he would not have, at the same time that he wills and acts for it. For if he prefers it in his present thoughts, before any other, 'tis plain he then thinks better of it, and would have it before any other; unless he can have, and not have it; will, and not will it, at the same time; a contradiction too manifest to be admitted.

"If we look upon those superior beings above us, who enjoy perfect happiness, we shall have reason to judge, that they are more steadily determined in their choice of good than we; and yet we have no reason to think they are less happy, or less free, than we are. And if it were fit for such poor finite creatures as we are, to pronounce what infinite wisdom and goodness could do, I think we might say, that God himself cannot choose what is not good. *The freedom of the Almighty hinders not his being determined by what is best.*

infinite *power;* whereby he is able to do what he pleases, without control, without any confinement of that power, without any subjection in the least measure to any other power; and so without any hindrance or restraint, that it should be either impossible, or at all difficult, for him to accomplish his will; and without any dependence of his power on any other power, from whence it should be derived, or which it should stand in any need of: so far from this, that all other

---

"But to give a right view of this mistaken part of liberty, let me ask, would anyone be a changeling, because he is less determined by wise determinations [Locke has "considerations"], than a wise man? Is it worth the name of freedom, to be at liberty to play the fool, and draw shame and misery upon a man's self? If to break loose from the conduct of reason, and to want that restraint of examination and judgment, that keeps us from doing or choosing the worse, be liberty, true liberty, mad men and fools are the only free men. Yet I think nobody would choose to be mad, for the sake of such liberty, but he that is mad already." Locke, *Essay,* Bk. II, ch. 21, nos. 48–51; *1,* 345–7.

"This Being having all things always necessarily in view, must always, and eternally will, according to his infinite comprehension of things; that is, must will all things that are wisest and best to be done. There is no getting free of this consequence. If it can will at all, it must will this way. To be capable of knowing, and not capable of willing, is not to be understood. And to be capable of willing otherwise than what is wisest and best, contradicts that knowledge which is infinite. Infinite knowledge must direct the will without error. *Here then is the origin of moral necessity; and that is really, of freedom.* . . . Perhaps it may be said, when the divine will is determined, from the consideration of the eternal aptitudes of things, it is as necessarily determined, as if it were physically impelled, if that were possible. But it is unskillfulness, to suppose this an objection. The great principle is once established, vis. that the divine will is determined by the eternal reason and aptitudes of things [By this Baxter means, determined by "the intuition of the eternal relations of its own ideas, which are the archetypes of things"], instead of being physically impelled; and after that, the more strong and necessary this determination is, the more perfect the Deity must be allowed to be: it is this that makes him an amiable and adorable being, whose will and power are constantly, immutably determined, by the consideration of what is wisest and best; instead of a surd being, with power, but without discerning and reason. *It is the beauty of this necessity, that it is strong as fate itself, with all the advantage of reason and goodness.* . . . It is strange, to see men contend, that the Deity is not free, because he is necessarily rational, immutably good and wise; when a man is allowed still the perfecter being, the more fixedly and constantly his will is determined by reason and truth." Andrew Baxter, *An Enquiry into the Nature of the Human Soul, Wherein the Immateriality of the Soul is Evinced from the Principles of Reason and Philosophy,* 3d ed., *2,* 403 f. [The passage is from a long concluding footnote, which I have checked in the one-volume 1st ed. (London, 1730?), p. 372–3, and in the 2d ed. (London, 1737), *2,* 431–3].

power is derived from him, and is absolutely dependent on him. (2) That he has supreme *authority;* absolute and most perfect right to do what he wills, without subjection to any superior authority, or any derivation of authority from any other, or limitation by any distinct independent authority, either superior, equal, or inferior; he being the head of all dominion, and fountain of all authority; and also without restraint by any obligation, implying either subjection, derivation, or dependence, or proper limitation. (3) That his *will* is supreme, underived, and independent on anything without himself; being in everything determined by his own counsel, having no other rule but his own wisdom; his will not being subject to, or restrained by the will of any other, and others' wills being perfectly subject to his. (4) That his *wisdom,* which determines his will, is supreme, perfect, underived, self-sufficient, and independent; so that it may be said as in Is. 40:14, "With whom took he counsel? And who instructed him and taught him in the path of judgment, and taught him knowledge, and showed him the way of understanding?" —There is no other divine sovereignty but this: and this is properly *absolute sovereignty:* no other is desirable; nor would any other be honorable, or happy: and indeed there is no other conceivable or possible. 'Tis the glory and greatness of the divine sovereignty, that God's will is determined by his own infinite all-sufficient wisdom in everything; and in nothing at all is either directed by any inferior wisdom, or by no wisdom; whereby it would become senseless arbitrariness, determining and acting without reason, design or end.

If God's will is steadily and surely determined in everything by *supreme* wisdom, then it is in everything necessarily determined to that which is *most* wise. And certainly it would be a disadvantage and indignity, to be otherwise. For if the divine will was not necessarily determined to that which in every case is wisest and best, it must be subject to some degree of undesigning contingence; and so in the same degree liable to evil. To suppose the divine will liable to be carried hither and thither at random, by the uncertain wind of blind contingence, which is guided by no wisdom, no motive, no intelligent dictate whatsoever (if any such thing were possible), would certainly argue a great degree of imperfection and meanness, infinitely unworthy of the deity. If it be a disadvantage, for the divine will to be attended with this moral necessity, then the more free from it, and the more left at random, the greater dignity and advantage. And consequently to be perfectly free from the direction of understanding, and universally and entirely left to senseless unmeaning contingence, to act absolutely at random, would be the supreme glory.

It no more argues any dependence of God's will, that his supremely wise volition is necessary, than it argues a dependence of his being, that his existence is necessary. If it be something too low, for the supreme Being to have his will determined by moral necessity, so as necessarily, in every case, to will in the highest degree holily and happily; then why is it not also something too low, for him to have his existence, and the infinite perfection of his nature, and his infinite happiness determined by necessity? It is no more to God's dishonor, to be necessarily wise, than to be necessarily holy. And if neither of them be to his dishonor, then it is not to his dishonor necessarily to act holily and wisely. And if it be not dishonorable, to be necessarily holy and wise, in the highest possible degree, no more is it mean or dishonorable, necessarily to act holily and wisely in the highest possible degree; or (which is the same thing) to do that, in every case, which above all other things is wisest and best.

The reason why it is not dishonorable, to be necessarily *most* holy, is, because holiness in itself is an excellent and honorable thing. For the same reason, it is no dishonor to be necessarily *most* wise, and in every case to act most wisely, or do the thing which is the wisest of all; for wisdom is also in itself excellent and honorable.

The forementioned author of the *Essay on the Freedom of Will*, etc., as has been observed, represents that doctrine of the divine will's being in everything necessarily determined by superior fitness, as making the blessed God a kind of almighty minister and mechanical medium of fate: and he insists (pp. 93, 94),[3] that this moral necessity and impossibility is in effect the same thing with physical and natural necessity and impossibility: and in pp. 54, 55 [4] he says,

> The scheme which determines the will always and certainly by the understanding, and the understanding by the appearance of things, seems to take away the true nature of vice and virtue. For the sublimest of virtues, and the vilest of vices, seem rather to be matters of fate and necessity, flowing naturally and necessarily from the existence, the circumstances, and present situation of persons and things: for this existence and situation necessarily

3. [Watts, *Essay*, Sec. 7, *dif.* 3; in *Works, 6,* 275.]
4. [Ibid., Sec. 5, *adv.* 4; in *Works, 6,* 260. See above, Intro., Pt. 5, no. 18.]

makes such an appearance to the mind; from this appearance flows a necessary perception and judgment, concerning these things; this judgment necessarily determines the will: and thus by this chain of necessary causes, virtue and vice would lose their nature, and become natural ideas, and necessary things, instead of moral and free actions.

And yet this same author allows (pp. 30, 31),[5] that a perfectly wise being will constantly and certainly choose what is most fit; and says (pp. 102, 103),[6] "I grant, and always have granted, that wheresoever there is such an antecedent superior fitness of things, God acts according to it, so as never to contradict it; and particularly, in all his judicial proceedings, as a governor, and distributer of rewards and punishments." Yea, he says expressly (p. 42),[7] "That it is not possible for God to act otherwise, than according to this fitness and goodness in things."

So that according to this author, putting these several passages of his *Essay* together, there is *no virtue, nor anything of a moral nature,* in the most sublime and glorious acts and exercises of God's holiness, justice, and faithfulness; and he never does anything which is in itself supremely worthy, and above all other things fit and excellent, but only as a kind of mechanical medium of fate; and in what he does as the judge, and *moral governor* of the world, he exercises no moral excellency; exercising no freedom in these things, because he acts by moral necessity, which is in effect the same with physical or natural necessity; and therefore he only acts by an Hobbistical fatality; as "a being indeed of vast understanding, as well as power and efficiency (as he said before) but without a will to choose, being a kind of almighty minister of fate, acting under its supreme influence." For he allows, that in all these things God's will is determined constantly and certainly by a superior fitness, and that it is not possible for him to act otherwise. And if these things are so, what glory or praise belongs to God for doing holily and justly, or taking the most fit, holy, wise and excellent course, in any one instance? Whereas, according to the Scriptures, and also the common sense of mankind, it don't in the least derogate from the honor of any being, that through the moral perfection of his nature, he necessarily acts with supreme

5. [Ibid., Sec. 3, *prop.* 4; in *Works, 6,* 251.]
6. [Ibid., Sec. 7, *dif.* 6; in *Works, 6,* 278.]
7. [Ibid., Sec. 4, *prop.* 11; in *Works, 6,* 255.]

wisdom and holiness: but on the contrary, his praise is the greater: herein consists the height of his glory.[8]

The same author (p. 56) [9] supposes, that herein appears the excellent "character of a wise and good man, that though he can choose contrary to the fitness of things, yet he does not; but suffers himself to be directed by fitness"; and that in this conduct "he imitates the blessed God." And yet he supposes 'tis contrariwise with the blessed God; not that he suffers himself to be directed by fitness, when he can choose contrary to the fitness of things, but that "he cannot choose contrary to the fitness of things"; as he says (p. 42), "That it is not possible for God to act otherwise, than according to this fitness, where there is any fitness or goodness in things": yea, he supposes (p. 31) [1] that if a man "were perfectly wise and good, he could not do otherwise than be constantly and certainly determined by the fitness of things."

One thing more I would observe, before I conclude this section; and that is, that if it derogates nothing from the glory of God, to be necessarily determined by superior fitness in some things, then neither does it to be thus determined in all things; from anything in the nature of such necessity, as at all detracting from God's freedom, independence, absolute supremacy, or any dignity or glory of his nature, state, or manner of acting; or as implying any infirmity, restraint, or subjection. And if the thing be such as well consists with God's glory, and has nothing tending at all to detract from it; then we need not be afraid of ascribing it to God in too many things, lest thereby we should detract from God's glory too much.

8. [See above, Intro., Pt. 5, no. 16.]
9. [*Essay*, Sec. 5, *adv.* 5; in *Works, 6,* 260.]
1. [Ibid., Sec. 3, *prop.* 4; in *Works, 6,* 251.]

SECTION 8. SOME FURTHER OBJECTIONS AGAINST THE MORAL NECESSITY OF GOD'S VOLITIONS CONSIDERED

THE AUTHOR last cited, as has been observed, owns that God, being perfectly wise, will constantly and certainly choose what appears most fit, where there is a superior fitness and goodness in things; and that it is not possible for him to do otherwise. So that it is in effect confessed, that in those things where there is any real preferableness, 'tis no dishonor, nothing in any respect unworthy of God, for him to act from necessity; notwithstanding all that can be objected from the agreement of such a necessity, with the fate of the Stoics, and the necessity maintained by Mr. Hobbes. From which it will follow, that if it were so, that in all the different things, among which God chooses, there were evermore a superior fitness or preferableness on one side, then it would be no dishonor, or anything, in any respect, unworthy, or unbecoming of God, for his will to be necessarily determined in everything. And if this be allowed, it is a giving up entirely the argument, from the unsuitableness of such a necessity to the liberty, supremacy, independence and glory of the divine Being; and a resting the whole weight of the affair on the decision of another point wholly diverse; viz. *whether it be so indeed,* that in all the various possible things which are in God's view, and may be considered as capable objects of his choice, there is not evermore a preferableness in one thing above another. This is denied by this author; who supposes, that in many instances, between two or more possible things, which come within the view of the divine mind, there is a perfect indifference and equality as to fitness, or tendency to attain any good end which God can have in view, or to answer any of his designs. Now therefore I would consider whether this be evident.

The arguments brought to prove this, are of two kinds. (1) It is urged, that in many instances we must suppose there is absolutely no difference between various possible objects of choice, which God has in view: and (2) that the difference between many things is so in-considerable, or of such a nature, that it would be unreasonable to suppose it to be of any consequence; or to suppose that any of God's wise designs would not be answered in one way as well as the other.

Therefore,

I. The first thing to be considered is, whether there are any in-stances wherein there is a perfect likeness, and absolutely no differ-ence, between different objects of choice, that are proposed to the divine understanding?

And here in the first place, it may be worthy to be considered, whether the contradiction there is in the *terms* of the question pro-posed, don't give reason to suspect that there is an inconsistence in the *thing* supposed. 'Tis inquired, whether *different* objects of choice mayn't be absolutely *without difference?* If they are absolutely *with-out difference,* then how are they *different* objects of choice? If there be absolutely *no difference* in any respect, then there is *no variety* or *distinction:* for distinction is only by some difference. And if there be no *variety* among proposed *objects* of choice, then there is no opportunity for *variety of choice,* or difference of determination. For that determination of a thing which is not different in any respect, is not a different determination, but the same. That this is no quibble, may appear more fully anon.

The arguments, to prove that the most High, in some instances, chooses to do one thing rather than another, where the things them-selves are perfectly without difference, are two.

1. That the various parts of infinite time and space, absolutely considered, are perfectly alike, and don't differ at all one from an-other: and that therefore, when God determined to create the world in such a part of infinite duration and space, rather than others, he determined and preferred among various objects, between which there was no preferableness, and absolutely no difference.

Answer. This objection supposes an infinite length of time before the world was created, distinguished by successive parts, properly and truly so; or a succession of limited and measurable [1] periods of time, following one another, in an infinitely long series: which must needs be a groundless imagination. The eternal duration which was before the world, being only the eternity of God's existence; which is noth-ing else but his immediate, perfect and invariable possession of the whole of his unlimited life, together and at once; *vitæ interminabilis,*

1. [The 1754 ed. reads "*un*measurable."]

tota, simul et perfecta possessio. Which is so generally allowed, that I need not stand to demonstrate it.[2]

So this objection supposes an extent of space beyond the limits of the creation, of an infinite length, breadth and depth, truly and properly distinguished into different measurable parts, limited at certain stages, one beyond another, in an infinite series. Which notion of absolute and infinite space is doubtless as unreasonable, as that now mentioned, of absolute and infinite duration. 'Tis as improper, to imagine that the immensity and omnipresence of God is distinguished by a series of miles and leagues, one beyond another; as that the infinite duration of God is distinguished by months and years, one after another. A diversity and order of distinct parts, limited by certain periods, is as conceivable, and does as naturally obtrude itself on our imagination, in one case as the other; and there is equal reason in each case, to suppose that our imagination deceives us. 'Tis equally improper, to talk of months and years of the divine existence,

2. "If all created beings were taken away, all possibility of any mutation or succession of one thing to another would appear to be also removed. Abstract succession in eternity is scarce to be understood. What is it that succeeds? One minute to another perhaps, *velut unda supervenit undam.* But when we imagine this, we fancy that the minutes are things separately existing. This is the common notion; and yet it is a manifest prejudice. Time is nothing but the existence of created successive beings, and eternity the necessary existence of the Deity. Therefore, if this necessary Being hath no change or succession in his nature, his existence must of course be unsuccessive. We seem to commit a double oversight in this case; *first,* we find succession in the necessary nature and existence of the Deity himself: which is wrong, if the reasoning above be conclusive. And *then* we ascribe this succession to eternity, considered abstractedly from the eternal Being; and suppose it, one knows not what, a thing subsisting by itself, and flowing, one minute after another. This is the work of pure imagination, and contrary to the reality of things. Hence the common metaphorical expressions: 'time runs apace,' 'let us lay hold on the present minute,' and the like. The philosophers themselves mislead us by their illustrations; they compare eternity to the motion of a point running on forever, and making a traceless infinite line. Here the point is supposed a thing actually subsisting, representing the present minute; and then they ascribe motion or succession to it: that is, they ascribe motion to a mere non-entity, to illustrate to us a successive eternity made up of finite successive parts. . . . If once we allow an all-perfect Mind, which hath an eternal immutable and infinite comprehension of all things, always (and allow it we must) the distinction of past and future vanishes with respect to such a mind. . . . In a word, if we proceed step by step, as above, the eternity or existence of the Deity will appear to be *vitæ interminabilis, tota, simul et perfecta possessio;* how much soever this may have been a paradox hitherto." Baxter, 3d ed. 2, 409 ff. [1st ed., pp. 375–6; 2d ed. 2, 438–9].

and mile-squares of deity: and we equally deceive ourselves, when we talk of the world's being differently fixed with respect to either of these sorts of measures. I think, we know not what we mean, if we say, the world might have been differently placed from what it is, in the broad expanse of infinity; or, that it might have been differently fixed in the long line of eternity: and all arguments and objections which are built on the imaginations we are apt to have of infinite extension or duration, are buildings founded on shadows, or castles in the air.

2. The second argument, to prove that the most High wills one thing rather than another, without any superior fitness or preferableness in the thing preferred, is God's actually placing in different parts of the world, particles or atoms of matter that are perfectly equal and alike. The forementioned author says (p. 78,[3] etc.), "If one would descend to the minute specific particles, of which different bodies are composed, we should see abundant reason to believe that there are thousands of such little particles or atoms of matter, which are perfectly equal and alike, and could give no distinct determination to the will of God, where to place them." He there instances in particles of water, of which there are such immense numbers, which compose the rivers and oceans of this world; and the infinite myriads of the luminous and fiery particles, which compose the body of the sun; so many, that it would be very unreasonable to suppose no two of them should be exactly equal and alike.

Answer (1). To this I answer: that as we must suppose matter to be infinitely divisible, 'tis very unlikely that any two of all these particles are exactly equal and alike; so unlikely, that it is a thousand to one, yea, an infinite number to one, but it is otherwise: and that although we should allow a great similarity between the different particles of water and fire, as to their general nature and figure; and however small we suppose those particles to be, 'tis infinitely unlikely, that any two of them should be exactly equal in dimensions and quantity of matter. If we should suppose a great many globes of the same nature with the globe of the earth, it would be very strange, if there were any two of them that had exactly the same number of particles of dust and water in them. But infinitely less strange, than that two particles of light should have just the same quantity of matter. For a particle of light (according to the doctrine of the infinite divisibility of matter) is composed of infinitely more

3. [Watts, *Essay,* Sec. 6, *ans.* to *obj.* 6; in *Works, 6,* 269.]

assignable parts, than there are particles of dust and water in the globe of the earth. And as it is infinitely unlikely, that any two of these particles should be *equal;* so it is, that they should be *alike* in other respects: to instance, in the configuration of their surfaces. If there were very many globes, of the nature of the earth, it would be very unlikely that any two should have exactly the same number of particles of dust, water and stone, in their surfaces, and all posited exactly alike, one with respect to another, without any difference, in any part discernible either by the naked eye or microscope; but infinitely less strange, than that two particles of light should be perfectly of the same figure. For there are infinitely more assignable real parts on the surface of a particle of light, than there are particles of dust, water and stone, on the surface of the terrestrial globe.

Answer (2). But then, supposing that there are two particles or atoms of matter perfectly equal and alike, which God has placed in different parts of the creation; as I will not deny it to be possible for God to make two bodies perfectly alike, and put them in different places; yet it will not follow, that two different or distinct acts or effects of the divine power have exactly the same fitness for the same ends. For these two different bodies are not different or distinct, in any other respects than those wherein they *differ:* they are two in no other respects than those wherein there is a difference. If they are perfectly equal and alike *in themselves,* then they can be distinguished, or be distinct, only in those things which are called *circumstances;* as, place, time, rest, motion, or some other present or past circumstances or relations. For 'tis difference only, that constitutes distinction. If God makes two bodies *in themselves* every way equal and alike, and agreeing perfectly in all other circumstances and relations, but only *their place;* then in this only is there any distinction or duplicity. The figure is the same, the measure is the same, the solidity and resistance are the same, and everything the same, but only the place. Therefore what the will of God determines, is this, namely, that there should be the same figure, the same extension, the same resistance, etc. in two different places. And for this determination he has some reason. There is some end, for which such a determination and act has a peculiar fitness, above all other acts. Here is no one thing determined without an end, and no one thing without a fitness for that end, superior to anything else. If it be the pleasure of God to cause the same resistance, and the same figure, to be in two different places and situations, we can no more justly argue from it, that here must be some determination or act of God's will, that is wholly without motive or end, than [4] we can argue that whenever, in any case, it is a man's will to speak the same words, or make the same sounds at two different times; there must be some determination or act of his will, without any motive or end. The difference of place, in the former case, proves no more than the difference of time does in the other. If anyone should say with regard to the former case, that there must be something determined without an end; viz. that of those two similar bodies, this in particular should be made in this place, and the other in the other, and should inquire why the creator did not make them in a transposition, when both are alike, and each would equally have suited either place? The inquiry supposes something that is not true; namely, that the two bodies differ and are distinct in other respects besides their place. So that with this distinction, *inherent* in them, they might in their first creation have been transposed, and each might have begun its existence in the place of the other.

Let us for clearness' sake suppose, that God had at the beginning made two globes, each of an inch diameter, both perfect spheres, and perfectly solid without pores, and perfectly alike in every respect, and placed them near one to another, one towards the right hand, and the other towards the left, without any difference as to time, motion or rest, past or present, or any circumstance, but only their place; and the question should be asked, Why God in their creation placed 'em so? Why that which is made on the right hand, was not made on the left, and *vice versa?* Let it be well considered, whether there be any sense in such a question; and whether the inquiry don't suppose something false and absurd. Let it be considered, what the creator must have done otherwise than he did, what different act of will or power he must have exerted, in order to the thing proposed. All that could have been done, would have been to have made two spheres, perfectly alike, in the same places where he has made them, without any difference of the things made, either in themselves, or in any circumstance; so that the whole effect would have been without any difference, and therefore just the same. By the supposition, the two spheres are different in no other respect but their place; and therefore in other respects they are the same. Each has the same roundness: it is not a distinct rotundity, in any other respect but its situation. There are also the same dimensions, differing in nothing but

4. [The 1754 ed. reads "then."]

their place. And so of their resistance, and everything else that belongs to them.

Here if any chooses to say, "that there is a difference in another respect, viz. that they are not *numerically* the same: that it is thus with all the qualities that belong to them: that it is confessed they are in some respects the same; that is, they are both exactly alike; but yet *numerically* they differ. Thus the roundness of one is not the same *numerical, individual* roundness with that of the other." Let this be supposed; then the question about the determination of the divine will in the affair, is, why did God will, that this individual roundness should be at the right hand, and the other individual roundness at the left? Why did not he make them in a contrary position? Let any rational person consider, whether such questions be not words without a meaning; as much as if God should see fit for some ends to cause the same sounds to be repeated, or made at two different times; the sounds being perfectly the same in every other respect, but only one was a minute after the other; and it should be asked upon it, why God caused these sounds, numerically different, to succeed one the other in such a manner? why he did not make that individual sound which was in the first minute, to be in the second? and the individual sound of the last minute to be in the first? Which inquiries would be even ridiculous; as I think every person must see at once, in the case proposed of two sounds, being only the same repeated, absolutely without any difference, but that one circumstance of time. If the most High sees it will answer some good end, that the same sound should be made by lightning at two distinct times, and therefore wills that it should be so, must it needs therefore be, that herein there is some act of God's will without any motive or end? God saw fit often, at distinct times, and on different occasions, to say the very same words to Moses; namely those, "I am Jehovah." And would it not be unreasonable, to infer as a certain consequence from this, that here must be some act or acts of the divine will, in determining and disposing these words exactly alike at different times, wholly without aim or inducement? But it would be no more unreasonable than to say, that there must be an act of God's without any inducement, if he sees it best, and for some reason, determines that there shall be the same resistance, the same dimensions, and the same figure, in several distinct places.

If in the instance of the two spheres, perfectly alike, it be supposed possible that God might have made them in a contrary position; that which is made at the right hand, being made at the left; then I ask, whether it is not evidently equally possible, if God had made but one of them, and that in the place of the right-hand globe, that he might have made that numerically different from what it is, and numerically different from what he did make it; though perfectly alike, and in the same place; and at the same time, and in every respect, in the same circumstances and relations? Namely, whether he might not have made it numerically the same with that which he has now made at the left hand; and so have left that which is now created at the right hand, in a state of nonexistence? And if so, whether it would not have been possible to have made one in that place, perfectly like these, and yet numerically differing from both? And let it be considered, whether from this notion of a numerical difference in bodies, perfectly equal and alike, which numerical difference is something inherent in the bodies themselves, and diverse from the difference of place or time, or any circumstance whatsoever; it will not follow, that there is an infinite number of numerically different possible bodies, perfectly alike, among which God chooses, by a self-determining power, when he goes about to create bodies.

Therefore let us put the case thus: supposing that God in the beginning had created but one perfectly solid sphere, in a certain place; and it should be inquired, why God created that individual sphere, in that place, at that time? And why he did not create another sphere perfectly like it, but numerically different, in the same place, at the same time? Or why he chose to bring into being there, that very body, rather than any of the infinite number of other bodies, perfectly like it; either of which he could have made there as well, and would have answered his end as well? Why he caused to exist, at that place and time, that individual roundness, rather than any other of the infinite number of individual rotundities, just like it? Why that individual resistance, rather than any other of the infinite number of possible resistances just like it? And it might as reasonably be asked, why, when God first caused it to thunder, he caused that individual sound then to be made, and not another just like it? Why did he make choice of this very sound, and reject all the infinite number of other possible sounds just like it, but numerically differing from it, and all differing one from another? I think, everybody must be sensible of the absurdity and nonsense of what is supposed in such inquiries. And if we calmly attend to the matter, we shall be convinced, that all such kind of objections as I am answering, are founded on nothing but the imperfection of our manner of conceiving of things, and the obscureness of language, and great want of clearness and precision in the signification of terms.

If any shall find fault with this reasoning, that it is going a great length into metaphysical niceties and subtleties; I answer, the objection which they are in reply to, is a metaphysical subtlety, and must be treated according to the nature of it.[5]

II. Another thing alleged is, that innumerable things which are determined by the divine will, and chosen and done by God rather than others, differ from those that are not chosen in so inconsiderable a manner, that it would be unreasonable to suppose the difference to be of any consequence, or that there is any superior fitness or goodness, that God can have respect to in the determination.

To which I answer; it is impossible for us to determine with any certainty or evidence, that because the difference is very small, and appears to us of no consideration, therefore there is absolutely no superior goodness, and no valuable end which can be proposed by the creator and governor of the world, in ordering such a difference. The forementioned author mentions many instances. One is, there being one atom in the whole universe more, or less. But I think it would be unreasonable to suppose, that God made one atom in vain, or without any end or motive. He made not one atom but what was a work of his almighty power, as much as the whole globe of the earth, and requires as much of a constant exertion of almighty power to uphold it; and was made and is upheld understandingly, and on design, as much as if no other had been made but that. And it would be as unreasonable to suppose, that he made it without anything really aimed at in so doing, as much as to suppose that he made the planet Jupiter without aim or design.

'Tis possible, that the most minute effects of the creator's power, the smallest assignable differences between the things which God has made, may be attended, in the whole series of events, and the whole compass and extent of their influence, with very great and important consequences. If the laws of motion and gravitation, laid down by Sir Isaac Newton, hold universally, there is not one atom, nor the least assignable part of an atom, but what has influence, every moment, throughout the whole material universe, to cause every part to be

5. "For men to have recourse to subtleties, in raising difficulties, and then complain, that they should be taken off by minutely examining these subtleties, is a strange kind of procedure." Baxter, 2, 331 [1st ed., p. 340–1; 2d ed., 2, 355–6].

otherwise than it would be, if it were not for that particular corporeal existence. And however the effect is insensible for the present, yet it may in length of time become great and important.

To illustrate this, let us suppose two bodies moving the same way, in straight lines, perfectly parallel one to another; but to be diverted from this parallel course, and drawn one from another, as much as might be by the attraction of an atom, at the distance of one of the furthest of the fixed stars from the earth; these bodies being turned out of the lines of their parallel motion, will, by degrees, get further and further distant, one from the other; and though the distance may be imperceptible for a long time, yet at length it may become very great. So the revolution of a planet round the sun being retarded or accelerated, and the orbit of its revolution made greater or less, and more or less elliptical, and so its periodical time longer or shorter, no more than may be by the influence of the least atom, might in length of time perform a whole revolution sooner or later than other-wise it would have done; which might make a vast alteration with regard to millions of important events. So the influence of the least particle may, for ought we know, have such effect on something in the constitution of some human body, as to cause another thought to arise in the mind at a certain time, than otherwise would have been; which in length of time (yea, and that not very great) might occa-sion a vast alteration through the whole world of mankind. And so innumerable other ways might be mentioned, wherein the least assignable alteration may possibly be attended with great conse-quences.

Another argument, which the forementioned author brings against a necessary determination of the divine will by a superior fitness, is, that such doctrine derogates from the *freeness* of God's *grace* and *goodness,* in choosing the objects of his favor and bounty, and from the obligation upon men to *thankfulness* for special benefits (p. 89,[6] etc.).

In answer to this objection, I would observe,

1. That it derogates no more from the goodness of God, to sup-pose the exercise of the benevolence of his nature to be determined by wisdom, than to suppose it determined by chance, and that his favors are bestowed altogether at random, his will being determined by nothing but perfect accident, without any end or design whatso-ever; which must be the case, as has been demonstrated, if volition be

6. [Watts, *Essay,* Sec. 5, *adv.* 8; in *Works, 6,* 262. See above, Intro., Pt. 5, no. 17.]

not determined by a prevailing motive. That which is owing to perfect contingence, wherein neither previous inducement, nor antecedent choice has any hand, is not owing more to goodness or benevolence, than that which is owing to the influence of a wise end.

2. 'Tis acknowledged, that if the motive that determines the will of God, in the choice of the objects of his *favors,* be any moral quality in the object, recommending that object to his benevolence above others, his choosing that object is not so great a manifestation of the freeness and sovereignty of his grace, as if it were otherwise. But there is no necessity of supposing this, in order to our supposing that he has some wise end in view, in determining to bestow his favors on one person rather than another. We are to distinguish between the *merit* of the *object* of God's favor, or a moral qualification of the object attracting that favor and recommending to it, and the *natural fitness* of such a determination of the *act* of God's goodness, to answer some wise design of his own, some end in the view of God's omniscience. 'Tis God's own act, that is the proper and immediate object of his volition.

3. I suppose that none will deny, but that in some instances, God acts from wise design in determining the particular subjects of his favors: none will say, I presume, that when God distinguishes by his bounty particular societies or persons, he never, in any instance, exercises any wisdom in so doing, aiming at some happy consequence. And if it be not denied to be so in some instances, then I would inquire, whether in these instances God's goodness is less manifested, than in those wherein God has no aim or end at all? And whether the subjects have less cause of thankfulness? And if so, who shall be thankful for the bestowment of distinguishing mercy, with that enhancing circumstance of the distinction's being made without an end? How shall it be known when God is influenced by some wise aim, and when not? It is very manifest with respect to the Apostle Paul, that God had wise ends in choosing him to be a Christian and an apostle, who had been a persecutor, etc. The Apostle himself mentions one end. I Tim. 1:15, 16: "Christ Jesus came into the world to save sinners, of whom I am chief. Howbeit, for this cause I obtained mercy, that in me first, Jesus Christ might show forth all long-suffering, for a pattern to them who should hereafter believe on him to life everlasting." But yet the Apostle never looked on it as a diminution of the freedom and riches of divine grace in his election, which he so often and so greatly magnifies. This brings me to observe,

4. Our supposing such a moral necessity in the acts of God's will as has been spoken of, is so far from necessarily derogating from the riches of God's grace to such as are the chosen objects of his favor, that in many instances, this moral necessity may arise from goodness, and from the great degree of it. God may choose this object rather than another, as having a superior fitness to answer the ends, designs and inclinations of his goodness; being more sinful, and so more miserable and necessitous than others; the inclinations of infinite mercy and benevolence may be more gratified, and the gracious design of God's sending his Son into the world may be more abundantly answered, in the exercises of mercy towards such an object, rather than another.

One thing more I would observe, before I finish what I have to say on the head of the necessity of the acts of God's will; and that is, that something much more like a servile subjection of the divine being to fatal necessity, will follow from Arminian principles, than from the doctrines which they oppose. For they (at least most of them) suppose, with respect to all events that happen in the moral world depending on the volitions of moral agents, which are the most important events of the universe, to which all others are subordinate; I say, they suppose with respect to these, that God has a certain foreknowledge of them, antecedent to any purposes or decrees of his about them. And if so, they have a fixed certain futurity, prior to any designs or volitions of his, and independent on them, and to which his volitions must be subject, as he would wisely accommodate his affairs to this fixed futurity of the state of things in the moral world. So that here, instead of a moral necessity of God's will, arising from or consisting in the infinite perfection and blessedness of the divine Being, we have a fixed unalterable state of things, properly distinct from the perfect nature of the divine mind, and the state of the divine will and design, and entirely independent on these things, and which they have no hand in, because they are prior to them; and which God's will is truly subject to, being obliged to conform or accommodate himself to it, in all his purposes and decrees, and in everything he does in his disposals and government of the world; the moral world being the end of the natural; so that all is in vain, that is not accommodated to that state of the moral world, which consists in, or depends upon the acts and state of the wills of moral agents, which had a fixed futurition from eternity. Such a subjection to necessity as this, would truly argue an inferiority and servitude, that would be unworthy of the supreme Being; and is much more agreeable to the notion which many of the heathen had of fate, as above the gods, than that moral necessity of fitness and wisdom which has been spoken of; and is truly repugnant to the absolute sovereignty of God, and inconsistent with the supremacy of his will; and really subjects the will of the most High to the will of his creatures, and brings him into dependence upon them.[7]

7. [See above, Intro., Pt. 5, nos. 19, 20, 21, for an analysis and final appraisal of the encounter between Watts and JE.]

SECTION 9. CONCERNING THAT OBJECTION AGAINST THE DOCTRINE WHICH HAS BEEN MAINTAINED, THAT IT MAKES GOD THE AUTHOR OF SIN

'TIS urged by Arminians, that the doctrine of the necessity of men's volitions, or their necessary connection with antecedent events and circumstances, makes the first cause, and supreme orderer of all things, the author of sin; in that he has so constituted the state and course of things, that sinful volitions become necessary, in consequence of his disposal. Dr. Whitby, in his "Discourse on the Freedom of the Will," [1] cites one of the ancients, as on his side, declaring that this opinion of the necessity of the will "absolves sinners, as doing nothing of their own accord which was evil, and would cast all the blame of all the wickedness committed in the world, upon God, and upon his providence, if that were admitted by the asserters of this fate; whether he himself did necessitate them to do these things, or ordered matters so that they should be constrained to do them by some other cause." And the Doctor says in another place,[2] "In the nature of the thing, and in the opinion of philosophers, *causa deficiens, in rebus necessariis, ad causam per se efficientem reducenda est*. In things necessary, the deficient cause must be reduced to the efficient. And in this case the reason is evident; because the not doing what is required, or not avoiding what is forbidden, being a defect, must follow from the position of the necessary cause of that deficiency."

Concerning this, I would observe the following things.

I. If there be any difficulty in this matter, 'tis nothing peculiar to this scheme; 'tis no difficulty or disadvantage wherein it is distinguished from the scheme of Arminians; and therefore not reasonably objected by them.

Dr. Whitby supposes, that if sin necessarily follows from God's

1. Whitby, *Discourse on the Five Points*, Dis. IV, ch. 4, no. 3; p. 361.
2. Ibid., Dis. VI, ch. 1, no. 4; p. 486.

withholding assistance, or if that assistance be not given which is absolutely necessary to the avoiding of evil; then in the nature of the thing, God must be as properly the author of that evil, as if he were the efficient cause of it. From whence, according to what he himself says of the devils and damned spirits, God must be the proper author of their perfect unrestrained wickedness: he must be the efficient cause of the great pride of the devils, and of their perfect malignity against God, Christ, his saints, and all that is good, and of the insatiable cruelty of their disposition. For he allows, that God has so forsaken them, and does so withhold his assistance from them, that they are incapacitated from doing good, and determined only to evil.[3] Our doctrine, in its consequence, makes God the author of men's sin in this world, no more, and in no other sense, than his doctrine, in its consequence, makes God the author of the hellish pride and malice of the devils. And doubtless the latter is as odious an effect as the former.

Again, if it will *follow at all,* that God is the author of sin, from what has been supposed of a sure and infallible connection between antecedents and consequents, it will *follow because of this,* viz. that for God to be the author or orderer of those things which he knows beforehand, will infallibly be attended with such a consequence, is the same thing in effect, as for him to be the author of that consequence. But if this be so, this is a difficulty which equally attends the doctrine of Arminians themselves; at least, of those of them who allow God's certain foreknowledge of all events. For on the supposition of such a foreknowledge, this is the case with respect to every sin that is committed: God knew, that if he ordered and brought to pass such and such events, such sins would infallibly follow. As for instance, God certainly foreknew, long before Judas was born, that if he ordered things so, that there should be such a man born, at such a time, and at such a place, and that his life should be preserved, and that he should, in divine providence, be led into acquaintance with Jesus; and that his heart should be so influenced by God's spirit or providence, as to be inclined to be a follower of Christ; and that he should be one of those twelve, which should be chosen constantly to attend him as his family; and that his health should be preserved so that he should go up to Jerusalem, at the last Passover in Christ's life; and it should be so ordered that Judas should see Christ's kind treatment of the woman which anointed him at Bethany, and have

3. Ibid., Dis. IV, ch. 1, no. 3; pp. 302, 305 [See above, Intro., Pt. 5, no. 10.]

that reproof from Christ, which he had at that time, and see and hear other things, which excited his enmity against his master, and other circumstances should be ordered, as they were ordered; it would be what would most certainly and infallibly follow, that Judas would betray his Lord, and would soon after hang himself, and die impenitent, and be sent to hell, for his horrid wickedness.

Therefore this supposed difficulty ought not to be brought as an objection against the scheme which has been maintained, as *disagreeing* with the Arminian scheme, seeing 'tis no difficulty owing to such a *disagreement;* but a difficulty wherein the Arminians share with us. That must be unreasonably made an objection against our differing from them, which we should not escape or avoid at all by agreeing with them.

And therefore I would observe,

II. They who object, that this doctrine makes God the author of sin, ought distinctly to explain what they mean by that phrase, "the author of sin." I know, the phrase, as it is commonly used, signifies something very ill. If by "the author of sin," be meant the sinner, the agent, or actor of sin, or the *doer* of a wicked thing; so it would be a reproach and blasphemy, to suppose God to be the author of sin. In this sense, I utterly deny God to be the author of sin; rejecting such an imputation on the most High, as what is infinitely to be abhorred; and deny any such thing to be the consequence of what I have laid down. But if by "the author of sin," is meant the permitter, or not a hinderer of sin; and at the same time, a disposer of the state of events, in such a manner, for wise, holy and most excellent ends and purposes, that sin, if it be permitted or not hindered, will most certainly and infallibly follow: I say, if this be all that is meant, by being the author of sin, I don't deny that God is the author of sin (though I dislike and reject the phrase, as that which by use and custom is apt to carry another sense), it is no reproach for the most High to be thus the author of sin. This is not to be the *actor* of sin, but on the contrary, of *holiness.* What God doth herein, is holy; and a glorious exercise of the infinite excellency of his nature. And I don't deny, that God's being thus the author of sin, follows from what I have laid down; and I assert, that it equally follows from the doctrine which is maintained by most of the Arminian divines.

That it is most certainly so, that God is in such a manner the disposer and orderer of sin, is evident, if any credit is to be given to the Scripture; as well as because it is impossible in the nature of things to be otherwise. In such a manner God ordered the obstinacy of Pharaoh, in his refusing to obey God's commands, to let the people go. Ex. 4:21: "I will harden his heart, and he shall not let the people go." Ch. 7:2–5: "Aaron thy brother shall speak unto Pharaoh, that he send the children of Israel out of his land. And I will harden Pharaoh's heart, and multiply my signs and my wonders in the land of Egypt. But Pharaoh shall not hearken unto you; that I may lay mine hand upon Egypt, by great judgments," etc. Ch. 9:12: "And the Lord hardened the heart of Pharaoh, and he hearkened not unto them, as the Lord had spoken unto Moses." Ch. 10:1, 2: "And the Lord said unto Moses, go in unto Pharaoh; for I have hardened his heart, and the heart of his servants, that I might shew these my signs before him, and that thou mayst tell it in the ears of thy son, and thy son's son, what things I have wrought in Egypt, and my signs which I have done amongst them, that ye may know that I am the Lord." Ch. 14:4: "And I will harden Pharaoh's heart, that he shall follow after them: and I will be honored upon Pharaoh, and upon all his host." Ver. 8: "And the Lord hardened the heart of Pharaoh King of Egypt, and he pursued after the children of Israel." And it is certain that in such a manner, God for wise and good ends, ordered that event, Joseph's being sold into Egypt by his brethren. Gen. 45:5: "Now therefore be not grieved, nor angry with yourselves, that ye sold me hither; for God did send me before you to preserve life." Ver. 7, 8: "God did send me before you to preserve a posterity in the earth, and to save your lives by a great deliverance: so that now it was not you, that sent me hither, but God." Ps. 105:17: "He sent a man before them, even Joseph, who was sold for a servant." 'Tis certain, that thus God ordered the sin and folly of Sihon King of the Amorites, in refusing to let the people of Israel pass by him peaceably. Deut. 2:30: "But Sihon King of Heshbon would not let us pass by him; for the Lord thy God hardened his spirit, and made his heart obstinate, that he might deliver him into thine hand." 'Tis certain, that God thus ordered the sin and folly of the kings of Canaan, that they attempted not to make peace with Israel, but with a stupid boldness and obstinacy, set themselves violently to oppose them and their God. Josh. 11:20: "For it was of the Lord, to harden their hearts, that they should come against Israel in battle, that he might destroy them utterly, and that they might have no favor; but that he might destroy them, as the Lord commanded Moses." 'Tis evident, that thus God ordered the treacherous rebellion of Zedekiah, against the King of Babylon. Jer. 52:3: "For through the anger of the Lord it came to pass in Jerusalem, and Judah, till he had cast them out from his presence, that Zedekiah rebelled against the King of Babylon." So II Kgs. 24:20. And 'tis exceeding manifest, that God thus ordered the rapine and unrighteous ravages of Nebuchadnezzar, in spoiling and ruining the nations round about. Jer. 25:9: "Behold, I will send and take all the families of the north, saith the Lord, and Nebuchadnezzar my servant, and will bring them against this land, and against all the nations round about; and will utterly destroy them, and make them an astonishment, and an hissing, and perpetual desolations." Ch. 43:10, 11: "I will send and take Nebuchadnezzar the King of Babylon, my servant; and I will set his throne upon these stones that I have hid, and he shall spread his royal pavilion over them. And when he cometh, he shall smite the land of Egypt, and deliver such as are for death to death, and such as are for captivity to captivity, and such as are for the sword to the sword." Thus God represents himself as *sending* for Nebuchadnezzar, and *taking* of him and his armies, and *bringing* him against the nations which were to be destroyed by him, to that very end, that he might utterly destroy them, and make them desolate; and as appointing the work that he should do, so particularly, that the very persons were designed, that he should kill with the sword; and those that should be killed with famine and pestilence, and those that should be carried into captivity; and that in doing all these things, he should act as his servant: by which, less can't be intended, than that he should serve his purposes and designs. And in Jer. 27:4, 5, 6, God declares how he would cause him thus to serve his designs, viz. by bringing this to pass in his sovereign disposals, as the great possessor and governor of the universe, that disposes all things just as pleases him: "Thus saith the Lord of Hosts, the God of Israel; I have made the earth, the man and the beast that are upon the ground, by my great power, and my stretched out arm, and have given it unto whom it seemed meet unto me: and now I have given all these lands into the hands of Nebuchadnezzar *my servant,* and the beasts of the field have I given also to serve him." And Nebuchadnezzar is spoken of as doing these things, by having his "arms strengthened" by God, and having "God's sword put into his hands, for this end" (Ezek. 30:24, 25, 26). Yea, God speaks of his terribly ravaging and wasting the nations, and cruelly destroying all sorts, without distinction of sex or age, as the weapon in God's hand, and the instrument of his indignation, which

God makes use of to fulfill his own purposes, and execute his own vengeance. Jer. 51:20, etc.: "Thou art my battle-axe, and weapons of war. For with thee will I break in pieces the nations, and with thee I will destroy kingdoms, and with thee I will break in pieces the horse and his rider, and with thee I will break in pieces the chariot and his rider; with thee also will I break in pieces man and woman; and with thee will I break in pieces old and young; and with thee will I break in pieces the young man and the maid," etc. 'Tis represented, that the designs of Nebuchadnezzar, and those that destroyed Jerusalem, never could have been accomplished, had not God determined them, as well as they; Lam. 3:37, "Who is he that saith, and it cometh to pass, and the Lord commandeth it not?" And yet the King of Babylon's thus destroying the nations, and especially the Jews, is spoken of as his great wickedness, for which God finally destroyed him (Is. 14:4, 5, 6, 12; Hab. 2:5–12; and Jer. ch. 50 and 51). 'Tis most manifest, that God, to serve his own designs, providentially ordered Shimei's cursing David. II Sam. 16:10, 11: "The Lord hath said unto him, curse David. . . . Let him curse, for the Lord hath bidden him."

'Tis certain, that God thus, for excellent, holy, gracious and glorious ends, ordered the fact which they committed, who were concerned in Christ's death; and that therein they did but fulfill God's designs. As, I trust, no Christian will deny it was the design of God, that Christ should be *crucified,* and that for this end, he came into the world. 'Tis very manifest by many scriptures, that the whole affair of Christ's crucifixion, with its circumstances, and the treachery of Judas, that made way for it, was ordered in God's providence, in pursuance of his purpose; notwithstanding the violence that is used with those plain Scriptures, to obscure and pervert the sense of 'em. Acts 2:23: "Him being delivered, by the determinate counsel and foreknowledge of God,[4] ye have taken, and with wicked hands, have crucified and slain." Luke 22:21, 22: [5] "But behold the hand of him

4. "Grotius, as well as Beza, observes, that πρόγνωσις must here signify 'decree'; and Elsner has shown that it has that signification, in approved Greek writers. And it is certain ἔκδοτος signifies one 'given up' into the hands of an enemy." Philip Doddridge, *The Family Expositor, or a Paraphrase and Version of the New Testament* (London, J. Waugh, 1739–48), *in loc.* Acts 2:23; 3, 23 n.

5. "As this passage is not liable to the ambiguities, which some have apprehended in Acts 2:23 and 4:28 (which yet seem on the whole to be parallel to it, in their most natural construction) I look upon it as an evident proof, that these things are, in the language of Scripture, said to be determined or decreed (or

that betrayeth me, is with me on the table: and truly the Son of man goeth, as it was determined." Acts 4:27, 28: "For of a truth, against thy holy child Jesus, whom thou hast anointed, both Herod, and Pontius Pilate, with the Gentiles, and the people of Israel, were gathered together, for to do whatsoever thy hand and thy counsel determined before to be done." Acts 3:17, 18: "And now brethren, I wot that through ignorance ye did it, as did also your rulers: but these things, which God before had showed by the mouth of all his prophets, that Christ should suffer, he hath so fulfilled." So that what these murderers of Christ did, is spoken of as what God brought to pass or ordered, and that by which he fulfilled his own word.

In Rev. 17:17, "the agreeing of the kings of the earth to give their kingdom to the beast," though it was a very wicked thing in them, is spoken of as "a fulfilling God's will," and what "God had put it into their hearts to do." 'Tis manifest, that God sometimes permits sin to be committed, and at the same time orders things so, that if he permits the fact, it will come to pass, because on some accounts he sees it needful and of importance that it should come to pass. Matt. 18:7: "It must needs be, that offences come; but woe to that man by whom the offence cometh." With I Cor. 11:19, "For there must also be heresies among you, that they which are approved, may be made manifest among you."

Thus it is certain and demonstrable, from the holy Scriptures, as well as the nature of things, and the principles of Arminians, that God permits sin; and at the same time, so orders things, in his providence, that it certainly and infallibly will come to pass, in consequence of his permission.

I proceed to observe in the next place,

III. That there is a great difference between God's being concerned thus, by his *permission,* in an event and act, which in the inherent subject and agent of it, is sin (though the event will certainly follow on his permission), and his being concerned in it by *producing* it and exerting the act of sin; or between his being the *orderer* of its certain existence, by *not hindering* it, under certain circumstances, and his being the proper *actor* or *author* of it, by a *positive agency* or *efficiency.* And this, notwithstanding what Dr.

---

exactly bounded and marked out by God, as the word ὁρίζω most naturally signifies) which he sees in fact will happen, in consequence of his volitions, without any necessitating agency; as well as those events of which he is properly the author." Doddridge *in loc.* Luke 22:22; *3,* 434 n.

Whitby offers about a saying of philosophers, that *causa deficiens, in rebus necessariis, ad causam per se efficientem reducenda est.* As there is a vast difference between the sun's being the cause of the lightsomeness and warmth of the atmosphere, and brightness of gold and diamonds, by its presence and positive influence; and its being the occasion of darkness and frost, in the night, by its motion, whereby it descends below the horizon. The motion of the sun is the occasion of the latter kind of events; but it is not the proper cause, efficient or producer of them; though they are necessarily consequent on that motion, under such circumstances: no more is any action of the divine Being the cause of the evil of men's wills. If the sun were the proper *cause* of cold and darkness, it would be the *fountain* of these things, as it is the fountain of light and heat: and then something might be argued from the nature of cold and darkness, to a likeness of nature in the sun; and it might be justly inferred, that the sun itself is dark and cold, and that his beams are black and frosty. But from its being the cause no otherwise than by its departure, no such thing can be inferred, but the contrary; it may justly be argued, that the sun is a bright and hot body, if cold and darkness are found to be the consequence of its withdrawment; and the more constantly and necessarily these effects are connected with, and confined to its absence, the more strongly does it argue the sun to be the fountain of light and heat. So, inasmuch as sin is not the fruit of any positive agency or influence of the most High, but on the contrary, arises from the withholding of his action and energy, and under certain circumstances, necessarily follows on the want of his influence; this is no argument that he is sinful, or his operation evil, or has anything of the nature of evil; but on the contrary, that he, and his agency, are altogether good and holy, and that he is the fountain of all holiness. It would be strange arguing indeed, because men never commit sin, but only when God leaves 'em *to themselves,* and necessarily sin, when he does so, that therefore their sin is not *from themselves,* but from God; and so, that God must be a sinful being: as strange as it would be to argue, because it is always dark when the sun is gone, and never dark when the sun is present, that therefore all darkness is from the sun, and that his disk and beams must needs be black.

IV. It properly belongs to the supreme and absolute Governor of the universe, to order all important events within his dominion, by his wisdom: but the events in the moral world are of the most important kind; such as the moral actions of intelligent creatures, and their consequences.

These events will be ordered by something. They will either be disposed by wisdom, or they will be disposed by chance; that is, they will be disposed by blind and undesigning causes, if that were possible, and could be called a disposal. Is it not better, that the good and evil which happens in God's world, should be ordered, regulated, bounded and determined by the good pleasure of an infinitely wise Being, who perfectly comprehends within his understanding and constant view, the universality of things, in all their extent and duration, and sees all the influence of every event, with respect to every individual thing and circumstance, throughout the grand system, and the whole of the eternal series of consequences; than to leave these things to fall out by chance, and to be determined by those causes which have no understanding or aim? Doubtless, in these important events, there is a better and a worse, as to the time, subject, place, manner and circumstances of their coming to pass, with regard to their influence on the state and course of things. And if there be, 'tis certainly best that they should be determined to that time, place, etc. which is best. And therefore 'tis in its own nature fit, that wisdom, and not chance, should order these things. So that it belongs to the Being, who is the possessor of infinite wisdom, and is the creator and owner of the whole system of created existences, and has the care of all; I say, it belongs to him, to take care of this matter; and he would not do what is proper for him, if he should neglect it. And it is so far from being unholy in him, to undertake this affair, that it would rather have been unholy to neglect it; as it would have been a neglecting what fitly appertains to him; and so it would have been a very unfit and unsuitable neglect.

Therefore the sovereignty of God doubtless extends to this matter; especially considering, that if it should be supposed to be otherwise, and God should leave men's volitions, and all moral events, to the determination and disposition of blind and unmeaning causes, or they should be left to happen perfectly without a cause; this would be no more consistent with liberty, in any notion of it, and particularly not in the Arminian notion of it, than if these events were subject to the disposal of divine providence, and the will of man were determined by circumstances which are ordered and disposed by divine wisdom; as appears by what has been already observed. But 'tis evident, that such a providential disposing and determining men's moral actions, though it infers a moral necessity of those actions, yet it does not in the least infringe the real liberty of mankind; the only liberty that common sense teaches to be necessary to moral agency, which, as has been demonstrated, is not inconsistent with such necessity.

On the whole, it is manifest, that God may be, in the manner which has been described, the orderer and disposer of that event, which in the inherent subject and agent is moral evil; and yet his so doing may be no moral evil. He may will the disposal of such an event, and its coming to pass for good ends, and his will not be an immoral or sinful will, but a perfectly holy will. And he may actually in his providence so dispose and permit things, that the event may be certainly and infallibly connected with such disposal and permission, and his act therein not be an immoral or unholy, but a perfectly holy act. Sin may be an evil thing, and yet that there should be such a disposal and permission, as that it should come to pass, may be a good thing. This is no contradiction, or inconsistence. Joseph's brethren's selling him into Egypt, consider it only as it was acted by them, and with respect to their views and aims which were evil, was a very bad thing; but it was a good thing, as it was an event of God's ordering, and considered with respect to his views and aims which were good. Gen. 50:20: "As for you, ye thought evil against me; but God meant it unto good." So the crucifixion of Christ, if we consider only those things which belong to the event as it proceeded from his murderers, and are comprehended within the compass of the affair considered as their act, their principles, dispositions, views and aims; so it was one of the most heinous things that ever was done; in many respects the most horrid of all acts: but consider it, as it was willed and ordered of God, in the extent of his designs and views, it was the most admirable and glorious of all events; and God's willing the event was the most holy volition of God, that ever was made known to men; and God's act in ordering it, was a divine act, which above all others, manifests the moral excellency of the divine Being.

The consideration of these things may help us to a sufficient answer to the cavils of Arminians concerning what has been supposed by many Calvinists, of a distinction between a *secret* and *revealed* will of God, and their diversity one from the other; supposing, that the Calvinists herein ascribe inconsistent wills to the most High: which is without any foundation. God's *secret* and *revealed* will, or in other words, his *disposing* and *preceptive* will may be diverse, and exercised in dissimilar acts, the one in disapproving and opposing, the other in willing and determining, without any inconsistence. Because, although these dissimilar exercises of the divine will may in some respects relate to the same things, yet in strictness they have different and contrary objects, the one evil and the other good. Thus for instance, the crucifixion of Christ was a thing contrary to the revealed or preceptive will of God; because, as it was viewed and done by his malignant murderers, it was a thing infinitely contrary to the holy nature of God, and so necessarily contrary to the holy inclination of his heart revealed in his Law. Yet this don't at all hinder but that the crucifixion of Christ, considered with all those glorious consequences, which were within the view of the divine omniscience, might be indeed, and therefore might appear to God to be, a glorious event; and consequently be agreeable to his will, though this will may be secret, i.e. not revealed in God's Law. And thus considered, the crucifixion of Christ was not evil, but good. If the secret exercises of God's will were of a kind that is dissimilar and contrary to his revealed will, respecting the same, or like objects; if the objects of both were good, or both evil; then indeed to ascribe contrary kinds of volition or inclination to God, respecting these objects, would be to ascribe an inconsistent will to God: but to ascribe to him different and opposite exercises of heart, respecting different objects, and objects contrary one to another, is so far from supposing God's will to be *inconsistent* with itself, that it can't be supposed *consistent* with itself any other way. For any being to have a will of choice respecting good, and at the same time a will of rejection and refusal respecting evil, is to be very consistent: but the contrary, viz. to have the same will towards these contrary objects, and to choose and love both good and evil at the same time, is to be very inconsistent.

There is no inconsistence in supposing, that God may hate a thing as it is in itself, and considered simply as evil, and yet that it may be his will it should come to pass, considering all consequences. I believe, there is no person of good understanding, who will venture to say, he is certain that it is impossible it should be best, taking in the whole compass and extent of existence, and all consequences in the endless series of events, that there should be such a thing as moral evil in the world.[6] And if so, it will certainly follow, that an infinitely

6. Here are worthy to be observed some passages of a late noted writer, of our nation, that nobody who is acquainted with him will suspect to be very favorable

wise Being, who always chooses what is best, must choose that there
should be such a thing. And if so, then such a choice is not an evil,
but a wise and holy choice. And if so, then that providence which is
agreeable to such a choice, is a wise and holy providence. Men do
will sin as sin, and so are the authors and actors of it: they love it as

---

to Calvinism. "It is difficult (says he) to handle the *necessity of evil* in such a manner, as not to stumble such as are not above being alarmed at propositions which
have an uncommon sound. But if philosophers will but reflect calmly on the matter, they will find, that consistently with the unlimited power of the supreme
Cause, it may be said, that in the best ordered system, *evils* must have place."
George Turnbull, *The Principles of Moral Philosophy, an Enquiry into the Wise
and Good Government of the Moral World* (London, 1740), pp. 327 f. in the
footnote. He is there speaking of *moral* evils, as may be seen. [It may also be seen
that Turnbull justifies the existence of moral evil not only by considering all the
consequences which God may have in his view, but by himself viewing moral evil
as an unavoidable result and risk of freedom, which great good everyone may
witness along with the evil, or else phrase as follows his "complaint against nature": "Nature hath dealt unkindly by us in making our happiness depend in
any measure on ourselves, and in making us capable of the pleasures of knowledge,
foresight, *self-direction,* and good management" (p. 326; italics mine).]
    Again the same author [George Turnbull], in his second volume entitled,
Christian Philosophy, [*The Principles of Moral and Christian Philosophy* (2 vols.
London, 1740), 2], 35, has these words: "If the Author and Governor of all things
be infinitely perfect, then whatever is, is right; of all possible systems he hath
chosen the best: and consequently there is *no absolute evil* in the universe. . . .
This being the case, all the seeming *imperfections* or *evils* in it are such only in a
partial view; and with respect to the *whole* system, they are *goods."*
    Ibid., p. 37: *"Whence then comes evil,* is the question that hath in all ages
been reckoned the Gordian knot in philosophy. And indeed, if we own the existence of evil in the world in an *absolute* sense, we diametrically contradict what
hath been just now proved of God. For if there be any *evil* in the system, that is
not good with respect to the *whole,* then is the *whole* not good, but evil: or at
best, very imperfect: and an *author* must be as his *workmanship* is; as is the effect,
such is the cause. But the solution of this difficulty is at hand; that *there is no evil
in the universe.* What! Are there no pains, no imperfections? Is there no misery,
no vice in the world? Or are not these *evils?* Evils indeed they are; that is, those
of one sort are hurtful, and those of the other sort are equally hurtful and
abominable: but they are *not* evil or mischievous with respect to the *whole."*
    Ibid., p. 42: "But He is at the same time said to *create* evil, darkness, con-
fusion; and yet to do no evil, but to be the author of good only. He is called the
'Father of lights,' the Author of every perfect and good gift, with whom there is
no variableness nor shadow of turning, who tempteth no man, but giveth to all
men liberally, and upbraideth not. And yet by the prophet Isaias he is introduced
saying of himself, 'I form light, and create darkness; I make peace, and create
evil: I the Lord do all these things.' What is the meaning, the plain language of

sin, and for evil ends and purposes. God don't will sin as sin, or for the sake of anything evil; though it be his pleasure so to order things, that he permitting, sin will come to pass; for the sake of the great good that by his disposal shall be the consequence. His willing to order things so that evil should come to pass, for the sake of the contrary good, is no argument that he don't hate evil, as evil: and if so, then it is no reason why he mayn't reasonably forbid evil as evil, and punish it as such.

The Arminians themselves must be obliged, whether they will or no, to allow a distinction of God's will, amounting to just the same thing that Calvinists intend by their distinction of a *secret* and *revealed* will. They must allow a distinction of those things which God thinks best should be, considering all circumstances and consequences, and so are agreeable to his disposing will, and those things which he loves, and are agreeable to his nature, in themselves considered. Who is there that will dare to say, that the hellish pride, malice and cruelty of devils, are agreeable to God, and what he likes and approves? And yet, I trust, there is no Christian divine but what will allow, that 'tis agreeable to God's will so to order and dispose things concerning them, so to leave them to themselves, and give them up to their own wickedness, that this perfect wickedness should be a necessary consequence. Be sure Dr. Whitby's words do plainly suppose and allow it.[7]

These following things may be laid down as maxims of plain truth, and indisputable evidence.

1. That God is a *perfectly happy* Being, in the most absolute and highest sense possible.

2. That it will follow from hence, that God is free from every thing that is *contrary to happiness;* and so, that in strict propriety of speech, there is no such thing as any pain, grief or trouble in God.

3. When any intelligent being is really crossed and disappointed, and things are contrary to what he truly desires, he is the *less pleased,* or has less pleasure, his pleasure and happiness is diminished, and he

---

all this, but that the Lord delighteth in goodness, and (as the Scripture speaks) evil is his *strange* work? He intends and pursues the universal *good* of his creation: and the *evil* which happens is not permitted for its own sake, or through any pleasure in evil, but because it is requisite to the *greater good* pursued."

7. *Discourse on the Five Points,* Dis. IV, ch. 1, nos. 1, 2, 5; pp. 300, 305, 309 [Here again JE cites the 2d ed., if indeed he ever left off doing so. See above, note 1 to Sec. 3, Pt. III, and the Intro., Pt. 5, no. 10].

suffers what is disagreeable to him, or is the subject of something that is of a nature contrary to joy and happiness, even pain and grief.[8]

From this last axiom it follows, that if no distinction is to be admitted between God's hatred of sin, and his will with respect to the event and the existence of sin, as the all-wise determiner of all events, under the view of all consequences through the whole compass and series of things; I say, then it certainly follows, that the coming to pass of every individual act of sin is truly, all things considered, contrary to his will, and that his will is really crossed in it; and this in proportion as he hates it. And as God's hatred of sin is infinite, by reason of the infinite contrariety of his holy nature to sin; so his will is infinitely crossed, in every act of sin that happens. Which is as much as to say, he endures that which is infinitely disagreeable to him, by means of every act of sin that he sees committed. And therefore, as appears by the preceding positions, he endures truly and really, infinite grief or pain from every sin. And so he must be infinitely crossed, and suffer infinite pain, every day, in millions of millions of instances: he must continually be the subject of an immense number of *real,* and truly infinitely *great* crosses and vexations. Which would be to make him infinitely the most miserable of all beings.

If any objector should say; all that these things amount to, is, that God may do evil that good may come; which is justly esteemed immoral and sinful in men; and therefore may be justly esteemed inconsistent with the moral perfections of God. I answer, that for God to dispose and permit evil, in the manner that has been spoken of, is not to do evil that good may come; for it is not to do evil at all. In order to a thing's being morally evil, there must be one of these things belonging to it: either it must be a thing *unfit* and *unsuitable* in its own nature; or it must have a *bad tendency;* or it must proceed from an *evil disposition,* and be done for an evil end. But neither of these things can be attributed to God's ordering and permitting such events, as the immoral acts of creatures, for good ends. (1) It is not *unfit in its own nature,* that he should do so. For it is in its own nature fit, that infinite wisdom, and not blind chance, should dispose

8. Certainly 'tis not less absurd and unreasonable, to talk of God's will and desire's being truly and properly crossed, without his suffering any uneasiness, or anything grievous or disagreeable, than it is to talk of something that may be called a *revealed* will, which may in some respect be different from a *secret* purpose; which purpose may be fulfilled, when the other is opposed.

moral good and evil in the world. And 'tis fit, that the Being who has infinite wisdom, and is the maker, owner, and supreme governor of the world, should take care of that matter. And therefore there is no unfitness, or unsuitableness in his doing it. It may be unfit, and so immoral, for any other beings to go about to order this affair; because they are not possessed of a wisdom, that in any manner fits them for it; and in other respects they are not fit to be trusted with this affair; nor does it belong to them, they not being the owners and lords of the universe.

We need not be afraid to affirm, that if a wise and good man knew with absolute certainty, it would be best, all things considered, that there should be such a thing as moral evil in the world, it would not be contrary to his wisdom and goodness, for him to choose that it should be so. 'Tis no evil desire, to desire good, and to desire that which, all things considered, is best. And it is no unwise choice, to choose that that should be, which it is best should be; and to choose the existence of that thing concerning which this is known, viz. that it is best it should be, and so is known in the whole to be most worthy to be chosen. On the contrary, it would be a plain defect in wisdom and goodness, for him not to choose it. And the reason why he might not *order* it, if he were able, would not be because he might not desire it, but only the ordering of that matter don't belong to him. But it is no harm for him who is by right, and in the greatest propriety, the supreme orderer of all things, to order everything in such a manner, as it would be a point of wisdom in him to choose that they should be ordered. If it would be a plain defect of wisdom and goodness in a being, not to choose that that should be, which he certainly knows it would, all things considered, be best should be (as was but now observed) then it must be impossible for a being who has no defect of wisdom and goodness, to do otherwise than choose it should be; and that, for this very reason, because he is perfectly wise and good. And if it be agreeable to perfect wisdom and goodness for him to choose that it should be, and the ordering of all things supremely and perfectly belongs to him, it must be agreeable to infinite wisdom and goodness, to order that it should be. If the choice is good, the ordering and disposing things according to that choice must also be good. It can be no harm in one to whom it belongs "to do his will in the armies of heaven, and amongst the inhabitants of the earth," to execute a good volition. If his will be good, and the object of his will be, all things considered, good and best, then the choosing or willing it is not *willing evil* that good may come. And if so, then his ordering according to that will is not *doing evil,* that good may come.

2. 'Tis not of a *bad tendency,* for the supreme Being thus to order and permit that moral evil to be, which it is best should come to pass. For that it is of good tendency, is the very thing supposed in the point now in question. Christ's crucifixion, though a most horrid fact in them that perpetrated it, was of most glorious tendency as permitted and ordered of God.

3. Nor is there any need of supposing, it *proceeds from any evil disposition or aim:* for by the supposition, what is aimed at is good, and good is the actual issue, in the final result of things.

SECTION 10. CONCERNING SIN'S FIRST ENTRANCE
INTO THE WORLD

THE THINGS which have already been offered, may serve to obviate or clear many of the objections which might be raised concerning sin's first coming into the world; as though it would follow from the doctrine maintained, that God must be the author of the first sin, through his so disposing things, that it should necessarily follow from his permission, that the sinful act should be committed, etc. I need not therefore stand to repeat what has been said already, about such a necessity's not proving God to be the author of sin, in any ill sense, or in any such sense as to infringe any liberty of man, concerned in his moral agency, or capacity of blame, guilt and punishment.

But if it should nevertheless be said, supposing the case so, that God, when he had made man, might so order his circumstances, that from these circumstances, together with his withholding further assistance and divine influence, his sin would infallibly follow, why might not God as well have first made man with a fixed prevailing principle of sin in his heart?

I answer, 1. It was meet, if sin did come into existence, and appear in the world, it should arise from the imperfection which properly belongs to a creature, as such, and should appear so to do, that it might appear not to be from God as the efficient or fountain. But this could not have been, if man had been made at first with sin in his heart; nor unless the abiding principle and habit of sin were first introduced by an evil act of the creature. If sin had not arose from the imperfection of the creature, it would not have been so visible, that it did not arise from God, as the positive cause, and real source of it.—But it would require room that can't be here allowed, fully to consider all the difficulties which have been started, concerning the first entrance of sin into the world.

And therefore,

413

2. I would observe, that objections against the doctrine that has been laid down, in opposition to the Arminian notion of liberty, from these difficulties, are altogether impertinent; because no additional difficulty is incurred, by adhering to a scheme in this manner differing from theirs, and none would be removed or avoided, by agreeing with, and maintaining theirs. Nothing that the Arminians say, about the contingence, or self-determining power of man's will, can serve to explain with less difficulty, how the first sinful volition of mankind could take place, and man be justly charged with the blame of it. To say, the will was self-determined, or determined by free choice, in that sinful volition; which is to say, that the first sinful volition was determined by a foregoing sinful volition; is no solution of the difficulty. It is an odd way of solving difficulties, to advance greater, in order to it. To say, two and two makes nine; or, that a child begat his father, solves no difficulty: no more does it, to say, the first sinful act of choice was before the first sinful act of choice, and chose and determined it, and brought it to pass. Nor is it any better solution, to say, the first sinful volition chose, determined and produced itself; which is to say, it was before it was. Nor will it go any further towards helping us over the difficulty, to say, the first sinful volition arose accidentally, without any cause at all; any more than it will solve that difficult question, How the world could be made out of nothing? to say, it came into being out of nothing, without any cause; as has been already observed. And if we should allow that that could be, that the first evil volition should arise by perfect accident, without any cause, it would relieve no difficulty, about God's laying the blame of it to man. For how was man to blame for perfect accident, which had no cause, and which therefore, he (to be sure) was not the cause of, any more than if it came by some external cause? Such kind of solutions are no better, than if some person, going about to solve some of the strange mathematical paradoxes, about infinitely great and small quantities; as, that some infinitely great quantities are infinitely greater than some other infinitely great quantities; and also that some infinitely small quantities are infinitely less than others, which yet are infinitely little; in order to a solution, should say, that mankind have been under a mistake, in supposing a greater quantity to exceed a smaller; and that a hundred multiplied by ten, makes but a single unit.

SECTION 11. OF A SUPPOSED INCONSISTENCE OF THESE PRINCIPLES, WITH GOD'S MORAL CHARACTER

THE THINGS which have been already observed, may be sufficient to answer most of the objections, and silence the great exclamations of Arminians against the Calvinists, from the supposed inconsistence of Calvinistic principles with the moral perfections of God, as exercised in his government of mankind. The consistence of such a doctrine of necessity as has been maintained, with the fitness and reasonableness of God's commands, promises and threatenings, rewards and punishments, has been particularly considered: the cavils of our opponents, as though our doctrine of necessity made God the author of sin, have been answered; and also their objection against these principles, as inconsistent with God's sincerity, in his counsels, invitations and persuasions, has been already obviated, in what has been observed, respecting the consistence of what Calvinists suppose concerning the *secret* and *revealed* will of God: by that it appears, there is no repugnance in supposing it may be the secret will of God, that his ordination and permission of events should be such that it shall be a certain consequence, that a thing never will come to pass; which yet it is man's duty to do, and so God's *preceptive* will, that he should do; and this is the same thing as to say, God may sincerely command and require him to do it. And if he may be sincere in commanding him, he may for the same reason be sincere in counseling, inviting and using persuasions with him to do it. Counsels and invitations are manifestations of God's preceptive will, or of what God loves, and what is in itself, and as man's act, agreeable to his heart; and not of his disposing will, and what he chooses as a part of his own infinite scheme of things. It has been particularly shown (Pt. III, Sec. 4) that such a necessity as has been maintained, is not inconsistent with the propriety and fitness of divine commands; and for the same reason, not inconsistent with the sincerity of invitations and counsels, in the corollary at the end of that section. Yea, it hath been

415

shewn (Pt. III, Sec. 7, *Corol. 1*) that this objection of Arminians, concerning the sincerity and use of divine exhortations, invitations and counsels, is demonstrably against themselves.

Notwithstanding, I would further observe, that the difficulty of reconciling the sincerity of counsels, invitations and persuasions, with such an antecedent known fixedness of all events, as has been supposed, is not peculiar to this scheme, as distinguished from that of the generality of Arminians, which acknowledge the absolute foreknowledge of God: and therefore, it would be unreasonably brought as an objection against my differing from them. The main seeming difficulty in the case is this: that God in counseling, inviting and persuading, makes a shew of aiming at, seeking and using endeavors for the thing exhorted and persuaded to; whereas, 'tis impossible for any intelligent being truly to seek, or use endeavors for a thing, which he at the same time knows most perfectly will not come to pass; and that it is absurd to suppose, he makes the obtaining of a thing his end, in his calls and counsels, which he at the same time infallibly knows will not be obtained by these means. Now, if God knows this, in the utmost certainty and perfection, the way by which he comes by this knowledge makes no difference. If he knows it by the necessity which he sees in things, or by some other means; it alters not the case. But it is in effect allowed by Arminians themselves, that God's inviting and persuading men to do things, which he at the same time certainly knows will not be done, is no evidence of insincerity; because they allow, that God has a certain foreknowledge of all men's sinful actions and omissions. And as this is thus implicitly allowed by most Arminians, so all that pretend to own the Scriptures to be the Word of God, must be constrained to allow it. God commanded and counseled Pharaoh to let his people go, and used arguments and persuasions to induce him to it; he laid before him arguments taken from his infinite greatness and almighty power (Ex. 7:16) and forewarned him of the fatal consequences of his refusal, from time to time (Ch. 8:1, 2, 20, 21; Ch. 9:1–5, 13–17; and 10:3, 6). He commanded Moses, and the elders of Israel, to go and beseech Pharaoh to let the people go; and at the same time told 'em, he knew surely that he would not comply to it. Ex. 3:18, 19: "And thou shalt come, thou and the elders of Israel, unto the king of Egypt, and you shall say unto him; the Lord God of the Hebrews hath met with us; and now let us go, we beseech thee, three days' journey into the wilderness, that we may sacrifice unto the Lord our

God": and, "I am sure that the king of Egypt will not let you go." So
our blessed Saviour, the evening wherein he was betrayed, knew that
Peter would shamefully deny him, before the morning; for he declares it to him with asseverations, to shew the certainty of it; and
tells the disciples, that all of them should be offended because of him
that night (Matt. 26:31–35; John 13: 38; Luke 22:31–34; John 16:32).
And yet it was their duty to avoid these things; they were very sinful
things, which God had forbidden, and which it was their duty to
watch and pray against; and they were obliged to do so from the
counsels and *persuasions* Christ used with them, at that very time, so
to do (Matt. 26:41), "Watch and pray, that ye enter not into temptation." So that whatever difficulty there can be in this matter, it can
be no objection against any principles which have been maintained
in opposition to the principles of Arminians; nor does it any more
concern me to remove the difficulty, than it does them, or indeed all
that call themselves Christians, and acknowledge the divine authority
of the Scriptures. Nevertheless, this matter may possibly (God allowing) be more particularly and largely considered, in some future discourse, on the doctrine of predestination.

But I would here observe, that however the defenders of that notion of liberty of will, which I have opposed, exclaim against the
doctrine of Calvinists, as tending to bring men into doubts, concerning the moral perfections of God; it is their scheme, and not the
scheme of Calvinists, that indeed is justly chargeable with this. For
'tis one of the most fundamental points of their scheme of things,
that a freedom of will, consisting in self-determination, without all
necessity, is essential to *moral agency.* This is the same thing as to
say, that such a determination of the will without all necessity, must
be in all intelligent beings, in those things, wherein they are *moral
agents,* or in their *moral acts:* and from this it will follow, that God's
will is not necessarily determined, in anything he does, as a moral
agent, or in any of his *acts* that are of a *moral nature.* So that in all
things, wherein he acts *holily, justly* and *truly,* he don't act necessarily; or his will is not necessarily determined to act holily and
justly; because if it were necessarily determined, he would not be a
moral agent in thus acting: his will would be attended with necessity;
which they say is inconsistent with moral agency: "He can act no
otherwise; he is at no liberty in the affair; he is determined by unavoidable invincible necessity: therefore such agency is no moral
agency; yea, no agency at all, properly speaking: a necessary agent is

no agent: he being passive, and subject to necessity, what he does is no act of his, but an effect of a necessity prior to any act of his." This is agreeable to their manner of arguing. Now then what is become of all our proof of the moral perfections of God? How can we prove, that God certainly will in any one instance do that which is just and holy; seeing his will is determined in the matter by no necessity? We have no other way of proving that anything *certainly* will be, but only by the necessity of the event. Where we can see no necessity, but that the thing may be, or may not be, there we are unavoidably left at a loss. We have no other way properly and truly to demonstrate the moral perfections of God, but the way that Mr. Chubb proves them, in pp. 252, 261, 262, 263 of his *Tracts;* [1] viz. that God must necessarily perfectly know what is most worthy and valuable in itself, which in the nature of things is best and fittest to be done. And as this is most eligible in itself, he being omniscient, must see it to be so; and being both omniscient and self-sufficient, cannot have any temptation to reject it; and so must necessarily will that which is best. And thus, by this necessity of the determination of God's will to what is good and best, we demonstrably establish God's moral character.

Corol. From things which have been observed, it appears, that most of the arguments from Scripture, which Arminians make use of to support their scheme, are no other than *begging the question.* For in these their arguments they determine in the first place, that without such a freedom of will as they hold, men can't be proper moral agents, nor the subjects of command, counsel, persuasion, invitation, promises, threatenings, expostulations, rewards and punishments; and that without such a freedom 'tis to no purpose for men to take any care, or use any diligence, endeavors or means, in order to their avoiding sin, or becoming holy, escaping punishment or obtaining happiness: and having supposed these things, which are grand things in question in the debate, then they heap up scriptures containing commands, counsels, calls, warnings, persuasions, expostulations, promises and threatenings (as doubtless they may find enough such; the Bible is confessedly full of them, from the beginning to the end); and then they glory, how full the Scripture is on their side, how many more texts there are that evidently favor their scheme, than such as seem to favor the contrary. But let them first make manifest the things in question, which they suppose and take for granted,

1. [See Intro., Pt. 5, no. 5.]

and shew them to be consistent with themselves, and produce clear evidence of their truth; and they have gained their point, as all will confess, without bringing one scripture. For none denies, that there are commands, counsels, promises, threatenings, etc. in the Bible. But unless they do these things, their multiplying such texts of Scripture is insignificant and vain.

It may further be observed, that such scriptures as they bring, are really against them, and not for them. As it has been demonstrated, that 'tis their scheme, and not ours, that is inconsistent with the use of motives and persuasives, or any moral means whatsoever, to induce men to the practice of virtue, or abstaining from wickedness: their principles, and not ours, are repugnant to moral agency, and inconsistent with moral government, with law or precept, with the nature of virtue or vice, reward or punishment, and with everything whatsoever of a moral nature, either on the part of the moral Governor, or in the state, actions, or conduct of the subject.

SECTION 12. OF A SUPPOSED TENDENCY OF THESE PRINCIPLES TO ATHEISM AND LICENTIOUSNESS

IF ANY OBJECT against what has been maintained, that it tends to atheism; I know not on what grounds such an objection can be raised, unless it be that some atheists have held a doctrine of necessity which they suppose to be like this. But if it be so, I am persuaded the Arminians would not look upon it just, that their notion of freedom and contingence should be charged with a tendency to all the errors that ever any embraced, who have held such opinions. The Stoic philosophers, whom the Calvinists are charged with agreeing with, were no atheists, but the greatest theists, and nearest akin to Christians in their opinions concerning the unity and the perfections of the Godhead, of all the heathen philosophers. And Epicurus, that chief father of atheism, maintained no such doctrine of necessity, but was the greatest maintainer of contingence.

The doctrine of necessity, which supposes a necessary connection of all events, on some antecedent ground and reason of their existence, is the only medium we have to prove the being of God. And the contrary doctrine of contingence, even as maintained by Arminians (which certainly implies or infers, that events may come into existence, or begin to be, without dependence on anything foregoing, as their cause, ground or reason) takes away all proof of the being of God; which proof is summarily expressed by the Apostle, in Rom. 1:20. And this is a tendency to atheism with a witness. So that indeed it is the doctrine of Arminians, and not of the Calvinists, that is justly charged with a tendency to atheism; it being built on a foundation that is the utter subversion of every demonstrative argument for the proof of a deity; as has been shewn (Pt. II, Sec. 3).

And whereas it has often been said, that the Calvinistic doctrine of necessity, saps the foundations of all religion and virtue, and tends to the greatest licentiousness of practice: this objection is built on the pretense, that our doctrine renders vain all means and endeavors, in order to be virtuous and religious. Which pretense has been already particularly considered in the 5th section of this part; where it has been demonstrated, that this doctrine has no such tendency; but that such a tendency is truly to be charged on the contrary doctrine: inasmuch as the notion of contingence, which their doctrine implies, in its certain consequences, overthrows all connection, in every degree, between endeavor and event, means and end.

And besides, if many other things which have been observed to belong to the Arminian doctrine, or to be plain consequences of it, be considered, there will appear just reason to suppose that it is *that,* which must rather tend to licentiousness. Their doctrine excuses all evil inclinations, which men find to be natural; because in such inclinations, they are not self-determined, as such inclinations are not owing to any choice or determination of their own wills. Which leads men wholly to justify themselves in all their wicked actions, so far as natural inclination has had a hand in determining their wills, to the commission of 'em. Yea, these notions which suppose moral necessity and inability to be inconsistent with blame or moral obligation, will directly lead men to justify the vilest acts and practices, from the strength of their wicked inclinations of all sorts; strong inclinations inducing a moral necessity; yea, to excuse every degree of evil inclination, so far as this has evidently prevailed, and been the thing which has determined their wills: because, so far as antecedent inclination determined the will, so far the will was without liberty of indifference and self-determination. Which at last will come to this, that men will justify themselves in all the wickedness they commit. It has been observed already, that this scheme of things does exceedingly diminish the guilt of sin, and the difference between the greatest and smallest offences: [1] and if it be pursued in its real consequences, it leaves room for no such thing, as either virtue or vice, blame or praise in the world.[2] And then again, how naturally does this notion of the sovereign self-determining power of the will, in all things, virtuous or vicious, and whatsoever deserves either reward or punishment, tend to encourage men to put off the work of religion and virtue, and turning from sin to God; it being that which they have a sovereign power to determine themselves to, just when they please; or if not, they are wholly excusable in going on in sin, because of their inability to do any other.

1. Part III, Sec. 6.
2. Pt. III, Secs. 6, 7; Pt. IV, Sec. 1; Pt. III, Sec. 3, *corol.* 1 after the first Head.

If it should be said, that the tendency of this doctrine of necessity, to licentiousness, appears by the improvement many at this day actually make of it, to justify themselves in their dissolute courses; I will not deny that some men do unreasonably abuse this doctrine, as they do many other things which are true and excellent in their own nature: but I deny that this proves, the doctrine itself has any tendency to licentiousness. I think, the tendency of doctrines, by what now appears in the world, and in our nation in particular, may much more justly be argued from the general effect which has been seen to attend the prevailing of the principles of Arminians, and the contrary principles; as both have had their turn of general prevalence in our nation. If it be indeed, as is pretended, that Calvinistic doctrines undermine the very foundation of all religion and morality, and enervate and disannul all rational motives, to holy and virtuous practice; and that the contrary doctrines give the inducements to virtue and goodness their proper force, and exhibit religion in a rational light, tending to recommend it to the reason of mankind, and enforce it in a manner that is agreeable to their natural notions of things: I say, if it be thus, 'tis remarkable, that virtue and religious practice should prevail most, when the former doctrines, so inconsistent with it, prevailed almost universally: and that ever since the latter doctrines, so happily agreeing with it, and of so proper and excellent a tendency to promote it, have been gradually prevailing, vice, profaneness, luxury and wickedness of all sorts, and contempt of all religion, and of every kind of seriousness and strictness of conversation, should proportionably prevail; and that these things should thus accompany one another, and rise and prevail one with another, now for a whole age together. 'Tis remarkable, that this happy remedy (discovered by the free inquiries, and superior sense and wisdom of this age) against the pernicious effects of Calvinism, so inconsistent with religion, and tending so much to banish all virtue from the earth, should on so long a trial, be attended with no good effect; but that the consequence should be the reverse of amendment; that in proportion, as the remedy takes place, and is thoroughly applied, so the disease should prevail; and the very same dismal effect take place, to the highest degree, which Calvinistic doctrines are supposed to have so great a tendency to; even the banishing of religion and virtue, and the prevailing of unbounded licentiousness of manners. If these things are truly so, they are very remarkable, and matter of very curious speculation!

SECTION 13. CONCERNING THAT OBJECTION AGAINST
THE REASONING, BY WHICH THE
CALVINISTIC DOCTRINE IS SUPPORTED,
THAT IT IS METAPHYSICAL
AND ABSTRUSE

IT HAS OFTEN been objected against the defenders of Calvinistic principles, that in their reasonings, they run into nice scholastic distinctions, and abstruse metaphysical subtleties, and set these in opposition to common sense. And 'tis possible, that after the former manner it may be alleged against the reasoning by which I have endeavored to confute the Arminian scheme of liberty and moral agency, that it is very abstracted and metaphysical. Concerning this, I would observe the following things.

I. If that be made an objection against the foregoing reasoning, that it is *metaphysical,* or may properly be reduced to the science of metaphysics, it is a very impertinent objection; whether it be so or no, is not worthy of any dispute or controversy. If the reasoning be good, 'tis as frivolous to inquire what science it is properly reduced to, as what language it is delivered in: and for a man to go about to confute the arguments of his opponent, by telling him, his arguments are "metaphysical" would be as weak as to tell him, his arguments could not be substantial, because they were written in French or Latin. The question is not, whether what is said be metaphysics, physics, logic, or mathematics, Latin, French, English, or Mohawk? [1] but, whether the reasoning be good, and the arguments truly conclusive? The foregoing arguments are no more metaphysical, than those which we use against the Papists, to disprove their doctrine of transubstantiation; alleging, it is inconsistent with the notion of corporeal identity, that it should be in ten thousand places at the same time. 'Tis by metaphysical arguments only we are able to prove, that the rational soul is not corporeal; that lead or sand can't think; that

1. [One of the tribes of Indians to which JE was missionary at Stockbridge while writing the *Inquiry*.]

thoughts are not square or round, or don't weigh a pound. The arguments by which we prove the being of God, if handled closely and distinctly, so as to shew their clear and demonstrative evidence, must be metaphysically treated. 'Tis by metaphysics only, that we can demonstrate, that God is not limited to a place, or is not mutable; that he is not ignorant, or forgetful; that it is impossible for him to lie, or be unjust; and that there is one God only, and not hundreds or thousands. And indeed we have no strict demonstration of anything, excepting mathematical truths, but by metaphysics. We can have no proof, that is properly demonstrative, of any one proposition, relating to the being and nature of God, his creation of the world, the dependence of all things on him, the nature of bodies or spirits, the nature of our own souls, or any of the great truths of morality and natural religion, but what is metaphysical. I am willing, my arguments should be brought to the test of the strictest and justest reason, and that a clear, distinct and determinate meaning of the terms I use, should be insisted on; but let not the whole be rejected, as if all were confuted, by fixing on it the epithet "metaphysical."

II. If the reasoning which has been made use of, be in some sense metaphysical, it will not follow, that therefore it must needs be abstruse, unintelligible, and akin to the jargon of the schools. I humbly conceive, the foregoing reasoning, at least as to those things which are most material belonging to it, depends on no abstruse definitions or distinctions, or terms without a meaning, or of very ambiguous and undetermined signification, or any points of such abstraction and subtlety, as tend to involve the attentive understanding in clouds and darkness. There is no high degree of refinement and abstruse speculation, in determining, that a thing is not before it is, and so can't be the cause of itself; or that the first act of free choice, has not another act of free choice going before that, to excite or direct it; or in determining, that no choice is made, while the mind remains in a state of absolute indifference; that preference and equilibrium never coexist; and that therefore no choice is made in a state of liberty, consisting in indifference: and that so far as the will is determined by motives, exhibited and operating previous to the act of the will, so far it is not determined by the act of the will itself; that nothing can begin to be, which before was not, without a cause, or some antecedent ground or reason, why it then begins to be; that effects depend on their causes, and are connected with them; that virtue is not the worse, nor sin the better, for the strength of inclination, with which it is practiced, and the difficulty which thence arises of doing otherwise; that when it is already infallibly known, that a thing will be, it is not a thing contingent whether it will ever be or no; or that it can be truly said, notwithstanding, that it is not necessary it should be, but it either may be, or may not be. And the like might be observed of many other things which belong to the foregoing reasoning.

If any shall still stand to it, that the foregoing reasoning is nothing but metaphysical sophistry; and that it must be so, that the seeming force of the arguments all depends on some fallacy and wile that is hid in the obscurity, which always attends a great degree of metaphysical abstraction and refinement; and shall be ready to say, "Here is indeed something that tends to confound the mind, but not to satisfy it: for who can ever be truly satisfied in it, that men are fitly blamed or commended, punished or rewarded, for those volitions which are not from themselves, and of whose existence they are not the causes. Men may refine, as much as they please, and advance their abstract notions, and make out a thousand seeming contradictions, to puzzle our understandings; yet there can be no satisfaction in such doctrine as this: the natural sense of the mind of man will always resist it." [2] I humbly conceive, that such an objector, if he has capac-

---

2. A certain noted author, of the present age, says, the arguments for *necessity* are nothing but "quibbling, or logomachy, using words without a meaning, or begging the question." I don't know what kind of necessity any authors he may have reference to, are advocates for; or whether they have managed their arguments well, or ill. As to the arguments I have made use of, if they are "quibbles," they may be shewn to be so: such knots are capable of being untied, and the trick and cheat may be detected and plainly laid open. If this be fairly done, with respect to the grounds and reasons I have relied upon, I shall have just occasion for the future to be silent, if not to be ashamed of my argumentations. I am willing, my proofs should be thoroughly examined; and if there be nothing but "begging the question," or mere "logomachy," or dispute of words, let it be made manifest, and shewn how the seeming strength of the argument depends on my "using words without a meaning," or arises from the ambiguity of terms, or my making use of words in an indeterminate and unsteady manner; and that the weight of my reasons rest mainly on such a foundation; and then, I shall either be ready to retract what I have urged, and thank the man that has done the kind part, or shall be justly exposed for my obstinacy.

The same author is abundant in appealing, in this affair, from what he calls "logomachy and sophistry," to "experience." A person can experience only what passes in his own mind. But yet, as we may well suppose, that all men have the same human faculties; so a man may well argue from his own experience to that of others, in things that shew the nature of those faculties, and the manner of their

ity and humility and calmness of spirit, sufficient impartially and thoroughly to examine himself, will find that he knows not really what he would be at; and that indeed his difficulty is nothing but a mere prejudice, from an inadvertent customary use of words, in a meaning that is not clearly understood, nor carefully reflected upon. Let the objector reflect again, if he has candor and patience enough, and don't scorn to be at the trouble of close attention in the affair. He would have a man's volition be *from himself*. Let it be *from himself,* most primarily and originally of any way conceivable; that is, from his own choice: how will that help the matter, as to his being justly blamed or praised, unless that choice itself be blame or praiseworthy? And how is the choice itself (an ill choice, for instance)

---

operation. But then one has as good right to allege his experience, as another. As to my own experience, I find, that in innumerable things I can do as I will; that the motions of my body, in many respects, instantaneously follow the acts of my will concerning those motions; and that my will has some command of my thoughts; and that the acts of my will are my own, i.e. that they are acts of my will, the volitions of my own mind; or in other words, that what I will, I will. Which, I presume, is the sum of what others experience in this affair. But as to finding by experience, that my will is originally determined by itself; or that my will first choosing what volition there shall be, the chosen volition accordingly follows; and that this is the first rise of the determination of my will in any affair; or that any volition arises in my mind contingently; I declare, I know nothing in myself, by experience, of this nature; and nothing that ever I experienced, carries the least appearance or shadow of any such thing, or gives me any more reason to suppose or suspect any such thing, than to suppose that my volitions existed twenty years before they existed. 'Tis true, I find myself possessed of my volitions before I can see the effectual power of any cause to produce them (for the power and efficacy of the cause is not seen but by the effect) and this, for ought I know, may make some imagine, that volition has no cause, or that it produces itself. But I have no more reason from hence to determine any such thing, than I have to determine that I gave myself my own being, or that I came into being accidentally without a cause, because I first found myself possessed of being, before I had knowledge of a cause of my being.

[From the opening words of this footnote, referring to "a certain noted author, of the present age" (cf. the words JE used when first citing George Turnbull: "a late noted writer, of our nation," Pt. IV, Sec. 9, note 6, above), and from the fact that in the Conclusion, note 1, below, JE says that he has had occasion several times to mention this "writer of the present age," we may conclude that the "author" is the same Turnbull. This identification is confirmed by Turnbull's frequent use of the expressions, "logomachy," "perplexing intricacies," "subtle sophistical resorts," "odd quibbles," "studied verbal labyrinths," and by his appeal to the facts of experience to silence his opponents (*The Principles of Moral and Christian Philosophy,* 2, 39, 198–200, 202, 206, and the table of contents at this place).]

blameworthy, according to these principles, unless that be from himself too, in the same manner; that is, from his own choice? But the original and first determining choice in the affair is not from his choice: his choice is not the cause of it. And if it be from himself some other way, and not from his choice, surely that will not help the matter: if it ben't from himself of choice, then it is not from himself voluntarily; and if so, he is surely no more to blame, than if it were not from himself at all. It is a vanity, to pretend it is a sufficient answer to this, to say, that it is nothing but metaphysical refinement and subtlety, and so attended with obscurity and uncertainty.

If it be the natural sense of our minds, that what is blameworthy in a man must be from himself, then it doubtless is also, that it must be from something *bad* in himself, a bad *choice,* or bad *disposition.* But then our natural sense is, that this bad choice or disposition is evil *in itself,* and the man blameworthy for it, on *its own account,* without taking into our notion of its blameworthiness, another bad choice, or disposition going before this, from whence this arises; for that is a ridiculous absurdity, running us into an immediate contradiction, which our natural sense of blameworthiness has nothing to do with, and never comes into the mind, nor is supposed in the judgment we naturally make of the affair. As was demonstrated before, natural sense don't place the moral evil of volitions and dispositions in the cause of them, but the nature of them. An evil thing's being "from" a man, or from something antecedent in him,[3] is not essential to the original notion we have of blameworthiness: but 'tis its being the choice of the heart; as appears by this, that if a thing be "from" us, and not from our choice, it has not the nature of blameworthiness or ill desert, according to our natural sense. When a thing is *from* a man, in that sense, that it is from his will or choice, he is to blame for it, because his will is *in it:* so far as the will is *in it,* blame is *in it,* and no further. Neither do we go any further in our notion of blame, to inquire whether the bad will be "from" a bad will: there is no consideration of the original of that bad will; because

3. [Here JE plays on the word "from." In the first meaning, FROM (which JE thus capitalizes in the first edition, and which we today would place in quotation marks to indicate a flavor of ironic rejection), the word means "without" or "from outside" the man, "from something antecedent to and not from the present act of choice itself," that is, not from some property or act of the soul. The second meaning, which is JE's own, is indicated when the word *from* is in italics, and here the emphasis is upon the act being from *within* will or choice, the will being *in* it, we *in* the choices and they *our* properties.]

according to our natural apprehension, blame *originally consists in it.* Therefore a thing's being "from" a man, is a secondary consideration, in the notion of blame or ill-desert. Because those things in our *external* actions, are most properly said to be *from* us, which are *from* our choice; and no other *external* actions but those that are from us in this sense, have the nature of blame; and they indeed, not so properly because they are *from* us, as because we are *in them,* i.e. our wills are in them; not so much because they are from some *property* of ours, as because they are our *properties.*

However, all these external actions being truly *from us,* as their cause; and we being so used, in ordinary speech, and in the common affairs of life, to speak of men's actions and conduct that we see, and that affect human society, as deserving ill or well, as worthy of blame or praise; hence it is come to pass, that philosophers have incautiously taken all their measures of good and evil, praise and blame, from the dictates of common sense, about these *overt acts* of men; to the running of everything into the most lamentable and dreadful confusion. And therefore I observe,

III. 'Tis so far from being true (whatever may be pretended) that the proof of the doctrine which has been maintained, depends on certain abstruse, unintelligible, metaphysical terms and notions; and that the Arminian scheme, without needing such clouds and darkness, for its defense, is supported by the plain dictates of common sense; that the very reverse is most certainly true, and that to a great degree. 'Tis fact, that they, and not we, have confounded things with metaphysical, unintelligible notions and phrases, and have drawn them from the light of plain truth, into the gross darkness of abstruse metaphysical propositions, and words without a meaning. Their pretended demonstrations depend very much on such unintelligible, metaphysical phrases, as "self-determination" and "sovereignty of the will"; and the metaphysical sense they put on such terms, as "necessary," "contingency," "action," "agency," etc. quite diverse from their meaning as used in common speech; and which, as they use them, are without any consistent meaning, or any manner of distinct consistent ideas; as far from it as any of the abstruse terms and perplexed phrases of the peripatetic philosophers, or the most unintelligible jargon of the schools, or the cant of the wildest fanatics. Yea, we may be bold to say, these metaphysical terms, on which they build so much, are what they use without knowing what they mean themselves; they are pure metaphysical sounds, without any ideas whatsoever in their minds to answer them; inasmuch as it has been demonstrated, that there cannot be any notion in the mind consistent with these expressions, as they pretend to explain them; because their explanations destroy themselves. No such notions as imply self-contradiction, and self-abolition, and this a great many ways, can subsist in the mind; as there can be no idea of a whole which is less than any of its parts, or of solid extension without dimensions, or of an effect which is before its cause. Arminians improve these terms, as terms of art, and in their metaphysical meaning, to advance and establish those things which are contrary to common sense, in a high degree. Thus, instead of the plain vulgar notion of liberty, which all mankind, in every part of the face of the earth, and in all ages, have; consisting in opportunity to do as one pleases; they have introduced a new strange liberty, consisting in indifference, contingence, and self-determination; by which they involve themselves and others in great obscurity, and manifold gross inconsistence. So, instead of placing virtue and vice, as common sense places them very much, in fixed bias and inclination, and greater virtue and vice in stronger and more established inclination; these, through their refinings and abstruse notions, suppose a liberty consisting in indifference, to be essential to all virtue and vice. So they have reasoned themselves, not by metaphysical distinctions, but metaphysical confusion, into many principles about moral agency, blame, praise, reward and punishment, which are, as has been shewn, exceeding contrary to the common sense of mankind; and perhaps to their own sense, which governs them in common life.

THE CONCLUSION

WHETHER the things which have been alleged, are liable to any tolerable answer in the ways of calm, intelligible and strict reasoning, I must leave others to judge: but I am sensible they are liable to one sort of answer. 'Tis not unlikely, that some who value themselves on the supposed rational and generous principles of the modern fashionable divinity, will have their indignation and disdain raised at the sight of this discourse, and on perceiving what things are pretended to be proved in it. And if they think it worthy of being read, or of so much notice as to say much about it, they may probably renew the usual exclamations, with additional vehemence and contempt, about the "fate" of the heathen, "Hobbes' necessity," and "making men mere machines"; accumulating the terrible epithets of "fatal," "unfrustrable," "inevitable," "irresistible," etc. and it may be, with the addition of "horrid" and "blasphemous"; and perhaps much skill may be used to set forth things which have been said, in colors which shall be shocking to the imaginations, and moving to the passions of those who have either too little capacity, or too much confidence of the opinions they have imbibed, and contempt of the contrary, to try the matter by any serious and circumspect examination.[1] Or difficulties may be started and insisted on which don't be-

1. A writer of the present age, whom I have several times had occasion to mention, speaks once and again of those who hold the doctrine of *necessity*, as scarcely worthy of the name of "philosophers." I don't know, whether he has respect to any particular notion of necessity, that some may have maintained; and if so, what doctrine of necessity it is that he means. Whether I am worthy of the name of a philosopher, or not, would be a question little to the present purpose. If any, and ever so many, should deny it, I should not think it worth the while to enter into a dispute on that question; though at the same time I might expect, some better answer should be given to the arguments brought for the truth of the doctrine I maintain; and I might further reasonably desire, that it might be considered, whether it don't become those who are *truly worthy* of the name of philosophers, to be sensible, that there is a difference between *argument* and *contempt;* yea, and a difference between the contemptibleness of the *person* that

long to the controversy; because, let them be more or less real, and hard to be resolved, they are not what are owing to anything distinguishing of this scheme from that of the Arminians, and would not be removed nor diminished by renouncing the former, and adhering to the latter. Or some particular things may be picked out, which they may think will sound harshest in the ears of the generality; and these may be glossed and descanted on, with tart and contemptuous words; and from thence, the whole treated with triumph and insult.

'Tis easy to see how the decision of most of the points in controversy, between Calvinists and Arminians, depends on the determination of this grand article concerning *the freedom of the will requisite to moral agency;* and that by clearing and establishing the Calvinistic doctrine in this point, the chief arguments are obviated, by which Arminian doctrines in general are supported, and the contrary doctrines demonstratively confirmed. Hereby it becomes manifest, that God's moral government over mankind, his treating them as moral agents, making them the objects of his commands, counsels, calls, warnings, expostulations, promises, threatenings, rewards and punishments, is not inconsistent with a determining disposal of all events, of every kind, throughout the universe, in his providence; either by positive efficiency, or permission. Indeed such an *universal, determining providence,* infers some kind of necessity of all events; such a necessity as implies an infallible previous fixedness of the futurity of the event: but no other necessity of moral events, or volitions of intelligent agents, is needful in order to this, than *moral* necessity; which does as much ascertain the futurity of the event, as any other necessity. But, as has been demonstrated, such a necessity is not at all repugnant to moral agency, and the reasonable use of commands, calls, rewards, punishments, etc. Yea, not only are objections of this kind against the doctrine of an universal determining providence, removed by what has been said; but the truth of such a doctrine is demonstrated. As it has been demonstrated, that the fu-

---

argues, and the inconclusiveness of the *arguments* he offers. [George Turnbull affirms that the error of that great genius Leibniz "consists in his saying *most unphilosophically,* that God could not do otherwise than he hath done"; he urges that "we keep to experience, and use words in a determinate, clear sense, *as philosophers ought to do";* and he asserts that the inward feeling of freedom "is only called in question by some *pretended philosophers"* (*Christian Philosophy,* pp. 38, 39, 198; italics mine).]

turity of all future events is established by previous necessity, either natural or moral; so 'tis manifest, that the sovereign Creator and Disposer of the world has ordered this necessity, by ordering his own conduct, either in designedly acting, or forbearing to act. For, as the being of the world is from God, so the circumstances in which it had its being at first, both negative and positive, must be ordered by him, in one of these ways; and all the necessary consequences of these circumstances, must be ordered by him. And God's active and positive interpositions, after the world was created, and the consequences of these interpositions; also every instance of his forbearing to interpose, and the sure consequences of this forbearance, must all be determined according to his pleasure. And therefore every event which is the consequence of anything whatsoever, or that is connected with any foregoing thing or circumstance, either positive or negative, as the ground or reason of its existence, must be ordered of God; either by a designed efficiency and interposition, or a designed forbearing to operate or interpose. But, as has been proved, all events whatsoever are necessarily connected with something foregoing, either positive or negative, which is the ground of its existence. It follows therefore, that the whole series of events is thus connected with something in the state of things, either positive or negative, which is original in the series; i.e. something which is connected with nothing preceding that, but God's own immediate conduct, either his acting or forbearing to act. From whence it follows, that as God designedly orders his own conduct, and its connected consequences, it must necessarily be, that he designedly orders all things.

The things which have been said, obviate some of the chief objections of Arminians against the Calvinistic doctrine of the *total depravity and corruption of man's nature,* whereby his heart is wholly under the power of sin, and he is utterly unable, without the interposition of sovereign grace, savingly to love God, believe in Christ, or do anything that is truly good and acceptable in God's sight. For the main objection against this doctrine is, that it is inconsistent with the freedom of man's will, consisting in indifference and self-determining power; because it supposes man to be under a necessity of sinning, and that God requires things of him, in order to his avoiding eternal damnation, which he is unable to do; and that this doctrine is wholly inconsistent with the sincerity of counsels, invitations, etc. Now this doctrine supposes *no other necessity* of sinning, than a moral necessity; which, as has been shewn, don't at all excuse sin;

and supposes *no other inability* to obey any command, or perform any duty, even the most spiritual and exalted, but a moral inability, which, as has been proved, don't excuse persons in the nonperformance of any good thing, or make 'em not to be the proper objects of commands, counsels and invitations. And moreover, it has been shewn, that there is not, and never can be, either in existence, or so much as in idea, any such freedom of will, consisting in indifference and self-determination, for the sake of which, this doctrine of original sin is cast out; and that no such freedom is necessary, in order to the nature of sin, and a just desert of punishment.

The things which have been observed, do also take off the main objections of Arminians against the doctrine of *efficacious grace;* and at the same time, prove the grace of God in a sinner's conversion (if there be any grace or divine influence in the affair) to be efficacious, yea, and *irresistible* too, if by irresistible is meant, that which is attended with a moral necessity, which it is impossible should ever be violated by any resistance. The main objection of Arminians against this doctrine is, that it is inconsistent with their self-determining freedom of will; and that it is repugnant to the nature of virtue, that it should be wrought in the heart by the determining efficacy and power of another, instead of its being owing to a self-moving power; that in that case, the good which is wrought, would not be *our* virtue, but rather *God's* virtue; because it is not the person in whom it is wrought, that is the determining author of it, but God that wrought it in him. But the things which are the foundation of these objections, have been considered; and it has been demonstrated, that the liberty of moral agents does not consist in self-determining power; and that there is no need of any such liberty, in order to the nature of virtue; nor does it at all hinder, but that the state or act of the will may be the virtue of the subject, though it be not from self-determination, but the determination of an extrinsic cause; even so as to cause the event to be morally necessary to the subject of it. And as it has been proved, that nothing in the state or acts of the will of man is contingent; but that on the contrary, every event of this kind is necessary, by a moral necessity; and has also been now demonstrated, that the doctrine of an universal determining providence, follows from that doctrine of necessity, which was proved before: and so, that God does decisively, in his providence, order all the volitions of moral agents, either by positive influence or permission: and it being allowed on all hands, that what God does in the affair of man's virtuous volitions, whether it be more or less, is by some positive influence, and not by mere permission, as in the affair of a sinful volition: if we put these things together, it will follow, that God's assistance or influence, must be determining and decisive, or must be attended with a moral necessity of the event; and so, that God gives virtue, holiness and conversion to sinners, by an influence which determines the effect, in such a manner, that the effect will infallibly follow by a moral necessity; which is what Calvinists mean by efficacious and irresistible grace.

The things which have been said, do likewise answer the chief objections against the doctrine of God's *universal* and *absolute decree*, and afford infallible proof of that doctrine; and of the doctrine of *absolute, eternal, personal election* in particular. The main objections against these doctrines are, that they infer a necessity of the volitions of moral agents, and of the future moral state and acts of men; and so are not consistent with those eternal rewards and punishments, which are connected with conversion and impenitence; nor can be made to agree with the reasonableness and sincerity of the precepts, calls, counsels, warnings and expostulations of the Word of God; or with the various methods and means of grace, which God uses with sinners, to bring 'em to repentance; and the whole of that moral government, which God exercises towards mankind: and that they infer an inconsistence between the *secret* and *revealed will* of God; and make God the author of sin. But all these things have been obviated in the preceding discourse. And the certain truth of these doctrines, concerning God's eternal purposes, will follow from what was just now observed concerning God's universal providence; how it infallibly follows from what has been proved, that God orders all events, and the volitions of moral agents amongst others, by such a decisive disposal, that the events are infallibly connected with his disposal. For if God disposes all events, so that the infallible existence of the events is decided by his providence, then he doubtless thus orders and decides things *knowingly,* and *on design.* God don't do what he does, nor order what he orders, accidentally and unawares; either *without,* or *beside* his intention. And if there be a foregoing *design* of doing and ordering as he does, this is the same with a purpose or *decree.* And as it has been shewn, that nothing is new to God, in any respect, but all things are perfectly and equally in his view from eternity; hence it will follow, that his designs or purposes are not things formed anew, founded on any new views or appearances, but are all eternal purposes. And as it has been now shewn, how the doctrine of determining efficacious grace certainly follows from things proved in the foregoing discourse; hence will necessarily follow the doctrine of particular, eternal, absolute election. For if men are made true saints, no otherwise than as God makes 'em so, and distinguishes 'em from others, by an efficacious power and influence of his, that decides and fixes the event; and God thus makes some saints, and not others, on design or purpose, and (as has been now observed) no designs of God are new; it follows, that God thus distinguished from others, all that ever become true saints, by his eternal design or decree. I might also shew, how God's certain foreknowledge must suppose an absolute decree, and how such a decree can be proved to a demonstration from it: but that this discourse mayn't be lengthened out too much, that must be omitted for the present.

From these things it will inevitably follow, that however Christ in some sense may be said to *die for all,* and to redeem all visible Christians, yea, the whole world by his death; yet there must be something *particular* in the design of his death, with respect to such as he intended should actually be saved thereby. As appears by what has been now shewn, God has the actual salvation or redemption of a certain number in his proper absolute design, and of a certain number only; and therefore such a design only can be prosecuted in anything God does, in order to the salvation of men. God pursues a proper design of the salvation of the elect in giving Christ to die, and prosecutes such a design with respect to no other, most strictly speaking; for 'tis impossible, that God should prosecute any other design than only such as he has: he certainly don't, in the highest propriety and strictness of speech, pursue a design that he has not. And indeed such a particularity and limitation of redemption will as infallibly follow from the doctrine of God's foreknowledge, as from that of the decree. For 'tis as impossible, in strictness of speech, that God should prosecute a design or aim at a thing, which he at the same time most perfectly knows will not be accomplished, as that he should use endeavors for that which is beside his decree.

By the things which have been proved, are obviated some of the main objections against the doctrine of the infallible and necessary *perseverance* of saints, and some of the main foundations of this doctrine are established. The main prejudices of Arminians against this doctrine seem to be these; they suppose such a necessary, infallible perseverance to be repugnant to the freedom of the will; that it must be owing to man's own self-determining power, that he *first becomes* virtuous and holy; and so in like manner, it must be left a thing contingent, to be determined by the same freedom of will, whether he will *persevere* in virtue and holiness; and that otherwise his continuing steadfast in faith and obedience would not be his virtue, or at all praiseworthy and rewardable; nor could his perseverance be properly the matter of divine commands, counsels and promises, nor his apostasy be properly threatened, and men warned against it. Whereas we find all these things in Scripture: there we find steadfastness and perseverance in true Christianity, represented as the virtue of the saints, spoken of as praiseworthy in them, and glorious rewards promised to it; and also find, that God makes it the subject of his commands, counsels and promises; and the contrary, of threatenings and warnings. But the foundation of these objections has been removed, in its being shewn that moral necessity and infallible certainty of events is not inconsistent with these things; and that, as to freedom of will lying in the power of the will to determine itself, there neither is any such thing, nor any need of it, in order to virtue, reward, commands, counsels, etc.

And as the doctrines of efficacious grace and absolute election do certainly follow from things which have been proved in the preceding discourse; so some of the main foundations of the doctrine of perseverance are thereby established. If the beginning of true faith and holiness, and a man's becoming a true saint at first, don't depend on the self-determining power of the will, but on the determining efficacious grace of God; it may well be argued, that it is so also with respect to men's being continued saints, or persevering in faith and holiness. The conversion of a sinner being not owing to a man's self-determination, but to God's determination, and eternal election, which is absolute, and depending on the sovereign will of God, and not on the free will of man; as is evident from what has been said: and it being very evident from the Scriptures, that the eternal election which there is of saints to faith and holiness, is also an election of them to eternal salvation; hence their appointment to salvation must also be absolute, and not depending on their contingent, self-determining will. From all which it follows, that it is absolutely fixed in God's decree, that all true saints shall persevere to actual eternal salvation.

But I must leave all these things to the consideration of the fair and impartial reader; and when he has maturely weighed them, I would propose it to his consideration, whether many of the first Reformers, and others that succeeded them, whom God in their day made the chief pillars of his church, and greatest instruments of their deliverance from error and darkness, and of the support of the cause of piety among them, have not been injured, in the contempt with which they have been treated by many late writers, for their teaching and maintaining such doctrines as are commonly called Calvinistic. Indeed some of these new writers, at the same time that they have represented the doctrines of these ancient and eminent divines, as in the highest degree ridiculous, and contrary to common sense, in an ostentation of a very generous charity, have allowed that they were honest well-meaning men: yea, it may be some of them, as though it were in great condescension and compassion to them, have allowed that they did pretty well for the day which they lived in, and considering the great disadvantages they labored under: when at the same time, their manner of speaking has naturally and plainly suggested to the minds of their readers, that they were persons, who through the lowness of their genius, and greatness of the bigotry, with which their minds were shackled, and thoughts confined, living in the gloomy caves of superstition, fondly embraced, and demurely and zealously taught the most absurd, silly and monstrous opinions, worthy of the greatest contempt of gentlemen possessed of that noble and generous freedom of thought, which happily prevails in this age of light and inquiry. When indeed such is the case, that we might, if so disposed, speak as big words as they, and on far better grounds. And really all the Arminians on earth might be challenged without arrogance or vanity, to make these principles of theirs wherein they mainly differ from their fathers, whom they so much despise, consistent with common sense; yea, and perhaps to produce any doctrine ever embraced by the blindest bigot of the church of Rome, or the most ignorant Mussulman, or extravagant enthusiast, that might be reduced to more, and more demonstrable inconsistencies, and repugnancies to common sense, and to themselves; though their inconsistencies indeed may not lie so deep, or be so artfully veiled by a deceitful ambiguity of words, and an indeterminate signification of phrases. I will not deny, that these gentlemen, many of them, are men of great abilities, and have been helped to higher attainments in philosophy, than those ancient divines, and have done great service to the church of God in some respects: but I humbly conceive, that their differing from their fathers with such magisterial assurance, in these points in divinity, must be owing to some other cause than superior wisdom.

It may also be worthy of consideration, whether the great alteration which has been made in the state of things in our nation, and some other parts of the Protestant world, in this and the past age, by the exploding so generally Calvinistic doctrines, that is so often spoken of as worthy to be greatly rejoiced in by the friends of truth, learning and virtue, as an instance of the great increase of light in the Christian Church; I say, it may be worthy to be considered, whether this be indeed a happy change, owing to any such cause as an increase of true knowledge and understanding in things of religion; or whether there is not reason to fear, that it may be owing to some worse cause.

And I desire it may be considered, whether the boldness of some writers may not be worthy to be reflected on, who have not scrupled to say, that if these and those things are true (which yet appear to be the demonstrable dictates of reason, as well as the certain dictates of the mouth of the most High) then God is unjust and cruel, and guilty of manifest deceit and double-dealing, and the like. Yea, some have gone so far, as confidently to assert, that if any book which pretends to be Scripture, teaches such doctrines, that alone is sufficient warrant for mankind to reject it, as what cannot be the Word of God. Some who have not gone so far, have said, that if the Scripture seems to teach any such doctrines, so contrary to reason, we are obliged to find out some other interpretation of those texts, where such doctrines seem to be exhibited. Others express themselves yet more modestly: they express a tenderness and religious fear, lest they should receive and teach anything that should seem to reflect on God's moral character, or be a disparagement to his methods of administration, in his moral government; and therefore express themselves as not daring to embrace some doctrines, though they seem to be delivered in Scripture, according to the more obvious and natural construction of the words. But indeed it would shew a truer modesty and humility, if they would more entirely rely on God's wisdom and discerning, who knows infinitely better than we, what is agreeable to his own perfections, and never intended to leave these matters to the decision of the wisdom and discerning of men; but by his own unerring instruction, to determine for us what the truth is; knowing how little our judgment is to be depended on, and how extremely prone, vain and blind men are, to err in such matters.

The truth of the case is, that if the Scripture plainly taught the opposite doctrines, to those that are so much stumbled at, viz. the Arminian doctrine of free will, and others depending thereon, it would be the greatest of all difficulties that attend the Scriptures, incomparably greater than its containing any, even the most mysterious of those doctrines of the first Reformers, which our late free thinkers have so superciliously exploded. Indeed it is a glorious argument of the divinity of the holy Scriptures, that they teach such doctrines, which in one age and another, through the blindness of men's minds, and strong prejudices of their hearts, are rejected, as most absurd and unreasonable, by the wise and great men of the world; which yet, when they are most carefully and strictly examined, appear to be exactly agreeable to the most demonstrable, certain, and natural dictates of reason. By such things it appears, that the "foolishness of God is wiser than men," and God does as is said in I Cor. 1:19, 20: "For it is written, I will destroy the wisdom of the wise; I will bring to nothing the understanding of the prudent. Where is the wise! Where is the Scribe! Where is the disputer of this world! Hath not God made foolish the wisdom of this world?" And as it used to be in time past, so it is probable it will be in time to come, as it is there written, in ver. 27, 28, 29, "But God hath chosen the foolish things of the world, to confound the wise: and God hath chosen the weak things of the world, to confound the things that are mighty: and base things of the world, and things which are despised, hath God chosen: yea, and things which are not, to bring to nought things that are; that no flesh should glory in his presence." Amen.

RELATED CORRESPONDENCE

Two of Edwards' letters to the Reverend John Erskine have bearing upon the argument of the *Inquiry into the Freedom of the Will* (and upon the controversy over this issue in Scotland in the years following publication) of such importance as to demand inclusion within the present volume. The first, sent from Stockbridge on July 25, 1757, was written for publication in Scotland and entitled, at Edwards' own suggestion, "Remarks on the *Essays on the Principles of Morality and Natural Religion*,[1] in a Letter to a Minister of the Church of Scotland." These "Remarks" were at once recognized as a significant statement and clarification of Edwards' position; and the letter was afterward reprinted as an "appendix" to the third edition (1768), and many subsequent editions, of Edwards' *Inquiry*. This letter, as here published, has been edited from the third edition of the *Inquiry*.

The second letter, dated one week later, August 3, 1757, concluded with Erskine the arrangements for the publication of the first. Yet Edwards looked upon both these letters—the second no less than the first—as of such importance that he sent duplicates of both, by different routes and couriers, lest one copy of either should fail to arrive. He composed the first letter (the "Remarks") in answer to Erskine's request that he comment upon Lord Kames' *Essays* and distinguish between his own and Kames' opinions, since Kames' defenders were citing Edwards' work as authority for the contention that the necessity of human volitions, as set forth in the *Essays,* is consistent with orthodox Christianity and productive of no ill effects upon morality or religion. Edwards composed the second letter in reply to an anonymous pamphlet entitled, *Objections to the "Essays on the Principles of Morality and Natural Religion" Examined,* in which a disciple of Kames seems to have argued that the truth about man's possessing no liberty of contingence or self-determination better be kept a secret from the generality of mankind, else they would no

1. By Henry Home, Lord Kames, 1st ed. Edinburgh, 1751.

longer regard themselves as worthy of praise or blame. In both replies, Edwards clearly and forcefully states his opinion that men have
no other inability than mere unwillingness. Yet, in the second letter
more than in the "Remarks" (perhaps because it was in answer to a
view more extreme even than that of Lord Kames) Edwards explains
the practical implications of his *Inquiry* in a fashion which throws
more light upon his viewpoint than is to be found elsewhere in his
writings. This letter is here reprinted from the *Life of President
Edwards,* by Sereno Dwight,[2] who correctly estimated its significance
when he wrote that it also "might well have been published at the
time, and circulated through the Church at large." [3]

Before studying this correspondence, the reader may need to know
more about the point of view expressed by Lord Kames in the third
essay, "On Liberty and Necessity," in the original edition of his
Essays on the Principles of Morality and Natural Religion,[4] and the
extensive revisions made of this essay in subsequent editions.[5] These
revisions clearly reflect the influence of Jonathan Edwards, and show,
in one instance, what a force the theologian from the wilderness of
America was in determining the currents of intellectual life in Scotland in the mid-eighteenth century.

Writing upon the subject of liberty and necessity in 1751, three
years before the publication of Edwards' treatise, Kames started from
the accepted view that among our perceptions of the natural world
there are "secondary qualities" or "deceitful impressions" to be distinguished from the "primary qualities" or the true nature of things.
He proposed to "carry on this speculation from the natural to the
moral world" and, thus entering into "an unbeaten tract," to establish that there are, also among our moral impressions, some that are
primary and others that are "secondary" and "deceitful." [6] In both
instances, he contends that the mind's view is "so adjusted, as to be
made subservient to correctness of action rather than of belief." The
feeling men have that their *actions* are volitionally self-determined
and also the feeling that *events* are contingent or uncertain in themselves are examples of impressions which are rooted in human nature
yet are delusive.

2. *Works* (1829), *1,* 558–63.
3. Ibid., p. 558. See above, Intro., Pt. 4, no. 8.
4. Above, n. 1.
5. Second ed. London, 1758; 3d ed. Edinburgh, 1779.
6. First ed., p. 155.

While impressions are often deceitful and "differ from the real truth," still, Kames wrote, we are "not thereby in the least misled. On the contrary, the ends of life and action are better provided for by such artifice, than if these perceptions were more exact copies of their objects." Our senses are wonderfully designed, so that, far from being "betrayed into anything that is hurtful," the life of action is better provided for and "fulfilled to more advantage than if we conducted ourselves by the strictest truth of things." Moreover, no bad consequences result from discovering the truth that actions are determined by prior causes and not by free choice or that events are necessary, any more than from discovering the true nature of other secondary qualities. "Our natural principles are too deeply rooted, to give way to philosophy. . . . A feeling of liberty, which I now scruple not to call deceitful, is so interwoven in our nature, that it has an equal effect in action, as if we were really endued with such a power." Indeed, Kames was confident that his philosophy would convince men all the more of the beauty of God's "artful contrivance" in marvelously endowing men with "all the prerogatives both of a necessary and [a] free agent." Kames' analysis of man's "artificial sense of liberty" demonstrates that virtue is "in a singular manner, the care of Deity; and a peculiar glory is thrown around it. . . . A sort of extraordinary machinery is introduced for its sake. Human nature is forced, as it were, out of its course, and made to receive a nice and artificial set of feelings; merely that conscience may have a commanding power, and virtue be set on a throne." [7]

It should be noted that Kames distinguishes between the impression we have of contingency in events and the impression of liberty in actions, and at the time he wrote the first edition he was of the opinion that both were deceitful. The deceitful impression of freedom consists of precisely that perception of a self-determining power to have acted otherwise, which Edwards says is no part of any man's experience. Moreover, in the original version of this chapter Kames rejects the idea, which was later Edwards', that praise and blame rest only on immediate approbation or disapprobation and not on the agent's supposition that "he might have forborn to do the ill thing." [8]

In subsequent revisions Kames cleaves to the one and forsakes the other of these two sorts of impressions. In the second edition (1758) he still held the opinion that men have a natural sense of contingency,

7. Ibid., pp. 150, 155, 214 f., 203–4, 216–17, 210–11.
8. Ibid., pp. 196–9.

which is delusive; [1] but he tried to show that there is not in human nature any impression of self-determining freedom to act against motives. Contrariwise, in the third edition (1779) Kames explains our belief in contingency as a mistaken conclusion drawn from ignorance of causes and not in any way a natural (delusive) impression; and he admits again the presence in human experience of a sense of self-determining freedom, and the utility of this sense, even though it is an impression that arises from passion and not from nature. In each case, Kames' opinions hinge upon changes in his analysis of the meaning of praise and blame. His views in the second edition are, on this matter, closest to those of Edwards, whose *Inquiry* may reasonably be supposed to have influenced him, even though he *may* not at the time of this revision have read Edwards' "Remarks."

Kames summarizes as follows the change of mind which led him to make extensive revision of the chapter "Of Liberty and Necessity" in the second edition:

> I acknowledge it to have been once my opinion, that we have a delusive sense of power to act against motives, or to act against our own inclination and choice, commonly termed *liberty of indifference*. I was carried along by the current of popular opinion; and I could not dream this sense to be a pure imagination when I found it vouched by so many grave writers. I had at the same time a thorough conviction, from the clearest evidence, that man is a necessary agent; and therefore I justly concluded, that the sense of liberty of indifference, like that of contingency, must be delusive. I yielded to another popular opinion, that the perceptions of the moral sense, praise and blame, merit and demerit, guilt and remorse, are inconsistent with necessity, and must be founded upon the delusive sense of liberty of indifference. . . . I was sensible of the odium of a doctrine that rests virtue in any measure upon a delusion. . . . I now cheerfully acknowledge my errors; and am happy in thinking, that I have at last got into the right track. It appears to me at present a harsh doctrine, that virtue in any part should be founded on a delusion, though formerly the supposed truth of the doctrine reconciled me to it. [2]

1. In this second edition Kames uses the term "delusive" more frequently than "deceitful," and concerning both words he appends the note, "I am sensible that these terms are unhappy, because they are generally taken in a bad sense" (p. 114 n.).

2. Second ed., p. 157 n.

In a long section, introduced for the first time in the second edition,[3] Kames now admits that "all our moral sentiments" of praise and blame for a man's action presuppose that "he could have abstained from it," or that he had a "power," he *"might* or *could* have done otherways." But "when we examine the nature of this power" and subject our moral sentiments to the "strictest analysis," we "find it to be a physical power only, viz. a power to act *according to our will,* not a power to act against it." To be worthy of praise and blame a man "must be free from *external coaction,* and at liberty to follow his own choice." He must be able to say, "I could have acted a different part *had I been so inclined"* or that the "action was *my own* choice and voluntary deed." Thus, in agreement with Edwards, Kames now understands our "intuitive consciousness of freedom" as an intuition "of a power existing in us to act *according* to our will and choice," while he grants that "with the bulk of mankind, a power *to choose,* and a power to act *according* to that choice, though essentially distinct, pass readily the one for the other." [4] Nevertheless, there is no such thing in the nature or experience of man as a (delusive) sense of a liberty of indifference or the self-determination of motives.

When he turns to the question, Whence proceeds the sense of contingency in events? Kames reaches the opposite conclusion. The sense of contingency cannot arise simply as a mistake in judgment about events that are uncertain and variable rather than uniform in their occurrence. This would naturally have no other effect than to produce in us a sense of ignorance.[5] "The sense of contingency, then, with respect to things uncertain, must be pronounced an original law of our nature. . . . Contingency in this view may justly be considered a secondary quality, which hath no real existence in things." [6]

Apparently Kames at this point believed there was more odium to a doctrine that rests virtue upon a delusive sense of freedom than to a doctrine that rests incentives to action upon a delusive sense of

3. Ibid., pp. 141–52. These paragraphs, explaining in Edwardean fashion that men do *not* have a sense of being able to act against motives, were dropped from the third edition, where they are replaced by Kames' explanation that the (now readmitted) impression of such a liberty arises from the indiscriminate suggestions and irregular effects of the passion of remorse, and not from nature.

4. Pages 143–4, 149 (italics mine).

5. In the third (1779) edition Kames accepts the explanation (here rejected) that our sense of contingency simply expresses in a mistaken way our ignorance of causes.

6. Second ed., p. 152.

contingency. He found no difficulty in affirming the latter to be more deeply rooted in nature than the former. A wise Creator has so framed human nature that a strictly erroneous sense of contingency is "the cause of all the labour, care, and industry of mankind." The world is not what it seems to the mind impressed by this as well as by other secondary qualities. "And, after all, seeing our happiness, in many instances, is placed under delusive perceptions, why should it puzzle us that our activity is promoted by the same means? No one considers it an imputation on the Deity, that we are so framed as to perceive what is not, viz. beauty, grandeur, colour, heat or cold, as existing in objects, when such perceptions, though delusive, contribute to our happiness: and yet our happiness depends greatly more on actions than on any of these perceptions." [1]

In the preface to the third edition Kames gives an account of his intellectual pilgrimage before "being at last relieved from so many distressing errors." These errors were the opinions expressed in the original essay on liberty and necessity, that (1) "there is in man a sense of being able to act against motives. . . . I was carried along in the current of popular opinion; and could not dream but that this sense really existed, when I found it vouched by so many grave writers"; (2) that praise and blame are inconsistent with necessity and must be founded on this same delusive sense of liberty; and (3) that there is also in human nature a (delusive) sense of chance or contingency. Before the second edition Kames became persuaded (by Edwards?) that praise and blame are perfectly consistent with moral necessity; and, this being so, he too hastily ventured to say that men have no notion of being able to act against motives. In the third edition he again acknowledged there is such a notion in the mind, but says that it is not a delusion of nature (contrived by nature's God) but a delusion of the passions only. Finally, the third edition denies that the notions we have of chance and contingency are actually delusive, an error in which he confesses he was still entangled when writing the second edition.[2]

In the last analysis, therefore—in the first edition and again in the third—Kames affirms what Edwards denies: that there is in human experience an impression that we are able to act otherwise, or that by prior act of will we could have chosen another choice against the motives then present. Kames' first explanation of this sense was

1. Ibid., pp. 150, 160.
2. Third ed., pp. v–viii.

that it is a deceitful, secondary quality of moral experience designed to provide incentives to action. Edwards' reply to this point was most telling: "the very thing that this great benefit of care and industry is given as a reason for, is God's deceiving men in this very point, in making them think their care and industry to be of great benefit to them, when indeed it is none at all; and if they saw the real truth, they would see all their endeavors to be wholly useless," [3] and their delusive sense of freedom useful only for maintaining perfectly useless endeavor. Thus one deception rests for justification upon the other.

Kames' explanation in the third edition is that a feeling of self-determination results from the irregular influence of passion, especially from the passion of remorse. It is the nature of remorse to produce this delusive notion of freedom. If a man becomes involved in an evil course of events, "remorse . . . makes the man odious in his own eyes: it gratifies his remorse to find himself guilty; and to leave him without excuse, the passion forces upon him the conviction that he might and ought to have done otherways." The notion men have of a "restraining power" that might have interposed against their motives is entirely the result of the irregular influence of the passion of remorse, for "remorse is gratified in the criminal by a conviction that it was in his power to have restrained his passion." Having thus explained "this formidable notion" of freedom of the will to act against motives, Kames rests with entire satisfaction in the conviction that the system of nature consists in a necessary chain of causes and effects.[4]

"It is now my opinion," Kames also announced in the third edition, "that there is no such thing in nature as a sense of chance or contingency, such as described above." Chance or contingency mean only "that we are ignorant of the cause, and for ought we know the event might have happened, or not happened," or that we cannot foresee whether a future event will happen or not. Contingency expresses only an awareness of our ignorance, not an awareness of any looseness in the course of nature. Moreover, Kames concludes, "a firm conviction of universal necessity has no tendency to make us relax in our pursuits, either for our own good or for that of others; more than a delusive sense of contingency would have." [5]

3. See below, p. 462.
4. Third ed., pp. 177–9.
5. Ibid., pp. 194–6.

There is, in Kames' first edition, a distinction between moral and natural necessity; and it seems that Edwards overlooks this in his "Remarks." "For moral necessity," wrote Kames in reply to Samuel Clarke, "being that sort of necessity which affects the mind, and physical necessity that which affects matter, it is plain, that in all reasonings concerning human liberty, moral necessity, and no other, is meant to be established." [6] Moral necessity arises "not from the laws of matter, but from the constitution of the mind." Kames also distinguishes necessity from compulsion or constraint.[7]

However, on close inspection this proves to be a distinction without real difference, or without as much difference as Kames was to introduce in later revisions; and Edwards concentrated upon this point in his reply. When a criminal walks to the scaffold in the midst of his guards, Kames asks, is this a physical or a moral necessity? Admitting that "the difference betwixt these two seems lost" (a phrase stricken out in the third edition), he nevertheless affirms that "strictly speaking, it is only a moral necessity: for it is the force of a motive which determines the criminal to walk to the scaffold; to wit, that resistance is vain, because the guards are neither to be forced nor corrupted." [1] Kames' "moral necessity" corresponds, it is clear, more to what Edwards calls a liberty of "coaction" than to what he understands by "moral necessity." In the case of a man with a strong desire to escape who finds his keepers gone, where Edwards would have stressed his freedom to *act* from motive or volition, Kames emphasizes that "his escape now is as necessary, i.e. as certain and infallible a consequence *of the circumstances* he finds himself in, as his confinement was before." [2] It is true that, when considering Clarke's position, Kames clearly distinguishes between physical and moral necessity. Yet this passage concludes with words which stress the similarity of all types of necessity: "To say that moral necessity is no necessity at all, because it is not physical necessity, which is all that the doctor's argument amounts to, is no better than to argue that physical necessity is no necessity at all, because it is not moral necessity." [3] This suggests the reduction of moral to physical necessity,

6. First ed., pp. 172–3.
7. Ibid., pp. 165, 167, 173.
1. Pages 165–6.
2. Pages 173–4 (italics mine).
3. Pages 172–3.

or at least that Kames has not yet, so clearly as Edwards, distinguished between the two.

In later editions of this essay Kames clarified this distinction in a passage several pages in length.[4] In the second edition he remarks concerning physical and moral necessity, "Formerly I showed their resemblance, in the article of necessity: I now again compare them, to show in what circumstances they differ." [5] There is, first, physical necessity which is involuntary, or against a man's inclination and will. Kames calls this "constraint or coaction." But since "force may be applied to bring about an event which is agreeable," physical necessity is not always involuntary. Thus, secondly, there is a type of physical necessity which is voluntary, when the necessity men are under corresponds with their desire, as when Elijah was taken to heaven in a chariot of fire. Edwards would have called this second sort of necessity, and not the first, by the name of "coaction." Finally, Kames comes to the only necessity that should be called "moral," and this "moral necessity is always *voluntary*. A moral cause operates not by force or coaction, but by solicitation and persuasion." [6] Thus in the second edition Kames comes to a statement of the contrast between physical and moral necessity only by the foregoing steps, gradually disentangling himself, as it were, from too great an actual identification of moral and physical necessity, despite his earlier use of these expressions. This indicates the degree to which his earlier thought upon the subject of liberty and necessity was, as Edwards charged, shaped by the idea of necessity as merely the force of circumstance, or by the idea of the "coaction" of the will and of natural causes. In the third edition no mention is made of physical necessity which is *also* voluntary; and instead, from the first, physical and moral necessity are more sharply contrasted, in that moral necessity is always in the strictest sense voluntary.[7]

If this be not enough to demonstrate the influence of Edwards upon Kames' revisions, doubt cannot remain in face of the Edwardean definition of liberty itself as the power to act according to will or inclination. Entirely absent from the first edition, this understanding of the freedom of the will was introduced, as we have

4. Second ed., pp. 132–6; and 3d ed., pp. 165–9: inserted at p. 177 of the 1st ed.
5. Second ed., p. 132.
6. Ibid., pp. 132–3.
7. Third ed., pp. 166–7.

seen, into the second edition when Kames rejected his earlier view
that there is in the human constitution a natural intuition of self-
determining freedom and that praise and blame depend upon such
a delusion of nature. The Edwardean definition of freedom of will
was, it is true, stricken from the third edition, when Kames rejected
his rejection of the opinion of the first edition that men actually have
a sense of being able to choose against their motives. Hereby, Kames'
position was considerably weakened, despite the interesting explanation, in the final edition, of the feeling of freedom as an impression
not of nature but of the passion of remorse. Still, Kames inserted
this same Edwardean analysis of the nature of freedom into his consideration of the views of Samuel Clarke, in the third edition where
it was not in the second; and this was precisely also a point where it
was much needed if his analysis was ever to make full use of the idea
of moral necessity distinct from natural necessity: "Man is a free
agent undoubtedly, because *he acts as he wills;* but he is equally a
necessary agent, as being necessarily influenced by motives to act.
. . . Man is a free agent, because *he acts according to his will.* He is
at the same time a necessary agent, because his will is necessarily influenced by motives. These are perfectly consistent." [8]

Despite the significant alterations in Kames' viewpoint, there is
never any mention of Edwards' *Inquiry into the Freedom of the Will*
as having been in part the occasion of them. Instead, the effort continued to be made simply to range Edwards on the side of Kames'
position. There was printed as an appendix to Part I of the *Essays*
in both the 1758 and the 1779 editions the substance of a pamphlet
written in defense of Kames' essay "Of Liberty and Necessity." [9] This
contains three pages discussing Edwards' work, with the assertion,
"Nothing can be better calculated than this book to answer all the
objections against our author's doctrine of moral necessity, to show
its consistency with reason and scripture, and the injustice of ascribing to it any bad tendency." [10]

P.R.

8. Ibid., pp. 162–3 (italics mine).

9. "Containing the substance of a pamphlet writ in defence of the foregoing
Essay," *Essays* (2d ed.), pp. 164–78; "Containing the substance of a pamphlet
wrote in defence of the third Essay," ibid. (3d ed.), pp. 207–21.

10. Ibid. (2d ed.), p. 170; (3d ed.), pp. 213–14.

REMARKS ON THE *Essays on the Principles of Morality and Natural Religion,* IN A LETTER TO A MINISTER OF THE CHURCH OF SCOTLAND: BY THE REVEREND MR. JONATHAN EDWARDS, PRESIDENT OF THE COLLEGE OF NEW JERSEY, AND AUTHOR OF THE LATE *Inquiry into the Modern Notions of the Freedom of the Will*

Rev. Sir,

The intimations you have given me of the use which has, by some, been made of what I have written on the *Freedom of the Will,* etc. to vindicate what is said on the subject of liberty and necessity by the author of the *Essays on the Principles of Morality and Natural Religion,* has occasioned my reading this author's *Essay* on that subject, with particular care and attention. And I think it must be evident to everyone, that has read both his *Essay* and my *Inquiry,* that our schemes are exceeding reverse from each other. The wide difference appears particularly in the following things.

This author supposes, that such a necessity takes place with respect to all men's actions, as is inconsistent with liberty,[1] and plainly denies that men have any liberty in acting. Thus in p. 168 after he had been speaking of the necessity of our determinations, as connected with motives, he concludes with saying, "In short, if motives are not under our power or direction, which is confessedly the fact, we can at bottom have—*no liberty.*" Whereas I have abundantly expressed it as my mind, that man, in his moral actions, has true liberty; and that the moral necessity which universally takes place, is not in the least inconsistent with anything that is properly called liberty, and with the utmost liberty that can be desired, or that can possibly exist or be conceived of.[2]

I find that some are apt to think, that in that kind of moral necessity of men's volitions, which I suppose to be universal, at least some degree of liberty is denied; that though it be true I allow a sort of liberty, yet those who maintain a self-determining power in the will, and a liberty of contingence and indifference, hold an higher sort of freedom than I do: but I think this is certainly a great mistake.

Liberty, as I have explained it, in p. 38 and other places, is "the

1. [Henry Home, Lord Kames,] *Essays on the Principles of Morality and Natural Religion* (Edinburgh, 1751), pp. 160, 161, 164, 165, and many other places.

2. *Inquiry,* see above, pp. 163–6, 272–3, 343–9, 358–9, 363, 377–83.

power, opportunity, or advantage that anyone has to do as he pleases,"
or "conducting, *in any respect,* according to his pleasure"; without
considering how his pleasure comes to be as it is. It is demonstrable,
and I think has been demonstrated, that no necessity of men's volitions that I maintain, is inconsistent with this liberty: and I think it
is impossible for anyone to rise higher in his conceptions of liberty
than this: if any imagine they desire higher, and that they conceive
of a higher and greater liberty than this, they are deceived, and de-
lude themselves with confused ambiguous words, instead of ideas.
If anyone should here say, "Yes, I conceive of a freedom above and
beyond the liberty a man has of conducting in any respect as he
pleases, viz. a liberty of *choosing* as he pleases": such an one, if he
reflected, would either blush or laugh at his own instance. For, is
not choosing as he pleases, conducting, *in some respect,* according to
his pleasure, and still without determining how he came by that
pleasure? If he says, "Yes, I came by that pleasure by my own choice":
if he be a man of common sense, by this time he will see his own
absurdity: for he must needs see that his notion or conception, even
of this liberty, don't contain any judgment or conception how he
comes by that choice, which first determines his pleasure, or which
originally fixed his own will respecting the affair. Or if any shall say,
that "a man exercises liberty in this, even in determining his own
choice, but not as he pleases, or not in consequence of any choice,
preference, or inclination of his own, but by a determination arising
contingently out of a state of absolute indifference"; this is not rising
higher in his conception of liberty: as such a determination of the
will would not be a voluntary determination of it. Surely he that
places liberty in a power of doing something not according to his
own choice, or from his choice, has not a higher notion of it, than
he that places it in doing as he pleases, or acting from his own election. If there were a power in the mind to determine itself, but not
by its choice or according to its pleasure, what advantage would it
give? and what liberty, worth contending for, would be exercised in
it? Therefore no Arminian, Pelagian, or Epicurean, can rise higher
in his conceptions of liberty, than the notion of it which I have explained: which notion is, apparently, perfectly consistent with the
whole of that necessity of men's actions, which I suppose takes place.
And I scruple not to say 'tis beyond all their wits to invent a higher
notion, or form a higher imagination of liberty; let them talk of
sovereignty of the will, self-determining power, self-motion, self-

direction, arbitrary decision, liberty *ad utrumvis,* power of choosing differently in given cases, etc., etc. as long as they will. 'Tis apparent that these men, in their strenuous affirmation, and dispute about these things, aim at they know not what, fighting for something they have no conception of, substituting a number of confused unmeaning words, instead of things, and instead of thoughts. They may be challenged clearly to explain what they would have: they never can answer the challenge.

The author of the *Essays,* through his whole "Essay on Liberty and Necessity," goes on that supposition, that, in order to the being of real liberty, a man must have a freedom that is opposed to moral necessity: and yet he supposes (p. 175) that such a liberty "must signify a power in the mind of acting without and against motives, a power of acting without any view, purpose or design, and even of acting in contradiction to our own desires and aversions, and to all our principles of action"; and is "an absurdity altogether inconsistent with a rational nature." Now whoever imagined such a liberty as this, a higher sort or degree of freedom, than a liberty of following one's own views and purposes, and acting agreeable to his own inclinations and passions? Who will ever reasonably suppose that liberty, which is an absurdity altogether inconsistent with a rational nature, to be a kind of liberty above that which is consistent with the nature of a rational intelligent designing agent.

The author of the *Essays* seems to suppose such a necessity to take place, as is inconsistent with some supposable "power of arbitrary choice"; [3] or that there is some liberty conceivable, whereby men's own actions might be more "properly in their power," [4] and by which events might be more "dependent on ourselves": [5] contrary to what I suppose to be evident in my *Inquiry.* [6] What way can be imagined, of our actions being more *in our power, from ourselves,* or *dependent on ourselves,* than their being from our power to fulfill our own choice, to act from our own inclination, pursue our own views, and execute our own designs? Certainly, to be able to act thus, is as properly having our actions in our power, and dependent on ourselves, as a being liable to be the subjects of acts and events, contingently and fortuitously, "without desire, view, purpose or design, or any

3. *Essays,* p. 169.
4. Ibid., pp. 191, 185, 197, 206.
5. Ibid., p. 183.
6. See above, pp. 426–8.

principle of action" within ourselves; as we must be, according to this author's own declared sense, if our actions are performed with that liberty that is opposed to moral necessity.

This author seems everywhere to suppose, that necessity, most properly so called, attends all men's actions; and that the terms "necessary," "unavoidable," "impossible," etc. are equally applicable to the case of moral and natural necessity. In p. 173, he says, "the idea of *necessary* and *unavoidable* equally agrees, both to moral and physical necessity." And in p. 184, "All things that fall out in the natural and moral world are alike necessary." P. 174: "This inclination and choice is *unavoidably* caused or occasioned by the prevailing motive. In this lies the necessity of our actions, that in such circumstances it was *impossible* we *could* act otherwise." He often expresses himself in like manner elsewhere, speaking in strong terms of men's actions as "unavoidable," what they "cannot" forbear, having "no power" over their own actions, the order of them being "unalterably" fixed, and "inseparably" linked together, etc.[7]

On the contrary, I have largely declared, that the connection between antecedent things and consequent ones, which takes place with regard to the acts of men's wills, which is called moral necessity, is called by the name of "necessity" improperly; and that all such terms as "must," "cannot," "impossible," "unable," "irresistible," "unavoidable," "invincible," etc. when applied here, are not applied in their proper signification, and are either used nonsensically, and with perfect insignificance, or in a sense quite diverse from their original and proper meaning, and their use in common speech: [8] and that such a necessity as attends the acts of men's wills, is more properly called "certainty," than "necessity"; it being no other than the certain connection between the subject and predicate of the proposition which affirms their existence.[9]

Agreeable to what is observed in my *Inquiry*,[1] I think it is evidently owing to a strong prejudice in persons' minds, arising from an insensible habitual perversion and misapplication of suchlike terms, as "necessary," "impossible," "unable," "unavoidable," "invincible," etc. that they are ready to think, that to suppose a certain connection of men's volitions without any foregoing motives or inclinations, or

7. *Essays*, pp. 180, 188, 193, 194, 195, 197, 198, 199, 205, 206.
8. *Inquiry*, see above, pp. 149–55, 158–62, 308, 350–3, 355–6, 361–4, 428–9.
9. Ibid., pp. 151–3.
1. Ibid., pp. 351–3.

any preceding moral influence whatsoever, is truly and properly to suppose such a strong irrefragable chain of causes and effects, as stands in the way of, and makes utterly vain, opposite desires and endeavors, like immovable and impenetrable mountains of brass; and impedes our liberty like walls of adamant, gates of brass, and bars of iron: whereas all such representations suggest ideas as far from the truth, as the east is from the west. Nothing that I maintain, supposes that men are at all hindered by any fatal necessity, from doing, and even willing and choosing as they please, with full freedom; yea, with the highest degree of liberty that ever was thought of, or that ever could possibly enter into the heart of any man to conceive. I know it is in vain to endeavor to make some persons believe this, or at least fully and steadily to believe it: for if it be demonstrated to them, still the old prejudice remains, which has been long fixed by the use of the terms "necessary," "must," "cannot," "impossible," etc.: the association with these terms of certain ideas inconsistent with liberty, is not broken; and the judgment is powerfully warped by it; as a thing that has been long bent and grown stiff, if it be straightened, will return to its former curvity again and again.

The author of the *Essays* most manifestly supposes, that if men had the truth concerning the real necessity of all their actions clearly in view, they would not appear to themselves, or one another, as at all praiseworthy or culpable, or under any moral obligation, or accountable for their actions: [2] which supposes, that men are not to be blamed or praised for any of their actions, and are not under any obligations, nor are truly accountable for anything they do, by reason of this necessity; which is very contrary to what I have endeavored to prove, throughout the third Part of my *Inquiry*. I humbly conceive it is there shewn, that this is so far from the truth, that the moral necessity of men's actions, which truly take place, is requisite to the being of virtue and vice, or anything praiseworthy or culpable: that the liberty of indifference and contingence, which is advanced in opposition to that necessity, is inconsistent with the being of these; as it would suppose that men are not determined in what they do, by any virtuous or vicious principles, nor act from any motives, intentions or aims whatsoever; or have any end, either good or bad, in acting. And is it not remarkable, that this author should suppose, that, in order to men's actions truly having any desert, they must be performed "without any view, purpose, design,

2. *Essays,* pp. 207, 209, and other places.

or desire," or "any principle of action," or anything "agreeable to a rational nature"? As it will appear that he does, if we compare, pp. 206, 207, with p. 175.

The author of the *Essays* supposes, that God has deeply implanted in man's nature, a strong and invincible apprehension, or feeling, as he calls it, of a liberty, and contingence of his own actions, opposite to that necessity which truly attends them; and which in truth don't agree with real fact,[3] is not agreeable to strict philosophic truth,[4] is contradictory to the truth of things,[5] and which truth contradicts,[6] not tallying with the real plan: [7] and that therefore such feelings are deceitful,[8] are in reality of the delusive kind.[9] He speaks of them as a wise delusion,[1] as nice artificial feelings, merely that conscience may have a commanding power: [2] meaning plainly, that these feelings are a cunning artifice of the Author of nature, to make men believe they are free, when they are not.[3] He supposes that by these feelings the moral world has a disguised appearance.[4] And other things of this kind he says. He supposes that all self-approbation, and all remorse of conscience, all commendation or condemnation of ourselves or others, all sense of desert, and all that is connected with this way of thinking, all the ideas, which at present are suggested by the words "ought," "should," arise from this delusion, and would entirely vanish without it.[5]

All which is very contrary to what I have abundantly insisted on and endeavored to demonstrate in my *Inquiry;* where I have largely shewn, that it is agreeable to the natural sense of mankind, that the moral necessity or certainty that attends men's actions, is consistent with praise and blame, reward and punishment; [6] and that it is agreeable to our natural notions, that moral evil, with its desert of dislike

3. Ibid., p. 200.
4. Ibid., p. 152.
5. Ibid., p. 183.
6. Ibid., p. 186.
7. Ibid., p. 205.
8. Ibid., pp. 203, 204, 211.
9. Ibid., p. 183.
1. Ibid., p. 209.
2. Ibid., p. 211.
3. Ibid., p. 153.
4. Ibid., p. 214.
5. Ibid., pp. 160, 194, 199, 205, 206, 207, 209.
6. *Inquiry,* see above, Pt. IV, Sec. 4, throughout.

and abhorrence, and all its other ill-deservings, consists in a certain
deformity in the nature of the dispositions and acts of the heart, and
not in the evil of something else, diverse from these, supposed to be
their cause or occasion.[7]

I might well ask here, whether anyone is to be found in the world
of mankind, who is conscious to a sense or feeling, naturally and
deeply rooted in his mind, that, in order to a man's performing any
action that is praise or blameworthy, he must exercise a liberty that
implies and signifies a power of acting without any motive, view, design, desire, or principle of action? For such a liberty this author supposes that must be which is opposed to moral necessity, as I have
already observed once and again. Supposing a man should actually
do good, independent of desire, aim, inducement, principle or end,
is it a dictate of invincible natural sense, that his act is more meritorious or praiseworthy than if he had performed it for some good end,
and had been governed in it by good principles and motives? And so
I might ask, on the contrary, with respect to evil actions.[8]

The author of the *Essays* supposes that the liberty without necessity which we have a natural feeling of, implies *contingence:* and
speaking of this contingence, he sometimes calls it by the name of
"chance." And 'tis evident, that his notion of it, or rather what he
says about it, implies things happening "loosely," "fortuitously," by
"accident," and "without a cause." [9] Now I conceive the slightest reflection may be sufficient to satisfy anyone, that such a contingence
of men's actions, according to our natural sense, is so far from being
essential to the morality or merit of those actions, that it would destroy it; and that, on the contrary, the dependence of our actions on
such causes, as inward inclinations, incitements and ends, is essential to the being of it. Natural sense teaches men, when they see anything done by others of a good or evil tendency, to inquire what their
intention was; what principles and views they were moved by, in
order to judge how far they are to be justified or condemned; and
not to determine, that, in order to their being approved or blamed
at all, the action must be performed altogether fortuitously, proceeding from nothing, arising from no cause. Concerning this matter, I
have fully expressed my mind in the *Inquiry.*[1]

7. Ibid., Sec. 1, throughout, and pp. 426–8.
8. See this matter illustrated in ibid., Sec. 4, esp. pp. 360–2.
9. *Essays,* pp. 156, 157, 158, 159, 177, 178, 181, 183, 184, 185.
1. See above, pp. 326–8, 332–3, 360–1, and other places.

If the liberty which we have a natural sense of as necessary to desert, consists in the mind's self-determination, without being determined by previous inclination or motive, then indifference is essential to it, yea, absolute indifference; as is observed in my *Inquiry*.[2] But men naturally have no notion of any such liberty as this, as essential to the morality or demerit of their actions; but, on the contrary, such a liberty, if it were possible, would be inconsistent with our natural notions of desert, as is largely shown in the *Inquiry*.[3] If it be agreeable to natural sense, that men must be indifferent in determining their own actions; then, according to the same, the more they are determined by inclination, either good or bad, the less they have of desert: the more good actions are performed from good dispositions, the less praiseworthy; and the more evil deeds are from evil dispositions, the less culpable; and in general, the more men's actions are from their hearts, the less they are to be commended or condemned: which all must know is very contrary to natural sense.

Moral necessity is owing to the power and government of the inclination of the heart, either habitual or occasional, excited by motive; but, according to natural and common sense, the more a man does anything with full inclination of heart, the more is it to be charged to his account for his condemnation, if it be an ill action, and the more to be ascribed to him for his praise, if it be good.

If the mind were determined to evil actions by contingence, from a state of indifference, then either there would be no fault in them, or else the fault would be in being so perfectly indifferent, that the mind was equally liable to a bad or good determination. And if this indifference be liberty, then the very essence of the blame or fault would lie in the liberty itself, or the wickedness would, primarily and summarily, lie in being a free agent. If there were no fault in being indifferent, then there would be no fault in the determination's being agreeable to such a state of indifference: that is, there could no fault be reasonably found with this, viz. that opposite determinations actually happen to take place *indifferently,* sometimes good and sometimes bad, as contingence governs and decides. And if it be a fault to be indifferent to good and evil, then such indifference is no indifference to good and evil, but is a determination to evil, or to a fault; and such an indifferent disposition would be an evil, faulty

2. Ibid., pp. 203–5.
3. Ibid., esp. in Pt. III, Secs. 6 and 7.

disposition, tendency or determination of mind. So inconsistent are these notions of liberty, as essential to praise or blame.

The author of the *Essays* supposes men's natural delusive sense of a liberty of contingence to be, in truth, the foundation of all the labor, care and industry of mankind;[4] and that if men's "practical ideas had been formed on the plan of universal necessity, the *ignava ratio,* the inactive doctrine of the Stoics, would have followed"; and that "there would have been no *room* for forethought about futurity, or any sort of industry and care":[5] plainly implying, that, in this case, men would see and know that all their industry and care signified nothing, was in vain, and to no purpose, or of no benefit; events being fixed in an irrefragable chain, and not at all *depending* on their care and endeavor; as he explains himself, particularly, in the instance of men's use of means to prolong life:[6] not only very contrary to what I largely maintain in my *Inquiry,*[7] but also very inconsistently with his own scheme, in what he supposes of the ends for which God has so deeply implanted this deceitful feeling in man's nature; in which he manifestly supposes men's care and industry not to be in vain and of no benefit, but of great use, yea, of absolute necessity, in order to the obtaining the most important ends and necessary purposes of human life, and to fulfill the ends of action to the "best advantage"; as he largely declares.[8] Now, how shall these things be reconciled? That, if men had "a clear view of real truth," they would see that there was "no room" for their care and industry, because they would see it to be in vain, and of no benefit; and yet that God, by having a clear view of real truth, sees that their being excited to care and industry, will be of excellent use to mankind, and greatly for the benefit of the world, yea, absolutely necessary in order to it: and that therefore the great wisdom and goodness of God to men appears, in artfully contriving to put them on care and industry for their good, which good could not be obtained without them; and yet both these things are maintained at once, and in the same sentences and words by this author. The very reason he gives, why God has put this deceitful feeling into men, contradicts and destroys itself; that

4. *Essays,* p. 184.
5. Ibid., p. 189.
6. Ibid., pp. 184, 185.
7. *Inquiry,* esp. Pt. IV, Sec. 5.
8. *Essays,* pp. 188–92, and in many other places.

God in his great goodness to men gave them such a deceitful feeling, because it was very useful and necessary for them, and greatly for their benefit, or excites them to care and industry for their own good, which care and industry is useful and necessary to that end: and yet the very thing that this great benefit of care and industry is given as a reason for, is God's deceiving men in this very point, in making them think their care and industry to be of great benefit to them, when indeed it is of none at all; and if they saw the real truth, they would see all their endeavors to be wholly useless, that there was "no room" for them, and that the event don't at all depend upon them.[9]

And besides, what this author says, plainly implies (as appears by what has been already observed) that it is necessary men should be deceived, by being made to believe that future events are contingent, and their own future actions free, with such a freedom, as signifies that their actions are not the fruit of their own desires, or designs, but altogether contingent, fortuitous and without a cause. But how should a notion of liberty, consisting in accident or loose chance, encourage care and industry? I should think it would rather entirely discourage everything of this nature. For surely, if our actions don't depend on our desires and designs, then they don't depend on our endeavors, flowing from our desires and designs. This author himself seems to suppose, that if men had indeed such a liberty of contingence, it would render all endeavors to determine or move men's future volitions, in vain: he says, that, in this case, "to exhort, to instruct, to promise, or to threaten, would be to no purpose."[1] Why? Because (as he himself gives the reason) then our will would be "capricious and arbitrary," and we should "be thrown loose altogether," and our arbitrary power could do us good or ill only "by accident."[2] But if such a loose fortuitous state would render vain others' endeavors upon us, for the same reason would it make useless our endeavors on ourselves: for events that are truly contingent and accidental, and altogether loose from and independent of all foregoing causes, are independent on every foregoing cause within ourselves, as well as in others.

I suppose that it is so far from being true, that our minds are naturally possessed with a notion of such liberty as this, so strongly, that it is impossible to root it out, that indeed men have no such

9. Ibid., pp. 188, 189, etc.
1. Ibid., pp. 178, 213, 214.
2. [Ibid., pp. 177–8.]

notion of liberty at all, and that it is utterly impossible, by any means whatsoever, to implant or introduce such a notion into the mind. As no such notions as imply self-contradiction and self-abolition can subsist in the mind, as I have shewn in my *Inquiry;* [3] I think a mature sensible consideration of the matter, sufficient to satisfy anyone, that even the greatest and most learned advocates themselves for liberty of indifference and self-determination, have no such notion; and that indeed they mean something wholly inconsistent with, and directly subversive of what they strenuously affirm, and earnestly contend for. By a man's having a power of determining his own will, they plainly mean a power of determining his will, as he pleases, or as he chooses; which supposes that the mind has a choice, prior to its going about to conform any action or determination to it. And if they mean that they determine even the original or prime choice, by their own pleasure or choice, as the thing that causes and directs it; I scruple not most boldly to affirm, that they speak they know not what, and that of which they have no manner of idea; because no such contradictory notion can come into, or have a moment's subsistence in the mind of any man living, as an original or first choice being caused, or brought into being, by choice. After all they say, they have no higher or other conception of liberty, than that vulgar notion of it, which I contend for, viz. a man's having power or opportunity to do as he chooses: or if they had a notion that every act of choice was determined by choice, yet it would destroy their notion of the contingence of choice; for then no one act of choice would arise contingently, or from a state of indifference, but every individual act, in all the series, would arise from foregoing bias or preference, and from a cause predetermining and fixing its existence, which introduces at once such a chain of causes and effects, each preceding link decisively fixing the following, as they would by all means avoid.

And such kind of delusion and self-contradiction as this don't arise in men's minds by nature: it is not owing to any natural feeling which God has strongly fixed in the mind and nature of man; but to false philosophy, and strong prejudice, from a deceitful abuse of words. It is "artificial"; not in the sense of the author of the *Essays,* supposing it to be a deceitful artifice of God; but artificial as opposed to natural, and as owing to an artificial deceitful management of terms, to darken and confound the mind. Men have no such thing when they

3. *Inquiry,* see above, pp. 325–6. See also pp. 174, 179, 190–1, 196, 270–3, 345–6, 357–60.

first begin to exercise reason; but must have a great deal of time to blind themselves with metaphysical confusion, before they can embrace, and rest in such definitions of liberty as are given, and imagine they understand them.

On the whole, I humbly conceive, that whosoever will give himself the trouble of weighing, what I have offered to consideration in my *Inquiry,* must be sensible, that such a moral necessity of men's actions as I maintain, is not at all inconsistent with any liberty that any creature has, or can have, as a free, accountable, moral agent, and subject of moral government; and that this moral necessity is so far from being inconsistent with praise and blame, and the benefit and use of men's own care and labor, that on the contrary it implies the very ground and reason, why men's actions are to be ascribed to them as their own, in that manner as to infer desert, praise and blame, approbation and remorse of conscience, reward and punishment; and that it establishes the moral system of the universe, and God's moral government, in every respect, with the proper use of motives, exhortations, commands, counsels, promises, and threatenings; and the use and benefit of endeavors, care and industry: and that therefore there is no need that the strict philosophic truth should be at all concealed from men; no danger in "contemplation" and "profound discovery" in these things. So far from this, that the truth in this matter is of vast importance, and extremely needful to be known; and that the more clearly and perfectly the real fact is known, and the more constantly it is in view, the better; and particularly, that the clear and full knowledge of that which is the true system of the universe, in these respects, would greatly establish the doctrines which teach the true Christian scheme of divine administration in the City of God, and the gospel of Jesus Christ, in its most important articles; and that these things never can be well established, and the opposite errors, so subversive of the whole gospel, which at this day so greatly and generally prevail, be well confuted, or the arguments by which they are maintained, answered, till these points are settled: while this is not done, it is, to me, beyond doubt, that the friends of those great gospel truths, will but poorly maintain their controversy with the adversaries of those truths: they will be obliged often to dodge, shuffle, hide, and turn their backs; and the latter will have a strong fort, from whence they never can be driven, and weapons to use, which those whom they oppose will find no shield to screen themselves from; and they will always puzzle, confound, and keep under the friends of sound doctrine; and glory, and vaunt themselves in their advantage over them; and carry their affairs with an high hand, as they have done already for a long time past.

I conclude, sir, with asking your pardon for troubling you with so much said in vindication of myself from the imputation of advancing a scheme of necessity, of a like nature with that of the author of the *Essays on the Principles of Morality and Natural Religion.* Considering that what I have said is not only in vindication of myself, but, as I think, of the most important articles of moral philosophy and religion; I trust in what I know of your candor, that you will excuse,

Your obliged friend and brother,
J. EDWARDS

Stockbridge,
July 25, 1757.

TO MR. ERSKINE [1]

Stockbridge, August 3, 1757

Rev. and Dear Sir,

In June last, I received a letter from you, dated January 22, 1757, with "Mr. Anderson's complaint verified," and "Objections to the Essays examined." For these things, I now return you my hearty thanks.

The conduct of the vindicator of the *Essays*, from objections made against them, seems to be very odd. Many things are produced from Calvin, and several Calvinistic writers, to defend what is not objected against. His book is almost wholly taken up about that, which is nothing to the purpose; perhaps only to amuse and blind the common people. According to your proposal, I have drawn up something, stating the difference between my hypothesis, and that of the *Essays;* which I have sent to you, to be printed in Scotland, if it be thought best; or to be disposed of as you think proper. I have written it in a letter to you: and if it be published, it may be as "A letter from me to a minister in Scotland." Lord Kames's notion of God's deceiving mankind, by a kind of invincible or natural instinct or feeling, leading them to suppose, that they have a liberty of *con-*

1. For a comment on the significance of the argument of this letter, see above, Intro., Pt. 5, no. 2, esp. pp. 71-3.

tingence and *self-determination of will,* in order to make them believe themselves and others worthy to be blamed or praised for what
they do, is a strange notion indeed; and it is hard for me to conjecture, what his views could be, in publishing such things to the world.

However, by what I have heard, some others seem to be so far of
the same mind, that they think, that if it be really true, that there is
no self-determining power in the will, as opposed to any such moral
necessity, as I speak of, consisting in a certain connection between
motives and volitions, it is of mischievous tendency to say anything
of it; and that it is best that the truth in this matter should not be
known, by any means. I cannot but be of an extremely different mind.
On the contrary, I think that the notion of liberty, consisting in a
contingent self-determination of the will, as necessary to the morality
of men's dispositions and actions, is almost inconceivably pernicious;
and that the contrary truth is one of the most important truths of
moral philosophy, that ever was discussed, and most necessary to be
known; and that for want of it, those schemes of morality and religion, which are a kind of infidel schemes, entirely diverse from the
virtue and religion of the Bible, and wholly inconsistent with, and
subversive of, the main things belonging to the gospel scheme, have
so vastly and so long prevailed, and have stood in such strength. And
I think, whoever imagines that he, or anybody else, shall ever see the
doctrines of grace effectually maintained against these adversaries,
till the truth in this matter be settled, imagines a vain thing. For,
allow these adversaries what they maintain in this point, and I think
they have strict demonstration against us. And not only have these
errors a most pernicious influence, in the public religious controversies, that are maintained in the world; but such sort of notions
have a more fatal influence many ways, on the minds of all ranks, in
all transactions between God and their souls. The longer I live, and
the more I have to do with the souls of men, in the work of the min-
istry, the more I see of this. Notions of this sort are one of the main
hindrances of the success of the preaching of the Word, and other
means of grace, in the conversion of sinners. This especially appears,
when the minds of sinners are affected with some concern for their
souls, and they are stirred up to seek their salvation. Nothing is more
necessary for men, in such circumstances, than thorough conviction
and humiliation; than that their consciences should be properly convinced of their real guilt and sinfulness in the sight of God, and their
deserving of his wrath. But who is there, that has had experience of

the work of a minister, in dealing with souls in such circumstances, that does not find that the thing, that mainly prevents this, is men's excusing themselves with their own inability, and the moral necessity of those things, wherein their exceeding guilt and sinfulness in the sight of God, most fundamentally and mainly consist: such as, living from day to day, without one spark of true love to the God of infinite glory, and the Fountain of all good; their having greater complacency, in the little vile things of this world, than in him; their living in a rejection of Christ, with all his glorious benefits and dying love; and after all the exhibition of his glory and grace, having their hearts still as cold as a stone towards him; and their living in such ingratitude, for that infinite mercy of his laying down his life for sinners. They, it may be, think of some instances of lewd behavior, lying, dishonesty, intemperance, profaneness, etc. But the grand principles of iniquity, constantly abiding and reigning, from whence all proceeds, are all overlooked. Conscience does not condemn them for those things, because they "cannot love God of themselves," they "cannot believe of themselves," and the like. They rather lay the blame of these things, and their other reigning wicked dispositions of heart, to God, and secretly charge him with all the blame. These things are very much, for want of being thoroughly instructed, in that great and important truth, that *a bad will, or an evil disposition of heart, itself, is wickedness.* It is wickedness, in its very being, nature and essence, and not merely the occasion of it, or the determining influence, that it was at first owing to. Some, it may be, will say, "They own it is their fault that they have so bad a heart, that they have no love to God, no true faith in Christ, no gratitude to him, because they have been careless and slothful in times past, and have not used means to obtain a better heart, as they should have done." And it may be, they are taught, "that they are to blame for their wickedness of heart, because they, as it were, brought it on themselves, in Adam, by the sin which he voluntarily committed, which sin is justly charged to their account"; which perhaps they do not deny. But how far are these things from being a proper conviction of their wickedness, in their enmity to God and Christ. To be convinced of the sin of something that, long ago, was the occasion of their enmity to God; and to be convinced of the wickedness of the enmity itself; are quite two things. And if sinners, under some awakening, find the exercise of corruption of heart, as it appears in a great many ways; in their meditations, prayers, and other religious duties, and on occasion of their fears of hell, etc., etc.; still, this notion of their inability to help it, excusing them, will keep them from proper conviction of sin herein. Fears of hell tend to convince men of the hardness of their hearts. But then, when they find how hard their hearts are, and how far from a proper sensibility and affection in things of religion; they are kept from properly condemning themselves for it, from the *moral necessity,* or *inability,* which attends it. For the very notion of hardness of heart, implies moral inability. The harder the heart is, the more dead is it in sin, and the more unable to exert good affections and acts. Thus the strength of sin, is made the excuse for sin. And thus I have known many under fears of hell, justifying, or excusing, themselves, at least implicitly, in horrid workings of enmity against God, in blasphemous thoughts, etc.

It is of great importance, that they, that are seeking their salvation, should be brought off from all dependence on their own righteousness: but these notions above all things prevent it. They justify themselves, in the sincerity of their endeavors. They say to themselves, that they do what they can; they take great pains; and though there be great imperfection in what they do, and many evil workings of heart arise, yet these they cannot help: here moral necessity, or inability, comes in as an excuse. Things of this kind have visibly been the main hindrance of the true humiliation and conversion of sinners, in the times of awakening, that have been in this land, everywhere, in all parts, as I have had opportunity to observe, in very many places. When the gospel is preached, and its offers, and invitations, and motives, most powerfully urged, and some hearts stand out, here is their stronghold, their sheet-anchor. Were it not for this, they would either comply; or their hearts would condemn them, for their horrid guilt in not complying. And if the law of God be preached in its strictness and spirituality, yet conscience is not properly convinced by it. They justify themselves with their *inability;* and the design and end of the law, as a schoolmaster, to fit them for Christ, is defeated. Thus both the law and the gospel are prevented from having their proper effect.

The doctrine of a self-determining will, as the ground of all moral good and evil, tends to prevent any proper exercises of faith in God and Christ, in the affair of our salvation, as it tends to prevent all dependence upon them. For, instead of this, it teaches a kind of absolute independence on all those things, that are of chief importance in this affair; our righteousness depending originally on our own acts, as self-determined. Thus our own holiness is from ourselves, as its determining cause, and its original and highest source. And as for imputed righteousness, that should have any merit at all in it, to be sure, there can be no such thing. For self-determination is necessary to praise and merit. But what is imputed from another is not from our self-determination or action. And truly, in this scheme, man is not dependent on God; but God is rather dependent on man in this affair: for he only operates consequentially in acts, in which he depends on what he sees we determine, and do first.

The nature of true faith implies a disposition, to give all the glory of our salvation to God and Christ. But this notion is inconsistent with it, for it in effect gives the glory wholly to man. For that is the very doctrine that is taught, that the merit and praise is his, whose is the original and effectual determination of the praiseworthy deed. So that, on the whole, I think it must be a miracle, if ever men are converted, that have imbibed such notions as these, and are under their influence in their religious concerns.

Yea, these notions tend effectually to prevent men's ever seeking after conversion, with any earnestness. It is manifest, that men never will be in earnest in this matter, till their consciences are awakened, and they are made sensible of God's anger, and their danger of suffering the terrible effects of it. But that stupidity, which is opposed to this awakening, is upheld chiefly by these two things: their insensibility of their guilt, in what is past, and present; and their flattering themselves, as to what is future. These notions of liberty of indifference, contingence, and self-determination, as essential to guilt or merit, tend to preclude all sense of any great guilt for past or present wickedness. As has been observed already, all wickedness of heart is excused, as what, in itself considered, brings no guilt. And all that the conscience has to recur to, to find any guilt, is the first wrong determination of the will, in some bad conduct, before that wickedness of heart existed, that was the occasion of introducing or confirming it. Which determination arose contingently from a state of indifference. And how small a matter does this at once bring men's guilt to, when all the main things, wherein their wickedness consists, are passed over. And indeed the more these principles are pursued, the more and more must guilt vanish, till at last it comes to nothing, as may easily be shown.

And with respect to self-flattery and presumption, as to what is future, nothing can possibly be conceived more directly tending to it, than a notion of a liberty, at all times possessed, consisting in a power to determine one's own will to good or evil; which implies a power men have, at all times, to determine them to repent and turn to God. And what can more effectually encourage the sinner, in present delays and neglects, and embolden him to go on in sin, in a presumption of having his own salvation at all times at his command? And this notion of self-determination and self-dependence, tends to prevent, or enervate, all prayer to God for converting grace; for why should men earnestly cry to God for his grace, to determine their hearts to that, which they must be determined to of themselves. And indeed it destroys the very notion of conversion itself. There can properly be no such thing, or anything akin to what the Scripture speaks of conversion, renovation of the heart, regeneration, etc. if growing good, by a number of self-determined acts, are all that is required, or to be expected.

Excuse me, sir, for troubling you with so much on this head. I speak from the fullness of my heart. What I have long seen of the dreadful consequences of these prevalent notions everywhere, and what I am convinced will still be their consequences so long as they continue to prevail, fills me with concern. I therefore wish that the affair were more thoroughly looked into, and searched to the very bottom.

I have reserved a copy of this letter, and also of my other to you, dated July 25, intending to send them to Mr. Burr, to be by him conveyed, by the way of New York or Philadelphia. Looking on these letters as of special importance, I send duplicates, lest one copy should fail. The pacquet, in which I enclose this, I cover to Mr. Gillies, and send to Boston, to the care of Mr. Hyslop, to be conveyed to Mr. Gillies. But yet have desired him, if he has a more direct opportunity, to convey the pacquet to Edinburgh, by the way of London, then to put a wrapper over the whole, inscribed to you; and to write to you, desiring you to break open the pacquet, and take out the letters which belong to you.

You will see, sir, something of our sorrowful state, on this side of the water, by my letter to Mr. M'Culloch. O, sir, pray for us; and pray in particular, for

Your affectionate and obliged
Friend and brother,
JONATHAN EDWARDS

Appetite: animal, 28 n.; comparison of hungers, 232

Aquinas, Thomas, 76, 228

Arbitrary: God's operation, in Watts' view, 99–105; and JE's, 108, 110–12; intercourse between man and God, 112

Arbitrium, 103, 110. *See also* Arbitrary; God, act of will

Arian (Arianism), 82, 90, 93; Chubb's defense of, 67

Arian Invited to the Orthodox Faith (Watts), 90

Aristotle, 13

Arminian, use of the name, 129–32

Arminian notion of liberty: point absolutely determining the dispute, 9, 289; implies contingency and acts of volition without a cause, 179, 183–5, 199 n., 216; impossible and inconceivable, 171–4, 238; anything can happen, 183–5; destroys itself in an infinite series of self-determining acts, 190–1; as the mind's power to have whatever dictates of the understanding it pleases, 222–3; freedom from evidence and understanding, 223–4; liableness to act at random, 272–3; and use of praise, 278–9; supposes God necessarily holy, 280; inconsistent in allowing greater difficulty for fallen man to be good, 297; or that it is impossible for fallen man to perform perfect goodness, 300–1; inconsistent with moral agency, 302–3. *See also* Indifference; Self-Determination

Arminianism: and Calvinism contrasted, 2–3; JE's project of writing against, 2–7; increasing stress on autonomy of will, 3, 83; spread of, 4, 5 n., 422, 437–8; distinction between foreknowledge and predetermination, 10, 262–3, 263 n., 265; spread of, accompanied by increased licentiousness, 422; and use of praise, 278–9; supposes God necessarily holy, 280; on general election, 286, 287 n.; difficulty of goodness, 297; and moral impossibility of perfect goodness in fallen man, 300–1. *See also* Arminian notion of liberty

Arminius, Jacobus, 3, 129, 131, 289 n.

Art, terms of, 39, 150 f., 155. *See also* Language, ethical

Athanasian Creed, 91

Atheism, tendency to, attributable to Arminianism, not to doctrine of necessity, 420

Atoms of matter, identical, 113–14, 387–92

Augustine, Saint, 41 n., 50 n., 94 n., 295 n.: on God determining the determining acts of the soul, 40–1; theological necessity distinct from compulsion, 40–1; and JE on willing and nilling, 50–1; on trinitarian formula, 93–4

Austin, Samuel (ed. Worcester edition), 127

"Austin, St.," 295 and n.

"Author of" (used for *Watts*), 94–5, 98–9, 132, 186, 263, 271

Author of an act, on being the, 21, 342. *See* Agency; Praise; Volition, act of

Author of sin. *See* Sin

Bailey, Derrick Sherwin, 329 n.

Balance, weights in, 232–3

Baptists, 91

Barclay, Robert, 73 n., 74

Baxter, Andrew: moral necessity determines the will to the wisest and best, 377 n.; no successiveness in God, or parts in eternity, 386 n.; on metaphysical subtleties, 392 n.

Beasts, men compared with, 28 n.

Beers, Nathan, 118 n.

Beginnings of Unitarianism in America (Wright), 69 n., 105 n.

Being, divine, 151, 259, 384, 395, 404 f.; supreme, 165, 396; perfect, 182; general and universal, 182; first, self-existent, 377

Belknap, Jeremy, 92 n., 93 n., 94 n.

Bellamy, Joseph, 14 n.

Beneficence to others, renders praise and thanks in lieu of rewarding God, 280

Berkeleian idealism, 36 n.

Berkeley, Bishop, 15

Best. *See* Good, greatest

Beza, Theodore, 402 n.

Bible. *See* Scripture

Bicentenary of Watts (1948), 95 n.

Blame (blameworthy, blameworthiness): Whitby on what deserves the name of sin or, 295; those whom God gives up to sin show that necessity does not make them blameless, 296; if necessity wholly excuses of blame, then difficulty partially excuses, 297–9; admitted to consist with necessity by Arminians who say fallen man unable to perform perfect obedience, 299–301. *See also* Praise

Bodies of Christians not suddenly made immortal, 192 and n.

Bondage of the Will (Luther), 42 n.

Book, God's certain knowledge written down in, 267; Volume of the, 287

Boston, 5 n., 7, 470

Boston *Gazette*, 14 n.

"Bracketing," 11 and n., 15 f., 20, 24

Choice *(continued)*
106–7, 112–13, 147, 178, 200–1, 394; between two indifferent things, 100–5, 112–13, 195, 197–201; necessary, 151; why we suppose nature has nothing to do with, 158–9; cannot determine the will without preceding act, 175–6; acting "according" to, imperfectly distinguishes doing from willing, 192–3; creates its own delight in the thing chosen, 196–8. *See also* Volition, act of

Christ. *See* Jesus Christ

Christian(s), 88, 129 f., 133, 192 and n., 239, 256, 278, 289 f.

Christian Philosophy (Turnbull), 217–18, 218 n., 407 n., 430 n.

Christianity, 69, 289

Chubb, Thomas, 6, 9, 69 n., 73, 76 n., 77 n., 78 n., 79 n., 80 n., 81 n., 98, 132, 232 f.: why chosen for extended refutation, 65–6; life and place in eighteenth century deism, 66–9; key to page citation of his tracts, 73 n.; repelled by Barclay's doctrine of sin, 74; plebian origin, 66, 75; on need for motives to excite action, 75–6, 78–80, 226–7; faculty psychology, 76–8, 79–80; on motives as passive ground or reason but not cause of exercise of the active faculty, 76–8, 228–30, 236; on suspension, 77–8; impossible for God to act other than perfectly, 79, 418; motives necessary to exertion of act of will, 80–1, 236–8; or production of an act of will, 80–1, 228, 237–8; will does not always follow strongest motive, 229–33; volition independent of motive, 232; necessary agency a contradiction in terms, 233–4; choosing to choose as well as to do, 234–5; act of choice the produce of a free act of choice, 235–6; the active faculty, 236–7; gross inconsistencies, 237–8; metaphysical notion of action or agency excludes all passiveness, 343–8

Clarke, Samuel, 18, 67, 93, 217, 224, 263; will and understanding not diverse, 49, 222; not selected for chief attention by JE, 65; on deity of Christ, 82; on determination of God's will by wisdom and superior fitness, 377 n.; and Kames on moral necessity, 450, 452

Clagett, William, 301 n.

Coaction, 203 n., 213, 269; as compulsion or natural necessity, 37, 164, 297; Whitby's definition, 213 n.; whether any other necessity than, removes praiseworthiness, 277–81, or destroys sin and blame, 295–6; Kames on, **450–1**

Collection of Papers Which Passed between the Late Learned Mr. Leibniz and Dr. Clarke (1715–16), 114 n.

Collection of Tracts on Various Subjects (Chubb), 67, 73, 76 n., 77 n., 78 n., 79 n., 80 n., 81 n., 226 and n., 343 n., 418; key to page citations in the text, 73 n.

Coleman, Benjamin, 96; on Watts' heterodoxy, 94; Watts to, 92, 97–8

College of New Jersey, 69

Collins, Anthony: on suspension, 63 n.; on Sherlock's mathematical proof of Trinity, 68; on Anglican Arminianism, 82; on Whitby, 89

Colonies, American, Watts' connection with, 89–90, 92, 96–8

Command: used to determine the will one way, 22–3; of God supposes freedom of man in state of trial, 86–7; of God agrees with necessity of volition as much as with prescience, 269, 416-17; Jesus subject to, yet not free to sin, 289–92; the will itself, not its actions, the proper object of, 302–3; first determining act required, not an act before this, 303; direct and indirect or remote subject of, 303; disobedience of first determining act shows moral inability, 304–6; state or act of will may be commanded which may not exist before or after, 308–9; inconsistent with natural inability, 309; cited from Scripture begs the question, 418–19. *See also* Inducements

Common sense: and principle of causality, 181–2; on necessity of motives to volition, 238

Communion, qualifications for, 4 f.

Compulsion, 12, 164. *See also* Coaction; Necessity, natural

Conducting as one pleases: defines freedom, 163–4, 445; includes forbearance, 163 n. *See also* Volition, act of

Confessions (Augustine), 50 n.

Confirmed spirits: freedom of confirmed angels and men and damned spirits, 84, 86–7, 203 n., 277 n., 323, 325

Connection, 11–12; cause as, 34–6, 118; as meaning of philosophical necessity, 36–7, 152; of subject and predicate of proposition affirming existence, 36–7, 152–4, 265; may be perfect between moral causes and volition, 38, 157–8; lying in the will, 40; full and certain in and of itself, 152 f.; full and certain consequentially, 153; contingency as undiscerned, 155; infallible, 213; freedom of will not lacking connection with

Jesus Christ (*continued*)
247; and future events dependent on the certainty of his own will, made as *Logos*, 287; and as man, 288–9.

In a state of trial his acts necessarily holy yet deserving of praise, 9, 85–6, 281, 293–4, 326; subject to commands and promises and, while not free to sin, worthy of praise for merit of his obedience, 289–92; and to be rewarded, 292–3
Johnson, Samuel, 90 and n., 91 n.
Johnson, T. H., 1 n., 14 n., 23 n., 52 n., 97 n.; editions of the *Inquiry*, 118–19, 119 n.
Jonathan Edwards (Miller), 31 n.
"Jonathan Edwards' Background of Reading" (Johnson), 97 n.
"Justification by Faith Alone" (JE's sermon), 74, 300 n.
Justin Martyr, 192

Kames (Henry Home), Lord, 14 n., 71 n., 118, 443–52 *passim*, 453 n.; occasion of JE's reply to his *Essays*, 443–4; freedom a deceitful impression, 444–5, 458, 465–7; changes of mind, 445–52; influence of JE upon, 447, 451–2; moral necessity and JE's coaction, 450–1; necessity excludes freedom, 455; and praiseworthiness, 457–8; contingency, 459; rests industriousness upon delusive sense of liberty, 461–2
Kierkegaard, Soren, 2
Knowledge: of God and of ourselves, 133, 306–7, 376–7; certainty of, 152; of immediate ideas, 183; of God from effects or creatures, 182–3; of any existence other than ideas, 183; of God, true virtue and religion, 246

Language, ethical: ordinary language inexact, 11; shaped to refer to the production of external action with supposable opposition to the will's endeavor, 27, 38, 341–2, 348–9, 351–5; this also shapes JE's reply, 29; relative terms, 39; error of using terms unaltered when speaking of volition itself, 39, 456–7; origin of such terms in childhood, 150–1, 352–3, 457–8; words with meanings very diverse from original import, 161–2; improving the benefit of language, 353 n.; imagination lends strength to errors in usage, 355–6; origin of error of associating necessity with faultlessness, 363
Laud, Archbishop, 82
Law: moral, 165; use of, puts will out of equilibrium, 304; end of laws is to bind

and bias the will one way, 304. *See also* Command; Inducements
Le Blanc, 263
Leeds edition of JE's Works, 119
Leibniz: on willing to will, 64 n.; and JE on identity of indiscernibles and sufficient reason, 114–15; moral necessity compatible with liberty, 115–16; and JE on whether this is the best of all possible worlds, 115–17
Leibniz-Clarke Correspondence (ed. Alexander), 114 n.
Lewis, H. D., 23 n.
Liberty. *See* Freedom; Indifference; Self-Determination; Volition, act of
Licentiousness, tendency to: attributable to Arminianism, not to doctrine of necessity, 420–1; the spread of modern notions of freedom far from improving morals, 422
Life and Character of the Late Reverend Mr. Jonathan Edwards (Hopkins), 1 n.
Life of President Edwards (Dwight), 2 n., 4 n., 5 n., 6 n., 7 n., 8 n., 14 n., 47 n., 444
Lives of the Most Eminent English Poets (Johnson), 90 n., 91 n.
Locke, John, 1, 10 n., 14, 47 n., 80 n., 97, 138 n., 139 n., 164 n., 189 n., 194 n.; distinction between volition and agent, 10 n., 164, 171; origin of simple ideas in impressions provides JE with way of expressing the efficacy of grace, 43 n.; possibility of God impressing the soul immediately, 43 n.; whether the man or the will be free, 47–8; the will as power of the mind, 47–8, 137–8, 163–4, 171–2, 175; rejection of faculty psychology, 48–9; whether choice is the same as preference or desire, 51–2, 60, 138–40; revision of chapter on power and second thoughts concerning liberty, 53–4, 58–9, 59 n., 60–1, 64; on uneasiness or greatest good determining the will, 53–5, 143; whether the will always follows last dictate of understanding, 56–7, 377 n.; Watts' criticism of Locke on uneasiness, 58; distinction between objects chosen and acts of choice, 58–60, 59 n., 99; the will conversant about suspending action, 60–2; absurdity of an act of will preceding first act, 63–5; Watts' interest in Locke, 90–1; on mixed modes, 353 and n.
Logomachy, 425 n.
Logos, 287
Luther, Martin: necessity of compulsion and necessity of immutability, 41–2, 42 n.; no medium between will and action to fetch will forth, 64 n.

INDEX OF BIBLICAL PASSAGES

OLD TESTAMENT

NEW TESTAMENT